Allen.

# Programmer's Quick Reference
## High Performance Animation in C for Windows

Continued from inside front cover

| Software Feature | Demo | Discussion |
|---|---|---|
| **REALTIME ANIMATION ENGINE** -- Use runtime creation and display of computer-generated images for realtime animation in interactive modes, including forward, reverse, freeze frame and single step. | realtime.c | Chapter 7 |
| **FRAME ANIMATION ENGINE** -- Create and save to disk each frame for an animation sequence, then play back the frames in interactive modes, including forward, reverse, freeze frame, and single step. | frame.c<br>blink.c<br>bouncing.c<br>panning.c<br>running.c<br>spatial.c | Chapter 8<br>Chapter 10<br>Chapter 13<br>Chapter 14<br>Chapter 15<br>Chapter 17 |
| **ANIMATION STORAGE TECHNIQUES** -- Manage a frame animation sequence using RAM or disk to store the frames. Use Windows memory in real, standard, and enhanced mode. | frame.c | Chapter 8 |
| **CHARACTER AND CARTOON ANIMATION** -- Use cel animation techniques to animate facial expressions, dialogue, hand movements, and more. | blink.c | Chapter 10 |
| **MOTION BLUR ANIMATION** -- Use advanced methods like motion blur, deformation, staggers, temporal anti-aliasing, run-cycles, and collisions to create believable motion. | bouncing.c | Chapter 13 |
| **BACKGROUND PANS** -- Build an oversized background on a hidden bitmap and pan across the image to create versatile scenes for your animation sequences. | panning.c | Chapter 14 |
| **TRACEBACKS AND KEYFRAMES** -- Use time-saving techniques like tweening, key frames, tracebacks, onionskin, and motion-tests to create powerful and arresting animation sequences. | running.c<br>blink.c | Chapter 15<br>Chapter 10 |
| **BEHAVIORAL AND KINEMATIC ANIMATION** -- Invoke simulation, forensic, and analytic animation techniques to make your application a productive tool for researchers, investigators, analysts, students, and others. | spatial.c | Chapter 17 |

A Lee Adams™ Book

# C FOR WINDOWS®
# ANIMATION PROGRAMMING

Windcrest®/McGraw-Hill

FIRST EDITION
FIRST PRINTING

**Library of Congress Cataloging-in-Publication Data**

Adams, Lee.
   C for windows animation programming / by Lee Adams.
     p.    cm.
   Includes index.
   ISBN 0-8306-3810-5
   1. Computer graphics.   2. C (Computer program language)
  3. Windows (Computer programs)  I. Title.
T385.A32   1992
006.6'762—dc20                 92-24351
                                      CIP

Acquisitions Editor: Ron D. Powers
Editor: Mark Vanderslice
Director of Production: Katherine G. Brown
Book Design: Jaclyn J. Boone
Cover Design: Sandra Blair Design, Harrisburg, Pa.      WP1

This book is warmly dedicated to my grandfather, a frontiersman and intrepid woodsman, finally swept aside by the relentless progress of civilization.

# Contents

―――――――――――――――― **PART ONE** ――――――――――――――――

# GRAPHICS PROGRAMMING

# *Preface*

---

Computer animation is built from a legacy of human innovation and inventive spirit—most primarily the pioneering skills of traditional film animators, whose own evolution dates back to 1824. That was the year France's Peter Roget (of thesaurus fame) originated the theory of persistence of vision.

Seven years later in 1831 Joseph Plateau introduced an animation device called the phenakistoscope. It was essentially a spinning disk that allowed drawings mounted on an interior drum to be viewed through numerous framing windows. Monsieur Plateau and his phenakistoscope are generally considered as the starting point for animation technology as we have come to know it.

Plateau's invention was a refinement of the so-called magic lanterns of the era. A magic lantern consisted of hand-drawn pictures fitted into a lamp shade. The pictures were manually lit in sequence in order to create a crude illusion of movement.

In 1834 an Englishman named Horner invented a device that further automated the process. His so-called zoetrope consisted of a rotating drum with individual drawings mounted on its inner surface. As the drum spun, audiences could view the individual frames that passed by a fixed framing slit. The illusion created by Horner's zoetrope was roughly equivalent to flipping a book's pages with your thumb.

Animation devices like the zoetrope and the phenakistoscope became very popular during the mid-1800s. Around 1860 the effect became more lifelike when Emile Reynaud, working in France, added a set of flipping mirrors to replace the viewing slits. The devices were produced and sold in quantity in Europe and North America.

As the technology continued to mature, small theaters came and went.

Clever American inventors like Henry Heyl continued to refine the devices. In 1870 Heyl perfected a set of flipping mirrors that acted as a shutter to allow projection by gaslight. His so-called phantasmatrope thrilled an audience of 1500 people at the Philadelphia Academy of Music.

Traditional animation did not appear, however, until after the introduction of Thomas Edison's kinetoscope—the first movie camera and film projection system. The kinetoscope was soon copied—and often improved upon—in other countries. The cinematographe, designed by the Lumiere brothers in France, became popular across much of Europe and audiences flocked to see the movies. By 1892 Emile Reynaud opened the first permanent (and commercially profitable) movie theater, La Theatre Optique in Paris. In 1896 the first permanent North American movie theater was opened in New York City.

Although Edison's kinetoscope was bulky and unsuited for single-frame exposure, the Lumiere brothers' cinematographe was a portable, hand-cranked camera that could be readily adapted for single-frame exposure— and the idea of animated movies was already beginning to germinate in a number of bright individuals, including some North American newspaper cartoonists.

Winsor McCay was drawing a daily comic strip called Little Nemo for the New York Herald newspaper. In 1912 he drew the artwork for a short animated movie. McCay originated the animation cycle, whereby a series of drawings is repeated in order to animate a repetitive motion like walking, running, chewing, and so on. In 1914 he produced *Gertie the Dinosaur*, an animated film that was almost as popular as Charlie Chaplin.

Soon other American newspaper cartoonists began to experiment with animated films. In 1913 a Canadian named Raoul Barre invented a registration system that made it possible to produce animated films in quantity. By punching registration holes in the drawing paper, each frame could be mounted on pegs on the drawing board, ensuring accurate positioning for filming. Soon after, American cartoonist John Bray established a commercial animation studio using Barre's registration methods, and in 1915 Bray hired cartoonist Earl Hurd of Kansas City, who had worked out the fundamentals of cel animation. The word cel was derived from the transparent sheets of celluloid on which individual frames were drawn. By stacking two or three celluloid sheets on top on each other, numerous foreground characters and backgrounds could be integrated into a single animation. If the background were drawn on an oversized celluloid sheet, it could be moved during single-frame filming, making panning backgrounds possible.

Film animation became an industry. Characters like Betty Boop and Felix the Cat became international celebrities. Max Fleischer and Dave Fleischer, creators of Betty Boop, perfected the art of sound effects. A young innovator named Walt Disney introduced animated characters named Donald Duck and Mickey Mouse (who first appeared as Steamboat Willie). By 1938 Disney had produced the first full-length animated movie, *Snow White and the Seven Dwarfs*. Disney's artists had used over 100,000 frames to create the movie, which was an immediate box office success. Disney Studios quickly followed up with *Fantasia* and *Pinocchio* in 1940, and *Dumbo* in 1941.

Large, established studios like Warner Brothers, Columbia, and Metro-Goldwyn-Mayer soon began to produce animated shorts. The Looney Tunes and Merrie Melodies series were huge commercial successes for Warner. Now-legendary names like Tex Avery, Chuck Jones, and Friz Freleng were soon creating characters like Bugs Bunny and Daffy Duck to compete with Disney's cast of Mickey Mouse, Donald Duck, and others. Film animation was also beginning to be used for serious enterprises like training, simulations, education, corporate public relations, government propaganda, and scientific research.

By the 1950s and 1960s traditional film animation had become a mature technology. Although most of the wrinkles had been ironed out of the production process, it remained labor intensive and time-consuming. First, a storyboard for the animation was laid out, incorporating a sequence of drawings that indicated the broad structure and primary ideas for the animation in outline form. Second, a soundtrack was recorded, complete with voices, sound effects, and musical score. Then, a more detailed layout was prepared in order to ensure that the drawings will match the timing of the soundtrack. Next, a series of key frames or key drawings were created by the main artists. Junior artists called *inbetweeners* created a set of intermediate frames according to instructions that the main artists placed on the key frames. Next, the tweens were gathered together and a trial film was made. (This trial film is called a *pencil test*.) After correcting any timing errors or position mistakes, the frames from the pencil test were copied by hand onto celluloid sheets called *cels*. With the invention of xerography and the advent of affordable photocopiers, animation studios began to simply photocopy the pencil-test frames onto the cels. Junior artists then added color to the cels by hand-painting each frame. A 16mm movie camera capable of single-frame exposures was used to photograph the cels, which were usually lit from below the stand on which they were mounted.

By the mid-1960s television had created an insatiable demand for animated cartoons. Warner Brothers Studios was marketing a stable of characters that included Bugs Bunny, Daffy Duck, Porky Pig, Tweety and Sylvester, the Tasmanian Devil, the Road Runner and Wile E. Coyote, Speedy Gonzales, Foghorn Leghorn, Yosemite Sam, Pepe Le Pew, Elmer Fudd, and others. Likewise, Hanna-Barbera Productions was enjoying commercial success with Tom and Jerry, Huckleberry Hound, Quick Draw McGraw and Baba Looey, Yogi Bear and Boo Boo Bear, the Flintstones, Scooby-Doo, the Jetsons, Magilla Gorilla, Snagglepuss, Top Cat, Augie Doggie and Daddie Doggie, the Smurfs, and others.

As early as 1970 a number of universities and research centers were experimenting with computer-assisted animation. Over the next 15 years software and hardware systems were developed to automate the inbetweening process, dramatically speeding up the production of intermediate images from key frames. Soon, even the camera itself was being controlled through software. By the 1980s entire animation sequences were being commercially produced using dedicated computer systems. Then, as computer hardware prices dropped—and as the personal computer became more powerful—animation became possible on desktop systems.

The evolution of animation has now come full circle. The individual inventors and innovators of the 1800s tinkered with animation player devices. The entrepreneurs and cartoonists of the early 1900s discovered and refined the art of hand-drawn, film animation. These early animation pioneers blazed a trail for the personal computer programmers of the 1990s, who now finally have the speed, power, and storage they need to experiment with digital animation on their desktops. These programmers will help open up the rich potential of computer-assisted 2D and 3D animation, simulation, and visualization—the new thinking tools of the knowledge revolution.

# Introduction

Whether you program for a living, or live for programming, this book can help you master the skills you need to create professional animation on today's personal computers.

## How to get the most from this book

*C for Windows Animation Programming* provides practical instruction and hands-on examples for programming animation sequences on today's PCs. You can use this book and your favorite C or C++ compiler to create animated software that takes full advantage of the powerful capabilities of personal computers running in the cooperative, multitasking operating environment of Windows.

### Three books in one

The book is really three books in one. First, it is an introduction to Windows graphics programming for personal computers. Second, it is a tutorial guide to high-performance animation skills. Third, it is an annotated collection of sample program listings.

### Source code

Inside are 19,000 lines of here-is-how-it's-done program listings—nearly 800K of source code if you are using the companion disk. All of the code is royalty-free, ready for you to paste into your own applications.

## Solutions

The book is a banquet of solutions. It helps you acquire marketable skills—and helps improve skills you may already have—so you can be more successful in today's increasingly competitive world. The text continues the practical, hands-on approach made popular in previous books in the Windcrest/McGraw-Hill graphics programming series. The book helps you master the skills you need to get things done in Windows.

# Who should use animation

Any programmer or developer who wants to improve the ability of their software to communicate should use animation. Even spot animation (which is what the pros have named occasional, brief, partial-screen animation sequences) can improve the impact of your software application, lofting it into the arena where the world-class competitors play.

## Practical uses for animation

There are many practical uses for animation, and for its two cousins, simulation and visualization. Markets for PC animation include education, training, simulation, entertainment, games, software demos, software tutorials, business presentations, point-of-purchase displays, disk-based advertising, and more.

PC animation is also a powerful tool for architectural design, industrial design, and engineering design. Typical animation sequences include walkthroughs, walk-bys, fly-pasts, rotating widgets, and assembly line sequences. Personal computer animation is also an important component of simulation and visualization, including scientific, biomedical, engineering, chemical, and mathematical. Even criminal and civil courts are relying more frequently on computer-based forensic animation to help them reconstruct and analyze important events.

Personal computer animation is becoming more significant in television production—both commercial and public access television—including program logos, opening sequences, television commercials and promos, special effects, corporate communications, and industrial promotion. In a growing variety of fields, computer animation is rapidly becoming an indispensable part of today's—and tomorrow's—software packages.

# Who should use the book

Anyone who wants to create animation sequences to run with the 10 million copies of Windows installed worldwide should read this book. More than 5000 Windows applications are already being marketed, many of them taking advantage of the rich capabilities for animation offered by the retail package of Windows.

If you are interested in course-ware authoring, tutorial authoring, or software demo authoring, then you need an understanding of the Windows animation skills demonstrated in this book.

If you are interested in creating multimedia presentations, disk-based advertising, computer-based training, or interactive video, then you need a sure grasp of the Windows animation techniques presented in this book.

If you want to write entertainment software, games, or simulation software, then you will want to ensure your programming toolkit is stocked with the Windows animation methods described in this book.

You will benefit from reading the book if one of the following categories fits you:

- Programmers and developers who are new to Windows graphics and Windows animation application development.
- Experienced programmers and experienced developers of Windows graphics applications.
- Technical managers of Windows programming environments, including the developers and programmers they supervise.
- Project managers who want to increase productivity.
- Programmers, developers, and technical managers who are selecting software tools for Windows application development.
- Software developers who plan to use animation sequences in their Windows applications.
- Consultants, researchers, and managers who want to track future trends in Windows graphics, animation, simulation, and visualization.
- Contract programmers who need a solid understanding of Windows graphics and animation in order to attract new clients and service existing clients in the marketplace.
- Corporate programmers who want to broaden the scope of Windows graphics features that they offer to their in-house clients and branch office locations.
- Independent developers who want to secure and maintain a competitive edge in Windows graphics and Windows animation techniques.
- Part-time programmers, including hobbyists, amateurs, and aficionados who simply enjoy programming and who want to broaden their Windows animation skills.

## Special features

The book has been carefully crafted to be a potent component of your programming environment. Practicality and usefulness were the buzzwords of the publisher's production team as the manuscript progressed from typesetting through pasteup and on to binding. You hold in your hands a tool designed to give you some clout in achieving your programming goals.

## A learning tool

The book's primary goal is to be useful to you in your quest to write animated Windows graphics applications. The book has been designed to be a learning tool. It is a programmer's toolkit. The book does not attempt to be complete, however, because no single book has enough pages to address every aspect of animation programming for Windows. Instead, the book attempts to be useful. It does this by example-rich text. Many programming examples and plenty of royalty-free source code demonstrate the animation techniques being discussed—and numerous hand-drawn illustrations support the text. In addition, the book emphasizes cross-compiler compatibility and device-independent graphics.

**Complete and unabridged**  The book is completely self-contained and unabridged. Nothing is missing. You get all the production files needed to build each of the sample applications. As a further convenience to you, all the program listings in the book are also provided on companion disks.

**Icons**  Throughout the book, icons located at the left margin are used to flag important sections of text. The icons help catch your attention when you are skimming pages looking for a topic of particular interest. Two types of icons are used in the book. These are topic indicators and code indicators.

**Topic indicators**  Topic indicators are used to accent the text, helping alert you to special information and topics, as shown in FIG. 1. The Tip icon signifies a tip to increase your productivity. The Fact icon indicates important background information. The Here's How icon provides a kernel of practical programming instruction. The Expert icon signals an apposite tip or practical technique for the experienced programmer or developer. The Sample App icon appears alongside a program listing for a sample application ready to build and run with your favorite C or C++ compiler. The User's Guide icon is placed next to instructions for running and using a sample application. The Demo icon indicates a discussion of demo program performance, features, and graphics output. The Code icon signifies a discussion of source code logic, algorithms, and functions. The Toolkit icon appears alongside text that describes companion disk material. The Disk icon indicates a discussion of disk activity by a sample application, usually image files used during an animation sequence.

**Code indicators**  Code indicators are used to identify the program listings for the production files that comprise each demonstration program, as shown in FIG. 2. The .def icon signifies the module definition file. The .h icon indentifies the include file that contains function prototypes and constant definitions. The .rc icon indicates the resource script file that declares the menus and other resources used by the sample application. The .c icon

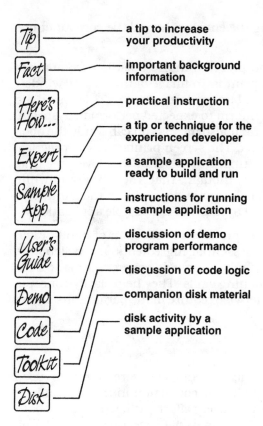

*Tip* — a tip to increase your productivity

*Fact* — important background information

*Here's How...* — practical instruction

*Expert* — a tip or technique for the experienced developer

*Sample App* — a sample application ready to build and run

*User's Guide* — instructions for running a sample application

*Demo* — discussion of demo program performance

*Code* — discussion of code logic

*Toolkit* — companion disk material

*Disk* — disk activity by a sample application

**1** Icons are used throughout the book to help you find the material you need.

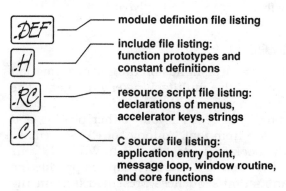

*.DEF* — module definition file listing

*.H* — include file listing: function prototypes and constant definitions

*.RC* — resource script file listing: declarations of menus, accelerator keys, strings

*.C* — C source file listing: application entry point, message loop, window routine, and core functions

**2** Each program listing in the book is captioned with an icon in the margin.

identifys the C source file containing the entry point and the core functions of the demo program.

**Screen images**  Each demonstration program in the book is accompanied by a number of screen prints. Each print is an image of the display window of the sample application, as produced on my laser printer. This visual aid helps you confirm that the demos conform to expected performance specifications on your own computer system. It also means you can study the book without having to be at your computer. The screen prints make it practical for you to use the book while commuting, travelling, or whenever free time becomes available. Please remember, though, that the black-and-white screen prints used throughout the book cannot do justice to the subtle and rich hues, shades, and gradients used by many of the sample applications.

**Illustrations**  The book contains a comprehensive collection of hand-drawn illustrations. These illustrations are essential ingredients and collaborate closely with the text discussion. They often provide concrete, practical examples of artistic, design, and cartooning skills. They help clarify concepts and technical details that would otherwise require many paragraphs of text to explain.

## A commitment to graphics

The hand-drawn illustrations, the icons, and the screen prints used throughout the book reflect my unshakeable conviction in the tremendous strength of graphics in communication. Every effort has been made by both publisher and myself to ensure that the material presented in this book is supported by graphics imagery. All in all, the book practices what it preaches and delivers plenty of graphics. As you might have already discovered to your chagrin, trying to master Windows programming with a graphics-impaired book is like a fly trying to conquer flypaper.

# How the book is organized

The book is organized to provide a practical, hands-on tutorial of animation programming in the Windows cooperative multitasking environment. The layout of the book does not force upon you any dogmatic approach to learning. You can use whatever approach is best for you—either picking and choosing what you want as you skip from topic to topic, or else systematically covering the material in the book from start to finish. Whatever your style of learning, the book will serve you well. Earlier chapters provide the underpinnings for advanced animation sequences presented later in the book, but each chapter has been crafted as a stand-alone module that can be studied independent of other chapters.

The book is organized into four parts. The book begins with the general and progresses to the specific.

## Graphics programming skills

The first part of the book introduces fundamental graphics programming skills, including managing the display window, display-independent graphics, persistent images, blitting, transparent PUT, 3D modeling and shading, and font titling. The images in FIG. 3 depict the images produced by some of the sample applications in Part 1.

## Computer animation

The second part of the book discusses hardware-dependent methods of animation, including real-time animation and frame animation engines that can be reconfigured and pasted into any Windows animation application. The images in FIG. 4 illustrate the graphics displays produced by these generic animation engine demos.

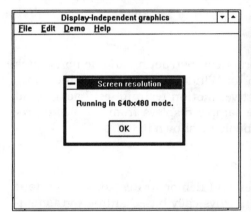
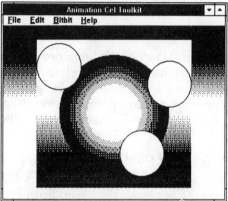
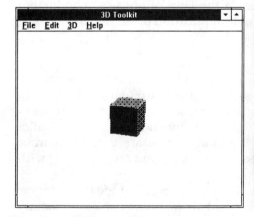
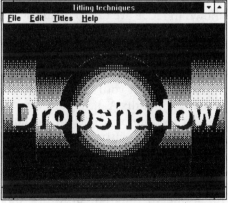

**3** Fundamental programming skills like display-independent graphics, bitblits, bitmaps, 3D modeling, titling, and text output are demonstrated by the sample applications in Part One of the book.

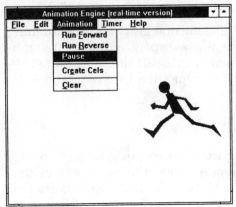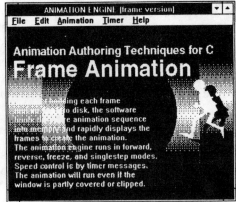

**4** Reconfigurable animation engines for creating realtime animation and frame animation in Windows using available hardware are demonstrated by the sample applications in Part Two of the book.

## Cel animation

The third part of the book provides practical instruction and demonstrates the implementation of cel animation for Windows applications, including character animation, layout, perspective, motion techniques, background panning, tweening, and more. Some sample displays from the demo programs provided in this section of the book are shown in FIG. 5.

## Physically based animation

The fourth part of the book describes and demonstrates some important aspects of physically based animation. Physically based animation is usually designed to conform more or less to the laws of physics. The images shown in FIG. 6 are taken from the sample application presented in Part 4.

## Appendix material

The appendix material provides information to help you build the sample applications on your own computer system. If you are using Microsoft C, consult appendix A. If you are working with QuickC for Windows, see appendix B. Check appendix C for Borland C++, and appendix D if you are building the demos with Turbo C++ for Windows. If you are using Symantec Zortech C++, see Appendix E. Refer to Appendix F if you are compiling with WATCOM C.

Appendix G provides helpful tips for testing your Windows prototype programs in different graphics modes and in different runtime memory modes. Appendix H introduces audio track considerations. A listing of selected animation schools is presented in appendix I. You can find a listing of selected sources for hardware and software tools for animation in appendix J, including magazines, catalogs, and directories.

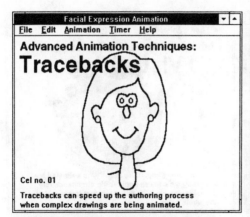

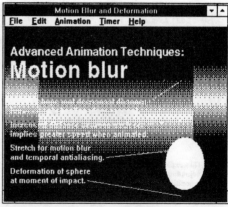

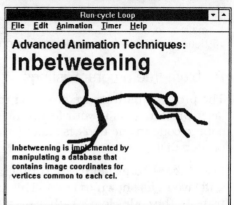

**5** Creative techniques like character animation, cel animation, motion blur, perspective, layout, background panning, run-cycles, tweening, keyframes, and animation production methods are discussed and selectively demonstrated by the sample applications in Part Three of the book.

## Glossary and index

A comprehensive glossary of important words and phrases ensures that you understand the text and helps you grasp the broader field of computer graphics programming in general and animation programming in particular. The index helps you find sections of text that discuss topics of immediate interest to you.

# About the program listings

A significant component of the book's content is the C source code, which has been rigorously tested in different display modes and memory modes using a variety of compilers.

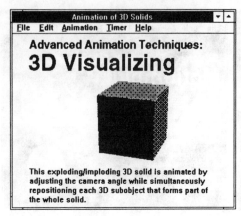
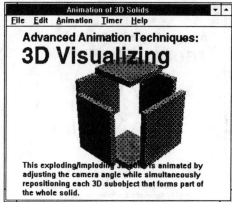

**6** Techniques for simulation and analysis, including behavioral animation, viewpoint animation, forward dynamics, and kinematic animation are discussed and selectively demonstrated by the sample applications in Part Four of the book.

## Problem-free program listings

The program listings are direct reproductions of printouts produced on my laser printer. This is your assurance of problem-free program listings. The source code in the book is exactly the same as the source files on the companion disks.

**Source code formatting**  Each program listing follows a consistent format and layout, as shown in FIG. 7. This uniform approach allows you to concentrate on the code's logic, rather than on the layout or style of the listing.

**Line numbering**  Every line of code in each program listing is numbered. Whenever the text refers to a statement, expression, or block of code, it refers to a line number. If you are new to C programming, remember that neither C nor C++ compilers recognize or tolerate line numbers in source files. The line numbers that appear throughout the book were added when the program listings were printed. Do not type the line numbers if you are typing the program listings. The line numbers do not appear in the source files on the companion disks.

## Program stability

Each sample application in the book follows a consistent set of conventions that make learning easy. The conventions also help minimize the possibility of conflicts with other Windows applications that may be running on your system.

**Common user interface**  As shown in FIG. 8, a common user interface is found in each sample application. The caption bar, menu bar, and menuing structure are similar throughout all the demo programs. Each sample application provides a message box that acts as a tutorial at runtime.

```
0001    case WM_PAINT:                    /* if image needs to be refreshed... */
0002      hDCpaint= BeginPaint(hWnd,&ps);              /* load structure */
0003      EndPaint(hWnd, &ps);                     /* validate client area */
0004      if (PaintImage==zBLANK) break;    /* if client area is blank */
0005      zCopyToDisplay(hWnd);    /* else copy hidden frame to display */
0006      break;
0007
0008
0009    /* ------------------hidden frame operations ------------------ */
0010    HDC hFrameDC;                /* memory display-context for hidden-frame */
0011    HBITMAP hFrame;                   /* handle to hidden-frame bitmap */
0012    HBITMAP hPrevFrame;                      /* default bitmap */
0013    BOOL FrameReady= FALSE;                   /* hidden-frame created? */
0014
0015
0016    /* ------- calculate screen position to center the window ------ */
0017    WindowX= (DisplayWidth - zWINDOW_WIDTH) / 2;         /* horizontal */
0018    WindowY= (DisplayHeight - zWINDOW_HEIGHT) /2;          /* vertical */
0019    if (WindowX < 0) WindowX= 0;
0020    if (WindowY < 0) WindowY= 0;
0021
0022
0023    GlobalCompact((DWORD)-1L);           /* maximize contiguous memory */
0024    hDisplayDC= GetDC(hWnd);                /* set the display-context */
0025    hFrameDC= CreateCompatibleDC(hDisplayDC);       /* create frame... */
0026    hFrame= CreateCompatibleBitmap(hDisplayDC,zFRAMEWIDE,zFRAMEHIGH);
0027    if (hFrame==NULL)
0028    {
0029      LoadString(hInst,IDS_NotReady,lpCaption,Max);
0030      LoadString(hInst,IDS_NoMem,lpMessage,MaxText);
0031      MessageBox(GetFocus(),lpMessage,lpCaption,MB_OK);
0032      DeleteDC(hFrameDC);
0033      FrameReady= FALSE;
0034      return;
0035    }
0036    hPrevFrame= SelectObject(hFrameDC,hFrame);  /* select the bitmap */
0037    zClearHiddenFrame();                    /* clear the hidden frame */
```

— blocks are indented

— general comments

— specific comments

— display-independent graphics

— careful memory management

— careful error management

— status reports to user

— careful resource management

— persistent graphics

**7**    The sample program listings in the book provide a here-is-how-its-done tutorial to animation programming in Windows. The source code has been designed to be accessible and understandable, ready for you to adapt for use in your own software projects.

**Common display frame**    As shown in FIG. 9, a common display frame is used by each demo program. The code logic ensures that the display window appears at the center of the screen. Measured in screen pixels, each sample application uses a standard-sized display frame. This commonality of display frame (or addressable image area) ensures that any image files saved to disk are of predictable size. Further, the $400 \times 300$ pixel dimensions of the image area mean you can easily adapt your animation sequences for the 4:3 aspect ratio of television and videotape.

**Persistent graphics**    Each sample application provides persistent graphics. This means that even animated programs can be moved around the screen by the user at runtime. You can cover a running animation with another application's window and the exposed portion of the animation will continue to run. You can move the window so part of it is clipped by the edge of the screen and the exposed portion of the animation will continue to run.

**Instancing**    If you double-click on an application's icon and attempt to run a second copy of the application while a first copy is already running, the code is smart enough to detect this and simply transfer control back to the already-running copy of the application. On a broader level, the demo programs are nominally designed to run exclusive of each other. For example, if you attempt to launch BOUNCING.EXE while BLINK.EXE is already running, the code logic will ensure that Windows simply passes control back to BLINK.EXE. This regime ensures that your computer system does not begin

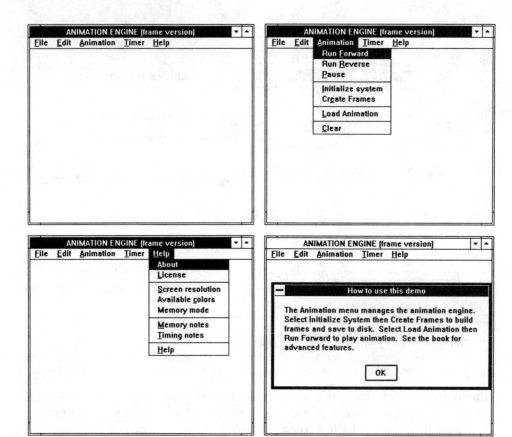

**8** Each sample application in the book adheres to a consistent user interface design that allows you to concentrate on graphics programming.

to thrash when Windows' built-in memory manager starts swapping data segments in its attempt to cope with excessive demands on system memory. You can, however, override this exclusivity feature by changing one line of code.

**Practical conventions** The naming conventions for variables and functions in Windows applications are not always strictly enforced in the demonstration programs. Error-trapping and inspection of function return values are not rigorously implemented either. The demos make no attempt to intercept Unrecoverable Application Error (UAE) conditions found in Windows 3.0 or General Protection Fault (GPF) conditions found in Windows 3.1. By relaxing these conventions, the book sustains an application-prototyping environment that is more conducive to teaching and learning.

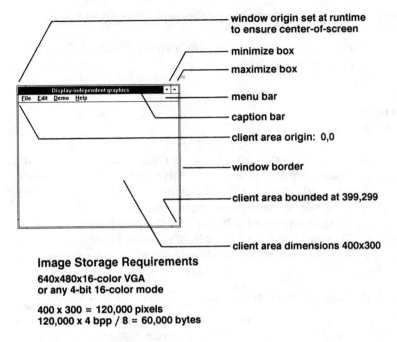

**window origin set at runtime to ensure center-of-screen**

**minimize box**

**maximize box**

**menu bar**

**caption bar**

**client area origin: 0,0**

**window border**

**client area bounded at 399,299**

**client area dimensions 400x300**

## Image Storage Requirements

**640x480x16-color VGA
or any 4-bit 16-color mode**

**400 x 300 = 120,000 pixels
120,000 x 4 bpp / 8 = 60,000 bytes**

**9** Each sample application in the book provides a graphics workspace whose 4:3 dimensions make it easy to develop your own applications for Windows, for multimedia PCs, and for videotape output.

## Hardware and software compatibility

If your authoring platform or your target platform is running Windows version 3.0 or 3.1 or newer, then your hardware system and your operating system is compatible with the program listings in the book (subject to the requirements discussed in "What you need to use this book").

**Validation suite** The sample applications in the book were created and tested on a personal computer equipped with a 33 MHz Intel 80386DX processor, 4Mb RAM, and a VGA display system. When Windows runs on a VGA it uses the default $640 \times 480 \times 16$-color mode. In addition, the demo programs were tested using the following Windows display modes:

- $640 \times 480 \times 16$ color VGA
- $640 \times 480 \times 2$ color mono VGA and MCGA
- $800 \times 600 \times 16$ color SVGA
- $1024 \times 768 \times 16$ color SVGA, XGA, and 8514/A
- $720 \times 348 \times 2$ color Hercules
- $640 \times 350 \times 16$ color EGA
- $640 \times 350 \times 2$ color mono EGA

Any demo that does not read or write image files will also run in the 640-×-480-×-256 color and other 256-color modes.

The program listings in the book were also tested in each of the following Windows runtime memory modes:

- Real mode.
- Standard mode.
- Enhanced mode.

In order to validate the demo programs in real mode and standard mode, a personal computer equipped with a 16 MHz Intex 80386SX processor and 2Mb RAM was used. Machine speed, available RAM, and graphics capabilities each play a role in animation performance. You should not, however, expect a 16 MHz machine with limited memory to perform as effectively as a 25 or 33 MHz machine with 4 or 8Mb of extended memory. See the discussion in chapter 6, "Animating in Windows," for more information.

## How to adapt the code for your own use

You can use the source code in this book for your own Windows application development, subject to the conditions of the License Agreement and Limited Warranty shown in FIG. 10. The code is royalty-free. Remember, however, that the sample applications in the book are advanced prototypes. They are not production code ready for commercial release. The code is optimized for teaching purposes. It is not optimized for speed or for efficient use of memory.

You can maximize your productivity by using the code as a starting point. Paste the code that you need into your own prototype to get your software up and running sooner. This a-la-carte approach can give you an advantage over your competition. It can increase your chances of meeting and beating deadlines imposed by your supervisor or by your client.

# What you need to use the book

If you use one of the popular C or C++ compilers that can generate Windows applications, then you likely have all the software you need to take full advantage of the book.

## Software

You can build all of the demo programs if you are using any of the following compiler packages:

- Microsoft C and the SDK.
- QuickC for Windows.
- Borland C++.

- Turbo C++ for Windows.
- Symantec Zortech C++.
- WATCOM C.

## License Agreement and Limited Warranty

Contains licensed material Copyright 1987-1992 Lee Adams (hereinafter called Author). All rights reserved except as noted below. This License Agreement governs the permitted uses of the source code (hereinafter called Program Code) published in Windcrest/McGraw-Hill book 4114 (hereinafter called the Book)and on the companion disk(s). This License Agreement does not diminish in any way the rights of the Author and publisher in the copyright of the Book and its companion disk(s). You acknowledge your acceptance of this License Agreement by using the Program Code as part of your software product. If you do not agree to the conditions of this License Agreement, then do not use the Program Code as part of your software product.

## License

As a purchaser of a new copy of the Book, you are granted and you accept a non-exclusive royalty-free license to reproduce and distribute executable files generated using the Program Code provided that: (a) you distribute the resulting executable code in conjunction with and as part of your software product, (b) you agree to indemnify, hold harmless, and defend the Author and publisher from and against any claims or lawsuits, including attorney's fees, that arise or result from the use or distribution of your software product, and (c) you agree to all conditions of the License Agreement and Limited Warranty as described in the Book. You further acknowledge that all rights, title, and interest in and to the Program Code are and shall remain with the Author. The Program Code in the Book and on the companion disk(s) is Copyright 1987-1992 Lee Adams. All other rights reserved. You further acknowledge that your use of the Program Code is subject to any copyright, trademark, and patent rights of others, and that it is your express responsibility to conduct reasonable search to determine the existence of any such rights of others. Neither the Author nor any person or entity acting on behalf of the Author warrants that the use of the Program Code is free from such privately-held rights.

## Limited Warranty

The best efforts of the Author have been used to prepare the information and Program Code contained in the Book and on the companion disk(s). These efforts include research, development, and testing of the information and the Program Code to determine their effectiveness and accuracy. In spite of this care, however, the Author does not warrant that the information and Program Code will solve your particular programming needs. You may find many techniques, routines, and algorithms in the Book and on the companion disk(s), but it is your express responsibility to thoroughly test the information and Program Code before you rely upon their accuracy. The Author makes no express or implied warranty and will not be liable for incidental or consequential damages arising from use of the information and Program Code and/or claims of productivity gains. The Author is not rendering legal, accounting, marketing, engineering, or management counselling service. If legal advice or other expert assistance is required, you should acquire the services of a professional. In particular, it is important that you understand you are responsible for ensuring your use or adaptation of the materials or Program Code does not infringe upon any copyright, patent, or trademark right of others. The Program Code contained in the Book and on the companion disk(s) is provided as is without warranty of any kind, either express or implied, including, but not limited to, the implied warranties of merchantability and fitness for a particular purpose. The entire risk related to the quality and performance of the Program Code is on you. In the event there is any defect, you assume the entire cost of all necessary servicing, repair, or correction. The Author does not warrant that the functions, routines, and data contained in the Program Code will meet your requirements or that the operation of the Program Code will be uninterrupted or error-free. In no event will the Author be liable to you for any damages (including any lost profits, savings, or other incidental or consequential damages arising out of the use of or inability to use such Program Code even if the Author has been advised of the possibility of such damages) or for any claim by any other party.

## Limitations of Reliance

The Book does not necessarily contain all information, knowledge, or expertise that is available to or known by the Author or publisher. Rather, the Book is intended as a supplement to other texts you may need in order to obtain sufficient information to satisfy your particular software development requirements. The Book may contain unintentional and inadvertent errors including, but not limited to, typographical errors, mistakes in context, mistatements of fact, incorrect charts and illustrations, and other erroneous information. The Book is intended as a general guide only, and should not be construed as a definitive source of information about computer animation in general or about Windows animation programming in particular.

## No Other Conditions Binding

This License Agreement and Limited Warranty constitutes the complete and exclusive statement of the conditions of the agreement between you and the Author of the Program Code. It supersedes and replaces any previous written or oral agreements and communications relating to the Program Code. No oral or written information or advice given by the Author or by his dealers, distributors, agents, or employees creates any warranty or in any way increases the scope of the warranty provided in this agreement, and you may not rely on any such information or advice. This License Agreement shall be construed and governed in accordance with the laws of British Columbia, Canada and in compliance with the Free Trade Agreement (FTA) between the USA and Canada, or any agreement superseding the FTA. Questions concerning the license may be directed to the Author in care of Windcrest/McGraw-Hill, TAB BOOKS Division of McGraw-Hill Inc., Blue Ridge Summit, PA, USA 17294-0850.

## U.S. Government Restricted Rights

The Program Code and its documentation are provided with restricted rights. The use, duplication, or disclosure by the Government is subject to restrictions set forth in subdivision (b)(3)(ii) of The Rights in Technical Data and Computer Software clause at 252.227-7013, or as set forth in other sections. The contractor/manufacturer is Lee Adams, c/o TAB BOOKS Division of McGraw-Hill Inc., 13311 Monterey Avenue, Blue Ridge Summit PA 17294, USA.

## Trademarks and Persona Rights

The name Lee Adams is a trademark. The persona of the Author is proprietary and commercial property. No photo or likeness of the Author may be used for commercial purpose without permission in writing from the Author. No product endorsement, whether by direct quote or paraphrase or otherwise, may be used for commercial purpose without permission in writing from the Author.

## Non-affiliation

The Author is not affiliated, associated, or otherwise connected with, and has not previously been affiliated, associated, or otherwise connected with, any software product other than the demonstration programs found on the companion disks to his books.

**10**   Your royalty-free license to use the source code in your own software development is provided by the License Agreement and Limited Warranty.

Refer to the appendices for a discussion of version numbers that have been explictly validated during testing of the sample applications.

## Hardware

If you have a VGA-equipped personal computer running MS-DOS and Microsoft Windows then you likely have the hardware and operating system software you need. The demo programs will also execute on computers equipped with EGA, Hercules, Super VGA, XGA, and 8514/A graphics adapters.

Each sample application in the book was validated on a VGA-equipped, 33 MHz Intel 80386DX personal computer with 4Mb RAM running MS-DOS 4.01 and Windows 3.0. Each demo program was also validated in various display modes on a Super VGA-equipped, 33 MHz Intel 83086DX personal computer with 4Mb RAM running MS-DOS 5.0 and Windows 3.0. All timing-sensitive animation code was also validated on a VGA-equipped, 16 MHz Intel 83086SX personal computer with 2Mb RAM running MS-DOS 3.30 and Windows 3.0. The executable for each demo program was also tested with Windows 3.1.

# List of demonstration programs

The program listings in the book contain all the source code needed to build the following sample applications.

- **TEMPLATE.C** Demonstrates an application template with menus, message boxes, intercepted system messages, mnemonic keys, and accelerator keys.
- **DETECT.C** Demonstrates display-independent graphics suitable for different graphics modes and persistent images that redraw themselves when the application's display window is unclipped or uncovered.
- **BLITTING.C** Demonstrates bitblt copying, raster operations, disk save and disk load functions, and a versatile transparent PUT function that can cleanly paste any multicolored, random-shaped bitblt over a multicolored background image.
- **IMAGE3D.C** Demonstrates and exercises LIB3D.C, a powerful 3D modeling and shading toolkit that you can use with any Windows graphics application you are building.
- **TITLES.C** Demonstrates font programming techniques, including color manipulation, transparent and opaque drawing modes, superimposition of text and titles, and special effects like dropshadows.
- **REALTIME.C** Demonstrates a reconfigurable real-time animation engine that can be used to drive a variety of Windows animation sequences. A two-legged run-cycle is presented.
- **FRAME.C** Demonstrates a reconfigurable frame animation engine that can be pasted into any Windows graphics application project and

used to drive a variety of animation sequences. A two-legged run-cycle is presented.

- **BLINK.C**   Demonstrates the subtleties of facial expression, timing, pacing, and design that are needed in order to effectively animate a character.
- **STORAGE.C**   Demonstrates a module that can be linked with any Windows graphics application project to provide disk input/output functions for animation images.
- **BOUNCING.C**   Demonstrates the techniques of motion blur and deformation in the realistic animation of a bouncing ball.
- **PANNING.C**   Demonstrates how to use an oversized, hidden bitmap to implement a smooth background pan.
- **RUNNING.C**   Demonstrates a four-legged run-cycle using an ordered database suitable for computer-assisted tweening.
- **SPATIAL.C**   Demonstrates the disassembly and reassembly of a 3D solid using moving-viewpoint animation and the LIB3D.C toolkit of 3D modeling and shading routines.

## Technical notes

In the time-honored tradition of the README.DOC files used by retail software packages, here is a selection of technical tips that you might find useful as you work with the sample applications in the book.

If you are using a VGA running in the Windows default $640 \times 480 \times$ 16-color mode, none of the following tips applies to your system.

**Window height in 640 × 350 modes**   If you are using an EGA to experiment with the sample applications, you can obtain a more pleasing image by redefining the height of the application's display window. Simply locate the appropriate line near the beginning of the C source module and change #define zWINDOW_HEIGHT 346 to #define zWINDOW_HEIGHT 342.

**Disk operations in 256-color modes**   The current implementation of the image file save/load functions is designed to work with the 16-color modes supported by the retail version of Windows. The source code uses a single-pass read/write algorithm, which limits the maximum size of the image file to about 64K. The display window for each sample application in the book has been especially sized to produce a working area that requires less than 64K to store an image on disk. Because of the memory-mapping scheme used by graphics drivers that support 256-color modes, attempting to save an image to disk in these modes will produce a file larger than 64K. To accommodate this, you will need to modify the code by adding a loop that keeps writing data to the disk file in 64K chunks until the entire image has been saved. See the discussion in chapter 3.

**Font display in 800×600 modes**   Because of the size of the caption bar font and menu bar font used in the 800×600 modes by some third-party graphics drivers, the bottom line of text in some sample applications might fall below the bottom of the display window. As the hucksters say, your mileage may vary.

**Font display in 640×350 modes**   Because of the cel box size of fonts in 640×350 modes, the larger width of characters results in some text being clipped at the right edge of the display window in some sample applications.

**Color text in 2-color modes**   Some font colors in some applications are invisible in 2-color modes. See the discussion in chapter 5. See also the program listing in chapter 16.

**Area fill in 2-color modes**   When running in a 2-color mode, a few of the sample applications use dithering instead of solid colors. This might result in a slight difference in appearance that does not otherwise affect the fundamental performance of the demo.

## Related material

**C programming**   If you find the material in this book helpful, you can find additional instruction in my earlier book about Windows graphics programming, published by Windcrest/McGraw-Hill. It is titled *High Performance C Graphics Programming for Windows*, published May 1992, ISBN 0-8306-3790-7, Windcrest/McGraw-Hill book number 4103.

**Visual Basic programming**   If you prefer a more abstract approach to Windows animation using a higher-level language, you can find additional instruction in my other book about Windows animation programming, published by Windcrest/McGraw-Hill. It is titled *Visual Basic: Animation Graphics Programming*, book number 4224, published simultaneously with the book you are reading.

# Part one

# Graphics programming

# 1

# Windows

Windows is a runtime environment. Once you understand the underpinnings of this special environment, you can begin to build animation applications that take full advantage of the features Windows offers.

At the same time Windows is running your program, your program is running Windows. As shown in FIG. 1-1, a message-based paradigm makes cooperative partners of your application and Windows at runtime.

## How Windows runs your program

*Here's How...* Windows is a referee in a game with many players; your application is one of those players. Windows provides a nurturing runtime environment for your application by performing three services. First, Windows loads and executes your program. This is called launching your application. Second, Windows manages the computer's memory so that your application (and any other Windows applications that may be running at the same time) have access to the memory and other system resources they need. Third, Windows handles most of the low-level input that your application requires.

### Launching an application

When the user selects your application's icon, Windows sets aside some memory for your program. Then it loads in the executable code and sets up a local stack. It downloads your application's data and any other special resources needed by your program at runtime. These special resources are unique to the Windows environment. They include a menu system, accelerator keys, dialog boxes, message boxes, icons, and bitmaps. Do not confuse

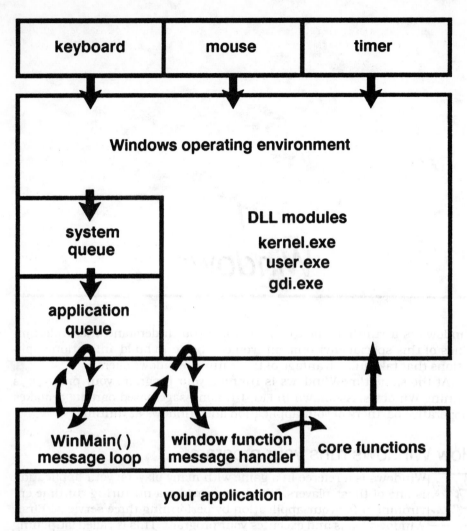

**1-1** A conceptual schematic showing how your application interacts with the Windows environment at runtime.

Windows resources with system resources like memory, disk access, keyboard and mouse input, and access to the display screen.

Every Windows application contains a function named WinMain(). This is the starting point for your program. When Windows launches your application, it begins program execution by calling WinMain().

## Managing system resources

If more than one Windows application is running, memory may be limited. Windows provides a built-in memory manager that acts in the background to ensure that each application has the memory it requires. Sometimes this means swapping code, data, and resources out of memory in order to make room for another application. Each of these three components—code, data, and resources—is organized into units called *segments*. Windows swaps or discards entire segments when it is managing memory.

## Managing input

Windows insulates your application from hardware dependence by providing a rich set of built-in input and output services. This makes it easier for you to develop applications because you do not need to make any special allowances for different computers, displays, printers, and so on. As shown in FIG. 1-1, Windows continually polls the keyboard, mouse, and timer. When an event occurs on one of these devices, Windows generates an appropriate message and places the message into the system queue. The system queue is a first-in first-out list of messages that corresponds to events received from the keyboard and mouse. Timer events are stored separately.

Windows is smart enough to know which message is intended for which application, even if more than one application is running. Other applications (and Windows itself) may send messages directly to your program at runtime. Messages for your application are stored in a separate queue that Windows maintains explicitly for your program.

**The message paradigm**  Understanding messages is the key to understanding Windows programming. Your application receives input by fetching messages from the queue that Windows maintains for your program. Your application can send messages to other applications and to Windows itself. It can also receive messages from other applications and from Windows itself.

Each message is a uniform kernel of data. The Windows #include file windows.h must be included at the beginning of every Windows application you create. This #include file declares a data structure called *MSG*. The MSG structure contains six members. They are hwnd, WM, wParam, lParam, time, and pt.

**The hwnd window handle**  The first member indicates the application that should receive the message. Every Windows application must have a main window, which is usually implemented as a rectangular area on the display screen. Each window is identified by a token called a *handle*, expressed as hwnd. This first member of the MSG structure contains a hwnd window handle.

**The WM message identifier**  The second member specifies the type of event that has occurred. This member is the message identifier. Every message identifier starts with the prefix WM_, an acronym for window message. If the user has selected a command from your application's menu system, for example, Windows will send a WM_COMMAND message to your application.

**wParam and lParam**   The third and fourth members contain additional parameters relevant to the message. In the case of a WM_COMMAND message, the third member of the MSG structure, called wParam, contains the identity of the menu item that was selected by the user. If a WM_KEYDOWN message is being received, it indicates that the user has pressed a key on the keyboard. In this case, wParam indicates which key was struck. If a WM_MOUSEMOVE message is being received, it indicates that the user has moved the mouse. In this case, the fourth member of the message, called lParam, contains the new coordinates of the mouse cursor.

**time and pt**   The fifth and sixth members of the MSG message structure are used less frequently. The fifth member, time, indicates the time when the message was placed into the queue. The sixth member, pt, contains the coordinates of the mouse cursor at the moment Windows placed the message into the queue.

## The message loop

Your application uses messages by fetching them from the queue. The loop that your program uses to read messages is called the *message loop*. The message loop is contained in your application's WinMain() function, which is also the starting point for your program.

If your application detects a message in the queue, it jumps out of the message loop in order to perform whatever activity you have programmed. Program control then returns to the message loop and begins checking the queue for the next incoming message.

Your application's message loop calls a built-in Windows function named GetMessage() that instructs Windows to check for messages. When GetMessage() is called, Windows first searches the application queue for messages, then searches the system queue for keyboard and mouse messages, then checks to see if any timer messages are present.

## The message handler

When your application detects an incoming message and calls the C functions that you have built into your program, it does so by sending a message through Windows to a special part of your program called a *message handler*, also called a *window procedure*. Every Windows application must have a message handler, because Windows associates each window with a message handler.

Windows does not permit your application to directly call other functions. This is because Windows is a cooperative multitasking environment where more than one application may be running. Other applications might want to send messages to your program. The most efficient way for them to do this is to send a message to your application's message handler, where it will receive immediate attention from your program. If the sender of the message posts a message to the queue that Windows maintains for your program, the message might be placed behind a long list of messages, and it might be a while before your program retrieves it from the queue. On the other hand, if the message is posted directly to your application's message handler, there is no delay. The built-in Windows functions that your application can call to pass messages are in fact called SendMessage() and PostMessage().

## How your program runs Windows

Many of the built-in operations performed by an application are implemented by calling functions that are built into the retail version of Windows. These callable routines are found in the Windows application programming interface (API). When it calls these functions, your program is in effect running Windows.

Your application can use the API to perform a variety of tasks. Your program can resize or move windows on the display screen. It can reconfigure menu systems while an application is running. Your application can copy images to the Windows clipboard, from which they can be pasted into other applications that are running. Your program can instruct Windows' print manager to create a hard copy of your graphics on the user's printer. You can use the Windows API to generate graphics in your application's main window, including animation.

### Dynamic-link libraries

The callable functions of the Windows API are contained in runtime libraries called *dynamic-link libraries* (DLLs). There are three DLLs provided with the retail version of Windows. They are kernel.exe, user.exe, and gdi.exe, as shown in FIG. 1-1.

The kernel.exe DLL provides functions for general window management and for supporting the entire Windows environment. The user.exe DLL provides system services like memory management and multitasking management. The graphics device interface, gdi.exe, provides a set of graphics routines, many of which are well-suited to animation. The demonstration programs in the book take advantage of the callable functions built into the gdi.exe graphics engine.

**How DLLs work.**   The three API libraries are called dynamic because your application is not linked to them until runtime. The linking occurs dynamically, hence the term dynamic-link library.

This method of linking is unlike static linking, which is the method used by C programs intended for execution under DOS. When you compile and link a DOS program, the object code from the runtime libraries is physically inserted into the resulting executable file. However, in a Windows application the linker inserts a block of object code called an *import library*. The import library is the gateway to the callable functions in the Windows API.

**The import library**   The import library contains information about the location of callable functions in kernel.exe, user.exe, and gdi.exe. At runtime your application uses the information in the import library to help it find and call the API routines. The import library for Microsoft C, WATCOM C, and Zortech C++ is named libw.lib. The import library for Borland C++ is named import.lib.

**The DLL advantage**   Because Windows uses dynamic-link libraries to provide callable functions, this means that only one copy of each library is kept in memory, even though more than one running application can call the API functions. This not only conserves system memory, but also means that the executable file for your application is smaller—many of the functions your program uses are located in the Windows API.

## Components of a typical Windows application

Windows application programming is multimodule programming. A number of source files are compiled and linked together to form a finished program, which is called a *Windows executable*.

The sample applications in the book are each built from a minimum of four source files. These source files include a module definition file, an #include file, a resource script file, and a C source file.

**The module definition file**   The module definition file contains information about the structure of the finished executable file. The information is used mainly by the linker. The module definition file, which carries a .def filename extension, describes options like the size of the local stack and the name of the message handler function.

**The #include file**   The #include file is a header file. It provides function prototypes, which declare the parameter lists and return values for the C functions you are building into your application. The #include file also defines assorted variables, including a list of menu identifiers called *ID constants* that make it possible for you to associate your core functions with specific menu items. The #include file uses an .h filename extension.

**The resource script file**   The resource script file, which carries the .rc filename extension, uses unique keywords to describe the resources your application will use at runtime. These resources include the menu system and its mnemonic keys. Other resources include accelerator keys, dialog boxes, and text strings.

**The C source file**   The C source file contains the core functions of your application. It also contains the mandatory WinMain() function, which is the starting point for execution. The message handler in your C source file is a switcher that calls the core functions you have built into your application. The C source file uses the .c filename extension.

# Compiling and linking a Windows application

In addition to the familiar C compiler and linker, a new development tool is required to build a typical Windows application. The new tool is the resource compiler. This triad of Windows programming tools provides the glue that binds together all the pieces of your application. If you are using a menu-driven, integrated development environment like QuickC for Windows or Turbo C++ for Windows, much of the compile process will be hidden from you, handled behind the scenes by the editor when you build your program prototype. Alternatively, if you are using Borland C++, Zortech C++, WATCOM C, or Microsoft C and the SDK, refer to FIG. 1-2 for a list of generic command lines you can use to compile and link a Windows application.

**Compiling**   Two compilers are needed to build a Windows application. They are the C compiler and the resource compiler. The C compiler collects together the .h #include file and the .c source file, and compiles them into .obj object code. The resource compiler collects together the .rc resource script file and the .h #include file, and compiles them into .res object code.

**Linking**   The linker combines .obj code modules and .lib code modules together to produce a Windows executable file with an .exe extension. First, the linker inspects the information in the .def module definition file. Next, it links your .obj code with the Windows import library and with any C functions from the runtime library that your code call. The linker uses a static link process to insert into your program the appropriate .obj modules from the C runtime library. However, a dynamic-link process is required for the Windows API functions that your application calls. The linker inserts the .obj code for the entire import library into your program. The API location information found in the import library allows dynamic linking of your application and Windows' DLL libraries at runtime.

The .exe file generated by the linker is still not yet ready to run. The resources must be attached to the executable.

**Resource binding**   The resource compiler attaches the .res object code to the executable file. The .res file contains the resources used by your application at runtime. The result is a Windows executable file.

**Stamping**   At the same time the resource compiler binds the resources to the executable file, it stamps the file with the Windows version number. Each Windows executable must have a version number embedded in its header. The retail version of Windows inspects the header at launch time. Windows will refuse to execute any file not carrying the correct Windows version number. Even if your application does not use any resources, you should still use the resource compiler to stamp the executable file generated by the linker.

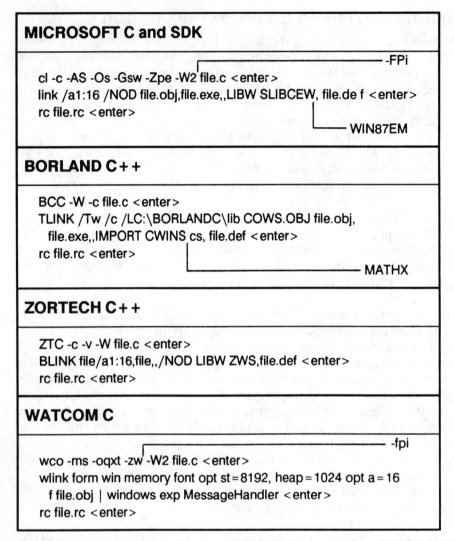

**MICROSOFT C and SDK**

```
                                                    ┌──────────── -FPi
                                                    │
cl -c -AS -Os -Gsw -Zpe -W2 file.c <enter>
link /a1:16 /NOD file.obj,file.exe,,LIBW SLIBCEW, file.de f <enter>
rc file.rc <enter>
                                                    │
                                                    └──── WIN87EM
```

**BORLAND C++**

```
BCC -W -c file.c <enter>
TLINK /Tw /c /LC:\BORLANDC\lib COWS.OBJ file.obj,
   file.exe,,IMPORT CWINS cs, file.def <enter>
rc file.rc <enter>
                        │
                        └──────────────── MATHX
```

**ZORTECH C++**

```
ZTC -c -v -W file.c <enter>
BLINK file/a1:16,file,,/NOD LIBW ZWS,file.def <enter>
rc file.rc <enter>
```

**WATCOM C**

```
                                                    ┌──────── -fpi
                                                    │
wco -ms -oqxt -zw -W2 file.c <enter>
wlink form win memory font opt st=8192, heap=1024 opt a=16
   f file.obj | windows exp MessageHandler <enter>
rc file.rc <enter>
```

**1-2** Sample command-lines for building the demonstration programs in the book using Microsoft C and the SDK, Borland C++, Symantec Zortech C++, and WATCOM C. If you are working with Turbo C++ for Windows or QuickC for Windows, use instead the integrated development environment (also called the IDE or simply the editor).

# Building the parts of a Windows application

Assembling the parts of a Windows application may seem complicated, but most programmers soon find themselves following familiar patterns as they build programs. Because all Windows applications must follow the Windows way of doing things, all applications are similar. You can use this similarity to your advantage by building a template, which is a set of generic files that you can easily modify to produce other specialized Windows applications, including animation.

A typical template contains code for the front-end (or user interface) of your program. This includes code that creates a main window, defines a set of menus, creates message boxes, creates and uses text strings in your program, and calls core C functions in your application.

## Creating a main window

Every Windows application must have a main window, although every application does not necessarily display its main window on the screen. Windows associates a hwnd window handle with each window.

In each demonstration program in the book, code for creating a main window is provided as a function named zInitMainWindow(). This function is called by WinMain(), which is the entry point for each application. In turn, zInitMainWindow() calls a function named CreateWindow(), which is located in the Windows graphics device interface DLL, gdi.exe.

## Creating a set of menus

The statements that define a menu system for your application are found in the .rc resource script file. The IDM_ constants used in the .rc file are defined in the .h #include file as menu ID constants. Each IDM_ constant refers to a menu item. These menu ID constants are used in a switch() block in the your C source file to permit your code to branch to appropriate core functions.

## Creating a message box

Message boxes are useful for providing information to your user at runtime. Windows' built-in MessageBox() function can be called by your application. You simply provide the strings to be displayed and the response buttons that you want. Windows takes care of all the low-level work. The buttons available for use in message boxes include Yes, No, Abort, Retry, Ignore, OK, and Cancel. Icons that can be automatically displayed by Windows in a message box include an exclamation point, question mark, stop sign, and information symbol.

Every message box returns a value that indicates the button selected by the user. Your code can use an if() statement to make a decision based on the user's selection.

## Creating and using strings

There are two different ways to use text strings in your Windows application. These are the *hard-coding method* and the *string resources method*.

Windows' built-in LoadString() function can be called to load a string that you have defined as a resource in the .rc resource script file. There are a number of advantages to this method. First, the string does not need to remain in memory when it is not being used because it is not intermingled with executable code. This gives Windows more flexibility in managing system memory. If the string is hard-coded into your C source file, it is always present in memory in the local heap. Second, putting all your strings into the .rc file means that all the runtime text used by your application can be found at a single location in the source files. This makes it a easier to modify the text for languages other than North American english, reducing the time and effort required to adapt your Windows application for the international marketplace.

Using hard-coded strings does have a few advantages, however. It is easier to read source code that contains embedded text strings. This can be helpful while you are building your prototype. If you are developing your Windows application for only the domestic market, you can safely use hard-coded strings, although it contradicts the underlying philosophy of Windows application development.

## Using core graphics functions

The core C code that you build into your Windows graphics application will likely involve graphics output. This imagery is generated by calls to the GDI, which is an acronym for the Windows graphics device interface. The callable functions of the GDI are found in the gdi.exe dynamic-link library.

Because the GDI can be called by any application that is running in the Windows environment, you must carefully describe to the GDI the context of any call you make. *Context* means the assumptions you are making about existing conditions when you call a GDI function. Windows recognizes different types of contexts, but the most important context for animation programmers is the display-context.

**The display-context**  The display-context specifies which window is to be used by the GDI for graphics output. It also defines the current pen color, brush color, clipping boundaries, background color, and so on. You must establish a display-context before calling any graphics functions in the GDI. Windows supports only a finite number of common display-contexts, so you should always release a display-context after you are finished with it. This usually means that you set a display-context at the beginning of your function and release the display-context before returning from your function. Animation programs often set a display-context at application startup and release it when the application ends.

**Typical code**  A typical block of C graphics code first creates drawing tools—these are the pens and brushes that will be used later. Then the code calls the GDI's GetDC() function in order to establish a display-context. The handle to the application's main window is passed to the GDI in the GetDC() parameter list. GetDC() returns a handle to the new display context.

Each time a display-context is established, Windows sets up a default set of drawing parameters. If your application needs a different pen color than the default black color, for example, then you must explicitly select another drawing tool into the display-context. You use the GDI's SelectObject() function to do this.

After creating the graphics and images you want, you must tidy up before returning from your function. First, you use the SelectObject() function to restore the default drawing tools to the display-context. Then you call the GDI function named ReleaseDC() to release the display-context that you were using. Finally, you destroy the custom drawing tools you created, freeing the memory they occupied.

## A sample application

*Sample App* The sample application presented in this chapter is a template. It demonstrates a front-end that can be used for any Windows graphics application, including animation. The sample application is in large part display-independent and provides a significant measure of cross-compiler compatibility. Like many of the sample applications in the book, the program has been tested with the compilers and display modes shown in FIG. 1-3.

The screen image in FIG. 1-4 illustrates the startup display of the sample application, which is named template.exe. The image in FIG. 1-5 shows the Demo menu from template.exe, which provides nominal graphics output.

### A reusable framework

The template.exe demonstration program is in fact a reconfigurable template, complete with a working menu system, mnemonic keys, accelerator keys, message boxes, and other elements that you can use to build more advanced applications.

The template.exe demo is built from four modules, including a .def module definition file, an .h #include file, an .rc resource script file, and a .c source module. All of these production files are presented as ready-to-use source code in the program listing later in the chapter. The source files are also provided on the companion disk. You can refer to the appropriate appendix for instructions on how to build template.exe with QuickC for Windows, Turbo C++ for Windows, Borland C++, Zortech C++, WATCOM C, and Microsoft C and the SDK.

## What the program does: A user's guide

*User's Guide* You can use either mouse or keyboard to experiment with the sample application. Simply point and click to navigate through the menus using a mouse. Use the arrow keys, enter key, and escape key to manually navigate through the menus using your keyboard. You can also use the underscored mnemonic keys from the keyboard, saving you the trouble of using the down-arrow key to scroll down a list of menu items.

| | VGA 640 x 480 16 clr | SVGA 640 x 480 256 clr | SVGA 800 x 600 16 clr | XGA 1024 x 768 2 clr | VGA 640 x 480 2 clr | EGA 640 x 350 16 clr |
|---|---|---|---|---|---|---|
| QUICK C for Windows | ✔ | ✔ | ✔ | ✔ | ✔ | ✔ |
| Turbo C++ for Windows | ✔ | ✔ | ✔ | ✔ | ✔ | ✔ |
| *Microsoft C and SDK | ✔ | ✔ | ✔ | ✔ | ✔ | ✔ |
| Borland C++ | ✔ | | | | | |
| Zortech C++ | ✔ | | | | | |
| WATCOM C | ✔ | | | | | |

**\*Microsoft C and SDK were used to validate the 640 x 350 x 2-clr EGA mode and the 720 x 348 x 2-clr Hercules mode.**

**1-3** The sample applications in the book have been subjected to rigorous quality assurance testing. Each program listing has been test-built using different compilers. The resulting executables have been test-run and validated under Windows in different screen modes.

After you have pulled down a menu, simply tap the mnemonic key to jump directly to the desired menu item.

The menus also support accelerator keys. An accelerator key is a shortcut key that can activate the feature it supports from anywhere in the program. You do not need to pull down a menu to access a menu item that is supported by an accelerator key. If a menu item is supported by an accelerator key, the keystroke combination is listed immediately to the right of the menu item in the menu.

## Menus and message boxes

The IBM System Application Architecture (SAA) Common User Access (CUA) document specifies a set of standards for programs that run in windowing environments. The template.exe demo program provides a number of SAA CUA-compliant menus and features.

**About** It has become customary for a Windows application to provide an About box that contains the program's name, copyright information, production credits, advertisements for other software products marketed by the publisher, and so on. You can click on the Help menu and select About to

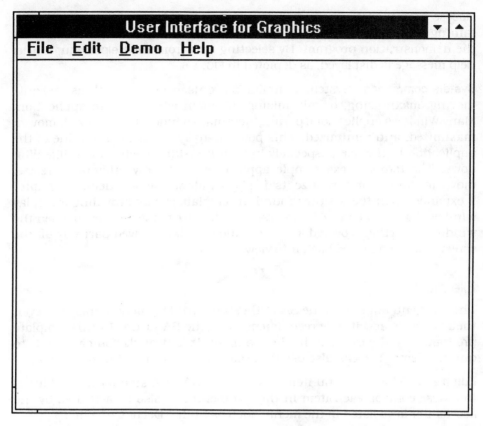

**1-4** The startup display window for the sample application. The image surface of the addressable client area measures 400 × 300 pixels.

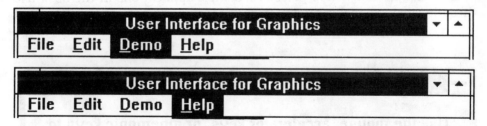

**1-5** Menu items from the sample application. The Demo menu provides interactive controls for experimenting with the application at runtime. The Help menu provides access to copyright and licensing notes, as well as a runtime help message.

cause the sample application to display its About box. Click on the OK button or press the Enter key to remove the message box.

**Help menu**   It has also become a tradition for Windows applications to offer a Help menu, usually as the last item on the main menu bar. Selecting

License from the Help menu will cause a message box to be displayed, containing information about the License Agreement and Limited Warranty for the demonstration program. By selecting Help from the Help menu, a brief help message is displayed, as depicted in FIG. 1-6.

**System commands**  System commands are user actions such as resizing, moving, maximizing, or minimizing the main window of an application. Many Windows applications permit their main window to be resized, moved, maximized, and minimized. This policy usually enhances the value of the application to the user, especially in a multitasking environment like Windows. The template.exe sample application traps any attempt to resize, move, maximize, or minimize its display window. The next demo in chapter 2 expands upon the features found in template.exe by providing a display window that can be moved and graphics that are persistent, even when the window is partially covered and then uncovered, or moved part way off the screen and then moved back into view.

## File menu

The File menu adheres to the SAA CUA standard. The menu items, and even their order, is specifically recommended by the SAA CUA. In this template program only the Exit item in the File menu is activated. You can use it to quit the demo. You can also use the system menu to stop the application.

**Edit menu**  The Edit menu items follow the SAA CUA standard. In addition to mouse control, each item in the Edit menu can also be activated by the accelerator keys listed in the menu, such as Shift + Del or Ctrl + Ins.

**Demo menu**  As shown in FIG. 1-5, you can use the menu items in the Demo menu to change the client area to black or to white. The size of the client area is fixed at 400 × 300 pixels. All sample applications in the book use these dimensions, making it easier for you to build animation programs and

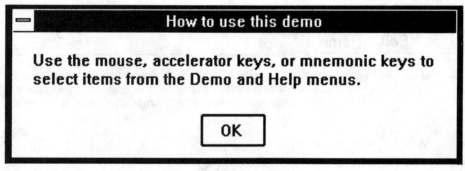

**1-6**  The About message box from the sample application.

export them to videotape or television, both of which conform to a 4:3 screen ratio.

While you are experimenting with template.exe, you can observe the non-persistent graphics by using the Demo menu to set the client area to black, then click on another program group to partially cover the template.exe window. When you click on the demo's window to bring it to the front, you can see how the client area was not refreshed correctly when the window is uncovered.

# How the source code works: A programmer's guide

The template.exe demonstration program provides a generic front-end by using the .rc file to define a menu system, accelerator keys, and string table. The menu and string IDs needed by the .c source file are defined in the .h file. The .c source file uses a message loop to fetch mouse and keystroke messages from the queue. It then dispatches a message to the message handler. The message handler uses a switch() statement to call the appropriate functions in the .c source file.

## How the .h file works

The program listing for the .h #include file is presented in FIG. 1-8. Function prototypes are provided in lines 0014 through 0018. This block is sandwiched by an #if !defined . . . #endif preprocessor directive.

This ensures that the function prototypes are not used in the .rc file, which has no need for them. The .h #include file is included by both the .rc file and by the .c file.

The menu ID constants are found in lines 0025 through 0043. It is good programming practice to use the prefix IDM_ for each constant. These constants are used by the message handler in the .c source file, which relies on a switch() block to compare them to incoming messages fetched from the queue.

Lines 0049 through 0057 contain the string ID constants. These will be used by the .rc file when it defines the text strings. They are also used by the .c source file when it loads the string resources at runtime.

## How the .rc file works

The program listing for the .rc resource script file is presented in FIG. 1-9. This file specifies resources that the sample application will use at runtime, including the menus, accelerator keys, and string resources. Note line 0010, which uses the #define preprocessor directive to define the variable zRCFILE before it attempts to #include template.h at line 0012. This ensures that the compiler does not attempt to declare function prototypes in the .rc file.

**Menus**    Lines 0018 through 0051 describe the menu system for the sample application. Notice how the IDM_ menu ID constants are assigned to each menu item, giving the .c file the tools it needs to identify specific menu items that can be selected by the user at runtime.

The & ampersand character signifies a mnemonic key. Windows will underscore mnemonic keys at runtime. The \t token causes Windows to tab over before displaying the menu text that describes accelerator keys. The pop-up Edit menu, described by lines 0029 through 0037, is the only menu that uses accelerator keys, which can be used from anywhere in the program at runtime. Unlike accelerator keys, the underscored mnemonic keys can be accessed only when the user is navigating the appropriate part of the menu system. The accelerator keys used by the Edit menu are defined at lines 0059 through 0063 in the .rc file. Note how an IDM_ menu ID constant is assigned to each VK_ virtual key ID.

The horizontal lines that appear in the menus at runtime are created by the SEPARATOR keyword, as shown in line 0042, for example.

**String resources**    The STRINGTABLE keyword at line 0075 indicates the beginning of string definitions, which run from line 0076 through line 0086. Each string is assigned an IDS_ string ID constant. The string ID constant will be used by the .c source file whenever it needs to load a string it needs at runtime.

The line endings that appear in the middle of strings in the string table are for publishing purposes only. They make the source code easier to read, but they are not permitted by the resource compiler. If you are typing the listings from the book, type each string on a single line with no line-breaks.

## How the .c file works

The program listing for the .c source file is presented in FIG. 1-10. This file contains the WinMain() function, which is the entry point for the application. WinMain() contains the message loop that fetches incoming messages from Windows. The .c source file also contains the message handler, a function that identifies incoming messages and calls the appropriate function in the .c source file.

**Included files**    Line 0036 #includes windows.h, which contains variable declarations, constant definitions, and function prototypes necessary for all Windows applications. Line 0037 #includes template.h, which contains function prototypes, menu ID constants, and string ID constants.

**Static variables**    Static variables are global variables that are visible throughout the .c source file. Lines 0043 through 0067 declare and occasionally initialize static variables for template.c.

Line 0044 defines the width of the window, expressed in pixels. Line 0045 defines the height. In their current implementation, zWINDOW_WIDTH and zWINDOW_HEIGHT produce a caption bar, menu bar, and borders that properly frame a 400 × 300 client area no matter which display mode is being used by Windows—640 × 480, 800 × 600, or 1024 × 768. (If you are working with an EGA, change line 0045 from a value of 346 to 342. The odd size of the default font used by Windows when running in the EGA 640 × 350 mode causes the caption bar and menu bar to occupy more raster lines at the expense of the client area.) The variables that are declared and initialized at lines 0064 through 0067 are used when the program loads strings for message boxes.

**The WinMain() function**  The WinMain() function is located at lines 0074 through 0129. This is the entry point for the application when Windows launches the program. The code at lines 0083 through 0088 uses the FindWindow() function to ensure that this is the only copy of the application that is running. This check is used because, in addition to Windows' ability to run more than one application at a time, it can also run more than one copy of the same application.

*Note*

The single-copy rule is enforced by all the demo programs in the book. Multiple instances of a Windows application can cause a variety of side effects (especially with resources), which can make more difficult to master the techniques of animation programming.

The code at lines 0090 through 0095 determines the capabilities of the screen display. First, a call to GetDesktopWindow() grabs the handle to the entire screen display. Then a call to GetDC() establishes a display-context for the entire screen. Subsequent calls to GetDeviceCaps() are used to determine the horizontal and vertical resolution of the screen.

The code at lines 0098 and 0099 uses the horizontal and vertical resolution of the screen to ensure that the application's window is centered on the screen.

The code at lines 0104 through 0109 builds and displays the main window. Line 0105 calls core function zInitClass() to create a class of window. Then line 0106 creates a main window with the attributes of the class. Line 0108 calls API function ShowWindow() to display the main window. Finally, line 0110 calls LoadAccelerators() to load the accelerator keys table that was defined in the .rc resource script file.

The code at lines 0113 through 0119 checks for the presence of a mouse. If the mouse hardware is not installed, the code at lines 0116 through 0118 displays a message box to inform the user. The template.exe demo will continue to run if no mouse is found.

**The message loop**  The message loop for the demonstration program is located at lines 0122 through 0127. A call to GetMessage() checks for incoming messages. Then DispatchMessage() is called to send a message to the application's message handler.

**The message handler**  The message handler for template.exe is located at line 0135. The switch() statement at line 0139 is used to identify the nature of the incoming message. Line 0142 detects WM_COMMAND messages, which signify menu items being selected by the user. Line 0194 detects if the application is being terminated by the user. Line 0198 detects if the user is attempting to invoke a system command like resizing, moving, minimizing, or maximizing the main window. Finally, lines 0216 and 0217 pass the message back to Windows if it is not usable by the application.

The case statements at lines 0157, 0163, and 0169 carry out appropriate processing when the user selects a menu item from the Demo menu. The GDI's PatBlt() function is called to change the client area to white or black as required.

**The window class**   The attributes of the class that describe the main window are defined by the function located at lines 0226 through 0240. Note in particular lines 0234 and 0235, which define the application's icon and mouse cursor. The icon and cursor used by template.exe are stock items provided by the retail version of Windows.

Line 0236 calls the GDI's CreateSolidBrush() function to set the window's background color to white. This function and other GDI routines are described in more detail in the next chapter.

**Creating the main window**   The function at lines 0247 through 0260 creates the display window of the application. Line 0250 loads a string resource that will become the caption (title) of the main window. Line 0253 implements the caption. Line 0256 instructs Windows where to locate the window on the screen. Line 0257 specifies the dimensions of the window, using constants defined at the beginning of the .c source file.

**Clearing the window**   The function at lines 0270 through 0277 blanks the client area of the main window. The comments along the right side of the program listing explain the purpose of each GDI call.

## Program listings for the sample application

*Code*   The program listings presented here contain all the source code you need to build and run the sample application. The module definition file is provided in FIG. 1-7. The #include file is found in FIG. 1-8. The resource script file is presented in FIG. 1-9. The C source file is contained in FIG. 1-10.

*Disk*   **Companion disk**   If you have the companion disk, the source files are provided as template.def, template.h, template.rc, and template.c.

*License*   **License**   You can paste the royalty-free source code into your own applications and distribute the resulting executable files under the conditions of the License Agreement and Limited Warranty in FIG. 10 in the introduction to the book.

**1-7**  The module definition file listing for the sample application.

```
0001   NAME           DEFDEMO
0002   DESCRIPTION    'Copyright 1992 Lee Adams.  All rights reserved.'
0003   EXETYPE        WINDOWS
0004   STUB           'WINSTUB.EXE'
0005   CODE           PRELOAD MOVEABLE
0006   DATA           PRELOAD MOVEABLE MULTIPLE
0007   HEAPSIZE       1024
0008   STACKSIZE      8192
0009   EXPORTS        zMessageHandler
```

**1-8**  The include file listing for the sample application.

```
0001   /*
0002   -----------------------------------------------------------------
0003                      Include file TEMPLATE.H
0004            Copyright 1992 Lee Adams.  All rights reserved.
0005      Include this file in the .RC resource script file and in the
0006      .C source file.  It contains function prototypes, menu ID
0007      constants, and string ID constants.
0008   -----------------------------------------------------------------
0009   -----------------------------------------------------------------
0010                         Function prototypes
0011   -----------------------------------------------------------------
0012                                                                 */
0013   #if !defined(zRCFILE)              /* if not an .RC file... */
0014      LONG FAR PASCAL zMessageHandler(HWND, unsigned, WORD, LONG);
0015      int PASCAL WinMain(HANDLE,HANDLE,LPSTR,int);
0016      HWND zInitMainWindow(HANDLE);
0017      BOOL zInitClass(HANDLE);
0018   static void zClear(HWND);               /* blank the viewport */
0019   #endif
0020   /*
0021   -----------------------------------------------------------------
0022                         Menu ID constants
0023   -----------------------------------------------------------------
0024                                                                 */
0025   #define IDM_New           1
0026   #define IDM_Open          2
0027   #define IDM_Save          3
0028   #define IDM_SaveAs        4
0029   #define IDM_Exit          5
0030
0031   #define IDM_Undo          6
0032   #define IDM_Cut           7
0033   #define IDM_Copy          8
0034   #define IDM_Paste         9
0035   #define IDM_Delete        10
0036
0037   #define IDM_Black         11
0038   #define IDM_White         12
0039   #define IDM_Clear         13
0040
0041   #define IDM_About         14
0042   #define IDM_License       15
0043   #define IDM_GeneralHelp   16
0044   /*
0045   -----------------------------------------------------------------
0046                         String ID constants
0047   -----------------------------------------------------------------
```

```
0048                                                                          */
0049   #define IDS_Caption        1
0050   #define IDS_Warning        2
0051   #define IDS_NoMouse        3
0052   #define IDS_About          4
0053   #define IDS_AboutText      5
0054   #define IDS_License        6
0055   #define IDS_LicenseText    7
0056   #define IDS_Help           8
0057   #define IDS_HelpText       9
0058   /*
0059   -----------------------------------------------------------------
0060                         End of include file
0061   -----------------------------------------------------------------
0062                                                                          */
```

**1-9** The resource script file listing for the sample application.

```
0001   /*
0002   -----------------------------------------------------------------
0003                  Resource script file TEMPLATE.RC
0004            Copyright 1992 Lee Adams.  All rights reserved.
0005     This file defines the menu resources, the accelerator key
0006     resources, and the string resources that will be used by the
0007     demonstration application at runtime.
0008   -----------------------------------------------------------------
0009                                                                          */
0010   #define zRCFILE
0011   #include <WINDOWS.H>
0012   #include "TEMPLATE.H"
0013   /*
0014   -----------------------------------------------------------------
0015                         Script for menus
0016   -----------------------------------------------------------------
0017                                                                          */
0018   MENUS1 MENU
0019     BEGIN
0020     POPUP "&File"
0021       BEGIN
0022         MENUITEM  "&New", IDM_New, GRAYED
0023         MENUITEM  "&Open...", IDM_Open, GRAYED
0024         MENUITEM  "&Save", IDM_Save, GRAYED
0025         MENUITEM  "Save &As...", IDM_SaveAs, GRAYED
0026         MENUITEM SEPARATOR
0027         MENUITEM  "E&xit", IDM_Exit
0028       END
0029     POPUP "&Edit"
0030       BEGIN
0031         MENUITEM  "&Undo\tAlt+BkSp", IDM_Undo, GRAYED
0032         MENUITEM SEPARATOR
0033         MENUITEM  "Cu&t\tShift+Del", IDM_Cut, GRAYED
0034         MENUITEM  "&Copy\tCtrl+Ins", IDM_Copy, GRAYED
0035         MENUITEM  "&Paste\tShift+Ins", IDM_Paste, GRAYED
0036         MENUITEM  "&Delete\tDel", IDM_Delete, GRAYED
0037       END
0038     POPUP "&Demo"
0039       BEGIN
0040         MENUITEM "&Blackness", IDM_Black
0041         MENUITEM "&Whiteness", IDM_White
0042         MENUITEM SEPARATOR
```

**1-9** Continued.

```
0043        MENUITEM "&Clear the display", IDM_Clear
0044      END
0045    POPUP "&Help"
0046      BEGIN
0047        MENUITEM "&About", IDM_About
0048        MENUITEM "&License", IDM_License
0049        MENUITEM "&Help", IDM_GeneralHelp
0050      END
0051    END
0052  /*
0053  -----------------------------------------------------------------
0054                    Script for accelerator keys
0055  -----------------------------------------------------------------
0056                                                              */
0057  KEYS1 ACCELERATORS
0058    BEGIN
0059    VK_BACK, IDM_Undo, VIRTKEY, ALT
0060    VK_DELETE, IDM_Cut, VIRTKEY, SHIFT
0061    VK_INSERT, IDM_Copy, VIRTKEY, CONTROL
0062    VK_INSERT, IDM_Paste, VIRTKEY, SHIFT
0063    VK_DELETE, IDM_Delete, VIRTKEY
0064    END
0065  /*
0066  -----------------------------------------------------------------
0067                        Script for strings
0068    Programmer's Notes:  If you are typing this listing, set your
0069    margins to a line length of 255 characters so you can create
0070    lengthy strings without embedded carriage returns.  The line
0071    wraparounds in the following STRINGTABLE script are used for
0072    readability only in this printout.
0073  -----------------------------------------------------------------
0074                                                              */
0075  STRINGTABLE
0076    BEGIN
0077      IDS_Caption      "User Interface for Graphics"
0078      IDS_Warning      "Graphics system warning"
0079      IDS_NoMouse      "No mouse found.  Some features of this
0080      demonstration program may require a mouse."
0080      IDS_About        "About this program"
0081      IDS_AboutText    "This is a demo from Windcrest McGraw-Hill
0081      book 4114.  Copyright 1992 Lee Adams.  All rights reserved."
0082      IDS_License      "License Agreement"
0083      IDS_LicenseText "You can use this code as part of your own
0083      software product subject to the License Agreement and Limited
0083      Warranty in Windcrest McGraw-Hill book 4114 and on its
0083      companion disk."
0084      IDS_Help         "How to use this demo"
0085      IDS_HelpText     "Use the mouse, accelerator keys, or mnemonic
0085      keys to select items from the Demo and Help menus."
0086    END
0087  /*
0088  -----------------------------------------------------------------
0089                    End of resource script file
0090  -----------------------------------------------------------------
0091                                                              */
```

**1-10** The C source file listing for the sample application, template.c. This demonstration program is ready to build using QuickC for Windows, Turbo C++ for Windows, Microsoft C and the SDK, Borland C++, Symantec Zortech C++, WATCOM C, and other compilers. See FIG. 1-2 for sample command-lines to build the program. Guidelines for using your compiler are provided in the appropriate appendix at the back of the book.

```
0001   /*
0002   ------------------------------------------------------------------
0003      Reusable template for Windows applications that use a hidden
0004      frame, display-independent graphics, and persistent images.
0005   ------------------------------------------------------------------
0006      Source file: TEMPLATE .C
0007      Release version:  1.00                  Programmer:  Lee Adams
0008      Type:   C source file for Windows application development.
0009      Compilers:  Microsoft C and SDK, Borland C++, Zortech C++,
0010        QuickC for Windows, Turbo C++ for Windows, WATCOM C.
0011      Memory model:   small.
0012      Dependencies:   TEMPLATE.DEF module definition file, TEMPLATE.H
0013                      include file, TEMPLATE.RC resource script file,
0014                      and TEMPLATE.C source file.
0015      Output and features:  Demonstrates a user-interface template
0016        suitable for graphics applications.
0017      Publication: Contains material from Windcrest/McGraw-Hill book
0018        4114 published by TAB BOOKS Division of McGraw-Hill Inc.
0019      License:  As purchaser of the book you are granted a royalty-
0020        free license to distribute executable files generated using
0021        this code provided you accept the conditions of the License
0022        Agreement and Limited Warranty described in the book and on
0023        the companion disk.  Government users:  This software and
0024        documentation are subject to restrictions set forth in The
0025        Rights in Technical Data and Computer Software clause at
0026        252.227-7013 and elsewhere.
0027   ------------------------------------------------------------------
0028         (c) Copyright 1992 Lee Adams.  All rights reserved.
0029         Lee Adams(tm) is a trademark of Lee Adams.
0030   ------------------------------------------------------------------
0031
0032   ------------------------------------------------------------------
0033                          Include files
0034   ------------------------------------------------------------------
0035                                                                   */
0036   #include <WINDOWS.H>
0037   #include "TEMPLATE.H"
0038   /*
0039   ------------------------------------------------------------------
0040            Static variables visible throughout this file
0041   ------------------------------------------------------------------
0042                                                                   */
0043   /* ------------------ window specifications ------------------ */
0044   #define zWINDOW_WIDTH 408                    /* width of window */
0045   #define zWINDOW_HEIGHT 346                  /* height of window */
0046   #define zFRAMEWIDE 400                 /* width of client area */
0047   #define zFRAMEHIGH 300                /* height of client area */
0048   int WindowX, WindowY;                   /* location of window */
0049
0050   /* -------------------- instance operations -------------------- */
0051   HANDLE hInst;                        /* handle to this instance */
0052   HWND MainhWnd;                   /* handle to the main window */
0053   HANDLE hAccel;              /* handle to accelerator keys table */
0054
0055   /* -------------------- mouse and cursor -------------------- */
```

```
0056  HCURSOR hPrevCursor;                    /* handle to default cursor */
0057  HCURSOR hHourGlass;                     /* handle to hourglass cursor */
0058  int MousePresent;               /* will indicate if mouse present */
0059
0060  /* ------------------- runtime conditions -------------------- */
0061  int DisplayWidth, DisplayHeight;          /* screen resolution */
0062
0063  /* ------------------- message box operations ----------------- */
0064  char lpCaption[51];       /* will hold caption for message boxes */
0065  int Max= 50;                       /* maximum length of caption */
0066  char lpMessage[250];       /* will hold text for message boxes */
0067  int MaxText= 249;                   /* maximum length of text */
0068
0069  /*
0070  -------------------------------------------------------------------
0071                  Entry point for the application
0072  -------------------------------------------------------------------
0073                                                                 */
0074  int PASCAL WinMain(HANDLE hInstance, HANDLE hPrevInstance,
0075                     LPSTR lpCmdLine, int nCmdShow)
0076  {
0077    MSG msg;                          /* will hold incoming messages */
0078    HWND hWndPrev;          /* handle to window of another instance */
0079    HWND hDesktopWnd;        /* handle to full-screen desktop window */
0080    HDC hDCcaps;             /* display-context of desktop window */
0081
0082  /* ------------ ensure only one instance is running ----------- */
0083  hWndPrev = FindWindow("DEMOCLASS", NULL);
0084  if (hWndPrev != NULL)         /* if another instance was found... */
0085    {
0086    BringWindowToTop(hWndPrev);             /* make it active... */
0087    return FALSE;               /* ...and terminate this instance */
0088    }
0089
0090  /* --------- determine capabilities of screen display ---------- */
0091  hDesktopWnd= GetDesktopWindow();
0092  hDCcaps= GetDC(hDesktopWnd);
0093  DisplayWidth= GetDeviceCaps(hDCcaps,HORZRES);
0094  DisplayHeight= GetDeviceCaps(hDCcaps,VERTRES);
0095  ReleaseDC(hDesktopWnd,hDCcaps);
0096
0097  /* ------- calculate screen position to center the window ------ */
0098  WindowX= (DisplayWidth - zWINDOW_WIDTH) / 2;      /* horizontal */
0099  WindowY= (DisplayHeight - zWINDOW_HEIGHT) /2;       /* vertical */
0100  if (WindowX < 0) WindowX= 0;
0101  if (WindowY < 0) WindowY= 0;
0102
0103  /* -------------- create and display the window --------------- */
0104  hInst= hInstance;                  /* remember the instance handle */
0105  if (!zInitClass(hInstance)) return FALSE;      /* create the class */
0106  MainhWnd= zInitMainWindow(hInstance);         /* create the window */
0107  if (!MainhWnd) return FALSE;    /* exit if no window was created */
0108  ShowWindow(MainhWnd, nCmdShow);             /* display the window */
0109  UpdateWindow(MainhWnd);                  /* send a paint message */
0110  hAccel= LoadAccelerators(hInstance,"KEYS1"); /* accelerator keys */
0111
0112  /* -------------------- check for mouse -------------------- */
0113  MousePresent= GetSystemMetrics(SM_MOUSEPRESENT);
0114  if (!MousePresent)                   /* if no active mouse found */
0115    {
0116    LoadString(hInst,IDS_Warning,lpCaption,Max);   /* load caption */
```

```
0117    LoadString(hInst,IDS_NoMouse,lpMessage,MaxText);  /* load text */
0118    MessageBox(GetFocus(),lpMessage,lpCaption,MB_OK);   /* message */
0119    }
0120
0121  /* ---------- begin retrieving messages for the window --------- */
0122  while (GetMessage(&msg,0,0,0))
0123    {
0124    if(TranslateAccelerator(MainhWnd, hAccel, &msg)) continue;
0125    TranslateMessage(&msg);
0126    DispatchMessage(&msg);
0127    }
0128  return(msg.wParam);
0129  }
0130  /*
0131  ----------------------------------------------------------------
0132                    Switcher for incoming messages
0133  ----------------------------------------------------------------
0134                                                                 */
0135  LONG FAR PASCAL zMessageHandler(HWND hWnd, unsigned message,
0136                                  WORD wParam, LONG lParam)
0137  {
0138    HDC hDC; /* local variable will hold handle to display-context */
0139  switch (message)
0140    {
0141
0142    case WM_COMMAND:        /* if user has selected a menu item... */
0143      switch(wParam)
0144        {
0145        case IDM_New:    break;
0146        case IDM_Open:   break;
0147        case IDM_Save:   break;
0148        case IDM_SaveAs: break;
0149        case IDM_Exit:   PostQuitMessage(0); break;
0150
0151        case IDM_Undo:   break;
0152        case IDM_Cut:    break;
0153        case IDM_Copy:   break;
0154        case IDM_Paste:  break;
0155        case IDM_Delete: break;
0156
0157        case IDM_Black:
0158                hDC= GetDC(hWnd);
0159                PatBlt(hDC,0,0,zFRAMEWIDE,zFRAMEHIGH,BLACKNESS);
0160                ReleaseDC(hWnd,hDC);
0161                MessageBeep(0);
0162                break;
0163        case IDM_White:
0164                hDC= GetDC(hWnd);
0165                PatBlt(hDC,0,0,zFRAMEWIDE,zFRAMEHIGH,WHITENESS);
0166                ReleaseDC(hWnd,hDC);
0167                MessageBeep(0);
0168                break;
0169        case IDM_Clear:
0170                zClear(hWnd);
0171                MessageBeep(0);
0172                break;
0173
0174        case IDM_About:
0175           LoadString(hInst,IDS_About,lpCaption,Max);
0176           LoadString(hInst,IDS_AboutText,lpMessage,MaxText);
```

```
0177            MessageBox(GetFocus(),lpMessage,lpCaption,MB_OK);
0178            break;
0179          case IDM_License:
0180            LoadString(hInst,IDS_License,lpCaption,Max);
0181            LoadString(hInst,IDS_LicenseText,lpMessage,MaxText);
0182            MessageBox(GetFocus(),lpMessage,lpCaption,MB_OK);
0183            break;
0184          case IDM_GeneralHelp:
0185            LoadString(hInst,IDS_Help,lpCaption,Max);
0186            LoadString(hInst,IDS_HelpText,lpMessage,MaxText);
0187            MessageBox(GetFocus(),lpMessage,lpCaption,MB_OK);
0188            break;
0189          default:
0190            return(DefWindowProc(hWnd, message, wParam, lParam));
0191        }
0192      break;
0193
0194    case WM_DESTROY:  /* if user is terminating the application... */
0195      PostQuitMessage(0);
0196      break;
0197
0198    case WM_SYSCOMMAND:      /* if user selects a system command... */
0199      if ((wParam & 0xfff0)== SC_SIZE)
0200        {              /* intercept any attempt to resize the window */
0201        MessageBeep(0); break;
0202        }
0203      if ((wParam & 0xfff0)== SC_MOVE)
0204        {                /* intercept any attempt to move the window */
0205        MessageBeep(0); break;
0206        }
0207      if ((wParam & 0xfff0)== SC_MINIMIZE)
0208        {            /* intercept any attempt to minimize the window */
0209        MessageBeep(0); break;
0210        }
0211      if ((wParam & 0xfff0)== SC_MAXIMIZE)
0212        {            /* intercept any attempt to maximize the window */
0213        MessageBeep(0); break;
0214        }
0215
0216    default:
0217      return(DefWindowProc(hWnd, message, wParam, lParam));
0218    }
0219  return FALSE;
0220  }
0221  /*
0222  -------------------------------------------------------------------
0223           Initialize the attributes of the window class
0224  -------------------------------------------------------------------
0225                                                                    */
0226  BOOL zInitClass(HANDLE hInstance)
0227  {
0228    WNDCLASS WndClass;
0229  WndClass.style= 0;                              /* class style */
0230  WndClass.lpfnWndProc= zMessageHandler;       /* callback function */
0231  WndClass.cbClsExtra= 0;            /* unused, no customized data */
0232  WndClass.cbWndExtra= 0;            /* unused, no customized data */
0233  WndClass.hInstance= hInstance;    /* application that owns class */
0234  WndClass.hIcon= LoadIcon(NULL,IDI_EXCLAMATION); /* minimize icon */
0235  WndClass.hCursor= LoadCursor(NULL,IDC_ARROW);    /* app's cursor */
0236  WndClass.hbrBackground= /* specifies background color of window */
```

```
0237                     CreateSolidBrush(RGB(255,255,255));
0238 WndClass.lpszMenuName= "MENUS1";    /* name of .RC menu resource */
0239 WndClass.lpszClassName= "DEMOCLASS";         /* name of the class */
0240 return RegisterClass(&WndClass);        /* registers the class */
0241 }
0242 /*
0243 ------------------------------------------------------------------
0244                      Create the main window
0245 ------------------------------------------------------------------
0246                                                                 */
0247 HWND zInitMainWindow(HANDLE hInstance)
0248 {
0249   HWND hWnd;
0250 LoadString(hInstance,IDS_Caption,lpCaption,Max); /* load caption */
0251 hHourGlass= LoadCursor(NULL,IDC_WAIT);   /* load the wait cursor */
0252 hWnd= CreateWindow("DEMOCLASS",   /* create window of this class */
0253      lpCaption,                                    /* caption */
0254      WS_OVERLAPPED | WS_THICKFRAME | WS_MINIMIZEBOX |  /* type */
0255       WS_MAXIMIZEBOX | WS_CLIPCHILDREN,
0256      WindowX,WindowY,                       /* screen location */
0257      zWINDOW_WIDTH,zWINDOW_HEIGHT,       /* window dimensions */
0258      0,0,                      /* parent handle, menu or child ID */
0259      hInstance,(LPSTR)NULL); /* app instance and unused pointer */
0260 return hWnd;
0261 }
0262 /*
0263 ------------------------------------------------------------------
0264          THE CORE FUNCTIONS OF THE APPLICATION
0265 ------------------------------------------------------------------
0266 ------------------------------------------------------------------
0267                   Clear the display window.
0268 ------------------------------------------------------------------
0269                                                                 */
0270 static void zClear(HWND hWnd)
0271 {
0272   HDC hDC;
0273 hDC= GetDC(hWnd);                        /* get the display-context */
0274 PatBlt(hDC,0,0,zFRAMEWIDE,zFRAMEHIGH,WHITENESS);   /* make white */
0275 ReleaseDC(hWnd,hDC);                 /* release the display-context */
0276 return;
0277 }
0278 /*
0279 ------------------------------------------------------------------
0280                  End of the C source file
0281 ------------------------------------------------------------------
0282                                                                 */
```

# 2
# *Graphics*

Microsoft Windows provides a built-in graphics library called the *graphics device interface* (GDI). The functions of the GDI can be called by your application at runtime. The callable functions are found in gdi.exe, one of the dynamic-link libraries that is included with each retail version of Windows.

The GDI provides powerful graphics routines that are optimized for Windows. In addition to standard line, ellipse, and fill routines, the GDI offers a selection of dithering, bitblt, and clipping functions. These three categories of functions are particularly well-suited for advanced graphics work. The bitblt functions are especially useful for animation.

## The GDI

The GDI is a Windows-hosted graphics engine. The functions of the GDI can be called by any application running in the Windows environment. The GDI can direct its graphics output to the screen, memory, printer, disk file, and other devices. Because of this flexibility of output, you must provide a context each time you call a function in the GDI. A context is a set of assumptions that both you and the GDI are making about the current output device. The word device has special meaning to the GDI.

### Devices

*Here's Why---* Devices are focal points of input and output. The keyboard, mouse, and timer are input devices. The screen, printer, plotter, disk drive, and modem are output devices. Output devices can also include simulated devices in memory such as bitmaps and metafiles. A *bitmap* is a simulated drawing surface in memory. A *metafile* is a collection of

GDI function calls that can be used to store the means for recreating an image.

Before calling a graphics function, you must provide device-context information to the GDI. You must inform the GDI where and how to write the graphics output. You do this by creating a device-context.

## Device-contexts

A *device-context* represents an output device and its device driver. A *device driver* is the software that directly manipulates the hardware device. The printer has a device driver. The graphics adapters has a device driver. The mouse has a device driver.

If you are running Windows on a VGA-equipped computer, the software that manipulates the display memory of the graphics adapter is located in a driver named vga.drv. This driver usually resides in the c:\windows\system directory on your hard disk. Windows loads this device driver into memory at startup. When your application calls the GDI to create graphics imagery on the screen, the GDI calls routines in vga.drv to manipulate the VGA graphics adapter. The VGA adapter is the device, and vga.drv is the driver.

Device-contexts can describe a variety of output devices. A display-context is one type of device-context.

## Display-contexts

A *display-context* specifies a window on the screen. In particular, a display-context describes how graphics output is to be written to the client area of a particular window. The client area is the interior part, or drawing surface, of the window (not including the caption, menu bar, and borders). Windows programmers often use the acronym DC to mean either a display-context or a device-context.

# The display-context

Whenever you initialize a display-context for a window, Windows resets the graphics origin to the upper left corner of the window's client area and resets the clipping rectangle to the dimensions of the client area. The *graphics origin* is the pixel location described by coordinates 0,0. The *clipping rectangle* is a viewport for drawing—the GDI will clip all graphics at the edge of the viewport and will not draw outside the clipping rectangle. The graphics origin and clipping rectangle are just two of the many default attributes of a display-context.

## Default attributes

A summary of default DC attributes is shown in FIG. 2-1. Although each of

| DEFAULT DC ATTRIBUTES | |
|---|---|
| background color | white |
| background mode | opaque |
| brush color | white |
| pen color | black |
| text color | black |
| font | system font, System, proportional |
| clipping region | client area |
| DC origin | 0,0  (upper left corner, client area) |
| pen position | 0,0 |
| brush position | 0,0 |

**2-1** The display window of your graphics application will exhibit these default attributes unless you specify others.

these attributes can be changed by your application, many DCs are used in their default condition.

- The default background color is white. This means the GDI assumes that the background of the window's client area is white.
- The default brush color is white. Any filled solids that the GDI draws, such as rectangles, will be filled with white.
- The default pen color is black. Any lines, rectangles, ellipses, and polygons that the GDI draws will appear black against the white background.
- The default text color is black. The GDI will write black characters on a white field.
- The background mode is opaque. The background portion of each character cel will be opaque, overwriting and obliterating any image already on the screen. Dashed and dotted lines will be drawn in black, but the white spaces between the dashes will overwrite any existing graphics.
- The default clipping region is the client area. This means that drawing activity outside the client area will not be visible. All lines, rectangles, bitblts, and text will be clipped at the edges of the client area.
- The default origin for the graphics coordinate system is the upper left corner of the client area and the current position of the pen and the brush is reset to this 0,0 position.

## Creating a display-context

**Here's How...** To create a display-context you usually call GetDC() and pass to the GDI the handle of the window you want to use for graphics output. A handle is simply a number from an internal table that Windows uses to identify different contexts that it may be maintaining. GetDC() returns a handle to the display-context that has been created for you. You pass this handle to graphics function that you call in the GDI.

## Releasing a display-context

Because Windows maintains a finite number of display contexts, you should always release a display-context after you are finished with it. If you do not, some other application may not be able to create a display-context and may be prevented from writing to the screen.

You release a display-context by calling ReleaseDC(). Well-behaved applications usually create a display-context at the beginning of a function that produces graphics output, and release the display-context at the end of the function. Some animation programs create a display-context when they are launched and release it when they are terminated. This is more efficient than creating and releasing a display-context for each frame in the animation sequence.

## Saving and restoring a display-context

**Expert** You can save and restore display-contexts by calling SaveDC(). This is convenient if your application has changed the default attributes. The SaveDC() function saves the display-context information on a context stack. SaveDC() returns a handle to the information that it has stored. To restore a previously-saved display-context, you call RestoreDC().

SaveDC() and RestoreDC() are often used in graphics applications that manipulate more than one display window. Saving and restoring DCs with SaveDC() and RestoreDC() is more efficient than reconfiguring the default attributes each time you need to use the DC.

## Compatible device-contexts

A *compatible device-context* is a simulated display-context. The compatible device-context refers to a block of memory configured as a bitmap. A bitmap is a rectangular array of bits on which you can draw and perform other graphics operations.

In order for the contents of the bitmap to be copied to the application's window on the screen, the bitmap must possess many of the same DC attributes as the window. The compatible device-context refers to a device in memory (the bitmap) that is compatible with the display-context (the window on the screen).

Bitmaps are especially useful for storing the frames for an animation sequence.

# Drawing tools

Drawing tools provided in gdi.exe include pens, brushes, and fonts. Pens draw lines and shapes. Brushes fill areas with color. Fonts provide text, captions, and titles.

Before you use a drawing tool you must create and select it. When you are finished using it, you must delete it. Drawing tool functions are specialized GDI routines that create, select, and delete drawing tools. Drawing attribute functions are specialized routines that modify the way the drawing tools work.

You use drawing tools to perform output operations. Pens, brushes, and fonts are drawing tools. Output operations include lines, polygons, rectangles, ellipses, text, bitblts, metafiles, and others.

## Drawing tool functions

*Here's How...* You use drawing tool functions to create, select, and delete drawing tools. Before you can use a red pen, for example, you must create it and select it into the display-context. When you are finished using the red pen you deselect it by restoring the default pen to the display-context. Then you delete (destroy) the red pen in order to release the memory that it occupied.

**Creating drawing tools**   To create a new pen you use CreatePen(). To create a solid brush you call CreateSolidBrush(). To create a patterned brush you call CreateHatchBrush() or CreatePatternBrush(). Any drawing tool you create is called a *custom drawing tool*.

You can also choose from a selection of built-in drawing tools that Windows maintains, called *stock objects*. They include tools like transparent brushes and dashed pens. You call GetStockObject() to use one of these stock objects.

**Using drawing tools**   To use a drawing tool that you have created, you must select it into the display-context. You call SelectObject() to do this.

**Deleting drawing tools**   After you are finished using a custom drawing tool, you should destroy it. Destroying a drawing tool frees the memory that it occupied. Well-behaved applications manage memory carefully because memory is a shared system resource. More important, however, you cannot safely release a display-context until you have deselected any drawing tools that you have selected into it.

To deselect a drawing tool you call SelectObject() and select a default drawing tool back into the display-context. To destroy the custom drawing tool you call DeleteObject().

## Drawing attribute functions

 *Drawing attribute functions* are specialized routines that modify the way drawing tools operate. Drawing functions can change the background, the drawing mode, text color, and bitblt behavior.

**Background attributes**   To set the background color you can call SetBkColor(). To set the background mode, you use SetBkMode(). If the background mode is opaque, any gaps in dashed lines and patterned fills will be set to the background color. Underlying images will be overwritten and obliterated. If the background mode is transparent, the GDI will not modify the pixels under these gaps when drawing styled lines, patterned fills, and hatched fills. The background mode also affects how text is written. The noncharacter portion of the text cel is either opaque or transparent, according to the current background mode.

**Drawing modes**   The default drawing mode is overwrite. Any graphics you draw will cover anything already existing on the display surface. You can use the SetROP2() function to change the drawing mode that the GDI uses for pens and filled objects. Supported drawing modes include OR, XOR, AND, NOT, and others. These Boolean operators are called *raster-operation codes* by Windows programmers. For example, the R2_NOT raster-operation code is an exclusive-or operator useful for rubberbanding cursors.

**Bitblt stretching attributes**   The GDI can stretch or compress any bitmap that you are copying with a bitblt function. If the image is larger than your application's main window you can call SetStretchBltMode() to to set the current stretch mode. The stretch mode defines which scan lines or pixels will be deleted when the source bitmap is compressed to fit the available space. SetStretchBltMode() affects the operation of the StretchBlt() copying function. It has no effect on the BitBlt() function, which copies a bitmap at the same size, without expansion or compression.

**Text color**   The default color for text output is black. To change the default text color you can call SetTextColor(). Subsequent text will be drawn in the new color.

## Pens

To create a pen drawing tool you normally use CreatePen() and specify the style, width, and color that you want. Six styles are supported by Windows, including solid, dashed, and transparent. The default width is one unit, but you can specify a thicker pen. You can call CreatePen() with any color argument, but Windows uses only solid hues when drawing with a pen. This means you are limited to 16 pen colors if you are running Windows on a VGA-equipped computer, 256 colors with a SVGA, XGA, or 8514/A.

## Brushes

To create a brush drawing tool you usually call CreateSolidBrush(). You can request any color and Windows will provide the exact color you want or a reasonable approximation using dithering. If you are running Windows on a VGA-equipped computer, the GDI will use dithering if your selection is not one of the 16 colors available on a VGA. Dithering means mixing pixels of different hues so that the overall pattern mimics a desired color. If you are running Windows in a 256-color mode using an SVGA, 8514/A, or XGA graphics adapter, the GDI will use the extended hardware palette to create the pure hue you want.

## Fonts

To display text you can call TextOut(), which uses the current font. The default font is named System, which is a sans serif, proportional-spaced typeface. A number of other stock fonts are also available, including serif, sans serif, fixed-spacing, and proportional-spaced typefaces. You load a font by calling GetStockObject(). You select the font into the display-context by calling SelectObject(). You can use different colors by calling SetTextColor(). To display the text, you call TextOut(). You can modify the way the GDI displays fonts by calling CreateFont() and specifing the size, style, weight, and other attributes you want.

# Color

Color is an attribute of pens, brushes, and fonts. You must specify a color when you create a pen or brush. The easiest way to specify a color is to call RGB() using the intensities of the RGB guns as arguments. RGB() is a macro that returns a COLORREF value. You can use COLORREF to specify color when you call other GDI functions.

## RGB descriptions

*Here's Why...* The RGB() macro takes three arguments which represent the red, green, and blue guns of the cathode ray tube of the display monitor hardware. Each argument is of type BYTE and can range in value from 0 to 255. A value of 0 turns a gun completely off. A value of 255 turns it on to brightest intensity. RGB(0,0,0) results in black, because all three guns are off. RGB(255,255,255) produces bright white.

If the color you want is in the hardware palette of the installed graphics card, the GDI provides it as a pure hue, otherwise the GDI simulates the color by dithering.

## Color palettes

A color palette is a group of colors. The default palette is called the *system palette*, or *hardware palette*. This is the palette that Windows uses to display and manipulate application windows, menus, message boxes, dialog boxes, and icons. Windows initializes this palette at startup. You can call SetSystemPaletteUse() to change the hardware colors in the palette, although Windows will retain two entries (black and white) for its own use in window management. Any changes you make to the system palette will affect the entire screen.

**Logical palettes** A logical palette is a set of colors that your application specifies for its own use. Figure 2-2 shows GDI functions useful for creating and using a logical palette. Windows uses different methods to build your palette depending upon the graphics adapter being used. If you are using a VGA and a palette color is not one of the 16 hardware colors available on the VGA, Windows will use dithering to simulate the color. The default VGA system palette is shown in FIG. 2-3.

To allocate memory for the palette data you call LocalAlloc(). To define the colors in the palette you use CreatePalette(). Before you can use the palette's colors you must call SelectPalette() to select the palette into the display-context. RealizePalette() is used to add new colors to the RGB hardware table of SVGA, 8514/A, and XGA graphics adapters. Figure 2-4 shows the relationship between your application, the color index table (logical palette), the hardware lookup table (system palette), and the display monitor. Figure 2-5 illustrates the dithering thresholds that Windows uses when a requested color is not available in the hardware palette.

| COLOR FUNCTIONS | |
|---|---|
| LocalAlloc( ) | allocate memory to hold a palette structure |
| CreatePalette( ) | create a logical palette |
| SelectPalette( ) | select a logical palette into a display-context |
| RealizePalette( ) | map the logical palette to the system palette or hardware |
| PALETTEINDEX( ) | macro that selects a color from a palette at runtime |
| RGB( ) | macro that selects a logical color (often dithered) created at runtime |

**2-2** You can call the GDI to set individual colors or an entire palette of colors.

## VGA System Palette

| color index | displayed color | RGB gun settings in hardware lookup table |
|:---:|:---:|:---|
| 0 | black | 0, 0, 0 |
| 1 | red | 127, 0, 0 |
| 2 | green | 0, 127, 0 |
| 3 | brown | 127, 127, 0 |
| 4 | blue | 0, 0, 127 |
| 5 | magenta | 127, 0, 127 |
| 6 | cyan | 0, 127, 127 |
| 7 | light gray | 191, 191, 191 |
| 8 | dark gray | 127, 127, 127 |
| 9 | bright red | 255, 0, 0 |
| 10 | bright green | 0, 0, 0 |
| 11 | yellow | 0, 0, 0 |
| 12 | bright blue | 0, 0, 0 |
| 13 | bright magenta | 0, 0, 0 |
| 14 | bright cyan | 0, 0, 0 |
| 15 | white | 0, 0, 0 |

**2-3** Windows rewrites the contents of the system palette at startup. The pure hues shown here are available to all applications in the Windows environment.

## Output operations

The Windows GDI provides a variety of output operations that includes line, rectangle, polygon, ellipse, bitmap, region, clipboard, metafile, font, and mapping.

You call MoveTo() to specify the current pen position. No graphics are drawn by MoveTo(). Any subsequent line that you draw will use the new pen position as its starting point.

The LineTo() function draws a line from the current pen position to a point you specify when you call LineTo(). The current pen position is updated

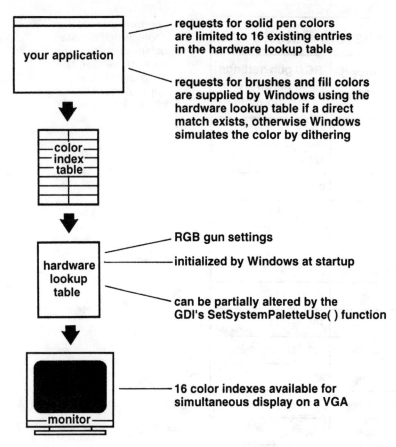

**2-4** A conceptual schematic showing how Windows fulfills requests for colors that your application makes.

and any subsequent line will start at the end of the previous line. The line is drawn using the current color, style, and thickness.

You can use Polyline() to draw a set of connected line segments. When you call Polyline(), you provide an array of coordinates representing the vertices of the polyline. The polyline is drawn using the current color, style, and thickness.

The Rectangle() function to draw a rectangle using four points that you provide as arguments. The rectangle is drawn using the color, style, and thickness of the current pen. The interior is filled using the current brush.

You can call RoundRect() to draw a round-cornered rectangle using four points that you provide as arguments. The rectangle is drawn using the color, style, and thickness of the current pen. The interior is filled using the current brush. The shape of the rounded corners is determined by ellipse parameters that you provide when you call RoundRect().

The Polygon() function creates a multisided polygon from an array of

## DITHERING THRESHOLDS

| | | | | |
|---|---|---|---|---|
| 255 | 203 | 151 | 99 | 47 |
| 251 | 199 | 147 | 95 | 43 |
| 247 | 195 | 143 | 91 | 39 |
| 243 | 191 | 139 | 87 | 35 |
| 239 | 187 | 135 | 83 | 31 |
| 235 | 183 | 131 | 79 | 27 |
| 231 | 179 | 127 | 75 | 23 |
| 227 | 175 | 123 | 71 | 19 |
| 223 | 171 | 119 | 67 | 15 |
| 219 | 167 | 115 | 63 | 11 |
| 215 | 163 | 111 | 59 | 7 |
| 211 | 159 | 107 | 55 | 3 |
| 207 | 155 | 103 | 51 | 0 |

- There are 64 dithered shades are available for each pure hue. Thresholding means that RGB (127, 0, 0), RGB (128, 0, 0), RGB (129, 0, 0), and RGB (130, 0, 0) are each displayed as normal -intensity red.

- 47 is the darkest shadow value in the lib3d 3D shading routines.

- 191 is solid light gray.

- 127 is solid dark gray and solid normal blue, green, cyan, red, magenta, and brown.

**2-5** Your application can use almost any color, because the GDI uses dithering to approximate a hue that is not present in the system palette.

points that you provide. If the final point does not close the polygon, Polygon() will close it for you by connecting the final point to the first point. The polygon is drawn using the color, style, and thickness of the current pen. The interior is filled with the current brush using a filling algorithm that you specify by calling SetPolyFillMode(). For most simple polygons, the default filling mode is satisfactory.

You can draw circles and ellipses by calling Ellipse(). You provide four sets of X-Y coordinates to specify the bounding box that circumscribes the circle or ellipse. If the bounding box is a square, the GDI draws a circle. If the bounding box is a rectangle, the GDI draws an ellipse. The shape is drawn using the color, style, and thickness of the current pen. The interior is filled using the current brush.

## Bitmaps

A bitmap is an array of bits in memory that represents an image. You can draw on a bitmap just like you draw on the screen. You can copy bitmaps from memory to the screen, from the screen to memory, and from memory to memory. A selection of useful bitmap functions is shown in FIG. 2-6.

*Here's How...* **Creating a bitmap**  To create a bitmap you first must create a compatible device-context in memory. This compatible device-context possesses attributes similar to the display-context of the screen. You create a compatible device-context by calling Create-CompatibleDC(). The newly-created context is also called a *memory-display context*. You then use the compatible device-display context to create a bitmap that is compatible with both the memory-display context and the display-context of the application's window on the screen. You call Create-CompatibleBitmap() to create the bitmap. Before you begin drawing on the bitmap you must select it into the memory-display context by calling Select-Object().

You can create graphics on a bitmap in the same way you draw on the application's window. You use the handle to the memory-display context (instead of the display-context) when you call the GDI. Another way to create graphics on a bitmap is to draw on your application's main window and copy the finished image to the bitmap. Copying in the reverse

| BITMAP FUNCTIONS | |
|---|---|
| CreateCompatibleDC( ) | create a memory-display context for hidden bitmap |
| CreateCompatibleBitmap( ) | create a bitmap compatible with the display-context |
| SelectObject( ) | select a bitmap into the display-context or into a memory-display context |
| BitBlt( ) | copy a bitmap from one display (or device) context to another |
| DeleteObject( ) | destroy a bitmap |
| StretchBlt( ) | copies and resizes a bitmap to fit the target display-context or device context |
| GetObject( ) | retrieve info from bitmap header concerning width, depth, et cetera |

**2-6**  The GDI provides a comprehensive assortment of functions to create, select, copy, inspect, and resize bitmaps.

direction, from the bitmap to the window, is an important part of Windows animation.

**Moving a bitmap** You can copy a bitmap from one location to another by calling BitBlt(). You can use different raster operations to produce different results, as shown in FIG. 2-7. The BitBlt() function is useful for frame animation, and for implementing undo and refresh functions by moving a hidden page bitmap to the visible window.

If the bitmap must be stretched or compressed in order to fit the destination, you can use StretchBlt(). Both StretchBlt() and BitBlt() can use raster operations to control the result when the bitmap is laid onto the existing image. StretchBlt() and BitBlt() can move a rectangular portion of the source

| BitBlt() Raster Operations | | | | |
|---|---|---|---|---|
| Source Bitmap | Target Bitmap | Raster Operation | Boolean Logic | Resulting Image |
| ○ | ▮ | SRCCOPY | overwrite | ○ |
| ○ | ▮ | SRCPAINT | OR | ◖ |
| ● | ▮ | MERGEPAINT | invert source, then OR | ◖ |
| ○ | ▮ | NOTSRCERASE | invert result of OR | ◖ |
| ○ | ▮ | SRCINVERT | XOR | ◐ |
| ○ | ▮ | SRCAND | AND | ◐ |
| ○ | ▯ | SRCERASE | invert target, then AND | ◐ |
| null | ▮ | BLACKNESS | pattern | ▮ |
| null | ▮ | WHITENESS | pattern | ▯ |

**2-7** Some of the many raster operations available with the GDI's BitBlt() function.

bitmap to a target bitmap. This is how the sample application in chapter 14 implements a panning background. It copies selected rectangles from a hidden bitmap that is larger than the window on the screen.

**Deleting a bitmap**   You can delete a bitmap after you are finished using it by calling DeleteObject(). This frees the memory used by the bitmap.

## Regions

Two categories of region functions are provided by the GDI. They are fill-regions and clipping regions. The fill-region functions create polygon-shaped regions that can be filled with a brush. The clipping regions are rectangular viewports that are used to clip graphics output.

**Creating a fill-region**   You can create a rectangular fill-region by calling CreateRectRgn(). To create a fill-region in the shape of a round-cornered rectangle call CreateRoundRectRgn(). To create an ellipse-shaped fill-region, call CreateEllipticRgn().

**Filling a region**   You can use FillRgn() to fill a fill-region with a brush that you pass as an argument. The brush does not need to be the current brush. Use PaintRgn() to fill a fill-region with the current brush. The 3D modeling and shading library that is demonstrated in chapter 4 uses FillRgn() to fill facets of solid objects.

**Using clipping regions**   To create a clipping region, first call CreateRectRgn() to create a region, then use SelectClipRgn() to select it as the current clipping region. Any subsequent graphics output will be clipped at the edges of the region.

## Fonts and text

The font functions provided by the GDI fall into two categories. They are font functions and text functions. Font functions create and select fonts. A font is a style of alphanumeric characters. Text functions display the characters on the screen. The retail version of Windows provides a number of built-in fonts that your application can use. The demonstration program in chapter 5 provides examples of fonts in different colors, sizes, and styles. Useful font and text functions are shown in FIG. 2-8.

## Mapping

The GDI provides a set of coordinate functions that map graphics from one coordinate system to another. In its default mapping mode, the GDI maps your X-Y coordinates on a one-to-one basis to the pixels in the application's window. The origin, represented by the coordinates (0,0), is located the

| FONT FUNCTIONS | |
|---|---|
| TextOut( ) | displays a text string using the current font |
| GetStockObject( ) | retrieve handle to a system font |
| SelectObject( ) | select a font into a display-context or device context |
| SetTextColor( ) | set the text color (foreground only) |
| SetBkColor( ) | set the text cel background color |
| SetBkMode( ) | set text cel background to opaque or transparent |
| CreateFont( ) | create a logical font with specific height, weight, style, et cetera |

**2-8** The GDI provides functions to select fonts with different styles, sizes, and colors.

upper left corner of the drawing surface. This coordinate system is called MM_TEXT.

Other coordinate systems are useful for specialized graphics applications like drafting, page layout, and so on. The MM_LOENGLISH mode maps each of your X-Y coordinates to .01 inch units on the display surface. The MM_LOMETRIC mode maps your X-Y coordinates to .1 millimeter units on the display surface.

 **Using viewports and scaling windows** The mapping modes use viewports and scaling windows. When discussing mapping, *window* does not mean an application's window, but instead refers to an abstract scaling rectangle.

A viewport is defined by physical coordinates. Viewports occupy physical-coordinate space. A scaling window, on the other hand, is defined by logical coordinates unrelated to the screen's pixels. These scaling windows are said to occupy logical-coordinate space. When you call a GDI graphics function you provide logical coordinates as arguments. The current mapping mode determines how the GDI maps those logical coordinates to the screen (which uses physical coordinates) or to the viewport (which is a clipping rectangle on the screen). By default it is a 1:1 mapping scheme. The logical coordinates you provide are mapped directly to physical-coordinate space. Your application's main window is in physical-coordinate space.

# A sample application

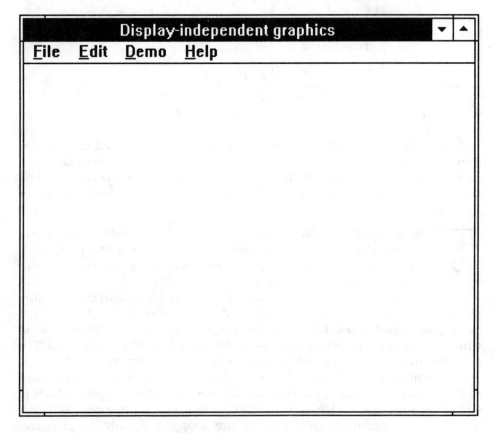

The screen image in FIG. 2-9 shows the startup display from the sample application detect.exe. This program exercises many of the GDI's graphics functions and provides a working example of persistent graphics in a cooperative multitasking environment.

The sample application will run in any Windows display mode, and its images will be properly refreshed when the window is moved, clipped, or uncovered. You can cover the detect.exe window with another application's window or with a program group, and when you uncover the window, its graphics will not be affected. You can move the detect.exe window off the edge of the screen, and when you move the window back on screen its graphics will be correctly displayed.

The sample application will also detect and report on the current screen resolution, maximum number of available hardware colors, and the current memory mode that Windows is using (real, standard, or enhanced).

**2-9** The display window from the sample application. The demonstration program provides nominal display-independent graphics imagery across different screen modes.

The detect.exe demo is built from four modules, including a .def module definition file, an .h #include file, an .rc resource script file, and a .c source file. All of these production files are presented as ready-to-use source code in the program listing later in the chapter. The source files are also provided on the companion disk. You can refer to the appropriate appendix for instructions on how to build detect.exe with QuickC for Windows, Turbo C++ for Windows, Borland C++, Zortech C++, WATCOM C, and Microsoft C and the SDK.

## What the program does: A user's guide

 You can use either a mouse or the keyboard to experiment with the sample application. The menus also support mnemonic keys.

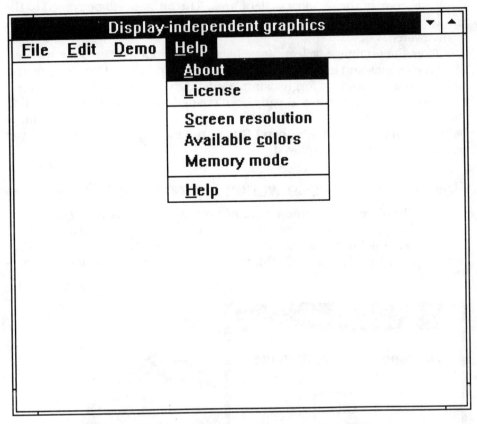

**2-10**  The Help menu from the sample application provides information about runtime conditions like the screen resolution, the maximum number of displayable colors, and the memory mode being use by Windows (real, standard, or enhanced).

## Device independence

As shown in FIG. 2-10, you can use the Help menu to obtain information about the screen resolution, the maximum number of hardware colors available for use, and the current memory mode being used by Windows. The screen image in FIG. 2-11 shows a typical message box that is displayed when you select Screen resolution from the Help menu. The image shown in FIG. 2-12 is a typical report that is displayed when you select Available colors from the Help menu. The screen image in FIG. 2-13 illustrates a typical message box that appears when you select Memory mode from the Help menu.

## Persistent graphics

You can select items from the Demo menu to experiment with persistent graphics, as shown in FIG. 2-14. To create an image, first select Create hidden frame from the Demo menu. Figure 2-15 shows the message box that appears after a hidden bitmap has been created. This bitmap will be used to store a duplicate copy of the window's client area. The bitmap will be copied to the window whenever the image needs refreshing after being unclipped, moved, or uncovered.

    To create an image, select Create background from the Demo menu. A set of subtle shades and gradients is drawn, as shown in FIG. 2-16. The application is smart enough to forgive simple mistakes. If you attempt to create a hidden frame after one has already been created, the message box shown in the upper part of FIG. 2-17 will be displayed. If you attempt to create an image before you have created a hidden bitmap, the message box shown in lower part of FIG. 2-17 will be displayed.

# How the source code works: A programmer's guide

 The detect.exe demonstration program provides a powerful platform for animation development. The persistent graphics make it possible to run animation sequences while other applications are running. The demo's ability to detect screen resolution and run-

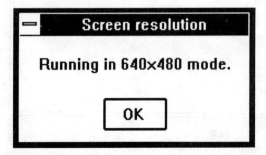

**2-11**  The screen resolution message box from the sample application.

**2-12** The available colors message box from the sample application.

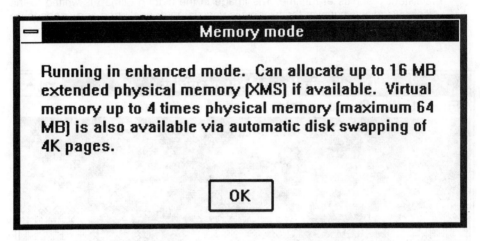

**2-13** The memory mode message box from the sample application.

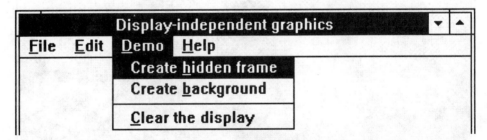

**2-14** The Demo menu from the sample application allows interactive experimentation with graphics that provide nominal display-independence.

time memory mode make it smart enough to decide whether to run an animation from disk or from memory. The detect.exe sample application provides a powerful foundation upon which all of the animated demos in the book are built.

The organization of the .h #include file and the .rc resource script file adhere to the format described in the previous chapter. A few new menu

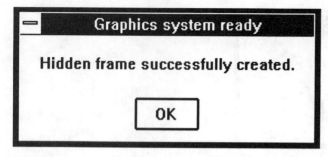

**Graphics system ready**

**Hidden frame successfully created.**

**OK**

**2-15** A message box provides a status report for the hidden bitmap that is used to store persistent graphics at runtime. The image in the hidden bitmap is written to the display window whenever the window is uncovered or unclipped and needs to be refreshed.

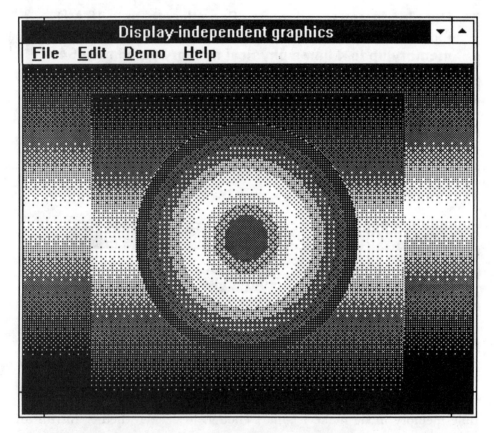

**Display-independent graphics**

<u>F</u>ile   <u>E</u>dit   <u>D</u>emo   <u>H</u>elp

**2-16** The dithered image created by the sample application. The image will persist and is correctly refreshed if the display window is unclipped by the edge of the screen or uncovered by another window's movement.

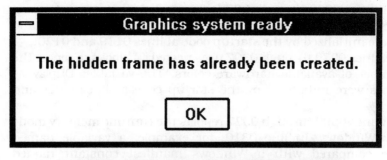

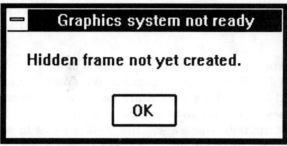

**2-17** Message boxes are used by the sample application to advise you of runtime exceptions (errors) that have been detected.

items and strings have been added to support the enhanced capabilities of detect.exe.

## How the .c file works

The program listing for the .c file is presented in FIG. 2-21.

**Static variables** Some new static variables have been added in order to support persistent graphics and hidden frame operations. The code at lines 0085 through 0087 defines two constants and a variable which are used to keep track of the type of refresh required at runtime. This ensures that if the window is blank, it will be refreshed as a blank image and not with the gradient graphics.

Lines 0090 through 0093 declare and initialize variables that are used for hidden bitmap operations.

**The message handler** Some new code has been added to the message handler function, which is located at lines 0174 through 0374.

Note the case statement at lines 0201 through 0213. This block of code corresponds to the Create background item in the Demo menu. An if() statement is used to check if the hidden frame has been created. If not, MessageBox() is called to advise the user before cancelling the order. If the hidden bitmap is ready, line 0210 calls a function to draw the image and line 0211 copies the finished image to the hidden frame, where it can be called when needed to refresh the display window.

The code at lines 0230 through 0277 uses nested if() statements to report on the current screen resolution. The variables DisplayWidth and DisplayHeight were initialized by the startup code at lines 0119 and 0120.

The code at lines 0279 through 0307 uses nested if() blocks to report the maximum number of available hardware colors. The variables DisplayBits and DisplayPlanes were initialized by the startup code at lines 0121 and 0122.

The code at lines 0309 through 0327 reports the runtime memory mode being used by Windows. In line 0310, for example, a variable named MemoryMode is compared with a Windows manifest constant named WF_ENHANCED to check if the computer is running in enhanced mode. The variable MemoryMode was initialed by the startup code at line 0132, which called GetWinFlags().

**case WM_PAINT**   The code at lines 0339 through 0344 manages the persistent graphics. If a WM_PAINT message is received, Windows is advised the application that something has happened that may have corrupted the application's window. Lines 0340 and 0341 validate the window, so that Windows will not reiterate the paint message. Line 0342 checks to see if the client area is blank. If so, it simply breaks out of the case block. If an image has been drawn and now needs to be refreshed, line 0343 calls a function that copies the contents of the hidden bitmap to the display window .

**Creating the hidden frame**   The function at lines 0424 through 0457 creates the hidden bitmap. The if() statement at lines 0428 through 0435 checks a variable named FrameReady to ensure that the hidden bitmap has not already been created. The call to GlobalCompact() at line 0436 forces Windows to perform a memory sort, creating as much contiguous memory as possible. Then the code at lines 0437 through 0439 sets a display-context, creates a memory-display context, and creates a compatible bitmap. The if() block at lines 0440 through 0448 issues a warning and cancels the operation if the call to CreateCompatibleBitmap() returned an invalid handle.

The code at line 0449 selects the newly-created bitmap into the memory-display context. Line 0459 calls a function to clear the hidden frame. Finally, a message box reports the successful creation of a hidden bitmap.

Before returning to the caller, line 0454 releases the display-context (but not the memory-display context) and line 0455 sets FrameReady to True. (If the function is called again the code at line 0428 will detect the user's error.)

**Clearing the display window**   The function at lines 0463 through 0470 clears the display window by calling PatBlt(). The constants zFRAMEWIDE and zFRAMEHIGH were initialized at lines 0051 and 0052. The constant WHITENESS is a Windows manifest constant defined in windows.h, which was #included at line 0041.

**Clearing the hidden frame**   The function at lines 0476 through 0481 clears the hidden frame by calling PatBlt().

**Copying the hidden frame**   The function at lines 0487 through 0495 copies the hidden bitmap to the display window. Note how line 0490 checks to ensure that a bitmap exists before attempting to copy it. The BitBlt() call at line 0492 copies the bitmap. The hDC property is the destination, and hFrameDC is the source.

**Backing up the display window**   The function at lines 0501 through 0509 copies the client area of the display window to the hidden bitmap. It works the same way as the code at lines 0487 through 0495.

**Drawing the image**   The function at lines 0515 through 0593 draws the gradient graphics. The code at lines 0517 through 0526 declares and initializes local variables.

Note in particular the use of the rectangle structure declared at line 0519. The members of this structure are initialized at lines 0529 through 0532.

The for() loop at lines 0534 through 0544 draws the background gradient. The code at line 0543 adjusts the value of the blue gun on each pass through the loop. The loop at lines 0559 through 0569 draws the gradient rectangle, and the loop at lines 0575 through 0587 draws the gradient circle. Note how each loop deletes the drawing tools that it uses.

## Program listings for the sample application

 The program listings presented here contain all the source code you need to build and run the sample application. The module definition file is provided in FIG. 2-18. The #include file is found in FIG. 2-19. The resource script file is presented in FIG. 2-20. The C source file is provided in FIG. 2-21.

 **Companion disk**   If you have the companion disk, the source files are presented as detect.def, detect.h, detect.rc, and detect.c.

**License**   You can paste the royalty-free source code into your own applications and distribute the resulting executable files under the conditions of the License Agreement and Limited Warranty in FIG. 10 in the introduction to the book.

**2-18**   The module definition file listing for the sample application.

```
0001   NAME          DEFDEMO
0002   DESCRIPTION   'Copyright 1992 Lee Adams.  All rights reserved.'
0003   EXETYPE       WINDOWS
0004   STUB          'WINSTUB.EXE'
0005   CODE          PRELOAD MOVEABLE
0006   DATA          PRELOAD MOVEABLE MULTIPLE
0007   HEAPSIZE      1024
0008   STACKSIZE     8192
0009   EXPORTS       zMessageHandler
```

**2-19** The include file listing for the sample application.

```
0001  /*
0002  --------------------------------------------------------------
0003                    Include file DETECT.H
0004           Copyright 1992 Lee Adams.  All rights reserved.
0005     Include this file in the .RC resource script file and in the
0006     .C source file.  It contains function prototypes, menu ID
0007     constants, and string ID constants.
0008  --------------------------------------------------------------
0009  --------------------------------------------------------------
0010                    Function prototypes
0011  --------------------------------------------------------------
0012                                                             */
0013  #if !defined(zRCFILE)                /* if not an .RC file... */
0014     LONG FAR PASCAL zMessageHandler(HWND, unsigned, WORD, LONG);
0015     int PASCAL WinMain(HANDLE,HANDLE,LPSTR,int);
0016     HWND zInitMainWindow(HANDLE);
0017     BOOL zInitClass(HANDLE);
0018  static void zClear(HWND);                   /* blank the viewport */
0019  static void zInitFrame(HWND);              /* creates hidden frame */
0020  static void zCopyToDisplay(HWND);       /* copies frame to display */
0021  static void zCopyToFrame(HWND);         /* copies display to frame */
0022  static void zClearHiddenFrame(void);       /* clears hidden frame */
0023  static void zDrawBg(HDC);               /* draws background scene */
0024  #endif
0025  /*
0026  --------------------------------------------------------------
0027                    Menu ID constants
0028  --------------------------------------------------------------
0029                                                             */
0030  #define IDM_New            1
0031  #define IDM_Open           2
0032  #define IDM_Save           3
0033  #define IDM_SaveAs         4
0034  #define IDM_Exit           5
0035
0036  #define IDM_Undo           6
0037  #define IDM_Cut            7
0038  #define IDM_Copy           8
0039  #define IDM_Paste          9
0040  #define IDM_Delete        10
0041
0042  #define IDM_InitFrame     11
0043  #define IDM_DrawBg        12
0044  #define IDM_Clear         13
0045
0046  #define IDM_About         14
0047  #define IDM_License       15
0048  #define IDM_Display       16
0049  #define IDM_Colors        17
0050  #define IDM_Mode          18
0051  #define IDM_GeneralHelp   19
0052  /*
0053  --------------------------------------------------------------
0054                    String ID constants
0055  --------------------------------------------------------------*/
0056                                                             */
0057  #define IDS_Caption       1
0058  #define IDS_Warning       2
0059  #define IDS_NoMouse       3
0060  #define IDS_About         4
0061  #define IDS_AboutText     5
```

**2-19** Continued.

```
0062   #define IDS_License      6
0063   #define IDS_LicenseText  7
0064   #define IDS_Help         8
0065   #define IDS_HelpText     9
0066   #define IDS_Completed    10
0067   #define IDS_Resolution   11
0068   #define IDS_ResVGA       12
0069   #define IDS_ResEGA       13
0070   #define IDS_ResCGA       14
0071   #define IDS_ResSVGA      15
0072   #define IDS_Res8514      16
0073   #define IDS_ResHerc      17
0074   #define IDS_ResCustom    18
0075   #define IDS_Color        19
0076   #define IDS_Color16      20
0077   #define IDS_Color256     21
0078   #define IDS_Color2       22
0079   #define IDS_ColorCustom  23
0080   #define IDS_Machine      24
0081   #define IDS_Enhanced     25
0082   #define IDS_Standard     26
0083   #define IDS_Real         27
0084   #define IDS_NoFrame      28
0085   #define IDS_Ready        29
0086   #define IDS_Already      30
0087   #define IDS_NotReady     31
0088   #define IDS_NoMem        32
0089   #define IDS_FrameOK      33
0090   /*
0091   ----------------------------------------------------------------
0092                          End of include file
0093   ----------------------------------------------------------------
0094                                                                  */
```

**2-20** The resource script file listing for the sample application.

```
0001   /*
0002   ----------------------------------------------------------------
0003                   Resource script file DETECT.RC
0004           Copyright 1992 Lee Adams.  All rights reserved.
0005   This file defines the menu resources, the accelerator key
0006   resources, and the string resources that will be used by the
0007   demonstration application at runtime.
0008   ----------------------------------------------------------------
0009                                                                  */
0010   #define zRCFILE
0011   #include <WINDOWS.H>
0012   #include "DETECT.H"
0013   /*
0014   ----------------------------------------------------------------
0015                          Script for menus
0016   ----------------------------------------------------------------
0017                                                                  */
0018   MENUS1 MENU
0019     BEGIN
0020     POPUP "&File"
0021       BEGIN
0022         MENUITEM    "&New", IDM_New, GRAYED
0023         MENUITEM    "&Open...", IDM_Open, GRAYED
0024         MENUITEM    "&Save", IDM_Save, GRAYED
```

```
0025          MENUITEM  "Save &As...", IDM_SaveAs, GRAYED
0026          MENUITEM SEPARATOR
0027          MENUITEM  "E&xit", IDM_Exit
0028        END
0029      POPUP "&Edit"
0030        BEGIN
0031        MENUITEM  "&Undo\tAlt+BkSp", IDM_Undo, GRAYED
0032        MENUITEM SEPARATOR
0033        MENUITEM  "Cu&t\tShift+Del", IDM_Cut, GRAYED
0034        MENUITEM  "&Copy\tCtrl+Ins", IDM_Copy, GRAYED
0035        MENUITEM  "&Paste\tShift+Ins", IDM_Paste, GRAYED
0036        MENUITEM  "&Delete\tDel", IDM_Delete, GRAYED
0037        END
0038      POPUP "&Demo"
0039        BEGIN
0040        MENUITEM "Create &hidden frame", IDM_InitFrame
0041        MENUITEM "Create &background", IDM_DrawBg
0042        MENUITEM SEPARATOR
0043        MENUITEM "&Clear the display", IDM_Clear
0044        END
0045      POPUP "&Help"
0046        BEGIN
0047        MENUITEM "&About", IDM_About
0048        MENUITEM "&License", IDM_License
0049        MENUITEM SEPARATOR
0050        MENUITEM "&Screen resolution", IDM_Display
0051        MENUITEM "Available &colors", IDM_Colors
0052        MENUITEM "Memory mode", IDM_Mode
0053        MENUITEM SEPARATOR
0054        MENUITEM "&Help", IDM_GeneralHelp
0055        END
0056      END
0057    /*
0058    ------------------------------------------------------------------
0059                      Script for accelerator keys
0060    ------------------------------------------------------------------
0061                                                                   */
0062    KEYS1 ACCELERATORS
0063      BEGIN
0064      VK_BACK, IDM_Undo, VIRTKEY, ALT
0065      VK_DELETE, IDM_Cut, VIRTKEY, SHIFT
0066      VK_INSERT, IDM_Copy, VIRTKEY, CONTROL
0067      VK_INSERT, IDM_Paste, VIRTKEY, SHIFT
0068      VK_DELETE, IDM_Delete, VIRTKEY
0069      END
0070    /*
0071    ------------------------------------------------------------------
0072                         Script for strings
0073       Programmer's Notes:  If you are typing this listing, set your
0074       margins to a line length of 255 characters so you can create
0075       lengthy strings without embedded carriage returns.  The line
0076       wraparounds in the following STRINGTABLE script are used for
0077       readability only in this printout.
0078    ------------------------------------------------------------------
0079                                                                   */
0080    STRINGTABLE
0081      BEGIN
0082      IDS_Caption      "Display-independent graphics"
0083      IDS_Warning      "Graphics system warning"
0084      IDS_NoMouse      "No mouse found.  Some features of this
           demonstration program may require a mouse."
```

```
0085      IDS_About        "About this program"
0086      IDS_AboutText    "This is a demo from Windcrest McGraw-Hill
          book 4114. Copyright 1992 Lee Adams. All rights reserved."
0087      IDS_License      "License Agreement"
0088      IDS_LicenseText "You can use this code as part of your own
          software product subject to the License Agreement and Limited
          Warranty in Windcrest McGraw-Hill book 4114 and on its
          companion disk."
0089      IDS_Help         "How to use this demo"
0090      IDS_HelpText     "Use Demo menu to create a persistent image.
          Test it by moving window off screen or cover with another
          window. Use Help menu to determine runtime conditions such as
          screen resolution, available colors, and memory mode."
0091      IDS_Resolution   "Screen resolution"
0092      IDS_ResVGA       "Running in 640x480 mode."
0093      IDS_ResEGA       "Running in 640x350 mode."
0094      IDS_ResCGA       "Running in 640x200 mode."
0095      IDS_ResSVGA      "Running in 800x600 mode."
0096      IDS_Res8514      "Running in 1024x768 mode."
0097      IDS_ResHerc      "Running in 720x348 mode."
0098      IDS_ResCustom    "Running in custom mode."
0099      IDS_Color        "Available colors"
0100      IDS_Color16      "Running in 16-color mode."
0101      IDS_Color256     "Running in 256-color mode."
0102      IDS_Color2       "Running in 2-color mode."
0103      IDS_ColorCustom "Running in a custom color mode."
0104      IDS_Machine      "Memory mode"
0105      IDS_Enhanced     "Running in enhanced mode. Can allocate up to
          16 MB extended physical memory (XMS) if available. Virtual
          memory up to 4 times physical memory (maximum 64 MB) is also
          available via automatic disk swapping of 4K pages."
0106      IDS_Standard     "Running in standard mode. Can allocate up to
          16 MB extended physical memory (XMS) if available."
0107      IDS_Real         "Running in real mode. Can allocate blocks of
          memory from the first 640K of RAM. Can also allocate blocks
          from expanded memory (EMS) if available."
0108      IDS_NoFrame      "Hidden frame not yet created."
0109      IDS_Ready        "Graphics system ready"
0110      IDS_Already      "The hidden frame has already been created."
0111      IDS_NotReady     "Graphics system not ready"
0112      IDS_NoMem        "Insufficient memory. Hidden frame not
          created."
0113      IDS_FrameOK      "Hidden frame successfully created."
0114   END
0115 /*
0116 ----------------------------------------------------------------
0117                    End of resource script file
0118 ----------------------------------------------------------------
0119                                                              */
```

**2-21**  The C source file listing for the sample application, detect.c. This demonstration program is ready to build using QuickC for Windows, Turbo C++ for Windows, Microsoft C and the SDK, Borland C++, Symantec Zortech C++, WATCOM C, and other compilers. See FIG. 1-2 for sample command-lines to build the program. Guidelines for using your compiler are provided in the appropriate appendix at the back of the book.

```
0001 /*
0002 ----------------------------------------------------------------
0003      Reusable template for Windows applications that use a hidden
```

```
0004      frame, display-independent graphics, and persistent images.
0005   ------------------------------------------------------------------
0006      Source file: DETECT.C
0007      Release version: 1.00              Programmer: Lee Adams
0008      Type: C source file for Windows application development.
0009      Compilers: Microsoft C and SDK, Borland C++, Zortech C++,
0010         QuickC for Windows, Turbo C++ for Windows, WATCOM C.
0011      Memory model: small.
0012      Dependencies: DETECT.DEF module definition file, DETECT.H
0013                       include file, DETECT.RC resource script file,
0014                       and DETECT.C source file.
0015      Output and features: Demonstrates a display-independent
0016         graphics application that can run in different screen modes.
0017         Demonstrates persistent graphics that are automatically
0018         refreshed when covered by another window or cropped by the
0019         edge of the screen. Demonstrates how to detect various
0020         runtime conditions such as screen resolution, number of
0021         available colors, and memory mode (real, standard, enhanced).
0022      Publication: Contains material from Windcrest/McGraw-Hill book
0023         4114 published by TAB BOOKS Division of McGraw-Hill Inc.
0024      License: As purchaser of the book you are granted a royalty-
0025         free license to distribute executable files generated using
0026         this code provided you accept the conditions of the License
0027         Agreement and Limited Warranty described in the book and on
0028         the companion disk. Government users: This software and
0029         documentation are subject to restrictions set forth in The
0030         Rights in Technical Data and Computer Software clause at
0031         252.227-7013 and elsewhere.
0032   ------------------------------------------------------------------
0033         (c) Copyright 1992 Lee Adams. All rights reserved.
0034         Lee Adams(tm) is a trademark of Lee Adams.
0035   ------------------------------------------------------------------
0036
0037   ------------------------------------------------------------------
0038                          Include files
0039   ------------------------------------------------------------------
0040                                                                   */
0041   #include <WINDOWS.H>
0042   #include "DETECT.H"
0043   /*
0044   ------------------------------------------------------------------
0045             Static variables visible throughout this file
0046   ------------------------------------------------------------------
0047                                                                   */
0048   /* ------------------- window specifications ------------------- */
0049   #define zWINDOW_WIDTH 408                      /* width of window */
0050   #define zWINDOW_HEIGHT 346                    /* height of window */
0051   #define zFRAMEWIDE 400                   /* width of client area */
0052   #define zFRAMEHIGH 300                  /* height of client area */
0053   int WindowX, WindowY;                      /* location of window */
0054
0055   /* ------------------- instance operations --------------------- */
0056   HANDLE hInst;                          /* handle to this instance */
0057   HWND MainhWnd;                       /* handle to the main window */
0058   HANDLE hAccel;                  /* handle to accelerator keys table */
0059   HMENU hMenu;                     /* handle to a menu at runtime */
0060   PAINTSTRUCT ps;          /* structure used by persistent graphics */
0061   int MessageRet;         /* will hold receive value returned by GDI */
0062
0063   /* --------------------- mouse and cursor --------------------- */
0064   HCURSOR hPrevCursor;                   /* handle to default cursor */
```

```
0065   HCURSOR hHourGlass;                    /* handle to hourglass cursor */
0066   int MousePresent;                     /* will indicate if mouse present */
0067
0068   /* ------------------ runtime conditions -------------------- */
0069   int DisplayWidth, DisplayHeight;          /* screen resolution */
0070   int DisplayBits;                      /* number of bits-per-pixel */
0071   int DisplayPlanes;                       /* number of bitplanes */
0072   DWORD MemoryMode;                       /* runtime memory mode */
0073
0074   /* ----------------- message box operations ----------------- */
0075   char lpCaption[51];        /* will hold caption for message boxes */
0076   int Max= 50;                       /* maximum length of caption */
0077   char lpMessage[250];       /* will hold text for message boxes */
0078   int MaxText= 249;                     /* maximum length of text */
0079
0080   /* -------------------- font operations -------------------- */
0081   HFONT hFont, hPrevFont;        /* handles to new, previous font */
0082   HDC hFontDC;                      /* display-context for font */
0083
0084   /* ------------- persistent image operations ----------------- */
0085   #define zBLANK 0
0086   #define zIMAGE 1
0087   int PaintImage= zBLANK;              /* indicates type of refresh */
0088
0089   /* -----------------hidden frame operations ------------------ */
0090   HDC hFrameDC;          /* memory display-context for hidden-frame */
0091   HBITMAP hFrame;               /* handle to hidden-frame bitmap */
0092   HBITMAP hPrevFrame;                        /* default bitmap */
0093   BOOL FrameReady= FALSE;                /* hidden-frame created? */
0094
0095   /*
0096   ------------------------------------------------------------------
0097                   Entry point for the application
0098   ------------------------------------------------------------------
0099                                                                   */
0100   int PASCAL WinMain(HANDLE hInstance, HANDLE hPrevInstance,
0101                   LPSTR lpCmdLine, int nCmdShow)
0102   {
0103     MSG msg;                          /* will hold incoming messages */
0104     HWND hWndPrev;          /* handle to window of another instance */
0105     HWND hDesktopWnd;       /* handle to full-screen desktop window */
0106     HDC hDCcaps;                 /* display-context of desktop window */
0107
0108   /* ----------- ensure only one instance is running ----------- */
0109   hWndPrev = FindWindow("DEMOCLASS", NULL);
0110   if (hWndPrev != NULL)         /* if another instance was found... */
0111     {
0112     BringWindowToTop(hWndPrev);                  /* make it active... */
0113     return FALSE;                /* ...and terminate this instance */
0114     }
0115
0116   /* --------- determine capabilities of screen display ---------- */
0117   hDesktopWnd= GetDesktopWindow();
0118   hDCcaps= GetDC(hDesktopWnd);
0119   DisplayWidth= GetDeviceCaps(hDCcaps,HORZRES);
0120   DisplayHeight= GetDeviceCaps(hDCcaps,VERTRES);
0121   DisplayBits= GetDeviceCaps(hDCcaps,BITSPIXEL);
0122   DisplayPlanes= GetDeviceCaps(hDCcaps,PLANES);
0123   ReleaseDC(hDesktopWnd,hDCcaps);
0124
0125   /* ------- calculate screen position to center the window ------ */
```

```
0126   WindowX= (DisplayWidth - zWINDOW_WIDTH) / 2;        /* horizontal */
0127   WindowY= (DisplayHeight - zWINDOW_HEIGHT) /2;          /* vertical */
0128   if (WindowX < 0) WindowX= 0;
0129   if (WindowY < 0) WindowY= 0;
0130
0131   /* ---- determine memory mode (enhanced, standard, or real) ---- */
0132   MemoryMode= GetWinFlags();              /* will read this value later */
0133
0134   /* -------------- create and display the window --------------- */
0135   hInst= hInstance;                       /* remember the instance handle */
0136   if (!zInitClass(hInstance)) return FALSE;      /* create the class */
0137   MainhWnd= zInitMainWindow(hInstance);          /* create the window */
0138   if (!MainhWnd) return FALSE;      /* exit if no window was created */
0139   ShowWindow(MainhWnd, nCmdShow);             /* display the window */
0140   UpdateWindow(MainhWnd);                  /* send a paint message */
0141   hAccel= LoadAccelerators(hInstance,"KEYS1"); /* accelerator keys */
0142   hFontDC= GetDC(MainhWnd);               /* get a display-context */
0143   hFont= GetStockObject(SYSTEM_FONT);        /* grab handle to font */
0144   hPrevFont= SelectObject(hFontDC,hFont);    /* select font into DC */
0145   SetTextColor(hFontDC,RGB(191,191,191));     /* set new text color */
0146   TextOut(hFontDC,10,280,"- Copyright 1992 Lee Adams.",27);/* text */
0147   SetTextColor(hFontDC,RGB(255,255,255));    /* restore text color */
0148   SelectObject(hFontDC,hPrevFont);         /* restore previous font */
0149   ReleaseDC(MainhWnd,hFontDC);             /* release display-context */
0150
0151   /* --------------------- check for mouse --------------------- */
0152   MousePresent= GetSystemMetrics(SM_MOUSEPRESENT);
0153   if (!MousePresent)                      /* if no active mouse found */
0154     {
0155     LoadString(hInst,IDS_Warning,lpCaption,Max);    /* load caption */
0156     LoadString(hInst,IDS_NoMouse,lpMessage,MaxText);  /* load text */
0157     MessageBox(GetFocus(),lpMessage,lpCaption,MB_OK);   /* message */
0158     }
0159
0160   /* ---------- begin retrieving messages for the window --------- */
0161   while (GetMessage(&msg,0,0,0))
0162     {
0163     if(TranslateAccelerator(MainhWnd, hAccel, &msg)) continue;
0164     TranslateMessage(&msg);
0165     DispatchMessage(&msg);
0166     }
0167   return(msg.wParam);
0168   }
0169   /*
0170   ----------------------------------------------------------------
0171                    Switcher for incoming messages
0172   ----------------------------------------------------------------
0173                                                                   */
0174   LONG FAR PASCAL zMessageHandler(HWND hWnd, unsigned message,
0175                                   WORD wParam, LONG lParam)
0176   {
0177     HDC hDCpaint;        /* display-context for persistent graphics */
0178
0179   switch (message)
0180     {
0181
0182     case WM_COMMAND:         /* if user has selected a menu item... */
0183       switch(wParam)
0184         {
0185         case IDM_New:    break;
0186         case IDM_Open:   break;
```

```
0187        case IDM_Save:    break;
0188        case IDM_SaveAs: break;
0189        case IDM_Exit:    PostQuitMessage(0); break;
0190
0191        case IDM_Undo:    break;
0192        case IDM_Cut:     break;
0193        case IDM_Copy:    break;
0194        case IDM_Paste:   break;
0195        case IDM_Delete: break;
0196
0197        case IDM_InitFrame: zInitFrame(hWnd);
0198                            zClear(hWnd);
0199                            break;
0200
0201        case IDM_DrawBg:
0202                if (FrameReady==FALSE)
0203                  {
0204                  MessageBeep(0);
0205                  LoadString(hInst,IDS_NotReady,lpCaption,Max);
0206                  LoadString(hInst,IDS_NoFrame,lpMessage,MaxText);
0207                  MessageBox(GetFocus(),lpMessage,lpCaption,MB_OK);
0208                  break;
0209                  }
0210                zDrawBg(hFrameDC);
0211                zCopyToDisplay(hWnd);
0212                PaintImage= zIMAGE;
0213                break;
0214
0215        case IDM_Clear: zClear(hWnd); PaintImage= zBLANK;
0216                        break;
0217
0218        case IDM_About:
0219          LoadString(hInst,IDS_About,lpCaption,Max);
0220          LoadString(hInst,IDS_AboutText,lpMessage,MaxText);
0221          MessageBox(GetFocus(),lpMessage,lpCaption,MB_OK);
0222          break;
0223
0224        case IDM_License:
0225          LoadString(hInst,IDS_License,lpCaption,Max);
0226          LoadString(hInst,IDS_LicenseText,lpMessage,MaxText);
0227          MessageBox(GetFocus(),lpMessage,lpCaption,MB_OK);
0228          break;
0229
0230        case IDM_Display:
0231          if (DisplayWidth==640)
0232            {
0233            if (DisplayHeight==480)
0234              {
0235              LoadString(hInst,IDS_Resolution,lpCaption,Max);
0236              LoadString(hInst,IDS_ResVGA,lpMessage,MaxText);
0237              MessageBox(GetFocus(),lpMessage,lpCaption,MB_OK);
0238              }
0239            if (DisplayHeight==350)
0240              {
0241              LoadString(hInst,IDS_Resolution,lpCaption,Max);
0242              LoadString(hInst,IDS_ResEGA,lpMessage,MaxText);
0243              MessageBox(GetFocus(),lpMessage,lpCaption,MB_OK);
0244              }
0245            if (DisplayHeight==200)
0246              {
0247              LoadString(hInst,IDS_Resolution,lpCaption,Max);
0248              LoadString(hInst,IDS_ResCGA,lpMessage,MaxText);
```

```
0249                    MessageBox(GetFocus(),lpMessage,lpCaption,MB_OK);
0250                    }
0251                  break;
0252                  }
0253              if (DisplayWidth==800)
0254                  {
0255                  LoadString(hInst,IDS_Resolution,lpCaption,Max);
0256                  LoadString(hInst,IDS_ResSVGA,lpMessage,MaxText);
0257                  MessageBox(GetFocus(),lpMessage,lpCaption,MB_OK);
0258                  break;
0259                  }
0260              if (DisplayWidth==1024)
0261                  {
0262                  LoadString(hInst,IDS_Resolution,lpCaption,Max);
0263                  LoadString(hInst,IDS_Res8514,lpMessage,MaxText);
0264                  MessageBox(GetFocus(),lpMessage,lpCaption,MB_OK);
0265                  break;
0266                  }
0267              if (DisplayWidth==720)
0268                  {
0269                  LoadString(hInst,IDS_Resolution,lpCaption,Max);
0270                  LoadString(hInst,IDS_ResHerc,lpMessage,MaxText);
0271                  MessageBox(GetFocus(),lpMessage,lpCaption,MB_OK);
0272                  break;
0273                  }
0274              LoadString(hInst,IDS_Resolution,lpCaption,Max);
0275              LoadString(hInst,IDS_ResCustom,lpMessage,MaxText);
0276              MessageBox(GetFocus(),lpMessage,lpCaption,MB_OK);
0277              break;
0278
0279          case IDM_Colors:
0280              if (DisplayBits==1)
0281                  {
0282                  if (DisplayPlanes==4)
0283                      {
0284                      LoadString(hInst,IDS_Color,lpCaption,Max);
0285                      LoadString(hInst,IDS_Color16,lpMessage,MaxText);
0286                      MessageBox(GetFocus(),lpMessage,lpCaption,MB_OK);
0287                      break;
0288                      }
0289                  if (DisplayPlanes==1)
0290                      {
0291                      LoadString(hInst,IDS_Color,lpCaption,Max);
0292                      LoadString(hInst,IDS_Color2,lpMessage,MaxText);
0293                      MessageBox(GetFocus(),lpMessage,lpCaption,MB_OK);
0294                      break;
0295                      }
0296                  }
0297              if (DisplayBits==8)
0298                  {
0299                  LoadString(hInst,IDS_Color,lpCaption,Max);
0300                  LoadString(hInst,IDS_Color256,lpMessage,MaxText);
0301                  MessageBox(GetFocus(),lpMessage,lpCaption,MB_OK);
0302                  break;
0303                  }
0304              LoadString(hInst,IDS_Color,lpCaption,Max);
0305              LoadString(hInst,IDS_ColorCustom,lpMessage,MaxText);
0306              MessageBox(GetFocus(),lpMessage,lpCaption,MB_OK);
0307              break;
0308
0309          case IDM_Mode:
0310              if (MemoryMode & WF_ENHANCED)
```

```
0311              {
0312              LoadString(hInst,IDS_Machine,lpCaption,Max);
0313              LoadString(hInst,IDS_Enhanced,lpMessage,MaxText);
0314              MessageBox(GetFocus(),lpMessage,lpCaption,MB_OK);
0315              break;
0316              }
0317          if (MemoryMode & WF_STANDARD)
0318              {
0319              LoadString(hInst,IDS_Machine,lpCaption,Max);
0320              LoadString(hInst,IDS_Standard,lpMessage,MaxText);
0321              MessageBox(GetFocus(),lpMessage,lpCaption,MB_OK);
0322              break;
0323              }
0324          LoadString(hInst,IDS_Machine,lpCaption,Max);
0325          LoadString(hInst,IDS_Real,lpMessage,MaxText);
0326          MessageBox(GetFocus(),lpMessage,lpCaption,MB_OK);
0327          break;
0328
0329        case IDM_GeneralHelp:
0330          LoadString(hInst,IDS_Help,lpCaption,Max);
0331          LoadString(hInst,IDS_HelpText,lpMessage,MaxText);
0332          MessageBox(GetFocus(),lpMessage,lpCaption,MB_OK);
0333          break;
0334        default:
0335          return(DefWindowProc(hWnd, message, wParam, lParam));
0336        }
0337      break;
0338
0339    case WM_PAINT:              /* if image needs to be refreshed... */
0340      hDCpaint= BeginPaint(hWnd,&ps);            /* load structure */
0341      EndPaint(hWnd, &ps);              /* validate client area */
0342      if (PaintImage==zBLANK) break;     /* if client area is blank */
0343      zCopyToDisplay(hWnd);   /* else copy hidden frame to display */
0344      break;
0345
0346    case WM_DESTROY:  /* if user is terminating the application... */
0347      if (FrameReady==TRUE)
0348        {                          /* remove the hidden frame bitmap */
0349        SelectObject(hFrameDC,hPrevFrame);
0350        DeleteObject(hFrame);
0351        DeleteDC(hFrameDC);
0352        }
0353      PostQuitMessage(0);
0354      break;
0355
0356    case WM_SYSCOMMAND:     /* intercept resize, minimize, maximize */
0357      if ((wParam & 0xfff0)== SC_SIZE)
0358        {
0359        MessageBeep(0); break;
0360        }
0361      if ((wParam & 0xfff0)== SC_MINIMIZE)
0362        {
0363        MessageBeep(0); break;
0364        }
0365      if ((wParam & 0xfff0)== SC_MAXIMIZE)
0366        {
0367        MessageBeep(0); break;
0368        }
0369
0370    default:
0371      return(DefWindowProc(hWnd, message, wParam, lParam));
```

```
0372     }
0373   return FALSE;
0374   }
0375   /*
0376   -----------------------------------------------------------------
0377               Initialize the attributes of the window class
0378   -----------------------------------------------------------------
0379                                                                  */
0380   BOOL zInitClass(HANDLE hInstance)
0381   {
0382     WNDCLASS WndClass;
0383   WndClass.style= 0;                              /* class style */
0384   WndClass.lpfnWndProc= zMessageHandler;      /* callback function */
0385   WndClass.cbClsExtra= 0;            /* unused, no customized data */
0386   WndClass.cbWndExtra= 0;            /* unused, no customized data */
0387   WndClass.hInstance= hInstance;      /* application that owns class */
0388   WndClass.hIcon= LoadIcon(NULL,IDI_EXCLAMATION); /* minimize icon */
0389   WndClass.hCursor= LoadCursor(NULL,IDC_ARROW);    /* app's cursor */
0390   WndClass.hbrBackground= /* specifies background color of window */
0391                     CreateSolidBrush(RGB(255,255,255));
0392   WndClass.lpszMenuName= "MENUS1";    /* name of .RC menu resource */
0393   WndClass.lpszClassName= "DEMOCLASS";       /* name of the class */
0394   return RegisterClass(&WndClass);       /* registers the class */
0395   }
0396   /*
0397   -----------------------------------------------------------------
0398                    Create the main window
0399   -----------------------------------------------------------------
0400                                                                  */
0401   HWND zInitMainWindow(HANDLE hInstance)
0402   {
0403     HWND hWnd;
0404   LoadString(hInstance,IDS_Caption,lpCaption,Max); /* load caption */
0405   hHourGlass= LoadCursor(NULL,IDC_WAIT);   /* load the wait cursor */
0406   hWnd= CreateWindow("DEMOCLASS",   /* create window of this class */
0407         lpCaption,                                    /* caption */
0408         WS_OVERLAPPED | WS_THICKFRAME | WS_MINIMIZEBOX |   /* type */
0409          WS_MAXIMIZEBOX | WS_CLIPCHILDREN,
0410         WindowX,WindowY,                     /* screen location */
0411         zWINDOW_WIDTH,zWINDOW_HEIGHT,        /* window dimensions */
0412         0,0,                     /* parent handle, menu or child ID */
0413         hInstance,(LPSTR)NULL); /* app instance and unused pointer */
0414   return hWnd;
0415   }
0416   /*
0417   -----------------------------------------------------------------
0418              THE CORE FUNCTIONS OF THE APPLICATION
0419   -----------------------------------------------------------------
0420   -----------------------------------------------------------------
0421                    Create the hidden frame.
0422   -----------------------------------------------------------------
0423                                                                  */
0424   static void zInitFrame(HWND hWnd)
0425   {
0426     HDC hDisplayDC;                           /* display-context */
0427
0428   if (FrameReady==TRUE)
0429     {                        /* if hidden frame already created... */
0430     MessageBeep(0);
0431     LoadString(hInst,IDS_Ready,lpCaption,Max);
0432     LoadString(hInst,IDS_Already,lpMessage,MaxText);
```

```
0433   MessageBox(GetFocus(),lpMessage,lpCaption,MB_OK);
0434   return;
0435   }
0436 GlobalCompact((DWORD)-1L);            /* maximize contiguous memory */
0437 hDisplayDC= GetDC(hWnd);                   /* set the display-context */
0438 hFrameDC= CreateCompatibleDC(hDisplayDC);     /* create frame... */
0439 hFrame= CreateCompatibleBitmap(hDisplayDC,zFRAMEWIDE,zFRAMEHIGH);
0440 if (hFrame==NULL)
0441   {
0442   LoadString(hInst,IDS_NotReady,lpCaption,Max);
0443   LoadString(hInst,IDS_NoMem,lpMessage,MaxText);
0444   MessageBox(GetFocus(),lpMessage,lpCaption,MB_OK);
0445   DeleteDC(hFrameDC);
0446   FrameReady= FALSE;
0447   return;
0448   }
0449 hPrevFrame= SelectObject(hFrameDC,hFrame);  /* select the bitmap */
0450 zClearHiddenFrame();                     /* clear the hidden frame */
0451 LoadString(hInst,IDS_Ready,lpCaption,Max);
0452 LoadString(hInst,IDS_FrameOK,lpMessage,MaxText);
0453 MessageBox(GetFocus(),lpMessage,lpCaption,MB_OK);
0454 ReleaseDC(hWnd,hDisplayDC);         /* release the display-context */
0455 FrameReady= TRUE;                        /* set a global token */
0456 return;
0457 }
0458 /*
0459 ------------------------------------------------------------------
0460                      Clear the display window.
0461 ------------------------------------------------------------------
0462                                                                  */
0463 static void zClear(HWND hWnd)
0464 {
0465   HDC hDC;
0466 hDC= GetDC(hWnd);
0467 PatBlt(hDC,0,0,zFRAMEWIDE,zFRAMEHIGH,WHITENESS);
0468 ReleaseDC(hWnd,hDC);
0469 return;
0470 }
0471 /*
0472 ------------------------------------------------------------------
0473                       Clear the hidden frame.
0474 ------------------------------------------------------------------
0475                                                                  */
0476 static void zClearHiddenFrame(void)
0477 {
0478 if (FrameReady==FALSE) return;
0479 PatBlt(hFrameDC,0,0,zFRAMEWIDE,zFRAMEHIGH,WHITENESS);
0480 return;
0481 }
0482 /*
0483 ------------------------------------------------------------------
0484          Copy the hidden frame to the display window.
0485 ------------------------------------------------------------------
0486                                                                  */
0487 static void zCopyToDisplay(HWND hWnd)
0488 {
0489   HDC hDC;
0490 if (FrameReady==FALSE) return;
0491 hDC= GetDC(hWnd);
0492 BitBlt(hDC,0,0,zFRAMEWIDE,zFRAMEHIGH,hFrameDC,0,0,SRCCOPY);
0493 ReleaseDC(hWnd,hDC);
```

```
0494   return;
0495   }
0496   /*
0497   ------------------------------------------------------------------
0498                  Copy the display window to the hidden frame.
0499   ------------------------------------------------------------------
0500                                                                  */
0501   static void zCopyToFrame(HWND hWnd)
0502   {
0503     HDC hDC;
0504   if (FrameReady==FALSE) return;
0505   hDC= GetDC(hWnd);
0506   BitBlt(hFrameDC,0,0,zFRAMEWIDE,zFRAMEHIGH,hDC,0,0,SRCCOPY);
0507   ReleaseDC(hWnd,hDC);
0508   return;
0509   }
0510   /*
0511   ------------------------------------------------------------------
0512                        Draw a background image.
0513   ------------------------------------------------------------------
0514                                                                  */
0515   static void zDrawBg(HDC hDC)
0516   {
0517     HBRUSH hPrevBrush, hSwatchBrush;                    /* brushes */
0518     HPEN hPrevPen, hBorderPen;                            /* pens */
0519     RECT rcSwatch;                           /* rectangle structure */
0520     int iWidth= zFRAMEWIDE, iDepth= 4;        /* swatch dimensions */
0521     int iSwatchX= 0, iSwatchY= 0;              /* swatch location */
0522     BYTE bRed= 0, bGreen= 0, bBlue= 0;     /* rgb gun intensities */
0523     int iCount;                                   /* loop counter */
0524     int iX1= 100, iY1= 50, iX2= 300, iY2= 250;   /* ellipse coords */
0525     BYTE bGradient= 20;                   /* shading gradient factor */
0526     int iResize= 10;                            /* sizing factor */
0527
0528   /* ----------------- draw gradient background ---------------- */
0529   rcSwatch.left= iSwatchX;
0530   rcSwatch.top= iSwatchY;
0531   rcSwatch.right= rcSwatch.left + iWidth;
0532   rcSwatch.bottom= rcSwatch.top + iDepth;
0533   bRed= 0; bGreen= 0; bBlue= 3;
0534   for (iCount= 0; iCount < 64; iCount++)
0535     {
0536     hSwatchBrush= CreateSolidBrush(RGB(bRed,bGreen,bBlue));
0537     hPrevBrush= SelectObject(hDC,hSwatchBrush);
0538     FillRect(hDC,&rcSwatch,hSwatchBrush);
0539     SelectObject(hDC,hPrevBrush);
0540     DeleteObject(hSwatchBrush);
0541     rcSwatch.top= rcSwatch.top + iDepth;
0542     rcSwatch.bottom= rcSwatch.bottom + iDepth;
0543     bBlue= bBlue + (BYTE) 4;
0544     }
0545   bBlue= 255; rcSwatch.bottom= 300;
0546   hSwatchBrush= CreateSolidBrush(RGB(bRed,bGreen,bBlue));
0547   hPrevBrush= SelectObject(hDC,hSwatchBrush);
0548   FillRect(hDC,&rcSwatch,hSwatchBrush);
0549   SelectObject(hDC,hPrevBrush); DeleteObject(hSwatchBrush);
0550
0551   /* ----------------- draw gradient rectangle ---------------- */
0552   bRed= 0; bGreen= 0; bBlue= 255;
0553   iWidth= 280; iDepth= 4;
0554   iSwatchX= 60; iSwatchY= 24;
```

```
0555   rcSwatch.left= iSwatchX;
0556   rcSwatch.top= iSwatchY;
0557   rcSwatch.right= rcSwatch.left + iWidth;
0558   rcSwatch.bottom= rcSwatch.top + iDepth;
0559   for (iCount= 0; iCount < 64; iCount++)
0560     {
0561     hSwatchBrush= CreateSolidBrush(RGB(bRed,bGreen,bBlue));
0562     hPrevBrush= SelectObject(hDC,hSwatchBrush);
0563     FillRect(hDC,&rcSwatch,hSwatchBrush);
0564     SelectObject(hDC,hPrevBrush);
0565     DeleteObject(hSwatchBrush);
0566     rcSwatch.top= rcSwatch.top + iDepth;
0567     rcSwatch.bottom= rcSwatch.bottom + iDepth;
0568     bBlue= bBlue - (BYTE) 4;
0569     }
0570
0571   /* -------------------- draw gradiant circle -------------------- */
0572   hBorderPen= CreatePen(PS_NULL,1,RGB(0,0,255));
0573   hPrevPen= SelectObject(hDC,hBorderPen);   /* use transparent pen */
0574   bRed= 0; bGreen= 0; bBlue= 31;            /* reset rgb intensities */
0575   for (iCount= 1; iCount <= 9; iCount++)
0576     {   /* draw 7 ellipses, decreasing size, increasing brightness */
0577     hSwatchBrush= CreateSolidBrush(RGB(bRed,bGreen,bBlue));
0578     hPrevBrush= SelectObject(hDC,hSwatchBrush);
0579     Ellipse(hDC,iX1,iY1,iX2,iY2);
0580     bBlue+= bGradiant;
0581     iX1+= iResize;
0582     iY1+= iResize;
0583     iX2-= iResize;
0584     iY2-= iResize;
0585     SelectObject(hDC,hPrevBrush);
0586     DeleteObject(hSwatchBrush);
0587     }
0588
0589   /* -------------------- tidy up and exit -------------------- */
0590   SelectObject(hDC,hPrevPen); SelectObject(hDC,hPrevBrush);
0591   DeleteObject(hBorderPen); DeleteObject(hSwatchBrush);
0592   return;
0593   }
0594   /*
0595   ----------------------------------------------------------------
0596                      End of the C source file
0597   ----------------------------------------------------------------
0598                                                                */
```

# 3
# *Blitting*

The Windows graphics device interface contains bitmap functions and bitblt functions that can be used to create powerful animation functions such as the so-called transparent put function and image file functions.

## Transparent put

Expert | By careful manipulation of bitblt raster operators, an odd-shaped, multicolored bitmap can be cleanly pasted onto a multicolored background. This feature closely mimics the transparent cels used in traditional film animation. This so-called transparent put function or transparent cel function is the workhorse of many commercial animation and multimedia authoring software programs. Using transparent put, you can layer images on top of each other to create numerous actors and objects in front of a complex background.

A sampling of the numerous raster operators supported by the GDI's BitBlt() function is shown in FIG. 3-1. A raster operator is included in the argument list when your application calls BitBlt(). As FIG. 3-1 illustrates, a source bitmap can be written to a target bitmap in a variety of ways that produce dramatically different results, all made possible by the Boolean logic of the raster operators.

The conceptual schematic in FIG. 3-2 shows how raster operators can be used to build a transparent put function. This algorithm requires only one prerequisite: the cel bitmap must be comprised of a color image against a black background.

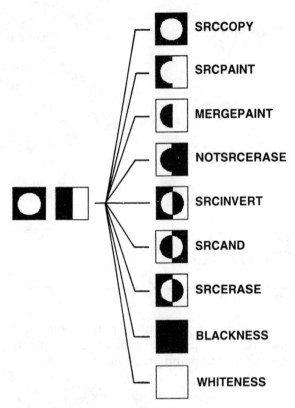

**3-1** A sampling of bitblt raster operators supported by the GDI.

## Image file functions

 The ability to save an image to disk in binary file format is an important feature of any Windows animation application. If each frame of an animation sequence can be written to disk, it can be downloaded later for editing or for playback. The animation engines demonstrated later in the book are smart enough to load an entire animation sequence into RAM if enough memory is available. Alternatively, they will run the animation from disk, loading each frame as it is needed for display during playback.

Together, the transparent put function and the image file functions are cornerstones of animation in Windows. They are an integral element in every animation programmer's toolkit.

## A sample application

The screen image in FIG. 3-3 shows the runtime menu display from the sample application blitting.exe. This program provides a working example of the transparent put function. It also demonstrates

## 5-step Transparent PUT

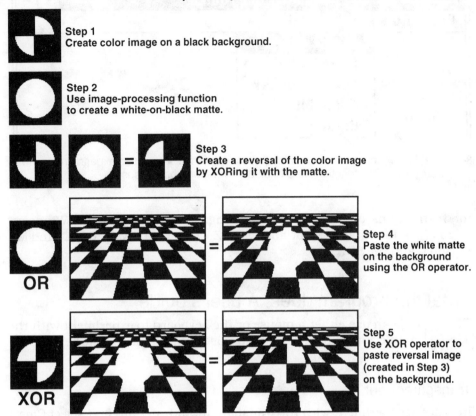

**Step 1**
Create color image on a black background.

**Step 2**
Use image-processing function
to create a white-on-black matte.

**Step 3**
Create a reversal of the color image
by XORing it with the matte.

**OR**

**Step 4**
Paste the white matte
on the background
using the OR operator.

**XOR**

**Step 5**
Use XOR operator to
paste reversal image
(created in Step 3)
on the background.

**3-2** The transparent PUT algorithm can cleanly paste an odd-shaped, multicolored bitblt on a multicolored image.

how to save a bitblt to disk as an image file in binary format, and how to load and display a previously-saved image from disk.

The transparent put function can be pasted into any Windows animation application that requires clean blitting of an odd-shaped, multicolored image over a multicolored background. This algorithm is also called a *transparent cel function*, because of the manner in which it mimics the transparent cels of traditional film animation. The image file functions can be pasted into any Windows graphics application that requires file I/O capabilities to store bitblts, bitmaps, or animation frames to disk.

The blitting.exe demo is built from four modules, including a .def module definition file, an .h #include file, an .rc resource script file, and a .c source file. All of these production files are presented as ready-to-use source code in the program listing later in this chapter. The source files are also provided on the companion disk. You can refer to the appropriate appendix

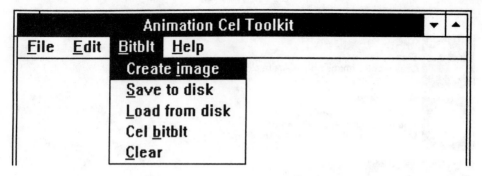

**3-3** The Bitblt menu from the sample application permits interactive experimentation with transparent PUT functions and bitblt disk save/load operations.

for instructions on how to build blitting.exe with QuickC for Windows, Turbo C++ for Windows, Borland C++, Zortech C++, WATCOM C, and Microsoft C and the SDK.

## What the program does: A user's guide

 You can use either a mouse or the keyboard to experiment with the sample application. The menus also support mnemonic keys.

### Transparent put

In order to experiment with the transparent put function, first select Create image from the Bitblt menu. A gradient image will be drawn, as shown in FIG. 3-4. Next select Cel bitblt from the Bitblt menu. A cel bit will be cleanly pasted over the multicolored background in three different locations, as shown in FIG. 3-5.

### Disk files

To experiment with the file save and file load features of the application program, first create a background and paste the cel bitmaps onto it as described in the previous paragraph. Next, select Save to disk from the Bitblt menu. If you have neglected to create the background image a message box will appear, as shown in FIG. 3-6.

To load a bitmap from disk, first select Clear from the Bitblt menu to blank the display window, then select Load from disk from the Bitblt menu. If the hidden bitmap has not yet been created, a warning will appear, as shown in FIG. 3-7 (top). If a disk error occurred or if the file could not be found, a message advisory will appear, as shown in FIG. 3-7 (bottom). If the file save

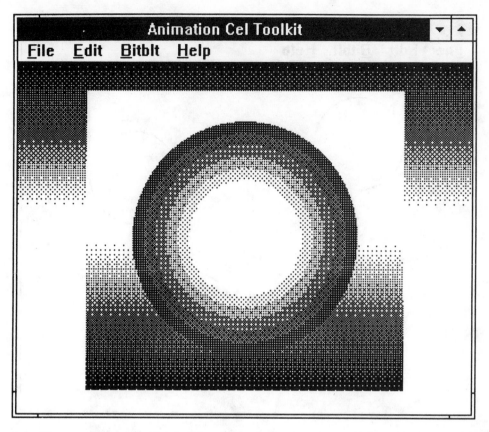

**3-4** The sample application builds a dithered image, over which multicolored, non-rectangular bitblts will be cleanly pasted.

and file load functions are successful, the program displays messages as shown in FIG. 3-8.

## How the source code works: A programmer's guide

The blitting.exe demonstration program provides a platform that exercises two powerful functions for animation development. The transparent put function makes it possible to cleanly paste any odd-shaped, multicolored bitblt over any multicolored background. The file save and file load functions make it possible to store bitblts, bitmaps, or frames on disk for later editing or animation playback.

The organization of the .h #include file and the .rc resource script file follow the format established in earlier sample applications. A few new menu items and strings have been added to support the enhanced capabilities of blitting.exe. See chapter 1 for a detailed discussion of the mechanics of the .h #include file and the .rc resource script file.

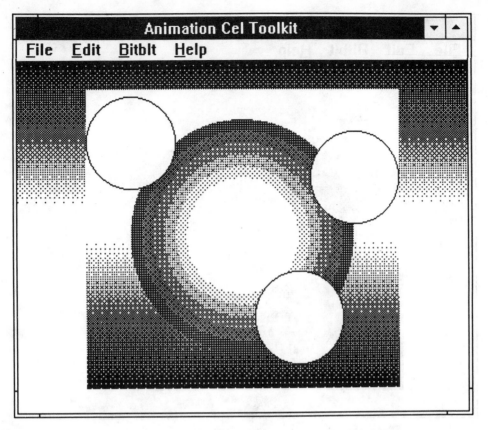

**3-5** Three instances of a multicolored, non-rectangular bitblt have been cleanly pasted over the multicolored, dithered background image shown here. The transparent PUT function uses a key color (a frisket metaphor) to write the bitblt over the background scene.

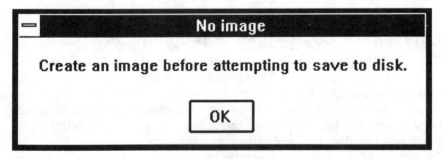

**3-6** File save operations are carefully monitored by the sample application in order to trap exceptions.

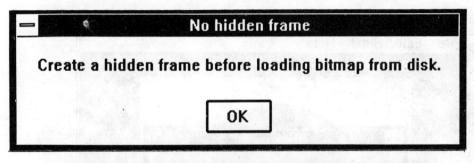

**3-7** The sample application monitors the status of memory and the disk drive during file load operations.

## How the .c file works

The program listing for the .c file is presented in FIG. 3-12.

**Static variables** The static variables for the .c file are located at lines 0049 through 0101. The code at lines 0091 through 0095 declares and initializes variables for disk file operations. Two Boolean variables named bImageExists and bBitmapExists are used in order to keep track of whether a bitmap exists to be saved and whether an image has been drawn on the bitmap. Two more Boolean variables named bFrameSaved and bFrameLoaded are used to keep track of whether the frame has already been saved to disk during the current work session and whether the frame has already been loaded and displayed during the current work session.

The code at lines 0098 through 0101 declares and initializes variables for the transparent cel operation. A Boolean variable named bTestBitbltExists keeps track of whether the user has created a bitblt that can pasted onto the package. Variables at lines 0100 and 0101 are used to manage the bitblt itself. hTestDC is the memory-display context for the bitmap that holds the bitblt. hTest is the handle to the bitmap. hPrevTest is the default handle for the hTestDC memory-display context, which is restored after the program is finished with the hTest handle.

**Managing the transparent cel** The message handler for the sample application is located at lines 0182 through 0293. The case block at lines 0226

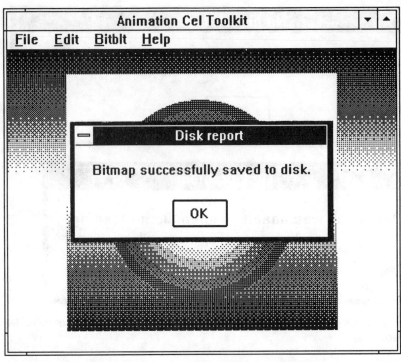

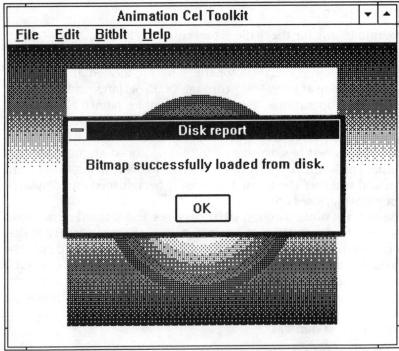

**3-8** The sample application uses message boxes to report the status of successful bitblt file save/load operations.

through 0233 manages the transparent put operations. Note how the if() statement at line 0227 tests to ensure that a working bitmap (background) has been created and that a test bitblt is ready. Then the code makes three calls to the zCelBlt() function in order to cleanly paste the test bitblt onto the multicolored background at three different locations. The multicolored background is shown in FIG. 3-4. The results of the transparent put function are shown in FIG. 3-5.

**Transparent put function**   The transparent put function is located at lines 0651 through 0756. The function, named zCelBlt(), adheres to the six-step method depicted earlier in FIG. 3-2. It does all its work on a33. Mercier, *Tableau de Paris*, 1:78. hidden bitmap called a *hidden frame*. First, zCelBlt() creates a bitblt consisting of a white matte on a black background. Next, it creates a reverse image of the cel bitmap (the test bitblt). Then it pastes the white matte onto the scene (the background bitmap) using OR logic. Next, it pastes the reverse image bitblt onto the scene using XOR logic, which results in a true image of the original cel bitmap on the scene. Finally, zCelBlt() copies the hidden frame (the work space) to the display window, destroys the various temporary display contexts, handles, and bitmaps it used, and returns to the caller.

**Creating a white matte**   The code that creates a white matte is located at lines 0677 through 0715. The call to GetObject() at line 0678 grabs a copy of the cel bitmap's data structure. The cel bitmap is the bitblt that is to be cleanly placed on the background scene. The code at lines 0687 and 0688 captures the dimensions of the cel bitmap. The code at lines 0689 through 0700 creates a compatible display-context, a compatible bitmap, and selects the compatible bitmap into the compatible display-context, where it is ready to be used. The call to BitBlt() at line 0701 copies the cel bitmap into the newly created bitmap. Next, the for() loop at lines 0706 through 0715 sets all non-background pixels to white. It can easily do this because the cel bitmap passed in the argument list (when zCelBlt() was called) is composed of a black background. So any pixel element that is not black is non-background.

The resulting white matte is a frisket that protects the scene from being overwritten by the background portion (clear portion) of the cel bitmap.

**Creating a reversal**   The code at lines 0717 through 0734 creates a reverse image of the cel bitmap. First, the code at lines 0718 through 0732 creates a copy of the white matte. Then the call to BitBlt() at line 0733 uses the SRCINVERT raster operator to copy the cel bitmap onto the white matte to create a reversal (as shown in FIG. 3-2, Step 3).

**Pasting the cel onto the scene**   The code at lines 0736 through 0738 copies the white matte onto the scene (the background bitmap). Then the code at lines 0740 through 0742 uses the SRCINVERT raster operator to paste the reversal onto the white matte (which has already been pasted onto the scene). The result is a positive image of the original cel bitmap, correctly positioned on the scene. The code then copies the work space (the hidden frame) to the application's display window.

**Saving an image to disk**  The function that saves a bitmap file to disk in binary format is located at lines 0413 through 0524. The local variables for this function are declared at lines 0415 through 0425. The comments in the source code explain the intended use of each variable.

The if() statement at lines 0427 through 0433 checks to see if Windows is running in a 256-color mode. If so, it advises the user that the code is intended for 16-color modes.

Next the code checks to determine if an image exists on the bitmap (at line 0435). If so, the call to GetObject() at line 0442 grabs a copy of the bitmap's data structure. The code at lines 0451 through 0453 captures the dimensions of the bitmap and the number of bitplanes in the bitmap.

**Monitoring the length**  The code at lines 0454 and 0455 calculates the length (in bytes) of the data in the bitmap. If the bitmap data is lengthier than 65,534 bytes then the if() statement at line 0456 detects this and issues an explanatory message. Otherwise, the code at line 0462 casts the LONG TestLength variable into a WORD NumBytes variable.

**Writing the data to disk**  In order to write the data from the bitmap to disk, the function must create a memory buffer, lock it, copy the data from the bitmap to the buffer, open a file, write the data from the buffer to the file, close the file, and discard the buffer. At each step in this process, the code carefully checks to ensure that no runtime errors have occurred that could lock up the computer system.

The code at line 0464 calls GlobalAlloc() to create a memory buffer by allocating memory in the global heap. Next, a call to GlobalLock() at line 0471 ensures that the buffer will not be moved by Windows' built-in memory manager. Then the handle returned by GlobalLock() is used in a call to Get-BitmapBits() at line 0472, which copies the raw bits from the bitmap to the memory buffer. Again, note how the if() statement at lines 0473 through 0479 tests for the occurrence of an error and cleanly tidies up before returning if an error was detected.

The code at lines 0481 through 0491 checks for the existence of a file. If the file already exists the user is given the option of overwriting it or cancelling the operation. The MB_YESNO argument in the call to MessageBox() provides feedback that the program uses to make a branching decision.

*Market*  The code at lines 0493 through 0500 opens the file for writing. Then the code at lines 0502 through 0510 writes the data from the memory buffer to the disk file. The _lwrite() function can write a maximum of 65,534 bytes, which was why the code checked the length of the bitmap data earlier at line 0456. If Windows is running in a 16-color mode (or a 2-color mode), the display window of the sample application will require 60,000 bytes of storage. However, if Windows is running in a 256-color mode, the display window requires 120,000 bytes of storage. You can modify the code to support 256-color bitmaps by creating a loop which keeps calling _lwrite() until all the bytes in the memory buffer have been written to disk.

Finally, the code at line 0512 closes the file. The call to GlobalUnlock() at line 0521 discards the pointer to the buffer and unlocks the block of memory. The call to GlobalFree() at line 0522 frees the block, making it available for use by other applications.

**Loading an image from disk**   The function at lines 0530 through 0641 loads a binary bitmap image from disk. This function performs many of the same checks that were described in the file save function. The if() statement at line 0545 ensures that Windows is not running in a 256-color mode. The code at line 0553 ensures that a bitmap exists to receive the image that will be downloaded from disk. The code at lines 0561 through 0581 determines the dimensions of the bitmap and calculates the number of bytes it holds.

Next, the code at lines 0583 through 0590 creates a memory buffer and locks it. A call to OpenFile() at line 0592 opens the file for reading. The if() statement at lines 0593 through 0599 gracefully cancels the operation if the file does not exist.

The call to _lread() at line 0601 reads the data from the disk. (Again, if you want to support 256-color modes, you would create a loop to repeatedly call _lread() until the entire file had been read into the buffer.) Note in particular the if() statement at lines 0610 through 0617, which checks the number of bytes read from the file against the expected number.

Next, the code calls _lclose() at line 0619 to close the file. A call to SetBitmapBits() at line 0628 copies the raw data from the memory buffer into the bitmap. Then the code at lines 0637 through 0640 unlocks the memory buffer, frees it, sets the Boolean variable bImageExists to TRUE, and returns to the caller.

## Program listings for the sample application

The program listings presented here contain all the source code you need to build and run the sample application. The module definition file is provided in FIG. 3-9. The #include file is found in FIG. 3-10. The resource script file is presented in FIG. 3-11. The C source file is provided in FIG. 3-12.

**Companion disk**   If you have the companion disk, the source files are presented as blitting.def, blitting.h. blitting.rc, and blitting.c.

**License**   You can paste the royalty-free source code into your own applications and distribute the resulting executable files under the conditions of the License Agreement and Limited Warranty in FIG. 10 in the introduction to the book.

**3-9** The module definition file listing for the sample application.

```
0001   NAME           DEFDEMO
0002   DESCRIPTION    'Copyright 1992 Lee Adams.  All rights reserved.'
0003   EXETYPE        WINDOWS
0004   STUB           'WINSTUB.EXE'
0005   CODE           PRELOAD MOVEABLE
0006   DATA           PRELOAD MOVEABLE MULTIPLE
0007   HEAPSIZE       1024
0008   STACKSIZE      8192
0009   EXPORTS        zMessageHandler
```

**3-10** The include file listing for the sample application.

```
0001   /*
0002   ------------------------------------------------------------------
0003                       Include file BLITTING.H
0004            Copyright 1992 Lee Adams.  All rights reserved.
0005      Include this file in the .RC resource script file and in the
0006      .C source file.  It contains function prototypes, menu ID
0007      constants, and string ID constants.
0008   ------------------------------------------------------------------
0009   ------------------------------------------------------------------
0010                       Function prototypes
0011   ------------------------------------------------------------------
0012                                                                    */
0013   #if !defined(zRCFILE)                  /* if not an .RC file... */
0014      LONG FAR PASCAL zMessageHandler(HWND, unsigned, WORD, LONG);
0015      int PASCAL WinMain(HANDLE,HANDLE,LPSTR,int);
0016      HWND zInitMainWindow(HANDLE);
0017      BOOL zInitClass(HANDLE);
0018   static void zClear(HWND);              /* blank the display window */
0019   static void zCreateImage(HWND);          /* creates test graphics */
0020   static void zDrawBg(HDC);              /* draws background scene */
0021   static BOOL zSaveFrame(HBITMAP, LPSTR);   /* save frame to disk */
0022   static BOOL zLoadFrame(HBITMAP, LPSTR);  /* load frame from disk */
0023   static BOOL zCelBlt(HWND,HDC,HDC,             /* transparent PUT */
0024                       HBITMAP,int,int);
0025   #endif
0026   /*
0027   ------------------------------------------------------------------
0028                       Menu ID constants
0029   ------------------------------------------------------------------
0030                                                                    */
0031   #define IDM_New            1
0032   #define IDM_Open           2
0033   #define IDM_Save           3
0034   #define IDM_SaveAs         4
0035   #define IDM_Exit           5
0036
0037   #define IDM_Undo           6
0038   #define IDM_Cut            7
0039   #define IDM_Copy           8
0040   #define IDM_Paste          9
0041   #define IDM_Delete         10
0042
0043   #define IDM_CreateFrame    11
0044   #define IDM_SaveFrame      12
0045   #define IDM_LoadFrame      13
0046   #define IDM_CelBlt         14
0047   #define IDM_Clear          15
0048
```

**3-10** Continued.

```
0049    #define IDM_About              16
0050    #define IDM_License            17
0051    #define IDM_GeneralHelp        18
0052    /*
0053    -------------------------------------------------------------------
0054                          String ID constants
0055    -------------------------------------------------------------------
0056                                                                     */
0057    #define IDS_Caption       1
0058    #define IDS_Warning       2
0059    #define IDS_NoMouse       3
0060    #define IDS_About         4
0061    #define IDS_AboutText     5
0062    #define IDS_License       6
0063    #define IDS_LicenseText   7
0064    #define IDS_Help          8
0065    #define IDS_HelpText      9
0066    /*
0067    -------------------------------------------------------------------
0068                          End of include file
0069    -------------------------------------------------------------------
0070                                                                     */
```

**3-11** The resource script file listing for the sample application.

```
0001    /*
0002    -------------------------------------------------------------------
0003                    Resource script file BLITTING.RC
0004            Copyright 1992 Lee Adams.  All rights reserved.
0005      This file defines the menu resources, the accelerator key
0006      resources, and the string resources that will be used by the
0007      demonstration application at runtime.
0008    -------------------------------------------------------------------
0009                                                                     */
0010    #define zRCFILE
0011    #include <WINDOWS.H>
0012    #include "BLITTING.H"
0013    /*
0014    -------------------------------------------------------------------
0015                          Script for menus
0016    -------------------------------------------------------------------
0017                                                                     */
0018    MENUS1 MENU
0019      BEGIN
0020      POPUP "&File"
0021        BEGIN
0022          MENUITEM   "&New", IDM_New, GRAYED
0023          MENUITEM   "&Open...", IDM_Open, GRAYED
0024          MENUITEM   "&Save", IDM_Save, GRAYED
0025          MENUITEM   "Save &As...", IDM_SaveAs, GRAYED
0026          MENUITEM SEPARATOR
0027          MENUITEM   "E&xit", IDM_Exit
0028        END
0029      POPUP "&Edit"
0030        BEGIN
0031          MENUITEM   "&Undo\tAlt+BkSp", IDM_Undo, GRAYED
0032          MENUITEM SEPARATOR
0033          MENUITEM   "Cu&t\tShift+Del", IDM_Cut, GRAYED
0034          MENUITEM   "&Copy\tCtrl+Ins", IDM_Copy, GRAYED
0035          MENUITEM   "&Paste\tShift+Ins", IDM_Paste, GRAYED
```

```
0036         MENUITEM  "&Delete\tDel", IDM_Delete, GRAYED
0037       END
0038    POPUP "&Bitblt"
0039      BEGIN
0040        MENUITEM "Create &image", IDM_CreateFrame
0041        MENUITEM "&Save to disk", IDM_SaveFrame
0042        MENUITEM "&Load from disk", IDM_LoadFrame
0043        MENUITEM "Cel &bitblt", IDM_CelBlt
0044        MENUITEM "&Clear", IDM_Clear
0045      END
0046    POPUP "&Help"
0047      BEGIN
0048        MENUITEM "&About", IDM_About
0049        MENUITEM "&License", IDM_License
0050        MENUITEM SEPARATOR
0051        MENUITEM  "&Help", IDM_GeneralHelp
0052      END
0053    END
0054  /*
0055  -----------------------------------------------------------------
0056                    Script for accelerator keys
0057  -----------------------------------------------------------------
0058                                                                 */
0059  KEYS1 ACCELERATORS
0060    BEGIN
0061    VK_BACK, IDM_Undo, VIRTKEY, ALT
0062    VK_DELETE, IDM_Cut, VIRTKEY, SHIFT
0063    VK_INSERT, IDM_Copy, VIRTKEY, CONTROL
0064    VK_INSERT, IDM_Paste, VIRTKEY, SHIFT
0065    VK_DELETE, IDM_Delete, VIRTKEY
0066    END
0067  /*
0068  -----------------------------------------------------------------
0069                        Script for strings
0070    Programmer's Notes:  If you are typing this listing, set your
0071    margins to a line length of 255 characters so you can create
0072    lengthy strings without embedded carriage returns.  The line
0073    wraparounds in the following STRINGTABLE script are used for
0074    readability only in this printout.
0075  -----------------------------------------------------------------
0076                                                                 */
0077  STRINGTABLE
0078    BEGIN
0079      IDS_Caption      "Animation Cel Toolkit"
0080      IDS_Warning      "Graphics system warning"
0081      IDS_NoMouse      "No mouse found.  Some features of this
          demonstration program may require a mouse."
0082      IDS_About        "About this program"
0083      IDS_AboutText    "This is a demo from Windcrest McGraw-Hill
          book 4114.  Copyright 1992 Lee Adams.  All rights reserved."
0084      IDS_License      "License Agreement"
0085      IDS_LicenseText "You can use this code as part of your own
          software product subject to the License Agreement and Limited
          Warranty in Windcrest McGraw-Hill book 4114 and on its
          companion disk."
0086      IDS_Help         "How to use this demo"
0087      IDS_HelpText     "First, select Create Image from the Bitblt
          menu.  Choose Cel Bitblt to PUT a non-rectangular bitblt over
          a multicolor image.  You can also save the bitmap to disk and
          load a previously-saved image."
0088    END
```

**3-11** Continued.

```
0089  /*
0090  ------------------------------------------------------------------
0091                     End of resource script file
0092  ------------------------------------------------------------------
0093                                                                  */
```

**3-12** The C source file listing for the sample application, blitting.c. This demonstration program is ready to build using QuickC for Windows, Turbo C++ for Windows, Microsoft C and the SDK, Borland C++, Symantec Zortech C++, WATCOM C, and other compilers. See FIG. 1-2 for sample command-lines to build the program. Guidelines for using your compiler are provided in the appropriate appendix at the back of the book.

```
0001  /*
0002  ------------------------------------------------------------------
0003               Bitmap toolkit for Windows applications that use
0004               real-time animation or frame animation functions.
0005  ------------------------------------------------------------------
0006     Source file:  BLITTING.C
0007     Release version:  1.00                   Programmer:  Lee Adams
0008     Type:  C source file for Windows application development.
0009     Compilers:  Microsoft C and SDK, Borland C++, Zortech C++,
0010        QuickC for Windows, Turbo C++ for Windows, WATCOM C.
0011     Memory model:  small.
0012     Dependencies:  BLITTING.DEF module definition file, BLITTING.H
0013                    include file, BLITTING.RC resource script file,
0014                    and BLITTING.C source file.
0015     Output and features:  Demonstrates transparent PUT, whereby
0016        a non-rectangular, multicolored bitblt can be cleanly placed
0017        over a multicolor image using a frisket metaphor that causes
0018        the bitblt background to remain transparent. This method is
0019        useful for placing cels on a scene.  Also demonstrates how
0020        to save a bitmap to disk and load a bitmap file from disk.
0021     Publication: Contains material from Windcrest/McGraw-Hill book
0022        4114 published by TAB BOOKS Division of McGraw-Hill Inc.
0023     License:  As purchaser of the book you are granted a royalty-
0024        free license to distribute executable files generated using
0025        this code provided you accept the conditions of the License
0026        Agreement and Limited Warranty described in the book and on
0027        the companion disk.  Government users:  This software and
0028        documentation are subject to restrictions set forth in The
0029        Rights in Technical Data and Computer Software clause at
0030        252.227-7013 and elsewhere.
0031  ------------------------------------------------------------------
0032           (c) Copyright 1992 Lee Adams.  All rights reserved.
0033           Lee Adams(tm) is a trademark of Lee Adams.
0034  ------------------------------------------------------------------
0035
0036  ------------------------------------------------------------------
0037                           Include files
0038  ------------------------------------------------------------------
0039                                                                  */
0040  #include <WINDOWS.H>
0041  #include <SYS\TYPES.H>                /* supports disk operations */
0042  #include <SYS\STAT.H>                 /* supports disk operations */
0043  #include "BLITTING.H"
0044  /*
0045  ------------------------------------------------------------------
0046               Static variables visible throughout this file
```

```
0047  ------------------------------------------------------------------
0048                                                                  */
0049  /* ----------------- window specifications ------------------ */
0050  #define zWINDOW_WIDTH 408                    /* width of window */
0051  #define zWINDOW_HEIGHT 346                   /* height of window */
0052  #define zFRAMEWIDE 400                  /* width of client area */
0053  #define zFRAMEHIGH 300                 /* height of client area */
0054  int WindowX, WindowY;                   /* location of window */
0055
0056  /* ------------------- instance operations ------------------- */
0057  HANDLE hInst;                     /* handle to this instance */
0058  HWND MainhWnd;                    /* handle to the main window */
0059  HANDLE hAccel;              /* handle to accelerator keys table */
0060  HMENU hMenu;                  /* handle to a menu at runtime */
0061  PAINTSTRUCT ps;      /* structure used by persistent graphics */
0062
0063  /* -------------------- mouse and cursor --------------------- */
0064  HCURSOR hPrevCursor;              /* handle to default cursor */
0065  HCURSOR hHourGlass;             /* handle to hourglass cursor */
0066  int MousePresent;           /* will indicate if mouse present */
0067
0068  /* ------------------- runtime conditions -------------------- */
0069  int DisplayWidth, DisplayHeight;       /* screen resolution */
0070  int DisplayBits;                /* number of bits-per-pixel */
0071  int DisplayPlanes;                 /* number of bitplanes */
0072  DWORD MemoryMode;                  /* runtime memory mode */
0073
0074  /* ------------------ message box operations ----------------- */
0075  char lpCaption[51];     /* will hold caption for message boxes */
0076  int Max= 50;                   /* maximum length of caption */
0077  char lpMessage[250];        /* will hold text for message boxes */
0078  int MaxText= 249;              /* maximum length of text */
0079
0080  /* -------------------- font operations ---------------------- */
0081  HFONT hFont, hPrevFont;         /* handles to new, previous font */
0082  HDC hFontDC;                     /* display-context for font */
0083
0084  /* ------------------hidden frame operations ----------------- */
0085  HDC hFrameDC;            /* memory display-context for hidden-frame */
0086  HBITMAP hFrame;                 /* handle to hidden-frame bitmap */
0087  HBITMAP hPrevFrame;                   /* default bitmap */
0088  BOOL FrameReady= FALSE;             /* hidden-frame created? */
0089
0090  /* ----------------- variables for disk I/O ----------------- */
0091  BOOL bImageExists= FALSE;                 /* status indicator */
0092  BOOL bBitmapExists= FALSE;                /* status indicator */
0093  int RetVal;                               /* return value */
0094  BOOL bFrameSaved;                         /* status indicator */
0095  BOOL bFrameLoaded;                        /* status indicator */
0096
0097  /* ------------- variables for transparent bitblts ------------- */
0098  BOOL bCelBlt= TRUE;              /* result of transparent put */
0099  BOOL bTestBitbltExists= FALSE;        /* TRUE if bitblt exists */
0100  HDC hTestDC;                     /* memory display-context */
0101  HBITMAP hTest, hPrevTest;             /* handle to bitmap */
0102
0103  /*
0104  ------------------------------------------------------------------
0105                Entry point for the application
0106  ------------------------------------------------------------------
0107                                                                  */
```

```
0108  int PASCAL WinMain(HANDLE hInstance, HANDLE hPrevInstance,
0109                    LPSTR lpCmdLine, int nCmdShow)
0110  {
0111    MSG msg;                            /* will hold incoming messages */
0112    HWND hWndPrev;           /* handle to window of another instance */
0113    HWND hDesktopWnd;        /* handle to full-screen desktop window */
0114    HDC hDCcaps;               /* display-context of desktop window */
0115
0116  /* ----------- ensure only one instance is running ----------- */
0117  hWndPrev = FindWindow("DEMOCLASS", NULL);
0118  if (hWndPrev != NULL)          /* if another instance was found... */
0119    {
0120    BringWindowToTop(hWndPrev);              /* make it active... */
0121    return FALSE;               /* ...and terminate this instance */
0122    }
0123
0124  /* --------- determine capabilities of screen display ---------- */
0125  hDesktopWnd= GetDesktopWindow();
0126  hDCcaps= GetDC(hDesktopWnd);
0127  DisplayWidth= GetDeviceCaps(hDCcaps,HORZRES);
0128  DisplayHeight= GetDeviceCaps(hDCcaps,VERTRES);
0129  DisplayBits= GetDeviceCaps(hDCcaps,BITSPIXEL);
0130  DisplayPlanes= GetDeviceCaps(hDCcaps,PLANES);
0131  ReleaseDC(hDesktopWnd,hDCcaps);
0132
0133  /* ------- calculate screen position to center the window ------ */
0134  WindowX= (DisplayWidth - zWINDOW_WIDTH) / 2;        /* horizontal */
0135  WindowY= (DisplayHeight - zWINDOW_HEIGHT) /2;         /* vertical */
0136  if (WindowX < 0) WindowX= 0;
0137  if (WindowY < 0) WindowY= 0;
0138
0139  /* ---- determine memory mode (enhanced, standard, or real) ---- */
0140  MemoryMode= GetWinFlags();          /* will read this value later */   32 bit value
0141
0142  /* -------------- create and display the window ---------------- */
0143  hInst= hInstance;                    /* remember the instance handle */
0144  if (!zInitClass(hInstance)) return FALSE;     /* create the class */
0145  MainhWnd= zInitMainWindow(hInstance);          /* create the window */
0146  if (!MainhWnd) return FALSE;     /* exit if no window was created */
0147  ShowWindow(MainhWnd, nCmdShow);            /* display the window */
0148  UpdateWindow(MainhWnd);                  /* send a paint message */
0149  hAccel= LoadAccelerators(hInstance,"KEYS1"); /* accelerator keys */
0150  hFontDC= GetDC(MainhWnd);              /* get a display-context */
0151  hFont= GetStockObject(SYSTEM_FONT);        /* grab handle to font */
0152  hPrevFont= SelectObject(hFontDC,hFont);   /* select font into DC */
0153  SetTextColor(hFontDC,RGB(191,191,191));     /* set new text color */
0154  TextOut(hFontDC,10,280,"- Copyright 1992 Lee Adams.",27);/* text */
0155  SetTextColor(hFontDC,RGB(255,255,255));    /* restore text color */
0156  SelectObject(hFontDC,hPrevFont);        /* restore previous font */
0157  ReleaseDC(MainhWnd,hFontDC);         /* release display-context */
0158
0159  /* -------------------- check for mouse -------------------- */
0160  MousePresent= GetSystemMetrics(SM_MOUSEPRESENT);
0161  if (!MousePresent)                   /* if no active mouse found */
0162    {
0163    LoadString(hInst,IDS_Warning,lpCaption,Max);   /* load caption */
0164    LoadString(hInst,IDS_NoMouse,lpMessage,MaxText);  /* load text */
0165    MessageBox(GetFocus(),lpMessage,lpCaption,MB_OK);  /* message */
0166    }
0167
0168  /* ---------- begin retrieving messages for the window --------- */
```

```
0169  while (GetMessage(&msg,0,0,0))
0170     {
0171     if(TranslateAccelerator(MainhWnd, hAccel, &msg)) continue;
0172     TranslateMessage(&msg);
0173     DispatchMessage(&msg);
0174     }
0175  return(msg.wParam);
0176  }
0177  /*
0178  -------------------------------------------------------------------
0179                    Switcher for incoming messages
0180  -------------------------------------------------------------------
0181                                                                  */
0182  LONG FAR PASCAL zMessageHandler(HWND hWnd, unsigned message,
0183                        WORD wParam, LONG lParam)
0184  {
0185     HDC hDC;
0186  switch (message)
0187     {
0188     case WM_COMMAND:          /* if user has selected a menu item... */
0189       switch(wParam)
0190          {
0191          case IDM_New:          break;
0192          case IDM_Open:         break;
0193          case IDM_Save:         break;
0194          case IDM_SaveAs:       break;
0195          case IDM_Exit:         PostQuitMessage(0); break;
0196
0197          case IDM_Undo:         break;
0198          case IDM_Cut:          break;
0199          case IDM_Copy:         break;
0200          case IDM_Paste:        break;
0201          case IDM_Delete:       break;
0202
0203          case IDM_CreateFrame: zCreateImage(hWnd); break;
0204          case IDM_SaveFrame:
0205               bFrameSaved= zSaveFrame(hFrame,(LPSTR)"FRAME1.BIT");
0206               if (bFrameSaved==TRUE)
0207                  {
0208                  MessageBox(GetFocus(),
0209                     "Bitmap successfully saved to disk.",
0210                     "Disk report", MB_OK);
0211                  }
0212               break;
0213          case IDM_LoadFrame:
0214               bFrameLoaded= zLoadFrame(hFrame,(LPSTR)"FRAME1.BIT");
0215               if (bFrameLoaded==TRUE)
0216                  {
0217                  hDC= GetDC(hWnd);
0218                  BitBlt(hDC,0,0,
0219                     zFRAMEWIDE,zFRAMEHIGH,hFrameDC,0,0,SRCCOPY);
0220                  ReleaseDC(hWnd,hDC);
0221                  MessageBox(GetFocus(),
0222                     "Bitmap successfully loaded from disk.",
0223                     "Disk report", MB_OK);
0224                  }
0225               break;
0226          case IDM_CelBlt:
0227            if ( (bBitmapExists==TRUE) && (bTestBitbltExists==TRUE) )
0228               {
0229               bCelBlt= zCelBlt(hWnd,hFrameDC,hTestDC,hTest,200,170);
```

```
0230              bCelBlt= zCelBlt(hWnd,hFrameDC,hTestDC,hTest,50,20);
0231              bCelBlt= zCelBlt(hWnd,hFrameDC,hTestDC,hTest,250,50);
0232              }
0233          break;
0234        case IDM_Clear: zClear(hWnd); break;
0235
0236        case IDM_About:
0237          LoadString(hInst,IDS_About,lpCaption,Max);
0238          LoadString(hInst,IDS_AboutText,lpMessage,MaxText);
0239          MessageBox(GetFocus(),lpMessage,lpCaption,MB_OK);
0240          break;
0241        case IDM_License:
0242          LoadString(hInst,IDS_License,lpCaption,Max);
0243          LoadString(hInst,IDS_LicenseText,lpMessage,MaxText);
0244          MessageBox(GetFocus(),lpMessage,lpCaption,MB_OK);
0245          break;
0246        case IDM_GeneralHelp:
0247          LoadString(hInst,IDS_Help,lpCaption,Max);
0248          LoadString(hInst,IDS_HelpText,lpMessage,MaxText);
0249          MessageBox(GetFocus(),lpMessage,lpCaption,MB_OK);
0250          break;
0251        default:
0252          return(DefWindowProc(hWnd, message, wParam, lParam));
0253        }
0254      break;
0255
0256    case WM_DESTROY:   /* if user is terminating the application... */
0257      if (bBitmapExists==TRUE)
0258        {
0259        SelectObject(hFrameDC, hPrevFrame);
0260        DeleteObject(hFrame);
0261        DeleteDC(hFrameDC);
0262        bBitmapExists= FALSE;
0263        bImageExists= FALSE;
0264        }
0265      if (bTestBitbltExists==TRUE)
0266        {
0267        SelectObject(hTestDC, hPrevTest);
0268        DeleteObject(hTest);
0269        DeleteDC(hTestDC);
0270        bTestBitbltExists= FALSE;
0271        }
0272      PostQuitMessage(0);
0273      break;
0274
0275    case WM_SYSCOMMAND:     /* intercept resize, minimize, maximize */
0276      if ((wParam & 0xfff0)== SC_SIZE)
0277        {
0278        MessageBeep(0); break;
0279        }
0280      if ((wParam & 0xfff0)== SC_MINIMIZE)
0281        {
0282        MessageBeep(0); break;
0283        }
0284      if ((wParam & 0xfff0)== SC_MAXIMIZE)
0285        {
0286        MessageBeep(0); break;
0287        }
0288
0289    default:
0290      return(DefWindowProc(hWnd, message, wParam, lParam));
```

```
0291     }
0292  return FALSE;
0293  }
0294  /*
0295  ----------------------------------------------------------------
0296          Initialize the attributes of the window class
0297  ----------------------------------------------------------------
0298                                                              */
0299  BOOL zInitClass(HANDLE hInstance)
0300  {
0301    WNDCLASS WndClass;
0302  WndClass.style= 0;                              /* class style */
0303  WndClass.lpfnWndProc= zMessageHandler;     /* callback function */
0304  WndClass.cbClsExtra= 0;          /* unused, no customized data */
0305  WndClass.cbWndExtra= 0;          /* unused, no customized data */
0306  WndClass.hInstance= hInstance;   /* application that owns class */
0307  WndClass.hIcon= LoadIcon(NULL,IDI_EXCLAMATION); /* minimize icon */
0308  WndClass.hCursor= LoadCursor(NULL,IDC_ARROW);    /* app's cursor */
0309  WndClass.hbrBackground=  /* specifies background color of window */
0310                      CreateSolidBrush(RGB(255,255,255));
0311  WndClass.lpszMenuName= "MENUS1";    /* name of .RC menu resource */
0312  WndClass.lpszClassName= "DEMOCLASS";       /* name of the class */
0313  return RegisterClass(&WndClass);        /* registers the class */
0314  }
0315  /*
0316  ----------------------------------------------------------------
0317                     Create the main window
0318  ----------------------------------------------------------------
0319                                                              */
0320  HWND zInitMainWindow(HANDLE hInstance)
0321  {
0322    HWND hWnd;
0323  LoadString(hInstance,IDS_Caption,lpCaption,Max); /* load caption */
0324  hHourGlass= LoadCursor(NULL,IDC_WAIT);  /* load the wait cursor */
0325  hWnd= CreateWindow("DEMOCLASS",   /* create window of this class */
0326        lpCaption,                             /* caption */
0327        WS_OVERLAPPED | WS_THICKFRAME | WS_MINIMIZEBOX |   /* type */
0328         WS_MAXIMIZEBOX | WS_CLIPCHILDREN,
0329        WindowX,WindowY,                  /* screen location */
0330        zWINDOW_WIDTH,zWINDOW_HEIGHT,      /* window dimensions */
0331        0,0,              /* parent handle, menu or child ID */
0332        hInstance,(LPSTR)NULL); /* app instance and unused pointer */
0333  return hWnd;
0334  }
0335  /*
0336  ----------------------------------------------------------------
0337            THE CORE FUNCTIONS OF THE APPLICATION
0338  ----------------------------------------------------------------
0339  ----------------------------------------------------------------
0340       Create hidden frame, a test image, and a test cel.
0341  ----------------------------------------------------------------
0342                                                              */
0343  static void zCreateImage(HWND hWnd)
0344  {
0345    HDC hDC;
0346    HPEN RedPen, PrevTestPen;
0347    HBRUSH RedBrush, PrevTestBrush;
0348
0349  hDC= GetDC(hWnd);                         /* get a display-context */
0350
0351  /* -------------------- create a test image -------------------- */
```

```
0352    zDrawBg(hDC);
0353
0354    /* ------------------ create a hidden frame ------------------ */
0355    if (bBitmapExists==FALSE)   /* if no hidden bitmap yet created... */
0356      {
0357      hFrameDC= CreateCompatibleDC(hDC);          /* create a memory DC */
0358      hFrame= CreateCompatibleBitmap(hDC,          /* create bitmap */
0359              zFRAMEWIDE, zFRAMEHIGH);
0360      if (hFrame==0)                     /* if cannot create bitmap... */
0361        {                      /* ...issue message, tidy up, and exit */
0362        MessageBeep(0); MessageBox(GetFocus(),
0363          "Unable to create hidden bitmap.  Possible memory error.",
0364          "Graphics system status", MB_OK);
0365        DeleteDC(hFrameDC);
0366        bBitmapExists= FALSE;
0367        bImageExists= FALSE;
0368        ReleaseDC(hWnd,hDC);
0369        return;
0370        }
0371      hPrevFrame= SelectObject(hFrameDC,hFrame);   /* select bitmap */
0372      bBitmapExists= TRUE;                 /* set the status indicator */
0373      }
0374    BitBlt(hFrameDC,0,0,                  /* copy image to hidden frame */
0375           zFRAMEWIDE,zFRAMEHIGH,hDC,0,0,SRCCOPY);
0376
0377    /* -------------------- create a test cel -------------------- */
0378    if (bTestBitbltExists==FALSE)         /* if no cel yet created... */
0379      {
0380      hTestDC= CreateCompatibleDC(hDC);          /* create a memory DC */
0381      hTest= CreateCompatibleBitmap(hDC,100,100);  /* create bitmap */
0382      if (hTest==0)                     /* if cannot create bitmap... */
0383        {                      /* ...issue message, tidy up, and exit */
0384        MessageBeep(0); MessageBox(GetFocus(),
0385          "Unable to create test bitblt.  Possible memory error.",
0386          "Graphics system status", MB_OK);
0387        DeleteDC(hTestDC); ReleaseDC(hWnd,hDC);
0388        bTestBitbltExists= FALSE; return;
0389        }
0390      hPrevTest= SelectObject(hTestDC,hTest);       /* select bitmap */
0391      PatBlt(hTestDC,0,0,100,100,BLACKNESS);       /* draw black bg */
0392      RedPen= CreatePen(PS_SOLID,1,RGB(255,0,0));
0393      RedBrush= CreateSolidBrush(RGB(127,0,0));
0394      PrevTestPen= SelectObject(hTestDC,RedPen);
0395      PrevTestBrush= SelectObject(hTestDC,RedBrush);
0396      Ellipse(hTestDC,10,10,90,90);            /* draw green ellipse */
0397      SelectObject(hTestDC,PrevTestBrush);
0398      SelectObject(hTestDC,PrevTestPen);
0399      DeleteObject(RedBrush); DeleteObject(RedPen);
0400      bTestBitbltExists= TRUE;           /* set the status indicator */
0401      }
0402
0403    /* -------------------- tidy up and return -------------------- */
0404    ReleaseDC(hWnd,hDC);                 /* release the display-context */
0405    bImageExists= TRUE;                      /* set a runtime token */
0406    return;
0407    }
0408    /*
0409    --------------------------------------------------------------
0410                      Save a bitmap file to disk.
0411    --------------------------------------------------------------
```

```
0412                                                                    */
0413    static BOOL zSaveFrame(HBITMAP hBitmap, LPSTR lpFileName)
0414    {
0415      BITMAP bmImage;                      /* bitmap data structure */
0416      short BytesPerLine;                    /* width of bitmap */
0417      short RasterLines;                     /* height of bitmap */
0418      BYTE NumPlanes;                      /* number of bitplanes */
0419      LPSTR lpImageData;    /* pointer to buffer that holds bit array */
0420      GLOBALHANDLE hMem;    /* handle to buffer that holds bit array */
0421      WORD NumBytes;                  /* length of array, in bytes */
0422      LONG TestLength;                         /* hash value */
0423      DWORD BytesCopied;        /* value returned by GetBitmapBits() */
0424      int hFile;                             /* DOS file handle */
0425      OFSTRUCT FileStruct;             /* data structure for file */
0426
0427    if(DisplayBits==8)           /* if running in 256-color mode... */
0428      {
0429      MessageBeep(0); MessageBox(GetFocus(),
0430      "Reset your system to 16-color mode to run this animation.
          Otherwise recompile the source files to run in 256-color mode.
           See the book for source code changes or use Windows Setup to
           change to a 16-color display.",
0431      "256-color support", MB_OK|MB_ICONINFORMATION);
0432      return FALSE;
0433      }
0434
0435    if (bImageExists==FALSE)              /* if no test image exists... */
0436      {
0437      MessageBeep(0); MessageBox(GetFocus(),
0438        "Create an image before attempting to save to disk.",
0439        "No image", MB_OK); return FALSE;
0440      }
0441
0442    RetVal= GetObject(hBitmap,          /* grab bitmap data structure */
0443            sizeof(BITMAP),(LPSTR)&bmImage);
0444    if (RetVal==0)
0445      {
0446      MessageBeep(0); MessageBox(GetFocus(),
0447        "Unable to retrieve bitmap data structure.",
0448        "GDI problem", MB_OK); return FALSE;
0449      }
0450
0451    BytesPerLine= bmImage.bmWidthBytes;            /* width of bitmap */
0452    RasterLines= bmImage.bmHeight;                /* height of bitmap */
0453    NumPlanes= bmImage.bmPlanes;              /* number of bitplanes */
0454    TestLength=                            /* calculate length of data */
0455              (LONG)(BytesPerLine * RasterLines * NumPlanes);
0456    if (TestLength > 65534) /* if too large for single-pass write... */
0457      {
0458      MessageBeep(0); MessageBox(GetFocus(),
0459        "Bit array is too large to save to disk in a single pass.",
0460        "Algorithm limitation", MB_OK); return FALSE;
0461      }
0462    NumBytes= (WORD) TestLength;      /* initialize arg for _lwrite() */
0463
0464    hMem= GlobalAlloc(GMEM_MOVEABLE, NumBytes);   /* create a buffer */
0465    if (hMem==0)
0466      {
0467      MessageBeep(0); MessageBox(GetFocus(),
0468        "GlobalAlloc() error: Cannot create memory buffer.",
0469        "Internal error", MB_OK); return FALSE;
```

```
0470    }
0471    lpImageData= GlobalLock(hMem);    /* lock buffer and grab pointer */
0472    BytesCopied= GetBitmapBits(hBitmap,NumBytes,lpImageData);
0473    if (BytesCopied==0)         /* if unable to copy bits to buffer... */
0474      {
0475      MessageBeep(0); MessageBox(GetFocus(),
0476        "GetBitmapBits() error:  No bits copied to buffer.",
0477        "GDI problem", MB_OK);
0478        GlobalUnlock(hMem); GlobalFree(hMem); return FALSE;
0479      }
0480
0481    hFile= OpenFile(lpFileName,&FileStruct,OF_EXIST);       /* exists? */
0482    if (hFile >= 0)
0483      {
0484      MessageBeep(0); RetVal= MessageBox(GetFocus(),
0485        "File already exists.  Overwrite existing file?",
0486        "Disk status", MB_YESNO);
0487      if (RetVal==IDNO)     /* if user does not want to overwrite... */
0488        {
0489        GlobalUnlock(hMem); GlobalFree(hMem); return FALSE;
0490        }
0491      }
0492
0493    hFile= OpenFile(lpFileName,&FileStruct,OF_CREATE|OF_WRITE);
0494    if (hFile==-1)
0495      {
0496      MessageBeep(0); MessageBox(GetFocus(),
0497        "OpenFile() was unable to open the file for writing.",
0498        "Disk problem", MB_OK);
0499      GlobalUnlock(hMem); GlobalFree(hMem); return FALSE;
0500      }
0501
0502    RetVal= _lwrite(hFile,lpImageData,NumBytes);    /* write to disk */
0503    if (RetVal==-1)
0504      {
0505      MessageBeep(0); MessageBox(GetFocus(),
0506        "_lwrite() was unable to write to the opened file.",
0507        "Disk problem", MB_OK);
0508      _lclose(hFile);
0509      GlobalUnlock(hMem); GlobalFree(hMem); return FALSE;
0510      }
0511
0512    RetVal= _lclose(hFile);                         /* close the file */
0513    if (RetVal==-1)                      /* if unable to close file... */
0514      {
0515      MessageBeep(0); MessageBox(GetFocus(),
0516        "_lclose() was unable to close the file after writing.",
0517        "Disk problem", MB_OK);
0518      GlobalUnlock(hMem); GlobalFree(hMem); return FALSE;
0519      }
0520
0521    GlobalUnlock(hMem);           /* discard the pointer to the buffer */
0522    GlobalFree(hMem);                         /* discard the buffer */
0523    return TRUE;
0524    }
0525    /*
0526    ----------------------------------------------------------------
0527                      Load a bitmap file from disk.
0528    ----------------------------------------------------------------
0529                                                              */
0530    static BOOL zLoadFrame(HBITMAP hBitmap, LPSTR lpFileName)
```

```
0531   {
0532     HDC hDC;                              /* handle to display-context */
0533     BITMAP bmImage;                          /* bitmap data structure */
0534     short BytesPerLine;                         /* width of bitmap */
0535     short RasterLines;                         /* height of bitmap */
0536     BYTE NumPlanes;                         /* number of bitplanes */
0537     LPSTR lpImageData;   /* pointer to buffer that holds bit array */
0538     GLOBALHANDLE hMem;    /* handle to buffer that holds bit array */
0539     WORD NumBytes;                      /* length of array, in bytes */
0540     LONG TestLength;                              /* hash value */
0541     DWORD BytesCopied;        /* value returned by GetBitmapBits() */
0542     int hFile;                                /* DOS file handle */
0543     OFSTRUCT FileStruct;                /* data structure for file */
0544
0545   if(DisplayBits==8)             /* if running in 256-color mode... */
0546     {
0547     MessageBeep(0); MessageBox(GetFocus(),
0548     "Reset your system to 16-color mode to run this animation.
0549        Otherwise recompile the source files to run in 256-color mode.
0550         See the book for source code changes or use Windows Setup to
0551        change to a 16-color display.",
0549   "256-color support", MB_OK|MB_ICONINFORMATION);
0550   return FALSE;
0551     }
0552
0553   if (bBitmapExists==FALSE)        /* if no target bitmap exists... */
0554     {
0555     MessageBeep(0); MessageBox(GetFocus(),
0556      "Create a hidden frame before loading bitmap from disk.",
0557      "No hidden frame", MB_OK);
0558     return FALSE;
0559     }
0560
0561   RetVal= GetObject(hBitmap,            /* grab bitmap data structure */
0562          sizeof(BITMAP),(LPSTR)&bmImage);
0563   if (RetVal==0)
0564     {
0565     MessageBeep(0); MessageBox(GetFocus(),
0566      "Unable to retrieve bitmap data structure.",
0567      "GDI problem", MB_OK); return FALSE;
0568     }
0569
0570   BytesPerLine= bmImage.bmWidthBytes;           /* width of bitmap */
0571   RasterLines= bmImage.bmHeight;                /* height of bitmap */
0572   NumPlanes= bmImage.bmPlanes;           /* number of bitplanes */
0573   TestLength=                           /* calculate length of data */
0574          (LONG)(BytesPerLine * RasterLines * NumPlanes);
0575   if (TestLength > 60000)         /* if larger than hardcoded value */
0576     {
0577     MessageBeep(0); MessageBox(GetFocus(),
0578      "Target bit array is larger than animation frame.",
0579      "Algorithm limitation", MB_OK); return FALSE;
0580     }
0581   NumBytes= (WORD) TestLength;        /* initialize arg for _lread() */
0582
0583   hMem= GlobalAlloc(GMEM_MOVEABLE, NumBytes);   /* create a buffer */
0584   if (hMem==0)
0585     {
0586     MessageBeep(0); MessageBox(GetFocus(),
0587      "GlobalAlloc() error:  Cannot create memory buffer.",
0588      "Internal error", MB_OK); return FALSE;
```

```
0589    }
0590    lpImageData= GlobalLock(hMem);    /* lock buffer and grab pointer */
0591
0592    hFile= OpenFile(lpFileName,&FileStruct,OF_READ);
0593    if (hFile==-1)
0594      {
0595      MessageBeep(0); MessageBox(GetFocus(),
0596        "OpenFile() was unable to open file for reading.",
0597        "Disk problem", MB_OK);
0598      GlobalUnlock(hMem); GlobalFree(hMem); return FALSE;
0599      }
0600
0601    RetVal= _lread(hFile,lpImageData,NumBytes);    /* read from disk */
0602    if (RetVal==-1)
0603      {
0604      MessageBeep(0); MessageBox(GetFocus(),
0605        "An error occurred while reading the opened file.",
0606        "Disk problem", MB_OK);
0607      _lclose(hFile);
0608      GlobalUnlock(hMem); GlobalFree(hMem); return FALSE;
0609      }
0610    if ((unsigned)RetVal < NumBytes)
0611      {
0612      MessageBeep(0); MessageBox(GetFocus(),
0613        "Possible error.  The frame file was shorter than specified.",
0614        "Algorithm limitation", MB_OK);
0615      _lclose(hFile);
0616      GlobalUnlock(hMem); GlobalFree(hMem); return FALSE;
0617      }
0618
0619    RetVal= _lclose(hFile);                         /* close the file */
0620    if (RetVal==-1)                      /* if unable to close file... */
0621      {
0622      MessageBeep(0); MessageBox(GetFocus(),
0623        "_lclose() was unable to close the file after reading.",
0624        "Disk problem", MB_OK);
0625      GlobalUnlock(hMem); GlobalFree(hMem); return FALSE;
0626      }
0627
0628    BytesCopied= SetBitmapBits(hBitmap,NumBytes,lpImageData);
0629    if (BytesCopied==0)         /* if unable to copy bits to bitmap... */
0630      {
0631      MessageBeep(0); MessageBox(GetFocus(),
0632        "SetBitmapBits() error:  No bits copied to bitmap.",
0633        "GDI problem", MB_OK);
0634        GlobalUnlock(hMem); GlobalFree(hMem); return FALSE;
0635      }
0636
0637    GlobalUnlock(hMem);             /* discard the pointer to the buffer */
0638    GlobalFree(hMem);                        /* discard the buffer */
0639    bImageExists= TRUE;
0640    return TRUE;
0641    }
0642    /*
0643    -----------------------------------------------------------------
0644                         Transparent PUT
0645      Bitblts a bitmap image using a transparent background paradigm.
0646      Useful for cleanly placing cels onto a background scene.
0647      Function expects the cel to possess a black background.
0648      Function creates/destroys a matte bitmap and a reversal bitmap.
0649    -----------------------------------------------------------------
```

```
0650                                                                  */
0651  static BOOL zCelBlt(
0652          HWND hWnd,                   /* handle to display window */
0653          HDC hSceneDC,                        /* hidden frame DC */
0654          HDC hCelDC,                            /* cel bitmap DC */
0655          HBITMAP hCel,               /* handle to cel bitmap */
0656          int SceneX, int SceneY)      /* xy installation location */
0657  {
0658    HDC hDC;                                    /* display-context */
0659    BITMAP bmImage;           /* will hold bitmap data structure */
0660    short CelWidth;                            /* width of bitblt */
0661    short CelHeight;                          /* height of bitblt */
0662    HDC hMatteDC;                          /* memory DC for matte */
0663    HBITMAP hMatte;                    /* handle to matte bitmap */
0664    HBITMAP hPrevMatte;       /* default bitmap of matte DC */
0665    HDC hReversalDC;                    /* memory DC for reversal */
0666    HBITMAP hReversal;                /* handle to reversal bitmap */
0667    HBITMAP hPrevRev;        /* default bitmap of reversal DC */
0668    COLORREF Black, White;                  /* RGB color values */
0669    DWORD CurrentColor;                        /* existing color */
0670    int ScanLine;                          /* current scan line */
0671    int Position;              /* position along current scan line */
0672
0673    hDC= GetDC(hWnd);                   /* set the display-context */
0674    SetCapture(hWnd);                          /* lock the mouse */
0675    hPrevCursor= SetCursor(hHourGlass);     /* set hourglass cursor */
0676
0677  /* --------- STEP ONE:  Create white matte on black bg --------- */
0678  RetVal= GetObject(hCel,sizeof(BITMAP),(LPSTR)&bmImage);
0679  if (RetVal==0)   /* if cannot grab copy of bitmap data struct... */
0680    {
0681    MessageBeep(0); MessageBox(GetFocus(),
0682      "Unable to retrieve bitmap data structure.",
0683      "Cel problem", MB_OK);
0684    SetCursor(hPrevCursor); ReleaseCapture();
0685    ReleaseDC(hWnd,hDC); return FALSE;
0686    }
0687  CelWidth= bmImage.bmWidth;         /* grab bitblt dimensions... */
0688  CelHeight= bmImage.bmHeight;
0689  hMatteDC= CreateCompatibleDC(hDC);              /* create DC */
0690  hMatte= CreateCompatibleBitmap(hDC,CelWidth, CelHeight);
0691  if (hMatte==0)           /* if cannot create bitmap for matte... */
0692    {
0693    MessageBeep(0); MessageBox(GetFocus(),
0694      "Unable to create a white matte bitmap.",
0695      "Cel problem", MB_OK);
0696    DeleteDC(hMatteDC);
0697    SetCursor(hPrevCursor); ReleaseCapture();
0698    ReleaseDC(hWnd,hDC); return FALSE;
0699    }
0700  hPrevMatte= SelectObject(hMatteDC,hMatte);    /* select into DC */
0701  BitBlt(hMatteDC,0,0,CelWidth,CelHeight,
0702          hCelDC,0,0,SRCCOPY);         /* grab copy of cel bitmap */
0703  Black= RGB(0,0,0); White= RGB(255,255,255);   /* define colors */
0704
0705  /* --------- set all non-background pixels to white ----------- */
0706  for (ScanLine= 0; ScanLine < CelHeight; ScanLine++)
0707    {                          /* for each scan line in the bitmap... */
0708    for (Position= 0; Position < CelWidth; Position++)
0709      {                  /* for each position along the scan line... */
0710      CurrentColor= GetPixel(hMatteDC,             /* read the color */
```

```
0711                    Position, ScanLine);
0712       if (CurrentColor != Black)        /* if pixel not bg color... */
0713         SetPixel(hMatteDC,Position,ScanLine, White);  /* ...whiten */
0714       }
0715     }
0716
0717 /* --------- STEP TWO:  Create reversal of cel bitmap ---------- */
0718 hReversalDC= CreateCompatibleDC(hDC);
0719 hReversal= CreateCompatibleBitmap(hDC,CelWidth,CelHeight);
0720 if (hReversal==0)
0721    {
0722    MessageBeep(0); MessageBox(GetFocus(),
0723      "Unable to create a reversal bitmap.",
0724      "Cel problem", MB_OK);
0725    SelectObject(hMatteDC,hPrevMatte); DeleteObject(hMatte);
0726    DeleteDC(hMatteDC); DeleteDC(hReversalDC);
0727    SetCursor(hPrevCursor); ReleaseCapture();
0728    ReleaseDC(hWnd,hDC); return FALSE;
0729    }
0730 hPrevRev= SelectObject(hReversalDC,hReversal);
0731 BitBlt(hReversalDC,0,0,CelWidth,CelHeight,
0732       hMatteDC,0,0,SRCCOPY);          /* create copy of white matte */
0733 BitBlt(hReversalDC,0,0,CelWidth,CelHeight,
0734       hCelDC,0,0,SRCINVERT);    /* create reversal of cel bitmap */
0735
0736 /* ---------- STEP THREE:  Place white matte on scene ---------- */
0737 BitBlt(hSceneDC,SceneX,SceneY,CelWidth,CelHeight,
0738       hMatteDC,0,0,SRCPAINT);
0739
0740 /* ------- STEP FOUR:  Place transparent bitblt on scene ------- */
0741 BitBlt(hSceneDC,SceneX,SceneY,CelWidth,CelHeight,
0742       hReversalDC,0,0,SRCINVERT);
0743
0744 /* ------ STEP FIVE:  Copy hidden frame to display window ------ */
0745 BitBlt(hDC,0,0,zFRAMEWIDE,zFRAMEHIGH,hFrameDC,0,0,SRCCOPY);
0746
0747 /* --------------- STEP SIX:  Tidy up and return -------------- */
0748 SelectObject(hMatteDC,hPrevMatte);
0749 SelectObject(hReversalDC,hPrevRev);
0750 DeleteObject(hReversal); DeleteObject(hMatte);
0751 DeleteDC(hReversalDC); DeleteDC(hMatteDC);
0752 SetCursor(hPrevCursor);              /* restore the previous cursor */
0753 ReleaseCapture();                         /* unlock the mouse */
0754 ReleaseDC(hWnd,hDC);              /* release the display-context */
0755 return TRUE;
0756 }
0757 /*
0758 ----------------------------------------------------------------
0759                  Blank the client area of the window.
0760 ----------------------------------------------------------------
0761                                                                */
0762 static void zClear(HWND hWnd)
0763 {
0764    HDC hDC;
0765 hDC= GetDC(hWnd);
0766 PatBlt(hDC,0,0,zFRAMEWIDE,zFRAMEHIGH,WHITENESS);
0767 ReleaseDC(hWnd,hDC);
0768 return;
0769 }
0770 /*
0771 ----------------------------------------------------------------
```

```
0772                        Draw a background image.
0773      ------------------------------------------------------------------
0774                                                                        */
0775    static void zDrawBg(HDC hDC)
0776    {
0777      HBRUSH hPrevBrush, hSwatchBrush;                        /* brushes */
0778      HPEN hPrevPen, hBorderPen;                                 /* pens */
0779      RECT rcSwatch;                            /* rectangle structure */
0780      int iWidth= zFRAMEWIDE, iDepth= 4;        /* swatch dimensions */
0781      int iSwatchX= 0, iSwatchY= 0;               /* swatch location */
0782      BYTE bRed= 0, bGreen= 0, bBlue= 0;     /* rgb gun intensities */
0783      int iCount;                                      /* loop counter */
0784      int iX1= 100, iY1= 50, iX2= 300, iY2= 250;   /* ellipse coords */
0785      BYTE bGradiant= 20;                    /* shading gradient factor */
0786      int iResize= 10;                              /* sizing factor */
0787
0788    /* ----------------- draw gradiant background ----------------- */
0789    rcSwatch.left= iSwatchX;
0790    rcSwatch.top= iSwatchY;
0791    rcSwatch.right= rcSwatch.left + iWidth;
0792    rcSwatch.bottom= rcSwatch.top + iDepth;
0793    bRed= 0; bGreen= 0; bBlue= 3;
0794    for (iCount= 0; iCount < 64; iCount++)
0795      {
0796      hSwatchBrush= CreateSolidBrush(RGB(bRed,bGreen,bBlue));
0797      hPrevBrush= SelectObject(hDC,hSwatchBrush);
0798      FillRect(hDC,&rcSwatch,hSwatchBrush);
0799      SelectObject(hDC,hPrevBrush);
0800      DeleteObject(hSwatchBrush);
0801      rcSwatch.top= rcSwatch.top + iDepth;
0802      rcSwatch.bottom= rcSwatch.bottom + iDepth;
0803      bBlue= bBlue + (BYTE) 4;
0804      }
0805    bBlue= 255; rcSwatch.bottom= 300;
0806    hSwatchBrush= CreateSolidBrush(RGB(bRed,bGreen,bBlue));
0807    hPrevBrush= SelectObject(hDC,hSwatchBrush);
0808    FillRect(hDC,&rcSwatch,hSwatchBrush);
0809    SelectObject(hDC,hPrevBrush); DeleteObject(hSwatchBrush);
0810
0811    /* ------------------- draw gradiant rectangle ---------------- */
0812    bRed= 0; bGreen= 0; bBlue= 255;
0813    iWidth= 280; iDepth= 4;
0814    iSwatchX= 60; iSwatchY= 24;
0815    rcSwatch.left= iSwatchX;
0816    rcSwatch.top= iSwatchY;
0817    rcSwatch.right= rcSwatch.left + iWidth;
0818    rcSwatch.bottom= rcSwatch.top + iDepth;
0819    for (iCount= 0; iCount < 64; iCount++)
0820      {
0821      hSwatchBrush= CreateSolidBrush(RGB(bRed,bGreen,bBlue));
0822      hPrevBrush= SelectObject(hDC,hSwatchBrush);
0823      FillRect(hDC,&rcSwatch,hSwatchBrush);
0824      SelectObject(hDC,hPrevBrush);
0825      DeleteObject(hSwatchBrush);
0826      rcSwatch.top= rcSwatch.top + iDepth;
0827      rcSwatch.bottom= rcSwatch.bottom + iDepth;
0828      bBlue= bBlue - (BYTE) 4;
0829      }
0830
0831    /* ------------------- draw gradiant circle ------------------- */
0832    hBorderPen= CreatePen(PS_NULL,1,RGB(0,0,255));
```

**3-12** Continued.

```
0833   hPrevPen= SelectObject(hDC,hBorderPen);      /* use transparent pen */
0834   bRed= 0; bGreen= 0; bBlue= 31;               /* reset rgb intensities */
0835   for (iCount= 1; iCount <= 9; iCount++)
0836     {   /* draw 7 ellipses, decreasing size, increasing brightness */
0837     hSwatchBrush= CreateSolidBrush(RGB(bRed,bGreen,bBlue));
0838     hPrevBrush= SelectObject(hDC,hSwatchBrush);
0839     Ellipse(hDC iY1 iY1 iY2 iY2).
0840     bBlu
0841     iX1+
0842     iY1+
0843     iX2-
0844     iY2-
0845     Sele
0846     Dele
0847     }
0848
0849   /* ---                                                          */
0850   Select(
0851   Delete(
0852   return;
0853   }
0854   /*
0855   -------                                                       --
0856
0857   -------                                                       --
0858                                                                 */
```

# 4
# *Modeling*

3D objects can add an element of realism to your Windows animation application. An understanding of 3D geometry and the ability to use a 3D graphics library is an asset for any animation programmer. The Windows graphics device interface (GDI) is well-suited for 3D programming, and offers four particularly useful tools:

- The RGB() macro.
- The CreateSolidBrush() function.
- The CreatePolygonRgn() function.
- Built-in dithering capabilities.

Because the RGB() macro provides precise control over each of the three rgb guns, it is easy to specify rendering colors for 3D objects during the illumination process. Applying color to a 3D object is further facilitated by Windows' built-in dithering capabilities when running in VGA mode. Dithering is activated when your application creates brushes with the CreateSolidBrush() function. Rendering a shape of a facet (polygon) on the surface of a 3D object is easily implemented by using the CreatePolygonRgn() function to create a fill region.

## A 3D primer

There are two commonly used methods for building 3D models. They are b-rep and CSG. The difference between the two approaches is depicted in FIG. 4-1.

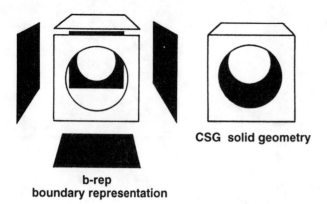

**CSG solid geometry**

**b-rep**
**boundary representation**

**4-1** Boundary representation (b-rep) considers only the skin or boundary of a 3D object. Constructive solid geometry (CSG) considers the whole solid.

## B-rep modeling

B-rep is an acronym for boundary-representation. Only the outer skin or boundary of the object is drawn. The surfaces of a b-rep model are constructed of facets or polygons. Groups of facets can be joined together to create different shapes, curves, and complex models.

B-rep modeling is easy to implement on a personal computer. It is fast and it can produce realistic imagery with the Windows GDI. Hidden surface removal can be accomplished using a number of different algorithms.

The b-rep technique has a few limitations, however. It is mathematically difficult to join two models together or to create a cavity in an existing model. The b-rep model considers only the boundaries of the object, not solid volumes or internal composition.

## CSG modeling

CSG is an acronym for constructive solid geometry. CSG models are built from 3D primitives like cubes, parallelepipeds, cylinders, spheres, and others. Because each of these primitives is also a 3D solid, these sub-objects can be combined together to produce more complex objects. CSG considers the volumetric structure of an object. This means the software can drill a hole into a model or perform other solid-based operations. To drill a hole, for example, the software mathematically subtracts a cylinder from the model and displays the result. This type of 3D logical operation is called a *3D Boolean* (or *Euler*) operation. 3D Euler operations are named after mathematician Leonard Euler (1707-1783), who described a connection between trigonometric functions and the exponential function. In 1972, Stanford University computer scientist B.G. Baumgart originated a set of so-called Euler operators that manipulate two 3D objects in a way that satisfies Euler's formula.

CSG modeling is used in applications where specific gravity, mass, moment of inertia, density, and other engineering considerations are important.

# Modeling functions

A typical 3D graphics library gives the programmer the ability to modify the modeling parameters during the creation of 3D objects. This interaction often relies upon stretching, moving, and spinning a 3D object. Stretching is called *extrusion*, moving is called *translation*, and spinning is called *rotation*.

## Revolve, extrude, sweep

3D functions like revolve, extrude, and sweep are used to build 3D objects from a 2D outline.

**Revolving** To implement a revolve operation, the programmer specifies a 2D shape and then indicates which direction to revolve the outline and how many degrees to rotate. The 3D library is responsible for generating the 3D object. This revolving or revolution function works equally well with both b-rep and CSG models.

**Extruding** The extrude function also takes a 2D outline and turns it into a 3D object. The programmer specifies how far and in which direction to stretch (or extrude) the shape. The extrude function also works with both b-rep and CSG models.

**Sweeping** The sweep function is similar to extrude, except that the stretching occurs along a curve rather than along a straight line.

## Primitives

Revolve, extrude, and sweep all rely upon input from the programmer. Some software takes a different approach, providing ready-to-use sub-objects. The programmer selects a desired sub-object and then advises the 3D library where to position the sub-object. sub-objects become building blocks that are used to construct more complex models. This is the approach that is used by the 3D graphics library presented later in this chapter.

**Sub-objects** Typical sub-objects (or primitives) include cylinders, cones, spheres, hyperboloids, paraboloids, wedges, parallelepipeds, pyramids, laminas, toruses, and others. In a typical 3D library, the programmer can manipulate the scale and dimensions of each primitive.

## Curved surfaces

Smoothly-curved surfaces can be constructed by both the b-rep and the CSG modeling systems. A ruled surface is a surface created by constructing a set of straight lines between two curved lines in 3D space. These two curved lines are usually parametric curves whose end points and control points have been specified by the programmer. Unlike a ruled surface which is bounded by two curved lines, a cubic patch surface is bounded by four curved edges.

## Euler operations

Euler operations, also called 3D Boolean operations, simulate the way the real world works. Euler operations include joining, intersection, and subtraction. *Joining* means attaching two solids to each other. *Intersection* means the common volume between two solids. *Subtraction* means the void occupying the common volume between two solids.

Leonard Euler was an 18th-century European mathematician who is credited with discovering a connection between trignometric functions and the exponential function. The so-called *Euler characteristic* is a constant that describes a surface by the sum of v-e+f, where v, e, and f represent the numbers of vertices, edges, and facets in a 3D surface.

# 3D coordinates

3D libraries use X-Y-Z coordinates to describe shapes and environments. When the environment or object is observed from directly in front, the X dimension describes left-right measurements, the Y dimension describes up-down, and the Z dimension describes near-far.

## Object coordinates and world coordinates

Object coordinates are X-Y-Z values that describe the manifest shape of a 3D object. They define the object.

World coordinates are X-Y-Z values that describe the object if it were positioned in a simulated 3D environment at a certain location (translation) and orientation (rotation). These coordinates are called *world coordinates* because the 3D environment is often referred to as a 3D world.

## Camera coordinates

Camera coordinates are X-Y-Z values that describe how a 3D object would appear to an observer (or camera) at a specified location or viewpoint in the 3D environment. The section of 3D space that is visible from the viewpoint is called the *3D perspective view volume.* Human eyes view the real world as two odd-shaped conical view volumes. Most 3D software uses a right-side pyramid as a view volume.

### Image plane coordinates

Image plane coordinates refer to the X-Y coordinates that are produced when the 3D camera coordinates are projected onto a two-dimensional image plane. The *image plane*, also called a *view plane* (or, more precisely, a view plane window) is a perpendicular slice of the 3D perspective view volume. The relationship between world coordinates, camera coordinates, and image plane coordinates is depicted in FIG. 4-2.

### Screen coordinates

*Screen coordinates*, also called *raster coordinates*, are X-Y coordinates on the client area of your application's main window on the screen. Screen coordinates display coordinates and viewport coordinates, are the result of scaling the image plane coordinates to fit a rectangular viewport on the display screen. The rectangular viewport is usually the main window of your application.

Calculating each set of coordinates in this 3D transformation cycle involves sine and cosine formulas derived from matrix math.

## 3D programming concepts

To create 3D images that can be used in an animation sequence, you need a working understanding of 3D graphics programming concepts and terminology. Like any other discipline in the field of computer graphics, 3D graphics has its own syntax.

**Modeling**   Modeling refers to the act of drawing the shape of the 3D object. Modeling is concerned with getting the shape right.

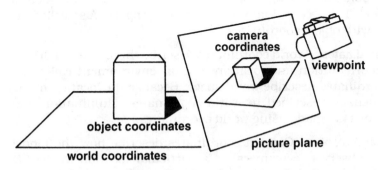

**4-2**   World coordinates define a model's orientation in a 3D scene. The model itself is defined by object coordinates. Camera coordinates describe how the 3D scene appears to a camera located at a particular viewpoint.

**Coordinates**   Coordinates are the X-Y-Z coordinates that represent a specific point on the 3D object. The coordinate system is an X-Y-Z axis system that provides measurements of width, height, and depth—or X, Y, and Z, the three dimensions of 3D.

**Rendering**   Rendering means the application of shading or coloring to the 3D object. Rendering simulates the effect of illumination in the scene.

**Hidden surfaces**   Hidden surface removal and visible surface detection refer to techniques for drawing 3D objects so that back-facing surfaces are discarded (*back-face culling*) and surfaces hidden by other objects are correctly represented.

**Solid modeling**   Solid modeling refers to 3D algorithms that treat each object as a solid with mass. Constructive solid geometry (CSG) uses solid modeling. Conversely, boundary representation modeling (b-rep) uses facets to build 3D objects using only the boundary or outer surface of the object.

## 3D transformation sequence

3D graphics programming uses X-Y-Z coordinates to describe a unique location in 3D space. There are different types of 3D space, however. An object must follow an evolutionary path through each type of 3D space before the object can be displayed on the screen. This path is called a *transformation sequence*, because one type of coordinates is transformed into other types of coordinates as it passes through the sequence.

A typical 3D transformation sequence involves five steps. These steps involve object coordinates, world coordinates, camera coordinates, image plane coordinates, and display coordinates. Extra steps are required if the objects are to be clipped in 3D before being displayed, or if the z-buffer method of visible surface detection is used to display the finished scene.

**Step 1—object coordinates**   Object coordinates define the fundamental shape of the model. These coordinates describe object space. A so-called 3D database is filled with object coordinates.

**Step 2—world coordinates**   World coordinates describe the shape of a 3D object at a specific orientation and location in a 3D environment called the *world*. World coordinates describe world space. Because the location of the light source is usually described in world coordinates, illumination and lighting calculations are made using world coordinates.

**Step 3—camera coordinates**   Camera coordinates describe how the model would look to an observer (or camera) at a particular location in the 3D world. This location is called the *viewpoint*. Viewing distance refers to the distance between the viewpoint and the object. The location of the viewpoint determines which surfaces and objects in a scene are hidden, because hidden surface calculations are usually made in camera space. In advanced 3D libraries, the camera coordinates are clipped to fit the 3D perspective view volume, which is the 3D space that can be seen from the viewpoint. The 3D perspective view volume is shaped like a pyramid, with the viewpoint located at the point of the pyramid. The far plane of the view volume is called the *far clipping plane*. A nearer plane is called the *near clipping plane*. Any object outside the clipping planes and outside the sides of the view volume is hidden. 3D clipping makes it possible to animate walk-throughs and fly-pasts of 3D scenes. If objects are not clipped to the 3D view volume, objects that are behind the viewpoint will be displayed on the screen upside down and backwards by the 3D graphics library.

**Step 4—view plane window coordinates**  If an imaginary pane of glass is placed between the viewer and the model, geometry can be used to determine how a 2D image of the 3D object would be drawn on the so-called image plane. These image plane coordinates are also called window coordinates and projection plane coordinates. They are device-independent. They are not scaled to the main window of your application, but rather are still scaled to the 3D world environment being used. Some 3D libraries normalize the 3D perspective view volume so it is one unit in depth and each edge of the far clipping plane is one unit from the viewing axis. In such a case, the normalized 3D perspective view volume is called a *canonical view volume*. A normalized view volume simplifies the math required for 3D clipping.

**Step 5—display coordinates**  Display coordinates are also called screen coordinates and raster coordinates. They are the X-Y coordinates that are used to draw the finished image in the client area of your application's window. This output rectangle is often called a viewport by 3D programmers. The GDI's built-in clipping formulas trim the image at the boundaries of the your application's window. Display coordinates are often described as device-dependent. If a visible surface detection method like the z-buffer algorithm is used, it normally does its work with display coordinates that are compared to camera coordinates that have been deliberately transformed to a 3D parallel projection.

## Coordinate systems

**Right-hand system**  The standard right-hand coordinate system is the most widely used 3D coordinate system. It specifies positive Z as nearer, positive Y as higher, and positive X as right. The ground plane is represented by X-Z coordinates. The 3D library presented in this chapter uses the right-hand coordinate system. Conversely, the left-hand system specifies negative Z as nearer.

## B-rep components

3D objects are usually constructed of four-sided polygons or three-sided polygons called *facets*. Each border of a facet is called a *halfedge*. Neither facets nor halfedges exist in the real world. This is because real objects have three dimensions- -width, depth, and height, whereas a facet possesses no thickness.

When a facet shares a halfedge with another facet (as part of a 3D solid, for example) the intersection is called an *edge*. A 3D object that is built of facets can be defined by the attributes listed below.

- A vertex is a corner where three or more edges meet.
- An edge is the boundary between two facets.
- A facet is a plane on the surface of the model.
- A hidden surface is any facet that is hidden from view either because it faces away from the viewer or because it is obscured by other facets.

## Modeling formulas

The mathematical formulas needed to manipulate a 3D object in order to produce a set of display coordinates are based on matrix multiplication. Rotation formulas can be broken down into three components—yaw, roll, and pitch. Translation formulas can be broken down into three components— near-far, left-right, and up-down. By selectively manipulating these parameters in the 3D formulas, the object, world, and viewpoint can be rotated and translated, independent of each other.

## Rendering methods

The three methods of rendering are wire-frame, solid, and shaded. Shaded 3D objects are rendered using shading methods. Shading methods include Lambert shading, Gouraud shading, Phong shading, ray tracing, and radiosity shading. Lambert shading is also called facet shading or constant shading. Gouraud shading is also called smooth shading and color interpolation shading.

**Wire-frame models**  Wire-frame models are built using only edges. No attempt is made to detect or remove hidden surfaces. If a wire-frame model is built using facets, the facets are not shaded, but are left transparent.

**Solid models**  Solid models are built using opaque facets. Hidden surfaces are detected and are removed, usually by back-face culling. The model appears solid like it would appear in the real world, as shown in FIG. 4-3. No attempt is made to shade the model to match existing lighting conditions.

**Shaded models**  Shaded models are built using facets that have been shaded according to the intensity of light striking each facet. On a VGA-equipped computer, the built-in dithering capabilities of the Windows GDI can be used as a convenient method for shading a facet.

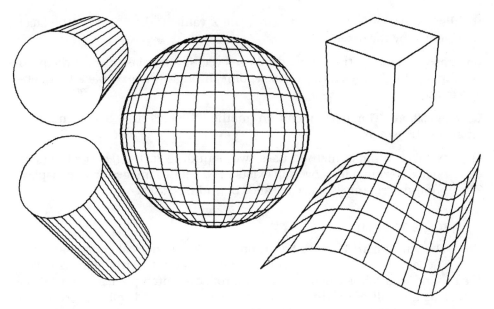

**4-3** Facets can be used to create a variety of fundamental 3D subobjects.

## Hidden surface removal

There are a variety of different algorithms used for hidden surface removal. Some are effective only when used in combination with other schemes. Typical methods include back-face culling, separation plane, z-buffer, ray tracing, radiosity, decomposition, and minmax.

**Back-face culling** The back-face culling method is also called the plane equation method and the backplane removal method. In a simple convex 3D solidlike a cube, facets that face away from the viewer are hidden from view. The back-face culling method uses surface normals (that are perpendicular to the each facet) and vector cross-products to determine which side of the facet is facing the observer.

**Separation plane** The separation plane method uses an imaginary plane positioned between two 3D objects. Vector formulas are used to determine on which side of the separation plane each object resides. The formulas can identify the object farthest from the viewpoint and therefore hidden from view by the nearer object. Vector math using half-planes can simplify the calculations.

**z-buffer** The z-buffer method compares the Z coordinate (or depth) for each pixel of each facet in the scene. Whenever a nearer value is encountered, it is written into the z-buffer, ensuring that only the nearest facet is drawn. A frame buffer is created in memory to store the color value for each pixel on the display. A z-buffer is used to store the Z value of the point on the facet represented by the pixel.

**Ray tracing**   The ray tracing method uses vector formulas to trace the path of individual light rays from the viewpoint through the pixel back to an object in the scene.

**Decomposition**   The decomposition method divides the 3D scene into smaller cubic solids.

**Minmax**   The minmax method uses two bounding rectangles (rectangular extents) to determine if an overlap exists between two images on the display. The bounding rectangles are also called bounding boxes.

## Yaw, roll, and pitch

The 3D environment is often based on an X-Y-Z spherical coordinate system. The viewpoint is always located at position 0,0,0. This point is called the origin. Rotation is calculated in yaw, roll, and pitch planes. Translation occurs as a result of moving the object coordinates and world coordinates through the spherical coordinate system.

## The light source

The position of the light source is expressed in world coordinates. Illumination calculations are made after the object coordinates have been transformed into world coordinates. If the world is rotated the position of the light source remains constant in relation to the position of the world. (When a new viewpoint is requested, the 3D library moves the world, not the camera, which remains fixed at 0,0,0.)

## Illumination

The level of illumination falling on a facet is usually calculated by comparing the incoming light vector to the surface perpendicular of the facet. The smaller the angle, the more light rays striking the surface, and the brighter the surface will appear. If the angle exceeds 90 degrees the surface is not illuminated by the light source, but is lit by only ambient light, reflected from other objects in the scene. The most common illumination algorithms used in 3D computer programming are Lambert shading, Gouraud shading, Phong shading, and ray tracing.

**Specific surface normal—Lambert shading**   Lambert shading is named after 18th-century mathematician Johann Heinrich Lambert (1728–1777). It is also called facet shading, faceted shading, flat shading, and constant shading. Facet shading uses facet-resolution color interpolation to shade the 3D model. Dithering is used to shade each facet on the object according to the relationship between the angle of the incoming light ray and the surface normal of the facet.

**Average surface normal—Gouraud shading**   Gouraud shading is named after French motorcar designer Henri Gouraud. It is also called smooth shading, color interpolation shading, and intensity interpolation shading. Gouraud shading uses color interpolation on individual pixels to achieve a smooth effect that reduces the harsh edges between facets.

**Individual normal interpolation—Phong shading**   Phong shading is named after computer science researcher Bui T. Phong. It is also called normal-vector interpolation shading. Phong shading is noted for its ability to produce highlights (specular reflections). Phong shading is founded upon the relationships between a surface normal, an incoming light ray, and the line of sight.

**Cosine power specular reflection—ray tracing**   Ray tracing is also called ray casting. It works by following individual paths of reflected light and refracted light through the 3D scene. Ray tracing makes it possible to generate subtle effects like reflections and shadows.

## A sample application

The screen images in FIG. 4-4 show the startup displays from the sample application image3d.exe. This program provides a runtime environment that exercises some of the routines in the 3D library, lib3d.c, whose complete source code is provided later in the chapter. Each 3D object that is created by the application is shaded according to the level of illumination striking each facet, and back-face culling is used to remove hidden surfaces.

The 3D management code in the C source file and the 3D functions in the 3D library can be pasted into any Windows animation application that uses 3D images. The animated demo in chapter 16 uses the same 3D library that is demonstrated in this chapter.

The image3d.exe demo is built from six modules, including a .def module definition file, an .h #include file, an .rc resource script file, a .c source file, an .h 3D library #include file, and a 3D library .c source file. All of these production files are presented as ready-to-use source code in the program listing later in this chapter. The source files are also provided on the companion disk. You can refer to the appropriate appendix for instructions on how to build image3d.exe with QuickC for Windows, Turbo C++ for Windows, Borland C++, Zortech C++, WATCOM C, and Microsoft C and the SDK.

## What the program does: A user's guide

The sample application provides an environment that exercises some of the features of the 3D library, lib3d.c. You can use either a mouse or the keyboard to experiment with the demo program. The menus also support mnemonic keys. To view a runtime help message, as shown in FIG. 4-5, select Help from the Help menu.

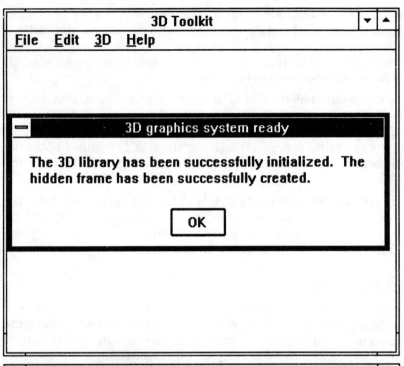

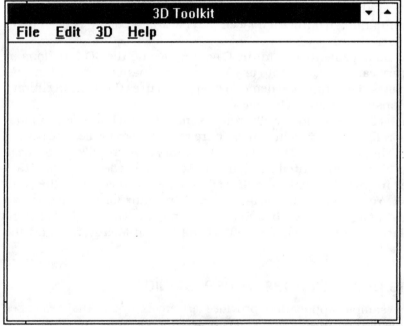

**4-4** Startup images from the sample application. Above, a message box confirms the successful initialization of the 3D library, lib3d.c. Below, the display window of the application after initialization, ready for 3D modeling and rendering.

## 3D objects

You can select menu items from the 3D menu, shown in FIG. 4-5, to experiment with 3D objects. Select Draw Carton from the 3D menu to cause the sample application to display a simple solid box, as shown in FIG. 4-6 (top). Select Clear the display to blank the display surface. Select other menu items to view the effects of extrusion on the solid box, as shown in FIG. 4-6 (bottom). Note that the first menu item, Draw Carton, also sets the orientation of the 3D solid. If you select either Variant 1 or Variant 2 before selecting Draw Carton, the box will be drawn using the default startup instancing angles, resulting in a head-on view of the 3D solid.

# How the source code works: A programmer's guide

*Hands On* The image3d.exe demonstration program provides a platform that exercises some of the functions of the 3D library, lib3d.c. The 3D library makes it possible for you to build 3D images that can be animated in Windows using the techniques described later in the book.

The organization of the .h #include file and the .rc resource script file follow the format established in earlier sample applications. A few new menu items and strings have been added to support the 3D capabilities of image3d.exe. See chapter 1 for a detailed discussion of the mechanics of the .h #include file and the .rc resource script file.

## How the .c file works

*.C* The program listing for the .c file is presented in FIG. 4-7.

**Include files**   The code at lines 0037 through 0039 includes three files: windows.h, image3d.h, and lib3d.h. The image3d.h include file supports the menuing system and string resources. The lib3d.h include file supports the 3D graphics library functions.

**Static variables**   The static variables that are visible through image3d.c are declared and initialized by the code at lines 0045 through 0090. These variables are for the most part unchanged from the code in chapter 2.

**WinMain()**   The WinMain() function is located at lines 0097 through 0169. Note in particular the code at lines 0157 through 0159 which initializes the 3D environment. The call to zInitialize3D() at line 0158 initializes the 3D variables internal to lib3d.c. The call to zInitFrame() at line 0159 creates the hidden frame bitmap that is used for persistent graphics.

**Switcher**   The message handler function is located at lines 0175 through 0381. The three case statements at lines 0198 through 0218 manipulate the 3D library, lib3d.c. The case block that begins at line 0198 corresponds to the first menu item in the 3D menu, named Draw Carton. The call to zSetCameraDistance() initializes the camera-to-subject distance. The call to

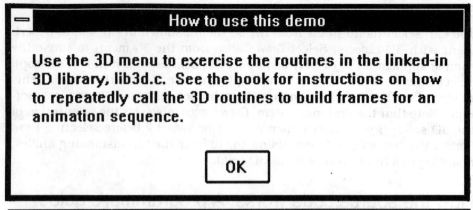

# How to use this demo

**Use the 3D menu to exercise the routines in the linked-in 3D library, lib3d.c. See the book for instructions on how to repeatedly call the 3D routines to build frames for an animation sequence.**

OK

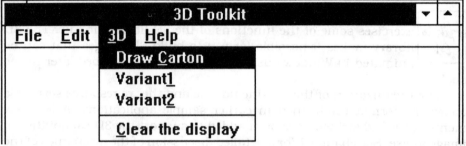

**3D Toolkit**

| File | Edit | 3D | Help |

Draw Carton

Variant1

Variant2

Clear the display

**4-5** Shown above is the Help message box from the sample application. Below, the 3D menu provides examples of runtime calls to the 3D routines in lib3d.c.

zSetCameraHeading() sets the orientation of the camera, expressed in compass heading degrees.

The call to zSetCameraPitch sets the pitch tilt of the camera, expressed in degrees. The call to zSetSubjectLocation() at line 0202 sets the translation instance of the 3D object, which is specified in this example as 0,0,0—the center of the 3D world. The call to zSetSubjectAttitude() at line 0203 sets the yaw, roll, and pitch orientation of the 3D object, expressed in degrees. In this example, yaw is set to 0 degrees, roll is set to 0 degrees, and pitch is set to 0 degrees, which results in no change to the default object coordinates which form the manifest definition of the 3D object. The call to zSetSubjectSize() at line 0204 defines the extrusion parameters to be used.

The argument list is 15,15,15. This means the 3D object is extruded (stretched) 15 units to the left and 15 units to the right of the origin along the X axis. The object is stretched 15 units up and 15 units down from the origin along the vertical Y axis. The 3D object is extruded 15 units forward and 15 units back from the origin along the near-far Z axis. Because each extrusion parameter is equal, the resulting 3D object will be a cube. (Note lines 0209 and 0214, which draw rectangular boxes.)

After specifying the parameters of the 3D object about to be drawn, the code calls zDrawCube() to build the object at the correct rotation and trans-

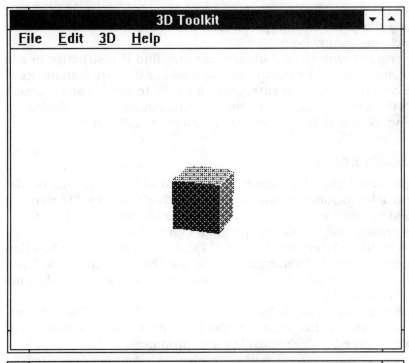

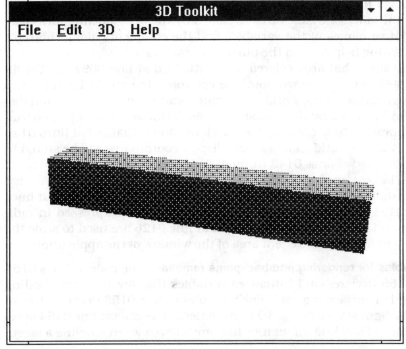

**4-6** Two examples of 3D models produced by the sample application.

lation in the 3D world. Then a variable named PaintImage is assigned a value that ensures the persistent graphics code will refresh the window if it is moved , unclipped, or uncovered.

To experiment with the 3D library, you may find it instructive to add code that manipulates the camera and the object in the case statements at lines 0208 and 0213. In each case, add your calls to zSetCameraDistance(), zSetCameraHeading(), zSetCameraPitch, zSetSubjectLocation(), zSetSubject-Attitude(), and zSetSubjectSize() immediately before the call to zDrawCube().

## How the 3D library works

The program listing for lib3d.h is presented in FIG. 4-11. This header file must be included in any application that uses the 3D routines in lib3d.c. Constants are defined at lines 0006 through 0012. These definitions ensure that the calling program can specify colors in a format understood by the 3D routines. Lines 0014 through 0022 provide function prototypes for routines in lib3d.c that can be called by the application. There are other routines in lib3d.c, but they are designed to be called by only functions resident in lib3d.c.

The program listing for lib3d.c is presented in FIG. 4-12. This file contains the 3D routines that maintain the three-dimensional environment and that manipulate 3D objects inside the environment.

**Static variables for 3D modeling**   The code at lines 0097 through 0145 declares and initializes variables that are used by the 3D modeling formulas. The descriptive names of the variables and the comments along the right side of the listing help explain the purpose of each variable.

The variables that are declared and initialized at line 0097 are the dimensions of the view plane window. The variables that are declared at lines 0098 through 0109 are the world coordinates, camera coordinates, and display coordinates used by the transformation formulas. The object coordinates are found in the array cubeObj[], declared and initialized at lines 0140 through 0142. The world, camera, and display coordinates will be stored in the arrays declared at lines 0143 through 0145.

The variable named focal_length that is declared and initialized at line 0113 is the distance from the viewpoint to the view plane. The code at lines 0120 and 0121 specifies the orientation of the camera, expressed in radians. The rx and ry ratio variables declared at line 0126 are used to scale the view plane window to fit the client area of the window of the application.

**Static variables for rendering and backplane removal**   The code at lines 0151 through 0165 declares and initializes variables that are used for shading and for hidden surface removal. The variables at line 0153 describe the location of the light source in the 3D environment. The code at line 0154 specifies the range of shading intensities that are allowed when shading a facet.

**Static variables for pixel operations**  The code at lines 0171 through 0178 declares and initializes variables that are used while the application is drawing on the client area of the application's main window.

**Initializing the 3D environment**  The function at lines 0187 through 0235 initializes a set of variables for the 3D runtime environment. Note how the code from lines 0197 through 0206 calculates the rx and ry ratio values that are needed to scale the view plane window to the display (the client area of the application's window). The code at line 0202 refers to the dimensions of the view plane window.

The variable at line 0213 refers to the distance from the camera to the view plane. The variable named viewheight at line 0214 can be reset to a value of 5 or 6 to simulate a viewing position of 5 or 6 feet above the groundplane. The variable at line 0215 specifies the distance from the camera to the origin of the 3D world in which the sub-objects reside. The code at line 0216 sets the camera orientation at straight ahead, expressed in radians. The two variables at line 0217 can be altered by the caller at runtime, and are expressed in degrees. The location of the camera is specified by the variables at line 0221. Note the negative value of zCam, which corresponds to the absolute value of dist at line 0215.

The orientation (rotation) and location (translation) of the 3D object is defined at lines 0223 through 0226. This is called the *instance* of the object. The code at lines 0228 through 0230 is provided for programmers who want to modify the code for interactive CAD use (see *High Performance C Graphics Programming for Windows*, by Lee Adams, Windcrest/McGraw-Hill book 4103).

**Camera heading**  The function at lines 0241 through 0275 resets the camera heading when called at runtime. After the camera is rotated, the code carefully repositions the 3D world so the camera continues to point at the center of the world. The code also maintains a consistent camera-to-subject distance.

**Camera pitch**  The function at lines 0281 through 0297 resets the camera pitch when called at runtime. The code at lines 0291 through 0295 ensures that the camera-to-subject distance remains consistent.

**Camera-to-subject distance**  The function at lines 0303 is callable at runtime. It resets the camera-to-subject distance by adjusting the hypotenuse and two sides of a triangle in 3D space.

**Instancing translation**  The function at lines 0320 through 0331 sets the location of the sub-object in the 3D world. Lines 0323 through 0328 inhibit the maximum translation allowed to 100 units. This is a work-around to ensure that all sub-objects remain inside the 3D view volume without the necessity of burdening the code with the 3D clipping routines.

**Instancing rotation**   The function at lines 0337 through 0357 sets the orientation of the sub-object, expressed as yaw, roll, and pitch. This function is callable at runtime.

**Instancing extrusion**   The function at lines 0363 through 0376 scales (stretches or shrinks) the sub-object. Note how the code at lines 0366 through 0371 limits the range of extrusion.

**Hidden surface removal**   The function at lines 0393 through 0401 uses the standard equation for a plane to detect back-facing facets. This is called back-face culling.

**Transformations**   The functions at lines 0407 through 0513 form the 3D transformation sequence described earlier in this chapter. Every 3D point must pass through these transformations before it can be drawn on the screen. The function at lines 0493 through 0499 calculates the view plane window coordinates. The function at lines 0505 through 0513 calculates the viewport coordinates (or raster coordinates).

**Drawing a facet**   The function at lines 0519 through 0571 draws a 3D facet on the client area of the application's window. The switch() block at lines 0530 through 0559 uses the current shading color to decide how to adjust the three rgb guns. If the current shading color is red, for example, only the red gun is set to the appropriate brightness level. If the current shading color is gray, all three guns are set to an appropriate intensity. The code at lines 0560 through 0564 uses a region for the fill operation. The call to CreatePolygonRgn() at line 0560 creates a region. It is selected into the display-context by the call to SelectObject() at line 0563. The code at lines 0565 through 0569 deselects the drawing tools, releases the display-context , and deletes the custom drawing tools.

**Calculating illumination**   The function at lines 0577 through 0600 uses vector math to compare the angle of the incoming light ray with the surface normal of the facet being considered. The code at line 0597 adjusts the light intensity to a Windows-specific format, in the range of 0 to 255, which is supported by the RGB() macro of the GDI. The if() statement at line 0599 specifies the shade to be used for facets facing away from the light source.

**Setting the shading color**   The function at lines 0607 through 0614 resets the current shading color. The variable that remembers this color, zShadingColor, is used by the switch() statement at line 0530 in the zDrawFacet() function.

**Drawing an object**   The code that draws a 3D parallelepiped is located at lines 0620 through 0644. Notice the for() loop at lines 0633 through 0642. This loop passes the cursor's object coordinates through the 3D transformation sequence by calling zGetWorldCoords(), zGetCameraCoords(), zGetImageCoords(), and zGetScreenCoords(). The function at lines 0646 through 0742 manages the actual building of the parallelepiped, ensuring that all six facets are drawn or hidden, as the case may require.

# Program listings for the sample application

The program listings presented here contain all the source code you need to build and run the sample application. The module definition file is provided in FIG. 4-7. The #include file is found in FIG. 4-8. The resource script file is presented in FIG. 4-9. The C source file is provided in FIG. 4-10. The 3D library #include file is presented in FIG. 4-11. The 3D library C source file is provided in FIG. 4-12.

**Companion disk** If you have the companion disk, the source files are presented as image3d.def, image3d.h, image3d.rc, image3d.c, lib3d.h, and lib3d.c.

**License** You can paste the royalty-free source code into your own applications and distribute the resulting executable files under the conditions of the License Agreement and Limited Warranty in FIG. 10 in the introduction to the book.

**4-7** The module definition file listing for the sample application.

```
0001   NAME          DEFDEMO
0002   DESCRIPTION   'Copyright 1992 Lee Adams.  All rights reserved.'
0003   EXETYPE       WINDOWS
0004   STUB          'WINSTUB.EXE'
0005   CODE          PRELOAD MOVEABLE
0006   DATA          PRELOAD MOVEABLE MULTIPLE
0007   HEAPSIZE      1024
0008   STACKSIZE     8192
0009   EXPORTS       zMessageHandler
```

**4-8** The include file listing for the sample application.

```
0001   /*
0002   --------------------------------------------------------------
0003                   Include file IMAGE3D.H
0004           Copyright 1992 Lee Adams.  All rights reserved.
0005    Include this file in the .RC resource script file and in the
0006    .C source file.  It contains function prototypes, menu ID
0007    constants, and string ID constants.
0008   --------------------------------------------------------------
0009   --------------------------------------------------------------
0010                   Function prototypes
0011   --------------------------------------------------------------
0012                                                              */
0013   #if !defined(zRCFILE)              /* if not an .RC file... */
0014     LONG FAR PASCAL zMessageHandler(HWND, unsigned, WORD, LONG);
0015     int PASCAL WinMain(HANDLE,HANDLE,LPSTR,int);
0016     HWND zInitMainWindow(HANDLE);
0017     BOOL zInitClass(HANDLE);
0018   static void zClear(HWND);                  /* blank the viewport */
0019   static void zInitFrame(HWND);              /* creates hidden frame */
0020   static void zCopyToDisplay(HWND);     /* copies frame to display */
0021   static void zCopyToFrame(HWND);       /* copies display to frame */
0022   static void zClearHiddenFrame(void);      /* clears hidden frame */
0023   #endif
0024   /*
0025   --------------------------------------------------------------
```

**4-8** Continued.

```
0026                           Menu ID constants
0027    --------------------------------------------------------------------
0028                                                                     */
0029    #define IDM_New              1
0030    #define IDM_Open             2
0031    #define IDM_Save             3
0032    #define IDM_SaveAs           4
0033    #define IDM_Exit             5
0034
0035    #define IDM_Undo             6
0036    #define IDM_Cut              7
0037    #define IDM_Copy             8
0038    #define IDM_Paste            9
0039    #define IDM_Delete           10
0040
0041    #define IDM_DrawCarton       11
0042    #define IDM_Variant1         12
0043    #define IDM_Variant2         13
0044    #define IDM_Clear            14
0045
0046    #define IDM_About            15
0047    #define IDM_License          16
0048    #define IDM_Display          17
0049    #define IDM_Colors           18
0050    #define IDM_Mode             19
0051    #define IDM_GeneralHelp      20
0052    /*
0053    --------------------------------------------------------------------
0054                           String ID constants
0055    --------------------------------------------------------------------
0056                                                                     */
0057    #define IDS_Caption      1
0058    #define IDS_Warning      2
0059    #define IDS_NoMouse      3
0060    #define IDS_About        4
0061    #define IDS_AboutText    5
0062    #define IDS_License      6
0063    #define IDS_LicenseText  7
0064    #define IDS_Help         8
0065    #define IDS_HelpText     9
0066    #define IDS_Completed    10
0067    #define IDS_Resolution   11
0068    #define IDS_ResVGA       12
0069    #define IDS_ResEGA       13
0070    #define IDS_ResCGA       14
0071    #define IDS_ResSVGA      15
0072    #define IDS_Res8514      16
0073    #define IDS_ResHerc      17
0074    #define IDS_ResCustom    18
0075    #define IDS_Color        19
0076    #define IDS_Color16      20
0077    #define IDS_Color256     21
0078    #define IDS_Color2       22
0079    #define IDS_ColorCustom  23
0080    #define IDS_Machine      24
0081    #define IDS_Enhanced     25
0082    #define IDS_Standard     26
0083    #define IDS_Real         27
0084    #define IDS_Ready        29
0085    #define IDS_NotReady     31
0086    #define IDS_NoMem        32
```

**4-8** Continued.

```
0087    #define IDS_FrameOK        33
0088    /*
0089    -----------------------------------------------------------------
0090                        End of include file
0091    -----------------------------------------------------------------
0092                                                                    */
```

**4-9** The resource script file listing for the sample application.

```
0001    /*
0002    -----------------------------------------------------------------
0003                    Resource script file IMAGE3D.RC
0004             Copyright 1992 Lee Adams.  All rights reserved.
0005    This file defines the menu resources, the accelerator key
0006    resources, and the string resources that will be used by the
0007    demonstration application at runtime.
0008    -----------------------------------------------------------------
0009                                                                    */
0010    #define zRCFILE
0011    #include <WINDOWS.H>
0012    #include "IMAGE3D.H"
0013    /*
0014    -----------------------------------------------------------------
0015                        Script for menus
0016    -----------------------------------------------------------------
0017                                                                    */
0018    MENUS1 MENU
0019      BEGIN
0020      POPUP "&File"
0021        BEGIN
0022          MENUITEM  "&New", IDM_New, GRAYED
0023          MENUITEM  "&Open...", IDM_Open, GRAYED
0024          MENUITEM  "&Save", IDM_Save, GRAYED
0025          MENUITEM  "Save &As...", IDM_SaveAs, GRAYED
0026          MENUITEM SEPARATOR
0027          MENUITEM  "E&xit", IDM_Exit
0028        END
0029      POPUP "&Edit"
0030        BEGIN
0031          MENUITEM  "&Undo\tAlt+BkSp", IDM_Undo, GRAYED
0032          MENUITEM SEPARATOR
0033          MENUITEM  "Cu&t\tShift+Del", IDM_Cut, GRAYED
0034          MENUITEM  "&Copy\tCtrl+Ins", IDM_Copy, GRAYED
0035          MENUITEM  "&Paste\tShift+Ins", IDM_Paste, GRAYED
0036          MENUITEM  "&Delete\tDel", IDM_Delete, GRAYED
0037        END
0038      POPUP "&3D"
0039        BEGIN
0040          MENUITEM  "Draw &Carton", IDM_DrawCarton
0041          MENUITEM  "Variant&1", IDM_Variant1
0042          MENUITEM  "Variant&2", IDM_Variant2
0043          MENUITEM SEPARATOR
0044          MENUITEM "&Clear the display", IDM_Clear
0045        END
0046      POPUP "&Help"
0047        BEGIN
0048          MENUITEM "&About", IDM_About
0049          MENUITEM "&License", IDM_License
0050          MENUITEM SEPARATOR
```

```
0051        MENUITEM "&Screen resolution", IDM_Display
0052        MENUITEM "Available &colors", IDM_Colors
0053        MENUITEM "Memory mode", IDM_Mode
0054        MENUITEM SEPARATOR
0055        MENUITEM "&Help", IDM_GeneralHelp
0056     END
0057   END
0058 /*
0059 ------------------------------------------------------------------
0060                    Script for accelerator keys
0061 ------------------------------------------------------------------
0062                                                                */
0063 KEYS1 ACCELERATORS
0064   BEGIN
0065   VK_BACK, IDM_Undo, VIRTKEY, ALT
0066   VK_DELETE, IDM_Cut, VIRTKEY, SHIFT
0067   VK_INSERT, IDM_Copy, VIRTKEY, CONTROL
0068   VK_INSERT, IDM_Paste, VIRTKEY, SHIFT
0069   VK_DELETE, IDM_Delete, VIRTKEY
0070   END
0071 /*
0072 ------------------------------------------------------------------
0073                       Script for strings
0074   Programmer's Notes:  If you are typing this listing, set your
0075   margins to a line length of 255 characters so you can create
0076   lengthy strings without embedded carriage returns.  The line
0077   wraparounds in the following STRINGTABLE script are used for
0078   readability only in this printout.
0079 ------------------------------------------------------------------
0080                                                                */
0081 STRINGTABLE
0082   BEGIN
0083     IDS_Caption      "3D Toolkit"
0084     IDS_Warning      "Graphics system warning"
0085     IDS_NoMouse      "No mouse found.  Some features of this
          demonstration program may require a mouse."
0086     IDS_About        "About this program"
0087     IDS_AboutText    "This is a demo from Windcrest McGraw-Hill
          book 4114.  Copyright 1992 Lee Adams.  All rights reserved."
0088     IDS_License      "License Agreement"
0089     IDS_LicenseText "You can use this code as part of your own
          software product subject to the License Agreement and Limited
          Warranty in Windcrest McGraw-Hill book 4114 and on its
          companion disk."
0090     IDS_Help         "How to use this demo"
0091     IDS_HelpText     "Use the 3D menu to exercise the routines in
          the linked-in 3D library, lib3d.c.  See the book for
          instructions on how to repeatedly call the 3D routines to
          build frames for an animation sequence."
0092     IDS_Resolution  "Screen resolution"
0093     IDS_ResVGA       "Running in 640x480 mode."
0094     IDS_ResEGA       "Running in 640x350 mode."
0095     IDS_ResCGA       "Running in 640x200 mode."
0096     IDS_ResSVGA      "Running in 800x600 mode."
0097     IDS_Res8514      "Running in 1024x768 mode."
0098     IDS_ResHerc      "Running in 720x348 mode."
0099     IDS_ResCustom    "Running in custom mode."
0100     IDS_Color        "Available colors"
0101     IDS_Color16      "Running in 16-color mode."
0102     IDS_Color256     "Running in 256-color mode."
0103     IDS_Color2       "Running in 2-color mode."
```

```
0104     IDS_ColorCustom "Running in a custom color mode."
0105     IDS_Machine     "Memory mode"
0106     IDS_Enhanced    "Running in enhanced mode.  Can allocate up to
         16 MB extended physical memory (XMS) if available.  Virtual
         memory up to 4 times physical memory (maximum 64 MB) is also
         available via automatic disk swapping of 4K pages."
0107     IDS_Standard    "Running in standard mode.  Can allocate up to
         16 MB extended physical memory (XMS) if available."
0108     IDS_Real        "Running in real mode.  Can allocate blocks of
         memory from the first 640K of RAM.  Can also allocate blocks
         from expanded memory (EMS) if available."
0109     IDS_Ready       "3D graphics system ready"
0110     IDS_NotReady    "3D graphics system not ready"
0111     IDS_NoMem       "Insufficient memory.  Hidden frame not
         created.  Any 3D images you create will not be preserved if
         the window is covered or clipped.  Close other applications to
         free memory and restart this demo."
0112     IDS_FrameOK     "The 3D library has been successfully
         initialized.  The hidden frame has been successfully created."
0113   END
0114 /*
0115 ----------------------------------------------------------------
0116                    End of resource script file
0117 ----------------------------------------------------------------
0118                                                              */
```

**4-10** The C source file listing for the sample application, image3d.c. This demonstration program is ready to build using QuickC for Windows, Turbo C++ for Windows, Microsoft C and the SDK, Borland C++, Symantec Zortech C++, WATCOM C, and other compilers. See FIG. 1-2 for sample command-lines to build the program. Guidelines for using your compiler are provided in the appropriate appendix at the back of the book.

```
0001 /*
0002 ----------------------------------------------------------------
0003         Reusable template for Windows applications that use
0004              3D images in animation sequences.
0005 ----------------------------------------------------------------
0006   Source file: IMAGE3D.C
0007   Release version: 1.00              Programmer: Lee Adams
0008   Type:  C source file for Windows application development.
0009   Compilers: Microsoft C and SDK, Borland C++, Zortech C++,
0010     QuickC for Windows, Turbo C++ for Windows, WATCOM C.
0011   Memory model:  small.
0012   Dependencies:   IMAGE3D.DEF module definition file, IMAGE3D.H
0013                   include file, IMAGE3D.RC resource script file,
0014                   IMAGE3D.C source file, LIB3D.H and LIB3D.C.
0015   Output and features:  Demonstrates a display-independent
0016     3D modeling and shading toolkit that can be used to build
0017     scenes for use in animation sequences.
0018   Publication: Contains material from Windcrest/McGraw-Hill book
0019     4114 published by TAB BOOKS Division of McGraw-Hill Inc.
0020   License:  As purchaser of the book you are granted a royalty-
0021     free license to distribute executable files generated using
0022     this code provided you accept the conditions of the License
0023     Agreement and Limited Warranty described in the book and on
0024     the companion disk.  Government users:  This software and
0025     documentation are subject to restrictions set forth in The
```

```
0026          Rights in Technical Data and Computer Software clause at
0027          252.227-7013 and elsewhere.
0028   -----------------------------------------------------------------
0029              (c) Copyright 1992 Lee Adams.  All rights reserved.
0030              Lee Adams(tm) is a trademark of Lee Adams.
0031   -----------------------------------------------------------------
0032
0033   -----------------------------------------------------------------
0034                           Include files
0035   -----------------------------------------------------------------
0036                                                                   */
0037   #include <WINDOWS.H>
0038   #include "IMAGE3D.H"
0039   #include "LIB3D.H"
0040   /*
0041   -----------------------------------------------------------------
0042           Static variables visible throughout this file
0043   -----------------------------------------------------------------
0044                                                                   */
0045   /* ------------------ window specifications ------------------ */
0046   #define zWINDOW_WIDTH 408                    /* width of window */
0047   #define zWINDOW_HEIGHT 346                  /* height of window */
0048   #define zFRAMEWIDE 400                /* width of client area */
0049   #define zFRAMEHIGH 300               /* height of client area */
0050   int WindowX, WindowY;                    /* location of window */
0051
0052   /* ------------------- instance operations ------------------- */
0053   HANDLE hInst;                      /* handle to this instance */
0054   HWND MainhWnd;                     /* handle to the main window */
0055   HANDLE hAccel;              /* handle to accelerator keys table */
0056   HMENU hMenu;                    /* handle to a menu at runtime */
0057   PAINTSTRUCT ps;        /* structure used by persistent graphics */
0058   int MessageRet;       /* will hold receive value returned by GDI */
0059
0060   /* ------------------- mouse and cursor ------------------- */
0061   HCURSOR hPrevCursor;                /* handle to default cursor */
0062   HCURSOR hHourGlass;               /* handle to hourglass cursor */
0063   int MousePresent;            /* will indicate if mouse present */
0064
0065   /* ------------------ runtime conditions ------------------ */
0066   int DisplayWidth, DisplayHeight;         /* screen resolution */
0067   int DisplayBits;                 /* number of bits-per-pixel */
0068   int DisplayPlanes;                  /* number of bitplanes */
0069   DWORD MemoryMode;                   /* runtime memory mode */
0070
0071   /* ------------------ message box operations ------------------ */
0072   char lpCaption[51];      /* will hold caption for message boxes */
0073   int Max= 50;                    /* maximum length of caption */
0074   char lpMessage[250];     /* will hold text for message boxes */
0075   int MaxText= 249;                  /* maximum length of text */
0076
0077   /* -------------------- font operations -------------------- */
0078   HFONT hFont, hPrevFont;       /* handles to new, previous font */
0079   HDC hFontDC;                   /* display-context for font */
0080
0081   /* -------------- persistent image operations ---------------- */
0082   #define zBLANK 0
0083   #define zIMAGE 1
0084   int PaintImage= zBLANK;          /* indicates type of refresh */
0085
0086   /* -----------------hidden frame operations ------------------ */
```

```
0087  HDC hFrameDC;              /* memory display-context for hidden-frame */
0088  HBITMAP hFrame;                    /* handle to hidden-frame bitmap */
0089  HBITMAP hPrevFrame;                       /* default bitmap */
0090  BOOL FrameReady= FALSE;            /* hidden-frame created? */
0091
0092  /*
0093  --------------------------------------------------------------------
0094                  Entry point for the application
0095  --------------------------------------------------------------------
0096                                                                    */
0097  int PASCAL WinMain(HANDLE hInstance, HANDLE hPrevInstance,
0098                  LPSTR lpCmdLine, int nCmdShow)
0099  {
0100    MSG msg;                        /* will hold incoming messages */
0101    HWND hWndPrev;          /* handle to window of another instance */
0102    HWND hDesktopWnd;       /* handle to full-screen desktop window */
0103    HDC hDCcaps;               /* display-context of desktop window */
0104
0105  /* ----------- ensure only one instance is running ----------- */
0106  hWndPrev = FindWindow("DEMOCLASS", NULL);
0107  if (hWndPrev != NULL)        /* if another instance was found... */
0108    {
0109    BringWindowToTop(hWndPrev);              /* make it active... */
0110    return FALSE;              /* ...and terminate this instance */
0111    }
0112
0113  /* --------- determine capabilities of screen display ---------- */
0114  hDesktopWnd= GetDesktopWindow();
0115  hDCcaps= GetDC(hDesktopWnd);
0116  DisplayWidth= GetDeviceCaps(hDCcaps,HORZRES);
0117  DisplayHeight= GetDeviceCaps(hDCcaps,VERTRES);
0118  DisplayBits= GetDeviceCaps(hDCcaps,BITSPIXEL);
0119  DisplayPlanes= GetDeviceCaps(hDCcaps,PLANES);
0120  ReleaseDC(hDesktopWnd,hDCcaps);
0121
0122  /* ------- calculate screen position to center the window ------ */
0123  WindowX= (DisplayWidth - zWINDOW_WIDTH) / 2;       /* horizontal */
0124  WindowY= (DisplayHeight - zWINDOW_HEIGHT) /2;        /* vertical */
0125  if (WindowX < 0) WindowX= 0;
0126  if (WindowY < 0) WindowY= 0;
0127
0128  /* ---- determine memory mode (enhanced, standard, or real) ---- */
0129  MemoryMode= GetWinFlags();          /* will read this value later */
0130
0131  /* -------------- create and display the window --------------- */
0132  hInst= hInstance;                  /* remember the instance handle */
0133  if (!zInitClass(hInstance)) return FALSE;     /* create the class */
0134  MainhWnd= zInitMainWindow(hInstance);        /* create the window */
0135  if (!MainhWnd) return FALSE;     /* exit if no window was created */
0136  ShowWindow(MainhWnd, nCmdShow);             /* display the window */
0137  UpdateWindow(MainhWnd);                  /* send a paint message */
0138  hAccel= LoadAccelerators(hInstance,"KEYS1"); /* accelerator keys */
0139  hFontDC= GetDC(MainhWnd);               /* get a display-context */
0140  hFont= GetStockObject(SYSTEM_FONT);       /* grab handle to font */
0141  hPrevFont= SelectObject(hFontDC,hFont);   /* select font into DC */
0142  SetTextColor(hFontDC,RGB(191,191,191));   /* set new text color */
0143  TextOut(hFontDC,10,280,"- Copyright 1992 Lee Adams.",27);/* text */
0144  SetTextColor(hFontDC,RGB(255,255,255));   /* restore text color */
0145  SelectObject(hFontDC,hPrevFont);        /* restore previous font */
0146  ReleaseDC(MainhWnd,hFontDC);             /* release display-context */
0147
```

```
0148   /* ---------------------- check for mouse --------------------- */
0149   MousePresent= GetSystemMetrics(SM_MOUSEPRESENT);
0150   if (!MousePresent)                    /* if no active mouse found */
0151     {
0152     LoadString(hInst,IDS_Warning,lpCaption,Max);    /* load caption */
0153     LoadString(hInst,IDS_NoMouse,lpMessage,MaxText);  /* load text */
0154     MessageBox(GetFocus(),lpMessage,lpCaption,MB_OK);    /* message */
0155     }
0156
0157   /* -------------- initialize the 3D environment --------------- */
0158   zInitialize3D(MainhWnd);            /* initialize the 3D variables */
0159   zInitFrame(MainhWnd);              /* initialize the hidden frame */
0160
0161   /* ---------- begin retrieving messages for the window --------- */
0162   while (GetMessage(&msg,0,0,0))
0163     {
0164     if(TranslateAccelerator(MainhWnd, hAccel, &msg)) continue;
0165     TranslateMessage(&msg);
0166     DispatchMessage(&msg);
0167     }
0168   return(msg.wParam);
0169   }
0170   /*
0171   ------------------------------------------------------------------
0172                   Switcher for incoming messages
0173   ------------------------------------------------------------------
0174                                                                   */
0175   LONG FAR PASCAL zMessageHandler(HWND hWnd, unsigned message,
0176                                   WORD wParam, LONG lParam)
0177   {
0178     HDC hDCpaint;        /* display-context for persistent graphics */
0179
0180   switch (message)
0181     {
0182
0183     case WM_COMMAND:          /* if user has selected a menu item... */
0184       switch(wParam)
0185         {
0186         case IDM_New:     break;
0187         case IDM_Open:    break;
0188         case IDM_Save:    break;
0189         case IDM_SaveAs:  break;
0190         case IDM_Exit:    PostQuitMessage(0); break;
0191
0192         case IDM_Undo:    break;
0193         case IDM_Cut:     break;
0194         case IDM_Copy:    break;
0195         case IDM_Paste:   break;
0196         case IDM_Delete:  break;
0197
0198         case IDM_DrawCarton:
0199           zSetCameraDistance(360);
0200           zSetCameraHeading(340);
0201           zSetCameraPitch(340);
0202           zSetSubjectLocation(0,0,0);
0203           zSetSubjectAttitude(0,0,0);
0204           zSetSubjectSize(15,15,15);
0205           zDrawCube(); PaintImage= zIMAGE;
0206           if (FrameReady==TRUE) zCopyToFrame(hWnd);
0207           break;
0208         case IDM_Variant1:
```

**4-10** Continued.

```
0209              zSetSubjectSize(100,15,15);
0210              zDrawCube(); PaintImage= zIMAGE;
0211              if (FrameReady==TRUE) zCopyToFrame(hWnd);
0212              break;
0213          case IDM_Variant2:
0214              zSetSubjectSize(15,15,4);
0215              zDrawCube();
0216              PaintImage= zIMAGE;
0217              if (FrameReady==TRUE) zCopyToFrame(hWnd);
0218              break;
0219          case IDM_Clear: zClear(hWnd);
0220                          PaintImage= zBLANK;
0221                          if (FrameReady==TRUE) zCopyToFrame(hWnd);
0222                          break;
0223
0224          case IDM_About:
0225            LoadString(hInst,IDS_About,lpCaption,Max);
0226            LoadString(hInst,IDS_AboutText,lpMessage,MaxText);
0227            MessageBox(GetFocus(),lpMessage,lpCaption,MB_OK);
0228            break;
0229
0230          case IDM_License:
0231            LoadString(hInst,IDS_License,lpCaption,Max);
0232            LoadString(hInst,IDS_LicenseText,lpMessage,MaxText);
0233            MessageBox(GetFocus(),lpMessage,lpCaption,MB_OK);
0234            break;
0235
0236          case IDM_Display:
0237            if (DisplayWidth==640)
0238              {
0239              if (DisplayHeight==480)
0240                {
0241                LoadString(hInst,IDS_Resolution,lpCaption,Max);
0242                LoadString(hInst,IDS_ResVGA,lpMessage,MaxText);
0243                MessageBox(GetFocus(),lpMessage,lpCaption,MB_OK);
0244                }
0245              if (DisplayHeight==350)
0246                {
0247                LoadString(hInst,IDS_Resolution,lpCaption,Max);
0248                LoadString(hInst,IDS_ResEGA,lpMessage,MaxText);
0249                MessageBox(GetFocus(),lpMessage,lpCaption,MB_OK);
0250                }
0251              if (DisplayHeight==200)
0252                {
0253                LoadString(hInst,IDS_Resolution,lpCaption,Max);
0254                LoadString(hInst,IDS_ResCGA,lpMessage,MaxText);
0255                MessageBox(GetFocus(),lpMessage,lpCaption,MB_OK);
0256                }
0257              break;
0258              }
0259            if (DisplayWidth==800)
0260              {
0261              LoadString(hInst,IDS_Resolution,lpCaption,Max);
0262              LoadString(hInst,IDS_ResSVGA,lpMessage,MaxText);
0263              MessageBox(GetFocus(),lpMessage,lpCaption,MB_OK);
0264              break;
0265              }
0266            if (DisplayWidth==1024)
0267              {
0268              LoadString(hInst,IDS_Resolution,lpCaption,Max);
0269              LoadString(hInst,IDS_Res8514,lpMessage,MaxText);
```

```
0270              MessageBox(GetFocus(),lpMessage,lpCaption,MB_OK);
0271              break;
0272            }
0273          if (DisplayWidth==720)
0274            {
0275            LoadString(hInst,IDS_Resolution,lpCaption,Max);
0276            LoadString(hInst,IDS_ResHerc,lpMessage,MaxText);
0277            MessageBox(GetFocus(),lpMessage,lpCaption,MB_OK);
0278            break;
0279            }
0280          LoadString(hInst,IDS_Resolution,lpCaption,Max);
0281          LoadString(hInst,IDS_ResCustom,lpMessage,MaxText);
0282          MessageBox(GetFocus(),lpMessage,lpCaption,MB_OK);
0283          break;
0284
0285        case IDM_Colors:
0286          if (DisplayBits==1)
0287            {
0288            if (DisplayPlanes==4)
0289              {
0290              LoadString(hInst,IDS_Color,lpCaption,Max);
0291              LoadString(hInst,IDS_Color16,lpMessage,MaxText);
0292              MessageBox(GetFocus(),lpMessage,lpCaption,MB_OK);
0293              break;
0294              }
0295            if (DisplayPlanes==1)
0296              {
0297              LoadString(hInst,IDS_Color,lpCaption,Max);
0298              LoadString(hInst,IDS_Color2,lpMessage,MaxText);
0299              MessageBox(GetFocus(),lpMessage,lpCaption,MB_OK);
0300              break;
0301              }
0302            }
0303          if (DisplayBits==8)
0304            {
0305            LoadString(hInst,IDS_Color,lpCaption,Max);
0306            LoadString(hInst,IDS_Color256,lpMessage,MaxText);
0307            MessageBox(GetFocus(),lpMessage,lpCaption,MB_OK);
0308            break;
0309            }
0310          LoadString(hInst,IDS_Color,lpCaption,Max);
0311          LoadString(hInst,IDS_ColorCustom,lpMessage,MaxText);
0312          MessageBox(GetFocus(),lpMessage,lpCaption,MB_OK);
0313          break;
0314
0315        case IDM_Mode:
0316          if (MemoryMode & WF_ENHANCED)
0317            {
0318            LoadString(hInst,IDS_Machine,lpCaption,Max);
0319            LoadString(hInst,IDS_Enhanced,lpMessage,MaxText);
0320            MessageBox(GetFocus(),lpMessage,lpCaption,MB_OK);
0321            break;
0322            }
0323          if (MemoryMode & WF_STANDARD)
0324            {
0325            LoadString(hInst,IDS_Machine,lpCaption,Max);
0326            LoadString(hInst,IDS_Standard,lpMessage,MaxText);
0327            MessageBox(GetFocus(),lpMessage,lpCaption,MB_OK);
0328            break;
0329            }
0330          LoadString(hInst,IDS_Machine,lpCaption,Max);
```

```
0331            LoadString(hInst,IDS_Real,lpMessage,MaxText);
0332            MessageBox(GetFocus(),lpMessage,lpCaption,MB_OK);
0333            break;
0334
0335          case IDM_GeneralHelp:
0336            LoadString(hInst,IDS_Help,lpCaption,Max);
0337            LoadString(hInst,IDS_HelpText,lpMessage,MaxText);
0338            MessageBox(GetFocus(),lpMessage,lpCaption,MB_OK);
0339            break;
0340          default:
0341            return(DefWindowProc(hWnd, message, wParam, lParam));
0342        }
0343      break;
0344
0345    case WM_PAINT:              /* if image needs to be refreshed... */
0346      hDCpaint= BeginPaint(hWnd,&ps);            /* load structure */
0347      EndPaint(hWnd, &ps);                /* validate client area */
0348      if (PaintImage==zBLANK) break;     /* if client area is blank */
0349      if (FrameReady==FALSE) break;         /* if no hidden frame */
0350      zCopyToDisplay(hWnd);    /* else copy hidden frame to display */
0351      break;
0352
0353    case WM_DESTROY:  /* if user is terminating the application... */
0354      if (FrameReady==TRUE)
0355        {                         /* remove the hidden frame bitmap */
0356        SelectObject(hFrameDC,hPrevFrame);
0357        DeleteObject(hFrame);
0358        DeleteDC(hFrameDC);
0359        }
0360      PostQuitMessage(0);
0361      break;
0362
0363    case WM_SYSCOMMAND:     /* intercept resize, minimize, maximize */
0364      if ((wParam & 0xfff0)== SC_SIZE)
0365        {
0366        MessageBeep(0); break;
0367        }
0368      if ((wParam & 0xfff0)== SC_MINIMIZE)
0369        {
0370        MessageBeep(0); break;
0371        }
0372      if ((wParam & 0xfff0)== SC_MAXIMIZE)
0373        {
0374        MessageBeep(0); break;
0375        }
0376
0377    default:
0378      return(DefWindowProc(hWnd, message, wParam, lParam));
0379    }
0380  return FALSE;
0381  }
0382  /*
0383  ------------------------------------------------------------------
0384            Initialize the attributes of the window class
0385  ------------------------------------------------------------------
0386                                                                  */
0387  BOOL zInitClass(HANDLE hInstance)
0388  {
0389    WNDCLASS WndClass;
0390  WndClass.style= 0;                             /* class style */
0391  WndClass.lpfnWndProc= zMessageHandler;    /* callback function */
```

```
0392   WndClass.cbClsExtra= 0;                /* unused, no customized data */
0393   WndClass.cbWndExtra= 0;                /* unused, no customized data */
0394   WndClass.hInstance= hInstance;      /* application that owns class */
0395   WndClass.hIcon= LoadIcon(NULL,IDI_EXCLAMATION); /* minimize icon */
0396   WndClass.hCursor= LoadCursor(NULL,IDC_ARROW);       /* app's cursor */
0397   WndClass.hbrBackground=  /* specifies background color of window */
0398                           CreateSolidBrush(RGB(255,255,255));
0399   WndClass.lpszMenuName= "MENUS1";    /* name of .RC menu resource */
0400   WndClass.lpszClassName= "DEMOCLASS";        /* name of the class */
0401   return RegisterClass(&WndClass);          /* registers the class */
0402   }
0403   /*
0404   -------------------------------------------------------------------
0405                        Create the main window
0406   -------------------------------------------------------------------
0407                                                                  */
0408   HWND zInitMainWindow(HANDLE hInstance)
0409   {
0410     HWND hWnd;
0411   LoadString(hInstance,IDS_Caption,lpCaption,Max); /* load caption */
0412   hHourGlass= LoadCursor(NULL,IDC_WAIT);   /* load the wait cursor */
0413   hWnd= CreateWindow("DEMOCLASS",   /* create window of this class */
0414        lpCaption,                               /* caption */
0415        WS_OVERLAPPED | WS_THICKFRAME | WS_MINIMIZEBOX |  /* type */
0416          WS_MAXIMIZEBOX | WS_CLIPCHILDREN,
0417        WindowX,WindowY,                      /* screen location */
0418        zWINDOW_WIDTH,zWINDOW_HEIGHT,       /* window dimensions */
0419        0,0,                /* parent handle, menu or child ID */
0420        hInstance,(LPSTR)NULL); /* app instance and unused pointer */
0421   return hWnd;
0422   }
0423   /*
0424   -------------------------------------------------------------------
0425             THE CORE FUNCTIONS OF THE APPLICATION
0426   -------------------------------------------------------------------
0427   -------------------------------------------------------------------
0428                     Create the hidden frame.
0429   -------------------------------------------------------------------
0430                                                                  */
0431   static void zInitFrame(HWND hWnd)
0432   {
0433     HDC hDisplayDC;                          /* display-context */
0434
0435   GlobalCompact((DWORD)-1L);          /* maximize contiguous memory */
0436   hDisplayDC= GetDC(hWnd);                /* set the display-context */
0437   hFrameDC= CreateCompatibleDC(hDisplayDC);     /* create frame... */
0438   hFrame= CreateCompatibleBitmap(hDisplayDC,zFRAMEWIDE,zFRAMEHIGH);
0439   if (hFrame==NULL)
0440     {
0441     LoadString(hInst,IDS_NotReady,lpCaption,Max);
0442     LoadString(hInst,IDS_NoMem,lpMessage,MaxText);
0443     MessageBox(GetFocus(),lpMessage,lpCaption,MB_OK);
0444     DeleteDC(hFrameDC);
0445     FrameReady= FALSE;
0446     return;
0447     }
0448   hPrevFrame= SelectObject(hFrameDC,hFrame);  /* select the bitmap */
0449   zClearHiddenFrame();                    /* clear the hidden frame */
0450   LoadString(hInst,IDS_Ready,lpCaption,Max);
0451   LoadString(hInst,IDS_FrameOK,lpMessage,MaxText);
0452   MessageBox(GetFocus(),lpMessage,lpCaption,MB_OK);
```

```
0453    ReleaseDC(hWnd,hDisplayDC);          /* release the display-context */
0454    FrameReady= TRUE;                              /* set a global token */
0455    return;
0456    }
0457    /*
0458    -----------------------------------------------------------------------
0459                        Clear the display window.
0460    -----------------------------------------------------------------------
0461                                                                        */
0462    static void zClear(HWND hWnd)
0463    {
0464       HDC hDC;
0465    hDC= GetDC(hWnd);
0466    PatBlt(hDC,0,0,zFRAMEWIDE,zFRAMEHIGH,WHITENESS);
0467    ReleaseDC(hWnd,hDC);
0468    return;
0469    }
0470    /*
0471    -----------------------------------------------------------------------
0472                        Clear the hidden frame.
0473    -----------------------------------------------------------------------
0474                                                                        */
0475    static void zClearHiddenFrame(void)
0476    {
0477    if (FrameReady==FALSE) return;
0478    PatBlt(hFrameDC,0,0,zFRAMEWIDE,zFRAMEHIGH,WHITENESS);
0479    return;
0480    }
0481    /*
0482    -----------------------------------------------------------------------
0483              Copy the hidden frame to the display window.
0484    -----------------------------------------------------------------------
0485                                                                        */
0486    static void zCopyToDisplay(HWND hWnd)
0487    {
0488       HDC hDC;
0489    if (FrameReady==FALSE) return;
0490    hDC= GetDC(hWnd);
0491    BitBlt(hDC,0,0,zFRAMEWIDE,zFRAMEHIGH,hFrameDC,0,0,SRCCOPY);
0492    ReleaseDC(hWnd,hDC);
0493    return;
0494    }
0495    /*
0496    -----------------------------------------------------------------------
0497              Copy the display window to the hidden frame.
0498    -----------------------------------------------------------------------
0499                                                                        */
0500    static void zCopyToFrame(HWND hWnd)
0501    {
0502       HDC hDC;
0503    if (FrameReady==FALSE) return;
0504    hDC= GetDC(hWnd);
0505    BitBlt(hFrameDC,0,0,zFRAMEWIDE,zFRAMEHIGH,hDC,0,0,SRCCOPY);
0506    ReleaseDC(hWnd,hDC);
0507    return;
0508    }
0509    /*
0510    -----------------------------------------------------------------------
0511                        End of the C source file
0512    -----------------------------------------------------------------------
0513                                                                        */
```

**4-11**  The include file listing for the sample library of 3D routines.

```
0001  /*
0002  ----------------------------------------------------------------
0003                            LIB3D.H
0004  ----------------------------------------------------------------
0005                                                              */
0006  #define zRED      1
0007  #define zGREEN    2
0008  #define zBROWN    3
0009  #define zBLUE     4
0010  #define zMAGENTA  5
0011  #define zCYAN     6
0012  #define zGRAY     7
0013
0014  void zInitialize3D(HWND);          /* initialize 3D configuration */
0015  void zDrawCube(void);                        /* draw 3D cube */
0016  void zSetShadingColor(int);                  /* dithering hue */
0017  void zSetCameraHeading(int);       /* sets camera heading angle */
0018  void zSetCameraPitch(int);           /* sets camera pitch angle */
0019  void zSetCameraDistance(int); /* sets camera-to-subject distance */
0020  void zSetSubjectLocation(int,int,int);   /* instance translation */
0021  void zSetSubjectAttitude(int,int,int);     /* instance rotation */
0022  void zSetSubjectSize(int,int,int);        /* instance extrusion */
0023  /*
0024  ----------------------------------------------------------------
0025                     End of LIB3D.H header file.
0026  ----------------------------------------------------------------
0027                                                              */
```

**4-12**  The C source file listing for the sample library of 3D routines, lib3d.c, providing facet shading and automatic backplane removal.

```
0001  /*
0002  ----------------------------------------------------------------
0003      Library of 3D routines for Windows animation sequences
0004  ----------------------------------------------------------------
0005      Source file:  LIB3D.C
0006      Release version:  1.00          Programmer:  Lee Adams
0007      Type:  C source file for Windows multimodule applications.
0008      Compilers:  Microsoft C and SDK, Borland C++, Zortech C++,
0009        QuickC for Windows, Turbo C++ for Windows, WATCOM C.
0010      Memory model:  small.
0011      Dependencies:  LIB3D.H include file.  Compile this file and
0012        link the resulting .OBJ file to your compiled main .C file.
0013        Include LIB3D.H in your main .C file.  The 3D routines use
0014        floating-point variables and floating-point math routines,
0015        so you must use the -FPi option on the compiler command-line
0016        and you must explicitly name the WIN87EM library on the
0017        linker command-line if you are using MSC 6.0A and the SDK.
0018      Output and features:  Provides control over camera pitch,
0019        camera heading, and camera-to-subject distance.  Provides
0020        precise control over the size, location, attitude, and
0021        color of each 3D object being drawn.  Provides automatic
0022        hidden surface removal using the backplane algorithm.
0023        Shades each surface according to its illumination level
0024        resulting from a point light source located above, behind,
0025        and to the left of the camera position.
0026      Publication: Contains material from Windcrest/McGraw-Hill book
0027        4114 published by TAB BOOKS Division of McGraw-Hill Inc.
```

**4-12** Continued.

```
0028        License: As purchaser of the book you are granted a royalty-
0029        free license to distribute executable files generated using
0030        this code provided you accept the conditions of the License
0031        Agreement and Limited Warranty described in the book and on
0032        the companion disk.  Government users:  This software and
0033        documentation are subject to restrictions set forth in The
0034        Rights in Technical Data and Computer Software clause at
0035        252.227-7013 and elsewhere.
0036   ------------------------------------------------------------------
0037           (c) Copyright 1992 Lee Adams.  All rights reserved.
0038             Lee Adams(tm) is a trademark of Lee Adams.
0039   ------------------------------------------------------------------
0040                                                                   */
0041   #define zRED            1                    /* shading colors... */
0042   #define zGREEN          2
0043   #define zBROWN          3
0044   #define zBLUE           4
0045   #define zMAGENTA        5
0046   #define zCYAN           6
0047   #define zGRAY           7
0048   #define zMAX_LOCATION 100                    /* max translation */
0049   #define zMAX_HEADING  360              /* max camera heading */
0050   #define zMIN_HEADING  0                /* min camera heading */
0051   #define zMAX_PITCH    360                /* max camera pitch */
0052   #define zMIN_PITCH    270                /* min camera pitch */
0053   #define zMAX_DISTANCE 700      /* max camera-to-subject distance */
0054   #define zMIN_DISTANCE 100      /* min camera-to-subject distance */
0055   /*
0056   ------------------------------------------------------------------
0057                            Include files
0058   ------------------------------------------------------------------
0059                                                                   */
0060   #include <WINDOWS.H>
0061   #include <math.h>
0062   /*
0063   ------------------------------------------------------------------
0064        Function prototypes:  low-level 3D graphics routines
0065   ------------------------------------------------------------------
0066                                                                   */
0067   /* ----- callable from both outside and inside this module ----- */
0068   void zInitialize3D(HWND);           /* initialize 3D configuration */
0069   void zDrawCube(void);                            /* draw 3D cube */
0070   void zSetShadingColor(int);                /* sets shading color */
0071   void zSetCameraHeading(int);         /* sets camera heading angle */
0072   void zSetCameraPitch(int);             /* sets camera pitch angle */
0073   void zSetCameraDistance(int); /* sets camera-to-subject distance */
0074   void zSetSubjectLocation(int,int,int);    /* instance translation */
0075   void zSetSubjectAttitude(int,int,int);      /* instance rotation */
0076   void zSetSubjectSize(int,int,int);         /* instance extrusion */
0077
0078   /* ----------- callable from only inside this module ----------- */
0079   static void zGetCameraCoords(void); /* wrld coords to cam coords */
0080   static void zGetImageCoords(void);  /* cam coords to imge coords */
0081   static void zGetScreenCoords(void); /* maps imge plane to screen */
0082   static void zGetWorldCoords(void);  /* obj coords to wrld coords */
0083   static void zVisibilityTest(void);       /* back-plane visibility */
0084   static void zGetBrightness(void); /* finds brightness of a facet */
0085   static void zGetCubeCoords(void); /* cam coords & display coords */
0086   static void zSetObjAngle(void); /* sine, cosine rotation factors */
0087   static void zSetCamAngle(void); /* sine, cosine rotation factors */
```

```
0088    static void zPutObjToScreen(void);      /* object to screen coords */
0089    static void zPutWorldToScreen(void);    /* world to screen coords */
0090    static void zDrawFacet(void);                      /* draws facet */
0091    static void zShowMessage(void);         /* shows debugging message */
0092    /*
0093    ------------------------------------------------------------------
0094          Declaration of static variables for 3D modeling
0095    ------------------------------------------------------------------
0096                                                                     */
0097    static double DomainWidth= 800, DomainDepth= 600;   /* 3D domain */
0098    static double x=0.0,y=0.0,z=0.0;/* wrld coords in,cam coords out */
0099    static double xc1=0.0,xc2=0.0,xc3=0.0,xc4=0.0,xc5=0.0,
0100           xc6=0.0,xc7=0.0,yc1=0.0,yc2=0.0,yc3=0.0,
0101           yc4=0.0,yc5=0.0,yc6=0.0,yc7=0.0,zc1=0.0,
0102           zc2=0.0,zc3=0.0,zc4=0.0,zc5=0.0,zc6=0.0,
0103           zc7=0.0;                         /* camera coords of facet */
0104    static double sx1=0.0,sx2=0.0,sx3=0.0,sx4=0.0,sx5=0.0,
0105           sy1=0.0,sy2=0.0,sy3=0.0,
0106           sy4=0.0,sy5=0.0;            /* display coords of facet */
0107    static double xw1=0,xw2=0,xw3=0,yw1=0,yw2=0,yw3=0,
0108       zw1=0,zw2=0,zw3=0;      /* raw world coords for brightness */
0109    static double sx3D=0.0,sy3D=0.0;       /* output of 3D formulas */
0110    static double cursorx=10,cursory=10,
0111           cursorz=10;                     /* volume of 3D cursor */
0112    static double xa=0.0,ya=0.0,za=0.0;  /* temporary in 3D formulas */
0113    static double focal_length=1200.0; /* angular perspective factor */
0114    static double ObjYaw=6.28319,ObjRoll=6.28319,
0115           ObjPitch=6.28319;             /* object rotation angles */
0116    static double sOYaw=0.0,cOYaw=0.0;
0117    static double sORoll=0.0,cORoll=0.0;
0118    static double sOPitch=0.0,cOPitch=0.0;
0119    static double xObj=0.0,yObj=0.0,zObj=0.0;     /* obj trans values */
0120    static double CamYaw=6.28319,CamRoll=6.28319,
0121           CamPitch=6.28319;                        /* camera */
0122    static double sCYaw=0.0,sCRoll=0.0,sCPitch=0.0;
0123    static double cCYaw=0.0,cCRoll=0.0,cCPitch=0.0;
0124    static double xCam=0.0,yCam=0.0,
0125           zCam=-360.0;               /* world translation values */
0126    static double rx=0.0,ry=0.0;       /* ratios used in windowing */
0127    static double hcenter=0.0,vcenter=0.0;     /* center of viewport */
0128    static double viewheight=0; /* viewer's height 0 ft above ground */
0129    static double dist=360;   /* viewer's virtual distance from scene */
0130    static double yawdist=360;/* viewer's actual distance from scene */
0131    static int pitchheading=360,yawheading=0;  /* cam angle, degrees */
0132    static int viewchg=2;            /* degrees to change camera angle */
0133    static double yawdelta=0,pitchdelta=0;/* current absolute change */
0134    static double planex=80,planey=0,
0135           planez=60;                  /* volume of groundplane */
0136    static double cursorxchg=0,cursorychg=0,
0137           cursorzchg=0;            /* extrude cursor and object */
0138    static double signmx=1,signmy=-1,
0139           signmz=-1;                  /* coord system tweaking */
0140    static double cubeObj[][3]={             /* cube xyz object coords */
0141           10,-10,10,    10,10,10,   -10,10,10,   -10,-10,10,
0142           10,10,-10,   -10,10,-10,   -10,-10,-10,   10,-10,-10};
0143    static double cubeWorld[8][3];/* xw1,yw1,zw1 vertex world coords */
0144    static double camcoords[8][3];   /* xc1,yc1,zc1 vertex cam coords */
0145    static double displaycoords[8][2]; /* sx1,sy1 vertex disp coords */
0146    /*
0147    ------------------------------------------------------------------
0148       Declaration of static variables: rendering & backplane removal
```

```
0149    ----------------------------------------------------------------
0150                                                                  */
0151    static double visible=0.0;                  /* visibility factor */
0152    static double sp1=0.0,sp2=0.0,sp3=0.0;          /* temp values of sp */
0153    static double xLight=-.1294089,yLight=.8660256,zLight=.4829627;
0154    static double illum_range= 255;             /* Windows-dependent range */
0155    static double normalized_illum=0.0; /* illum factor 0 to 1 range */
0156    static double xu=0.0,yu=0.0,zu=0.0;         /* vector vertex 1 to 2 */
0157    static double xv=0.0,yv=0.0,zv=0.0;         /* vector vertex 1 to 3 */
0158    static double x_surf_normal=0.0,
0159                  y_surf_normal=0.0,z_surf_normal=0.0;
0160    static double v1=0.0,v2=0.0;          /* length, surface perp vector */
0161    static double v3=0.0;               /* ratio, surf perp to unit vector */
0162    static double x_unit_vector=0.0,
0163                  y_unit_vector=0.0,z_unit_vector=0.0;
0164    static int zDeviceIllum=0;           /* Windows-dependent brightness */
0165    static int zShadingColor= 4;                   /* dithering hue */
0166    /*
0167    ----------------------------------------------------------------
0168            Declaration of static pixel-based variables
0169    ----------------------------------------------------------------
0170                                                                  */
0171    static HWND hWnd;              /* will hold handle to active window */
0172    static BOOL bInitialized= FALSE;        /* 3D system initialized? */
0173    static int clipx1=0, clipy1=0;              /* client area coords */
0174    static int clipx2=639, clipy2=479;          /* client area coords */
0175    static int ViewportWidth= 640;          /* width of client area */
0176    static int VirtualWidth= 640;           /* to preserve 4:3 ratio */
0177    static int ViewportDepth= 480;          /* depth of client area */
0178    static double ViewportTemp= 0;              /* temporary value */
0179    /*
0180    ----------------------------------------------------------------
0181                   3 D   R O U T I N E S
0182    ----------------------------------------------------------------
0183    ----------------------------------------------------------------
0184            Initialize and configure the 3D environment
0185    ----------------------------------------------------------------
0186                                                                  */
0187    void zInitialize3D(hWndow)
0188      HWND hWndow;                      /* handle to the active window */
0189    {
0190      RECT rcClientArea;   /* data structure of 4 xy coords for rect */
0191
0192    hWnd= hWndow;   /* store global handle that all routines can use */
0193    GetClientRect(hWnd, &rcClientArea);     /* fetch bounding coords */
0194    clipx1= rcClientArea.left; clipy1= rcClientArea.top;
0195    clipx2= rcClientArea.right; clipy2= rcClientArea.bottom;
0196
0197    /* ---------------------- viewport ---------------------- */
0198    ViewportWidth= clipx2 - clipx1;             /* width of viewport */
0199    ViewportDepth= clipy2 - clipy1;             /* depth of viewport */
0200    ViewportTemp= ViewportDepth * 1.3333;          /* 4:3 ratio */
0201    VirtualWidth= (int) ViewportTemp;   /* width of virtual viewport */
0202    DomainWidth= 800; DomainDepth= 600;         /* size of 3D domain */
0203    rx= VirtualWidth / DomainWidth;             /* mapping ratio */
0204    ry= ViewportDepth / DomainDepth;            /* mapping ratio */
0205    hcenter= ViewportWidth / 2;             /* center of viewport */
0206    vcenter= ViewportDepth / 2;             /* center of viewport */
0207
0208    /* ---------------------- illumination ---------------------- */
0209    xLight= -.21131; yLight= .86603; zLight= .45315; /* light source */
```

```
0210  illum_range= 255;                      /* surface brightness 0 to 255 */
0211
0212  /* ---------------------- camera -------------------------- */
0213  focal_length= 1200.0;                  /* angular perspective factor */
0214  viewheight= 0;          /* 0 for camera, else 5 or 6 for android */
0215  dist= 360;                             /* camera-to-subject distance */
0216  CamYaw= 0.0; CamRoll= 0.0; CamPitch= 6.28319;
0217  pitchheading= 360; yawheading= 0;                /* camera direction */
0218  viewchg= 2;
0219  yawdelta= 0; pitchdelta= 0;
0220  zSetCamAngle();
0221  xCam= 0.0; yCam= 0.0; zCam= -360.0;              /* camera location */
0222
0223  /* ---------------------- models ------------------------- */
0224  ObjYaw= 0.0; ObjRoll= 0.0; ObjPitch= 0.0;   /* model orientation */
0225  zSetObjAngle();
0226  xObj= 0.0; yObj= 0.0; zObj= 0.0;                 /* model location */
0227
0228  /* ------------------ virtual 3D cursors ------------------ */
0229  cursorx= 15; cursory= 15; cursorz= 15;   /* 3D volumetric cursor */
0230  planex= 100; planey= 0; planez= 75;              /* 3D groundplane */
0231
0232  /* ------------------ set a status indicator --------------- */
0233  bInitialized= TRUE;
0234  return;
0235  }
0236  /*
0237  -----------------------------------------------------------------
0238                    Set the camera heading.
0239  -----------------------------------------------------------------
0240                                                                  */
0241  void zSetCameraHeading(int Heading)
0242  {                  /* call with Heading in degrees range 0 to 360 */
0243  if (bInitialized==FALSE) {zShowMessage(); return;}
0244  if (Heading > zMAX_HEADING) return;
0245  if (Heading < zMIN_HEADING) return;
0246  yawheading= Heading;
0247  CamYaw= ((double)yawheading)*.0175433;
0248  if (yawheading==360) CamYaw= 6.28319;
0249  if (yawheading==0) CamYaw= 0.0;
0250  zSetCamAngle();
0251  if ((CamYaw >= 4.71239) && (CamYaw <= 6.28319))
0252    {
0253    signmx= -1; signmz= -1; yawdelta= 6.28319 - CamYaw;
0254    goto calccamyaw1;
0255    }
0256  if ((CamYaw >= 0) && (CamYaw < 1.57079))
0257    {
0258    signmx= 1; signmz= -1; yawdelta= CamYaw;
0259    goto calccamyaw1;
0260    }
0261  if ((CamYaw >= 1.57079) && (CamYaw < 3.14159))
0262    {
0263    signmx= 1; signmz= 1; yawdelta= 3.14159 - CamYaw;
0264    goto calccamyaw1;
0265    }
0266  if ((CamYaw >= 3.14159) && (CamYaw < 4.71239))
0267    {
0268    signmx= -1; signmz= 1; yawdelta= CamYaw - 3.14159;
0269    goto calccamyaw1;
0270    }
```

**4-12** Continued.

```
0271  calccamyaw1:
0272  xCam= sin(yawdelta) * yawdist * signmx;
0273  zCam= cos(yawdelta) * yawdist * signmz;
0274  return;
0275  }
0276  /*
0277  ------------------------------------------------------------------
0278                        Set the camera pitch.
0279  ------------------------------------------------------------------
0280                                                                   */
0281  void zSetCameraPitch(int Pitch)
0282  {              /* call with Pitch in range 270 to 360 (horizontal) */
0283  if (bInitialized==FALSE) {zShowMessage(); return;}
0284  if (Pitch > zMAX_PITCH) return;  /* do not penetrate groundplane */
0285  if (Pitch < zMIN_PITCH) return;        /* do not exceed vertical */
0286  pitchheading= Pitch;
0287  CamPitch= ((double)pitchheading) * .0174533;      /* make radians */
0288  if (pitchheading==360) CamPitch= 6.28319;
0289  if (pitchheading==0) CamPitch= 0.0;
0290  zSetCamAngle();
0291  pitchdelta= 6.28319 - CamPitch; /* change in pitch from start-up */
0292  yCam=sin(pitchdelta) * dist * signmy;        /* new y translation */
0293  yawdist=sqrt((dist * dist) - (yCam * yCam));       /* hypotenuse */
0294  xCam=sin(yawdelta) * yawdist * signmx;       /* new x translation */
0295  zCam=sqrt((yawdist * yawdist) - (xCam * xCam)) * signmz;   /* z */
0296  return;
0297  }
0298  /*
0299  ------------------------------------------------------------------
0300                  Set the camera-to-subject distance.
0301  ------------------------------------------------------------------
0302                                                                   */
0303  void zSetCameraDistance(int Range)
0304  {
0305  if (bInitialized==FALSE) {zShowMessage(); return;}
0306  if (Range < zMIN_DISTANCE) Range= zMIN_DISTANCE;
0307  if (Range > zMAX_DISTANCE) Range= zMAX_DISTANCE;
0308  dist= (double) Range;
0309  yCam=sin(pitchdelta) * dist * signmy;        /* new y translation */
0310  yawdist=sqrt((dist * dist) - (yCam * yCam));       /* hypotenuse */
0311  xCam=sin(yawdelta) * yawdist * signmx;       /* new x translation */
0312  zCam=sqrt((yawdist * yawdist) - (xCam * xCam)) * signmz;   /* z */
0313  return;
0314  }
0315  /*
0316  ------------------------------------------------------------------
0317                  Set the location of the subject.
0318  ------------------------------------------------------------------
0319                                                                   */
0320  void zSetSubjectLocation(int SSLx, int SSLy, int SSLz)
0321  {
0322  if (bInitialized==FALSE) {zShowMessage(); return;}
0323  if (SSLx > zMAX_LOCATION) return;
0324  if (SSLx < -zMAX_LOCATION) return;
0325  if (SSLy > zMAX_LOCATION) return;
0326  if (SSLy < -zMAX_LOCATION) return;
0327  if (SSLz > zMAX_LOCATION) return;
0328  if (SSLz < -zMAX_LOCATION) return;
0329  xObj= (double) SSLx; yObj= (double) SSLy; zObj= (double) SSLz;
0330  return;
0331  }
```

```
0332  /*
0333  ------------------------------------------------------------------
0334                   Set the attitude of the subject.
0335  ------------------------------------------------------------------
0336                                                              */
0337  void zSetSubjectAttitude(int Yaw, int Roll, int Pitch)
0338  {
0339  if (bInitialized==FALSE) {zShowMessage(); return;}
0340  if (Yaw < 0) return;                      /* trap illegal values... */
0341  if (Yaw > 360) return;
0342  if (Roll < 0) return;
0343  if (Roll > 360) return;
0344  if (Pitch < 0) return;
0345  if (Pitch > 360) return;
0346  ObjYaw=    ((double)Yaw) * .0175433;    /* convert to radians... */
0347  ObjRoll=   ((double)Roll) * .0175433;
0348  ObjPitch=  ((double)Pitch) * .0175433;
0349  if (Yaw==360) ObjYaw= 6.28319;       /* tidy up boundary values... */
0350  if (Yaw==0) ObjYaw= 0.0;
0351  if (Roll==360) ObjRoll= 6.28319;
0352  if (Roll==0) ObjRoll= 0.0;
0353  if (Pitch==360) ObjPitch= 6.28319;
0354  if (Pitch==0) ObjPitch= 0.0;
0355  zSetObjAngle();                       /* set sine and cosine factors */
0356  return;
0357  }
0358  /*
0359  ------------------------------------------------------------------
0360                   Set the extrusion of the subject.
0361  ------------------------------------------------------------------
0362                                                              */
0363  void zSetSubjectSize(int Width, int Height, int Depth)
0364  {
0365  if (bInitialized==FALSE) {zShowMessage(); return;}
0366  if (Width < 2) Width= 2;                     /* inhibit the range... */
0367  if (Width > 100) Width= 100;
0368  if (Height < 2) Height= 2;
0369  if (Height > 100) Height= 100;
0370  if (Depth < 2) Depth= 2;
0371  if (Depth > 100) Depth= 100;
0372  cursorx= (double) Width;           /* set the extrusion factors... */
0373  cursory= (double) Height;
0374  cursorz= (double) Depth;
0375  return;
0376  }
0377  /*
0378  ------------------------------------------------------------------
0379          Display debugging message if system not initialized.
0380  ------------------------------------------------------------------
0381                                                              */
0382  static void zShowMessage(void)
0383  {
0384  MessageBox(GetFocus(), "3D routines not yet initialized.",
0385    "3D programming error", MB_OK);
0386  return;
0387  }
0388  /*
0389  ------------------------------------------------------------------
0390                   Perform the backplane visibility test
0391  ------------------------------------------------------------------
0392                                                              */
```

**4-12** Continued.

```
0393  static void zVisibilityTest(void)
0394  {
0395     /* Enter with 3 vertices as camera coords.
0396        Exit with visibility token.                    */
0397  sp1=xc1*(yc2*zc3-yc3*zc2);sp1=(-1)*sp1;
0398  sp2=xc2*(yc3*zc1-yc1*zc3);sp3=xc3*(yc1*zc2-yc2*zc1);
0399  visible=sp1-sp2-sp3;
0400  return;
0401  }
0402  /*
0403  ------------------------------------------------------------
0404            Calculate object sine and cosine rotation factors
0405  ------------------------------------------------------------
0406                                                         */
0407  static void zSetObjAngle(void)
0408  {
0409     /* Enter with ObjYaw,ObjRoll,ObjPitch object rotation angles.
0410        Exit with sine, cosine object rotation factors.   */
0411  sOYaw=sin(ObjYaw);cOYaw=cos(ObjYaw);
0412  sORoll=sin(ObjRoll);cORoll=cos(ObjRoll);
0413  sOPitch=sin(ObjPitch);cOPitch=cos(ObjPitch);
0414  return;
0415  }
0416  /*
0417  ------------------------------------------------------------
0418            Calculate camera sine and cosine rotation factors
0419  ------------------------------------------------------------
0420                                                         */
0421  static void zSetCamAngle(void)
0422  {
0423     /* Enter with Yaw,Roll,Pitch world rotation angles.
0424        Exit with sine, cosine world rotation factors.   */
0425  sCYaw=sin(CamYaw);sCRoll=sin(CamRoll);sCPitch=sin(CamPitch);
0426  cCYaw=cos(CamYaw);cCRoll=cos(CamRoll);cCPitch=cos(CamPitch);
0427  return;
0428  }
0429  /*
0430  ------------------------------------------------------------
0431            Transform object coords to screen coords
0432  ------------------------------------------------------------
0433                                                         */
0434  static void zPutObjToScreen(void)
0435  {
0436     /* Enter with xyz object coordinates.  This routine transforms
0437        the obj coords to world coords to image plane coords to
0438        sx3D,sy3D physical screen coords.                */
0439  zGetWorldCoords();zGetCameraCoords();zGetImageCoords();
0440  zGetScreenCoords();
0441  return;
0442  }
0443  /*
0444  ------------------------------------------------------------
0445            Transform world coords to screen coords
0446  ------------------------------------------------------------
0447                                                         */
0448  static void zPutWorldToScreen(void)
0449  {
0450     /* Enter with xyz world coordinates.  This routine transforms
0451        the world coords to image plane coords to sx3D,sy3D physical
0452        screen coords.                                   */
0453  zGetCameraCoords();zGetImageCoords();zGetScreenCoords();
```

```
0454   return;
0455   }
0456   /*
0457   ---------------------------------------------------------------
0458               Calculate world coords from object coords
0459   ---------------------------------------------------------------
0460                                                               */
0461   static void zGetWorldCoords(void)
0462   {
0463     /* Enter with xyz unclipped object coordinates.
0464        Exit with unclipped xyz world coordinates.            */
0465   xa=cORoll*x+sORoll*y;ya=cORoll*y-sORoll*x;       /* roll rotate */
0466   x=cOYaw*xa-sOYaw*z;za=sOYaw*xa+cOYaw*z;            /* yaw rotate */
0467   z=cOPitch*za-sOPitch*ya;y=sOPitch*za+cOPitch*ya; /* pitch rotate */
0468   x=x+xObj;y=y+yObj;z=z+zObj;                  /* lateral movement */
0469   return;
0470   }
0471   /*
0472   ---------------------------------------------------------------
0473               Calculate camera coords from world coords
0474   ---------------------------------------------------------------
0475                                                               */
0476   static void zGetCameraCoords(void)
0477   {
0478     /* Enter with unclipped xyz world coordinates.
0479        Exit with unclipped xyz camera coordinates.           */
0480   x=(-1)*x;              /* adjust for cartesian coords of 2D screen */
0481   y=y-viewheight;        /* adjust world coords to height of viewer */
0482   x=x-xCam;y=y+yCam;z=z+zCam;                  /* lateral movement */
0483   xa=cCYaw*x-sCYaw*z;za=sCYaw*x+cCYaw*z;             /* yaw rotate */
0484   z=cCPitch*za-sCPitch*y;ya=sCPitch*za+cCPitch*y;  /* pitch rotate */
0485   x=cCRoll*xa+sCRoll*ya;y=cCRoll*ya-sCRoll*xa;      /* roll rotate */
0486   return;
0487   }
0488   /*
0489   ---------------------------------------------------------------
0490               Calculate dipslay coords from camera coords
0491   ---------------------------------------------------------------
0492                                                               */
0493   static void zGetImageCoords(void)
0494   {
0495     /* Enter with clipped xyz camera coordinates.
0496        Exit with unclipped sx3D,sy3D display coordinates.     */
0497   sx3D=focal_length*(x/z); sy3D=focal_length*(y/z);
0498   return;
0499   }
0500   /*
0501   ---------------------------------------------------------------
0502               Calculate screen coords from display coords
0503   ---------------------------------------------------------------
0504                                                               */
0505   static void zGetScreenCoords(void)
0506   {
0507     /* Enter with unclipped sx3D,sy3D display coordinates.
0508        Exit with sx3D,sy3D device-dependent display coordinates
0509        scaled to the world range with correct aspect ratio.   */
0510   sx3D=sx3D*rx;sy3D=sy3D*ry;
0511   sx3D=sx3D+hcenter;sy3D=sy3D+vcenter;
0512   return;
0513   }
0514   /*
```

**4-12** Continued.

```
0515   -----------------------------------------------------------------
0516                        Draw a four-sided polygon
0517   -----------------------------------------------------------------
0518                                                                   */
0519   static void zDrawFacet(void)
0520   {
0521     HDC hDC;
0522     HBRUSH hPrevBrush, hFacetBrush;
0523     HRGN hPrevRegion, hFacetRegion;
0524     POINT Points[4];
0525   Points[0].x= (int) sx1; Points[0].y= (int) sy1;
0526   Points[1].x= (int) sx2; Points[1].y= (int) sy2;
0527   Points[2].x= (int) sx3; Points[2].y= (int) sy3;
0528   Points[3].x= (int) sx4; Points[3].y= (int) sy4;
0529   zGetBrightness();                /* get brightness factor of facet */
0530   switch (zShadingColor)            /* set the dithering pattern... */
0531     {
0532     case zRED:
0533       hFacetBrush= CreateSolidBrush(RGB(zDeviceIllum,0,0));
0534       break;
0535     case zGREEN:
0536       hFacetBrush= CreateSolidBrush(RGB(0,zDeviceIllum,0));
0537       break;
0538     case zBROWN:
0539       hFacetBrush=
0540         CreateSolidBrush(RGB(zDeviceIllum,zDeviceIllum,0));
0541       break;
0542     case zBLUE:
0543       hFacetBrush= CreateSolidBrush(RGB(0,0,zDeviceIllum));
0544       break;
0545     case zMAGENTA:
0546       hFacetBrush=
0547         CreateSolidBrush(RGB(zDeviceIllum,0,zDeviceIllum));
0548       break;
0549     case zCYAN:
0550       hFacetBrush=
0551         CreateSolidBrush(RGB(0,zDeviceIllum,zDeviceIllum));
0552       break;
0553     case zGRAY:
0554       hFacetBrush=
0555         CreateSolidBrush(RGB(zDeviceIllum,zDeviceIllum,zDeviceIllum));
0556       break;
0557     default:
0558       hFacetBrush= CreateSolidBrush(RGB(0,0,zDeviceIllum));
0559     }
0560   hFacetRegion= CreatePolygonRgn(Points,4,WINDING);     /* region */
0561   hDC= GetDC(hWnd);                             /* set display-context */
0562   hPrevBrush= SelectObject(hDC,hFacetBrush);        /* select brush */
0563   hPrevRegion= SelectObject(hDC,hFacetRegion);     /* select region */
0564   PaintRgn(hDC,hFacetRegion);                      /* fill the region */
0565   SelectObject(hDC,hPrevBrush);                   /* deselect brush */
0566   SelectObject(hDC,hPrevRegion);                 /* deselect region */
0567   ReleaseDC(hWnd,hDC);                    /* release display-context */
0568   DeleteObject(hFacetRegion);                     /* destroy region */
0569   DeleteObject(hFacetBrush);                       /* destroy brush */
0570   return;
0571   }
0572   /*
0573   -----------------------------------------------------------------
0574              Calculate the brightness level of a facet
0575   -----------------------------------------------------------------
```

```
0576                                                              */
0577    static void zGetBrightness(void)
0578    {
0579       /* Enter with facet world coordinates.
0580          Exit with illumination level token.                 */
0581    xu=xw2-xw1;yu=yw2-yw1;zu=zw2-zw1; /* vector vertex 1 to vertex 2 */
0582    xv=xw3-xw1;yv=yw3-yw1;zv=zw3-zw1; /* vector vertex 1 to vertex 3 */
0583    x_surf_normal=(yu*zv)-(zu*yv);
0584    y_surf_normal=(zu*xv)-(xu*zv);
0585    z_surf_normal=(xu*yv)-(yu*xv);
0586    y_surf_normal=y_surf_normal*(-1);
0587    z_surf_normal=z_surf_normal*(-1); /* convert to cartesian system */
0588    v1=(x_surf_normal*x_surf_normal)+(y_surf_normal*y_surf_normal)
0589       +(z_surf_normal*z_surf_normal);
0590    v2=sqrt(v1);           /* magnitude of surface perpendicular vector */
0591    v3=1/v2;               /* ratio of magnitude to length of unit vector */
0592    x_unit_vector=v3*x_surf_normal;
0593    y_unit_vector=v3*y_surf_normal;
0594    z_unit_vector=v3*z_surf_normal;/* surf perpendicular unit vector */
0595    normalized_illum=(x_unit_vector*xLight)+(y_unit_vector*yLight)
0596       +(z_unit_vector*zLight);              /* illumination factor 0 to 1 */
0597    normalized_illum=normalized_illum*illum_range;/* expand 0 to 255 */
0598    zDeviceIllum= (int) normalized_illum;             /* cast to int */
0599    if (zDeviceIllum < 47) zDeviceIllum= 47;      /* deepest shadow */
0600    return;
0601    }
0602    /*
0603    -----------------------------------------------------------------
0604                    Set the current shading color for facets
0605    -----------------------------------------------------------------
0606                                                              */
0607    void zSetShadingColor(int iHue)
0608    {
0609    if (bInitialized==FALSE) {zShowMessage(); return;}
0610    if (iHue < 1) return;
0611    if (iHue > 7) return;
0612    zShadingColor= iHue;
0613    return;
0614    }
0615    /*
0616    -----------------------------------------------------------------
0617                    Draw an instance of a parallelepiped
0618    -----------------------------------------------------------------
0619                                                              */
0620    static void zGetCubeCoords(void)         /* called by zDrawCube() */
0621    {
0622       int t= 0;
0623       double negx,negy,negz;
0624    negx=(-1)*(cursorx);negy=(-1)*(cursory);negz=(-1)*(cursorz);
0625    cubeObj[0][0]=cursorx;cubeObj[0][1]=negy;cubeObj[0][2]=cursorz;
0626    cubeObj[1][0]=cursorx;cubeObj[1][1]=cursory;cubeObj[1][2]=cursorz;
0627    cubeObj[2][0]=negx;cubeObj[2][1]=cursory;cubeObj[2][2]=cursorz;
0628    cubeObj[3][0]=negx;cubeObj[3][1]=negy;cubeObj[3][2]=cursorz;
0629    cubeObj[4][0]=cursorx;cubeObj[4][1]=cursory;cubeObj[4][2]=negz;
0630    cubeObj[5][0]=negx;cubeObj[5][1]=cursory;cubeObj[5][2]=negz;
0631    cubeObj[6][0]=negx;cubeObj[6][1]=negy;cubeObj[6][2]=negz;
0632    cubeObj[7][0]=cursorx;cubeObj[7][1]=negy;cubeObj[7][2]=negz;
0633    for (t=0;t<=7;t++)
0634       {
0635       x=cubeObj[t][0];y=cubeObj[t][1];z=cubeObj[t][2];
0636       zGetWorldCoords();
```

```
0637    cubeWorld[t][0]=x;cubeWorld[t][1]=y;cubeWorld[t][2]=z;
0638    zGetCameraCoords();
0639    camcoords[t][0]=x;camcoords[t][1]=y;camcoords[t][2]=z;
0640    zGetImageCoords();zGetScreenCoords();
0641    displaycoords[t][0]=sx3D;displaycoords[t][1]=sy3D;
0642    }
0643 return;
0644 }
0645
0646 void zDrawCube(void)            /* draw box at current 3D position */
0647 {
0648 if (bInitialized==FALSE) {zShowMessage(); return;}
0649 zGetCubeCoords();              /* get camera coords and display coords */
0650 surface0:
0651    xc1=camcoords[7][0];yc1=camcoords[7][1];zc1=camcoords[7][2];
0652    xc2=camcoords[0][0];yc2=camcoords[0][1];zc2=camcoords[0][2];
0653    xc3=camcoords[3][0];yc3=camcoords[3][1];zc3=camcoords[3][2];
0654    xc4=camcoords[6][0];yc4=camcoords[6][1];zc4=camcoords[6][2];
0655    zVisibilityTest();
0656    if (visible > 0) goto surface1;
0657    sx1=displaycoords[7][0];sy1=displaycoords[7][1];
0658    sx2=displaycoords[0][0];sy2=displaycoords[0][1];
0659    sx3=displaycoords[3][0];sy3=displaycoords[3][1];
0660    sx4=displaycoords[6][0];sy4=displaycoords[6][1];
0661    xw3=cubeWorld[7][0];yw3=cubeWorld[7][1];zw3=cubeWorld[7][2];
0662    xw2=cubeWorld[0][0];yw2=cubeWorld[0][1];zw2=cubeWorld[0][2];
0663    xw1=cubeWorld[3][0];yw1=cubeWorld[3][1];zw1=cubeWorld[3][2];
0664    zDrawFacet();
0665 surface1:
0666    xc1=camcoords[6][0];yc1=camcoords[6][1];zc1=camcoords[6][2];
0667    xc2=camcoords[5][0];yc2=camcoords[5][1];zc2=camcoords[5][2];
0668    xc3=camcoords[4][0];yc3=camcoords[4][1];zc3=camcoords[4][2];
0669    xc4=camcoords[7][0];yc4=camcoords[7][1];zc4=camcoords[7][2];
0670    zVisibilityTest();
0671    if (visible > 0) goto surface2;
0672    sx1=displaycoords[6][0];sy1=displaycoords[6][1];
0673    sx2=displaycoords[5][0];sy2=displaycoords[5][1];
0674    sx3=displaycoords[4][0];sy3=displaycoords[4][1];
0675    sx4=displaycoords[7][0];sy4=displaycoords[7][1];
0676    xw3=cubeWorld[6][0];yw3=cubeWorld[6][1];zw3=cubeWorld[6][2];
0677    xw2=cubeWorld[5][0];yw2=cubeWorld[5][1];zw2=cubeWorld[5][2];
0678    xw1=cubeWorld[4][0];yw1=cubeWorld[4][1];zw1=cubeWorld[4][2];
0679    zDrawFacet();
0680 surface2:
0681    xc1=camcoords[3][0];yc1=camcoords[3][1];zc1=camcoords[3][2];
0682    xc2=camcoords[2][0];yc2=camcoords[2][1];zc2=camcoords[2][2];
0683    xc3=camcoords[5][0];yc3=camcoords[5][1];zc3=camcoords[5][2];
0684    xc4=camcoords[6][0];yc4=camcoords[6][1];zc4=camcoords[6][2];
0685    zVisibilityTest();
0686    if (visible > 0) goto surface3;
0687    sx1=displaycoords[3][0];sy1=displaycoords[3][1];
0688    sx2=displaycoords[2][0];sy2=displaycoords[2][1];
0689    sx3=displaycoords[5][0];sy3=displaycoords[5][1];
0690    sx4=displaycoords[6][0];sy4=displaycoords[6][1];
0691    xw3=cubeWorld[3][0];yw3=cubeWorld[3][1];zw3=cubeWorld[3][2];
0692    xw2=cubeWorld[2][0];yw2=cubeWorld[2][1];zw2=cubeWorld[2][2];
0693    xw1=cubeWorld[5][0];yw1=cubeWorld[5][1];zw1=cubeWorld[5][2];
0694    zDrawFacet();
0695 surface3:
0696    xc1=camcoords[0][0];yc1=camcoords[0][1];zc1=camcoords[0][2];
0697    xc2=camcoords[1][0];yc2=camcoords[1][1];zc2=camcoords[1][2];
```

```
0698    xc3=camcoords[2][0];yc3=camcoords[2][1];zc3=camcoords[2][2];
0699    xc4=camcoords[3][0];yc4=camcoords[3][1];zc4=camcoords[3][2];
0700    zVisibilityTest();
0701    if (visible > 0) goto surface4;
0702    sx1=displaycoords[0][0];sy1=displaycoords[0][1];
0703    sx2=displaycoords[1][0];sy2=displaycoords[1][1];
0704    sx3=displaycoords[2][0];sy3=displaycoords[2][1];
0705    sx4=displaycoords[3][0];sy4=displaycoords[3][1];
0706    xw3=cubeWorld[0][0];yw3=cubeWorld[0][1];zw3=cubeWorld[0][2];
0707    xw2=cubeWorld[1][0];yw2=cubeWorld[1][1];zw2=cubeWorld[1][2];
0708    xw1=cubeWorld[2][0];yw1=cubeWorld[2][1];zw1=cubeWorld[2][2];
0709    zDrawFacet();
0710 surface4:
0711    xc1=camcoords[7][0];yc1=camcoords[7][1];zc1=camcoords[7][2];
0712    xc2=camcoords[4][0];yc2=camcoords[4][1];zc2=camcoords[4][2];
0713    xc3=camcoords[1][0];yc3=camcoords[1][1];zc3=camcoords[1][2];
0714    xc4=camcoords[0][0];yc4=camcoords[0][1];zc4=camcoords[0][2];
0715    zVisibilityTest();
0716    if (visible > 0) goto surface5;
0717    sx1=displaycoords[7][0];sy1=displaycoords[7][1];
0718    sx2=displaycoords[4][0];sy2=displaycoords[4][1];
0719    sx3=displaycoords[1][0];sy3=displaycoords[1][1];
0720    sx4=displaycoords[0][0];sy4=displaycoords[0][1];
0721    xw3=cubeWorld[7][0];yw3=cubeWorld[7][1];zw3=cubeWorld[7][2];
0722    xw2=cubeWorld[4][0];yw2=cubeWorld[4][1];zw2=cubeWorld[4][2];
0723    xw1=cubeWorld[1][0];yw1=cubeWorld[1][1];zw1=cubeWorld[1][2];
0724    zDrawFacet();
0725 surface5:
0726    xc1=camcoords[1][0];yc1=camcoords[1][1];zc1=camcoords[1][2];
0727    xc2=camcoords[4][0];yc2=camcoords[4][1];zc2=camcoords[4][2];
0728    xc3=camcoords[5][0];yc3=camcoords[5][1];zc3=camcoords[5][2];
0729    xc4=camcoords[2][0];yc4=camcoords[2][1];zc4=camcoords[2][2];
0730    zVisibilityTest();
0731    if (visible > 0) goto surfaces_done;
0732    sx1=displaycoords[1][0];sy1=displaycoords[1][1];
0733    sx2=displaycoords[4][0];sy2=displaycoords[4][1];
0734    sx3=displaycoords[5][0];sy3=displaycoords[5][1];
0735    sx4=displaycoords[2][0];sy4=displaycoords[2][1];
0736    xw3=cubeWorld[1][0];yw3=cubeWorld[1][1];zw3=cubeWorld[1][2];
0737    xw2=cubeWorld[4][0];yw2=cubeWorld[4][1];zw2=cubeWorld[4][2];
0738    xw1=cubeWorld[5][0];yw1=cubeWorld[5][1];zw1=cubeWorld[5][2];
0739    zDrawFacet();
0740 surfaces_done:
0741 return;
0742 }
0743 /*
0744 ------------------------------------------------------------------
0745 End of LIB3D.C library of 3D routines for Windows applications.
0746 ------------------------------------------------------------------
0747                                                                */
```

# 5
# *Titling*

---

The Windows runtime environment provides functions that your application can call to display text in various typefaces, sizes, and colors. Your animation program can create text in three ways. First, you can use the fonts and typefaces built into the retail version of Windows. Second, you can create your own logical fonts. Third, you can use fonts from third-party add-on packages.

## Using text in your animation images

Each time you call GetDC() to set a new display-context for graphics output, a default font is made available by the Windows API for your program to use. This is a sans serif, proportional-spaced, bitmapped font called System. It is this font that Windows uses in menu systems and windows.

### Displaying text with TextOut()

 To display a text string at a specified location in your application's window, you can call TextOut(). The following sample illustrates a typical call.

```
TextOut(hDC,10,6,"This is animation.",18);
```

Here is what the sample arguments in the TextOut() parameter list mean. The GDI will send the string output to the display-context referenced by the handle named hDC. The starting point for writing the text, as shown in FIG. 5-1, will be 10 lines down and 6 characters over to the right from the origin. TextOut() will display 18 characters, consisting of the string, This is animation.

141

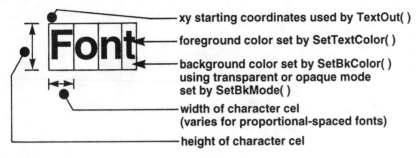

**5-1**  Font mechanics for the GDI's TextOut() function.

## Color text

The default color for font output is black. The default color of the character cel background is white. Your application can alter both attributes.

**Displaying color text**  You can call SetTextColor() to specify the color to be used by the API for text output. The new text color remains in effect until you release the display-context, or until you reset the color by another call to SetTextColor().

**Background attributes**  You can call SetBkColor() to indicate which color the API will use for the background portion of the character cel, as shown in FIG. 5-1. If the background mode is opaque, the background part of the character cel will overwrite existing graphics. If the background mode is transparent, the background part of the character cel will not be drawn, no matter what color has been passed to SetBkColor(). You can toggle between the OPAQUE and TRANSPARENT modes by calling SetBkMode(). SetBkMode() also affects other graphics primitives, including dashed lines, pattern fills, and others.

## Using Windows' built-in fonts

When you use TextOut() to display text, you can choose from a variety of different typefaces in many different sizes. A typeface is a particular design of characters in normal, bold, and italic variations. A specific typeface in a particular size is usually called a font. The retail version of Windows 3.0 provides bitmapped fonts and stroked fonts. The Windows 3.1 retail package includes bitmapped fonts, stroked fonts, and outline fonts.

**Bitmapped fonts**  A *bitmapped font* is built from patterns of pixels. Each character is positioned in a rectangular matrix of bits. Any attempt to enlarge a bitmapped character tends to produce a chunky appearance, so each size is usually provided as a separate font file containing the appropriate matrix designs. Bitmapped fonts are also called screen fonts.

**Stroked fonts**  A *stroked font* is created by a vector description of each character. Stroked fonts can be scaled larger or smaller, but their simple design is more suited for plotter output than the screen or printer. Stroked fonts are also called *plotter fonts*.

**Outline fonts** *Outline fonts* are typefaces. A file for an outline font contains the manifest design specifications for the font as well as the code that draws each character. An outline font can be scaled larger or smaller with no loss of quality, providing true WYSIWYG output on both the screen and your printer. The code that draws each character can be customized by application programmers by tapping into hooks called hints. The hints are like parameters that advise Windows how to adjust proportional spacing (kerning), serif emphasis, and more. The retail version of Windows 3.1 includes a small selection of outline fonts. The Microsoft TrueType Font Pack for Windows, which is available as an optional add-on, provides another 44 outline fonts, and third-party seamless add-on kits are also available. Alternative technology like Adobe Type Manager and Bitstream's Facelift provide equally facile capabilities. (All names are trademarks or registered trademarks.)

## Character sets

The fonts that are built into Windows are categorized by character sets. A character set defines the various printable characters found in a typeface, such as upper-case and lower-case characters, punctuation marks, numbers, and other symbols.

There are three character sets with which a Windows graphics programmer should be familiar. They are ANSI, OEM (sometimes called ASCII), and SYMBOL.

**ANSI** The ANSI character set is the default set used by Windows. Displayable characters 32 through 126 include all the standard keyboard keys (which are identical to the ASCII character set). Extended characters 128 through 255 provide special characters like fractions, currency symbols, mathematical symbols, and international language characters. Line-drawing characters are not supported.

**OEM** The OEM character set is hardware-specific. It is stored in ROM and is used by the operating system for text output. Displayable characters 32 to 126 adhere to the ASCII standard, representing all keys on the keyboard. Characters 128 through 255, called the extended set, include an assortment of line-drawing characters, including scientific characters, math symbols, and international characters.

**SYMBOL** The SYMBOL character set contains mathematical and scientific symbols, operators, and characters.

## Categories of stock fonts

The fonts that are built into the retail version of Windows are called *stock fonts*. They can be grouped into a number of categories, derived from the

ANSI, OEM, and SYMBOL character sets. You select a stock font by calling GetStockObject() with an arguments such as ANSI_FIXED_FONT, ANSI_VAR_FONT, DEVICE_DEFAULT_FONT, OEM_FIXED_FONT, SYSTEM_FONT, and so on. Each bitmap stock font is provided in a particular typeface at a predetermined size, expressed by its height in pixels. Each stroked stock font is scalable. Each outline font is scalable. On a typical Windows system, these stock font files are found in the c:\windows\system directory.

## Built-in bitmap fonts

The bitmap font files that are built into Windows include Courier, Helv, Tms Rmn, and Symbol. Some of these fonts are used to provide the stock fonts returned by GetStockObject(). You can use each of these typefaces in different sizes, as explained later in the chapter, by calling CreateFont() and SelectObject() instead of GetStockObject().

## Built-in stroked fonts

Windows provides a variety of built-in stroked typefaces, including Modern, Roman, Script, and others. Each font file contains a vector-based description of how to built the character set.

## Built-in outline fonts

The outline fonts that are bundled with the retail version of Windows 3.1 include Arial, Courier New, and Times New Roman. Arial is similar to the bitmapped Helv that is included with Windows 3.0 and 3.1. Courier New is similar to the bitmapped Courier. Times New Roman is the outline font version of the bitmapped Tms Rmn. A Symbol font is also provided.

# Specialized text functions

If your application requires more formatting than is provided by the TextOut() function, you can use other Windows API functions to display text in an opaque rectangle, a clipping rectangle, tabular format, and in justified format.

## Using ExtTextOut() to display text

The ExtTextOut() function displays a specified text string within a rectangle. You specify the dimensions of the rectangle in the parameter list when you call ExtTextOut(). If you use the ETO_OPAQUE parameter, the text is displayed against an opaque rectangle which is the same color as the current background color. The GDI organizes the text into lines that fit inside the rectangle. If you use the ETO_CLIPPED parameter when you call ExtTextOut(), the rectangle will be a transparent clipping region. The GDI will clip your text string at the edges of the rectangle.

## Advanced text output

 Windows provides a number of other functions useful for text output. You will not usually require these routines in your animation sequence.

**SetTextAlign()**  The SetTextAlign() function can be used to set a group of text-alignment flags. It mainly concerns offset distances from the starting point for the string, including whether or not the current position is updated after each call to TextOut() or ExtTextOut().

**SetTextJustification()**  The SetTextJustification() function is used to expand the spaces between words in order to make a line of text fit the left and right margins of the available space. You need to first call GetTextExtent() in order to determine the default size of the line of text. The difference between the default size and the available space is what you pass to SetTextJustification().

**GetTextExtent()**  The GetTextExtent() function returns the height and width of the line of text your application is getting ready to display.

**TabbedTextOut()**  The TabbedTextOut() function can be used to create tabular output. Before calling TabbedTextOut() you create an array of tab stop positions, which are expressed as pixel offsets. If each tab in your text uses the same distance, you define only one tab stop position, no matter how many tabs or text columns your text material uses.

## Using logical fonts

You can display Windows' built-in fonts in a variety of different sizes. To do so you must create a logical font that describes the attributes of the typeface you want. This means you must possess a better understanding of font mechanics than was required to call TextOut() using a stock font. As soon as you begin to display text in different sizes you need to concern yourself with details like pixel size and leading. Leading (pronounced *ledding*) is the spacing between each line of text.

## Text cel attributes

When you request a typeface in a particular size, you need to be aware how Windows uses the character size and internal leading as part of the pixel height specification, as shown in FIG. 5-2. Internal leading is built into each character cel to allow room for accents, tildes, and other character set peculiarities. The complete character is composed of the ascent and descent of the character. The full text cel occupied by a character is often two or more pixels higher than the character itself.

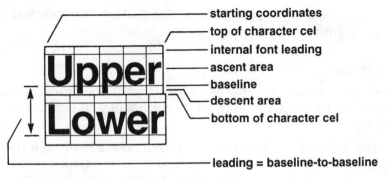

starting coordinates
top of character cel
internal font leading
ascent area
baseline
descent area
bottom of character cel

leading = baseline-to-baseline

**5-2**  Font positioning under Windows.

**Kerning**  The horizontal spacing between individual characters is called called kerning. Kerning is handled automatically for you by Windows, meaning that narrower characters will be placed into narrow character cels. This results in text that is easier to read.

**Leading**  The programmer is responsible for specifying that amount of leading to use between each line of text. In traditional phototypesetting, for example, 16-point type is often set to a leading of 17 or 18. The result, called 16-on-18, places type that is 16 points tall into a vertical space of 18 points, leaving 2 points of space (the leading) between each line of type.

The character cel specifications used by Windows are not fully compatible with traditional phototypesetting methods. Windows uses pixels instead of points to measure type. Windows uses the character's ascent, descent, and internal leading to define the height of the character cel. For example, a font of bitmapped characters sized at 12 pixels height is often provided as character cels a few pixels taller, with an internal leading of 2 pixels built-in.

If the background mode is set to opaque, the internal leading of a line of text can overwrite the descenders of the previous line when using bitmapped fonts. This occurs mainly while using larger-sized fonts.

## Using different type sizes and typefaces

To specify a typeface in a particular size you can call SelectObject(). You typically provide an argument specifying a font you have described earlier by a call to CreateFont(), called a *logical font*.

## Using a logical font

A font file contains physical fonts that actually exist, but a logical font is nothing more than a description of a font that may (or may not) exist in the Windows runtime environment. Using logical fonts is how Windows provides device independence to your application.

Windows uses an algorithm when it attempts to match the font you have described in your call to CreateFont(). It strives to match your request to the fonts that actually reside on the hard disk. If an exact match is found, Windows uses it. If not, Windows uses a next-best algorithm. In most cases your application will be provided with a font that is a reasonable approximation of the desired font. The broad assortment of serif, sans serif, fixed-space, proportional-spaced, bitmapped, stroked, and outine fonts that is built into Windows provides an inventory able to meet most requests.

The Createfont() function permits you to specify the height, aspect ratio, display angle, weight, character set, pitch, family, and typeface. It is a complicated call that is demonstrated when the demonstration program is being discussed.

## A sample application

The screen image in FIG. 5-3 shows the Titles menu from the sample application titles.exe. This program demonstrates bitmapped font techniques that are useful for adding text, captions, and titles to images for animation sequences. Advanced effects like color text and dropshadows are also demonstrated. The sample application is de-signed to run equally well on either Windows 3.0 or Windows 3.1.

The titles.exe demo is built from four modules, including a .def module definition file, an .h #include file, an .rc resource script file, and a .c source file. All of these production files are presented as ready-to-use source code in the program listing later in this chapter. The source files are also provided on the companion disk. You can refer to the appropriate appendix for instructions on how to build image3d.exe with QuickC for Windows, Turbo C++ for Windows, Borland C++, Zortech C++, WATCOM C, and Microsoft C and the SDK.

## What the program does: A user's guide

The sample application provides an environment that exercises some of the font features provided by the Windows graphics device interface. You can use either a mouse or the keyboard to experiment with the demo program. The menus also support mnemonic keys. To view a runtime help message, select Help from the Help menu.

### Stock fonts and colors

Select Stock fonts from the Titles menu to view a display of stock fonts that are bundled into the retail version of Windows, as shown in FIG. 5-4. Select Font colors from the Titles menu to display a font in different foreground and background colors.

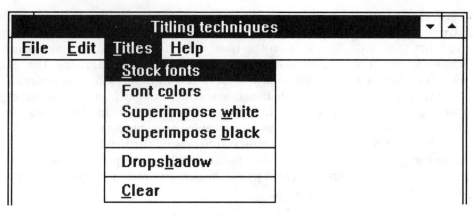

**5-3** The Titles menu from the sample application provides examples of different font output, including colors, superimposition, and dropshadows.

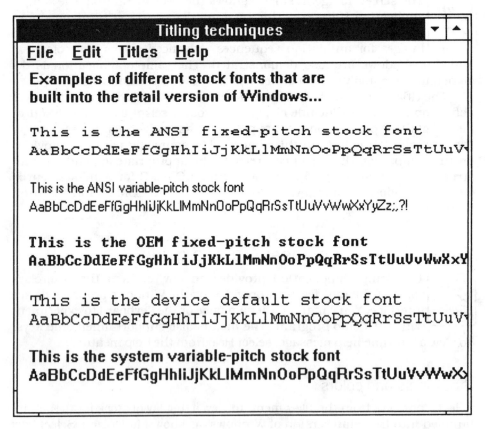

**5-4** Output from the sample application, showing stock fonts provided by the retail version of Windows.

## Superimposed text

Select Superimpose white from the Titles menu to experiment with white text superimposed over a complex background, as shown in FIG. 5-5 (top). To view black text superimposed over the same background, as shown in FIG. 5-5 (bottom), select Superimpose black from the Titles menu.

## Dropshadows

Select Dropshadow from the Titles menu to place a colored title and its drop-shadow over a complex background, as shown in FIG. 5-6. This effect is created by first writing a string of text in black to the window, then shifting the starting coordinates left and upwards before re-writing the same string in color.

# How the source code works: A programmer's guide

*Hands On* The titles.exe demonstration program exercises some of the font functions supported by the GDI. Using the techniques illustrated in the source code, you can easily add text, captions, and titles to your animation sequence.

The organization of the .h #include file and the .rc resource script file follow the format established in earlier sample applications. A few new menu items and strings have been added to support the font features of titles.exe. See chapter 1 for a detailed discussion of the mechanics of the .h #include file and the .rc resource script file.

### How the .c file works

*.C* The program listing for the .c file is presented in FIG. 5-10.

**Static variables** The static variables visible throughout the .c file are declared and initialized at lines 0044 through 0089. These variables conform to the format established by the persistent graphics demo program in chapter 2. Static variables for font operations are declared at lines 0076 through 0078.

**Switcher** The message handler function is located at lines 0173 through 0414. The case blocks located at lines 0196 through 0253 manage the font output when you experiment with menu items from the Titles menu.

The case IDM_Typeface statement at line 0196 calls a function named zTypeface() to display stock fonts that are built into the retail version of Windows. The case IDM_TypeColor statement at line 0207 calls a function named zTypeColor() to display a font in a variety of foreground and background colors. The case IDM_Super1 statement at line 0218 calls a function named zSuper1() to superimpose white text over a complex background. The case IDM_Super2 statement at line 0230 calls a function named zSuper2() to superimpose black text over a complex background. The case IDM_DropShadow

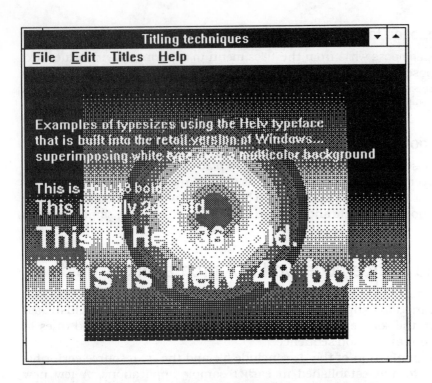

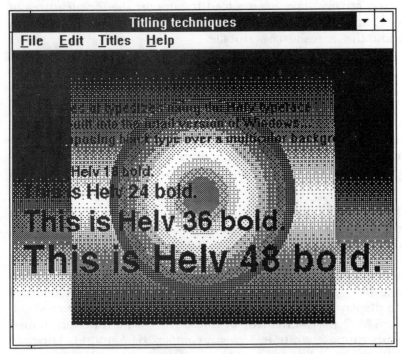

**5-5** The sample application provides examples of font superimposition in white and black.

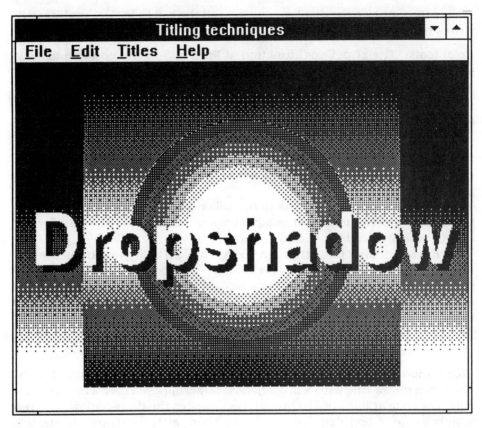

**5-6** An example of a black dropshadow over a multicolored background is provided by the sample application.

statement at line 0242 calls a function named zDropShadow() to display a yellow title with a dropshadow over a complex background. In each of these case blocks, note how the code either clears the display window or redraws the background before writing the fonts to the screen. Note also the call to zCopyToFrame(), which ensures that a backup copy of the display window is available for refreshing the screen if the window is moved, unclipped, or uncovered.

**Stock fonts** The zTypeface() function at lines 0464 through 0532 displays a selection of stock fonts that are built into the retail version of Windows. The starting point for the text is specified by two variables named Position and Line, declared at lines 0472 and 0473. The variable named Leading, declared and initialized at line 0474, defines how much space is left between each line of type. The default stock font, called System, is displayed by the code at lines 0477 through 0482. Then, a call to GetStockObject() at line 0485 grabs the handle to a different stock font. The call to SelectObject() at line 0486 selects the font into the display-context, and the call to TextOut() at line 0487 writes the text string. This code format is repeated for another four fonts.

**Color fonts**   The zTypeColor() function at lines 0538 through 0628 displays the default font in a variety of different foreground and background colors. The call to SetTextColor(), for example, at line 0558, sets the foreground text color to red . The call to SetBkColor(), for example, at line 0610, sets the background of each character cel to green.

**Superimposed text**   The zSuper1() function at lines 0634 through 0711 superimposes white text over a complex background. The most important GDI call in this function is at line 0649, where a call to SetBkMode() sets the write mode to transparent.

Before the function returns to the caller, another call to SetBkMode() at line 0706 restores the default opaque background mode. The color for text output is set by a call to SetTextColor() at line 0647.

The code at lines 0664 through 0678 is broken apart so you can see how to use CreateFont() to request a specific font in a specific size. The height is specified at line 0665. The font is specified at line 0678. The subsequent calls to CreateFont(), at line 0685, for example, adhere to the same argument format, but the code has been tightened up.

The zSuper2() function at lines 0717 through 0794 operates in similar fashion, except that the superimposed text is written in black.

**Dropshadow text**   The zDropShadow() function at lines 0800 through 0851 displays a yellow title with a dropshadow, superimposed over a complex display. The code at lines 0816 through 0833 writes the dropshadow, which is simply a line of text displayed in black. Then, after resetting the starting position at line 0836, the code at lines 0837 through 0843 writes the title itself. It is a combination of color differentiation and offset positioning that gives the dropshadow effect. You might find it interesting to tinker with this function by adjusting the values at line 0836.

## Program listings for the sample application

*Code*   The program listings presented here contain all the source code you need to build and run the sample application. The module definition file is provided in FIG. 5-7. The #include file is found in FIG. 5-8. The resource script file is presented in FIG. 5-9. The C source file is provided in FIG. 5-10.

*Disk*   **Companion disk**   If you have the companion disk, the source files are presented as titles.def, titles.h, titles.rc, and titles.c.

*License*   **License**   You can paste the royalty-free source code into your own applications and distribute the resulting executable files under the conditions of the License Agreement and Limited Warranty in FIG. 10 in the introduction to the book.

**5-7** The module definition file listing for the sample application.

```
0001   NAME           DEFDEMO
0002   DESCRIPTION    'Copyright 1992 Lee Adams.  All rights reserved.'
0003   EXETYPE        WINDOWS
0004   STUB           'WINSTUB.EXE'
0005   CODE           PRELOAD MOVEABLE
0006   DATA           PRELOAD MOVEABLE MULTIPLE
0007   HEAPSIZE       1024
0008   STACKSIZE      8192
0009   EXPORTS        zMessageHandler
```

**5-8** The include file listing for the sample application.

```
0001   /*
0002   ------------------------------------------------------------------
0003                       Include file TITLES.H
0004           Copyright 1992 Lee Adams.  All rights reserved.
0005     Include this file in the .RC resource script file and in the
0006     .C source file.  It contains function prototypes, menu ID
0007     constants, and string ID constants.
0008   ------------------------------------------------------------------
0009   ------------------------------------------------------------------
0010                       Function prototypes
0011   ------------------------------------------------------------------
0012                                                                   */
0013   #if !defined(zRCFILE)                  /* if not an .RC file... */
0014     LONG FAR PASCAL zMessageHandler(HWND, unsigned, WORD, LONG);
0015     int PASCAL WinMain(HANDLE,HANDLE,LPSTR,int);
0016     HWND zInitMainWindow(HANDLE);
0017     BOOL zInitClass(HANDLE);
0018   static void zClear(HWND);                   /* blank the viewport */
0019   static void zInitFrame(HWND);               /* creates hidden frame */
0020   static void zCopyToDisplay(HWND);     /* copies frame to display */
0021   static void zCopyToFrame(HWND);       /* copies display to frame */
0022   static void zClearHiddenFrame(void);     /* clears hidden frame */
0023   static void zDrawBg(HDC);              /* draws background scene */
0024   static BOOL zTypeface(HWND);    /* overwrites different typefaces */
0025   static BOOL zTypeColor(HWND);        /* overwrites text in color */
0026   static BOOL zSuper1(HWND);          /* superimposes black type */
0027   static BOOL zSuper2(HWND);          /* superimposes white type */
0028   static BOOL zDropShadow(HWND);           /* dropshadowed type */
0029   #endif
0030   /*
0031   ------------------------------------------------------------------
0032                       Menu ID constants
0033   ------------------------------------------------------------------
0034                                                                   */
0035   #define IDM_New           1
0036   #define IDM_Open          2
0037   #define IDM_Save          3
0038   #define IDM_SaveAs        4
0039   #define IDM_Exit          5
0040
0041   #define IDM_Undo          6
0042   #define IDM_Cut           7
0043   #define IDM_Copy          8
0044   #define IDM_Paste         9
0045   #define IDM_Delete        10
0046
0047   #define IDM_Typeface      11
```

```
0048    #define IDM_TypeColor        12
0049    #define IDM_Super1           13
0050    #define IDM_Super2           14
0051    #define IDM_DropShadow       15
0052    #define IDM_Clear            16
0053
0054    #define IDM_About            17
0055    #define IDM_License          18
0056    #define IDM_Display          19
0057    #define IDM_Colors           20
0058    #define IDM_Mode             21
0059    #define IDM_GeneralHelp      22
0060    /*
0061    ------------------------------------------------------------------
0062                            String ID constants
0063    ------------------------------------------------------------------
0064                                                                    */
0065    #define IDS_Caption       1
0066    #define IDS_Warning       2
0067    #define IDS_NoMouse       3
0068    #define IDS_About         4
0069    #define IDS_AboutText     5
0070    #define IDS_License       6
0071    #define IDS_LicenseText   7
0072    #define IDS_Help          8
0073    #define IDS_HelpText      9
0074    #define IDS_Completed     10
0075    #define IDS_Resolution    11
0076    #define IDS_ResVGA        12
0077    #define IDS_ResEGA        13
0078    #define IDS_ResCGA        14
0079    #define IDS_ResSVGA       15
0080    #define IDS_Res8514       16
0081    #define IDS_ResHerc       17
0082    #define IDS_ResCustom     18
0083    #define IDS_Color         19
0084    #define IDS_Color16       20
0085    #define IDS_Color256      21
0086    #define IDS_Color2        22
0087    #define IDS_ColorCustom   23
0088    #define IDS_Machine       24
0089    #define IDS_Enhanced      25
0090    #define IDS_Standard      26
0091    #define IDS_Real          27
0092    #define IDS_NoFrame       28
0093    #define IDS_NotReady      29
0094    #define IDS_NoMem         30
0095    /*
0096    ------------------------------------------------------------------
0097                            End of include file
0098    ------------------------------------------------------------------
0099                                                                    */
```

**5-9** The resource script file listing for the sample application.

```
0001    /*
0002    ------------------------------------------------------------------
0003                    Resource script file TITLES.RC
0004            Copyright 1992 Lee Adams.  All rights reserved.
0005      This file defines the menu resources, the accelerator key
```

```
0006      resources, and the string resources that will be used by the
0007      demonstration application at runtime.
0008      --------------------------------------------------------------
0009                                                                   */
0010   #define zRCFILE
0011   #include <WINDOWS.H>
0012   #include "TITLES.H"
0013   /*
0014      --------------------------------------------------------------
0015                           Script for menus
0016      --------------------------------------------------------------
0017                                                                   */
0018   MENUS1 MENU
0019     BEGIN
0020     POPUP "&File"
0021       BEGIN
0022         MENUITEM  "&New", IDM_New, GRAYED
0023         MENUITEM  "&Open...", IDM_Open, GRAYED
0024         MENUITEM  "&Save", IDM_Save, GRAYED
0025         MENUITEM  "Save &As...", IDM_SaveAs, GRAYED
0026         MENUITEM SEPARATOR
0027         MENUITEM  "E&xit", IDM_Exit
0028       END
0029     POPUP "&Edit"
0030       BEGIN
0031         MENUITEM  "&Undo\tAlt+BkSp", IDM_Undo, GRAYED
0032         MENUITEM SEPARATOR
0033         MENUITEM  "Cu&t\tShift+Del", IDM_Cut, GRAYED
0034         MENUITEM  "&Copy\tCtrl+Ins", IDM_Copy, GRAYED
0035         MENUITEM  "&Paste\tShift+Ins", IDM_Paste, GRAYED
0036         MENUITEM  "&Delete\tDel", IDM_Delete, GRAYED
0037       END
0038     POPUP "&Titles"
0039       BEGIN
0040         MENUITEM "&Stock fonts", IDM_Typeface
0041         MENUITEM "Font c&olors", IDM_TypeColor
0042         MENUITEM "Superimpose &white", IDM_Super2
0043         MENUITEM "Superimpose &black", IDM_Super1
0044         MENUITEM SEPARATOR
0045         MENUITEM "Drops&hadow", IDM_DropShadow
0046         MENUITEM SEPARATOR
0047         MENUITEM "&Clear", IDM_Clear
0048       END
0049     POPUP "&Help"
0050       BEGIN
0051         MENUITEM "&About", IDM_About
0052         MENUITEM "&License", IDM_License
0053         MENUITEM SEPARATOR
0054         MENUITEM "&Screen resolution", IDM_Display
0055         MENUITEM "Available &colors", IDM_Colors
0056         MENUITEM "&Memory mode", IDM_Mode
0057         MENUITEM SEPARATOR
0058         MENUITEM "&Help", IDM_GeneralHelp
0059       END
0060     END
0061   /*
0062      --------------------------------------------------------------
0063                       Script for accelerator keys
0064      --------------------------------------------------------------
0065                                                                   */
0066   KEYS1 ACCELERATORS
```

```
0067    BEGIN
0068    VK_BACK, IDM_Undo, VIRTKEY, ALT
0069    VK_DELETE, IDM_Cut, VIRTKEY, SHIFT
0070    VK_INSERT, IDM_Copy, VIRTKEY, CONTROL
0071    VK_INSERT, IDM_Paste, VIRTKEY, SHIFT
0072    VK_DELETE, IDM_Delete, VIRTKEY
0073    END
0074    /*
0075    -------------------------------------------------------------------
0076                        Script for strings
0077    Programmer's Notes:  If you are typing this listing, set your
0078    margins to a line length of 255 characters so you can create
0079    lengthy strings without embedded carriage returns.  The line
0080    wraparounds in the following STRINGTABLE script are used for
0081    readability only in this printout.
0082    -------------------------------------------------------------------
0083                                                                   */
0084    STRINGTABLE
0085    BEGIN
0086        IDS_Caption      "Titling techniques"
0087        IDS_Warning      "Graphics system warning"
0088        IDS_NoMouse      "No mouse found.  Some features of this
                demonstration program may require a mouse."
0089        IDS_About        "About this program"
0090        IDS_AboutText    "This is a demo from Windcrest McGraw-Hill
                book 4114.  Copyright 1992 Lee Adams.  All rights reserved."
0091        IDS_License      "License Agreement"
0092        IDS_LicenseText "You can use this code as part of your own
                software product subject to the License Agreement and Limited
                Warranty in Windcrest McGraw-Hill book 4114 and on its
                companion disk."
0093        IDS_Help         "How to use this demo"
0094        IDS_HelpText     "Use the Titles menu to experiment with
                different font techniques, including superimposition and
                dropshadow.  See the book for detailed explanations."
0095        IDS_Resolution  "Screen resolution"
0096        IDS_ResVGA       "Running in 640x480 mode."
0097        IDS_ResEGA       "Running in 640x350 mode."
0098        IDS_ResCGA       "Running in 640x200 mode."
0099        IDS_ResSVGA      "Running in 800x600 mode."
0100        IDS_Res8514      "Running in 1024x768 mode."
0101        IDS_ResHerc      "Running in 720x348 mode."
0102        IDS_ResCustom    "Running in custom mode."
0103        IDS_Color        "Available colors"
0104        IDS_Color16      "Running in 16-color mode."
0105        IDS_Color256     "Running in 256-color mode."
0106        IDS_Color2       "Running in 2-color mode."
0107        IDS_ColorCustom "Running in a custom color mode."
0108        IDS_Machine      "Memory mode"
0109        IDS_Enhanced     "Running in enhanced mode.  Can allocate up to
                16 MB extended physical memory (XMS) if available.  Virtual
                memory up to 4 times physical memory (maximum 64 MB) is also
                available via automatic disk swapping of 4K pages."
0110        IDS_Standard     "Running in standard mode.  Can allocate up to
                16 MB extended physical memory (XMS) if available."
0111        IDS_Real         "Running in real mode.  Can allocate blocks of
                memory from the first 640K of RAM.  Can also allocate blocks
                from expanded memory (EMS) if available."
0112        IDS_NoFrame      "Hidden frame not created at startup.  Close
                other applications to free more memory then restart this demo."
0113        IDS_NotReady     "Graphics system not ready"
```

**5-9** Continued.

```
0114    IDS_NoMem        "Insufficient memory.  Hidden frame not
        created.  Close other applications to free more memory then
        restart this demo."
0115    END
0116  /*
0117  ------------------------------------------------------------------
0118                    End of resource script file
0119  ------------------------------------------------------------------
0120                                                                  */
```

**5-10** The C source file listing for the sample application, titles.c. This demonstration program is ready to build using QuickC for Windows, Turbo C++ for Windows, Microsoft C and the SDK, Borland C++, Symantec Zortech C++, WATCOM C, and other compilers. See FIG. 1-2 for sample command-lines to build the program. Guidelines for using your compiler are provided in the appropriate appendix at the back of the book.

```
0001  /*
0002  ------------------------------------------------------------------
0003      Reusable template for Windows applications that use a hidden
0004      frame, display-independent graphics, and persistent images.
0005  ------------------------------------------------------------------
0006      Source file:  TITLES.C
0007      Release version:  1.00                  Programmer:  Lee Adams
0008      Type:  C source file for Windows application development.
0009      Compilers:  Microsoft C and SDK, Borland C++, Zortech C++,
0010        QuickC for Windows, Turbo C++ for Windows, WATCOM C.
0011      Memory model:  small.
0012      Dependencies:  TITLES.DEF module definition file, TITLES.H
0013                     include file, TITLES.RC resource script file,
0014                     and TITLES.C source file.
0015      Output and features:  Demonstrates display-independent
0016        techniques for font output, including superimposition and
0017        dropshadow, which are useful for captioning animation images.
0018      Publication: Contains material from Windcrest/McGraw-Hill book
0019        4114 published by TAB BOOKS Division of McGraw-Hill Inc.
0020      License:  As purchaser of the book you are granted a royalty-
0021        free license to distribute executable files generated using
0022        this code provided you accept the conditions of the License
0023        Agreement and Limited Warranty described in the book and on
0024        the companion disk.  Government users:  This software and
0025        documentation are subject to restrictions set forth in The
0026        Rights in Technical Data and Computer Software clause at
0027        252.227-7013 and elsewhere.
0028  ------------------------------------------------------------------
0029        (c) Copyright 1992 Lee Adams.  All rights reserved.
0030          Lee Adams(tm) is a trademark of Lee Adams.
0031  ------------------------------------------------------------------
0032
0033  ------------------------------------------------------------------
0034                            Include files
0035  ------------------------------------------------------------------
0036                                                                  */
0037  #include <WINDOWS.H>
0038  #include "TITLES.H"
0039  /*
0040  ------------------------------------------------------------------
0041            Static variables visible throughout this file
```

```
0042   ----------------------------------------------------------------
0043                                                                 */
0044   /* ----------------- window specifications ----------------- */
0045   #define zWINDOW_WIDTH 408              /* width of window */
0046   #define zWINDOW_HEIGHT 346             /* height of window */
0047   #define zFRAMEWIDE 400          /* width of client area */
0048   #define zFRAMEHIGH 300         /* height of client area */
0049   int WindowX, WindowY;              /* location of window */
0050
0051   /* ----------------- instance operations ----------------- */
0052   HANDLE hInst;                   /* handle to this instance */
0053   HWND MainhWnd;                 /* handle to the main window */
0054   HANDLE hAccel;           /* handle to accelerator keys table */
0055   HMENU hMenu;                /* handle to a menu at runtime */
0056   PAINTSTRUCT ps;       /* structure used by persistent graphics */
0057   int MessageRet;      /* will hold receive value returned by GDI */
0058
0059   /* ----------------- mouse and cursor ----------------- */
0060   HCURSOR hPrevCursor;             /* handle to default cursor */
0061   HCURSOR hHourGlass;            /* handle to hourglass cursor */
0062   int MousePresent;         /* will indicate if mouse present */
0063
0064   /* ----------------- runtime conditions ----------------- */
0065   int DisplayWidth, DisplayHeight;        /* screen resolution */
0066   int DisplayBits;              /* number of bits-per-pixel */
0067   int DisplayPlanes;              /* number of bitplanes */
0068   DWORD MemoryMode;               /* runtime memory mode */
0069
0070   /* ----------------- message box operations ----------------- */
0071   char lpCaption[51];       /* will hold caption for message boxes */
0072   int Max= 50;                 /* maximum length of caption */
0073   char lpMessage[250];       /* will hold text for message boxes */
0074   int MaxText= 249;             /* maximum length of text */
0075
0076   /* ----------------- font operations ----------------- */
0077   HFONT hFont, hPrevFont;     /* handles to new, previous font */
0078   HDC hFontDC;                /* display-context for font */
0079
0080   /* --------------- persistent image operations ----------------- */
0081   #define zBLANK 0
0082   #define zIMAGE 1
0083   int PaintImage= zBLANK;           /* indicates type of refresh */
0084
0085   /* -----------------hidden frame operations ----------------- */
0086   HDC hFrameDC;          /* memory display-context for hidden-frame */
0087   HBITMAP hFrame;             /* handle to hidden-frame bitmap */
0088   HBITMAP hPrevFrame;                    /* default bitmap */
0089   BOOL FrameReady= FALSE;           /* hidden-frame created? */
0090
0091   /*
0092   ----------------------------------------------------------------
0093                   Entry point for the application
0094   ----------------------------------------------------------------
0095                                                                 */
0096   int PASCAL WinMain(HANDLE hInstance, HANDLE hPrevInstance,
0097                   LPSTR lpCmdLine, int nCmdShow)
0098   {
0099     MSG msg;                      /* will hold incoming messages */
0100     HWND hWndPrev;         /* handle to window of another instance */
0101     HWND hDesktopWnd;      /* handle to full-screen desktop window */
0102     HDC hDCcaps;             /* display-context of desktop window */
```

```
0103
0104   /* ------------ ensure only one instance is running ------------ */
0105   hWndPrev = FindWindow("DEMOCLASS", NULL);
0106   if (hWndPrev != NULL)          /* if another instance was found... */
0107     {
0108     BringWindowToTop(hWndPrev);                /* make it active... */
0109     return FALSE;              /* ...and terminate this instance */
0110     }
0111
0112   /* --------- determine capabilities of screen display ---------- */
0113   hDesktopWnd= GetDesktopWindow();
0114   hDCcaps= GetDC(hDesktopWnd);
0115   DisplayWidth= GetDeviceCaps(hDCcaps,HORZRES);
0116   DisplayHeight= GetDeviceCaps(hDCcaps,VERTRES);
0117   DisplayBits= GetDeviceCaps(hDCcaps,BITSPIXEL);
0118   DisplayPlanes= GetDeviceCaps(hDCcaps,PLANES);
0119   ReleaseDC(hDesktopWnd,hDCcaps);
0120
0121   /* ------- calculate screen position to center the window ------ */
0122   WindowX= (DisplayWidth - zWINDOW_WIDTH) / 2;       /* horizontal */
0123   WindowY= (DisplayHeight - zWINDOW_HEIGHT) /2;        /* vertical */
0124   if (WindowX < 0) WindowX= 0;
0125   if (WindowY < 0) WindowY= 0;
0126
0127   /* ---- determine memory mode (enhanced, standard, or real) ---- */
0128   MemoryMode= GetWinFlags();         /* will read this value later */
0129
0130   /* -------------- create and display the window --------------- */
0131   hInst= hInstance;                    /* remember the instance handle */
0132   if (!zInitClass(hInstance)) return FALSE;     /* create the class */
0133   MainhWnd= zInitMainWindow(hInstance);       /* create the window */
0134   if (!MainhWnd) return FALSE;   /* exit if no window was created */
0135   ShowWindow(MainhWnd, nCmdShow);            /* display the window */
0136   UpdateWindow(MainhWnd);              /* send a paint message */
0137   hAccel= LoadAccelerators(hInstance,"KEYS1"); /* accelerator keys */
0138   hFontDC= GetDC(MainhWnd);              /* get a display-context */
0139   hFont= GetStockObject(SYSTEM_FONT);       /* grab handle to font */
0140   hPrevFont= SelectObject(hFontDC,hFont);    /* select font into DC */
0141   SetTextColor(hFontDC,RGB(191,191,191));     /* set new text color */
0142   TextOut(hFontDC,10,280,"- Copyright 1992 Lee Adams.",27);/* text */
0143   SetTextColor(hFontDC,RGB(255,255,255));     /* restore text color */
0144   SelectObject(hFontDC,hPrevFont);        /* restore previous font */
0145   ReleaseDC(MainhWnd,hFontDC);          /* release display-context */
0146
0147   /* --------------------- check for mouse ---------------------- */
0148   MousePresent= GetSystemMetrics(SM_MOUSEPRESENT);
0149   if (!MousePresent)                 /* if no active mouse found */
0150     {
0151     LoadString(hInst,IDS_Warning,lpCaption,Max);   /* load caption */
0152     LoadString(hInst,IDS_NoMouse,lpMessage,MaxText);  /* load text */
0153     MessageBox(GetFocus(),lpMessage,lpCaption,MB_OK);   /* message */
0154     }
0155
0156   /* ----------------- set up the hidden frame ----------------- */
0157   zInitFrame(MainhWnd);
0158
0159   /* ---------- begin retrieving messages for the window -------- */
0160   while (GetMessage(&msg,0,0,0))
0161     {
0162     if(TranslateAccelerator(MainhWnd, hAccel, &msg)) continue;
0163     TranslateMessage(&msg);
```

```
0164    DispatchMessage(&msg);
0165      }
0166   return(msg.wParam);
0167   }
0168   /*
0169   --------------------------------------------------------------------
0170                     Switcher for incoming messages
0171   --------------------------------------------------------------------
0172                                                                      */
0173   LONG FAR PASCAL zMessageHandler(HWND hWnd, unsigned message,
0174                                   WORD wParam, LONG lParam)
0175   {
0176     HDC hDCpaint;          /* display-context for persistent graphics */
0177
0178   switch (message)
0179     {
0180
0181     case WM_COMMAND:         /* if user has selected a menu item... */
0182       switch(wParam)
0183         {
0184         case IDM_New:     break;
0185         case IDM_Open:    break;
0186         case IDM_Save:    break;
0187         case IDM_SaveAs:  break;
0188         case IDM_Exit:    PostQuitMessage(0); break;
0189
0190         case IDM_Undo:    break;
0191         case IDM_Cut:     break;
0192         case IDM_Copy:    break;
0193         case IDM_Paste:   break;
0194         case IDM_Delete:  break;
0195
0196         case IDM_Typeface:    /* Windows retail product stock fonts */
0197                 if (FrameReady==FALSE)
0198                 {
0199                 MessageBeep(0);
0200                 LoadString(hInst,IDS_NotReady,lpCaption,Max);
0201                 LoadString(hInst,IDS_NoFrame,lpMessage,MaxText);
0202                 MessageBox(GetFocus(),lpMessage,lpCaption,MB_OK);
0203                 break;
0204                 }
0205                 zClear(hWnd); zTypeface(hWnd); zCopyToFrame(hWnd);
0206                 PaintImage= zIMAGE; break;
0207         case IDM_TypeColor:            /* overwrite various colors */
0208                 if (FrameReady==FALSE)
0209                 {
0210                 MessageBeep(0);
0211                 LoadString(hInst,IDS_NotReady,lpCaption,Max);
0212                 LoadString(hInst,IDS_NoFrame,lpMessage,MaxText);
0213                 MessageBox(GetFocus(),lpMessage,lpCaption,MB_OK);
0214                 break;
0215                 }
0216                 zClear(hWnd); zTypeColor(hWnd); zCopyToFrame(hWnd);
0217                 PaintImage= zIMAGE; break;
0218         case IDM_Super1:                   /* superimpose black type */
0219                 if (FrameReady==FALSE)
0220                 {
0221                 MessageBeep(0);
0222                 LoadString(hInst,IDS_NotReady,lpCaption,Max);
0223                 LoadString(hInst,IDS_NoFrame,lpMessage,MaxText);
0224                 MessageBox(GetFocus(),lpMessage,lpCaption,MB_OK);
```

```
0225                        break;
0226                        }
0227                   zDrawBg(hFrameDC); zCopyToDisplay(hWnd);
0228                   zSuper1(hWnd); zCopyToFrame(hWnd);
0229                   PaintImage= zIMAGE; break;
0230         case IDM_Super2:                    /* superimpose white type */
0231                   if (FrameReady==FALSE)
0232                        {
0233                        MessageBeep(0);
0234                        LoadString(hInst,IDS_NotReady,lpCaption,Max);
0235                        LoadString(hInst,IDS_NoFrame,lpMessage,MaxText);
0236                        MessageBox(GetFocus(),lpMessage,lpCaption,MB_OK);
0237                        break;
0238                        }
0239                   zDrawBg(hFrameDC); zCopyToDisplay(hWnd);
0240                   zSuper2(hWnd); zCopyToFrame(hWnd);
0241                   PaintImage= zIMAGE; break;
0242         case IDM_DropShadow:  /* yellow type with black dropshadow */
0243                   if (FrameReady==FALSE)
0244                        {
0245                        MessageBeep(0);
0246                        LoadString(hInst,IDS_NotReady,lpCaption,Max);
0247                        LoadString(hInst,IDS_NoFrame,lpMessage,MaxText);
0248                        MessageBox(GetFocus(),lpMessage,lpCaption,MB_OK);
0249                        break;
0250                        }
0251                   zDrawBg(hFrameDC); zCopyToDisplay(hWnd);
0252                   zDropShadow(hWnd); zCopyToFrame(hWnd);
0253                   PaintImage= zIMAGE; break;
0254         case IDM_Clear: zClear(hWnd); PaintImage= zBLANK;
0255                        break;
0256
0257         case IDM_About:
0258           LoadString(hInst,IDS_About,lpCaption,Max);
0259           LoadString(hInst,IDS_AboutText,lpMessage,MaxText);
0260           MessageBox(GetFocus(),lpMessage,lpCaption,MB_OK);
0261           break;
0262
0263         case IDM_License:
0264           LoadString(hInst,IDS_License,lpCaption,Max);
0265           LoadString(hInst,IDS_LicenseText,lpMessage,MaxText);
0266           MessageBox(GetFocus(),lpMessage,lpCaption,MB_OK);
0267           break;
0268
0269         case IDM_Display:
0270           if (DisplayWidth==640)
0271             {
0272             if (DisplayHeight==480)
0273               {
0274               LoadString(hInst,IDS_Resolution,lpCaption,Max);
0275               LoadString(hInst,IDS_ResVGA,lpMessage,MaxText);
0276               MessageBox(GetFocus(),lpMessage,lpCaption,MB_OK);
0277               }
0278             if (DisplayHeight==350)
0279               {
0280               LoadString(hInst,IDS_Resolution,lpCaption,Max);
0281               LoadString(hInst,IDS_ResEGA,lpMessage,MaxText);
0282               MessageBox(GetFocus(),lpMessage,lpCaption,MB_OK);
0283               }
0284             if (DisplayHeight==200)
0285               {
```

```
0286                    LoadString(hInst,IDS_Resolution,lpCaption,Max);
0287                    LoadString(hInst,IDS_ResCGA,lpMessage,MaxText);
0288                    MessageBox(GetFocus(),lpMessage,lpCaption,MB_OK);
0289                    }
0290                  break;
0291                  }
0292              if (DisplayWidth==800)
0293                  {
0294                  LoadString(hInst,IDS_Resolution,lpCaption,Max);
0295                  LoadString(hInst,IDS_ResSVGA,lpMessage,MaxText);
0296                  MessageBox(GetFocus(),lpMessage,lpCaption,MB_OK);
0297                  break;
0298                  }
0299              if (DisplayWidth==1024)
0300                  {
0301                  LoadString(hInst,IDS_Resolution,lpCaption,Max);
0302                  LoadString(hInst,IDS_Res8514,lpMessage,MaxText);
0303                  MessageBox(GetFocus(),lpMessage,lpCaption,MB_OK);
0304                  break;
0305                  }
0306              if (DisplayWidth==720)
0307                  {
0308                  LoadString(hInst,IDS_Resolution,lpCaption,Max);
0309                  LoadString(hInst,IDS_ResHerc,lpMessage,MaxText);
0310                  MessageBox(GetFocus(),lpMessage,lpCaption,MB_OK);
0311                  break;
0312                  }
0313              LoadString(hInst,IDS_Resolution,lpCaption,Max);
0314              LoadString(hInst,IDS_ResCustom,lpMessage,MaxText);
0315              MessageBox(GetFocus(),lpMessage,lpCaption,MB_OK);
0316              break;
0317
0318            case IDM_Colors:
0319              if (DisplayBits==1)
0320                  {
0321                  if (DisplayPlanes==4)
0322                      {
0323                      LoadString(hInst,IDS_Color,lpCaption,Max);
0324                      LoadString(hInst,IDS_Color16,lpMessage,MaxText);
0325                      MessageBox(GetFocus(),lpMessage,lpCaption,MB_OK);
0326                      break;
0327                      }
0328                  if (DisplayPlanes==1)
0329                      {
0330                      LoadString(hInst,IDS_Color,lpCaption,Max);
0331                      LoadString(hInst,IDS_Color2,lpMessage,MaxText);
0332                      MessageBox(GetFocus(),lpMessage,lpCaption,MB_OK);
0333                      break;
0334                      }
0335                  }
0336              if (DisplayBits==8)
0337                  {
0338                  LoadString(hInst,IDS_Color,lpCaption,Max);
0339                  LoadString(hInst,IDS_Color256,lpMessage,MaxText);
0340                  MessageBox(GetFocus(),lpMessage,lpCaption,MB_OK);
0341                  break;
0342                  }
0343              LoadString(hInst,IDS_Color,lpCaption,Max);
0344              LoadString(hInst,IDS_ColorCustom,lpMessage,MaxText);
0345              MessageBox(GetFocus(),lpMessage,lpCaption,MB_OK);
0346              break;
```

```
0347
0348        case IDM_Mode:
0349          if (MemoryMode & WF_ENHANCED)
0350            {
0351            LoadString(hInst,IDS_Machine,lpCaption,Max);
0352            LoadString(hInst,IDS_Enhanced,lpMessage,MaxText);
0353            MessageBox(GetFocus(),lpMessage,lpCaption,MB_OK);
0354            break;
0355            }
0356          if (MemoryMode & WF_STANDARD)
0357            {
0358            LoadString(hInst,IDS_Machine,lpCaption,Max);
0359            LoadString(hInst,IDS_Standard,lpMessage,MaxText);
0360            MessageBox(GetFocus(),lpMessage,lpCaption,MB_OK);
0361            break;
0362            }
0363          LoadString(hInst,IDS_Machine,lpCaption,Max);
0364          LoadString(hInst,IDS_Real,lpMessage,MaxText);
0365          MessageBox(GetFocus(),lpMessage,lpCaption,MB_OK);
0366          break;
0367
0368        case IDM_GeneralHelp:
0369          LoadString(hInst,IDS_Help,lpCaption,Max);
0370          LoadString(hInst,IDS_HelpText,lpMessage,MaxText);
0371          MessageBox(GetFocus(),lpMessage,lpCaption,MB_OK);
0372          break;
0373        default:
0374          return(DefWindowProc(hWnd, message, wParam, lParam));
0375        }
0376      break;
0377
0378    case WM_PAINT:              /* if image needs to be refreshed... */
0379      hDCpaint= BeginPaint(hWnd,&ps);           /* load structure */
0380      EndPaint(hWnd, &ps);                /* validate client area */
0381      if (PaintImage==zBLANK) break;    /* if client area is blank */
0382      if (FrameReady==FALSE) break;          /* if no hidden frame */
0383      zCopyToDisplay(hWnd);   /* else copy hidden frame to display */
0384      break;
0385
0386    case WM_DESTROY:  /* if user is terminating the application... */
0387      if (FrameReady==TRUE)
0388        {                       /* remove the hidden frame bitmap */
0389        SelectObject(hFrameDC,hPrevFrame);
0390        DeleteObject(hFrame);
0391        DeleteDC(hFrameDC);
0392        }
0393      PostQuitMessage(0);
0394      break;
0395
0396    case WM_SYSCOMMAND:     /* intercept resize, minimize, maximize */
0397      if ((wParam & 0xfff0)== SC_SIZE)
0398        {
0399        MessageBeep(0); break;
0400        }
0401      if ((wParam & 0xfff0)== SC_MINIMIZE)
0402        {
0403        MessageBeep(0); break;
0404        }
0405      if ((wParam & 0xfff0)== SC_MAXIMIZE)
0406        {
0407        MessageBeep(0); break;
```

```
0408          }
0409
0410    default:
0411      return(DefWindowProc(hWnd, message, wParam, lParam));
0412    }
0413  return FALSE;
0414  }
0415  /*
0416  ---------------------------------------------------------------
0417          Initialize the attributes of the window class
0418  ---------------------------------------------------------------
0419                                                          */
0420  BOOL zInitClass(HANDLE hInstance)
0421  {
0422    WNDCLASS WndClass;
0423  WndClass.style= 0;                           /* class style */
0424  WndClass.lpfnWndProc= zMessageHandler;    /* callback function */
0425  WndClass.cbClsExtra= 0;          /* unused, no customized data */
0426  WndClass.cbWndExtra= 0;          /* unused, no customized data */
0427  WndClass.hInstance= hInstance;    /* application that owns class */
0428  WndClass.hIcon= LoadIcon(NULL,IDI_EXCLAMATION); /* minimize icon */
0429  WndClass.hCursor= LoadCursor(NULL,IDC_ARROW);    /* app's cursor */
0430  WndClass.hbrBackground=  /* specifies background color of window */
0431                      CreateSolidBrush(RGB(255,255,255));
0432  WndClass.lpszMenuName= "MENUS1";    /* name of .RC menu resource */
0433  WndClass.lpszClassName= "DEMOCLASS";       /* name of the class */
0434  return RegisterClass(&WndClass);        /* registers the class */
0435  }
0436  /*
0437  ---------------------------------------------------------------
0438                    Create the main window
0439  ---------------------------------------------------------------
0440                                                          */
0441  HWND zInitMainWindow(HANDLE hInstance)
0442  {
0443    HWND hWnd;
0444  LoadString(hInstance,IDS_Caption,lpCaption,Max); /* load caption */
0445  hHourGlass= LoadCursor(NULL,IDC_WAIT);   /* load the wait cursor */
0446  hWnd= CreateWindow("DEMOCLASS",   /* create window of this class */
0447        lpCaption,                            /* caption */
0448        WS_OVERLAPPED | WS_THICKFRAME | WS_MINIMIZEBOX |   /* type */
0449          WS_MAXIMIZEBOX | WS_CLIPCHILDREN,
0450        WindowX,WindowY,                    /* screen location */
0451        zWINDOW_WIDTH,zWINDOW_HEIGHT,        /* window dimensions */
0452        0,0,                    /* parent handle, menu or child ID */
0453        hInstance,(LPSTR)NULL); /* app instance and unused pointer */
0454  return hWnd;
0455  }
0456  /*
0457  ---------------------------------------------------------------
0458          THE CORE FUNCTIONS OF THE APPLICATION
0459  ---------------------------------------------------------------
0460  ---------------------------------------------------------------
0461                  Display the stock fonts.
0462  ---------------------------------------------------------------
0463                                                          */
0464  static BOOL zTypeface(HWND hWnd)
0465  {
0466    HDC hDC;                              /* display-context */
0467    int Position, Line;      /* x,y location of displayed text */
0468    int Leading;              /* spacing between lines of text */
```

```
0469    HFONT Font;                                  /* handle to stock font */
0470    HFONT PrevFont;                            /* handle to default font */
0471  hDC= GetDC(hWnd);                            /* set the display-context */
0472  Position= 10;                    /* set the horizontal pixel position */
0473  Line= 4;                           /* set the vertical pixel position */
0474  Leading= 16;                    /* set the VGA vertical line spacing */
0475
0476  /* --------------- display the default font ------------------ */
0477  TextOut(hDC,Position,Line,                    /* display some text... */
0478    "Examples of different stock fonts that are",42);
0479  Line+= Leading;                 /* ...then move to the next text line */
0480  TextOut(hDC,Position,Line,
0481    "built into the retail version of Windows...",43);
0482  Line+= Leading; Line+= Leading;
0483
0484  /* --------------- display different stock fonts ------------- */
0485  Font= GetStockObject(ANSI_FIXED_FONT);     /* grab handle to font */
0486  PrevFont= SelectObject(hDC,Font);               /* select the font */
0487  TextOut(hDC,Position,Line,                   /* display some text... */
0488    "This is the ANSI fixed-pitch stock font",39);
0489  Line+= Leading;                 /* ...then move to the next text line */
0490  TextOut(hDC,Position,Line,
0491    "AaBbCcDdEeFfGgHhIiJjKkLlMmNnOoPpQqRrSsTtUuVvWwXxYyZz;,?!",56);
0492  Line+= Leading; Line+= Leading;
0493
0494  Font= GetStockObject(ANSI_VAR_FONT);
0495  SelectObject(hDC,Font);
0496  TextOut(hDC,Position,Line,
0497    "This is the ANSI variable-pitch stock font",42);
0498  Line+= Leading;
0499  TextOut(hDC,Position,Line,
0500    "AaBbCcDdEeFfGgHhIiJjKkLlMmNnOoPpQqRrSsTtUuVvWwXxYyZz;,?!",56);
0501  Line+= Leading; Line+= Leading;
0502
0503  Font= GetStockObject(OEM_FIXED_FONT);
0504  SelectObject(hDC,Font);
0505  TextOut(hDC,Position,Line,
0506    "This is the OEM fixed-pitch stock font",38);
0507  Line+= Leading;
0508  TextOut(hDC,Position,Line,
0509    "AaBbCcDdEeFfGgHhIiJjKkLlMmNnOoPpQqRrSsTtUuVvWwXxYyZz;,?!",56);
0510  Line+= Leading; Line+= Leading;
0511
0512  Font= GetStockObject(DEVICE_DEFAULT_FONT);
0513  SelectObject(hDC,Font);
0514  TextOut(hDC,Position,Line,
0515    "This is the device default stock font",37);
0516  Line+= Leading;
0517  TextOut(hDC,Position,Line,
0518    "AaBbCcDdEeFfGgHhIiJjKkLlMmNnOoPpQqRrSsTtUuVvWwXxYyZz;,?!",56);
0519  Line+= Leading; Line+= Leading;
0520
0521  Font= GetStockObject(SYSTEM_FONT);
0522  SelectObject(hDC,Font);
0523  TextOut(hDC,Position,Line,
0524    "This is the system variable-pitch stock font",44);
0525  Line+= Leading;
0526  TextOut(hDC,Position,Line,
0527    "AaBbCcDdEeFfGgHhIiJjKkLlMmNnOoPpQqRrSsTtUuVvWwXxYyZz;,?!",56);
0528
0529  SelectObject(hDC,PrevFont);                     /* restore default font */
```

```
0530   ReleaseDC(hWnd,hDC);              /* release the display-context */
0531   return TRUE;
0532   }
0533   /*
0534   ------------------------------------------------------------------
0535                    Display different font colors.
0536   ------------------------------------------------------------------
0537                                                                   */
0538   static BOOL zTypeColor(HWND hWnd)
0539   {
0540     HDC hDC;                                      /* display-context */
0541     int Position, Line;         /* x,y location of displayed text */
0542     int Leading;                /* spacing between lines of text */
0543   hDC= GetDC(hWnd);                      /* set the display-context */
0544   Position= 10;              /* set the horizontal pixel position */
0545   Line= 10;                   /* set the vertical pixel position */
0546   Leading= 16;                /* set the VGA vertical line spacing */
0547
0548   /* --------------- display the default font ------------------ */
0549   TextOut(hDC,Position,Line,                /* display some text... */
0550     "Examples of text colors using the default Helv font",51);
0551   Line+= Leading;                /* ...then move to the next text line */
0552   TextOut(hDC,Position,Line,
0553     "that is built into the retail version of Windows...",51);
0554   Line+= Leading;
0555
0556   /* -------------- display text in different colors ------------- */
0557   Line+= Leading;
0558   SetTextColor(hDC, RGB(255,0,0));
0559   TextOut(hDC,Position,Line,
0560     "This is displayed in red.",25);
0561
0562   Line+= Leading;
0563   SetTextColor(hDC, RGB(0,255,0));
0564   TextOut(hDC,Position,Line,
0565     "This is displayed in green.",27);
0566
0567   Line+= Leading;
0568   SetTextColor(hDC, RGB(0,0,255));
0569   TextOut(hDC,Position,Line,
0570     "This is displayed in blue.",26);
0571
0572   Line+= Leading;
0573   SetTextColor(hDC, RGB(0,255,255));
0574   TextOut(hDC,Position,Line,
0575     "This is displayed in cyan.",26);
0576
0577   Line+= Leading;
0578   SetTextColor(hDC, RGB(0,127,127));
0579   TextOut(hDC,Position,Line,
0580     "This is displayed in dull cyan.",31);
0581
0582   Line+= Leading;
0583   SetTextColor(hDC, RGB(255,0,255));
0584   TextOut(hDC,Position,Line,
0585     "This is displayed in magenta.",29);
0586
0587   Line+= Leading;
0588   SetTextColor(hDC, RGB(0,0,0));
0589   TextOut(hDC,Position,Line,
0590     "This is displayed in black.",27);
```

```
0591
0592   Line+= Leading;
0593   SetTextColor(hDC, RGB(127,127,127));
0594   TextOut(hDC,Position,Line,
0595     "This is displayed in dark gray.",31);
0596
0597   Line+= Leading;
0598   SetTextColor(hDC, RGB(191,191,191));
0599   TextOut(hDC,Position,Line,
0600     "This is displayed in light gray.",32);
0601
0602   Line+= Leading;
0603   SetTextColor(hDC, RGB(255,255,255));
0604   SetBkColor(hDC, RGB(0,0,0));
0605   TextOut(hDC,Position,Line,
0606     "This is white against a black background.",41);
0607
0608   Line+= Leading;
0609   SetTextColor(hDC, RGB(255,255,0));
0610   SetBkColor(hDC, RGB(0,255,0));
0611   TextOut(hDC,Position,Line,
0612     "This is yellow against a green background.",42);
0613
0614   Line+= Leading;
0615   SetTextColor(hDC, RGB(255,0,0));
0616   SetBkColor(hDC, RGB(127,0,0));
0617   TextOut(hDC,Position,Line,
0618     "This is red on red.",19);
0619
0620   Line+= Leading;
0621   SetTextColor(hDC, RGB(191,191,191));
0622   SetBkColor(hDC, RGB(127,127,127));
0623   TextOut(hDC,Position,Line,
0624     "This is gray on gray.",21);
0625
0626   ReleaseDC(hWnd,hDC);                      /* release the display-context */
0627   return TRUE;
0628   }
0629   /*
0630   ------------------------------------------------------------------
0631         Superimpose black type over a multicolor background.
0632   ------------------------------------------------------------------
0633                                                                  */
0634   static BOOL zSuper1(HWND hWnd)
0635   {
0636     HDC hDC;                                        /* display-context */
0637     int Position, Line;          /* x,y location of displayed text */
0638     int Leading;                 /* spacing between lines of text */
0639     HFONT Font;                                /* handle to logical font */
0640     HFONT PrevFont;                            /* handle to default font */
0641     DWORD PrevFontColor;              /* remembers default font color */
0642     DWORD PrevBkColor;          /* remembers default background color */
0643   hDC= GetDC(hWnd);                          /* set the display-context */
0644   Position= 10;                 /* set the horizontal pixel position */
0645   Line= 50;                     /* set the vertical pixel position */
0646   Leading= 16;                  /* set the vertical line spacing */
0647   PrevFontColor= SetTextColor(hDC,RGB(0,0,0));     /* set font color */
0648   PrevBkColor= SetBkColor(hDC,RGB(255,255,255));   /* set bg color */
0649   SetBkMode(hDC,TRANSPARENT);                    /* use superimposition */
0650
0651   /* --------------- display the default font ------------------ */
```

```
0652  TextOut(hDC,Position,Line,                    /* display some text... */
0653     "Examples of typesizes using the Helv typeface",45);
0654  Line+= Leading;               /* ...then move to the next text line */
0655  TextOut(hDC,Position,Line,
0656     "that is built into the retail version of Windows...",51);
0657  Line+= Leading;
0658  TextOut(hDC,Position,Line,
0659     "superimposing black type over a multicolor background",53);
0660  Line+= Leading;
0661  Line+= Leading;
0662
0663  /* -------------- display different sizes of text -------------- */
0664  Font= CreateFont(
0665        18,                                     /* height, in pixels */
0666        0,                        /* use aspect ratio to pick width */
0667        0,                       /* angle of textline, in .1 degrees */
0668        0,                   /* angle of each character, in .1 degrees */
0669        FW_BOLD,                       /* or FW_LIGHT or FW_NORMAL */
0670        FALSE,                          /* TRUE if italic desired */
0671        FALSE,                       /* TRUE if underscore desired */
0672        FALSE,                       /* TRUE if strikeout desired */
0673        ANSI_CHARSET,                      /* ANSI character set */
0674        OUT_DEFAULT_PRECIS,                /* method of matching */
0675        CLIP_DEFAULT_PRECIS,               /* method of clipping */
0676        DRAFT_QUALITY,                      /* scaling activated */
0677        VARIABLE_PITCH | FF_SWISS,          /* pitch and family */
0678        "Helv");                            /* name of typeface */
0679  PrevFont= SelectObject(hDC,Font);            /* select the font */
0680  TextOut(hDC,Position,Line,
0681     "This is Helv 18 bold.",21);                     /* display */
0682  Leading= 18;                    /* reset the line spacing factor */
0683  Line+= Leading;                                    /* next line */
0684
0685  Font= CreateFont(24, 0, 0, 0, FW_BOLD, FALSE, FALSE, FALSE,
0686        ANSI_CHARSET, OUT_DEFAULT_PRECIS, CLIP_DEFAULT_PRECIS,
0687        DRAFT_QUALITY, VARIABLE_PITCH | FF_SWISS, "Helv");
0688  SelectObject(hDC,Font);
0689  TextOut(hDC,Position,Line,"This is Helv 24 bold.",21);
0690  Leading= 24; Line+= Leading;
0691
0692  Font= CreateFont(36, 0, 0, 0, FW_BOLD, FALSE, FALSE, FALSE,
0693        ANSI_CHARSET, OUT_DEFAULT_PRECIS, CLIP_DEFAULT_PRECIS,
0694        DRAFT_QUALITY, VARIABLE_PITCH | FF_SWISS, "Helv");
0695  SelectObject(hDC,Font);
0696  TextOut(hDC,Position,Line,"This is Helv 36 bold.",21);
0697  Leading= 32; Line+= Leading;
0698
0699  Font= CreateFont(48, 0, 0, 0, FW_BOLD, FALSE, FALSE, FALSE,
0700        ANSI_CHARSET, OUT_DEFAULT_PRECIS, CLIP_DEFAULT_PRECIS,
0701        DRAFT_QUALITY, VARIABLE_PITCH | FF_SWISS, "Helv");
0702  SelectObject(hDC,Font);
0703  TextOut(hDC,Position,Line,"This is Helv 48 bold.",21);
0704
0705  SelectObject(hDC,PrevFont);              /* restore default font */
0706  SetBkMode(hDC,OPAQUE);                 /* restore overwrite mode */
0707  SetBkColor(hDC,PrevBkColor);      /* restore default font bg color */
0708  SetTextColor(hDC,PrevFontColor);   /* restore default font color */
0709  ReleaseDC(hWnd,hDC);               /* release the display-context */
0710  return TRUE;
0711  }
0712  /*
```

```
0713  ------------------------------------------------------------
0714          Superimpose white type over a multicolor background.
0715  ------------------------------------------------------------
0716                                                              */
0717  static BOOL zSuper2(HWND hWnd)
0718  {
0719    HDC hDC;                                   /* display-context */
0720    int Position, Line;            /* x,y location of displayed text */
0721    int Leading;                   /* spacing between lines of text */
0722    HFONT Font;                              /* handle to logical font */
0723    HFONT PrevFont;                          /* handle to default font */
0724    DWORD PrevFontColor;           /* remembers default font color */
0725    DWORD PrevBkColor;          /* remembers default background color */
0726  hDC= GetDC(hWnd);                        /* set the display-context */
0727  Position= 10;                /* set the horizontal pixel position */
0728  Line= 50;                      /* set the vertical pixel position */
0729  Leading= 16;                     /* set the vertical line spacing */
0730  PrevFontColor= SetTextColor(hDC,RGB(255,255,255)); /* font color */
0731  PrevBkColor= SetBkColor(hDC,RGB(0,0,0));    /* set font bg color */
0732  SetBkMode(hDC,TRANSPARENT);                /* use superimposition */
0733
0734  /* --------------- display the default font ------------------ */
0735  TextOut(hDC,Position,Line,                /* display some text... */
0736    "Examples of typesizes using the Helv typeface",45);
0737  Line+= Leading;                /* ...then move to the next text line */
0738  TextOut(hDC,Position,Line,
0739    "that is built into the retail version of Windows...",51);
0740  Line+= Leading;
0741  TextOut(hDC,Position,Line,
0742    "superimposing white type over a multicolor background",53);
0743  Line+= Leading;
0744  Line+= Leading;
0745
0746  /* -------------- display different sizes of text ------------- */
0747  Font= CreateFont(
0748      18,                                    /* height, in pixels */
0749      0,                          /* use aspect ratio to pick width */
0750      0,                          /* angle of textline, in .1 degrees */
0751      0,                        /* angle of each character, in .1 degrees */
0752      FW_BOLD,                        /* or FW_LIGHT or FW_NORMAL */
0753      FALSE,                             /* TRUE if italic desired */
0754      FALSE,                          /* TRUE if underscore desired */
0755      FALSE,                          /* TRUE if strikeout desired */
0756      ANSI_CHARSET,                        /* ANSI character set */
0757      OUT_DEFAULT_PRECIS,                  /* method of matching */
0758      CLIP_DEFAULT_PRECIS,                 /* method of clipping */
0759      DRAFT_QUALITY,                       /* scaling activated */
0760      VARIABLE_PITCH | FF_SWISS,           /* pitch and family */
0761      "Helv");                             /* name of typeface */
0762  PrevFont= SelectObject(hDC,Font);            /* select the font */
0763  TextOut(hDC,Position,Line,
0764    "This is Helv 18 bold.",21);                      /* display */
0765  Leading= 18;                    /* reset the line spacing factor */
0766  Line+= Leading;                                     /* next line */
0767
0768  Font= CreateFont(24, 0, 0, 0, FW_BOLD, FALSE, FALSE, FALSE,
0769      ANSI_CHARSET, OUT_DEFAULT_PRECIS, CLIP_DEFAULT_PRECIS,
0770      DRAFT_QUALITY, VARIABLE_PITCH | FF_SWISS, "Helv");
0771  SelectObject(hDC,Font);
0772  TextOut(hDC,Position,Line,"This is Helv 24 bold.",21);
0773  Leading= 24; Line+= Leading;
```

```
0774
0775    Font= CreateFont(36, 0, 0, 0, FW_BOLD, FALSE, FALSE, FALSE,
0776        ANSI_CHARSET, OUT_DEFAULT_PRECIS, CLIP_DEFAULT_PRECIS,
0777        DRAFT_QUALITY, VARIABLE_PITCH | FF_SWISS, "Helv");
0778    SelectObject(hDC,Font);
0779    TextOut(hDC,Position,Line,"This is Helv 36 bold.",21);
0780    Leading= 32; Line+= Leading;
0781
0782    Font= CreateFont(48, 0, 0, 0, FW_BOLD, FALSE, FALSE, FALSE,
0783        ANSI_CHARSET, OUT_DEFAULT_PRECIS, CLIP_DEFAULT_PRECIS,
0784        DRAFT_QUALITY, VARIABLE_PITCH | FF_SWISS, "Helv");
0785    SelectObject(hDC,Font);
0786    TextOut(hDC,Position,Line,"This is Helv 48 bold.",21);
0787
0788    SelectObject(hDC,PrevFont);             /* restore default font */
0789    SetBkMode(hDC,OPAQUE);                 /* restore overwrite mode */
0790    SetBkColor(hDC,PrevBkColor);      /* restore default font bg color */
0791    SetTextColor(hDC,PrevFontColor);  /* restore default font color */
0792    ReleaseDC(hWnd,hDC);                /* release the display-context */
0793    return TRUE;
0794    }
0795    /*
0796    -----------------------------------------------------------------
0797                    Superimpose dropshadowed type.
0798    -----------------------------------------------------------------
0799                                                                    */
0800    static BOOL zDropShadow(HWND hWnd)
0801    {
0802        HDC hDC;                               /* display-context */
0803        int Position, Line;        /* x,y location of displayed text */
0804        HFONT Font;                      /* handle to logical font */
0805        HFONT PrevFont;                  /* handle to default font */
0806        DWORD PrevFontColor;           /* remembers default font color */
0807        DWORD PrevBkColor;       /* remembers default background color */
0808    hDC= GetDC(hWnd);                      /* set the display-context */
0809    Position= 30;            /* set the horizontal pixel position */
0810    Line= 120;                   /* set the vertical pixel position */
0811    PrevFontColor= SetTextColor(hDC,RGB(0,0,0));    /* set font color */
0812    PrevBkColor= SetBkColor(hDC,RGB(255,255,255));   /* set bg color */
0813    SetBkMode(hDC,TRANSPARENT);            /* use superimposition */
0814
0815    /* ------------------ write the dropshadow ------------------- */
0816    Font= CreateFont(
0817        48,                                 /* height, in pixels */
0818        0,                         /* use aspect ratio to pick width */
0819        0,                      /* angle of textline, in .1 degrees */
0820        0,                /* angle of each character, in .1 degrees */
0821        FW_BOLD,                    /* or FW_LIGHT or FW_NORMAL */
0822        FALSE,                          /* TRUE if italic desired */
0823        FALSE,                     /* TRUE if underscore desired */
0824        FALSE,                      /* TRUE if strikeout desired */
0825        ANSI_CHARSET,                   /* ANSI character set */
0826        OUT_DEFAULT_PRECIS,             /* method of matching */
0827        CLIP_DEFAULT_PRECIS,            /* method of clipping */
0828        DRAFT_QUALITY,                  /* scaling activated */
0829        VARIABLE_PITCH | FF_SWISS,      /* pitch and family */
0830        "Helv");                        /* name of typeface */
0831    PrevFont= SelectObject(hDC,Font);       /* select the font */
0832    TextOut(hDC,Position,Line,
0833      "Dropshadow 48 pt.",17);                      /* display */
0834
```

```
0835  /* ----------------- write the foreground text ----------------- */
0836  Position-= 6; Line-= 6;            /* adjust the starting position */
0837  SetTextColor(hDC,RGB(255,255,0));   /* set font foreground color */
0838  SetBkColor(hDC,RGB(0,0,0));          /* set font background color */
0839  Font= CreateFont(48, 0, 0, 0, FW_BOLD, FALSE, FALSE, FALSE,
0840       ANSI_CHARSET, OUT_DEFAULT_PRECIS, CLIP_DEFAULT_PRECIS,
0841       DRAFT_QUALITY, VARIABLE_PITCH | FF_SWISS, "Helv");
0842  SelectObject(hDC,Font);
0843  TextOut(hDC,Position,Line,"Dropshadow 48 pt.",17);
0844
0845  SelectObject(hDC,PrevFont);                  /* restore default font */
0846  SetBkMode(hDC,OPAQUE);                    /* restore overwrite mode */
0847  SetBkColor(hDC,PrevBkColor);     /* restore default font bg color */
0848  SetTextColor(hDC,PrevFontColor);   /* restore default font color */
0849  ReleaseDC(hWnd,hDC);                  /* release the display-context */
0850  return TRUE;
0851  }
0852  /*
0853  --------------------------------------------------------------
0854                        Create the hidden frame.
0855  --------------------------------------------------------------
0856                                                                 */
0857  static void zInitFrame(HWND hWnd)
0858  {
0859    HDC hDisplayDC;                                /* display-context */
0860
0861  GlobalCompact((DWORD)-1L);           /* maximize contiguous memory */
0862  hDisplayDC= GetDC(hWnd);              /* set the display-context */
0863  hFrameDC= CreateCompatibleDC(hDisplayDC);       /* create frame... */
0864  hFrame= CreateCompatibleBitmap(hDisplayDC,zFRAMEWIDE,zFRAMEHIGH);
0865  if (hFrame==NULL)
0866    {
0867    LoadString(hInst,IDS_NotReady,lpCaption,Max);
0868    LoadString(hInst,IDS_NoMem,lpMessage,MaxText);
0869    MessageBox(GetFocus(),lpMessage,lpCaption,MB_OK);
0870    DeleteDC(hFrameDC);
0871    FrameReady= FALSE;
0872    return;
0873    }
0874  hPrevFrame= SelectObject(hFrameDC,hFrame);  /* select the bitmap */
0875  zClearHiddenFrame();                       /* clear the hidden frame */
0876  ReleaseDC(hWnd,hDisplayDC);        /* release the display-context */
0877  FrameReady= TRUE;                           /* set a global token */
0878  return;
0879  }
0880  /*
0881  --------------------------------------------------------------
0882                        Clear the display window.
0883  --------------------------------------------------------------
0884                                                                 */
0885  static void zClear(HWND hWnd)
0886  {
0887    HDC hDC;
0888  hDC= GetDC(hWnd);
0889  PatBlt(hDC,0,0,zFRAMEWIDE,zFRAMEHIGH,WHITENESS);
0890  ReleaseDC(hWnd,hDC);
0891  return;
0892  }
0893  /*
0894  --------------------------------------------------------------
0895                        Clear the hidden frame.
```

```
0896    --------------------------------------------------------------
0897                                                                */
0898    static void zClearHiddenFrame(void)
0899    {
0900    if (FrameReady==FALSE) return;
0901    PatBlt(hFrameDC,0,0,zFRAMEWIDE,zFRAMEHIGH,WHITENESS);
0902    return;
0903    }
0904    /*
0905    --------------------------------------------------------------
0906              Copy the hidden frame to the display window.
0907    --------------------------------------------------------------
0908                                                                */
0909    static void zCopyToDisplay(HWND hWnd)
0910    {
0911       HDC hDC;
0912    if (FrameReady==FALSE) return;
0913    hDC= GetDC(hWnd);
0914    BitBlt(hDC,0,0,zFRAMEWIDE,zFRAMEHIGH,hFrameDC,0,0,SRCCOPY);
0915    ReleaseDC(hWnd,hDC);
0916    return;
0917    }
0918    /*
0919    --------------------------------------------------------------
0920              Copy the display window to the hidden frame.
0921    --------------------------------------------------------------
0922                                                                */
0923    static void zCopyToFrame(HWND hWnd)
0924    {
0925       HDC hDC;
0926    if (FrameReady==FALSE) return;
0927    hDC= GetDC(hWnd);
0928    BitBlt(hFrameDC,0,0,zFRAMEWIDE,zFRAMEHIGH,hDC,0,0,SRCCOPY);
0929    ReleaseDC(hWnd,hDC);
0930    return;
0931    }
0932    /*
0933    --------------------------------------------------------------
0934                     Draw a background image.
0935    --------------------------------------------------------------
0936                                                                */
0937    static void zDrawBg(HDC hDC)
0938    {
0939       HBRUSH hPrevBrush, hSwatchBrush;                  /* brushes */
0940       HPEN hPrevPen, hBorderPen;                          /* pens */
0941       RECT rcSwatch;                           /* rectangle structure */
0942       int iWidth= zFRAMEWIDE, iDepth= 4;      /* swatch dimensions */
0943       int iSwatchX= 0, iSwatchY= 0;              /* swatch location */
0944       BYTE bRed= 0, bGreen= 0, bBlue= 0;     /* rgb gun intensities */
0945       int iCount;                                /* loop counter */
0946       int iX1= 100, iY1= 50, iX2= 300, iY2= 250;   /* ellipse coords */
0947       BYTE bGradiant= 20;                      /* shading gradiant factor */
0948       int iResize= 10;                            /* sizing factor */
0949
0950    /* ----------------- draw gradiant background ----------------- */
0951    rcSwatch.left= iSwatchX;
0952    rcSwatch.top= iSwatchY;
0953    rcSwatch.right= rcSwatch.left + iWidth;
0954    rcSwatch.bottom= rcSwatch.top + iDepth;
0955    bRed= 0; bGreen= 0; bBlue= 3;
```

```
0956  for (iCount= 0; iCount < 64; iCount++)
0957    {
0958    hSwatchBrush= CreateSolidBrush(RGB(bRed,bGreen,bBlue));
0959    hPrevBrush= SelectObject(hDC,hSwatchBrush);
0960    FillRect(hDC,&rcSwatch,hSwatchBrush);
0961    SelectObject(hDC,hPrevBrush);
0962    DeleteObject(hSwatchBrush);
0963    rcSwatch.top= rcSwatch.top + iDepth;
0964    rcSwatch.bottom= rcSwatch.bottom + iDepth;
0965    bBlue= bBlue + (BYTE) 4;
0966    }
0967  bBlue= 255; rcSwatch.bottom= 300;
0968  hSwatchBrush= CreateSolidBrush(RGB(bRed,bGreen,bBlue));
0969  hPrevBrush= SelectObject(hDC,hSwatchBrush);
0970  FillRect(hDC,&rcSwatch,hSwatchBrush);
0971  SelectObject(hDC,hPrevBrush); DeleteObject(hSwatchBrush);
0972
0973  /* ------------------ draw gradiant rectangle ---------------- */
0974  bRed= 255; bGreen= 0; bBlue= 0;
0975  iWidth= 280; iDepth= 4;
0976  iSwatchX= 60; iSwatchY= 24;
0977  rcSwatch.left= iSwatchX;
0978  rcSwatch.top= iSwatchY;
0979  rcSwatch.right= rcSwatch.left + iWidth;
0980  rcSwatch.bottom= rcSwatch.top + iDepth;
0981  for (iCount= 0; iCount < 64; iCount++)
0982    {
0983    hSwatchBrush= CreateSolidBrush(RGB(bRed,bGreen,bBlue));
0984    hPrevBrush= SelectObject(hDC,hSwatchBrush);
0985    FillRect(hDC,&rcSwatch,hSwatchBrush);
0986    SelectObject(hDC,hPrevBrush);
0987    DeleteObject(hSwatchBrush);
0988    rcSwatch.top= rcSwatch.top + iDepth;
0989    rcSwatch.bottom= rcSwatch.bottom + iDepth;
0990    bRed= bRed - (BYTE) 4;
0991    }
0992
0993  /* ------------------- draw gradiant circle ------------------ */
0994  hBorderPen= CreatePen(PS_NULL,1,RGB(0,0,255));
0995  hPrevPen= SelectObject(hDC,hBorderPen);   /* use transparent pen */
0996  bRed= 31; bGreen= 31; bBlue= 0;          /* reset rgb intensities */
0997  for (iCount= 1; iCount <= 9; iCount++)
0998    {  /* draw 7 ellipses, decreasing size, increasing brightness */
0999    hSwatchBrush= CreateSolidBrush(RGB(bRed,bGreen,bBlue));
1000    hPrevBrush= SelectObject(hDC,hSwatchBrush);
1001    Ellipse(hDC,iX1,iY1,iX2,iY2);
1002    bRed+= bGradiant; bGreen+= bGradiant;
1003    iX1+= iResize;
1004    iY1+= iResize;
1005    iX2-= iResize;
1006    iY2-= iResize;
1007    SelectObject(hDC,hPrevBrush);
1008    DeleteObject(hSwatchBrush);
1009    }
1010
1011  /* ------------------- tidy up and exit ------------------- */
1012  SelectObject(hDC,hPrevPen); SelectObject(hDC,hPrevBrush);
1013  DeleteObject(hBorderPen); DeleteObject(hSwatchBrush);
1014  return;
1015  }
```

```
1016    /*
1017    --------------------------------------------------------------
1018                    End of the C source file
1019    --------------------------------------------------------------
1020                                                               */
```

# Part two

# Computer animation

# 6

# *Animating in Windows*

The Microsoft Windows graphical environment offers a programming platform that is enriched with potential for animation. The field of computer-assisted animation is a rewarding and a profitable one—and it is expanding with dizzying speed.

Any thorough discussion of animation on personal computers must be organized into two fundamental categories. These categories are implementation and control. *Implementation* is concerned with the mechanics of creating the illusion of movement on the screen. *Control* is concerned with managing the objects and events that are being animated. Control is the tether that ties the subject matter to the software. Implementation is the conduit that connects the software to the hardware.

**Implementation**   Windows provides many different methods of implementing animation. The four most practical methods are:

- Fixed-loop animation.
- Idle-loop animation.
- Timer-based message-handler animation.
- Timer-based direct-call animation.

It is the two timer-based methods that produce well-behaved applications that can execute without conflicting with other Windows applications that may be running.

Each of these four methods of implementation can in turn be effected as real-time animation or as frame animation. Real-time animation uses dynamic images. Frame animation uses static images. During real-time animation (which is called *cast-based animation* by multimedia programmers), each image element is drawn by the software at the same time the animation is being displayed on the screen. Frame animation, on the other hand, fetches and displays images that have been previously completed and stored on disk. Whether you are using real-time animation or frame animation, each completed image is called a *frame*.

**Control**   If you understand how to implement animation on a personal computer that is running Windows, you can develop applications that provide explicit support for the three different categories of animation control. These three types of control are:

- Scripted animation.
- Procedural animation.
- Physically based animation.

Each method invokes a different paradigm to control the objects and events being animated.

## Computer-assisted animation

Applying the processing power of today's personal computer to the various fields of animation is opening up a motherlode of opportunity for creative expression, scientific research, marketing communications, entertainment, education, and training.

Computer-assisted animation is centered on the three disciplines of traditional animation, visualization, and simulation.

**Traditional animation**   *Traditional animation*, also called *film animation* and *cel animation*, is a mature technology that evolved from the so-called magic lantern parlor games of the 1820s. (See the Preface for a history of animation.) Traditional animation uses single-frame photography of individual celluloid sheets stacked on top of each other and illuminated from below. On each cel is a hand-drawn image of a character, a prop, or a background from the scene being animated. When computers are enjoined to assist in the production of traditional animation, it is called computer-assisted traditional animation (CATA).

**Visualization**   *Computer visualization* is visual thinking with computers. Visualization involves such diverse fields as 3D modeling and rendering, image analysis, computer vision, geometric processing, color analysis and retouching, before-and-after comparisons (ensemble processing), and much more. Computer visualization enhances our ability to solve complex problems and to realize creative ideas. It is an extension of our mind's thinking tools. Visualization can help us perceive and comprehend—especially when the image is animated.

Animated visualization sequences allow us to see how parts fit together, or how the timing of various events affects each other. Computer visualization is an important new thinking tool that has been made possible by the graphics capabilities of the personal computer. Animation can make visualization a reliable stand-in for a laboratory experiment, a physical prototype, or a mock-up.

**Simulation**   An animated visualization is often a simulation of some object or event that exists in the real world. Visualizing an object or event by means of computer animation often involves a database and rules of behavior taken from life. In many respects, animation and simulation are part and parcel of the same presentation.

## 4D space-time

Computer animation is the visual display of 4D space-time. The concept of 4D is derived from 3D. Objects in the real world possess the three dimensions of width, height, and depth. This is 3D, or three-dimensional modeling. When such an object is displayed by a computer, the image is presented in 3D space using X-Y-Z coordinates. When the same object is animated, a fourth dimension of time is added. Animation is movement over time. An animated 3D object is a display of 4D space-time using X-Y-Z-T coordinates.

In order to properly manage 4D space-time, a Windows animation application must continually monitor and update three sets of animation dynamics. These dynamics are:

- Motion
- Update
- Viewing

Taken together, these three sets of dynamics describe every aspect of an animation sequence, no matter whether the display is presented as 2D or 3D imagery.

**Motion dynamics**   Animation *motion dynamics*, also called *time-varying position*, refers to the location, orientation, and juxtaposition of individual objects. If the scene is rendered in 3D, motion dynamics are described by the rotation and translation of an object (see chapter 3, Modeling, for a primer on 3D modeling).

**Update dynamics**   Animation *update dynamics* are concerned with changes in shape, color, and texture. During a bouncing ball sequence, for example, the proper application of update dynamics will ensure that the ball is suitably deformed (squashed) each time it strikes the floor.

**Viewing dynamics**   Animation *viewing dynamics* involve changes in lighting, camera, and the viewpoint. During an animation sequence the camera can zoom in or zoom out, pan left or right, tilt up or down, truck in or truck out, or track alongside a moving object. Viewing dynamics concerns itself with these types of camera movements, as well as with changes in lighting and illumination, and special effects like soft-focus.

# Animation control

Methods for animation control fall into three categories. They are scripted animation, procedural animation, and physically based animation.

## Scripted animation

*Scripted animation* is the computer-assisted version of traditional film animation. Scripted animation is governed and directed by its namesake, the script. Typically, individual objects called *actors* are moved about in front of a background. Objects can include characters, props, and scenery elements. Multimedia developers refer to these objects as *cast-members* and the animation itself is called *cast-based animation*—especially if it is being produced using the techniques of real-time animation programming. This type of animation control is also called explicit control.

**Tricks of the trade**   Scripted animation is also called character animation, cel animation, conventional animation, traditional animation, and film animation. When computer software is used to assist in the production of scripted animation, the programmer is entering a milieu where the tricks of the trade are already well-documented and established (see chapter 9, Cel animation and Windows). Probably the most productive trick used by traditional animation studios is inbetweening (also called tweening).

**Interpolation**   *Tweening* is the creation of intermediate drawings from a set of so-called key drawings that have been prepared by the senior animator. Each key drawing represents an important moment in the animation sequence. Junior animators draw all the intermediate frames that must appear between two key drawings (also called key frames). Tweening is time-consuming, laborious work—and it is exactly the type of chore for which computers are well-suited, of course. When a personal computer is used to generate intermediate images from two key frames, the process is called *interpolation*. Computer-assisted interpolation can be used with both 2D and 3D animation. The interpolations can be programmed to follow a straight line (linear interpolation), or they can follow a curve (spline interpolation or curved interpolation).

**Rules of animation**   A number of so-called rules of animation have been discovered or invented during the 70-year history of film animation. The three most important categories of rules are:

- Deformation.
- Camera mechanics.
- Staging.

*Deformation*  Refers to the squashing and stretching of an object as it moves during the animation. A bouncing ball, for example, should be squashed (compressed) each time it strikes the floor, and should be stretched (extended) to simulate velocity as it bounces away. Subtle deformations like these add a magical, lifelike quality to any animation. They indicate that the animator or programmer has a sure grasp of the art of animation.

*Camera mechanics*  Rules of camera mechanics are concerned with viewpoint movement, or camera movement. For example, the slow-in/slow-out principle says that any camera movement must start very slowly and gradually build up to full speed, and then must reduce speed and end very slowly. This carefully choreographed slow-in/slow-out camera movement is the only way to avoid jerky camera pans and zooms.

*Staging*  Rules of staging are concerned with directing the animation. An animation sequence, after all, can be staged and directed just like an off-Broadway play. Pacing, cadence, plot development, dramatic lighting, actor entrances and exits, props, scenery, costume—these all fall into the domain of staging.

## Procedural animation

*Procedural animation*, or *actor animation*, is object-oriented animation. During animation playback, the software prepares the next frame by calculating the next position for each object in the scene. The calculations are often based on arbitrary, programmer-defined rules of behavior. The rules can describe not only an object's behavior in the scene itself, but also the object's behavior in relation to another object in the scene. When an object takes its cues from another object, the process is called *procedural interaction*.

**Procedural interaction**  Procedural control is best suited for simulations where the action is interdependent between objects in the scene. If, for example, your application is animating a conveyor belt assembly line, you could use procedural control to ensure that each box of widgets travels along with the conveyor belt until the end of the production line. A specialized routine in your code tracks the location of the conveyor belt from one frame to the next. The routine uses the updated location of the conveyor belt to reposition the box of widgets for the next frame. The location of the box of widgets (an object in the scene) is dependent upon the location of the conveyor belt (another object in the scene). This dependency between the two objects is called procedural interaction. The movement of the conveyor belt itself is governed by nominal rules of behavior defined by the programmer. These nominal rules are procedural control.

The objects, props, and background that make up a scene can be considered a cast of players in the animation sequence. Procedural animation shares similarities with cast-based animation, which is a technique used by multimedia programmers, as described during the previous discussion of scripted animation.

## Physically based animation

*Physically based animation*, or *contraint-based animation*, employs laws of physics to govern the motion of objects during animation playback. Motion in a constraint-based system is modeled using *constraints*. A constraint is a limiting condition or force.

Consider the animation of a bouncing tennis ball, for example. Gravity is one force among many that is acting on the ball. The ball is not being pushed up by gravity, it is being pushed down. This force is called a constraint. The motion of the tennis ball is being constrained (limited) by the force of gravity. When the ball hits the clay surface of the tennis court, it does not penetrate the surface, but instead bounces back. The tennis ball cannot pass through the surface. It is constrained to one side of the surface.

Physically based animation is concerned with positions, velocities, forces, mass, constraints, and so on. This method of animation control consists of four categories:

- Forward kinematics.
- Forward dynamics.
- Inverse kinematics.
- Inverse dynamics.

*Kinematics* refers to the positions and velocities of objects. *Dynamics* refers to laws of physics like force, mass, and so on that govern those positions and velocities.

**Forward kinematics**   *Forward kinematics* is the process of calculating the result of the application of velocity or acceleration to an object. Forward kinematics does not concern itself with forces or mass, but considers only the motion itself. You can use forward kinematics to check if two objects collide during an animation sequence.

**Forward dynamics**   *Forward dynamics* is the process of calculating the result of the application of force, loads, or constraints to an object. Dynamics concerns itself with the laws of physics that govern kinematics. You can use dynamic analysis to calculate the motion (kinematics) of an object resulting from forces acting on the object. You can also use dynamic analysis to calculate the forces resulting from the motion of the object. Like forward kinematics, forward dynamics can check if two objects collide, but forward dynamics can also calculate the forces resulting from the impact.

**Inverse kinematics**   *Inverse kinematics* is the process of calculating the velocity or acceleration required to move an object from one position to another over a fixed period of time. Whereas forward kinematics calculates the effect of velocity or acceleration and determines the resulting position of the object, inverse kinematics uses a programmer-defined position and calculates the amount of velocity or acceleration required to move the object to that position.

**Inverse dynamics**  *Inverse dynamics* is the process of calculating the forces or constraints required to move an object of a certain mass from one position to another over a fixed period of time. Whereas forward dynamics calculates the effect of forces, constraints, mass, and loads to determine the resulting position of an object, inverse dynamics uses a programmer-defined position and calculates the forces required to move the object to the position.

# Animation implementation

The Microsoft Windows graphical environment provides a number of low-level tools that make it possible to implement scripted animation, procedural animation, and physically based animation as either real-time animation or frame animation. In addition, the qualities of the C programming language and the message-based paradigm of Windows can be exploited to develop routines to manage animation playback using a variety of powerful algorithms. The four most useful algorithms are:

- Fixed-loop animation.
- Idle-loop animation.
- Timer-based message-handler animation.
- Timer-based direct-call animation.

## Low-level tools

The ability of the Windows GDI to manipulate and store graphic arrays provides a potent armory of low-level tools useful for animation The most effective of these tools are concerned with *graphic arrays*. A graphic array is a block of memory containing the information for a rectangular image. This image is called a *bitmap* or a *bitblt* (pronounced *bit-blit*). Larger images that are full-screen size or full-window size are often called bitmaps. Smaller images are often called bitblts. Some programmers and developers do not differentiate between the two.

**Blitting**  The process of pasting a bitblt onto the screen is called *blitting*. In practice, the GDI's BitBlt() function can be called to copy a bitblt from a memory location to the screen, from the screen to a memory location, from one memory location to another, or from one screen position to another screen position. Blitting provides the underpinnings for real-time animation. Refer back to chapter 3, Blitting, for a fuller discussion of the BitBlt() function.

**Page copying**   The process of copying a window-sized bitmap is called *page copying*. A page is a buffer in memory. It is also called a frame. The GDI's BitBlt() function can be called to copy the contents of the display window to a hidden frame in memory. It can also copy the contents of the hidden frame (the bitmap) back to the screen (the display window). Page copying provides the underpinnings for frame animation.

**Mattes and friskets**   In addition to pasting (copying a bitblt or bitmap from one location to another), the GDI can use *raster operators* to produce different visual effects when writing the bitmap or bitblt at the new location. These raster operators use Boolean logic. By careful application of the XOR and OR operators, a transparent PUT can be effected, as described and demonstrated in chapter 3. The transparent PUT operation uses a white matte to prepare the area where the image will be pasted. It uses a frisket to protect the existing scene from being overwritten by the background portion of the bitblt rectangle. Because the background portion of the rectangle does not show, it is called transparent. The transparent PUT algorithm provides you with the ability to manipulate numerous multicolored objects about a multicolored background.

## Real-time animation

A real-time animation sequence uses dynamic images. Each image element is drawn by the software at the same time the animation sequence is being displayed on the screen. Real-time animation can be implemented by three paradigms:

- On-screen bitblt to on-screen.
- Hidden frame bitblt to on-screen.
- Hidden frame drawn to on-screen.

Each of these methods offers advantages and disadvantages.

**On-screen bitblt to on-screen**   If a bitblt is copied or moved from one on-screen position to another on-screen position, the mechanics of preventing screen corruption often make the technique impractical. If the bitblt is being moved, the background at the previous position must be restored. Flickering is often unavoidable. Whether the bitblt is being copied or moved, a transparent PUT function must usually be invoked to ensure the bitblt is pasted cleanly at the new location.

**Hidden frame bitblt to on-screen**   If the bitblts have already been created and stored in memory, they can be used to build a completed image on a hidden frame. The hidden frame (hidden page) is copied to the display window as the next frame in the animation sequence. This method can produce optimum performance, but it sometimes limits the ability of the user to interact with the animation because all the images have been created in advance.

The more images (bitblts) your application has in inventory, the more runtime interaction you can offer to your user.

**Hidden frame drawn to on-screen**   The most versatile method of hardware implementation involves drawing each image on a hidden frame at runtime. Each completed image is copied to the display window during animation playback. This method provides the richest potential for user interaction with the animation at runtime, but the process of drawing each new frame can be time consuming.

## Frame animation

A frame animation sequence uses static images. During a frame animation sequence, the software fetches and displays previously completed full-window images that have been stored on disk. A typical frame animation engine is usually smart enough to attempt to load the entire animation sequence into memory for better playback performance if space permits. Frame animation authoring and playback can be implemented using three paradigms:

- On-screen bitblt to frame storage.
- On-screen drawn to frame storage.
- Frame playback to screen display.

**On-screen bitblt to frame storage**   Many programmers use bitblt images to build each completed frame on-screen in the display window. The software then saves the image from the screen to the hard disk. If the application needs to create new frames at runtime, the process can be made invisible to the user to building each new image on a hidden page and saving each new completed frame to the hard disk or to memory.

**On-screen drawn to frame storage**   Where previously created bitblt images are impractical, a developer will often use code that draws each frame from scratch on the screen. The software then saves each completed frame from the screen to the hard disk. If new frames are being created at runtime, the process can be concealed from the user by building each new frame on a hidden page and saving to hard disk or to memory.

**Frame playback to screen display**   Playback of a frame animation sequence is usually from disk to display or from memory to display. The frames that make up the animation sequence are usually stored on hard disk. If memory permits, the playback engine will usually strive to load all necessary frames into memory, from where they can be quickly displayed by copying them in sequence to the display window on-screen. If memory does not permit a preload, the animation engine is forced to load each frame from disk as required during playback—and animation performance is directly tied to hard disk performance.

# Coding an animation sequence

The C code that manages an animation sequence can exploit a fixed-loop or idle-loop algorithm—or it can rely upon timer-based algorithms.

## Loop algorithms

**Fixed loop**    A fixed loop is a block of C code that executes repeatedly for a predetermined number of iterations. The code is usually contained in one of the core functions of the application. While the loop is executing, other applications that may be running in the Windows environment are unable to share the CPU. Fixed-loop code is useful for short bursts of animation (called *spot animation*), where the brevity of the animation sequence will not adversely affect other applications that may be running.

**Idle loop**    Well-behaved applications modify their fixed loop blocks to produce idle-loop animation. You can do this by making calls to GetMessage() and DispatchMessage() in order to poll the application queue for user input during the loop—and to provide Windows with an opportunity to service other applications. Add the following code to your fixed loop to create an idle loop:

```
if (GetMessage(&msg,0,0,0))
{
if(TranslateAccelerator(MainhWnd,hAccel,&msg))
continue;
TranslateMessage(&msg);
DispatchMessage(&msg);
}
```

## Timer-based algorithms

Timer-based algorithms offer the most effective means of controlling the playback of an animation sequence. After you have specified a timing interval by a call to SetTimer(), Windows will send timer input to your application on each occasion that the interval elapses.

This timer input can take two forms. First, Windows can send a WM_TIMER message to your application by posting the message in the queue, from where it can be fetched by your application. This method is called *timer-based message-handler animation*. Second, Windows can call a particular function in your application on each timing interval. This method is called *timer-based direct-call animation*.

**Timer-based message-handler animation**    See FIG. 6-1 for a conceptual schematic that illustrates how timer-based message-handler animation works in the Windows cooperative multitasking environment. This method provides good runtime performance and it allows you to accurately control the playback speed by adjusting timing intervals with calls to the API's SetTimer()

# Timer-based animation

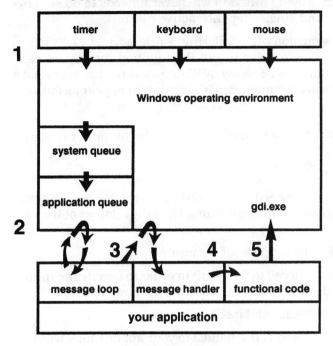

**1** The system timer chip is used to update a virtual timer managed by Windows.

**2** Windows posts a timer message in the queue, to be retrieved by your application's message loop.

**3** The message loop asks Windows to pass a message to your application's message handler function.

**4** The message handler function calls the appropriate core functions in your application.

**5** Core functions call the appropriate Windows DLL modules to draw graphics or manage resources.

**6-1** A conceptual schematic of timer-based animation in the Windows environment. The system clock is used to drive Windows' virtual timer, which posts a message in the queue, from where it is retrieved by your application's message loop. The message handler of your application then calls the appropriate function to display the next frame in the animation sequence.

function. The timer-based message-handler method also gives you good control over your application at runtime, because the logic flow is passing through your message handler's switch() block, which in turn calls a function to display the next frame. The message-handler method is also versatile because it provides two different ways to display the next frame. First, your message handler can call the appropriate function whenever a timer message is received from Windows. Second, any function in your application can call the frame-displaying function whenever it needs to do so. This is handy for freeze-frame and single-step interactive controls.

**Timer-based, direct-call animation**  By declaring a function as EXPORTS in your .def file, you can force Windows to call the function directly on each timer input. A function that can be called by Windows at runtime is called a *callback function*. A typical statement in a .def file might appear as follows:

```
EXPORTS zTimed
```

Next, you must declare the callback function in a header file or in the appropriate C source file.

```
FAR PROC lpfn zTimed;
```

When your application is launched, you should make a call to MakeProc-Instance() to allow Windows to initialize a thunk with the address of the callback function.

```
lpfnTimed = MakeProcInstance(zTimed, hInstance);
```

At runtime, your code makes a call to SetTimer() in order to specify the timing interval and to indicate the function that you want Windows to call.

```
SetTimer(hWnd, 1, wFrameRate, lpfnTimed)
```

In the example shown here hWnd is the handle to your application's window, wFrameRate is the timing interval (discussed later), and lpfnTimed is the name of the function to be called at each timer interval.

The definition for the function itself would appear in one of the C source files that makes up your application.

```
WORD FAR PASCAL zTimed(HWND hWnd, WORD Msg, WORD wParam, LONG
lParam)
{
. . .
return 0;
}
```

Each time Windows calls the EXPORTed function it passes a number of arguments. In the example shown here, hWnd is the handle to the window that you previously specified in a call to SetTimer(). Msg is the timer message. wParam is the timer ID number, and lParam is the address of the callback function.

Unlike the timer-based message-handler method, the timer-based direct-call method does not permit you to call the EXPORTed function directly.

**Timer settings**  The timer service that is provided by Windows operates by using the hardware timer chip, which issues an INT 08H approximately 18.2 times each second. This means that only a finite range of timer settings are actually implemented by timer input, as shown in FIG. 6-2.

| USABLE SetTimer( ) ARGUMENTS | | |
|---|---|---|
| INTERVAL (IN CLOCK TICKS) | INTERVAL (IN ms) | TIMER EVENTS PER SECOND |
| 1 | 55 ms | 1000/55 = 18.2 fps |
| 2 | 110 ms | 1000/110 = 9.1 fps |
| 3 | 165 ms | 1000/165 = 6.1 fps |
| 4 | 220 ms | 1000/220 = 4.5 fps |
| 5 | 275 ms | 1000/275 = 3.6 fps |
| 6 | 330 ms | 1000/330 = 3 fps |

The Windows GDI rounds down an argument to the nearest usable value. For example, if your application calls SetTimer( ) with an argument of 170, Windows will round it down to 165. The timer chip operates at 18.2 ticks per second, meaning each tick is 54.945 ms in duration (1000 divided by 18.2). Therefore 170 ms is 3.094 clock ticks (170 divided by 54.945). Windows rounds this down to exactly 3 clock ticks, which is equivalent to 165 ms.

**6-2** SetTimer() arguments can be used to implement message-based, timer-controlled, Windows-compliant animation.

For example, if you call SetTimer(170) you are setting the timer interval to 170 milliseconds (ms). There are 1000 ms in one second. But because the hardware timer chip operates at 18.2 clock ticks per second, each clock tick is 54.945 ms in duration (1000 divided by 18.2). This means that a request for 170 ms is actually a request for an interval of 3.094 clock ticks (170 divided by 54.945). Windows rounds this down to 3 clock ticks, or 165 ms. So even though you requested 170 ms in your call to SetTimer(), your application will receive a WM_TIMER message every 165 ms. The comparison in FIG. 6-2 also shows how timer input is directly related to animation speed, which is expressed as frames per second (fps).

## Animation platforms

The sample applications in the next two chapters provide reconfigurable animation engines that can be pasted into your own applications. Each of these animation engines provides a comprehensive animation platform composed of both an authoring platform and a delivery platform.

**Authoring platform** An *authoring platform* is the software that is used on the developer's computer system to design, build, and store an animation sequence. Authoring platforms are also called authoring tools and recording tools.

**Delivery platform**   A *delivery platform* is the software that is used to play the animation sequence on the user's computer. Delivery platforms are also called playback engines, animation engines, and players. The animation engines provided in the program listings in upcoming chapters provide many of the features found in Windows multimedia animation players, including loading an animation sequence, forward play, reverse play, freeze-frame, single-step forward, single-step reverse, and others.

## Animation authoring

Upcoming chapters in the book use sample applications to demonstrate the fundamental processes of animation authoring. These processes are:

- Creative processes.
- Production processes.
- Storage processes.

**Creative processes**   *Creative processes* are concerned with the creation, editing, and development of the storyline that is to be animated. An animation sequence will often be designed using the following creative processes:

- Script.
- Storyboard.
- Soundtrack.
- Bar sheet.
- Exposure sheet.

When these creative processes are complete, production processes are used to build the images for the animation sequence.

**Production processes**   *Production processes* are used to build preliminary images for the animation, test the prototype animation for performance and pacing, and then build the frames for the finished animation. An animation project will usually undergo the following production processes:

- Detailed storyboard.
- Key frames.
- Intermediate frames (tweening).
- Trial animation (pencil test).
- Inking and painting.

When these production processes are complete, storage processes are used to save the animation sequence for distribution and playback.

**Storage processes**   *Storage processes* are used to save the completed frames to hard disk, videotape (VTR), or film. Storage processes are concerned with:

- Storage of images.
- Delivery and playback.
- VTR output and NTSC animation.

Delivery and playback of an animation sequence can be from videotape, hard disk, or film projector. If your animation sequence is intended for television or videotape playback, you should pay careful attention to the timing requirements of NTSC videotape and television, as shown in FIG. 6-3. Television and videotape animation operates at 30 frames per second. This is called *animating on ones*. Each frame is shown for 1/30th second. The Windows SetTimer() function permits a maximum playback rate of 18.2 times per second, as shown previously in FIG. 6-2. For all practicable purposes this rate is equivalent to *animating on twos*—15 frames per second, which is the same as displaying each frame for 2/30th second.

## Performance considerations

Computer animation is hardware-dependent and a number of factors that are outside the author's control can directly affect the performance of your animation sequence at runtime. The most important of these factors are processor speed, display mode, amount of physical memory, and runtime memory mode.

| SetTimer( ) USABLE SETTINGS | | | NTSC VIDEOTAPE AND TELEVISION REQUIREMENTS | | |
|---|---|---|---|---|---|
| clock ticks | ms | fps | animated on ... | ms | fps |
| 1 | 55 | 18.2 | twos | 67 | 15 |
| 2 | 110 | 9.1 | threes | 100 | 10 |
| 3 | 165 | 6.1 | fours/fives | 133/167 | 7.5/6 |
| 4 | 220 | 4.5 | sixes | 200 | 5 |
| 5 | 275 | 3.6 | | | |
| 6 | 330 | 3 | tens | 333 | 3 |
| COMPUTER PLAYBACK | | | VTR PLAYBACK | | |

**6-3** A comparison of animation frame rates between Windows personal computer animation and television animation. The preferred TV and VTR animation rate is 30 frames per second (fps), equivalent to the NTSC screen refresh rate. Motion picture and film animation is usually produced at 24 fps.

**Processor speed**   The processor speed of the user's computer has a direct impact of the runtime performance of your animation sequence. A playback rate of 15 fps is easily achieved and maintained on 25 MHz and 33 MHz machines using the VGA's 640-×-480-×-16 color mode. A 16 MHz computer will have difficulty attaining this rate, however, and a phenomenon known as menu freeze-up may occur during animation playback. Because so much processing power is being used to simply move the next frame to the display, Windows may not be able to snatch enough cycles on the processor to permit it to display a menu that has been selected by the user. The sample applications in the upcoming chapters use a faisafe mechanism to detect if the user is selecting a menu during animation playback. If so, the animation engine idles for a brief interval to allow the Windows API enough time to display the menu.

**Windows memory modes**   The runtime memory mode being used by Windows has significant consequences for your animation sequence. Real mode (no longer supported by Windows 3.1) provides the most restrictive environment for animation. Only 640K of memory is available and the animation engine must often load frames from disk as needed during animation playback. Standard mode provides an improved environment for animation playback because up to 2 MB of memory is available and the processor is running in protected mode. Enhanced mode offers the best runtime environment for animation. Up to 16 MB of physical memory is available, and when physical memory is exhausted the processor provides virtual memory by swapping 4K blocks to the hard disk. The more extended memory available as physical memory on the playback computer, the more frames that can be loaded into RAM by the playback engine.

Properly designed code will produce satisfactory results on both high-end and low-end delivery platforms, however. The sample animations presented in upcoming chapters can generate professional displays on even 16 MHz 80386SX personal computers with only 2 MB RAM. On a computer running at 25 MHz or 33 MHz with 4 MB RAM, the animations are quick, smooth, and flicker-free.

# 7

# *Real-time animation engines*

Real-time animation, also called cast-based animation, uses dynamic images. During animation playback, each image element is drawn by the software at the same time the animation is being displayed on the screen.

The sample application in this chapter provides a working example of a real-time animation engine that you can paste into your own Windows applications. (See chapter 6, Animating in Windows, for a discussion of computer animation concepts and principles. See chapter 8, Frame animation engines, for a working example of a frame animation engine.)

The demo program provides full interactive control over an animated run-cycle, which is illustrated in FIG. 7-1. A *run-cycle* is a loop of images that is repeatedly cycled in order to simulate some form of repetitive movement like running, walking, chewing, blinking, and so on. (See chapter 13, Motion, for a detailed treatment of movement in animation sequences.)

## Preparation of the animation

*Here's How...* During preparation and design of the sample application, the individual drawings that make up the seven cels for the run-cycle were sketched with pencil on professional layout paper. The paper was translucent enough to permit comparison of drawings by superimposition over a portable light table. When the seven drawings were complete, each drawing in turn was placed over the animation grid shown in FIG. 7-2. The grid corresponds to the display window of the sample application. The X-Y coordinates of key elements for each drawing were noted for later use during program development and testing.

**7-1** The seven cels comprising the run-cycle that is demonstrated by the sample application.

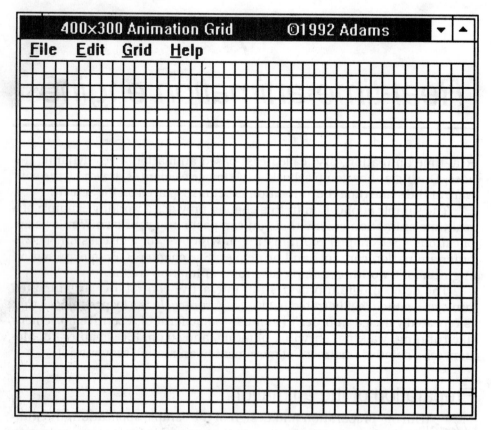

**7-2** The grid template that was used to calculate the X-Y coordinates for the seven cels of FIG. 7-1.

## About the grid

*Tip* The grid is measured in increments of ten pixels per unit. It was created by using the MoveTo() and LineTo() functions of the GDI in a program modified from the sample application presented in chapter 1, Windows. You can create your own personalized grid by building a function containing for() loops similar to the following fragment:

```
        HDC hDC;                                                      /* display-context */
        HPEN ColorPen, PrevPen;                                              /* pens */
        int Count;                                                     /*loop counter */
        int X1, Y1, X2, Y2;                                            /*line vertices */
        int Spacing = 10;                                            /* grid resolution */
        int Width, Depth;                                  /* dimensions of client area */
        RECT rcClientArea;                                     /* coords of client area */
        hDC = GetDC(hWnd);                                    /* set a display-context */
        ColorPen = CreatePen(PS_SOLID,1,RGB(25,0,0));                   /* new pen */
        PrevPen = SelectObject(hDC,ColorPen);                       /* select the pen */
        GetClientRect(hWnd, &rcClientArea);                       /* bounding coords */
        Width = rcClientArea.right;                           /* width of client area */
        Depth = rcClientArea.bottom;                          /* depth of client area */
        X1 = 0; X2 = 0; Y1 = 0; Y2 = Depth;                       /* reset the vertices */
        for (Count = Spacing; Count >= Width; Count + = Spacing) */
        {                                                      /* draw the vertical lines . . . . */
        X1 = Count; MoveTo(hDC,X1,Y1); LineTo(hDC,X1,Y2);
        }
        X1 = 0; X2 = Width; Y1 = 0; Y2 = 0;                       /* reset the vertices */
        for (Count = Spacing; Count <= Depth; Count + = Spacing)
        {                                                    /* draw the horizontal lines . . . */
        Y1 = Count; MoveTo(hDC,X1,Y1); LineTo(hDC,X2,Y1);
        }
        SelectObject(hDC,PrevPen);                             /* deselect the pen */
        DeleteObject(ColorPen);                                  /* delete the pen */
        ReleaseDC(hWnd,hDC);                           /* release the display-context */
```

When your grid meets the requirements of your software development project, print out a supply of grid sheets on your laser printer. Alternatively, you can draw a grid using pen and ink, taking care to preserve the 400 × 300 pixel resolution of the working surface. You can use a photocopier to make multiple copies of your hand-drawn grid.

## The animation algorithm

The real-time animation engine in the sample application is implemented by using a combination of bitblt actors and a hidden bitmap.

At program startup seven bitblts are created. Each bitblt contains the image for one of the seven cels that comprise the run-cycle shown in FIG. 7-1. During animation playback, these bitblts are pasted onto the hidden frame which is then copied to the display window.

For each frame in the animation sequence, the software clears the hidden bitmap, pastes the next bitblt onto the hidden bitmap at an appropriate location, and copies the finished frame to the display window. Whenever the user selects forward, reverse, pause, or single-step from the Animation menu, a runtime token is set by the software. The animation engine checks this token before it prepares the next frame in order to ensure that it is using the appropriate bitblt and location.

The real-time animation demo is implemented as scripted animation using the timer-based message-handler algorithm described in chapter 6, Animating in Windows. The paradigm that is being used is hidden frame bitblt to on-screen. This methodology can produce optimum performance, but it imposes limits on the ability of the user to interact with the animation because all the images have been created in advance. The user can make selections only from existing images.

## Sample application

*Sample App* The screen image in FIG. 7-3 shows the Animation menu from the sample application realtime.exe. This program demonstrates cast-based animation of a run-cycle in real-time. An interactive editor allows you to experiment with different animation player options, including full forward, full reverse, pause, freeze-frame, single-step forward, and single-step reverse. The animation will continue to execute even if the window is partially covered by another window or if the window is partially clipped by the edge of the screen.

The realtime.exe demo is built from four modules, including a .def module definition file, an .h #include file, an .rc resource script file, and a .c source file. All of these production files are presented as ready-to-use source code in the program listings later in this chapter. The source files are also provided on the companion disk. You can refer to the appropriate appendix for instructions on how to build realtime.exe with QuickC for Windows, Turbo C++ for Windows, Borland C++, Zortech C++, WATCOM C, and Microsoft C and the SDK.

## What the program does: A user's guide

*User's Guide* The sample application provides an interactive environment suitable for experimenting with real-time animation. You can use either a mouse or the keyboard to experiment with the demo program. The menus also support mnemonic keys. To view a runtime help message, select Help from the Help menu.

### Creating the cels

Select Create Cels from the Animation menu (see FIG. 7-3) to initialize the real-time animation engine. If you attempt to play the animation before initializing the system, an advisory warning is displayed in a message box, as shown in FIG. 7-4.

When you select Create Cels, the sample application first creates and initializes a hidden bitmap in memory. This is the hidden frame that will be

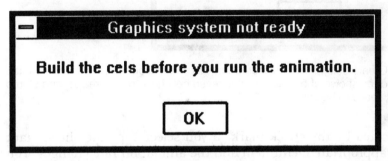

| Animation Engine (real-time version) | ▼ | ▲ |

**File   Edit   Animation   Timer   Help**

> **Run Forward**
> **Run Reverse**
> **Pause**
>
> **Create Cels**
>
> **Clear**

**7-3** The Animation menu from the sample application is used to build the cels and to provide interactive control over playback. Single-step control is provided by using the arrow keypad after selecting Pause from the Animation menu.

─  **Graphics system not ready**

**Build the cels before you run the animation.**

**OK**

**7-4** The realtime animation engine uses internal status flags to ensure the system is ready before an attempt is made to play the animation sequence.

used during animation playback. Next, the demo program draws each of the seven cels that make up the run-cycle. As each drawing is completed, it is stored in memory as a bitblt. The sample application provides status reports as it works, as shown in FIG. 7-5.

## Playing the animation

To play the animation sequence, select Run Forward from the Animation menu (see FIG. 7-3). A silhouette of a running character will dash across the screen from stage right to stage left. A sample image excerpted from the animation sequence is shown in FIG. 7-6. The character will continue running across the screen until you stop the animation.

### Adjusting the animation playback speed

You can increase or decrease the animation speed by selecting from the Timer menu, depicted in FIG. 7-7. At startup the rate is set to 18 frames per second

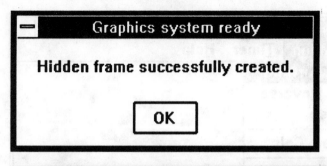

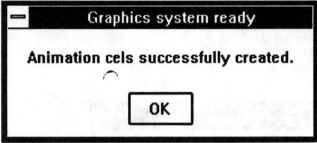

**7-5** When the Create cels items is selected from the Animation menu, a hidden bitmap is initialized, as shown above. Below, the seven cels have been created and stored in memory, ready to be animated.

(fps), as indicated by the check mark. If you select 6 fps the check mark moves to the appropriate menu item and the animation rate changes. You can adjust the playback speed when the animation is running forward, reverse, or paused.

Some slower computers may not be able to sustain a playback rate of 18 fps. An 80386SX running at 16 MHz, for example, is unable to exceed 6 fps when running in the 640-×-480-×-16-color VGA mode. An 80386DX running at 25 MHz or 33 MHz or faster can easily sustain the 18 fps rate. Selecting a rate that is faster than your computer can support will not result in any speed improvement, because the computer is already running at maximum display output.

If you attempt to reset the animation rate before you have initialized the animation engine, the application issues an advisory notice as shown in FIG. 7-8. To initialize the animation engine, select Create Cels from the Animation menu.

## Freeze-frame and single-step animation

**Pause** To pause the animation, select Pause from the Animation menu (see FIG. 7-3). Pause is also called freeze-frame by professional animators. To resume animation playback in full forward mode, select Run Forward from the

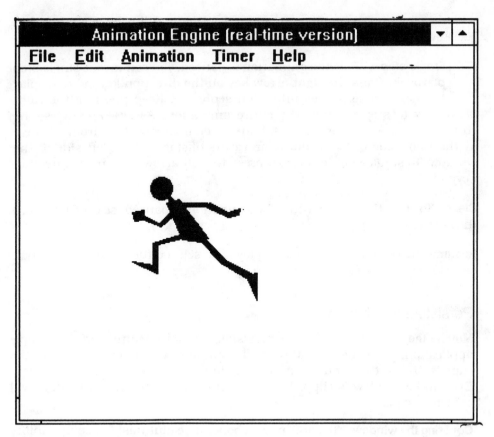

**7-6**  A freezeframe from the animated sample application.

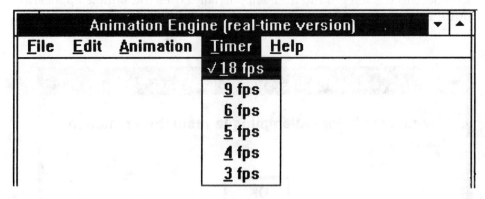

**7-7**  You can use the Timer menu to adjust the playback speed. The available frame speeds are a direct result of the attributes of the system timer chip (see FIG. 6-3 in chapter 6).

Animation menu. To resume animation playback in full reverse mode, select Run Reverse from the Animation menu.

**Single-step** While the animation is paused, you can invoke single-step playback. Press the right arrow key on the direction keypad to display the next frame in the animation sequence. Keep pressing the right arrow key to step through the entire animation. As FIG. 7-9 shows, the run-cycle wraps around. The silhouette character enters from offstage at the right side of the window, and exits offstage at the left side of the window. To single-step in reverse, press the left arrow key on the direction keypad.

**Clear** To clear the display while the animation is paused, select Clear from the Animation menu.

**Resume** To resume full animation playback, select either Run Forward or Run Reverse from the Animation menu.

## Persistent graphics

**Moving the window** To test the persistent graphics features of the sample application, start the animation and then move the window. Click on the caption bar of the window and drag it to another location on the screen. Even if the window is clipped by the edge of the screen the animation will continue to play.

**Covering the window** To confirm the cooperative multitasking compatibility of the sample application, position the window partially over a program group box. Then click on the program group box. The program group box will move to the foreground and will partially cover the sample application, but the animation will continue to run.

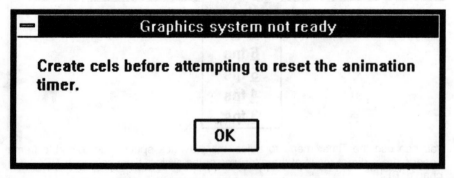

**7-8** The sample application traps any attempt to reset the timer before it has been initialized.

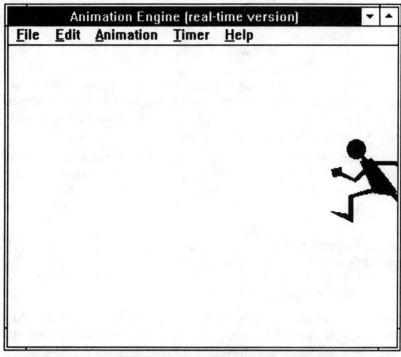

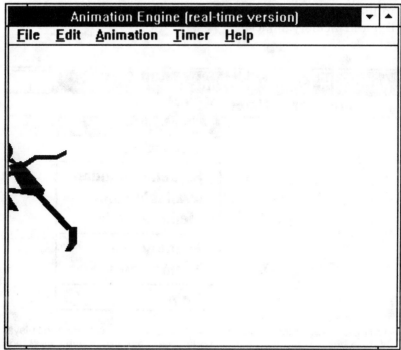

**7-9** The sample application provides an animation sequence that starts from off-stage right and finishes off-stage left.

**Using menus**   You can also select various menus from the sample application while the animation is running and the playback will be unaffected.

## Using the Help menu

You can use the Help menu to discover various facts about your system that are in effect at runtime. See FIG. 7-10. You can determine the current screen mode, the maximum number of available colors, the runtime memory mode (real, standard, or enhanced), and other facts.

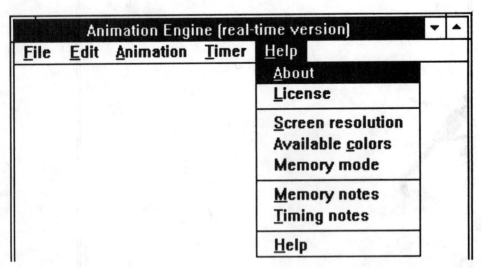 **Checking the screen resolution**   To find out the current screen mode, select Screen resolution from the Help menu. A message box will display the horizontal-by-vertical resolution. The sample application supports 640 × 480, 640 × 350, 800 × 600, and 1024 × 768 resolution displays.

**Maximum displayable colors**   To determine the maximum available colors that can be displayed simultaneously, select Available colors from the Help menu. A message box will indicate the mode. The sample application supports 16-color, 2- color, and 256-color displays.

**Determining the runtime memory mode**   To examine the current Windows runtime memory mode, select Memory mode from the Help menu. A message box will appear, containing an advisory notice describing the mode and its capabilities. The sample application supports real, standard, and enhanced memory modes.

**7-10**   The Help menu provides runtime access to screen resolution, maximum displayable colors, the current Windows memory mode (real, standard, or enhanced), animation memory requirements, and timing considerations.

**Animation memory requirements** To view an informative message concerning animation memory requirements, select Memory notes from the Help menu. The message box shown in FIG. 7-11 appears on the screen.

**Animation timing considerations** To view an informative message about animation playback rates, select Timing notes from the Help menu. The message box shown in FIG. 7-12 appears.

**General help** For a general help message at runtime, select Help from the Help menu.

## How the source code works: A programmer's guide

The realtime.exe demonstration program exercises many of the cast-based, real-time animation features supported by the Windows Graphics Device Interface (GDI). Using the techniques presented in the program listings, you can easily add interactive real-time capabilities to your own applications.

The organization of the .h #include file and the .rc resource script file follow the format established in earlier sample applications. See chapter 2, Graphics, for a prototype program listing for Windows graphics applications. A few new menu items and strings have been added to support the real-time animation features, persistent graphics features, and timing features of real-time.exe. See chapter 1, Windows, for a prototype program listing that demonstrates the mechanics of the .h #include file and the .rc resource script file.

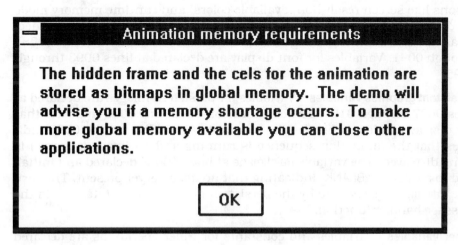

**7-11** The memory requirements message box.

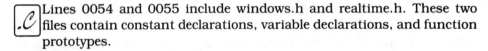

## Animation timing

**The Timer menu sets the animation display rate to 18.2, 9.1, 6.1, 4.5, 3.6, or 3 frames per second. Actual performance is limited by your computer's processor (25MHz or faster is recommended). See the book for details.**

OK

**7-12** The animation timing message box.

## How the .c file works

Lines 0054 and 0055 include windows.h and realtime.h. These two files contain constant declarations, variable declarations, and function prototypes.

**Static variables** Static variables that are visible throughout the .c file are declared at lines 0061 through 0228. Variables and constants that define the runtime appearance of the display window are declared at lines 0061 through 0066. Variables related to the operation of the window at its features are declared at lines 0068 through 0074. Variables for managing the window's cursor and a token that indicates if a mouse is present are declared at lines 0076 through 0079. Variables that will describe runtime conditions like screen resolution, available colors, and runtime memory mode are declared at lines 0081 through 0085. Variables (and arrays) that are necessary for operation of message boxes at runtime are declared at lines 0087 through 0091. Variables for font display are declared at lines 0093 through 0095.

**Persistent graphics variables** Variables for persistent images are declared at lines 0097 through 0100. The constant zBLANK at line 0098 indicates that the display window is blank. The constant zANIMATING at line 0099 indicates that the animation sequence is running and an image (a frame) is being displayed. The variable PaintImage at line 0100 is declared and initialized to a value of zBLANK, indicating that no image is yet present. The variable PaintImage is checked by the persistent graphics case statement in the message handler function.

**Timer variables** Variables and constants for timer operations are declared and initialized at lines 0102 through 0106. The variable TimerID1 at line

0103 identifies a unique timer that will be used by the application at run-time. Windows supports multiple timers among numerous applications that may be running. The constant zTIMER_PAUSE at line 0104 is assigned to a variable named TimerCounter at line 0105. This variable is activated at runtime if the user selects a menu while the animation is playing. The variable is decremented until it reaches zero, thereby forcing a brief pause that allows Windows enough processing time to display the menu. The Boolean variable TimerExists at line 0106 will be used at runtime to indicate that a timer has been set.

**Hidden frame variables**   Variables that support hidden bitmap operations are declared and initialized at lines 0108 through 0112. The HBITMAP handle hFrame at line 0110 is used throughout the .c file whenever an image is being drawn on the hidden frame and whenever the completed frame is being copied to the display window.

**The database**   The keyframe[] arrays that are declared and initialized at lines 0114 through 0199 contain the X-Y drawing coordinates for each of the seven cels that comprise the run-cycle that will be animated in real-time by the demo program. These X-Y coordinates were obtained by placing each pencil sketch over the animation grid described at the beginning of this chapter. The code at lines 0117 through 0132 is commented so you can see how the X-Y coordinates represent the elements of the running silhouette character. Because a similar format is used for each array in the database, the same core function (later in the .c file) can be used to draw each cel, even though the shape of the character in each cel is different, as was illustrated previously in FIG. 7-1.

**Cel variables**   Variables for managing the seven bitblts that hold the seven images are declared at lines 0201 through 0209. The pointer ArrayPtr will be used to point to the appropriate array of X-Y coordinates when the drawing function is called to build the cel images. The HBITMAP variables at lines 0204 through 0205 contain the handles for each of the seven bitblts. The animation engine will use these handles to paste the appropriate bitblt onto the hidden frame at a suitable location when the animation is playing. The Boolean variables declared and initialized at lines 0207 through 0209 are status flags that are used to manage the animation environment at runtime.

**Animation engine variables**   Variables and constants that are needed to support the animation engine are declared and initialized at lines 0211 through 0228. The variable wFrameRate at line 0213 initializes the default animation rate. If you are using a slower machine (such as a 16 MHz 80386SX, for example), you may want to change line 0213 to WORD wFrameRate = 165 ; instead. This will cause the animation to run at 6 frames per second, which is a rate that can be easily sustained by slower machines.

The constants zFORWARD and zREVERSE at lines 0215 and 0216 are used to indicate the direction of playback. The variable FrameDirection at line 0217 is set to zFORWARD, which is the default direction. The animation engine will check the value of FrameDirection when it decides which frame to next display on the screen.

The Boolean variable Redisplay at line 0218 is used whenever the image is being refreshed because of clipping or moving of the display window.

The variables SX1 and SY1 at lines 0219 and 0220 specify the starting position of the first cel in the animation sequence. SY1 does not change during animation playback, but SX1 does. The constant zMOVEHORIZ at line 0221 defines the value that will be used to increment or decrement SX1, depending on whether the animation is playing in forward or reverse. The zMAXLEFT and zMAXRIGHT constants at line 0224 and 0225 indicate the range of cel positions. If the animation is running forward, for example, when the SX1 cel position exceeds the zMAXLEFT value, the SX1 cel position will wrap around to stage right and will continue animating from the zMAXRIGHT position. The variable FrameNum at line 0226 will be used at runtime to keep track of the frame currently being displayed. If the animation is playing in the forward mode, FrameNum will be incremented for the next frame. If the animation is running in reverse, FrameNum will be decremented in order to decided which frame should be next displayed. The constants zFIRSTFRAME and zFINALFRAME at lines 0227 and 0228 are used by the animation engine to ensure that only existing frames are used in the animation.

**WinMain()**   The entry point for the application is the WinMain() function at lines 0234 through 0302. This block of code is similar to the prototype program listing discussed and demonstrated in chapter 2, Graphics.

**Switcher**   The message handler function is located at lines 0308 through 0650. Most of this lengthy function is comprised of overhead and housekeeping functions, including the case statements at lines 0411 through 0556 that manage the various features provided by the Help menu, which include message boxes for runtime help, licensing notes, screen resolution, available colors, runtime memory mode (real, standard, or enhanced), animation memory requirements, and timing notes.

The case WM_TIMER: statement at line 0316 is activated on each timer event. The variable TimerCounter is decremented and tested, then it is incremented. Under normal runtime circumstances, this means that TimerCounter will be maintained at a value of 1 and the call to zShowNextFrame() at line 0320 will execute. However, if the software has detected that the user is attempting to select a menu during animation playback, it will set TimerCounter to a value of zTIMER_PAUSE (refer to line 0105). This means that the code at lines 0317 and 0318 will need to be transversed twice before zShowNextFrame() can be called again by line 0320. This brief delay, consisting of three timed intervals, is required on slower machines in order to give the Windows API enough processing time to install the menu on the screen.

The delay is not needed by faster machines running at 25 MHz, 33 MHz, or faster—and is not noticeable because the animation is running so quickly.

The case blocks at lines 0338 through 0376 are activated when the user changes from forward to reverse or vice versa—or when the user resumes animation playback after the system has been paused. Note the inclusion of the if() statements at lines 0339 and 0354. This trap keeps the program from crashing if the user selects Run Forward or Run Reverse from the Animation menu before the cels have been created. Observe also how the variables Pause, PaintImage, and FrameDirection are reset before calling zShowNext-Frame() to display the next frame in the animation sequence.

The case block at lines 0386 through 0370 is activated whenever the user pauses the animation. The code resets the Pause variable and then calls zShowNextFrame().

The IDM_BuildCels case at lines 0371 through 0384 is invoked when the user selects Build Cels from the Animate menu. The if() statement at line 0372 ensures that the software does not attempt to rebuild cels that already exist. The call to zInitFrame() at line 0381 initializes the hidden bitmap that will be used as a hidden frame. The call to zBuildCels() at line 0383 draws and saves the cels at bitblts in memory.

The case statements from line 0392 to line 0409 are activated when the user resets the animation playback rate. After first storing the current frame rate in a variable named wPrevRate, the code resets wFrameRate to an appropriate value (see FIG. 6-2 in chapter 6, Animating in Windows). The code then calls a function named zSetFrameRate() to reset the timer.

The WM_INITMENUPOPUP case block at lines 0560 through 0564 is activated whenever the user attempts to select a menu during animation playback. Note line 0561, where TimerCounter is reset to a value of zTIMER_PAUSE. If you refer back to lines 0316 through 0321 you can see how this causes the animation to pause momentarily to give Windows enough processing time to display the menu on the screen. Also note lines 0562 and 0563 in the WM_INITMENUPOPUP case block. These lines remember the ID of the menu (if it was the Timer menu) and store it in the hMenu variable. The zSetFrameRate() function will use hMenu to help it reposition the check mark on the menu whenever a new animation rate is chosen by the user.

The WM_PAINT case block at lines 0566 through 0578 handles the persistent graphics operations. A WM_PAINT message is sent to the application by Windows whenever the client area (image area) of the window needs to be refreshed. This could result from moving, clipping, or uncovering the window at runtime. The code at lines 0570 through 0576 uses an if() statement to determine if the animation is paused. It sets Redisplay to TRUE before calling zShowNextFrame(), which will simply redisplay the current frame, otherwise the call to zShowNextFrame() at line 0577 will calculate the display the next frame in the animation sequence.

The WM_KEYDOWN case block at lines 0580 through 0610 detects the right arrow key and the left arrow key of the direction keypad. The case VK_LEFT statement at line 0583, for example, is activated if the left arrow key is pressed. The code first checks to ensure that the animation is paused. If so, it temporarily disables the Pause variable while it calls zShowNext-Frame() to display the next frame. If Pause was not disabled, the failsafe mechanism built into zShowNextFrame() would refuse to display any frame whatsoever.

The case block at lines 0612 through 0630 is invoked when the application is about to be terminated. If bitblts have been created in memory, the code at lines 0615 through 0620 deletes them. The call to KillTimer() at line 0621 releases the timer for use by other applications. If a hidden frame has been created, the code at lines 0625 through 0627 deletes it, freeing the memory for use by other applications.

**Creating the bitblts**   The zBuildCels() function at lines 0700 through 0873 draws the seven cels and stores them as bitblts in memory, ready to be animated. The manipulation of the CelsReady and CelsCalled variables at lines 0703 through 0705 ensure that zBuildCels() will be called only once during any working session. The call to GlobalCompact() at line 0706 causes the Windows memory manager to maximize contiguous memory, helping assure that enough memory will be available to store the bitblts.

A compatible memory-display context is created at line 0710. The code then creates a compatible bitmap and stores its handle in the Cel1 variable at line 0711. If the call to CreateCompatibleBitmap() fails, then the block of code at lines 0712 through 0721 tidies up and exits. This algorithm is repeated for each of the remaining cels.

After compatible bitmaps have been successfully created for each of the seven cels, the code at lines 0801 through 0835 draws an image and stores it in each cel. The code at lines 0801 through 0806 is commented to help you see what is happening. Note how the pointer named ArrayPtr is updated to point to the appropriate array of X-Y coordinates.

The code repeatedly calls zDrawOneCartoon() to draw the appropriate cel using the array of X-Y coordinates. The GDI's BitBlt() function is used to copy each completed cel to the appropriate bitblt in memory.

The timer is initialized by the code at lines 0840 through 0864. The call to SetTimer() at line 0840 uses the wFrameRate variable, which was initialized at line 0213. If the timer cannot be set, the if() statement at line 0842 causes an advisory message to be displayed, and the code then deletes the bitblts that have been created, tidies up, and exits.

Before returning to the caller, the zBuildCels() function sets the Boolean variables TimerExists, CelsReady, and Selected. It also sets FrameNum to a value of 1 at line 0868. The code at lines 0869 through 0871 displays a status report indicating successful initialization of the cels and bitblts.

**Drawing a cel**   The zDrawOneCartoon() function at lines 0879 through 0931 is called seven times by zBuildCels(). The zDrawOne-Cartoon() function uses the array pointed to by ArrayPtr to draw the appropriate cel image. Because each database array is organized in a similar manner, the same code can be used to draw each of the seven images, even though the shape of each image is different. The head is drawn using the GDI's Ellipse() function. The remaining elements are drawn using for() loops and the GDI's Polygon() function.

**Animation engine** The animation engine is contained in the zShowNextFrame() function at lines 0940 through 1004. This function calculates the next frame, builds the image by pasting the appropriate cel bitblt at the updated location on the hidden frame, and then copies the completed frame to the display window. The animation engine is smart enough to detect whether the animation is running forward or reverse. It can also detect whether the animation is paused or being single-stepped in forward or reverse.

The if() statements at lines 0944 through 0946 trap any runtime exceptions. If the bitblts are not ready, the function exits. If the animation is paused, the function exits. If a Redisplay is being requested, the code jumps ahead to line 0963 and simply redisplays the current frame.

The code at lines 0948 through 0961 calculates the next frame number and its updated location on the hidden frame. Line 0948, for example, is activated if the animation is running in forward mode. The variable FrameNum is incremented at line 0950. The if() statement at line 0951 ensures that only existing frame numbers are used. The zFINALFRAME and zFIRSTFRAME constants were defined at lines 0227 and 0228. The SX1 cel position variable is updated at line 0952. The if() statement at line 0953 wraps the position around to the other side of the window if required.

The code at lines 0963 through 0998 draws the next cel on the hidden frame. After first setting a display-context at line 0964, the code calls PatBlt() at line 0967 to clear the hidden frame. Then the switch() block at lines 0968 through 0998 tests FrameNum and jumps to the appropriate case block. The case block at lines 0982 through 0985, for example, pastes cel number four onto the hidden frame. First, a call to SelectObject() selects the appropriate bitblt into the memory-display context hMemoryDC. Then BitBlt() is called to copy the bitblt onto the hidden frame using the SRCCOPY raster operator.

The call to BitBlt() at line 1000 copies the completed frame to the display window. ReleaseDC() is called at line 1002 to release the display-context that was set at line 0964.

**Resetting the animation rate** The function at lines 1010 through 1050 resets the animation rate by resetting the timer. Note the switch() block at lines 1021 through 1029, which uses the hMenu menu ID to remove the check mark from the menu. The hMenu variable was initialized when the software detected that the user was accessing the Timer menu at line 0560 in the message handler function.

The call to KillTimer() at line 1030 disables the current timer. Then a call to SetTimer() at line 1031 sets a new timer using the wNewRate variable that was set in the message handler at lines 0392 through 0409 as a variable named wFrameRate. The code at line 1032 tidies up and exits if the call to SetTimer() failed.

The switch() block at lines 1040 through 1048 places a check mark on the menu. The check mark is located beside the new animation rate.

**Graphics system functions**   The functions from lines 1059 through 1144 perform general maintenance and housekeeping functions for the graphics system. The function zInitFrame() at lines 1059 through 1092 creates the hidden bitmap that acts as the hidden frame. The function zClear() at lines 1098 through 1105 clears the client area of the display window. The function zClearHiddenFrame() at lines 1111 through 1116 clears the hidden frame. The function zCopyToDisplay() at lines 1122 through 1130 copies the contents of the hidden frame to the display window. The function zCopyTo-Frame() at lines 1136 through 1144 copies the contents of the display window to the hidden frame.

# Program listings for the sample application

*Code*   The program listings presented here contain all the source code you need to build and run the sample application. The module definition file is provided in FIG. 7-13. The #include file is found in FIG. 7-14. The resource script file is presented in FIG. 7-15. The C source file is provided in FIG. 7-16.

*Disk*   **Companion disk**   If you have the companion disk, the source files are presented as realtime.def, realtime.h, realtime.rc, and realtime.c.

*License*   **License**   You can paste the royalty-free source code into your own applications and distribute the resulting executable files under the conditions of the License Agreement and Limited Warranty in FIG. 10 in the introduction to the book.

**7-13**   The module definition file listing for the sample application.

```
0001   NAME          DEFDEMO
0002   DESCRIPTION   'Copyright 1992 Lee Adams.  All rights reserved.'
0003   EXETYPE       WINDOWS
0004   STUB          'WINSTUB.EXE'
0005   CODE          PRELOAD MOVEABLE
0006   DATA          PRELOAD MOVEABLE MULTIPLE
0007   HEAPSIZE      1024
0008   STACKSIZE     8192
0009   EXPORTS       zMessageHandler
```

**7-14**   The include file listing for the sample application.

```
0001   /*
0002   -------------------------------------------------------------------
0003                    Include file REALTIME.H
0004           Copyright 1992 Lee Adams.  All rights reserved.
0005       Include this file in the .RC resource script file and in the
```

```
0006      .C source file.  It contains function prototypes, menu ID
0007      constants, and string ID constants.
0008    ------------------------------------------------------------------
0009    ------------------------------------------------------------------
0010                        Function prototypes
0011    ------------------------------------------------------------------
0012                                                                    */
0013    #if !defined(zRCFILE)                    /* if not an .RC file... */
0014      LONG FAR PASCAL zMessageHandler(HWND, unsigned, WORD, LONG);
0015      int PASCAL WinMain(HANDLE,HANDLE,LPSTR,int);
0016      HWND zInitMainWindow(HANDLE);
0017      BOOL zInitClass(HANDLE);
0018    static void zClear(HWND);                      /* blank the viewport */
0019    static void zInitFrame(HWND);                 /* creates hidden frame */
0020    static void zCopyToDisplay(HWND);      /* copies frame to display */
0021    static void zCopyToFrame(HWND);        /* copies display to frame */
0022    static void zClearHiddenFrame(void);        /* clears hidden frame */
0023    static void zBuildCels(HWND);        /* draws cels for animation */
0024    static void zShowNextFrame(HWND);           /* displays next frame */
0025    static void zDrawOneCartoon(HDC);               /* draws one cel */
0026    static void zSetFrameRate(HWND,WORD);        /* resets the timer */
0027    #endif
0028    /*
0029    ------------------------------------------------------------------
0030                        Menu ID constants
0031    ------------------------------------------------------------------
0032                                                                    */
0033    #define IDM_New              1
0034    #define IDM_Open             2
0035    #define IDM_Save             3
0036    #define IDM_SaveAs           4
0037    #define IDM_Exit             5
0038
0039    #define IDM_Undo             6
0040    #define IDM_Cut              7
0041    #define IDM_Copy             8
0042    #define IDM_Paste            9
0043    #define IDM_Delete          10
0044
0045    #define IDM_BuildCels       11
0046    #define IDM_RunForward      12
0047    #define IDM_RunReverse      13
0048    #define IDM_StopAnimation   14
0049    #define IDM_Clear           15
0050
0051    #define IDM_FPS182          16
0052    #define IDM_FPS91           17
0053    #define IDM_FPS61           18
0054    #define IDM_FPS45           19
0055    #define IDM_FPS36           20
0056    #define IDM_FPS30           21
0057
0058    #define IDM_About           22
0059    #define IDM_License         23
0060    #define IDM_Display         24
0061    #define IDM_Colors          25
0062    #define IDM_Mode            26
0063    #define IDM_Memory          27
0064    #define IDM_Timing          28
0065    #define IDM_GeneralHelp     29
0066    /*
```

**7-14**   Continued.

```
0067    -----------------------------------------------------------------
0068                          String ID constants
0069    -----------------------------------------------------------------
0070                                                                    */
0071    #define IDS_Caption      1
0072    #define IDS_Warning      2
0073    #define IDS_NoMouse      3
0074    #define IDS_About        4
0075    #define IDS_AboutText    5
0076    #define IDS_License      6
0077    #define IDS_LicenseText  7
0078    #define IDS_Help         8
0079    #define IDS_HelpText     9
0080    #define IDS_Memory       10
0081    #define IDS_MemText      11
0082    #define IDS_Timing       12
0083    #define IDS_TimingText   13
0084    #define IDS_NotReady     14
0085    #define IDS_Ready        15
0086    #define IDS_BuildBefore  16
0087    #define IDS_CelsAlready  17
0088    #define IDS_Already      18
0089    #define IDS_InsufMem1    19
0090    #define IDS_InsufMem2    20
0091    #define IDS_FrameOK      21
0092    #define IDS_CelsOK       22
0093    #define IDS_NoTimer      23
0094    #define IDS_NoReset      24
0095    #define IDS_CannotReset  25
0096    #define IDS_Resolution   26
0097    #define IDS_ResVGA       27
0098    #define IDS_ResEGA       28
0099    #define IDS_ResCGA       29
0100    #define IDS_ResSVGA      30
0101    #define IDS_Res8514      31
0102    #define IDS_ResHerc      32
0103    #define IDS_ResCustom    33
0104    #define IDS_Color        34
0105    #define IDS_Color16      35
0106    #define IDS_Color256     36
0107    #define IDS_Color2       37
0108    #define IDS_ColorCustom  38
0109    #define IDS_Machine      39
0110    #define IDS_Enhanced     40
0111    #define IDS_Standard     41
0112    #define IDS_Real         42
0113    /*
0114    -----------------------------------------------------------------
0115                          End of include file
0116    -----------------------------------------------------------------
0117                                                                    */
```

**7-15**   The resource script file listing for the sample application.

```
0001    /*
0002    -----------------------------------------------------------------
0003                    Resource script file REALTIME.RC
0004            Copyright 1992 Lee Adams.  All rights reserved.
0005       This file defines the menu resources, the accelerator key
```

```
0006      resources, and the string resources that will be used by the
0007      demonstration application at runtime.
0008    ------------------------------------------------------------------
0009                                                                    */
0010    #define zRCFILE
0011    #include <WINDOWS.H>
0012    #include "REALTIME.H"
0013    /*
0014    ------------------------------------------------------------------
0015                              Script for menus
0016    ------------------------------------------------------------------
0017                                                                    */
0018    MENUS1 MENU
0019      BEGIN
0020      POPUP "&File"
0021        BEGIN
0022          MENUITEM   "&New", IDM_New, GRAYED
0023          MENUITEM   "&Open...", IDM_Open, GRAYED
0024          MENUITEM   "&Save", IDM_Save, GRAYED
0025          MENUITEM   "Save &As...", IDM_SaveAs, GRAYED
0026          MENUITEM SEPARATOR
0027          MENUITEM   "E&xit", IDM_Exit
0028        END
0029      POPUP "&Edit"
0030        BEGIN
0031          MENUITEM   "&Undo\tAlt+BkSp", IDM_Undo, GRAYED
0032          MENUITEM SEPARATOR
0033          MENUITEM   "Cu&t\tShift+Del", IDM_Cut, GRAYED
0034          MENUITEM   "&Copy\tCtrl+Ins", IDM_Copy, GRAYED
0035          MENUITEM   "&Paste\tShift+Ins", IDM_Paste, GRAYED
0036          MENUITEM   "&Delete\tDel", IDM_Delete, GRAYED
0037        END
0038      POPUP "&Animation"
0039        BEGIN
0040          MENUITEM "Run &Forward", IDM_RunForward
0041          MENUITEM "Run &Reverse", IDM_RunReverse
0042          MENUITEM "&Pause", IDM_StopAnimation
0043          MENUITEM SEPARATOR
0044          MENUITEM "Cr&eate Cels", IDM_BuildCels
0045          MENUITEM SEPARATOR
0046          MENUITEM "&Clear", IDM_Clear
0047        END
0048      POPUP "&Timer"
0049        BEGIN
0050          MENUITEM "&18 fps", IDM_FPS182, CHECKED
0051          MENUITEM " &9 fps", IDM_FPS91
0052          MENUITEM " &6 fps", IDM_FPS61
0053          MENUITEM " &5 fps", IDM_FPS45
0054          MENUITEM " &4 fps", IDM_FPS36
0055          MENUITEM " &3 fps", IDM_FPS30
0056        END
0057      POPUP "&Help"
0058        BEGIN
0059          MENUITEM "&About", IDM_About
0060          MENUITEM "&License", IDM_License
0061          MENUITEM SEPARATOR
0062          MENUITEM "&Screen resolution", IDM_Display
0063          MENUITEM "Available &colors", IDM_Colors
0064          MENUITEM "Memory mode", IDM_Mode
0065          MENUITEM SEPARATOR
```

```
0066        MENUITEM "&Memory notes", IDM_Memory
0067        MENUITEM "&Timing notes", IDM_Timing
0068        MENUITEM SEPARATOR
0069        MENUITEM "&Help", IDM_GeneralHelp
0070      END
0071    END
0072  /*
0073  -----------------------------------------------------------------
0074                  Script for accelerator keys
0075  -----------------------------------------------------------------
0076                                                              */
0077  KEYS1 ACCELERATORS
0078    BEGIN
0079    VK_BACK, IDM_Undo, VIRTKEY, ALT
0080    VK_DELETE, IDM_Cut, VIRTKEY, SHIFT
0081    VK_INSERT, IDM_Copy, VIRTKEY, CONTROL
0082    VK_INSERT, IDM_Paste, VIRTKEY, SHIFT
0083    VK_DELETE, IDM_Delete, VIRTKEY
0084    END
0085  /*
0086  -----------------------------------------------------------------
0087                     Script for strings
0088    Programmer's Notes:  If you are typing this listing, set your
0089    margins to a line length of 255 characters so you can create
0090    lengthy strings without embedded carriage returns.  The line
0091    wraparounds in the following STRINGTABLE script are used for
0092    readability only in this printout.
0093  -----------------------------------------------------------------
0094                                                              */
0095  STRINGTABLE
0096    BEGIN
0097      IDS_Caption      "Animation Engine (real-time version)"
0098      IDS_Warning      "Graphics System Warning"
0099      IDS_NoMouse      "No mouse found.  Some features of this
      demonstration program may require a mouse."
0100      IDS_About        "About this program"
0101      IDS_AboutText    "This is a demo from Windcrest McGraw-Hill
      book 4114.  Copyright 1992 Lee Adams.  All rights reserved."
0102      IDS_License      "License Agreement"
0103      IDS_LicenseText "You can use this code as part of your own
      software product subject to the License Agreement and Limited
      Warranty in Windcrest McGraw-Hill book 4114 and on its
      companion disk."
0104      IDS_Help         "How to use this demo"
0105      IDS_HelpText     "The Animation menu manages the animation
      sequence. The Timer menu controls the display rate.  Select
      Create Cels from the Animation menu to begin.  See the book
      for single-step forward and single-step reverse controls."
0106      IDS_Memory       "Animation memory requirements"
0107      IDS_MemText      "The hidden frame and the cels for the
      animation are stored as bitmaps in global memory.  The demo
      will advise you if a memory shortage occurs.  To make more
      global memory available you can close other applications."
0108      IDS_Timing       "Animation timing"
0109      IDS_TimingText  "The Timer menu sets the animation display
      rate to 18.2, 9.1, 6.1, 4.5, 3.6, or 3 frames per second.
      Actual performance is limited by your computer's processor
      (25MHz or faster is recommended).  See the book for details."
0110      IDS_NotReady     "Graphics system not ready"
0111      IDS_Ready        "Graphics system ready"
0112      IDS_FrameOK      "Hidden frame successfully created."
```

**7-15** Continued.

```
0113      IDS_CelsOK        "Animation cels successfully created."
0114      IDS_BuildBefore   "Build the cels before you run the animation."
0115      IDS_CelsAlready   "The cels have already been created."
0116      IDS_Already       "The hidden frame has already been created."
0117      IDS_InsufMem1     "Insufficient memory.  Hidden frame not
          created."
0118      IDS_InsufMem2     "Insufficient memory.  Cel bitmaps not
          created."
0119      IDS_NoTimer       "Unable to create a timer.  Close other
          applications that may be using timers."
0120      IDS_NoReset       "Create cels before attempting to reset the
          animation timer."
0121      IDS_CannotReset   "Unable to reset the timer."
0122      IDS_Resolution    "Screen resolution"
0123      IDS_ResVGA        "Running in 640x480 mode."
0124      IDS_ResEGA        "Running in 640x350 mode."
0125      IDS_ResCGA        "Running in 640x200 mode."
0126      IDS_ResSVGA       "Running in 800x600 mode."
0127      IDS_Res8514       "Running in 1024x768 mode."
0128      IDS_ResHerc       "Running in 720x348 mode."
0129      IDS_ResCustom     "Running in custom mode."
0130      IDS_Color         "Available colors"
0131      IDS_Color16       "Running in 16-color mode."
0132      IDS_Color256      "Running in 256-color mode."
0133      IDS_Color2        "Running in 2-color mode."
0134      IDS_ColorCustom   "Running in a custom color mode."
0135      IDS_Machine       "Memory mode"
0136      IDS_Enhanced      "Running in enhanced mode.  Can allocate up to
          16 MB extended physical memory (XMS) if available.  Virtual
          memory up to 4 times physical memory (maximum 64 MB) is also
          available via automatic disk swapping of 4K pages."
0137      IDS_Standard      "Running in standard mode.  Can allocate up to
          16 MB extended physical memory (XMS) if available."
0138      IDS_Real          "Running in real mode.  Can allocate blocks of
          memory from the first 640K of RAM.  Can also allocate blocks
          from expanded memory (EMS) if available."
0139   END
0140   /*
0141   ------------------------------------------------------------------
0142                  End of resource script file
0143   ------------------------------------------------------------------
0144                                                                   */
```

**7-16** The C source file listing for the sample application, realtime.c. This demonstration program is ready to build using QuickC for Windows, Turbo C++ for Windows, Microsoft C and the SDK, Borland C++, Symantec Zortech C++, WATCOM C, and other compilers. See FIG. 1-2 for sample command-lines to build the program. Guidelines for using your compiler are provided in the appropriate appendix at the back of the book.

```
0001   /*
0002   ------------------------------------------------------------------
0003        Reconfigurable ANIMATION ENGINE for Windows applications
0004              that use real-time hidden-frame animation.
0005   ------------------------------------------------------------------
0006      Source file:  REALTIME.C
0007      Release version: 1.00          Programmer:  Lee Adams
0008      Type:  C source file for Windows application development.
```

```
0009      Compilers: Microsoft C and SDK, Borland C++, Zortech C++,
0010        QuickC for Windows, Turbo C++ for Windows, WATCOM C.
0011      Memory model: small.
0012      Dependencies: REALTIME.DEF module definition file, REALTIME.H
0013                    include file, REALTIME.RC resource script file,
0014                    and REALTIME.C source file.
0015      Output and features: Demonstrates an interactive playback
0016        engine for real-time hidden-frame animation, providing
0017        single-frame and full-motion in both forward and reverse.
0018        The window can be moved but not resized. Each new frame
0019        is assembled on a hidden bitmap that is copied to the
0020        display window when the frame is complete. The animation
0021        sequence will continue to run correctly when (a) menus and
0022        message boxes are displayed, (b) the window is partially
0023        covered by other windows or by program group boxes, or (c)
0024        the window is partially off the screen. The animation
0025        supports VGA, EGA, SuperVGA, 8514/A, XGA, CGA, and Hercules
0026        graphics modes under Windows. The animation plays correctly
0027        in Windows enhanced mode, standard mode, and real mode.
0028        The animation frame rate can be adjusted from 3 to 18 frames
0029        per second on computers from 16MHz to 33MHz.
0030      Animation subject: A seven-frame run-cycle in silhouette.
0031      Recommended hardware: 33 MHz 80386 or 80486, VGA graphics
0032        adapter and monitor, 4 MB memory, mouse.
0033      Minimum suggested hardware: 80386SX running at 16 MHz, VGA
0034        graphics adapter and monitor, 2 MB memory, mouse.
0035      Publication: Contains material from Windcrest/McGraw-Hill book
0036        4114 published by TAB BOOKS Division of McGraw-Hill Inc.
0037      License: As purchaser of the book you are granted a royalty-
0038        free license to distribute executable files generated using
0039        this code provided you accept the conditions of the License
0040        Agreement and Limited Warranty described in the book and on
0041        the companion disk. Government users: This software and
0042        documentation are subject to restrictions set forth in The
0043        Rights in Technical Data and Computer Software clause at
0044        252.227-7013 and elsewhere.
0045      ----------------------------------------------------------------
0046          (c) Copyright 1992 Lee Adams. All rights reserved.
0047          Lee Adams(tm) is a trademark of Lee Adams.
0048      ----------------------------------------------------------------
0049
0050      ----------------------------------------------------------------
0051                        Include files
0052      ----------------------------------------------------------------
0053                                                                  */
0054  #include <WINDOWS.H>
0055  #include "REALTIME.H"
0056  /*
0057  ----------------------------------------------------------------
0058          Static variables visible throughout this file
0059  ----------------------------------------------------------------
0060                                                                  */
0061  /* ------------------- window specifications ------------------- */
0062  #define zWINDOW_WIDTH 408                    /* width of window */
0063  #define zWINDOW_HEIGHT 346                   /* height of window */
0064  #define zFRAMEWIDE 400                 /* width of client area */
0065  #define zFRAMEHIGH 300                 /* height of client area */
0066  int WindowX, WindowY;                    /* location of window */
0067
0068  /* ------------------- instance operations ------------------- */
0069  HANDLE hInst;                         /* handle to this instance */
```

```
0070   HWND MainhWnd;                          /* handle to the main window */
0071   HANDLE hAccel;                   /* handle to accelerator keys table */
0072   HMENU hMenu;                        /* handle to a menu at runtime */
0073   PAINTSTRUCT ps;         /* structure used by persistent graphics */
0074   int MessageRet;             /* will receive value returned by GDI */
0075
0076   /* ------------------ mouse and cursor ---------------------- */
0077   HCURSOR hPrevCursor;                 /* handle to default cursor */
0078   HCURSOR hHourGlass;                /* handle to hourglass cursor */
0079   int MousePresent;          /* will indicate if mouse present */
0080
0081   /* ------------------ runtime conditions -------------------- */
0082   int DisplayWidth, DisplayHeight;       /* screen resolution */
0083   int DisplayBits;                /* number of bits-per-pixel */
0084   int DisplayPlanes;               /* number of bitplanes */
0085   DWORD MemoryMode;               /* runtime memory mode */
0086
0087   /* ----------------- message box operations ------------------- */
0088   char lpCaption[51];        /* will hold caption for message boxes */
0089   int Max= 50;                    /* maximum length of caption */
0090   char lpMessage[250];       /* will hold text for message boxes */
0091   int MaxText= 249;               /* maximum length of text */
0092
0093   /* --------------------- font operations --------------------- */
0094   HFONT hFont, hPrevFont;       /* handles to new, previous font */
0095   HDC hFontDC;                   /* display-context for font */
0096
0097   /* --------------- persistent image operations ---------------- */
0098   #define zBLANK 0                   /* indicates blank image */
0099   #define zANIMATING  1          /* indicates animation running */
0100   int PaintImage= zBLANK;           /* indicates current image */
0101
0102   /* -------------------- timer operations ------------------- */
0103   WORD TimerID1;                        /* identifies a timer */
0104   #define zTIMER_PAUSE 3     /* pauses timer for slow machines... */
0105   int TimerCounter= zTIMER_PAUSE;  /* ...so menus can be displayed */
0106   BOOL TimerExists= FALSE;                /* TRUE if timer is set */
0107
0108   /* ---------------- hidden frame operations ------------------ */
0109   HDC hFrameDC;           /* memory display-context for hidden-frame */
0110   HBITMAP hFrame;                 /* handle to hidden-frame bitmap */
0111   HBITMAP hPrevFrame;                    /* default bitmap */
0112   BOOL FrameReady= FALSE;         /* hidden-frame created? */
0113
0114   /* ---------------- database for cel images ------------------ */
0115   int keyframe1[]=           /* database of xy coords for cel 1... */
0116   {
0117   36,16,                                          /* circle */
0118   45,23,49,27,47,28,42,25,                        /* neck */
0119   54,26,78,54,76,60,57,57,42,30,                  /* torso */
0120   15,25,24,27,23,33,12,32,                    /* leading fist */
0121   22,32,30,44,26,46,20,35,                 /* leading forearm */
0122   45,35,48,38,25,46,23,44,                /* leading upper arm */
0123   55,28,69,20,70,23,58,31,               /* trailing upper arm */
0124   68,20,91,20,91,23,70,23,                /* trailing forearm */
0125   91,20,100,15,100,18,91,23,                 /* trailing hand */
0126   31,52,65,55,71,60,35,55,                   /* leading thigh */
0127   40,57,51,75,41,74,31,52,                   /* leading calf */
0128   46,68,51,75,22,72,40,68,                   /* leading foot */
0129   76,60,106,92,101,94,69,60,                /* trailing thigh */
0130   76,60,106,92,101,94,69,60,                /* trailing calf */
```

```
0131    104,92,111,92,111,108,104,106,                    /* trailing foot */
0132    111,108,105,115,100,115,104,107                   /* trailing toe */
0133    };
0134    int keyframe2[]=
0135    {
0136    36,13,44,20,48,24,43,24,41,21,51,22,77,55,71,58,54,56,40,25,
0137    20,31,20,39,12,40,10,33,20,36,34,43,35,45,20,39,
0138    44,32,46,36,35,45,34,42,54,25,76,25,76,28,54,28,
0139    78,25,95,33,95,37,74,28,95,33,105,30,104,35,95,37,
0140    52,52,54,55,32,60,28,59,28,59,32,60,32,85,28,78,
0141    32,78,32,85,10,75,28,78,75,56,92,73,88,76,70,57,
0142    92,74,116,86,112,90,88,76,116,86,120,85,120,108,112,90,
0143    116,86,120,85,120,108,112,90
0144    };
0145    int keyframe3[]=
0146    {
0147    38,10,45,16,48,21,44,22,41,17,52,20,75,55,70,56,53,54,40,22,
0148    20,36,24,44,17,47,13,40,22,40,40,43,40,47,22,44,
0149    37,43,44,31,47,36,40,47,55,25,76,29,74,31,55,29,
0150    76,29,90,45,85,48,74,31,90,45,100,45,95,49,85,49,
0151    53,54,55,58,35,72,30,69,35,72,16,96,17,85,30,69,
0152    17,85,20,90,17,96,0,80,75,55,92,70,88,74,70,57,
0153    92,70,121,77,122,81,87,73,121,77,126,75,139,95,122,81,
0154    121,77,126,75,139,95,122,81
0155    };
0156    int keyframe4[]=
0157    {
0158    38,13,45,19,48,23,44,25,41,20,52,22,70,56,64,60,46,60,40,26,
0159    32,43,36,46,34,51,27,48,36,46,50,44,50,48,36,49,
0160    36,46,50,44,50,48,36,49,55,35,69,45,62,50,55,40,
0161    55,35,69,45,62,50,55,40,55,35,69,45,62,50,55,40,
0162    46,59,51,60,31,75,26,73,26,73,31,76,25,105,22,97,
0163    22,97,26,99,25,105,0,95,58,60,64,60,58,78,50,78,
0164    58,78,75,85,74,89,50,78,75,85,80,85,80,103,74,88,
0165    75,85,80,85,80,103,74,88
0166    };
0167    int keyframe5[]=
0168    {
0169    38,18,45,25,49,28,43,30,42,26,54,28,56,64,45,66,34,64,40,31,
0170    27,58,26,63,18,58,21,55,28,58,40,56,40,60,25,63,
0171    28,58,40,56,40,60,25,63,54,28,57,48,60,46,54,38,
0172    60,48,66,48,52,53,50,50,60,48,66,48,52,53,50,50,
0173    34,65,40,66,14,76,12,74,22,74,40,78,38,82,12,76,
0174    40,78,46,76,45,96,38,82,40,68,45,66,27,85,20,84,
0175    27,85,33,114,25,107,20,84,25,107,31,107,32,115,5,115,
0176    25,107,31,107,32,115,5,115
0177    };
0178    int keyframe6[]=
0179    {
0180    38,22,41,29,45,35,39,35,39,30,38,36,49,33,60,68,52,70,39,70,
0181    12,48,16,54,11,59,5,51,15,52,34,55,38,59,15,56,
0182    33,55,40,40,50,38,60,50,38,65,50,60,50,50,43,
0183    60,50,65,50,60,67,58,63,60,50,65,50,60,67,58,63,
0184    38,66,39,70,16,80,15,76,22,77,49,85,36,85,16,80,
0185    40,83,49,86,32,102,36,86,45,72,52,70,43,91,38,90,
0186    41,89,62,104,54,103,38,92,53,104,63,104,54,115,49,112,
0187    52,112,53,115,43,115,49,112
0188    };
0189    int keyframe7[]=
0190    {
0191    38,19,45,25,48,30,43,31,42,26,51,30,69,62,60,65,49,61,40,32,
```

```
0192  14,33,15,41,6,42,4,34,15,38,30,45,30,50,15,41,
0193  30,45,41,38,42,42,30,50,53,32,73,36,71,39,55,36,
0194  73,37,83,53,80,55,71,40,83,53,93,55,89,57,80,55,
0195  49,61,60,65,22,65,23,61,31,65,53,81,40,80,23,65,
0196  48,77,53,81,27,89,40,79,61,65,67,63,68,84,63,85,
0197  68,83,84,99,80,101,63,85,81,98,89,98,85,113,80,111,
0198  89,111,85,112,80,115,76,115
0199  };
0200
0201  /* ---------------------- cel imagery ---------------------- */
0202  int * ArrayPtr;                      /* points to array of coords */
0203  HDC hMemoryDC;                /* memory display-context for cels */
0204  HBITMAP Cel1, Cel2, Cel3, Cel4,    /* handles to cel bitmaps... */
0205          Cel5, Cel6, Cel7;
0206  HBITMAP hPrevBitmap;                        /* default bitmap */
0207  BOOL CelsReady= FALSE;                  /* cel bitmaps ready? */
0208  BOOL CelsCalled= FALSE;                 /* cel routine called? */
0209  BOOL Selected= FALSE;              /* bitmap selected into DC? */
0210
0211  /* -------------------- animation engine ---------------------- */
0212  BOOL Pause= TRUE;                         /* animation running? */
0213  WORD wFrameRate= 55;               /* arbitrary rate of 18.2 fps */
0214  WORD wPrevRate= 55;           /* previous frame rate at runtime */
0215  #define zFORWARD 1
0216  #define zREVERSE 0
0217  int FrameDirection= zFORWARD;              /* forward or reverse */
0218  BOOL Redisplay= FALSE;             /* frame redisplay wanted? */
0219  int SX1= 238;                      /* horizontal position of cel */
0220  int SY1= 90;                         /* vertical position of cel */
0221  #define zMOVEHORIZ 26      /* distance to move each cel on frame */
0222  #define zWIDE 164                            /* width of cel */
0223  #define zHIGH 116                           /* height of cel */
0224  #define zMAXLEFT -164      /* left-most legal position of cel */
0225  #define zMAXRIGHT 400      /* right-most legal position of cel */
0226  int FrameNum= 0;                   /* current frame identifier */
0227  #define zFIRSTFRAME 1      /* first frame in animation sequence */
0228  #define zFINALFRAME 7      /* final frame in animation sequence */
0229  /*
0230  -----------------------------------------------------------------
0231                    Entry point for the application
0232  -----------------------------------------------------------------
0233                                                                  */
0234  int PASCAL WinMain(HANDLE hInstance, HANDLE hPrevInstance,
0235                     LPSTR lpCmdLine, int nCmdShow)
0236  {
0237    MSG msg;                        /* will hold incoming messages */
0238    HWND hWndPrev;          /* handle to window of another instance */
0239    HWND hDesktopWnd;       /* handle to full-screen desktop window */
0240    HDC hDCcaps;                /* display-context of desktop window */
0241
0242  /* ----------- ensure only one instance is running ----------- */
0243  hWndPrev = FindWindow("DEMOCLASS", NULL);
0244  if (hWndPrev != NULL)          /* if another instance was found... */
0245    {
0246    BringWindowToTop(hWndPrev);                 /* make it active... */
0247    return FALSE;                 /* ...and terminate this instance */
0248    }
0249
0250  /* --------- determine capabilities of screen display ---------- */
0251  hDesktopWnd= GetDesktopWindow();
0252  hDCcaps= GetDC(hDesktopWnd);
```

```
0253   DisplayWidth= GetDeviceCaps(hDCcaps,HORZRES);
0254   DisplayHeight= GetDeviceCaps(hDCcaps,VERTRES);
0255   DisplayBits= GetDeviceCaps(hDCcaps,BITSPIXEL);
0256   DisplayPlanes= GetDeviceCaps(hDCcaps,PLANES);
0257   ReleaseDC(hDesktopWnd,hDCcaps);
0258
0259   /* ------- calculate screen position to center the window ------ */
0260   WindowX= (DisplayWidth - zWINDOW_WIDTH) / 2;          /* horizontal */
0261   WindowY= (DisplayHeight - zWINDOW_HEIGHT) /2;           /* vertical */
0262   if (WindowX < 0) WindowX= 0;
0263   if (WindowY < 0) WindowY= 0;
0264
0265   /* ---- determine memory mode (enhanced, standard, or real) ---- */
0266   MemoryMode= GetWinFlags();          /* will read this value later */
0267
0268   /* ------------- create and display the window --------------- */
0269   hInst= hInstance;                   /* remember the instance handle */
0270   if (!zInitClass(hInstance)) return FALSE;     /* create the class */
0271   MainhWnd= zInitMainWindow(hInstance);       /* create the window */
0272   if (!MainhWnd) return FALSE;     /* exit if no window was created */
0273   ShowWindow(MainhWnd, nCmdShow);             /* display the window */
0274   UpdateWindow(MainhWnd);                    /* send a paint message */
0275   hAccel= LoadAccelerators(hInstance,"KEYS1"); /* accelerator keys */
0276   hFontDC= GetDC(MainhWnd);              /* get a display-context */
0277   hFont= GetStockObject(SYSTEM_FONT);       /* grab handle to font */
0278   hPrevFont= SelectObject(hFontDC,hFont);   /* select font into DC */
0279   SetTextColor(hFontDC,RGB(191,191,191));     /* set new text color */
0280   TextOut(hFontDC,10,280,"- Copyright 1992 Lee Adams.",27);/* text */
0281   SetTextColor(hFontDC,RGB(255,255,255));    /* restore text color */
0282   SelectObject(hFontDC,hPrevFont);         /* restore previous font */
0283   ReleaseDC(MainhWnd,hFontDC);          /* release display-context */
0284
0285   /* --------------------- check for mouse --------------------- */
0286   MousePresent= GetSystemMetrics(SM_MOUSEPRESENT);
0287   if (!MousePresent)                   /* if no active mouse found */
0288     {
0289     LoadString(hInst,IDS_Warning,lpCaption,Max);   /* load caption */
0290     LoadString(hInst,IDS_NoMouse,lpMessage,MaxText);  /* load text */
0291     MessageBox(GetFocus(),lpMessage,lpCaption,MB_OK);  /* message */
0292     }
0293
0294   /* ---------- begin retrieving messages for the window --------- */
0295   while (GetMessage(&msg,0,0,0))
0296     {
0297     if(TranslateAccelerator(MainhWnd, hAccel, &msg)) continue;
0298     TranslateMessage(&msg);
0299     DispatchMessage(&msg);
0300     }
0301   return(msg.wParam);
0302   }
0303   /*
0304   -------------------------------------------------------------------
0305                     Switcher for incoming messages
0306   -------------------------------------------------------------------
0307                                                                     */
0308   LONG FAR PASCAL zMessageHandler(HWND hWnd, unsigned message,
0309                          WORD wParam, LONG lParam)
0310   {
0311     HDC hDCpaint;       /* display-context for persistent graphics */
0312
0313   switch (message)
```

```
0314    {
0315
0316    case WM_TIMER:                                /* if a timer event... */
0317      TimerCounter--;
0318      if (TimerCounter > 0) break;
0319      TimerCounter++;
0320      zShowNextFrame(hWnd);
0321      break;
0322
0323    case WM_COMMAND:            /* if user has selected a menu item... */
0324      switch(wParam)
0325        {
0326        case IDM_New:          break;
0327        case IDM_Open:         break;
0328        case IDM_Save:         break;
0329        case IDM_SaveAs:       break;
0330        case IDM_Exit:         PostQuitMessage(0); break;
0331
0332        case IDM_Undo:         break;
0333        case IDM_Cut:          break;
0334        case IDM_Copy:         break;
0335        case IDM_Paste:        break;
0336        case IDM_Delete:       break;
0337
0338        case IDM_RunForward:
0339            if (CelsReady==FALSE)
0340              {
0341              MessageBeep(0);
0342              LoadString(hInst,IDS_NotReady,lpCaption,Max);
0343              LoadString(hInst,IDS_BuildBefore,lpMessage,MaxText);
0344              TimerCounter= zTIMER_PAUSE;
0345              MessageBox(GetFocus(),lpMessage,lpCaption,MB_OK);
0346              break;
0347              }
0348            Pause= FALSE;
0349            PaintImage= zANIMATING;
0350            FrameDirection= zFORWARD;
0351            zShowNextFrame(hWnd);
0352            break;
0353        case IDM_RunReverse:
0354            if (CelsReady==FALSE)
0355              {
0356              MessageBeep(0);
0357              LoadString(hInst,IDS_NotReady,lpCaption,Max);
0358              LoadString(hInst,IDS_BuildBefore,lpMessage,MaxText);
0359              TimerCounter= zTIMER_PAUSE;
0360              MessageBox(GetFocus(),lpMessage,lpCaption,MB_OK);
0361              break;
0362              }
0363            Pause= FALSE;
0364            PaintImage= zANIMATING;
0365            FrameDirection= zREVERSE;
0366            zShowNextFrame(hWnd);
0367            break;
0368        case IDM_StopAnimation: Pause= TRUE;
0369                                zShowNextFrame(hWnd);
0370                                break;
0371        case IDM_BuildCels:
0372          if (CelsReady==TRUE)        /* if cels already created... */
0373            {
0374            MessageBeep(0);
```

```
0375                 LoadString(hInst,IDS_Ready,lpCaption,Max);
0376                 LoadString(hInst,IDS_CelsAlready,lpMessage,MaxText);
0377                 TimerCounter= zTIMER_PAUSE;
0378                 MessageBox(GetFocus(),lpMessage,lpCaption,MB_OK);
0379             break;
0380             }
0381         zInitFrame(hWnd);
0382         if (FrameReady==FALSE) break;
0383         zBuildCels(hWnd);
0384         break;
0385     case IDM_Clear:  if (Pause==TRUE)
0386                         {
0387                         zClear(hWnd);
0388                         PaintImage= zBLANK;
0389                         }
0390                     break;
0391
0392     case IDM_FPS182: wPrevRate= wFrameRate;
0393                     wFrameRate= (WORD)55;
0394                     zSetFrameRate(hWnd, wFrameRate); break;
0395     case IDM_FPS91:  wPrevRate= wFrameRate;
0396                     wFrameRate= (WORD)110;
0397                     zSetFrameRate(hWnd, wFrameRate); break;
0398     case IDM_FPS61:  wPrevRate= wFrameRate;
0399                     wFrameRate= (WORD)165;
0400                     zSetFrameRate(hWnd, wFrameRate); break;
0401     case IDM_FPS45:  wPrevRate= wFrameRate;
0402                     wFrameRate= (WORD) 220;
0403                     zSetFrameRate(hWnd, wFrameRate); break;
0404     case IDM_FPS36:  wPrevRate= wFrameRate;
0405                     wFrameRate= (WORD) 275;
0406                     zSetFrameRate(hWnd, wFrameRate); break;
0407     case IDM_FPS30:  wPrevRate= wFrameRate;
0408                     wFrameRate= (WORD) 330;
0409                     zSetFrameRate(hWnd, wFrameRate); break;
0410
0411     case IDM_About:
0412       LoadString(hInst,IDS_About,lpCaption,Max);
0413       LoadString(hInst,IDS_AboutText,lpMessage,MaxText);
0414       TimerCounter= zTIMER_PAUSE;
0415       MessageBox(GetFocus(),lpMessage,lpCaption,MB_OK);
0416       break;
0417     case IDM_License:
0418       LoadString(hInst,IDS_License,lpCaption,Max);
0419       LoadString(hInst,IDS_LicenseText,lpMessage,MaxText);
0420       TimerCounter= zTIMER_PAUSE;
0421       MessageBox(GetFocus(),lpMessage,lpCaption,MB_OK);
0422       break;
0423
0424     case IDM_Display:
0425       if (DisplayWidth==640)
0426         {
0427         if (DisplayHeight==480)
0428           {
0429           LoadString(hInst,IDS_Resolution,lpCaption,Max);
0430           LoadString(hInst,IDS_ResVGA,lpMessage,MaxText);
0431           TimerCounter= zTIMER_PAUSE;
0432           MessageBox(GetFocus(),lpMessage,lpCaption,MB_OK);
0433           }
0434         if (DisplayHeight==350)
0435           {
```

```
0436                    LoadString(hInst,IDS_Resolution,lpCaption,Max);
0437                    LoadString(hInst,IDS_ResEGA,lpMessage,MaxText);
0438                    TimerCounter= zTIMER_PAUSE;
0439                    MessageBox(GetFocus(),lpMessage,lpCaption,MB_OK);
0440                  }
0441              if (DisplayHeight==200)
0442                  {
0443                    LoadString(hInst,IDS_Resolution,lpCaption,Max);
0444                    LoadString(hInst,IDS_ResCGA,lpMessage,MaxText);
0445                    TimerCounter= zTIMER_PAUSE;
0446                    MessageBox(GetFocus(),lpMessage,lpCaption,MB_OK);
0447                  }
0448              break;
0449                }
0450            if (DisplayWidth==800)
0451                {
0452                LoadString(hInst,IDS_Resolution,lpCaption,Max);
0453                LoadString(hInst,IDS_ResSVGA,lpMessage,MaxText);
0454                TimerCounter= zTIMER_PAUSE;
0455                MessageBox(GetFocus(),lpMessage,lpCaption,MB_OK);
0456                break;
0457                }
0458            if (DisplayWidth==1024)
0459                {
0460                LoadString(hInst,IDS_Resolution,lpCaption,Max);
0461                LoadString(hInst,IDS_Res8514,lpMessage,MaxText);
0462                TimerCounter= zTIMER_PAUSE;
0463                MessageBox(GetFocus(),lpMessage,lpCaption,MB_OK);
0464                break;
0465                }
0466            if (DisplayWidth==720)
0467                {
0468                LoadString(hInst,IDS_Resolution,lpCaption,Max);
0469                LoadString(hInst,IDS_ResHerc,lpMessage,MaxText);
0470                TimerCounter= zTIMER_PAUSE;
0471                MessageBox(GetFocus(),lpMessage,lpCaption,MB_OK);
0472                break;
0473                }
0474            LoadString(hInst,IDS_Resolution,lpCaption,Max);
0475            LoadString(hInst,IDS_ResCustom,lpMessage,MaxText);
0476            TimerCounter= zTIMER_PAUSE;
0477            MessageBox(GetFocus(),lpMessage,lpCaption,MB_OK);
0478            break;
0479
0480        case IDM_Colors:
0481            if (DisplayBits==1)
0482                {
0483                if (DisplayPlanes==4)
0484                    {
0485                    LoadString(hInst,IDS_Color,lpCaption,Max);
0486                    LoadString(hInst,IDS_Color16,lpMessage,MaxText);
0487                    TimerCounter= zTIMER_PAUSE;
0488                    MessageBox(GetFocus(),lpMessage,lpCaption,MB_OK);
0489                    break;
0490                    }
0491                if (DisplayPlanes==1)
0492                    {
0493                    LoadString(hInst,IDS_Color,lpCaption,Max);
0494                    LoadString(hInst,IDS_Color2,lpMessage,MaxText);
0495                    TimerCounter= zTIMER_PAUSE;
0496                    MessageBox(GetFocus(),lpMessage,lpCaption,MB_OK);
```

```
0497              break;
0498                }
0499            }
0500        if (DisplayBits==8)
0501            {
0502          LoadString(hInst,IDS_Color,lpCaption,Max);
0503          LoadString(hInst,IDS_Color256,lpMessage,MaxText);
0504          TimerCounter= zTIMER_PAUSE;
0505          MessageBox(GetFocus(),lpMessage,lpCaption,MB_OK);
0506          break;
0507            }
0508        LoadString(hInst,IDS_Color,lpCaption,Max);
0509        LoadString(hInst,IDS_ColorCustom,lpMessage,MaxText);
0510        TimerCounter= zTIMER_PAUSE;
0511        MessageBox(GetFocus(),lpMessage,lpCaption,MB_OK);
0512        break;
0513
0514      case IDM_Mode:
0515        if (MemoryMode & WF_ENHANCED)
0516            {
0517          LoadString(hInst,IDS_Machine,lpCaption,Max);
0518          LoadString(hInst,IDS_Enhanced,lpMessage,MaxText);
0519          TimerCounter= zTIMER_PAUSE;
0520          MessageBox(GetFocus(),lpMessage,lpCaption,MB_OK);
0521          break;
0522            }
0523        if (MemoryMode & WF_STANDARD)
0524            {
0525          LoadString(hInst,IDS_Machine,lpCaption,Max);
0526          LoadString(hInst,IDS_Standard,lpMessage,MaxText);
0527          TimerCounter= zTIMER_PAUSE;
0528          MessageBox(GetFocus(),lpMessage,lpCaption,MB_OK);
0529          break;
0530            }
0531        LoadString(hInst,IDS_Machine,lpCaption,Max);
0532        LoadString(hInst,IDS_Real,lpMessage,MaxText);
0533        TimerCounter= zTIMER_PAUSE;
0534        MessageBox(GetFocus(),lpMessage,lpCaption,MB_OK);
0535        break;
0536
0537      case IDM_Memory:
0538        LoadString(hInst,IDS_Memory,lpCaption,Max);
0539        LoadString(hInst,IDS_MemText,lpMessage,MaxText);
0540        TimerCounter= zTIMER_PAUSE;
0541        MessageBox(GetFocus(),lpMessage,lpCaption,MB_OK);
0542        break;
0543      case IDM_Timing:
0544        LoadString(hInst,IDS_Timing,lpCaption,Max);
0545        LoadString(hInst,IDS_TimingText,lpMessage,MaxText);
0546        TimerCounter= zTIMER_PAUSE;
0547        MessageBox(GetFocus(),lpMessage,lpCaption,MB_OK);
0548        break;
0549      case IDM_GeneralHelp:
0550        LoadString(hInst,IDS_Help,lpCaption,Max);
0551        LoadString(hInst,IDS_HelpText,lpMessage,MaxText);
0552        TimerCounter= zTIMER_PAUSE;
0553        MessageBox(GetFocus(),lpMessage,lpCaption,MB_OK);
0554        break;
0555      default:
0556        return(DefWindowProc(hWnd, message, wParam, lParam));
```

```
0557      }
0558    break;
0559
0560  case WM_INITMENUPOPUP:        /* if menu about to be displayed... */
0561    TimerCounter= zTIMER_PAUSE;       /* suspend the timer events */
0562    if (lParam == 3)                          /* if Timer menu... */
0563      hMenu= wParam;                    /* remember the menu handle */
0564    break;
0565
0566  case WM_PAINT:               /* if image needs to be refreshed... */
0567    hDCpaint= BeginPaint(hWnd,&ps);            /* load structure */
0568    EndPaint(hWnd, &ps);                /* validate client area */
0569    if (PaintImage==zBLANK) break;    /* if client area is blank */
0570    if (Pause==TRUE)                       /* if a freezeframe... */
0571      {
0572      Redisplay= TRUE;
0573      zShowNextFrame(hWnd);
0574      Redisplay= FALSE;
0575      break;
0576      }
0577    zShowNextFrame(hWnd);               /* if animation is running */
0578    break;
0579
0580  case WM_KEYDOWN:            /* if user has pressed a keystroke... */
0581    switch (wParam)
0582      {
0583      case VK_LEFT:     if (Pause==TRUE)
0584                          {
0585                          if (FrameDirection==zFORWARD)
0586                            {
0587                            FrameDirection= zREVERSE;
0588                            }
0589                          Pause= FALSE;
0590                          zShowNextFrame(hWnd);
0591                          Pause= TRUE;
0592                          PaintImage= zANIMATING;
0593                          }
0594                        break;
0595      case VK_RIGHT:    if (Pause==TRUE)
0596                          {
0597                          if (FrameDirection==zREVERSE)
0598                            {
0599                            FrameDirection= zFORWARD;
0600                            }
0601                          Pause= FALSE;
0602                          zShowNextFrame(hWnd);
0603                          Pause= TRUE;
0604                          PaintImage= zANIMATING;
0605                          }
0606                        break;
0607      default:      /* otherwise pass message to default handler */
0608              return(DefWindowProc(hWnd, message, wParam, lParam));
0609      }
0610    break;
0611
0612  case WM_DESTROY: /* if user is terminating the application... */
0613    if (CelsReady == TRUE)              /* if cels were created... */
0614      {
0615      SelectObject(hMemoryDC,hPrevBitmap);     /* deselect bitmap */
0616      DeleteObject(Cel1);              /* delete the cel bitmaps... */
```

```
0617          DeleteObject(Cel2); DeleteObject(Cel3);
0618          DeleteObject(Cel4); DeleteObject(Cel5);
0619          DeleteObject(Cel6); DeleteObject(Cel7);
0620          DeleteDC(hMemoryDC);              /* delete the memory DC */
0621          KillTimer(hWnd,1);               /* and release the timer */
0622          }
0623       if (FrameReady == TRUE)     /* if hidden frame was created... */
0624          {
0625          SelectObject(hFrameDC,hPrevFrame);       /* deselect bitmap */
0626          DeleteObject(hFrame);          /* delete the hidden frame */
0627          DeleteDC(hFrameDC);            /* delete the memory DC */
0628          }
0629       PostQuitMessage(0);              /* tidy up and terminate */
0630       break;
0631
0632     case WM_SYSCOMMAND:     /* intercept resize, minimize, maximize */
0633       if ((wParam & 0xfff0)== SC_SIZE)
0634          {
0635          MessageBeep(0); break;
0636          }
0637       if ((wParam & 0xfff0)== SC_MINIMIZE)
0638          {
0639          MessageBeep(0); break;
0640          }
0641       if ((wParam & 0xfff0)== SC_MAXIMIZE)
0642          {
0643          MessageBeep(0); break;
0644          }
0645
0646     default:
0647       return(DefWindowProc(hWnd, message, wParam, lParam));
0648     }
0649   return FALSE;
0650   }
0651   /*
0652   -----------------------------------------------------------------
0653              Initialize the attributes of the window class
0654   -----------------------------------------------------------------
0655                                                                   */
0656   BOOL zInitClass(HANDLE hInstance)
0657   {
0658     WNDCLASS WndClass;
0659   WndClass.style= 0;                               /* class style */
0660   WndClass.lpfnWndProc= zMessageHandler;       /* callback function */
0661   WndClass.cbClsExtra= 0;            /* unused, no customized data */
0662   WndClass.cbWndExtra= 0;            /* unused, no customized data */
0663   WndClass.hInstance= hInstance;     /* application that owns class */
0664   WndClass.hIcon= LoadIcon(NULL,IDI_EXCLAMATION); /* minimize icon */
0665   WndClass.hCursor= LoadCursor(NULL,IDC_ARROW);   /* app's cursor */
0666   WndClass.hbrBackground= /* specifies background color of window */
0667                          CreateSolidBrush(RGB(255,255,255));
0668   WndClass.lpszMenuName= "MENUS1";     /* name of .RC menu resource */
0669   WndClass.lpszClassName= "DEMOCLASS";        /* name of the class */
0670   return RegisterClass(&WndClass);        /* registers the class */
0671   }
0672   /*
0673   -----------------------------------------------------------------
0674                      Create the main window
0675   -----------------------------------------------------------------
0676                                                                   */
0677   HWND zInitMainWindow(HANDLE hInstance)
```

```
0678  {
0679    HWND hWnd;
0680  LoadString(hInstance,IDS_Caption,lpCaption,Max); /* load caption */
0681  hHourGlass= LoadCursor(NULL,IDC_WAIT);    /* load the wait cursor */
0682  hWnd= CreateWindow("DEMOCLASS",   /* create window of this class */
0683        lpCaption,                             /* caption */
0684        WS_OVERLAPPED | WS_THICKFRAME | WS_MINIMIZEBOX |   /* type */
0685          WS_MAXIMIZEBOX | WS_CLIPCHILDREN,
0686        WindowX,WindowY,                      /* screen location */
0687        zWINDOW_WIDTH,zWINDOW_HEIGHT,         /* window dimensions */
0688        0,0,                      /* parent handle, menu or child ID */
0689        hInstance,(LPSTR)NULL); /* app instance and unused pointer */
0690  return hWnd;
0691  }
0692  /*
0693  ------------------------------------------------------------------
0694                       ANIMATION FUNCTIONS
0695  ------------------------------------------------------------------
0696  ------------------------------------------------------------------
0697                  Create the bitmaps for the cels.
0698  ------------------------------------------------------------------
0699
0700  static void zBuildCels(HWND hWnd)
0701  {
0702    HDC hDisplayDC;                            /* display-context */
0703  if (CelsReady == TRUE) return;           /* cels already created */
0704  if (CelsCalled == TRUE) return;    /* if this func already called */
0705  CelsCalled= TRUE;               /* this func callable once only */
0706  GlobalCompact((DWORD)-1L);          /* maximize contiguous memory */
0707  hDisplayDC= GetDC(hWnd);                 /* set the display-context */
0708
0709  /* --------------------- create the cels --------------------- */
0710  hMemoryDC= CreateCompatibleDC(hDisplayDC);     /* create cels... */
0711  Cel1= CreateCompatibleBitmap(hDisplayDC,zWIDE,zHIGH);
0712  if (Cel1==NULL)
0713    {
0714    LoadString(hInst,IDS_NotReady,lpCaption,Max);
0715    LoadString(hInst,IDS_InsufMem2,lpMessage,MaxText);
0716    MessageBox(GetFocus(),lpMessage,lpCaption,MB_OK);
0717    DeleteDC(hMemoryDC);
0718    SelectObject(hFrameDC,hPrevFrame);
0719    DeleteObject(hFrame); DeleteDC(hFrameDC);
0720    TimerExists= FALSE; CelsReady= FALSE; Selected= FALSE; return;
0721    }
0722  Cel2= CreateCompatibleBitmap(hDisplayDC,zWIDE,zHIGH);
0723  if (Cel2==NULL)
0724    {
0725    LoadString(hInst,IDS_NotReady,lpCaption,Max);
0726    LoadString(hInst,IDS_InsufMem2,lpMessage,MaxText);
0727    MessageBox(GetFocus(),lpMessage,lpCaption,MB_OK);
0728    DeleteObject(Cel1);
0729    DeleteDC(hMemoryDC);
0730    SelectObject(hFrameDC,hPrevFrame);
0731    DeleteObject(hFrame); DeleteDC(hFrameDC);
0732    TimerExists= FALSE; CelsReady= FALSE; Selected= FALSE; return;
0733    }
0734  Cel3= CreateCompatibleBitmap(hDisplayDC,zWIDE,zHIGH);
0735  if (Cel3==NULL)
0736    {
0737    LoadString(hInst,IDS_NotReady,lpCaption,Max);
0738    LoadString(hInst,IDS_InsufMem2,lpMessage,MaxText);
```

```
0739    MessageBox(GetFocus(),lpMessage,lpCaption,MB_OK);
0740    DeleteObject(Cel1); DeleteObject(Cel2);
0741    DeleteDC(hMemoryDC);
0742    SelectObject(hFrameDC,hPrevFrame);
0743    DeleteObject(hFrame); DeleteDC(hFrameDC);
0744    TimerExists= FALSE; CelsReady= FALSE; Selected= FALSE; return;
0745    }
0746    Cel4= CreateCompatibleBitmap(hDisplayDC,zWIDE,zHIGH);
0747    if (Cel4==NULL)
0748    {
0749    LoadString(hInst,IDS_NotReady,lpCaption,Max);
0750    LoadString(hInst,IDS_InsufMem2,lpMessage,MaxText);
0751    MessageBox(GetFocus(),lpMessage,lpCaption,MB_OK);
0752    DeleteObject(Cel1); DeleteObject(Cel2);
0753    DeleteObject(Cel3);
0754    DeleteDC(hMemoryDC);
0755    SelectObject(hFrameDC,hPrevFrame);
0756    DeleteObject(hFrame); DeleteDC(hFrameDC);
0757    TimerExists= FALSE; CelsReady= FALSE; Selected= FALSE; return;
0758    }
0759    Cel5= CreateCompatibleBitmap(hDisplayDC,zWIDE,zHIGH);
0760    if (Cel5==NULL)
0761    {
0762    LoadString(hInst,IDS_NotReady,lpCaption,Max);
0763    LoadString(hInst,IDS_InsufMem2,lpMessage,MaxText);
0764    MessageBox(GetFocus(),lpMessage,lpCaption,MB_OK);
0765    DeleteObject(Cel1); DeleteObject(Cel2);
0766    DeleteObject(Cel3); DeleteObject(Cel4);
0767    DeleteDC(hMemoryDC);
0768    SelectObject(hFrameDC,hPrevFrame);
0769    DeleteObject(hFrame); DeleteDC(hFrameDC);
0770    TimerExists= FALSE; CelsReady= FALSE; Selected= FALSE; return;
0771    }
0772    Cel6= CreateCompatibleBitmap(hDisplayDC,zWIDE,zHIGH);
0773    if (Cel6==NULL)
0774    {
0775    LoadString(hInst,IDS_NotReady,lpCaption,Max);
0776    LoadString(hInst,IDS_InsufMem2,lpMessage,MaxText);
0777    MessageBox(GetFocus(),lpMessage,lpCaption,MB_OK);
0778    DeleteObject(Cel1); DeleteObject(Cel2);
0779    DeleteObject(Cel3); DeleteObject(Cel4);
0780    DeleteObject(Cel5);
0781    DeleteDC(hMemoryDC);
0782    SelectObject(hFrameDC,hPrevFrame);
0783    DeleteObject(hFrame); DeleteDC(hFrameDC);
0784    TimerExists= FALSE; CelsReady= FALSE; Selected= FALSE; return;
0785    }
0786    Cel7= CreateCompatibleBitmap(hDisplayDC,zWIDE,zHIGH);
0787    if (Cel7==NULL)
0788    {
0789    LoadString(hInst,IDS_NotReady,lpCaption,Max);
0790    LoadString(hInst,IDS_InsufMem2,lpMessage,MaxText);
0791    MessageBox(GetFocus(),lpMessage,lpCaption,MB_OK);
0792    DeleteObject(Cel1); DeleteObject(Cel2);
0793    DeleteObject(Cel3); DeleteObject(Cel4);
0794    DeleteObject(Cel5); DeleteObject(Cel6);
0795    DeleteDC(hMemoryDC);
0796    SelectObject(hFrameDC,hPrevFrame);
0797    DeleteObject(hFrame); DeleteDC(hFrameDC);
0798    TimerExists= FALSE; CelsReady= FALSE; Selected= FALSE; return;
0799    }
```

```
0800
0801    ArrayPtr= keyframe1;                            /* point to first array */
0802    zDrawOneCartoon(hDisplayDC);                        /* draw the cel */
0803    hPrevBitmap= SelectObject(hMemoryDC,Cel1);  /* select the bitmap */
0804    BitBlt(hMemoryDC,0,0,zWIDE,zHIGH, /* copy image to hidden bitmap */
0805          hDisplayDC,0,0,SRCCOPY);
0806    zClear(hWnd);
0807    ArrayPtr= keyframe2;
0808    zDrawOneCartoon(hDisplayDC);
0809    SelectObject(hMemoryDC,Cel2);
0810    BitBlt(hMemoryDC,0,0,zWIDE,zHIGH,hDisplayDC,0,0,SRCCOPY);
0811    zClear(hWnd);
0812    ArrayPtr= keyframe3;
0813    zDrawOneCartoon(hDisplayDC);
0814    SelectObject(hMemoryDC,Cel3);
0815    BitBlt(hMemoryDC,0,0,zWIDE,zHIGH,hDisplayDC,0,0,SRCCOPY);
0816    zClear(hWnd);
0817    ArrayPtr= keyframe4;
0818    zDrawOneCartoon(hDisplayDC);
0819    SelectObject(hMemoryDC,Cel4);
0820    BitBlt(hMemoryDC,0,0,zWIDE,zHIGH,hDisplayDC,0,0,SRCCOPY);
0821    zClear(hWnd);
0822    ArrayPtr= keyframe5;
0823    zDrawOneCartoon(hDisplayDC);
0824    SelectObject(hMemoryDC,Cel5);
0825    BitBlt(hMemoryDC,0,0,zWIDE,zHIGH,hDisplayDC,0,0,SRCCOPY);
0826    zClear(hWnd);
0827    ArrayPtr= keyframe6;
0828    zDrawOneCartoon(hDisplayDC);
0829    SelectObject(hMemoryDC,Cel6);
0830    BitBlt(hMemoryDC,0,0,zWIDE,zHIGH,hDisplayDC,0,0,SRCCOPY);
0831    zClear(hWnd);
0832    ArrayPtr= keyframe7;
0833    zDrawOneCartoon(hDisplayDC);
0834    SelectObject(hMemoryDC,Cel7);
0835    BitBlt(hMemoryDC,0,0,zWIDE,zHIGH,hDisplayDC,0,0,SRCCOPY);
0836
0837    zClear(hWnd);                                   /* clear the window */
0838    ReleaseDC(hWnd,hDisplayDC);        /* release the display-context */
0839
0840    TimerID1= SetTimer(hWnd,1,wFrameRate,           /* set the timer */
0841                  (FARPROC) NULL);
0842    if (TimerID1 == 0)              /* if unable to initialize timer... */
0843       {
0844       LoadString(hInst,IDS_NotReady,lpCaption,Max);
0845       LoadString(hInst,IDS_NoTimer,lpMessage,MaxText);
0846       MessageBox(GetFocus(),lpMessage,lpCaption,MB_OK);
0847       SelectObject(hMemoryDC,hPrevBitmap);   /* deselect cel bitmaps */
0848       DeleteObject(Cel1);                       /* delete the cels... */
0849       DeleteObject(Cel2);
0850       DeleteObject(Cel3);
0851       DeleteObject(Cel4);
0852       DeleteObject(Cel5);
0853       DeleteObject(Cel6);
0854       DeleteObject(Cel7);
0855       DeleteDC(hMemoryDC);                     /* delete the memory DC */
0856       SelectObject(hFrameDC,hPrevFrame);     /* deselect frame bitmap */
0857       DeleteObject(hFrame);                      /* delete the frame */
0858       DeleteDC(hFrameDC);                      /* delete the memory DC */
0859       TimerExists= FALSE;
0860       CelsReady= FALSE;
```

```
0861   Selected= FALSE;
0862   return;                                    /* ...and return */
0863   }
0864 TimerExists= TRUE;
0865 CelsReady= TRUE;
0866 SelectObject(hMemoryDC,Cel1);
0867 Selected= TRUE;
0868 FrameNum= 1;
0869 LoadString(hInst,IDS_Ready,lpCaption,Max);
0870 LoadString(hInst,IDS_CelsOK,lpMessage,MaxText);
0871 MessageBox(GetFocus(),lpMessage,lpCaption,MB_OK);
0872 return;
0873 }
0874 /*
0875 ------------------------------------------------------------------
0876                          Draw one cel.
0877 ------------------------------------------------------------------
0878                                                                  */
0879 static void zDrawOneCartoon(HDC hDC)
0880 {            /* uses display-context received as an argument */
0881   int Count;                                  /* loop counter */
0882   int Repeat;                                 /* loop counter */
0883   int DrawPtr;           /* dynamic index into array of coords */
0884   HBRUSH ColorBrush, PrevBrush;                     /* brushes */
0885   HPEN ColorPen, PrevPen;                              /* pens */
0886   POINT Shape[6];                          /* array of points */
0887
0888 ColorPen= CreatePen(PS_SOLID,1,RGB(0,128,0));     /* create pen */
0889 ColorBrush= CreateSolidBrush(RGB(0,128,0));     /* create brush */
0890 PrevPen= SelectObject(hDC,ColorPen);             /* select pen */
0891 PrevBrush= SelectObject(hDC,ColorBrush);       /* select brush */
0892
0893 /* --------------------- draw the head --------------------- */
0894 Ellipse(hDC,ArrayPtr[0]-10,ArrayPtr[1]-10,
0895           ArrayPtr[0]+10,ArrayPtr[1]+10);
0896
0897 /* --------------------- draw the neck --------------------- */
0898 DrawPtr= 2;              /* update the index into database array */
0899 for (Count= 0; Count <= 3; Count++)
0900   {            /* fetch four vertices from the database... */
0901   Shape[Count].x= ArrayPtr[DrawPtr]; DrawPtr++;
0902   Shape[Count].y= ArrayPtr[DrawPtr]; DrawPtr++;
0903   }
0904 Polygon(hDC,Shape,4);
0905
0906 /* -------------------- draw the torso --------------------- */
0907 for (Count= 0; Count <= 4; Count++)
0908   {            /* fetch five vertices from the database... */
0909   Shape[Count].x= ArrayPtr[DrawPtr]; DrawPtr++;
0910   Shape[Count].y= ArrayPtr[DrawPtr]; DrawPtr++;
0911   }
0912 Polygon(hDC,Shape,5);                    /* ...and draw a polygon */
0913
0914 /* ---------------- draw remaining body parts --------------- */
0915 for (Repeat= 1; Repeat<= 13; Repeat++)
0916   {                    // for each of the remaining body parts...
0917   for (Count= 0; Count <= 3; Count++)
0918     {           /* ...fetch four vertices from the database... */
0919     Shape[Count].x= ArrayPtr[DrawPtr]; DrawPtr++;
0920     Shape[Count].y= ArrayPtr[DrawPtr]; DrawPtr++;
0921     }
```

```
0922      Polygon(hDC,Shape,4);                        /* ...and draw a polygon */
0923      }
0924
0925  /* -------------------- tidy up and return -------------------- */
0926  SelectObject(hDC,PrevPen);                        /* deselect pen */
0927  SelectObject(hDC,PrevBrush);                      /* deselect brush */
0928  DeleteObject(ColorPen);                           /* delete pen */
0929  DeleteObject(ColorBrush);                         /* delete brush */
0930  return;
0931  }
0932  /*
0933  --------------------------------------------------------------------
0934                    REAL-TIME ANIMATION ENGINE.
0935    This function builds the next frame of the animation sequence
0936    on a hidden bitmap.  When completed, the finished frame is
0937    then copied to the display window.
0938  --------------------------------------------------------------------
0939                                                                    */
0940  static void zShowNextFrame(HWND hWnd)
0941  {                        /* this function uses global variable FrameNum */
0942    HDC hDC;                                         /* display-context */
0943
0944  if (CelsReady==FALSE) return;          /* cancel if cels not ready */
0945  if (Redisplay==TRUE) goto DISPLAY_FRAME;    /* if a refresh only */
0946  if (Pause==TRUE) return;               /* cancel if animation paused */
0947
0948  if (FrameDirection==zFORWARD)
0949      {
0950      FrameNum++;                        /* increment the frame number */
0951      if (FrameNum > zFINALFRAME) FrameNum= zFIRSTFRAME;
0952      SX1= SX1 - zMOVEHORIZ;             /* adjust the cel position */
0953      if (SX1 < zMAXLEFT) SX1= zMAXRIGHT;
0954      }
0955  if (FrameDirection==zREVERSE)
0956      {
0957      FrameNum--;                        /* decrement the frame number
0958      if (FrameNum < zFIRSTFRAME) FrameNum= zFINALFRAME;
0959      SX1= SX1 + zMOVEHORIZ;             /* adjust the cel position
0960      if (SX1 > zMAXRIGHT) SX1= zMAXLEFT;
0961      }
0962
0963  DISPLAY_FRAME:
0964  hDC= GetDC(hWnd);                             /* set the display-context */
0965
0966  /* ---------- draw the next image on the hidden frame ---------- */
0967  PatBlt(hFrameDC,0,0,zFRAMEWIDE,zFRAMEHIGH,WHITENESS);
0968  switch (FrameNum)
0969      {
0970      case 1:  SelectObject(hMemoryDC,Cel1);
0971               BitBlt(hFrameDC,SX1,SY1,zWIDE,zHIGH,
0972                 hMemoryDC,0,0,SRCCOPY);
0973               break;
0974      case 2:  SelectObject(hMemoryDC,Cel2);
0975               BitBlt(hFrameDC,SX1,SY1,zWIDE,zHIGH,
0976                 hMemoryDC,0,0,SRCCOPY);
0977               break;
0978      case 3:  SelectObject(hMemoryDC,Cel3);
0979               BitBlt(hFrameDC,SX1,SY1,zWIDE,zHIGH,
0980                 hMemoryDC,0,0,SRCCOPY);
```

```
0981           break;
0982    case 4:  SelectObject(hMemoryDC,Cel4);
0983            BitBlt(hFrameDC,SX1,SY1,zWIDE,zHIGH,
0984              hMemoryDC,0,0,SRCCOPY);
0985           break;
0986    case 5:  SelectObject(hMemoryDC,Cel5);
0987            BitBlt(hFrameDC,SX1,SY1,zWIDE,zHIGH,
0988              hMemoryDC,0,0,SRCCOPY);
0989           break;
0990    case 6:  SelectObject(hMemoryDC,Cel6);
0991            BitBlt(hFrameDC,SX1,SY1,zWIDE,zHIGH,
0992              hMemoryDC,0,0,SRCCOPY);
0993           break;
0994    case 7:  SelectObject(hMemoryDC,Cel7);
0995            BitBlt(hFrameDC,SX1,SY1,zWIDE,zHIGH,
0996              hMemoryDC,0,0,SRCCOPY);
0997           break;
0998    }
0999 /* ---------- copy hidden frame to the display window ---------- */
1000 BitBlt(hDC,0,0,zFRAMEWIDE,zFRAMEHIGH,hFrameDC,0,0,SRCCOPY);
1001
1002 ReleaseDC(hWnd,hDC);                    /* release the display-context */
1003 return;
1004 }
1005 /*
1006 ------------------------------------------------------------------
1007                      Reset the animation frame rate.
1008 ------------------------------------------------------------------
1009                                                                  */
1010 static void zSetFrameRate(HWND hWnd, WORD wNewRate)
1011 {
1012 if (TimerExists==FALSE)
1013   {                                     /* if no timer exists... */
1014   wFrameRate= wPrevRate;   /* ...restore the frame rate value... */
1015   MessageBeep(0);
1016   LoadString(hInst,IDS_NotReady,lpCaption,Max);
1017   LoadString(hInst,IDS_NoReset,lpMessage,MaxText);
1018   MessageBox(GetFocus(),lpMessage,lpCaption,MB_OK);
1019   return;                                   /* ... and return */
1020   }
1021 switch (wPrevRate)     /* depending on the previous frame rate... */
1022   {                     /* ...uncheck the the appropriate menu item */
1023   case 55:  CheckMenuItem(hMenu,IDM_FPS182,MF_UNCHECKED); break;
1024   case 110: CheckMenuItem(hMenu,IDM_FPS91,MF_UNCHECKED); break;
1025   case 165: CheckMenuItem(hMenu,IDM_FPS61,MF_UNCHECKED); break;
1026   case 220: CheckMenuItem(hMenu,IDM_FPS45,MF_UNCHECKED); break;
1027   case 275: CheckMenuItem(hMenu,IDM_FPS36,MF_UNCHECKED); break;
1028   case 330: CheckMenuItem(hMenu,IDM_FPS30,MF_UNCHECKED); break;
1029   }
1030 KillTimer(hWnd,1);                        /* release existing timer */
1031 TimerID1= SetTimer(hWnd,1,wNewRate,(FARPROC) NULL); /* new timer */
1032 if (TimerID1==0)
1033   {                            /* if unable to set a new timer... */
1034   LoadString(hInst,IDS_NotReady,lpCaption,Max);
1035   LoadString(hInst,IDS_CannotReset,lpMessage,MaxText);
1036   MessageBox(GetFocus(),lpMessage,lpCaption,MB_OK);
1037   CelsReady= FALSE;
1038   return;
1039   }
1040 switch (wFrameRate)        /* depending on the new frame rate... */
1041   {                        /* ...check the appropriate menu item */
```

**7-16** Continued.

```
1042    case 55:  CheckMenuItem(hMenu,IDM_FPS182,MF_CHECKED); break;
1043    case 110: CheckMenuItem(hMenu,IDM_FPS91,MF_CHECKED); break;
1044    case 165: CheckMenuItem(hMenu,IDM_FPS61,MF_CHECKED); break;
1045    case 220: CheckMenuItem(hMenu,IDM_FPS45,MF_CHECKED); break;
1046    case 275: CheckMenuItem(hMenu,IDM_FPS36,MF_CHECKED); break;
1047    case 330: CheckMenuItem(hMenu,IDM_FPS30,MF_CHECKED); break;
1048    }
1049 return;
1050 }
1051 /*
1052 -------------------------------------------------------------------
1053                   RUNTIME GRAPHICS SYSTEM FUNCTIONS
1054 -------------------------------------------------------------------
1055 -------------------------------------------------------------------
1056                       Create the hidden frame.
1057 -------------------------------------------------------------------
1058                                                                  */
1059 static void zInitFrame(HWND hWnd)
1060 {
1061    HDC hDisplayDC;                                /* display-context */
1062
1063 if (FrameReady==TRUE)
1064    {                           /* if hidden frame already created... */
1065    MessageBeep(0);
1066    LoadString(hInst,IDS_Ready,lpCaption,Max);
1067    LoadString(hInst,IDS_Already,lpMessage,MaxText);
1068    MessageBox(GetFocus(),lpMessage,lpCaption,MB_OK);
1069    return;
1070    }
1071 GlobalCompact((DWORD)-1L);        /* maximize contiguous memory */
1072 hDisplayDC= GetDC(hWnd);             /* set the display-context */
1073 hFrameDC= CreateCompatibleDC(hDisplayDC);    /* create frame... */
1074 hFrame= CreateCompatibleBitmap(hDisplayDC,zFRAMEWIDE,zFRAMEHIGH);
1075 if (hFrame==NULL)
1076    {
1077    LoadString(hInst,IDS_NotReady,lpCaption,Max);
1078    LoadString(hInst,IDS_InsufMem1,lpMessage,MaxText);
1079    MessageBox(GetFocus(),lpMessage,lpCaption,MB_OK);
1080    DeleteDC(hFrameDC);
1081    FrameReady= FALSE;
1082    return;
1083    }
1084 hPrevFrame= SelectObject(hFrameDC,hFrame);  /* select the bitmap */
1085 zClearHiddenFrame();                     /* clear the hidden frame */
1086 LoadString(hInst,IDS_Ready,lpCaption,Max);
1087 LoadString(hInst,IDS_FrameOK,lpMessage,MaxText);
1088 MessageBox(GetFocus(),lpMessage,lpCaption,MB_OK);
1089 ReleaseDC(hWnd,hDisplayDC);          /* release the display-context */
1090 FrameReady= TRUE;                        /* set a global token */
1091 return;
1092 }
1093 /*
1094 -------------------------------------------------------------------
1095                       Clear the display window.
1096 -------------------------------------------------------------------
1097                                                                  */
1098 static void zClear(HWND hWnd)
1099 {
1100    HDC hDC;
1101 hDC= GetDC(hWnd);
1102 PatBlt(hDC,0,0,zFRAMEWIDE,zFRAMEHIGH,WHITENESS);
```

```
1103  ReleaseDC(hWnd,hDC);
1104  return;
1105  }
1106  /*
1107  ------------------------------------------------------------------
1108                      Clear the hidden frame.
1109  ------------------------------------------------------------------
1110                                                                  */
1111  static void zClearHiddenFrame(void)
1112  {
1113  if (FrameReady==FALSE) return;
1114  PatBlt(hFrameDC,0,0,zFRAMEWIDE,zFRAMEHIGH,WHITENESS);
1115  return;
1116  }
1117  /*
1118  ------------------------------------------------------------------
1119            Copy the hidden frame to the display window.
1120  ------------------------------------------------------------------
1121                                                                  */
1122  static void zCopyToDisplay(HWND hWnd)
1123  {
1124     HDC hDC;
1125  if (FrameReady==FALSE) return;
1126  hDC= GetDC(hWnd);
1127  BitBlt(hDC,0,0,zFRAMEWIDE,zFRAMEHIGH,hFrameDC,0,0,SRCCOPY);
1128  ReleaseDC(hWnd,hDC);
1129  return;
1130  }
1131  /*
1132  ------------------------------------------------------------------
1133            Copy the display window to the hidden frame.
1134  ------------------------------------------------------------------
1135                                                                  */
1136  static void zCopyToFrame(HWND hWnd)
1137  {
1138     HDC hDC;
1139  if (FrameReady==FALSE) return;
1140  hDC= GetDC(hWnd);
1141  BitBlt(hFrameDC,0,0,zFRAMEWIDE,zFRAMEHIGH,hDC,0,0,SRCCOPY);
1142  ReleaseDC(hWnd,hDC);
1143  return;
1144  }
1145  /*
1146  ------------------------------------------------------------------
1147                      End of the C source file
1148  ------------------------------------------------------------------
1149                                                                  */
```

# 8
# *Frame animation engines*

Frame animation uses static images. During animation playback, the software fetches and displays images that have been previously completed and stored on disk. Frame animation engines are often smart enough to load an entire animation sequence into memory if there is enough physical memory available. Otherwise the engine will load each frame directly from disk as each frame is needed during playback.

The sample application in this chapter provides a working example of a frame animation engine that you can paste into your own Windows applications. (See chapter 6, Animating in Windows, for a discussion of computer animation concepts and principles. See chapter 7, Real-time animation engines, for a working example of a real-time animation engine.)

The frame animation demo program provides full interactive control over a run-cycle, as shown in FIG. 8-1. The run-cycle is animated in front of a complex scene consisting of a gradient background, a text title, and text captions. (A run-cycle is a loop of images that is repeatedly cycled in order to simulate some form of repetitive movement like running and walking. See chapter 13, Motion, for a detailed treatment of movement in animation sequences.)

The run-cycle used by the sample application consists of seven different cel images. The entire animation sequence comprises 19 different frames, however. This discrepancy occurs because nearly three run-cycle loops are needed in order to ensure that the sprinting character travels completely across the display area of the window.

**8-1** The run-cycle cels that are used to build the 19 frames in the sample application.

# Preparation of the animation

During preparation and design of the sample application, the individual drawings that make up the seven cels for the run-cycle were sketched with pencil on professional layout paper. The paper was translucent and permitted comparison of the drawings by superimposing them on a portable light table. When the seven drawings were complete, each drawing in turn was placed over the animation grid shown in FIG. 8-2. The grid corresponds to the display window of the sample application. The X-Y coordinates for each drawing were recorded for later use during program development.

## About the grid

The grid is measured in increments of ten pixels per unit. It was created by using the MoveTo() and LineTo() functions of the Graphics Device Interface in a program that was directly modified from the sample application presented in chapter 1, Windows. You can create your own personalized grid by using the code fragment presented in chapter 7, Real-time animation engines.

## The animation algorithm

The frame animation engine in the sample application is implemented by using a combination of bitblt actors and a hidden bitmap. The demo program contains a function to assemble the background, text, title, and run-cycle character for each frame in the animation sequence. The application also contains high-level functions to oversee disk operations. These high-level services include a function to save the entire 19-frame animation sequence to disk and a function to load a previously saved animation sequence from disk into memory. The frame animation engine also contains low-level functions to read and write individual image files in binary format.

The frame animation demo is implemented as scripted animation using the timer-based message-handler algorithm. The sample application uses a separate authoring paradigm and delivery paradigm. The authoring paradigm builds each frame on a hidden page using a combination of bitblt and drawn images. Each completed frame is copied to the display window, from

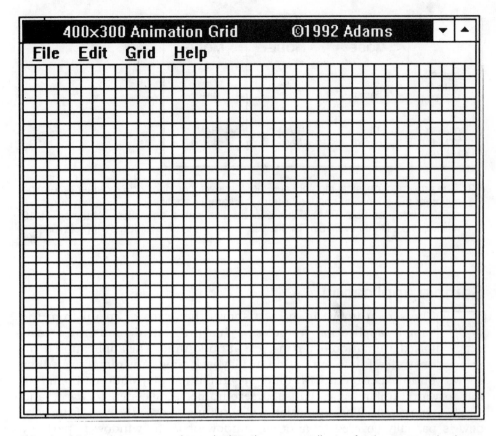

**8-2** A grid template was used to calculate the x-y coordinates for the seven cels shown in FIG. 8-1. The grid was also used to help determine the instancing coordinates of each cel as the actor is animated across the display window.

where it is saved to hard disk. The delivery paradigm is frame playback to screen display. Different computer configurations will result in different implementations of the delivery paradigm, as shown in FIG. 8-3. Any computer that is running Windows in real mode will use disk-based frame animation when the sample application is running. Each individual frame will be explicitly loaded from disk as needed during animation playback. Any computer with 2MB or less of physical memory will also use disk-based frame animation, because the 19 frames of the animation sequence require 1.2 MB of memory.

Personal computers having 4 MB of memory and running Windows in either standard mode or enhanced mode will exhibit the smoothest animation performance, because the frame animation engine will load all 19 frames into memory before playing the animation.

For a more detailed explanation of scripted animation and the implementation paradigms, see chapter 6, Animating in Windows.

|  | REAL MODE | STANDARD MODE | ENHANCED MODE |
|---|---|---|---|
| 80386SX 16 MHz 2 MB RAM | Disk-Based | Disk-Based | Disk-Based |
| 80386DX 33 MHz 4 MB RAM | Disk-Based | RAM-Based | RAM-Based |

**8-3** The amount of physical memory and the Windows memory mode together determine whether the animation sequence from the sample application will be run from disk (disk-based) or from RAM (RAM-based). The entire animation sequence of 19 frames must fit into available RAM if disk reads are to be avoided during playback.

## Sample application

The screen image in FIG. 8-4 shows the Animation menu from the sample application frame.exe. This program demonstrates cast-based animation of a run-cycle at build-time. The application demonstrates frame animation at playback time. An interactive editor allows you to experiment with different animation play options, including full forward, full reverse, pause, freeze-frame, single-step forward, and single-step reverse. The animation will continue to execute even if the window is partially covered by another window or if the window is partially clipped by the edge of the screen.

The frame.exe demo is built from four modules, including a .def module definition file, an .h #include file, an .rc resource script file, and a .c source file. All of these production files are presented as ready-to-use source code in the program listings later in this chapter. The source files are also provided on the companion disk. You can refer to the appropriate appendix for instructions on how to build frame.exe with QuickC for Windows, Turbo C++ for Windows, Borland C++, Zortech C++, WATCOM C, and Microsoft C and the SDK.

## What the program does: A user's guide

The sample application provides an interactive environment suitable for experimenting with frame animation. You can use either a mouse or the keyboard to experiment with the demo program. The menus also support mnemonic keys. To view a runtime help message, select Help from the Help menu.

```
┌─────────────────────────────────────────────────────────────┐
│        ANIMATION ENGINE (frame version)        ▼ ▲           │
│  File   Edit   Animation   Timer   Help                      │
│                 Run Forward                                  │
│                 Run Reverse                                  │
│                 Pause                                        │
│                ─────────────────                             │
│                 Initialize system                            │
│                 Create Frames                                │
│                ─────────────────                             │
│                 Load Animation                               │
│                ─────────────────                             │
│                 Clear                                        │
└─────────────────────────────────────────────────────────────┘
```

**8-4**  The Animation menu of the sample application is used to create the hidden bitmap, to build 19 frames, to save the animation sequence to disk, and to load a previously saved animation sequence into memory from disk. The first three menu items provide forward, reverse, and single-step playback control.

## Initializing the system

Select Initialize system from the Animation menu to initialize the hidden frame. None of the authoring or playback features of the Animation menu will function until the hidden frame has been created.

## Creating the frames

Select Create Frames from the Animation menu (see FIG. 8-4) to create the animation sequence and store it on disk. The sample application will build each frame in turn on the hidden page, copy the completed frame to the display window, and then save the image to disk as a binary image file. If you have already saved the 19 frames to disk, the demo program will present the advisory message shown at the top of FIG. 8-5. The software gives you the option of overwriting the existing file with the new image file. If you choose not to overwrite the existing file, the build sequence is stopped and no further frames are constructed. If not enough free space exists on your hard disk to store the image files the demo program displaysthe advisory message shown at the bottom of FIG. 8-5.

The sample application reports the successful completion of the Create Frames operation by displaying the message box shown in FIG. 8-6.

## Loading the animation

Before you can play an animation sequence that you have saved to disk, you must load it. If you saved the animation sequence during the current

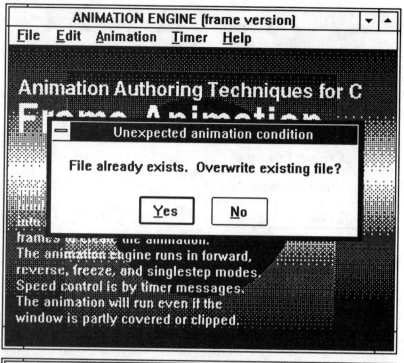

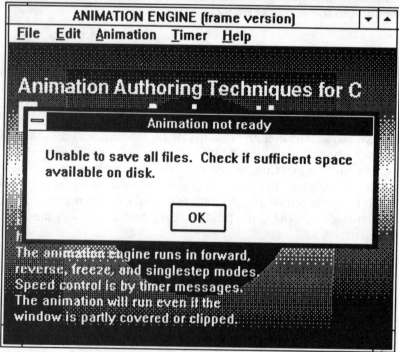

**8-5** The frame animation engine traps runtime exceptions during frame-building and disk-write operations.

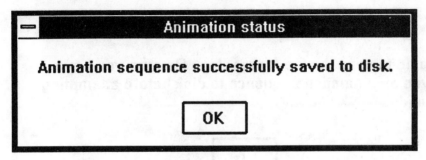

**8-6** An animation status message box reports the successful frame-storage operation, whereby 19 frames are written to disk as image files.

working session, simply select Load Animation from the Animation menu. If you saved the animation during a previous working session, you must select Initialize system from the Animation menu before selecting Load Animation.

If the software is unable to find the frame files on disk, it displays the advisory message that is depicted in FIG. 8-7. If you attempt to play an animation before loading it from disk, the sample application will display the message box shown in the top of FIG. 8-8. If you attempt to play an animation before selecting Initialize system from the Animation menu, the demo program will display the message box shown in the bottom of FIG. 8-8.

Under normal circumstances the sample application will load each frame file into the hidden frame, from where it is stored in memory. After all 19 frames have been loaded from disk, the program displays the message box shown in FIG. 8-9.

## Playing the animation

To play the animation sequence, select Run Forward from the Animation menu (see FIG. 8-4). A silhouette of a running character will dash across the screen from stage right to stage left. A sample image excerpted from the animation sequence is shown in FIG. 8-10. The character will continue running across the screen until you stop the animation. The character is accompanied by a dropshadow that covers the gradient background and the text caption, as shown in FIG. 8-11. The animation loop begins from off stage right and continues to off stage left, as illustrated by the two runtime screen prints in FIG. 8-12.

## Adjusting the animation playback speed

You can increase or decrease the animation speed by selecting from the Timer menu, depicted in FIG. 8-13. At startup the rate is set to 18 frames per second (fps), as indicated by the check mark. If you select 6 fps the check mark moves to the appropriate menu item and the animation rate changes. You can adjust the playback speed when the animation is running forward, reverse, or paused.

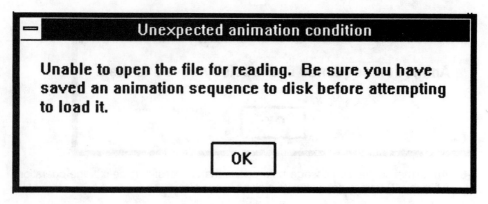

**8-7** The frame animation engine traps runtime exceptions during disk-read operations.

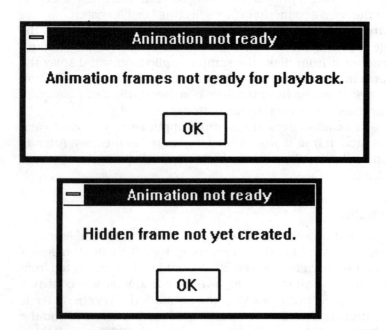

**8-8** The sample application uses message boxes to report any problems that may arise when you attempt to play the animation.

*Market* Some slower computers may not be able to sustain a playback rate of 18 fps. An 80386SX running at 16 MHz, for example, is unable to exceed 6 fps when running in the 640-×-480-×-16 color VGA mode. An 80386DX running at 25 MHz can sustain the 9 fps rate, and a computer running at 33 MHz or faster can sustain the 18 fps rate. Selecting a rate that is faster than your computer can support will not result in any speed improvement, because the computer is already running at maximum display output.

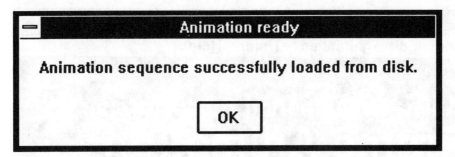

**8-9** A message box reports a successful frame-load operation, whereby 19 frames have been loaded into memory from disk, ready for playback.

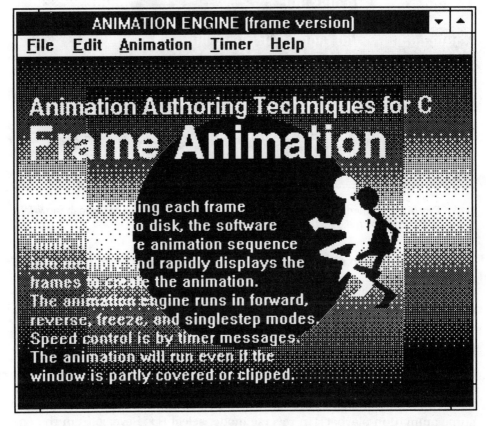

**8-10** A freezeframe from the animated sample application. The dithering process used by the author's laser printer to produce the screen print shown here does not convey the richness of hues produced by the sample application on a VGA display.

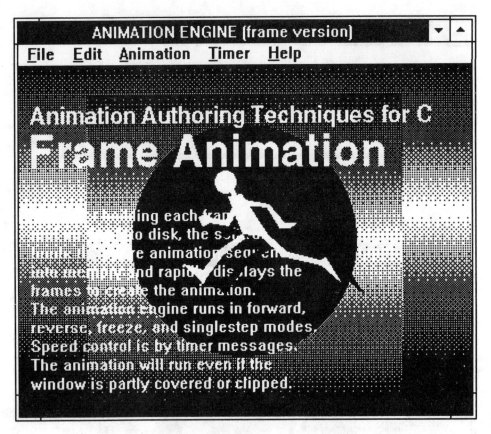

**8-11** The actor is animated in front of a complex background. The dropshadow falls across the text material during the animation sequence.

If you attempt to reset the animation rate before you have initialized the animation engine, the application issues an advisory notice as shown in FIG. 8-14. To initialize the animation engine, select Initialize system from the Animation menu.

## Freeze-frame and single-step animation

**Pause**  To pause the animation, select Pause from the Animation menu (see FIG. 8-4). Pause is also known as freeze-frame. To resume animation playback in forward mode, select Run Forward from the Animation menu. To resume animation playback in reverse mode, select Run Reverse from the Animation menu.

**Single-step**  While the animation is paused, you can invoke single-step playback. Press the right arrow key on the direction keypad to display the next frame in the animation sequence. Keep pressing the right arrow key to step through the entire animation. As FIG. 8-12 shows, the run-

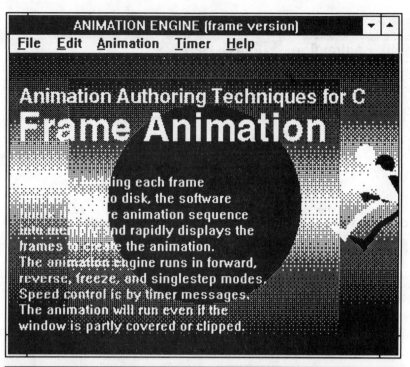

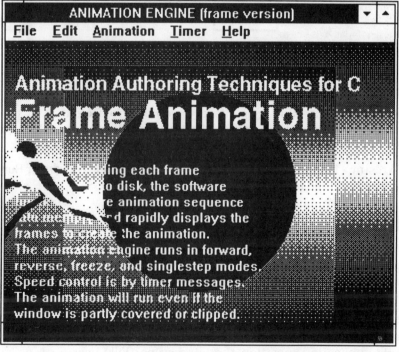

**8-12** The sample application provides an animation sequence that starts from off-stage right and ends at off-stage left.

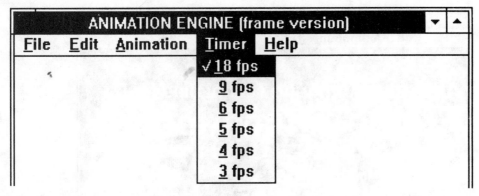

**8-13** You can use the Timer menu to adjust the playback speed. The available frame speeds are a direct result of the attributes of the system timer chip discussed in chapter 6 (see FIG. 6-3).

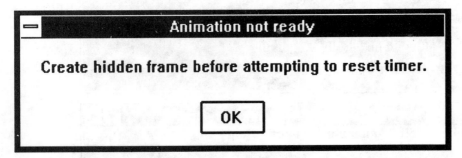

**8-14** The sample application traps any attempt to reset the timer before it has been initialized.

cycle wraps around. The silhouette character enters from offstage at the right side of the window, and exits offstage at the left side of the window. To single-step in reverse, press the left arrow key on the direction keypad.

**Resume**   To resume full animation playback, select either Run Forward or Run Reverse from the Animation menu.

## Persistent graphics

**Moving the window**   To test the persistent graphics features of the sample application, start the animation and then move the window. Click on the caption bar of the window and drag it to another location on the screen. Even if the window is clipped by the edge of the screen the animation will continue to play.

**Covering the window**   To confirm the cooperative multitasking compatibility of the sample application, position the window partially over a program group box. Then click on the program group box. The program group box will move to the foreground and will partially cover the sample application, but the animation will continue to run.

**Using menus**  You can also select various menus from the sample application while the animation is running and the playback will be unaffected.

## Using the Help menu

You can use the Help menu to discover various facts about your system that are in effect at runtime. See FIG. 8-15. You can determine the current screen mode, the maximum number of available colors, the runtime memory mode (real, standard, or enhanced), and other facts.

**Checking the screen resolution**  To find out the current screen mode, select Screen resolution from the Help menu. A message box will display the horizontal-by-vertical resolution. The sample application supports 640 × 480, 640 × 350, 800 × 600, and 1024 × 768 resolution displays.

**Maximum displayable colors**  To determine the maximum available colors that can be displayed simultaneously, select Available colors from the Help menu. A message box will indicate the mode. In its current implementation the sample application supports 16-color and 2-color displays. If you want to modify the source code to support 256-color displays, see the discussion in chapter 3, Blitting.

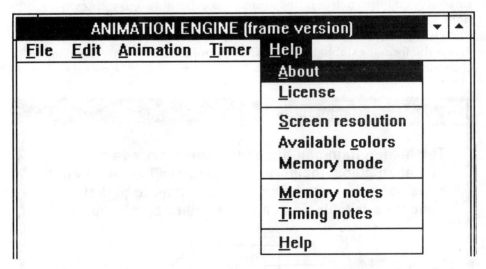

**8-15**  The Help menu provides runtime access to screen resolution, maximum displayable colors, the current Windows memory mode (real, standard, or enhanced), animation memory requirements, and timing considerations.

**Determining the runtime memory mode**  To examine the current Windows runtime memory mode, select Memory mode from the Help menu. A message box will appear, containing an advisory notice describing the mode and its capabilities. The sample application supports real, standard , and enhanced memory modes.

**Animation memory requirements**  To view an informative message concerning animation memory requirements, select Memory notes from the Help menu. The message box shown in FIG. 8-16 appears on the screen.

**Animation timing considerations**  To view an informative message about animation playback rates, select Timing notes from the Help menu. The message box shown in FIG. 8-17 appears.

**General help**  For a general help message at runtime, select Help from the Help menu. The sample application displays the message box shown in FIG. 8-18.

All of the messages provided by the Help menu are available during animation playback, as illustrated in FIG. 8-19. The animation continues to play beneath any message box that the Windows API has placed on the screen.

## How the source code works: A programmer's guide

The frame.exe demonstration program exercises many of the cast-based animation authoring features and frame animation playback features supported by the Windows Graphics Device Interface (GDI). Using the techniques presented in the program listings, you can easily add interactive frame animation capabilities to your own applications.

The organization of the .h #include file and the .rc resource script file follow the format established in earlier sample applications. See chapter 2, Graphics, for a prototype program listing for Windows graphics applica-

---

**Animation memory requirements**

**The hidden frame for the animation is stored as a bitmap in global memory. The demo will advise you if a memory shortage occurs. To make more global memory available you can close other applications.**

OK

**8-16**  The memory requirements message box.

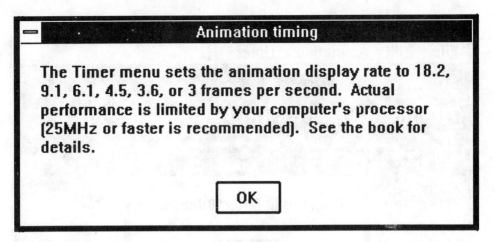

**8-17** The animation timing message box.

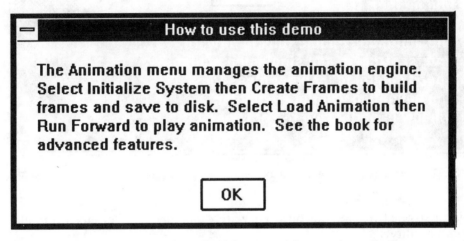

**8-18** The Help message box from the Help menu of the sample application.

tions. See chapter 7 , Real-time animation engines, for a set of listings adapted specifically for animation. A few new menu items and strings have been added to support the frame animation features, persistent graphics features, and timing features of frame.exe. See chapter 1, Windows, for a prototype program listing that demonstrates the mechanics of the .h #include file and the .rc resource script file.

## How the .c file works

Lines 0041 through 0044 include windows.h, types.h, stat.h, and frame.h. These files contain constant declarations, variable declarations, and function prototypes. The header files types.h and stat.h support file operations, although your particular compiler package may not

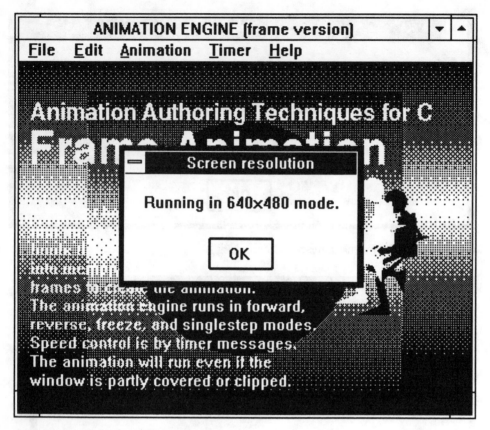

**8-19** The screen resolution message box from the Help menu of the sample application.

require these two #include files. They are #included here for cross-compiler compatibility.

**Static variables**  Static variables that are visible throughout the .c file are declared at lines 0050 through 0212. Variables and constants that define the runtime appearance of the display window are declared at lines 0051 through 0055. Variables related to the operation of the window and its features are declared at lines 0058 through 0063. Variables for managing the window's cursor and a token that indicates if a mouse is present are declared at lines 0066 through 0068. Variables that will describe runtime conditions like screen resolution, available colors, and runtime memory mode are declared at lines 0071 through 0074. Variables (and arrays) that are necessary for operation of message boxes at runtime are declared at lines 0087 through 0091. Variables for font display are declared at lines 0077 through 0080.

**Persistent graphics variables**  Variables for persistent images are declared at lines 0083 through 0085. The constant zBLANK at line 0083 indicates that the display window is blank. The constant zANIMATING at line 0084 indicates that the animation sequence is running and an image (a frame) is being displayed. The variable PaintImage at line 0085 is declared and initialized to a value of zBLANK, indicating that no image is yet present. The variable PaintImage is checked by the persistent graphics case statement in the message handler function whenever Windows sends a WM_PAINT message to the application at runtime.

**Timer variables** Variables and constants for timer operations are declared and initialized at lines 0088 through 0091. The variable TimerID1 at line 0091 identifies a unique timer that will be used by the application at runtime. Windows supports multiple timers among numerous applications that may be running. The constant zTIMER_PAUSE at line 0088 is assigned to a variable named TimerCounter at line 0089. This variable is activated at runtime if the user selects a menu while the animation is playing. The variable is decremented until it reaches zero, thereby forcing a brief pause that allows Windows enough processing time to display the menu. The Boolean variable TimerExists at line 0090 will be used at runtime to indicate that a timer has been set.

**Font variables** Variables that support font output are declared at lines 0094 and 0095. The startup code at lines 0260 through 0267 uses these handles to display the copyright notice. These handles are not used by the function at lines 0875 through 0923 that writes the title and caption on each frame image; the function uses its own local variables. $H = HIDDEN$.

**Hidden frame variables** Variables that support hidden bitmap operations are declared and initialized at lines 0098 through 0101. The HBITMAP handle hFrame at line 0099 is used throughout the .c file whenever an image is being draw on the hidden frame and whenever the completed frame is being copied to the display window.

**The database** The keyframe[] arrays that are declared and initialized at lines 0104 through 0180 contain the X-Y drawing coordinates for each of the seven cels that comprise the run-cycle that will be animated in front of a complex background as frame animation by the demo program. These X-Y coordinates were obtained by placing each pencil sketch over the animation grid described at the beginning of this chapter. The code at lines 0106 through 0113 is commented in the real- time version of the animation engine presented in the previous chapter. Refer back to the source code in chapter 7, Real-time animation engines, to see how the X-Y coordinates represent the elements of the running silhouette character. Because asimilar format is used for each array in the database, the same core function (later in the .c file) can be used to draw each cel, even though the shape of the character in each cel is different, as shown in FIG. 8-1.

**Animation engine variables** Variables and constants that are needed to support the animation engine are declared and initialized at lines 0183 through 0198. The variable wFrameRate at line

0184 initializes the default animation rate. If you are using a slower machine like a 16 MHz 80386SX, you may want to change line 0184 to WORD wFrameRate= 165; instead. This will cause the frame animation to run at 6 frames per second, which is a rate that can usually be sustained by slower machines.

The constants zFORWARD and zREVERSE at lines 0186 and 0187 are used to indicate the direction of playback. The variable FrameDirection at line 0188 is set to zFORWARD, which is the default direction. The animation engine will check the value of FrameDirection when it decides which frame to next display on the screen.

The Boolean variable Redisplay at line 0189 is used whenever the image is being refreshed because of clipping or moving of the display window.

The variables SX1 and SY1 at lines 0190 and 0191 specify the starting position of the first cel in the animation sequence. SY1 does not change while the animation sequence is being built, but SX1 does. The constant zMOVEHORIZ at line 0192 defines the value that will be used to increment SX1 as the character run-cycle is moved across the window in front of the complex background. The zMAXLEFT and zMAXRIGHT constants at line 0193 and 0194 indicate the range of legal cel positions.

The variable FrameNum at line 0195 will be used at runtime to keep track of the frame currently being displayed. If the animation is playing in the forward mode, FrameNum will be incremented for the next frame. If the animation is running in reverse, FrameNum will be decremented in order to decided which frame should be next displayed. The constants zFIRSTFRAME and zFINALFRAME at lines 0196 and 0197 are used by the animation engine to ensure that only existing frames are used in the animation. The variable FrameNum is initialized to a value of 1 at line 0743 when the graphics system is initialized at runtime.

**WinMain()**   The entry point for the application is the WinMain() function at lines 0218 through 0287. This block of code is similar to the prototype program listing discussed and demonstrated in chapter 2, Graphics. Refer to the program listing in chapter 7, Real-time animation engines, for fully commented code.

**Switcher**   The message handler function is located at lines 0293 through 0652. Most of this lengthy function is comprised of overhead and housekeeping functions, including the case statements at lines 0411 through 0556 that manage the various features provided by the Help menu, which include message boxes for runtime help, licensing notes, screen resolution, available colors, runtime memory mode (real, standard, or enhanced), animation memory requirements, and timing notes.

The case WM_TIMER: statement at line 0301 is activated on each timer event. The variable TimerCounter is decremented and tested, then it is incremented. Under normal runtime circumstances, this means that TimerCounter will be maintained at a value of 1 and the call to zShowNext-

Frame() at line 0305 will execute. However, if the software has detected that the user is attempting to select a menu during animation playback, it will set TimerCounter to a value of zTIMER_PAUSE(refer back to line 0088). This means that the code at lines 0301 and 0303 will need to execute twice before zShowNextFrame() can be called again by line 0305. This brief delay consists of three timed intervals. The delay is required on slower machines in order to give the Windows API enough processing time to install the menu on the screen. The delay is not needed by faster machines running at 25 MHz, 33 MHz, or faster.

The case blocks at lines 0323 through 0352 are activated when the user changes from forward to reverse or vice versa—or when the user resumes animation playback after the system has been paused. Note the inclusion of the if() statements at lines 0324 and 0339. This trap keeps the program from crashing if the user selects Run Forward or Run Reverse from the Animation menu before the cels have been created. Observe also how the variables Pause, PaintImage, and FrameDirection are reset before calling zShowNextFrame() to display the next frame in the animation sequence.

The case block at lines 0353 through 0365 is activated whenever the user pauses the animation. The code resets the Pause variable and then calls zShowNextFrame().

The case block at line 0366 creates the hidden frame and performs other general housekeeping operations to initialize the graphics system for use by the animation engine.

The IDM_SaveAnimation case block at lines 0367 through 0379 is invoked when the user selects Create Frames from the Animation menu, as shown in FIG. 8-4. The calls to SetCapture() and SetCursor() at line 0368 lock the mouse and change the mouse cursor to an hourglass during the operation. The call at line 0369 to the core function named zSaveAnimation() invokes processes that draw each frame and save the completed image to disk.

The if() statement at line 0371 checks to determine if any errors occurred during the building process. If so, the IDS_Disk26 message (refer to line 0147 in frame.h and to line 0169 in frame.rc) is displayed to advise the user that the Create Frames operation encountered a problem (see FIG. 8-5). Note also how the calls to SetCursor() and ReleaseCapture() at line 0370 restore the arrow cursor to an arrow and unlock the mouse.

The IDM_LoadAnimation case block at lines 0380 through 0384 calls a core function named zLoadAnimation() to load all 19 frames of the animation sequence into memory. SetCapture() and ReleaseCapture() are used to lock and unlock the mouse. Setcursor() is called twice to change the shape of the mouse cursor from an arrow to an hourglass, and back again. If the zLoadAnimation() function encounters any problems when it attempts to download the binary image files, it will display the message box shown in FIG. 8-7. Other low-level messages may also be displayed if a physical problem is discovered. If zLoadAnimation() is unable to fit all 19 frames into memory, it will display a message advising you that the frame animation will be managed by explicitly loading each frame from disk as needed during playback. (Refer again to FIG. 8-3.)

The case statements from line 0392 to line 0409 are activated when the user resets the animation playback rate. After first storing the current frame rate in a variable named wPrevRate, the code resets wFrameRate to an appropriate value (see FIG. 6-2 in chapter 6, Animating in Windows). The code then calls a function named zSetFrameRate() to reset the timer, passing as arguments the window handle and the desired timer interval.

The WM_INITMENUPOPUP case block at lines 0560 through 0564 is activated whenever the user attempts to select a menu during animation playback. Note line 0561, where TimerCounter is reset to a value of zTIMER_PAUSE. If you refer back to lines 0301 through 0306 you can see how this causes the animation to pause momentarily to give Windows enough processing time to display the menu on the screen. Also note lines 0562 and 0563 in the WM_INITMENUPOPUP case block. These lines remember the ID of the menu if it was the Timer menu and store it in the hMenu variable. The zSetFrameRate() core function will use hMenu to help it reposition the check mark on the Timer menu whenever a new animation rate is chosen by the user.

The WM_PAINT case block at lines 0566 through 0578 manages persistent graphics operations. A WM_PAINT message is sent to the application by Windows whenever the client area of the window needs to be refreshed. This could result from moving, clipping, or uncovering the window. The code at lines 0570 through 0576 uses an if() statement to determine if the animation is paused. It sets Redisplay to TRUE before calling zShowNextFrame(), which will then simply redisplay the current frame; otherwise the call to zShowNextFrame() at line 0577 will cause the animation engine to calculate and display the next frame in the animation sequence.

The WM_KEYDOWN case block at lines 0580 through 0610 detects the right arrow key and the left arrow key of the direction keypad. The case VK_LEFT statement at line 0583 is activated if the left arrow key is pressed. The code first checks to ensure that the animation is paused. If so, it temporarily disables the Pause variable while it calls zShowNextFrame() to display the next frame. If Pause was not disabled, a filter that is built into zShowNextFrame() would cause zShowNextFrame to refuse to display any frame whatsoever.

The case block at lines 0612 through 0632 is invoked when the application is about to be terminated. If a hidden frame has been created in memory, the code at lines 0615 through 0617 deletes it. The call to KillTimer() at line 0618 releases the timer for use by other applications. If bitmaps for the 19 frames have been created, the code at lines 0620 through 0630 deletes them, freeing the memory for use by other applications.

**Graphics system functions** The functions from lines 0698 through 0781 perform general maintenance and housekeeping functions for the graphics system. The function zInitFrame() at lines 0698 through 0745 creates the hidden bitmap that acts as the hidden frame. The function zClear() at lines 0774 through 0781 clears the client area of the display window. The function zClearHiddenFrame() at lines 0751 through 0755 clears the hidden frame. The function zCopyToDisplay() at lines 0761 through 0768 copies the contents of the hidden frame to the display window.

**Creating and saving the animation**  The zSaveAnimation() function at lines 0790 through 0869 manages the creation and storage of the 19-frame animation sequence. The if() statement at line 0792 ensures that a hidden frame has already been created (by selecting Initialize system from the Animation menu). The if() block at lines 0801 through 0809 cancels the operation if the frames have already been saved to disk during the current working session. (If the files were saved during a previous session, the software will detect their existence and will issue the warning advisory shown in FIG. 8-5 before overwriting them.) The if() statement at line 0811 cancels the operation if a previous attempt to create and save the frames failed. Finally, a flag named bPrevSaveAttempt is set to TRUE at line 0820. (This is the same variable that will be checked by line 0811 if zSaveAnimation() is called a second time.)

The code at lines 0822 through 0859 manages the pacing of the run-cycle and the frame file names. Observe line 0836, for example. The code calls a core function named zBuildFrame() that will create the image on the frame and save it to disk. The argument list includes the drawing1 array name, which indicates the the first cel in the run-cycle is to be used. If you check line 0834, you will see that the first seven frames have used the seven cels of the run-cycle, so the eighth frame will use the first cel of the run-cycle, which is a loop of images, of course. The argument list for zBuildFrame() also includes a LPSTR (long pointer to a string) variable that contains the file name. At line 0836, the file name is FRAME8.BIT. If you scan up and down the program listing, you can see how the file names are incremented from FRAME1.BIT to FRAME19.BIT. Note also how the call to zBuildFrame() returns a value and stores it in a variable named bFrameSaved. The next line of code uses an if() statement to test if any errors occurred and returns to the caller if the save was not successful. This premature return means that line 0861 would not execute, and the animation engine will remember that no animation has been saved during this working session.

**Building one frame**  The zBuildFrame() function at lines 0875 through 0923 is called 19 times by zSaveAnimation() as it creates and stores the entire animation sequence. Note the local font variables that are declared at lines 0879 and 0880. They are used by the block of code from lines 0887 through 0915 that writes the text title and text caption on the frame being built.

The zBuildFrame() function operates the same way each time it builds a frame. First, it clears the hidden frame (see line 0884). Second, it calls a core function to draw the gradient background on the hidden frame (see line

0885). Third, the block of code from 0887 through 0915 writes the text on the hidden frame. Fourth, it updates the cel position and calls a function to paste the cel onto the hidden frame (see lines 0917 and 0918). Fifth, it copies the completed image from the hidden frame to the display window (see line 0919). Finally, the code at line 0920 calls a function named zSaveFrame() to save the image to disk as a binary image file. Note how lines 0921 and 0922 return the result of the disk I/O operation to the caller.

**Drawing the background image** The zDrawBg() function at lines 0929 through 0997 draws the gradient background on the hidden page. This function is called by zBuildFrame(). The algorithm for gradient backgrounds was first introduced in the program listing in chapter 1, Windows.

**Drawing a cel** The zDoKeyDrawing() function at lines 1003 through 1080 is called 19 times by zBuildFrame(). The zDoKeyDrawing() function uses the array pointed to by ArrayPtr to draw the appropriate cel image. Because each database array is organized in a similar manner, the same code can be used to draw each of the seven images, even though the shape of each image is different. (Refer again to FIG. 8-1). The head is drawn using Ellipse(); the remaining elements are drawn using Polygon().

**Saving a frame to disk** The function at lines 1086 through 1209 saves a single frame to disk as a binary image file. Only the binary data that comprises the image from a bitmap is saved, not the bitmap header information.

Local variables are declared at lines 1088 through 1098. This block of code is fully commented so you can see the intended purpose of each variable.

The if() block at lines 1100 through 1106 cancels the save operation if Windows is running in a 256-color mode. In its current implementation the sample applicaton supports 16-color and 2-color modes in 640 × 480, 640 × 350, 800 × 600, and 1024 × 768 resolution. Refer to the discussion in chapter 3, Blitting, if you want to adapt the source code to support file I/O for 256-color images.

The if() statement at line 1108 ensures that a hidden frame is available.

The call to GetObject() at line 1117 grabs a copy of the bitmap data structure that is maintained by windows for the bitmap that comprises the client area of the display window. The if() statement at line 1119 kicks in if GetObject() returns any spurious values.

Using the data structure that was returned by GetObject(), the code at lines 1127 through 1140 calculates the width and height of the image, the number of bitplanes, and the corresponding length (in bytes) of the image data. A variable named NumBytes is initialized at line 1140 for future use by the low-level disk write function. Note also how the if() statement at line 1132 traps any image which is too large for a single-pass write to disk. (See chapter 3, Blitting, if you want to save larger images.)

The code that saves the image to disk operates by an eight-step algorithm that includes:

- Creating a buffer.
- Locking the buffer and grabbing a pointer to it.
- Copying the raw bits from the bitmap to the buffer.
- Opening a file.
- Writing the data from the buffer to the file.
- Closing the file.
- Unlocking the buffer and discarding the pointer.
- Discarding the buffer and freeing the memory it used.

Line 1142 calls GlobalAlloc() to allocate a moveable buffer in the far heap. The if() statement at line 1143 tests for memory allocation failures. The call to GlobalLock() at line 1151 locks the buffer and obtains a pointer to it. Then a call to GetBitmapBits() is used to copy the raw bits from the bitmap to the buffer. Again, an if() statement at line 1153 checks to ensure that everything went smoothly.

The application is now ready to write the image to disk. A call to Open-File() at line 1162 uses the OF_EXIST argument to test if the file already exists on disk. If so, the block of code at lines 1163 through 1173 uses a message box to ask the user if the software should overwrite the existing file with the new data. If not, the code at lines 1169 through 1172 tidies up and cancels the save function.

A call to OpenFile() at line 1174 using the OF_CREATE|OF_WRITE arguments opens a file for writing. A new file will be created if the file does not already exist. Notice the code that checks the return value at lines 1175 through 1182.

The image data is written to disk by the call to _lwrite() at line 1184. If any runtime errors occur, the IDS_DISK16 message is displayed (see line 0159 in the listing for frame.rc). Notice how the code carefully uses Global-Unlock() and GlobalFree() to tidy up all loose ends before cancelling.

A call to _lclose() at line 1196 closes the file after the data has been written to disk. Then lines 1206 and 1207 call GlobalUnlock() to discard the pointer to the buffer and GlobalFree() to discard the buffer and free the memory it occupied.

**Animation engine** The animation engine is contained in the zShowNextFrame() function at lines 1222 through 1340. This function calculates the next frame and then copies the appropriate bitmap to the display window. The animation engine is smart enough to detect whether the animation is running forward or reverse. It can also detect whether the animation is paused or being single-stepped in forward or reverse.

If Windows is running in real mode or if less than 2 MB of physical memory is available, the animation engine will load each frame from disk as needed during animation playback. Otherwise, the animation engine assumes that all 19 frames have already been loaded into memory and are ready for display. The code that loads the image files sets a variable named bUseDisk to indicate which algorithm is to be used for playback. The if() statement at line 1225 tests the value of bUseDisk and the code jumps ahead to line 1270 if disk-based playback is to be used.

The if() statements at lines 1228 through 1231 trap any runtime exceptions. If the animation is not ready, the function exits. If the animation is paused, the function exits. If a redisplay is being requested, the code jumps ahead to line 1242 and simply redisplays the current frame.

The code at lines 1232 through 1241 calculates the next frame number. For example, line 1234 is activated if the animation is running in forward mode and the variable FrameNum is incremented. The if() statement at line 1235 ensures that only existing frame numbers are used. The zFINALFRAME and zFIRSTFRAME constants were defined at lines 0196 and 0197.

The switch(FrameNum) block at lines 1244 through 1265 selects the appropriate bitmap into the hFDC memory-display context. Then the call to BitBlt() at line 1266 copies the bitmap to the display window. The function then returns to the caller.

If disk-based playback is being used, the code that traps runtime exceptions is located at lines 1271 through 1273. The code that calculates the next frame number is found at lines 1274 through 1283. The switch(FrameNum) block at lines 1286 through 1326 loads the appropriate image file from disk into the hidden frame bitmap. Then a call to BitBlt() at line 1337 copies the contents of the hidden frame to the display window. Note the trap at lines 1327 through 1336.

**Loading the animation** The zLoadAnimation() function at lines 1351 through 1513 loads all 19 frames from disk and stores them in memory. It calls zLoadFrame() (found later in the program listing at line 1565) 19 times. The block of code at lines 1384 through 1450 creates the bitmaps that will hold the images being downloaded from disk. Note the labels at lines 1426 through 1444. The code at lines 1387 through 1424 is structured to jump to the appropriate label if a memory allocation error occurs. It is important that DeleteObject() be called for every object created by CreateCompatible-Bitmap() before prematurely exiting the function. Note also how line 1384 makes a call to GlobalCompact() to force the Windows memory manager to reorganize memory to create the largest contiguous block possible. This improves the chances that the entire animation sequence will fit into memory on computers having more than 2 MB of memory.

The code at lines 1453 through 1500 loads the 19 frames from disk by repeatedly calling a core function named zLoadFrame() to load the data into a buffer and then to a bitmap. Note how if() statements are used to force the code to jumpt to the DISK_ERROR: label at line 1492 if any problems arise.

Before returning to the caller, the code at lines 1503 through 1512 selects the first frame into the hFDC memory-display context, sets a number of runtime flags to TRUE, and displays a message box to report the successful loading of the animation sequence.

**Resetting the animation rate**   The function at lines 1519 through 1559 resets the animation rate by resetting the timer. Note the switch() block at lines 1530 through 1538, which uses the hMenu menu ID to remove the check mark from the menu. The hMenu variable was initialized when the software detected that the user was accessing the Timer menu at line 0562 in the message handler function.

The call to KillTimer() at line 1539 disables the current timer. Then a call to SetTimer() at line 1540 sets a new timer using the wNewRate variable that was set in the message handler as a variable named wFrameRate. The code at line 1541 tidies up and exits if the call to SetTimer() failed.

The switch() block at lines 1549 through 1557 places a check mark on the menu. The check mark is located beside the new animation rate.

**Loading a single frame file**   The function named zLoadFrame() at lines 1565 through 1686 loads a single binary image file from disk. It operates by using an algorithm that is the reverse mirror image of the algorithm used by the file- save code at lines 1086 through 1209. The zLoadFrame() function follows eight steps:

- Create a buffer.
- Lock the buffer and grab a pointer to it.
- Open the file.
- Read the data from the file to the buffer.
- Close the file.
- Copy the raw bits from the buffer to the bitmap.
- Unlock the buffer and discard the pointer.
- Discard the buffer and free the memory it used.

## Program listings for the sample application

The program listings presented here contain all the source code you need to build and run the sample application. The module definition file is provided in FIG. 8-20. The #include file is found in FIG. 8-21. The resource script file is presented in FIG. 8-22. The C source file is provided in FIG. 8-23.

**Companion disk**   If you have the companion disk, the source files are presented as frame.def, frame.h, frame.rc, and frame.c.

**License**   You can paste the royalty-free source code into your own applications and distribute the resulting executable files under the conditions of the License Agreement and Limited Warranty in FIG. 10 in the introduction to the book.

**8-20** The module definition file listing for the sample application.

```
0001  NAME         DEFDEMO
0002  DESCRIPTION  'Copyright 1992 Lee Adams.  All rights reserved.'
0003  EXETYPE      WINDOWS
0004  STUB         'WINSTUB.EXE'
0005  CODE         PRELOAD MOVEABLE
0006  DATA         PRELOAD MOVEABLE MULTIPLE
0007  HEAPSIZE     1024
0008  STACKSIZE    8192
0009  EXPORTS      zMessageHandler
```

**8-21** The include file listing for the sample application.

```
0001  /*
0002  ------------------------------------------------------------------
0003                      Include file FRAME.H
0004          Copyright 1992 Lee Adams.  All rights reserved.
0005    Include this file in the .RC resource script file and in the
0006    .C source file.  It contains function prototypes, menu ID
0007    constants, and string ID constants.
0008  ------------------------------------------------------------------
0009  ------------------------------------------------------------------
0010                      Function prototypes
0011  ------------------------------------------------------------------
0012                                                                 */
0013  #if !defined(zRCFILE)                    /* if not an .RC file... */
0014    LONG FAR PASCAL zMessageHandler(HWND, unsigned, WORD, LONG);
0015    int PASCAL WinMain(HANDLE,HANDLE,LPSTR,int);
0016    HWND zInitMainWindow(HANDLE);
0017    BOOL zInitClass(HANDLE);
0018  static void zClear(HWND);              /* blank the display window */
0019  static void zInitFrame(HWND);             /* creates hidden frame */
0020  static void zShowNextFrame(HWND);        /* the playback engine */
0021  static void zDoKeyDrawing(HDC,int *);         /* draws one cel */
0022  static void zSetFrameRate(HWND,WORD);      /* resets the timer */
0023  static void zDrawBg(HDC);               /* draws the background */
0024  static void zSaveAnimation(HWND);      /* saves animation sequence */
0025  static BOOL zBuildFrame(int *,HWND,LPSTR);   /* builds one frame */
0026  static void zLoadAnimation(HWND);      /* loads animation sequence */
0027  static void zCopyToDisplay(HWND);      /* copies frame to display */
0028  static void zClearHiddenFrame(void);      /* clears hidden frame */
0029  static BOOL zSaveFrame(HBITMAP, LPSTR); /* saves a frame to disk */
0030  static BOOL zLoadFrame(HBITMAP, LPSTR);/* loads a frame from disk*/
0031  #endif
0032  /*
0033  ------------------------------------------------------------------
0034                      Menu ID constants
0035  ------------------------------------------------------------------
0036                                                                 */
0037  #define IDM_New           1
0038  #define IDM_Open          2
0039  #define IDM_Save          3
0040  #define IDM_SaveAs        4
0041  #define IDM_Exit          5
0042
0043  #define IDM_Undo          6
0044  #define IDM_Cut           7
0045  #define IDM_Copy          8
0046  #define IDM_Paste         9
0047  #define IDM_Delete        10
```

```
0048
0049    #define IDM_RunForward        11
0050    #define IDM_RunReverse        12
0051    #define IDM_StopAnimation     13
0052    #define IDM_InitFrame         14
0053    #define IDM_SaveAnimation     15
0054    #define IDM_LoadAnimation     16
0055    #define IDM_Clear             17
0056
0057    #define IDM_FPS182            18
0058    #define IDM_FPS91             19
0059    #define IDM_FPS61             20
0060    #define IDM_FPS45             21
0061    #define IDM_FPS36             22
0062    #define IDM_FPS30             23
0063
0064    #define IDM_About             24
0065    #define IDM_License           25
0066    #define IDM_Display           26
0067    #define IDM_Colors            27
0068    #define IDM_Mode              28
0069    #define IDM_Memory            29
0070    #define IDM_Timing            30
0071    #define IDM_GeneralHelp       31
0072    /*
0073    ----------------------------------------------------------------
0074                        String ID constants
0075    ----------------------------------------------------------------
0076                                                                  */
0077    #define IDS_Caption       1
0078    #define IDS_Warning       2
0079    #define IDS_NoMouse       3
0080    #define IDS_About         4
0081    #define IDS_AboutText     5
0082    #define IDS_License       6
0083    #define IDS_LicenseText   7
0084    #define IDS_Help          8
0085    #define IDS_HelpText      9
0086    #define IDS_Completed     10
0087    #define IDS_Error         11
0088    #define IDS_Memory        12
0089    #define IDS_MemText       13
0090    #define IDS_Timing        14
0091    #define IDS_TimingText    15
0092    #define IDS_NotReady      16
0093    #define IDS_Ready         17
0094    #define IDS_BuildBefore   18
0095    #define IDS_Already       19
0096    #define IDS_InsufMem1     20
0097    #define IDS_InsufMem2     21
0098    #define IDS_NoTimer       22
0099    #define IDS_NoReset       23
0100    #define IDS_CannotReset   24
0101    #define IDS_Resolution    25
0102    #define IDS_ResVGA        26
0103    #define IDS_ResEGA        27
0104    #define IDS_ResCGA        28
0105    #define IDS_ResSVGA       29
0106    #define IDS_Res8514       30
0107    #define IDS_ResHerc       31
0108    #define IDS_ResCustom     32
```

```
0109  #define IDS_Color        33
0110  #define IDS_Color16      34
0111  #define IDS_Color256     35
0112  #define IDS_Color2       36
0113  #define IDS_ColorCustom  37
0114  #define IDS_Machine      38
0115  #define IDS_Enhanced     39
0116  #define IDS_Standard     40
0117  #define IDS_Real         41
0118  #define IDS_NoFrame      42
0119  #define IDS_AnimReady    43
0120  #define IDS_Unexpected   44
0121  #define IDS_Status       45
0122  #define IDS_Disk1        46
0123  #define IDS_Disk2        47
0124  #define IDS_Disk3        48
0125  #define IDS_Disk4        49
0126  #define IDS_Disk5        50
0127  #define IDS_Disk6        51
0128  #define IDS_Disk7        52
0129  #define IDS_Disk8        53
0130  #define IDS_Disk9        54
0131  #define IDS_Disk10       55
0132  #define IDS_Disk11       56
0133  #define IDS_Disk12       57
0134  #define IDS_Disk13       58
0135  #define IDS_Disk14       59
0136  #define IDS_Disk15       60
0137  #define IDS_Disk16       61
0138  #define IDS_Disk17       62
0139  #define IDS_Disk18       63
0140  #define IDS_Disk19       64
0141  #define IDS_Disk20       65
0142  #define IDS_Disk21       66
0143  #define IDS_Disk22       67
0144  #define IDS_Disk23       68
0145  #define IDS_Disk24       69
0146  #define IDS_Disk25       70
0147  #define IDS_Disk26       71
0148  /*
0149  ------------------------------------------------------------
0150                      End of include file
0151  ------------------------------------------------------------
0152                                                          */
```

**8-22** The resource script file listing for the sample application.

```
0001  /*
0002  ------------------------------------------------------------
0003                  Resource script file FRAME.RC
0004              Copyright 1992 Lee Adams.  All rights reserved.
0005     This file defines the menu resources, the accelerator key
0006     resources, and the string resources that will be used by the
0007     demonstration application at runtime.
0008  ------------------------------------------------------------
0009                                                          */
0010  #define zRCFILE
0011  #include <WINDOWS.H>
0012  #include "FRAME.H"
0013  /*
```

**8-22** Continued.

```
0014    ---------------------------------------------------------------
0015                          Script for menus
0016    ---------------------------------------------------------------
0017                                                                  */
0018    MENUS1 MENU
0019      BEGIN
0020      POPUP "&File"
0021        BEGIN
0022          MENUITEM  "&New", IDM_New, GRAYED
0023          MENUITEM  "&Open...", IDM_Open, GRAYED
0024          MENUITEM  "&Save", IDM_Save, GRAYED
0025          MENUITEM  "Save &As...", IDM_SaveAs, GRAYED
0026          MENUITEM  SEPARATOR
0027          MENUITEM  "E&xit", IDM_Exit
0028        END
0029      POPUP "&Edit"
0030        BEGIN
0031          MENUITEM   "&Undo\tAlt+BkSp", IDM_Undo, GRAYED
0032          MENUITEM   SEPARATOR
0033          MENUITEM   "Cu&t\tShift+Del", IDM_Cut, GRAYED
0034          MENUITEM   "&Copy\tCtrl+Ins", IDM_Copy, GRAYED
0035          MENUITEM   "&Paste\tShift+Ins", IDM_Paste, GRAYED
0036          MENUITEM   "&Delete\tDel", IDM_Delete, GRAYED
0037        END
0038      POPUP "&Animation"
0039        BEGIN
0040          MENUITEM "Run &Forward", IDM_RunForward
0041          MENUITEM "Run &Reverse", IDM_RunReverse
0042          MENUITEM "&Pause", IDM_StopAnimation
0043          MENUITEM SEPARATOR
0044          MENUITEM "&Initialize system", IDM_InitFrame
0045          MENUITEM "Cr&eate Frames", IDM_SaveAnimation
0046          MENUITEM SEPARATOR
0047          MENUITEM "&Load Animation", IDM_LoadAnimation
0048          MENUITEM SEPARATOR
0049          MENUITEM "&Clear", IDM_Clear
0050        END
0051      POPUP "&Timer"
0052        BEGIN
0053          MENUITEM "&18 fps", IDM_FPS182, CHECKED
0054          MENUITEM " &9 fps", IDM_FPS91
0055          MENUITEM " &6 fps", IDM_FPS61
0056          MENUITEM " &5 fps", IDM_FPS45
0057          MENUITEM " &4 fps", IDM_FPS36
0058          MENUITEM " &3 fps", IDM_FPS30
0059        END
0060      POPUP "&Help"
0061        BEGIN
0062          MENUITEM "&About", IDM_About
0063          MENUITEM "&License", IDM_License
0064          MENUITEM SEPARATOR
0065          MENUITEM "&Screen resolution", IDM_Display
0066          MENUITEM "Available &colors", IDM_Colors
0067          MENUITEM "Memory mode", IDM_Mode
0068          MENUITEM SEPARATOR
0069          MENUITEM "&Memory notes", IDM_Memory
0070          MENUITEM "&Timing notes", IDM_Timing
0071          MENUITEM SEPARATOR
0072          MENUITEM "&Help", IDM_GeneralHelp
0073        END
0074    END
```

```
0075    /*
0076    ------------------------------------------------------------------
0077                       Script for accelerator keys
0078    ------------------------------------------------------------------
0079                                                                   */
0080    KEYS1 ACCELERATORS
0081      BEGIN
0082      VK_BACK, IDM_Undo, VIRTKEY, ALT
0083      VK_DELETE, IDM_Cut, VIRTKEY, SHIFT
0084      VK_INSERT, IDM_Copy, VIRTKEY, CONTROL
0085      VK_INSERT, IDM_Paste, VIRTKEY, SHIFT
0086      VK_DELETE, IDM_Delete,VIRTKEY
0087      END
0088    /*
0089    ------------------------------------------------------------------
0090                        Script for strings
0091      Programmer's Notes:  If you are typing this listing, set your
0092      margins to a line length of 255 characters so you can create
0093      lengthy strings without embedded carriage returns.  The line
0094      wraparounds in the following STRINGTABLE script are used for
0095      readability only in this printout.
0096    ------------------------------------------------------------------
0097                                                                   */
0098    STRINGTABLE
0099      BEGIN
0100        IDS_Caption      "ANIMATION ENGINE (frame version)"
0101        IDS_Warning      "Warning"
0102        IDS_NoMouse      "No mouse found.  Some features of this
                demonstration program may require a mouse."
0103        IDS_About        "About this program"
0104        IDS_AboutText    "This is a demo from Windcrest McGraw-Hill
                book 4114.  Copyright 1992 Lee Adams.  All rights reserved."
0105        IDS_License      "License Agreement"
0106        IDS_LicenseText "You can use this code as part of your own
                software product subject to the License Agreement and Limited
                Warranty in Windcrest McGraw-Hill book 4114 and on its
                companion disk."
0107        IDS_Help         "How to use this demo"
0108        IDS_HelpText     "The Animation menu manages the animation
                engine.  Select Initialize System then Create Frames to build
                frames and save to disk.  Select Load Animation then Run
                Forward to play animation.  See the book for advanced
                features."
0109        IDS_Completed    "Task completed OK"
0110        IDS_Error        "Runtime error"
0111        IDS_Memory       "Animation memory requirements"
0112        IDS_MemText      "The hidden frame for the animation is stored
                as a bitmap in global memory.  The demo will advise you if a
                memory shortage occurs.  To make more global memory available
                you can close other applications."
0113        IDS_Timing       "Animation timing"
0114        IDS_TimingText  "The Timer menu sets the animation display
                rate to 18.2, 9.1, 6.1, 4.5, 3.6, or 3 frames per second.
                Actual performance is limited by your computer's processor
                (25MHz or faster is recommended).  See the book for details."
0115        IDS_NotReady     "Animation not ready"
0116        IDS_Ready        "Animation ready"
0117        IDS_BuildBefore "Animation frames not ready for playback."
0118        IDS_Already      "The hidden frame has already been created."
0119        IDS_InsufMem1    "Insufficient global memory for frame bitmap."
```

**8-22** Continued.

```
0120    IDS_NoTimer      "Unable to create a timer.  Close other
        applications."
0121    IDS_NoReset      "Create hidden frame before attempting to
        reset timer."
0122    IDS_CannotReset  "Unable to reset the timer."
0123    IDS_Resolution   "Screen resolution"
0124    IDS_ResVGA       "Running in 640x480 mode."
0125    IDS_ResEGA       "Running in 640x350 mode."
0126    IDS_ResCGA       "Running in 640x200 mode."
0127    IDS_ResSVGA      "Running in 800x600 mode."
0128    IDS_Res8514      "Running in 1024x768 mode."
0129    IDS_ResHerc      "Running in 720x348 mode."
0130    IDS_ResCustom    "Running in custom mode."
0131    IDS_Color        "Available colors"
0132    IDS_Color16      "Running in 16-color mode."
0133    IDS_Color256     "Running in 256-color mode."
0134    IDS_Color2       "Running in 2-color mode."
0135    IDS_ColorCustom  "Running in a custom color mode."
0136    IDS_Machine      "Memory mode"
0137    IDS_Enhanced     "Running in enhanced mode.  Can allocate up to
        16 MB extended physical memory (XMS) if available.  Virtual
        memory up to 4 times physical memory (maximum 64 MB) is also
        available via automatic disk swapping of 4K pages."
0138    IDS_Standard     "Running in standard mode.  Can allocate up to
        16 MB extended physical memory (XMS) if available."
0139    IDS_Real         "Running in real mode.  Can allocate blocks of
        memory from the first 640K of RAM.  Can also allocate blocks
        from expanded memory (EMS) if available."
0140    IDS_NoFrame      "Hidden frame not yet created."
0141    IDS_AnimReady    "Animation ready"
0142    IDS_Unexpected   "Unexpected animation condition"
0143    IDS_Status       "Animation status"
0144    IDS_Disk1        "Animation files already saved to disk."
0145    IDS_Disk2        "Animation sequence successfully saved to
        disk."
0146    IDS_Disk3        "Unable to load next frame from disk.
        Animation halted."
0147    IDS_Disk4        "Animation sequence already loaded from disk."
0148    IDS_Disk5        "Previous load failed.  Cancelling this
        attempt."
0149    IDS_Disk6        "Not enough memory available.  Software will
        dynamically load each frame from disk during playback."
0150    IDS_Disk7        "Animation sequence successfully loaded from
        disk."
0151    IDS_Disk8        "Previous save failed.  Cancelling this
        attempt."
0152    IDS_Disk9        "No hidden-frame exists.  No frame saved to
        disk."
0153    IDS_Disk10       "Unable to retrieve bitmap data structure."
0154    IDS_Disk11       "Bit array is too long to save to disk in a
        single pass."
0155    IDS_Disk12       "Cannot create memory buffer for disk write."
0156    IDS_Disk13       "Unable to copy bits from bitmap to buffer."
0157    IDS_Disk14       "File already exists.  Overwrite existing
        file?"
0158    IDS_Disk15       "Unable to open the file for writing."
0159    IDS_Disk16       "Unable to write to the opened file."
0160    IDS_Disk17       "Unable to close the file after writing."
0161    IDS_Disk18       "No memory bitmap exists.  Unable to load from
        disk."
```

```
0162      IDS_Disk19      "Image file is larger than animation frame.
          No file loaded."
0163      IDS_Disk20      "Cannot create memory buffer for file read."
0164      IDS_Disk21      "Unable to open the file for reading.  Be sure
          you have saved an animation sequence to disk before attempting
          to load it."
0165      IDS_Disk22      "An error occurred while reading the file."
0166      IDS_Disk23      "The frame file was shorter than expected."
0167      IDS_Disk24      "Unable to close the file after reading."
0168      IDS_Disk25      "Unable to copy bits from buffer to bitmap."
0169      IDS_Disk26      "Unable to save all files.  Check if
          sufficient space available on disk."
0170   END
0171   /*
0172   --------------------------------------------------------------
0173                      End of resource script file
0174   --------------------------------------------------------------
0175                                                              */
```

**8-23**   The C source file listing for the sample application, frame.c. This demonstration program is ready to build using QuickC for Windows, Turbo C++ for Windows, Microsoft C and the SDK, Borland C++, Symantec Zortech C++, WATCOM C, and other compilers. See FIG. 1-2 for sample command-lines to build the program. Guidelines for using your compiler are provided in the appropriate appendix at the back of the book.

```
0001   /*
0002   --------------------------------------------------------------
0003        Reconfigurable ANIMATION ENGINE for Windows applications
0004        that use disk-based, hidden-page drawn, frame animation.
0005        The animation engine is comprised of an authoring system
0006        for creating cels, frames, and disk files -- and a playback
0007        engine for loading frames from disk files and displaying
0008        them as an animation sequence.
0009   --------------------------------------------------------------
0010   Source file: FRAME.C
0011   Release version: 1.00             Programmer: Lee Adams
0012   Type:  C source file for Windows application development.
0013   Compilers: Microsoft C and SDK, Borland C++, Zortech C++,
0014      QuickC for Windows, Turbo C++ for Windows, WATCOM C.
0015   Memory model:  small.
0016   Dependencies:  FRAME.DEF module definition file, FRAME.H
0017                  include file, FRAME.RC resource script file,
0018                  and FRAME.C source file.
0019   Output and features: Demonstrates interactive playback of
0020      disk-based hidden-page drawn frame animation.  Refer to
0021      REALTIME.C for fully-commented code.
0022   Publication: Contains material from Windcrest/McGraw-Hill book
0023      4114 published by TAB BOOKS Division of McGraw-Hill Inc.
0024   License:  As purchaser of the book you are granted a royalty-
0025      free license to distribute executable files generated using
0026      this code provided you accept the conditions of the License
0027      Agreement and Limited Warranty described in the book and on
0028      the companion disk.  Government users:  This software and
0029      documentation are subject to restrictions set forth in The
0030      Rights in Technical Data and Computer Software clause at
0031      252.227-7013 and elsewhere.
0032   --------------------------------------------------------------
```

**8-23** Continued.

```
0033            (c) Copyright 1992 Lee Adams.  All rights reserved.
0034              Lee Adams(tm) is a trademark of Lee Adams.
0035   -------------------------------------------------------------
0036
0037   -------------------------------------------------------------
0038                          Include files
0039   -------------------------------------------------------------
0040                                                              */
0041   #include <WINDOWS.H>
0042   #include <SYS\TYPES.H>
0043   #include <SYS\STAT.H>
0044   #include "FRAME.H"
0045   /*
0046   -------------------------------------------------------------
0047            Static variables visible throughout this file
0048   -------------------------------------------------------------
0049                                                              */
0050   /* -------------------- window specifications ---------------- */
0051   #define zWINDOW_WIDTH 408
0052   #define zWINDOW_HEIGHT 346
0053   #define zFRAMEWIDE 400
0054   #define zFRAMEHIGH 300
0055   int WindowX, WindowY;
0056
0057   /* -------------------- instance operations ------------------- */
0058   HANDLE hInst;
0059   HWND MainhWnd;
0060   HANDLE hAccel;
0061   HMENU hMenu;
0062   PAINTSTRUCT ps;
0063   int MessageRet;
0064
0065   /* -------------------- mouse and cursor -------------------- */
0066   HCURSOR hPrevCursor;
0067   HCURSOR hHourGlass;
0068   int MousePresent;
0069
0070   /* -------------------- runtime conditions ------------------- */
0071   int DisplayWidth, DisplayHeight;
0072   int DisplayBits;
0073   int DisplayPlanes;
0074   DWORD MemoryMode;
0075
0076   /* ------------------ message box operations ---------------- */
0077   char lpCaption[51];
0078   int Max= 50;
0079   char lpMessage[250];
0080   int MaxText= 249;
0081
0082   /* --------------- persistent image operations ------------- */
0083   #define zBLANK 0
0084   #define zANIMATING  1
0085   int PaintImage= zBLANK;
0086
0087   /* -------------------- timer operations -------------------- */
0088   #define zTIMER_PAUSE 3
0089   int TimerCounter= zTIMER_PAUSE;
0090   BOOL TimerExists= FALSE;
0091   WORD TimerID1;
0092
0093   /* -------------------- font operations -------------------- */
```

**8-23** Continued.

```
0094    HFONT hFont, hPrevFont;              /* handles to new, previous font */
0095    HDC hFontDC;                              /* display-context for font */
0096
0097    /* ----------------- hidden frame operations ----------------- */
0098    HDC hFrameDC;
0099    HBITMAP hFrame;
0100    HBITMAP hPrevFrame;
0101    BOOL FrameReady= FALSE;
0102
0103    /* ----------------- database for cel images ----------------- */
0104    int drawing1[]=
0105    {
0106    36,16,45,23,49,27,47,28,42,25,54,26,78,54,76,60,57,57,42,30,
0107    15,25,24,27,23,33,12,32,22,32,30,44,26,46,20,35,
0108    45,35,48,38,25,46,23,44,55,28,69,20,70,23,58,31,
0109    68,20,91,20,91,23,70,23,91,20,100,15,100,18,91,23,
0110    31,52,65,55,71,60,35,55,40,57,51,75,41,74,31,52,
0111    46,68,51,75,22,72,40,68,76,60,106,92,101,94,69,60,
0112    76,60,106,92,101,94,69,60,104,92,111,92,111,108,104,106,
0113    111,108,105,115,100,115,104,107
0114    };
0115    int drawing2[]=
0116    {
0117    36,13,44,20,48,24,43,24,41,21,51,22,77,55,71,58,54,56,40,25,
0118    20,31,20,39,12,40,10,33,20,36,34,43,35,45,20,39,
0119    44,32,46,36,35,45,34,42,54,25,76,25,76,28,54,28,
0120    78,25,95,33,95,37,74,28,95,33,105,30,104,35,95,37,
0121    52,52,54,55,32,60,28,59,28,59,32,60,32,85,28,78,
0122    32,78,32,85,10,75,28,78,75,56,92,73,88,76,70,57,
0123    92,74,116,86,112,90,88,76,116,86,120,85,120,108,112,90,
0124    116,86,120,85,120,108,112,90
0125    };
0126    int drawing3[]=
0127    {
0128    38,10,45,16,48,21,44,22,41,17,52,20,75,55,70,56,53,54,40,22,
0129    20,36,24,44,17,47,13,40,22,40,40,43,40,47,22,44,
0130    37,43,44,31,47,36,40,47,55,25,76,29,74,31,55,29,
0131    76,29,90,45,85,48,74,31,90,45,100,45,95,49,85,49,
0132    53,54,55,58,35,72,30,69,35,72,16,96,17,85,30,69,
0133    17,85,20,90,17,96,0,80,75,55,92,70,88,74,70,57,
0134    92,70,121,77,122,81,87,73,121,77,126,75,139,95,122,81,
0135    121,77,126,75,139,95,122,81
0136    };
0137    int drawing4[]=
0138    {
0139    38,13,45,19,48,23,44,25,41,20,52,22,70,56,64,60,46,60,40,26,
0140    32,43,36,46,34,51,27,48,36,46,50,44,50,48,36,49,
0141    36,46,50,44,50,48,36,49,55,35,69,45,62,50,55,40,
0142    55,35,69,45,62,50,55,40,55,35,69,45,62,50,55,40,
0143    46,59,51,60,31,75,26,73,26,73,31,76,25,105,22,97,
0144    22,97,26,99,25,105,0,95,58,60,64,60,58,78,50,78,
0145    58,78,75,85,74,89,50,78,75,85,80,85,80,103,74,88,
0146    75,85,80,85,80,103,74,88
0147    };
0148    int drawing5[]=
0149    {
0150    38,18,45,25,49,28,43,30,42,26,54,28,56,64,45,66,34,64,40,31,
0151    27,58,26,63,18,58,21,55,28,58,40,56,40,60,25,63,
0152    28,58,40,56,40,60,25,63,54,28,57,48,60,46,54,38,
0153    60,48,66,48,52,53,50,50,60,48,66,48,52,53,50,50,
0154    34,65,40,66,14,76,12,74,22,74,40,78,38,82,12,76,
```

```
0155   40,78,46,76,45,96,38,82,40,68,45,66,27,85,20,84,
0156   27,85,33,114,25,107,20,84,25,107,31,107,32,115,5,115,
0157   25,107,31,107,32,115,5,115
0158   };
0159   int drawing6[]=
0160   {
0161   38,22,41,29,45,35,39,35,39,30,38,36,49,33,60,68,52,70,39,70,
0162   12,48,16,54,11,59,5,51,15,52,34,55,38,59,15,56,
0163   33,55,40,40,40,50,38,60,50,38,65,50,60,50,50,43,
0164   60,50,65,50,60,67,58,63,60,50,65,50,60,67,58,63,
0165   38,66,39,70,16,80,15,76,22,77,49,85,36,85,16,80,
0166   40,83,49,86,32,102,36,86,45,72,52,70,43,91,38,90,
0167   41,89,62,104,54,103,38,92,53,104,63,104,54,115,49,112,
0168   52,112,53,115,43,115,49,112
0169   };
0170   int drawing7[]=
0171   {
0172   38,19,45,25,48,30,43,31,42,26,51,30,69,62,60,65,49,61,40,32,
0173   14,33,15,41,6,42,4,34,15,38,30,45,30,50,15,41,
0174   30,45,41,38,42,42,30,50,53,32,73,36,71,39,55,36,
0175   73,37,83,53,80,55,71,40,83,53,93,55,89,57,80,55,
0176   49,61,60,65,22,65,23,61,31,65,53,81,40,80,23,65,
0177   48,77,53,81,27,89,40,79,61,65,67,63,68,84,63,85,
0178   68,83,84,99,80,101,63,85,81,98,89,98,85,113,80,111,
0179   89,111,85,112,80,115,76,115
0180   };
0181
0182   /* ----------------- animation engine -------------------- */
0183   BOOL Pause= TRUE;
0184   WORD wFrameRate= 55;
0185   WORD wPrevRate= 55;
0186   #define zFORWARD 1
0187   #define zREVERSE 0
0188   int FrameDirection= zFORWARD;
0189   BOOL Redisplay= FALSE;
0190   int SX1= 406;
0191   int SY1= 90;
0192   #define zMOVEHORIZ 26
0193   #define zMAXLEFT -164
0194   #define zMAXRIGHT 400
0195   int FrameNum= 0;
0196   #define zFIRSTFRAME 1
0197   #define zFINALFRAME 19
0198   BOOL AnimationReady= FALSE;
0199
0200   /* --------------- disk save/load operations ---------------- */
0201   int RetVal;                              /* return value */
0202   BOOL bFrameSaved= FALSE;            /* frame saved to disk? */
0203   BOOL bFrameLoaded= FALSE;         /* frame loaded from disk? */
0204   BOOL bAnimationSaved= FALSE;       /* animation saved to disk? */
0205   BOOL bAnimationLoaded= FALSE;    /* animation loaded from disk? */
0206   BOOL bPrevSaveAttempt= FALSE;    /* previous save attempt made? */
0207   BOOL bPrevLoadAttempt= FALSE;    /* previous load attempt made? */
0208   HDC hFDC;                /* memory-display context for playback */
0209   HBITMAP hPrevF,hF1,hF2,hF3,hF4,hF5,   /* bitmaps for playback... */
0210    hF6,hF7,hF8,hF9,hF10,hF11,hF12,hF13,hF14,hF15,hF16,hF17,hF18,hF19;
0211   BOOL bUseDisk= FALSE;            /* load each frame as needed? */
0212   BOOL bAnimationHalted= FALSE;    /* disk error during animation? */
0213   /*
0214   -----------------------------------------------------------------
0215                    Entry point for the application
```

```
0216  -----------------------------------------------------------------
0217                                                                  */
0218  int PASCAL WinMain(HANDLE hInstance, HANDLE hPrevInstance,
0219                     LPSTR lpCmdLine, int nCmdShow)
0220  {
0221    MSG msg;
0222    HWND hWndPrev;
0223    HWND hDesktopWnd;
0224    HDC hDCcaps;
0225
0226  /* ----------- ensure only one instance is running ----------- */
0227  hWndPrev = FindWindow("DEMOCLASS", NULL);
0228  if (hWndPrev != NULL)
0229    {
0230    BringWindowToTop(hWndPrev);
0231    return FALSE;
0232    }
0233
0234  /* --------- determine capabilities of screen display ---------- */
0235  hDesktopWnd= GetDesktopWindow();
0236  hDCcaps= GetDC(hDesktopWnd);
0237  DisplayWidth= GetDeviceCaps(hDCcaps,HORZRES);
0238  DisplayHeight= GetDeviceCaps(hDCcaps,VERTRES);
0239  DisplayBits= GetDeviceCaps(hDCcaps,BITSPIXEL);
0240  DisplayPlanes= GetDeviceCaps(hDCcaps,PLANES);
0241  ReleaseDC(hDesktopWnd,hDCcaps);
0242
0243  /* ------- calculate screen position to center the window ------ */
0244  WindowX= (DisplayWidth - zWINDOW_WIDTH) / 2;
0245  WindowY= (DisplayHeight - zWINDOW_HEIGHT) /2;
0246  if (WindowX < 0) WindowX= 0;
0247  if (WindowY < 0) WindowY= 0;
0248
0249  /* ---- determine memory mode (enhanced, standard, or real) ---- */
0250  MemoryMode= GetWinFlags();
0251
0252  /* ---------------- create and show the window ---------------- */
0253  hInst = hInstance;
0254  if (!zInitClass(hInstance)) return FALSE;
0255  MainhWnd = zInitMainWindow(hInstance);
0256  if (!MainhWnd) return FALSE;
0257  ShowWindow(MainhWnd, nCmdShow);
0258  UpdateWindow(MainhWnd);
0259  hAccel= LoadAccelerators(hInstance,"KEYS1");
0260  hFontDC= GetDC(MainhWnd);
0261  hFont= GetStockObject(SYSTEM_FONT);
0262  hPrevFont= SelectObject(hFontDC,hFont);
0263  SetTextColor(hFontDC,RGB(191,191,191));
0264  TextOut(hFontDC,10,280,"- Copyright 1992 Lee Adams.",27);
0265  SetTextColor(hFontDC,RGB(0,0,0));
0266  SelectObject(hFontDC,hPrevFont);
0267  ReleaseDC(MainhWnd,hFontDC);
0268
0269  /* ---------------------- check for mouse --------------------- */
0270  MousePresent = GetSystemMetrics(SM_MOUSEPRESENT);
0271  if (!MousePresent)
0272    {
0273    LoadString(hInst,IDS_Warning,lpCaption,Max);
0274    LoadString(hInst,IDS_NoMouse,lpMessage,MaxText);
0275    MessageBox(GetFocus(),lpMessage,lpCaption,MB_OK);
0276    }
```

ENTRY POINT

```
0277
0278    /* ---------- begin retrieving messages for the window --------- */
0279    while (GetMessage(&msg,0,0,0))
0280      {
0281      if(TranslateAccelerator(MainhWnd, hAccel, &msg))
0282        continue;
0283      TranslateMessage(&msg);
0284      DispatchMessage(&msg);
0285      }
0286    return(msg.wParam);
0287    }
0288    /*
0289    ---------------------------------------------------------------------
0290                      Switcher for incoming messages
0291    ---------------------------------------------------------------------
0292                                                                     */
0293    LONG FAR PASCAL zMessageHandler(HWND hWnd, unsigned message,
0294                           WORD wParam, LONG lParam)
0295    {
0296      HDC hDCpaint;
0297
0298    switch (message)
0299      {
0300
0301      case WM_TIMER:
0302        TimerCounter--;
0303        if (TimerCounter > 0) break;
0304        TimerCounter++;
0305        zShowNextFrame(hWnd);
0306        break;
0307
0308      case WM_COMMAND:
0309        switch(wParam)
0310          {
0311          case IDM_New:     break;
0312          case IDM_Open:    break;
0313          case IDM_Save:    break;
0314          case IDM_SaveAs:  break;
0315          case IDM_Exit:    PostQuitMessage(0); break;
0316
0317          case IDM_Undo:    break;
0318          case IDM_Cut:     break;
0319          case IDM_Copy:    break;
0320          case IDM_Paste:   break;
0321          case IDM_Delete:  break;
0322
0323          case IDM_RunForward:
0324              if (AnimationReady==FALSE)
0325                {
0326                MessageBeep(0);
0327                LoadString(hInst,IDS_NotReady,lpCaption,Max);
0328                LoadString(hInst,IDS_BuildBefore,lpMessage,MaxText);
0329                TimerCounter= zTIMER_PAUSE;
0330                MessageBox(GetFocus(),lpMessage,lpCaption,MB_OK);
0331                break;
0332                }
0333              Pause= FALSE;
0334              PaintImage= zANIMATING;
0335              FrameDirection= zFORWARD;
0336              zShowNextFrame(hWnd);
0337              break;
```

```
0338        case IDM_RunReverse:
0339            if (AnimationReady==FALSE)
0340               {
0341               MessageBeep(0);
0342               LoadString(hInst,IDS_NotReady,lpCaption,Max);
0343               LoadString(hInst,IDS_BuildBefore,lpMessage,MaxText);
0344               TimerCounter= zTIMER_PAUSE;
0345               MessageBox(GetFocus(),lpMessage,lpCaption,MB_OK);
0346               break;
0347               }
0348            Pause= FALSE;
0349            PaintImage= zANIMATING;
0350            FrameDirection= zREVERSE;
0351            zShowNextFrame(hWnd);
0352            break;
0353        case IDM_StopAnimation:
0354            if (AnimationReady==FALSE)
0355               {
0356               MessageBeep(0);
0357               LoadString(hInst,IDS_NotReady,lpCaption,Max);
0358               LoadString(hInst,IDS_BuildBefore,lpMessage,MaxText);
0359               TimerCounter= zTIMER_PAUSE;
0360               MessageBox(GetFocus(),lpMessage,lpCaption,MB_OK);
0361               break;
0362               }
0363            Pause= TRUE;
0364            zShowNextFrame(hWnd);
0365            break;
0366        case IDM_InitFrame: zInitFrame(hWnd); break;
0367        case IDM_SaveAnimation:
0368            SetCapture(hWnd); hPrevCursor= SetCursor(hHourGlass);
0369            zSaveAnimation(hWnd);
0370            SetCursor(hPrevCursor); ReleaseCapture();
0371            if (bAnimationSaved==FALSE)
0372               {
0373               MessageBeep(0);
0374               LoadString(hInst,IDS_NotReady,lpCaption,Max);
0375               LoadString(hInst,IDS_Disk26,lpMessage,MaxText);
0376               TimerCounter= zTIMER_PAUSE;
0377               MessageBox(GetFocus(),lpMessage,lpCaption,MB_OK);
0378               }
0379            break;
0380        case IDM_LoadAnimation:
0381            SetCapture(hWnd); hPrevCursor= SetCursor(hHourGlass);
0382            zLoadAnimation(hWnd);
0383            SetCursor(hPrevCursor); ReleaseCapture();
0384            break;
0385        case IDM_Clear:  if (Pause==TRUE)
0386                            {
0387                            zClear(hWnd);
0388                            PaintImage= zBLANK;
0389                            }
0390                         break;
0391
0392        case IDM_FPS182: wPrevRate= wFrameRate;
0393                         wFrameRate= (WORD)55;
0394                         zSetFrameRate(hWnd, wFrameRate); break;
0395        case IDM_FPS91:  wPrevRate= wFrameRate;
0396                         wFrameRate= (WORD)110;
0397                         zSetFrameRate(hWnd, wFrameRate); break;
0398        case IDM_FPS61:  wPrevRate= wFrameRate;
```

```
0399                            wFrameRate= (WORD)165;
0400                            zSetFrameRate(hWnd, wFrameRate); break;
0401         case IDM_FPS45: wPrevRate= wFrameRate;
0402                            wFrameRate= (WORD) 220;
0403                            zSetFrameRate(hWnd, wFrameRate); break;
0404         case IDM_FPS36: wPrevRate= wFrameRate;
0405                            wFrameRate= (WORD) 275;
0406                            zSetFrameRate(hWnd, wFrameRate); break;
0407         case IDM_FPS30: wPrevRate= wFrameRate;
0408                            wFrameRate= (WORD) 330;
0409                            zSetFrameRate(hWnd, wFrameRate); break;
0410
0411         case IDM_About:
0412           LoadString(hInst,IDS_About,lpCaption,Max);
0413           LoadString(hInst,IDS_AboutText,lpMessage,MaxText);
0414           TimerCounter= zTIMER_PAUSE;
0415           MessageBox(GetFocus(),lpMessage,lpCaption,MB_OK);
0416           break;
0417         case IDM_License:
0418           LoadString(hInst,IDS_License,lpCaption,Max);
0419           LoadString(hInst,IDS_LicenseText,lpMessage,MaxText);
0420           TimerCounter= zTIMER_PAUSE;
0421           MessageBox(GetFocus(),lpMessage,lpCaption,MB_OK);
0422           break;
0423
0424         case IDM_Display:
0425           if (DisplayWidth==640)
0426             {
0427             if (DisplayHeight==480)
0428               {
0429               LoadString(hInst,IDS_Resolution,lpCaption,Max);
0430               LoadString(hInst,IDS_ResVGA,lpMessage,MaxText);
0431               TimerCounter= zTIMER_PAUSE;
0432               MessageBox(GetFocus(),lpMessage,lpCaption,MB_OK);
0433               }
0434             if (DisplayHeight==350)
0435               {
0436               LoadString(hInst,IDS_Resolution,lpCaption,Max);
0437               LoadString(hInst,IDS_ResEGA,lpMessage,MaxText);
0438               TimerCounter= zTIMER_PAUSE;
0439               MessageBox(GetFocus(),lpMessage,lpCaption,MB_OK);
0440               }
0441             if (DisplayHeight==200)
0442               {
0443               LoadString(hInst,IDS_Resolution,lpCaption,Max);
0444               LoadString(hInst,IDS_ResCGA,lpMessage,MaxText);
0445               TimerCounter= zTIMER_PAUSE;
0446               MessageBox(GetFocus(),lpMessage,lpCaption,MB_OK);
0447               }
0448             break;
0449             }
0450           if (DisplayWidth==800)
0451             {
0452             LoadString(hInst,IDS_Resolution,lpCaption,Max);
0453             LoadString(hInst,IDS_ResSVGA,lpMessage,MaxText);
0454             TimerCounter= zTIMER_PAUSE;
0455             MessageBox(GetFocus(),lpMessage,lpCaption,MB_OK);
0456             break;
0457             }
0458           if (DisplayWidth==1024)
0459             {
```

```
0460            LoadString(hInst,IDS_Resolution,lpCaption,Max);
0461            LoadString(hInst,IDS_Res8514,lpMessage,MaxText);
0462            TimerCounter= zTIMER_PAUSE;
0463            MessageBox(GetFocus(),lpMessage,lpCaption,MB_OK);
0464            break;
0465            }
0466          if (DisplayWidth==720)
0467            {
0468            LoadString(hInst,IDS_Resolution,lpCaption,Max);
0469            LoadString(hInst,IDS_ResHerc,lpMessage,MaxText);
0470            TimerCounter= zTIMER_PAUSE;
0471            MessageBox(GetFocus(),lpMessage,lpCaption,MB_OK);
0472            break;
0473            }
0474          LoadString(hInst,IDS_Resolution,lpCaption,Max);
0475          LoadString(hInst,IDS_ResCustom,lpMessage,MaxText);
0476          TimerCounter= zTIMER_PAUSE;
0477          MessageBox(GetFocus(),lpMessage,lpCaption,MB_OK);
0478          break;
0479
0480        case IDM_Colors:
0481          if (DisplayBits==1)
0482            {
0483            if (DisplayPlanes==4)
0484              {
0485              LoadString(hInst,IDS_Color,lpCaption,Max);
0486              LoadString(hInst,IDS_Color16,lpMessage,MaxText);
0487              TimerCounter= zTIMER_PAUSE;
0488              MessageBox(GetFocus(),lpMessage,lpCaption,MB_OK);
0489              break;
0490              }
0491            if (DisplayPlanes==1)
0492              {
0493              LoadString(hInst,IDS_Color,lpCaption,Max);
0494              LoadString(hInst,IDS_Color2,lpMessage,MaxText);
0495              TimerCounter= zTIMER_PAUSE;
0496              MessageBox(GetFocus(),lpMessage,lpCaption,MB_OK);
0497              break;
0498              }
0499            }
0500          if (DisplayBits==8)
0501            {
0502            LoadString(hInst,IDS_Color,lpCaption,Max);
0503            LoadString(hInst,IDS_Color256,lpMessage,MaxText);
0504            TimerCounter= zTIMER_PAUSE;
0505            MessageBox(GetFocus(),lpMessage,lpCaption,MB_OK);
0506            break;
0507            }
0508          LoadString(hInst,IDS_Color,lpCaption,Max);
0509          LoadString(hInst,IDS_ColorCustom,lpMessage,MaxText);
0510          TimerCounter= zTIMER_PAUSE;
0511          MessageBox(GetFocus(),lpMessage,lpCaption,MB_OK);
0512          break;
0513
0514        case IDM_Mode:
0515          if (MemoryMode & WF_ENHANCED)
0516            {
0517            LoadString(hInst,IDS_Machine,lpCaption,Max);
0518            LoadString(hInst,IDS_Enhanced,lpMessage,MaxText);
0519            TimerCounter= zTIMER_PAUSE;
0520            MessageBox(GetFocus(),lpMessage,lpCaption,MB_OK);
```

```
0521            break;
0522            }
0523         if (MemoryMode & WF_STANDARD)
0524            {
0525            LoadString(hInst,IDS_Machine,lpCaption,Max);
0526            LoadString(hInst,IDS_Standard,lpMessage,MaxText);
0527            TimerCounter= zTIMER_PAUSE;
0528            MessageBox(GetFocus(),lpMessage,lpCaption,MB_OK);
0529            break;
0530            }
0531         LoadString(hInst,IDS_Machine,lpCaption,Max);
0532         LoadString(hInst,IDS_Real,lpMessage,MaxText);
0533         TimerCounter= zTIMER_PAUSE;
0534         MessageBox(GetFocus(),lpMessage,lpCaption,MB_OK);
0535         break;
0536
0537       case IDM_Memory:
0538         LoadString(hInst,IDS_Memory,lpCaption,Max);
0539         LoadString(hInst,IDS_MemText,lpMessage,MaxText);
0540         TimerCounter= zTIMER_PAUSE;
0541         MessageBox(GetFocus(),lpMessage,lpCaption,MB_OK);
0542         break;
0543       case IDM_Timing:
0544         LoadString(hInst,IDS_Timing,lpCaption,Max);
0545         LoadString(hInst,IDS_TimingText,lpMessage,MaxText);
0546         TimerCounter= zTIMER_PAUSE;
0547         MessageBox(GetFocus(),lpMessage,lpCaption,MB_OK);
0548         break;
0549       case IDM_GeneralHelp:
0550         LoadString(hInst,IDS_Help,lpCaption,Max);
0551         LoadString(hInst,IDS_HelpText,lpMessage,MaxText);
0552         TimerCounter= zTIMER_PAUSE;
0553         MessageBox(GetFocus(),lpMessage,lpCaption,MB_OK);
0554         break;
0555       default:
0556         return(DefWindowProc(hWnd, message, wParam, lParam));
0557       }
0558     break;
0559
0560   case WM_INITMENUPOPUP:
0561     TimerCounter= zTIMER_PAUSE;
0562     if (lParam == 3)
0563       hMenu= wParam;
0564     break;
0565
0566   case WM_PAINT:
0567     hDCpaint= BeginPaint(hWnd,&ps);
0568     EndPaint(hWnd, &ps);
0569     if (PaintImage==zBLANK) break;
0570     if (Pause==TRUE)
0571       {
0572       Redisplay= TRUE;
0573       zShowNextFrame(hWnd);
0574       Redisplay= FALSE;
0575       break;
0576       }
0577     zShowNextFrame(hWnd);
0578     break;
0579
0580   case WM_KEYDOWN:
0581     switch (wParam)
```

```
0582            {
0583        case VK_LEFT:    if (Pause==TRUE)
0584                          {
0585                          if (FrameDirection==zFORWARD)
0586                           {
0587                            FrameDirection= zREVERSE;
0588                           }
0589                          Pause= FALSE;
0590                          zShowNextFrame(hWnd);
0591                          Pause= TRUE;
0592                          PaintImage= zANIMATING;
0593                          }
0594                        break;
0595        case VK_RIGHT:   if (Pause==TRUE)
0596                          {
0597                          if (FrameDirection==zREVERSE)
0598                           {
0599                            FrameDirection= zFORWARD;
0600                           }
0601                          Pause= FALSE;
0602                          zShowNextFrame(hWnd);
0603                          Pause= TRUE;
0604                          PaintImage= zANIMATING;
0605                          }
0606                        break;
0607        default:
0608                return(DefWindowProc(hWnd, message, wParam, lParam));
0609          }
0610     break;
0611
0612   case WM_DESTROY:
0613     if (FrameReady==TRUE)
0614        {
0615        SelectObject(hFrameDC,hPrevFrame);
0616        DeleteObject(hFrame);
0617        DeleteDC(hFrameDC);
0618        KillTimer(hWnd,1);
0619        }
0620     if (bAnimationLoaded==TRUE)
0621        {
0622        SelectObject(hFDC,hPrevF);
0623        DeleteObject(hF1); DeleteObject(hF2); DeleteObject(hF3);
0624        DeleteObject(hF4); DeleteObject(hF5); DeleteObject(hF6);
0625        DeleteObject(hF7); DeleteObject(hF8); DeleteObject(hF9);
0626        DeleteObject(hF10); DeleteObject(hF11); DeleteObject(hF12);
0627        DeleteObject(hF13); DeleteObject(hF14); DeleteObject(hF15);
0628        DeleteObject(hF16); DeleteObject(hF17); DeleteObject(hF18);
0629        DeleteObject(hF19); DeleteDC(hFDC);
0630        }
0631     PostQuitMessage(0);
0632     break;
0633
0634   case WM_SYSCOMMAND:
0635     if ((wParam & 0xfff0)== SC_SIZE)
0636        {
0637        MessageBeep(0); break;
0638        }
0639     if ((wParam & 0xfff0)== SC_MINIMIZE)
0640        {
0641        MessageBeep(0); break;
0642        }
```

```
0643       if ((wParam & 0xfff0)== SC_MAXIMIZE)
0644         {
0645         MessageBeep(0); break;
0646         }
0647
0648    default:
0649        return(DefWindowProc(hWnd, message, wParam, lParam));
0650     }
0651 return FALSE;
0652 }
0653 /*
0654 ------------------------------------------------------------------
0655              Initialize the attributes of the window class
0656 ------------------------------------------------------------------
0657                                                                 */
0658 BOOL zInitClass(HANDLE hInstance)
0659 {
0660   WNDCLASS WndClass;
0661 WndClass.style= 0;
0662 WndClass.lpfnWndProc= zMessageHandler;
0663 WndClass.cbClsExtra= 0;
0664 WndClass.cbWndExtra= 0;
0665 WndClass.hInstance= hInstance;
0666 WndClass.hIcon= LoadIcon(NULL,IDI_EXCLAMATION);
0667 WndClass.hCursor= LoadCursor(NULL,IDC_ARROW);
0668 WndClass.hbrBackground= CreateSolidBrush(RGB(255,255,255));
0669 WndClass.lpszMenuName= "MENUS1";
0670 WndClass.lpszClassName= "DEMOCLASS";
0671 return RegisterClass(&WndClass);
0672 }
0673 /*
0674 ------------------------------------------------------------------
0675                      Create the main window
0676 ------------------------------------------------------------------
0677                                                                 */
0678 HWND zInitMainWindow(HANDLE hInstance)
0679 {
0680   HWND hWnd;
0681 LoadString(hInstance,IDS_Caption,lpCaption,Max);
0682 hHourGlass= LoadCursor(NULL,IDC_WAIT);
0683 hWnd = CreateWindow("DEMOCLASS",lpCaption,
0684   WS_OVERLAPPED | WS_THICKFRAME | WS_MINIMIZEBOX |
0685     WS_MAXIMIZEBOX | WS_CLIPCHILDREN,
0686   WindowX,WindowY,zWINDOW_WIDTH,zWINDOW_HEIGHT,0,0,
0687   hInstance, (LPSTR)NULL);
0688 return hWnd;
0689 }
0690 /*
0691 ------------------------------------------------------------------
0692                     GRAPHICS SYSTEM Functions
0693 ------------------------------------------------------------------
0694 ------------------------------------------------------------------
0695                      Create the hidden frame.
0696 ------------------------------------------------------------------
0697                                                                 */
0698 static void zInitFrame(HWND hWnd)
0699 {
0700   HDC hDisplayDC;
0701
0702 if (FrameReady==TRUE)
0703   {
```

```
0704    MessageBeep(0);
0705    LoadString(hInst,IDS_Ready,lpCaption,Max);
0706    LoadString(hInst,IDS_Already,lpMessage,MaxText);
0707    TimerCounter= zTIMER_PAUSE;
0708    MessageBox(GetFocus(),lpMessage,lpCaption,MB_OK);
0709    return;
0710    }
0711 GlobalCompact((DWORD)-1L);
0712 hDisplayDC= GetDC(hWnd);
0713 hFrameDC= CreateCompatibleDC(hDisplayDC);
0714 hFrame= CreateCompatibleBitmap(hDisplayDC,zFRAMEWIDE,zFRAMEHIGH);
0715 if (hFrame==NULL)
0716    {
0717    LoadString(hInst,IDS_NotReady,lpCaption,Max);
0718    LoadString(hInst,IDS_InsufMem1,lpMessage,MaxText);
0719    MessageBox(GetFocus(),lpMessage,lpCaption,MB_OK);
0720    DeleteDC(hFrameDC);
0721    TimerExists= FALSE; FrameReady= FALSE; AnimationReady= FALSE;
0722    return;
0723    }
0724 hPrevFrame= SelectObject(hFrameDC,hFrame);
0725 zClear(hWnd);
0726 BitBlt(hFrameDC,0,0,zFRAMEWIDE,zFRAMEHIGH,hDisplayDC,0,0,SRCCOPY);
0727 ReleaseDC(hWnd,hDisplayDC);
0728
0729 TimerID1= SetTimer(hWnd,1,wFrameRate,(FARPROC) NULL);
0730 if (TimerID1 == 0)
0731    {
0732    LoadString(hInst,IDS_NotReady,lpCaption,Max);
0733    LoadString(hInst,IDS_NoTimer,lpMessage,MaxText);
0734    MessageBox(GetFocus(),lpMessage,lpCaption,MB_OK);
0735    SelectObject(hFrameDC,hPrevFrame);
0736    DeleteObject(hFrame);
0737    DeleteDC(hFrameDC);
0738    TimerExists= FALSE;
0739    return;
0740    }
0741 TimerExists= TRUE;
0742 FrameReady= TRUE;
0743 FrameNum= 1;
0744 return;
0745 }
0746 /*
0747 ----------------------------------------------------------------
0748                     Clear the hidden frame.
0749 ----------------------------------------------------------------
0750                                                              */
0751 static void zClearHiddenFrame(void)
0752 {
0753 PatBlt(hFrameDC,0,0,zFRAMEWIDE,zFRAMEHIGH,WHITENESS);
0754 return;
0755 }
0756 /*
0757 ----------------------------------------------------------------
0758          Copy the hidden frame to the display window.
0759 ----------------------------------------------------------------
0760                                                              */
0761 static void zCopyToDisplay(HWND hWnd)
0762 {
0763    HDC hDC;
0764 hDC= GetDC(hWnd);
```

```
0765  BitBlt(hDC,0,0,zFRAMEWIDE,zFRAMEHIGH,hFrameDC,0,0,SRCCOPY);
0766  ReleaseDC(hWnd,hDC);
0767  return;
0768  }
0769  /*
0770  ------------------------------------------------------------
0771                      Blank the display window.
0772  ------------------------------------------------------------
0773                                                           */
0774  static void zClear(HWND hWnd)
0775  {
0776    HDC hDC;
0777  hDC= GetDC(hWnd);
0778  PatBlt(hDC,0,0,zFRAMEWIDE,zFRAMEHIGH,WHITENESS);
0779  ReleaseDC(hWnd,hDC);
0780  return;
0781  }
0782  /*
0783  ------------------------------------------------------------
0784                     AUTHORING SYSTEM Functions
0785  ------------------------------------------------------------
0786  ------------------------------------------------------------
0787                   Create 19 frames and save to disk.
0788  ------------------------------------------------------------
0789                                                           */
0790  static void zSaveAnimation(HWND hWnd)
0791  {
0792  if (FrameReady==FALSE)          /* if no hidden-frame available... */
0793     {
0794     MessageBeep(0);
0795     LoadString(hInst,IDS_NotReady,lpCaption,Max);
0796     LoadString(hInst,IDS_NoFrame,lpMessage,MaxText);
0797     MessageBox(GetFocus(),lpMessage,lpCaption,MB_OK);
0798     return;
0799     }
0800
0801  if (bAnimationSaved==TRUE) /* if frames already saved to disk... */
0802     {
0803     MessageBeep(0);
0804     LoadString(hInst,IDS_Unexpected,lpCaption,Max);
0805     LoadString(hInst,IDS_Disk1,lpMessage,MaxText);
0806     TimerCounter= zTIMER_PAUSE;
0807     MessageBox(GetFocus(),lpMessage,lpCaption,MB_OK);
0808     return;
0809     }
0810
0811  if (bPrevSaveAttempt==TRUE)      /* if previous attempt failed... */
0812     {
0813     MessageBeep(0);
0814     LoadString(hInst,IDS_Unexpected,lpCaption,Max);
0815     LoadString(hInst,IDS_Disk8,lpMessage,MaxText);
0816     TimerCounter= zTIMER_PAUSE;
0817     MessageBox(GetFocus(),lpMessage,lpCaption,MB_OK);
0818     return;
0819     }
0820  bPrevSaveAttempt= TRUE;
0821
0822  bFrameSaved= zBuildFrame(drawing1,hWnd,(LPSTR)"FRAME1.BIT");
0823  if (bFrameSaved==FALSE) return;
0824  bFrameSaved= zBuildFrame(drawing2,hWnd,(LPSTR)"FRAME2.BIT");
0825  if (bFrameSaved==FALSE) return;
```

```
0826   bFrameSaved= zBuildFrame(drawing3,hWnd,(LPSTR)"FRAME3.BIT");
0827   if (bFrameSaved==FALSE) return;
0828   bFrameSaved= zBuildFrame(drawing4,hWnd,(LPSTR)"FRAME4.BIT");
0829   if (bFrameSaved==FALSE) return;
0830   bFrameSaved= zBuildFrame(drawing5,hWnd,(LPSTR)"FRAME5.BIT");
0831   if (bFrameSaved==FALSE) return;
0832   bFrameSaved= zBuildFrame(drawing6,hWnd,(LPSTR)"FRAME6.BIT");
0833   if (bFrameSaved==FALSE) return;
0834   bFrameSaved= zBuildFrame(drawing7,hWnd,(LPSTR)"FRAME7.BIT");
0835   if (bFrameSaved==FALSE) return;
0836   bFrameSaved= zBuildFrame(drawing1,hWnd,(LPSTR)"FRAME8.BIT");
0837   if (bFrameSaved==FALSE) return;
0838   bFrameSaved= zBuildFrame(drawing2,hWnd,(LPSTR)"FRAME9.BIT");
0839   if (bFrameSaved==FALSE) return;
0840   bFrameSaved= zBuildFrame(drawing3,hWnd,(LPSTR)"FRAME10.BIT");
0841   if (bFrameSaved==FALSE) return;
0842   bFrameSaved= zBuildFrame(drawing4,hWnd,(LPSTR)"FRAME11.BIT");
0843   if (bFrameSaved==FALSE) return;
0844   bFrameSaved= zBuildFrame(drawing5,hWnd,(LPSTR)"FRAME12.BIT");
0845   if (bFrameSaved==FALSE) return;
0846   bFrameSaved= zBuildFrame(drawing6,hWnd,(LPSTR)"FRAME13.BIT");
0847   if (bFrameSaved==FALSE) return;
0848   bFrameSaved= zBuildFrame(drawing7,hWnd,(LPSTR)"FRAME14.BIT");
0849   if (bFrameSaved==FALSE) return;
0850   bFrameSaved= zBuildFrame(drawing1,hWnd,(LPSTR)"FRAME15.BIT");
0851   if (bFrameSaved==FALSE) return;
0852   bFrameSaved= zBuildFrame(drawing2,hWnd,(LPSTR)"FRAME16.BIT");
0853   if (bFrameSaved==FALSE) return;
0854   bFrameSaved= zBuildFrame(drawing3,hWnd,(LPSTR)"FRAME17.BIT");
0855   if (bFrameSaved==FALSE) return;
0856   bFrameSaved= zBuildFrame(drawing4,hWnd,(LPSTR)"FRAME18.BIT");
0857   if (bFrameSaved==FALSE) return;
0858   bFrameSaved= zBuildFrame(drawing5,hWnd,(LPSTR)"FRAME19.BIT");
0859   if (bFrameSaved==FALSE) return;
0860
0861   bAnimationSaved= TRUE;
0862   bPrevLoadAttempt= FALSE;
0863   zClear(hWnd);
0864   MessageBeep(0);
0865   LoadString(hInst,IDS_Status,lpCaption,Max);
0866   LoadString(hInst,IDS_Disk2,lpMessage,MaxText);
0867   MessageBox(GetFocus(),lpMessage,lpCaption,MB_OK);
0868   return;
0869   }
0870   /*
0871   ------------------------------------------------------------------
0872                   Build one frame and save to disk.
0873   ------------------------------------------------------------------
0874                                                                  */
0875   static BOOL zBuildFrame(int * Drawing, HWND hWnd,
0876                   LPSTR lpFileName)
0877   {                    /* this function is called by zSaveAnimation() */
0878     BOOL bDiskResult;
0879     HFONT Font;
0880     HFONT PrevFont;
0881     DWORD PrevFontColor;
0882     DWORD PrevBkColor;
0883
0884   zClearHiddenFrame();                      /* clear hidden frame */
0885   zDrawBg(hFrameDC);            /* draw background on hidden frame */
0886
```

```
0887  PrevFontColor= SetTextColor(hFrameDC,RGB(255,255,255));
0888  PrevBkColor=  SetBkColor(hFrameDC,RGB(0,0,0));
0889  SetBkMode(hFrameDC,TRANSPARENT);
0890  Font= CreateFont(24, 0, 0, 0, FW_BOLD, FALSE, FALSE, FALSE,
0891       ANSI_CHARSET, OUT_DEFAULT_PRECIS, CLIP_DEFAULT_PRECIS,
0892       DRAFT_QUALITY, VARIABLE_PITCH | FF_SWISS, "Helv");
0893  PrevFont= SelectObject(hFrameDC,Font);
0894  TextOut(hFrameDC,10,30,"Animation Authoring Techniques for C",36);
0895  Font= CreateFont(48, 0, 0, 0, FW_BOLD, FALSE, FALSE, FALSE,
0896       ANSI_CHARSET, OUT_DEFAULT_PRECIS, CLIP_DEFAULT_PRECIS,
0897       DRAFT_QUALITY, VARIABLE_PITCH | FF_SWISS, "Helv");
0898  SelectObject(hFrameDC,Font);
0899  TextOut(hFrameDC,8,48,"Frame Animation",15);
0900  SelectObject(hFrameDC,PrevFont);
0901  TextOut(hFrameDC,10,120,"After first building each frame",31);
0902  TextOut(hFrameDC,10,136,"and saving it to disk, the software",35);
0903  TextOut(hFrameDC,10,152,"loads the entire animation sequence",35);
0904  TextOut(hFrameDC,10,168,"into memory and rapidly displays the",36);
0905  TextOut(hFrameDC,10,184,"frames to create the animation.",31);
0906  TextOut(hFrameDC,10,200,
0907    "The animation engine runs in forward,",37);
0908  TextOut(hFrameDC,10,216,
0909    "reverse, freeze, and singlestep modes.",38);
0910  TextOut(hFrameDC,10,232,"Speed control is by timer messages.",35);
0911  TextOut(hFrameDC,10,248,"The animation will run even if the",34);
0912  TextOut(hFrameDC,10,264,"window is partly covered or clipped.",36);
0913  SetBkMode(hFrameDC,OPAQUE);
0914  SetBkColor(hFrameDC,PrevBkColor);
0915  SetTextColor(hFrameDC,PrevFontColor);
0916
0917  SX1= SX1 - zMOVEHORIZ;                    /* update the cel position */
0918  zDoKeyDrawing(hFrameDC,Drawing);        /* place cel on hidden page */
0919  zCopyToDisplay(hWnd);                 /* copy hidden frame to display */
0920  bDiskResult= zSaveFrame(hFrame,lpFileName);           /* save file */
0921  if (bDiskResult==FALSE) return FALSE;            /* if disk error */
0922  return TRUE;
0923  }
0924  /*
0925  --------------------------------------------------------------------
0926                  Draw background image on the hidden frame.
0927  --------------------------------------------------------------------
0928                                                                    */
0929  static void zDrawBg(HDC hDC)
0930  {
0931    HBRUSH hPrevBrush, hSwatchBrush;
0932    HPEN hPrevPen, hBorderPen;
0933    RECT rcSwatch;
0934    int iWidth= 400, iDepth= 4;
0935    int iSwatchX= 0, iSwatchY=0;
0936    BYTE bRed= 0, bGreen= 0, bBlue= 0;
0937    int iCount;
0938
0939  if (FrameReady==FALSE)
0940    {
0941    MessageBeep(0);
0942    LoadString(hInst,IDS_NotReady,lpCaption,Max);
0943    LoadString(hInst,IDS_NoFrame,lpMessage,MaxText);
0944    MessageBox(GetFocus(),lpMessage,lpCaption,MB_OK);
0945    return;
0946    }
0947
```

```
0948  rcSwatch.left= iSwatchX;
0949  rcSwatch.top= iSwatchY;
0950  rcSwatch.right= rcSwatch.left + iWidth;
0951  rcSwatch.bottom= rcSwatch.top + iDepth;
0952  bRed= 0; bGreen= 0; bBlue= 3;
0953  for (iCount= 0; iCount < 64; iCount++)
0954    {
0955    hSwatchBrush= CreateSolidBrush(RGB(bRed,bGreen,bBlue));
0956    hPrevBrush= SelectObject(hDC,hSwatchBrush);
0957    FillRect(hDC,&rcSwatch,hSwatchBrush);
0958    SelectObject(hDC,hPrevBrush);
0959    DeleteObject(hSwatchBrush);
0960    rcSwatch.top= rcSwatch.top + iDepth;
0961    rcSwatch.bottom= rcSwatch.bottom + iDepth;
0962    bBlue= bBlue + (BYTE) 4;
0963    }
0964  bBlue= 255; rcSwatch.bottom= 300;
0965  hSwatchBrush= CreateSolidBrush(RGB(bRed,bGreen,bBlue));
0966  hPrevBrush= SelectObject(hDC,hSwatchBrush);
0967  FillRect(hDC,&rcSwatch,hSwatchBrush);
0968  SelectObject(hDC,hPrevBrush); DeleteObject(hSwatchBrush);
0969
0970  bRed= 0; bGreen= 0; bBlue= 255;
0971  iWidth= 280; iDepth= 4;
0972  iSwatchX= 60; iSwatchY= 24;
0973  rcSwatch.left= iSwatchX;
0974  rcSwatch.top= iSwatchY;
0975  rcSwatch.right= rcSwatch.left + iWidth;
0976  rcSwatch.bottom= rcSwatch.top + iDepth;
0977  for (iCount= 0; iCount < 64; iCount++)
0978    {
0979    hSwatchBrush= CreateSolidBrush(RGB(bRed,bGreen,bBlue));
0980    hPrevBrush= SelectObject(hDC,hSwatchBrush);
0981    FillRect(hDC,&rcSwatch,hSwatchBrush);
0982    SelectObject(hDC,hPrevBrush);
0983    DeleteObject(hSwatchBrush);
0984    rcSwatch.top= rcSwatch.top + iDepth;
0985    rcSwatch.bottom= rcSwatch.bottom + iDepth;
0986    bBlue= bBlue - (BYTE) 4;
0987    }
0988  hSwatchBrush= CreateSolidBrush(RGB(0,0,255));
0989  hPrevBrush= SelectObject(hDC,hSwatchBrush);
0990  hBorderPen= CreatePen(PS_SOLID,1,RGB(0,0,255));
0991  hPrevPen= SelectObject(hDC,hBorderPen);
0992  Ellipse(hDC,100,50,300,250);
0993
0994  SelectObject(hDC,hPrevPen); SelectObject(hDC,hPrevBrush);
0995  DeleteObject(hBorderPen); DeleteObject(hSwatchBrush);
0996  return;
0997  }
0998  /*
0999  --------------------------------------------------------------
1000          Draw one key drawing and place cel on hidden frame.
1001  --------------------------------------------------------------
1002                                                              */
1003  static void zDoKeyDrawing(HDC hDC, int * ArrayPtr)
1004  {
1005    int Count;
1006    int Repeat;
1007    int DrawPtr;
1008    HBRUSH ColorBrush, BlackBrush, PrevBrush;
```

```
1009    HPEN ColorPen, BlackPen, PrevPen;
1010    POINT Shape[6];
1011
1012  ColorPen= CreatePen(PS_SOLID,1,RGB(255,255,0));
1013  ColorBrush= CreateSolidBrush(RGB(255,255,0));
1014  BlackPen= CreatePen(PS_SOLID,1,RGB(0,0,0));
1015  BlackBrush= CreateSolidBrush(RGB(0,0,0));
1016
1017  /* ------------------- draw the dropshadow ------------------- */
1018  SetViewportOrg(hDC,SX1+20,SY1+10);        /* reset viewport origin */
1019  PrevPen= SelectObject(hDC,BlackPen);
1020  PrevBrush= SelectObject(hDC,BlackBrush);
1021  Ellipse(hDC,ArrayPtr[0]-10,ArrayPtr[1]-10,
1022            ArrayPtr[0]+10,ArrayPtr[1]+10);
1023  DrawPtr= 2;
1024  for (Count= 0; Count <= 3; Count++)
1025    {
1026    Shape[Count].x= ArrayPtr[DrawPtr]; DrawPtr++;
1027    Shape[Count].y= ArrayPtr[DrawPtr]; DrawPtr++;
1028    }
1029  Polygon(hDC,Shape,4);
1030  for (Count= 0; Count <= 4; Count++)
1031    {
1032    Shape[Count].x= ArrayPtr[DrawPtr]; DrawPtr++;
1033    Shape[Count].y= ArrayPtr[DrawPtr]; DrawPtr++;
1034    }
1035  Polygon(hDC,Shape,5);
1036  for (Repeat= 1; Repeat<= 13; Repeat++)
1037    {
1038    for (Count= 0; Count <= 3; Count++)
1039      {
1040      Shape[Count].x= ArrayPtr[DrawPtr]; DrawPtr++;
1041      Shape[Count].y= ArrayPtr[DrawPtr]; DrawPtr++;
1042      }
1043    Polygon(hDC,Shape,4);
1044    }
1045
1046  /* ----------------- draw foreground silhouette --------------- */
1047  SetViewportOrg(hDC,SX1,SY1);              /* reset viewport origin */
1048  SelectObject(hDC,ColorPen);
1049  SelectObject(hDC,ColorBrush);
1050  Ellipse(hDC,ArrayPtr[0]-10,ArrayPtr[1]-10,
1051            ArrayPtr[0]+10,ArrayPtr[1]+10);
1052  DrawPtr= 2;
1053  for (Count= 0; Count <= 3; Count++)
1054    {
1055    Shape[Count].x= ArrayPtr[DrawPtr]; DrawPtr++;
1056    Shape[Count].y= ArrayPtr[DrawPtr]; DrawPtr++;
1057    }
1058  Polygon(hDC,Shape,4);
1059  for (Count= 0; Count <= 4; Count++)
1060    {
1061    Shape[Count].x= ArrayPtr[DrawPtr]; DrawPtr++;
1062    Shape[Count].y= ArrayPtr[DrawPtr]; DrawPtr++;
1063    }
1064  Polygon(hDC,Shape,5);
1065  for (Repeat= 1; Repeat<= 13; Repeat++)
1066    {
1067    for (Count= 0; Count <= 3; Count++)
1068      {
1069      Shape[Count].x= ArrayPtr[DrawPtr]; DrawPtr++;
```

```
1070     Shape[Count].y= ArrayPtr[DrawPtr]; DrawPtr++;
1071     }
1072    Polygon(hDC,Shape,4);
1073    }
1074
1075  SetViewportOrg(hDC,0,0);        /* restore default viewport origin */
1076  SelectObject(hDC,PrevPen); SelectObject(hDC,PrevBrush);
1077  DeleteObject(ColorPen); DeleteObject(ColorBrush);
1078  DeleteObject(BlackPen); DeleteObject(BlackBrush);
1079  return;
1080  }
1081  /*
1082  ------------------------------------------------------------------
1083                      Save a frame file to disk.
1084  ------------------------------------------------------------------
1085                                                                  */
1086  static BOOL zSaveFrame(HBITMAP hBitmap, LPSTR lpFileName)
1087  {
1088    BITMAP bmImage;                      /* bitmap data structure */
1089    short BytesPerLine;                     /* width of bitmap */
1090    short RasterLines;                      /* height of bitmap */
1091    BYTE NumPlanes;                      /* number of bitplanes */
1092    LPSTR lpImageData;   /* pointer to buffer that holds bit array */
1093    GLOBALHANDLE hMem;   /* handle to buffer that holds bit array */
1094    WORD NumBytes;               /* length of array, in bytes */
1095    LONG TestLength;                            /* hash value */
1096    DWORD BytesCopied;       /* value returned by GetBitmapBits() */
1097    int hFile;                              /* DOS file handle */
1098    OFSTRUCT FileStruct;             /* data structure for file */
1099
1100  if(DisplayBits==8)              /* if running in 256-color mode... */
1101    {
1102    MessageBeep(0); MessageBox(GetFocus(),
1103    "Reset your system to 16-color mode to run this animation.
1104     Otherwise recompile the source files to run in 256-color mode.
1105      See the book for source code changes or use Windows Setup to
1106      change to a 16-color display.",
1104    "256-color support", MB_OK|MB_ICONINFORMATION);
1105    return FALSE;
1106    }
1107
1108  if (FrameReady==FALSE)             /* if no hidden-frame exists... */
1109    {
1110    MessageBeep(0);
1111    LoadString(hInst,IDS_Unexpected,lpCaption,Max);
1112    LoadString(hInst,IDS_Disk9,lpMessage,MaxText);
1113    MessageBox(GetFocus(),lpMessage,lpCaption,MB_OK);
1114    return FALSE;
1115    }
1116
1117  RetVal= GetObject(hBitmap,         /* grab bitmap data structure */
1118          sizeof(BITMAP),(LPSTR)&bmImage);
1119  if (RetVal==0)
1120    {
1121    MessageBeep(0);
1122    LoadString(hInst,IDS_Unexpected,lpCaption,Max);
1123    LoadString(hInst,IDS_Disk10,lpMessage,MaxText);
1124    MessageBox(GetFocus(),lpMessage,lpCaption,MB_OK);
1125    return FALSE;
1126    }
1127  BytesPerLine= bmImage.bmWidthBytes;              /* width of bitmap */
```

```
1128   RasterLines= bmImage.bmHeight;                    /* height of bitmap */
1129   NumPlanes= bmImage.bmPlanes;                  /* number of bitplanes */
1130   TestLength=                              /* calculate length of data */
1131              (LONG)(BytesPerLine * RasterLines * NumPlanes);
1132   if (TestLength > 65534) /* if too large for single-pass write... */
1133      {
1134      MessageBeep(0);
1135      LoadString(hInst,IDS_Unexpected,lpCaption,Max);
1136      LoadString(hInst,IDS_Disk11,lpMessage,MaxText);
1137      MessageBox(GetFocus(),lpMessage,lpCaption,MB_OK);
1138      return FALSE;
1139      }
1140   NumBytes= (WORD) TestLength;     /* initialize arg for _lwrite() */
1141
1142   hMem= GlobalAlloc(GMEM_MOVEABLE, NumBytes);   /* create a buffer */
1143   if (hMem==0)
1144      {
1145      MessageBeep(0);
1146      LoadString(hInst,IDS_Unexpected,lpCaption,Max);
1147      LoadString(hInst,IDS_Disk12,lpMessage,MaxText);
1148      MessageBox(GetFocus(),lpMessage,lpCaption,MB_OK);
1149      return FALSE;
1150      }
1151   lpImageData= GlobalLock(hMem);   /* lock buffer and grab pointer */
1152   BytesCopied= GetBitmapBits(hBitmap,NumBytes,lpImageData);
1153   if (BytesCopied==0)        /* if unable to copy bits to buffer... */
1154      {
1155      MessageBeep(0);
1156      LoadString(hInst,IDS_Unexpected,lpCaption,Max);
1157      LoadString(hInst,IDS_Disk13,lpMessage,MaxText);
1158      MessageBox(GetFocus(),lpMessage,lpCaption,MB_OK);
1159      GlobalUnlock(hMem); GlobalFree(hMem); return FALSE;
1160      }
1161
1162   hFile= OpenFile(lpFileName,&FileStruct,OF_EXIST);     /* exists? */
1163   if (hFile >= 0)
1164      {
1165      MessageBeep(0);
1166      LoadString(hInst,IDS_Unexpected,lpCaption,Max);
1167      LoadString(hInst,IDS_Disk14,lpMessage,MaxText);
1168      RetVal= MessageBox(GetFocus(),lpMessage,lpCaption,MB_YESNO);
1169      if (RetVal==IDNO)     /* if user does not want to overwrite... */
1170         {
1171         GlobalUnlock(hMem); GlobalFree(hMem); return FALSE;
1172         }
1173      }
1174   hFile= OpenFile(lpFileName,&FileStruct,OF_CREATE|OF_WRITE);
1175   if (hFile==-1)
1176      {
1177      MessageBeep(0);
1178      LoadString(hInst,IDS_Unexpected,lpCaption,Max);
1179      LoadString(hInst,IDS_Disk15,lpMessage,MaxText);
1180      MessageBox(GetFocus(),lpMessage,lpCaption,MB_OK);
1181      GlobalUnlock(hMem); GlobalFree(hMem); return FALSE;
1182      }
1183
1184   RetVal= _lwrite(hFile,lpImageData,NumBytes);     /* write to disk */
1185   if (RetVal==-1)
1186      {
1187      MessageBeep(0);
1188      LoadString(hInst,IDS_Unexpected,lpCaption,Max);
```

```
1189    LoadString(hInst,IDS_Disk16,lpMessage,MaxText);
1190
1191    MessageBox(GetFocus(),lpMessage,lpCaption,MB_OK);
1192    _lclose(hFile);
1193    GlobalUnlock(hMem); GlobalFree(hMem); return FALSE;
1194    }
1195
1196 RetVal= _lclose(hFile);                          /* close the file */
1197 if (RetVal==-1)                      /* if unable to close file... */
1198    {
1199    MessageBeep(0);
1200    LoadString(hInst,IDS_Unexpected,lpCaption,Max);
1201    LoadString(hInst,IDS_Disk17,lpMessage,MaxText);
1202    MessageBox(GetFocus(),lpMessage,lpCaption,MB_OK);
1203    GlobalUnlock(hMem); GlobalFree(hMem); return FALSE;
1204    }
1205
1206 GlobalUnlock(hMem);         /* discard the pointer to the buffer */
1207 GlobalFree(hMem);                          /* discard the buffer */
1208 return TRUE;
1209 }
1210 /*
1211 ------------------------------------------------------------------
1212                      ANIMATION PLAYBACK Functions
1213 ------------------------------------------------------------------
1214 ------------------------------------------------------------------
1215                        Display the next frame.
1216   This function is intelligent enough to discern between RAM-BASED
1217   FRAME ANIMATION (where all frames have already been loaded from
1218   disk and stored in RAM) and DISK-BASED FRAME ANIMATION (where
1219   each frame must be loaded from disk during playback).
1220 ------------------------------------------------------------------
1221                                                                  */
1222 static void zShowNextFrame(HWND hWnd)
1223 {
1224   HDC hDC;
1225 if (bUseDisk==TRUE) goto DISK_PLAYBACK;
1226
1227 RAM_PLAYBACK:        /* if all frames have been loaded into RAM... */
1228 if (AnimationReady==FALSE) return;
1229 if (bAnimationLoaded==FALSE) return;
1230 if (Redisplay==TRUE) goto DISPLAY_FRAME;
1231 if (Pause==TRUE) return;
1232 if (FrameDirection==zFORWARD)
1233    {
1234    FrameNum++;
1235    if (FrameNum > zFINALFRAME) FrameNum= zFIRSTFRAME;
1236    }
1237 if (FrameDirection==zREVERSE)
1238    {
1239    FrameNum--;
1240    if (FrameNum < zFIRSTFRAME) FrameNum= zFINALFRAME;
1241    }
1242 DISPLAY_FRAME:
1243 hDC= GetDC(hWnd);
1244 switch (FrameNum)
1245    {
1246    case 1:  SelectObject(hFDC,hF1); break;
1247    case 2:  SelectObject(hFDC,hF2); break;
1248    case 3:  SelectObject(hFDC,hF3); break;
1249    case 4:  SelectObject(hFDC,hF4); break;
```

```
1250    case 5:  SelectObject(hFDC,hF5);  break;
1251    case 6:  SelectObject(hFDC,hF6);  break;
1252    case 7:  SelectObject(hFDC,hF7);  break;
1253    case 8:  SelectObject(hFDC,hF8);  break;
1254    case 9:  SelectObject(hFDC,hF9);  break;
1255    case 10: SelectObject(hFDC,hF10); break;
1256    case 11: SelectObject(hFDC,hF11); break;
1257    case 12: SelectObject(hFDC,hF12); break;
1258    case 13: SelectObject(hFDC,hF13); break;
1259    case 14: SelectObject(hFDC,hF14); break;
1260    case 15: SelectObject(hFDC,hF15); break;
1261    case 16: SelectObject(hFDC,hF16); break;
1262    case 17: SelectObject(hFDC,hF17); break;
1263    case 18: SelectObject(hFDC,hF18); break;
1264    case 19: SelectObject(hFDC,hF19); break;
1265    }
1266  BitBlt(hDC,0,0,zFRAMEWIDE,zFRAMEHIGH,hFDC,0,0,SRCCOPY);
1267  ReleaseDC(hWnd,hDC);
1268  return;
1269
1270  DISK_PLAYBACK:    /* if loading each frame from disk as needed... */
1271  if (bAnimationHalted==TRUE) return;
1272  if (Redisplay==TRUE) goto SAME_FRAME;
1273  if (Pause==TRUE) return;
1274  if (FrameDirection==zFORWARD)
1275    {
1276    FrameNum++;
1277    if (FrameNum > zFINALFRAME) FrameNum= zFIRSTFRAME;
1278    }
1279  if (FrameDirection==zREVERSE)
1280    {
1281    FrameNum--;
1282    if (FrameNum < zFIRSTFRAME) FrameNum= zFINALFRAME;
1283    }
1284  SAME_FRAME:
1285  hDC= GetDC(hWnd);
1286  switch (FrameNum)
1287    {
1288    case 1:  bFrameLoaded= zLoadFrame(hFrame, (LPSTR) "FRAME1.BIT");
1289             break;
1290    case 2:  bFrameLoaded= zLoadFrame(hFrame, (LPSTR) "FRAME2.BIT");
1291             break;
1292    case 3:  bFrameLoaded= zLoadFrame(hFrame, (LPSTR) "FRAME3.BIT");
1293             break;
1294    case 4:  bFrameLoaded= zLoadFrame(hFrame, (LPSTR) "FRAME4.BIT");
1295             break;
1296    case 5:  bFrameLoaded= zLoadFrame(hFrame, (LPSTR) "FRAME5.BIT");
1297             break;
1298    case 6:  bFrameLoaded= zLoadFrame(hFrame, (LPSTR) "FRAME6.BIT");
1299             break;
1300    case 7:  bFrameLoaded= zLoadFrame(hFrame, (LPSTR) "FRAME7.BIT");
1301             break;
1302    case 8:  bFrameLoaded= zLoadFrame(hFrame, (LPSTR) "FRAME8.BIT");
1303             break;
1304    case 9:  bFrameLoaded= zLoadFrame(hFrame, (LPSTR) "FRAME9.BIT");
1305             break;
1306    case 10: bFrameLoaded= zLoadFrame(hFrame, (LPSTR) "FRAME10.BIT");
1307             break;
1308    case 11: bFrameLoaded= zLoadFrame(hFrame, (LPSTR) "FRAME11.BIT");
1309             break;
1310    case 12: bFrameLoaded= zLoadFrame(hFrame, (LPSTR) "FRAME12.BIT");
```

```
1311            break;
1312    case 13: bFrameLoaded= zLoadFrame(hFrame, (LPSTR) "FRAME13.BIT");
1313            break;
1314    case 14: bFrameLoaded= zLoadFrame(hFrame, (LPSTR) "FRAME14.BIT");
1315            break;
1316    case 15: bFrameLoaded= zLoadFrame(hFrame, (LPSTR) "FRAME15.BIT");
1317            break;
1318    case 16: bFrameLoaded= zLoadFrame(hFrame, (LPSTR) "FRAME16.BIT");
1319            break;
1320    case 17: bFrameLoaded= zLoadFrame(hFrame, (LPSTR) "FRAME17.BIT");
1321            break;
1322    case 18: bFrameLoaded= zLoadFrame(hFrame, (LPSTR) "FRAME18.BIT");
1323            break;
1324    case 19: bFrameLoaded= zLoadFrame(hFrame, (LPSTR) "FRAME19.BIT");
1325            break;
1326    }
1327 if (bFrameLoaded==FALSE)
1328    {
1329    bAnimationHalted= TRUE;
1330    MessageBeep(0);
1331    LoadString(hInst,IDS_Unexpected,lpCaption,Max);
1332    LoadString(hInst,IDS_Disk3,lpMessage,MaxText);
1333    TimerCounter= zTIMER_PAUSE;
1334    MessageBox(GetFocus(),lpMessage,lpCaption,MB_OK);
1335    return;
1336    }
1337 BitBlt(hDC,0,0,zFRAMEWIDE,zFRAMEHIGH,hFrameDC,0,0,SRCCOPY);
1338 ReleaseDC(hWnd,hDC);
1339 return;
1340 }
1341 /*
1342 --------------------------------------------------------------------
1343              Load the animation sequence from disk.
1344    If memory limitations prevent this function from loading the
1345    entire animation sequence into RAM, it sets a token to FALSE.
1346    In that case the playback function zShowNextFrame() will load
1347    each frame from disk as required during animation playback,
1348    otherwise all frames are expected to be in RAM.
1349 --------------------------------------------------------------------
1350                                                                  */
1351 static void zLoadAnimation(HWND hWnd)
1352 {
1353    HDC hDC;
1354
1355 if (FrameReady==FALSE)          /* if no hidden-frame available... */
1356    {
1357    MessageBeep(0);
1358    LoadString(hInst,IDS_NotReady,lpCaption,Max);
1359    LoadString(hInst,IDS_NoFrame,lpMessage,MaxText);
1360    MessageBox(GetFocus(),lpMessage,lpCaption,MB_OK);
1361    return;
1362    }
1363 if (bAnimationLoaded==TRUE)       /* if frames already loaded... */
1364    {
1365    MessageBeep(0);
1366    LoadString(hInst,IDS_Unexpected,lpCaption,Max);
1367    LoadString(hInst,IDS_Disk4,lpMessage,MaxText);
1368    TimerCounter= zTIMER_PAUSE;
1369    MessageBox(GetFocus(),lpMessage,lpCaption,MB_OK);
1370    return;
1371    }
```

```
1372   if (bPrevLoadAttempt==TRUE)        /* if previous attempt failed... */
1373     {
1374     MessageBeep(0);
1375     LoadString(hInst,IDS_Unexpected,lpCaption,Max);
1376     LoadString(hInst,IDS_Disk5,lpMessage,MaxText);
1377     TimerCounter= zTIMER_PAUSE;
1378     MessageBox(GetFocus(),lpMessage,lpCaption,MB_OK);
1379     return;
1380     }
1381   bPrevLoadAttempt= TRUE;
1382
1383   /* ------------- create bitmaps to hold the frames ------------ */
1384   GlobalCompact((DWORD)-1L);              /* maximize contiguous memory */
1385   hDC= GetDC(hWnd);
1386   hFDC= CreateCompatibleDC(hDC);
1387   hF1= CreateCompatibleBitmap(hDC,zFRAMEWIDE,zFRAMEHIGH);
1388   if (hF1==NULL) goto F1;
1389   hF2= CreateCompatibleBitmap(hDC,zFRAMEWIDE,zFRAMEHIGH);
1390   if (hF2==NULL) goto F2;
1391   hF3= CreateCompatibleBitmap(hDC,zFRAMEWIDE,zFRAMEHIGH);
1392   if (hF3==NULL) goto F3;
1393   hF4= CreateCompatibleBitmap(hDC,zFRAMEWIDE,zFRAMEHIGH);
1394   if (hF4==NULL) goto F4;
1395   hF5= CreateCompatibleBitmap(hDC,zFRAMEWIDE,zFRAMEHIGH);
1396   if (hF5==NULL) goto F5;
1397   hF6= CreateCompatibleBitmap(hDC,zFRAMEWIDE,zFRAMEHIGH);
1398   if (hF6==NULL) goto F6;
1399   hF7= CreateCompatibleBitmap(hDC,zFRAMEWIDE,zFRAMEHIGH);
1400   if (hF7==NULL) goto F7;
1401   hF8= CreateCompatibleBitmap(hDC,zFRAMEWIDE,zFRAMEHIGH);
1402   if (hF8==NULL) goto F8;
1403   hF9= CreateCompatibleBitmap(hDC,zFRAMEWIDE,zFRAMEHIGH);
1404   if (hF9==NULL) goto F9;
1405   hF10= CreateCompatibleBitmap(hDC,zFRAMEWIDE,zFRAMEHIGH);
1406   if (hF10==NULL) goto F10;
1407   hF11= CreateCompatibleBitmap(hDC,zFRAMEWIDE,zFRAMEHIGH);
1408   if (hF11==NULL) goto F11;
1409   hF12= CreateCompatibleBitmap(hDC,zFRAMEWIDE,zFRAMEHIGH);
1410   if (hF12==NULL) goto F12;
1411   hF13= CreateCompatibleBitmap(hDC,zFRAMEWIDE,zFRAMEHIGH);
1412   if (hF13==NULL) goto F13;
1413   hF14= CreateCompatibleBitmap(hDC,zFRAMEWIDE,zFRAMEHIGH);
1414   if (hF14==NULL) goto F14;
1415   hF15= CreateCompatibleBitmap(hDC,zFRAMEWIDE,zFRAMEHIGH);
1416   if (hF15==NULL) goto F15;
1417   hF16= CreateCompatibleBitmap(hDC,zFRAMEWIDE,zFRAMEHIGH);
1418   if (hF16==NULL) goto F16;
1419   hF17= CreateCompatibleBitmap(hDC,zFRAMEWIDE,zFRAMEHIGH);
1420   if (hF17==NULL) goto F17;
1421   hF18= CreateCompatibleBitmap(hDC,zFRAMEWIDE,zFRAMEHIGH);
1422   if (hF18==NULL) goto F18;
1423   hF19= CreateCompatibleBitmap(hDC,zFRAMEWIDE,zFRAMEHIGH);
1424   if (hF19==NULL) goto F19;
1425   goto BITMAPS_OK;
1426   F19: DeleteObject(hF18);
1427   F18: DeleteObject(hF17);
1428   F17: DeleteObject(hF16);
1429   F16: DeleteObject(hF15);
1430   F15: DeleteObject(hF14);
1431   F14: DeleteObject(hF13);
1432   F13: DeleteObject(hF12);
```

```
1433   F12: DeleteObject(hF11);
1434   F11: DeleteObject(hF10);
1435   F10: DeleteObject(hF9);
1436   F9:  DeleteObject(hF8);
1437   F8:  DeleteObject(hF7);
1438   F7:  DeleteObject(hF6);
1439   F6:  DeleteObject(hF5);
1440   F5:  DeleteObject(hF4);
1441   F4:  DeleteObject(hF3);
1442   F3:  DeleteObject(hF2);
1443   F2:  DeleteObject(hF1);
1444   F1:  DeleteDC(hFDC); ReleaseDC(hWnd,hDC);
1445        bUseDisk= TRUE; AnimationReady= TRUE;
1446        LoadString(hInst,IDS_Status,lpCaption,Max);
1447        LoadString(hInst,IDS_Disk6,lpMessage,MaxText);
1448        MessageBox(GetFocus(),lpMessage,lpCaption,MB_OK);
1449        return;
1450   BITMAPS_OK: ReleaseDC(hWnd,hDC);
1451
1452   /* ------------ load frame files into the bitmaps ------------ */
1453   bFrameLoaded= zLoadFrame(hF1, (LPSTR) "FRAME1.BIT");
1454   if (bFrameLoaded==FALSE) goto DISK_ERROR;
1455   bFrameLoaded= zLoadFrame(hF2, (LPSTR) "FRAME2.BIT");
1456   if (bFrameLoaded==FALSE) goto DISK_ERROR;
1457   bFrameLoaded= zLoadFrame(hF3, (LPSTR) "FRAME3.BIT");
1458   if (bFrameLoaded==FALSE) goto DISK_ERROR;
1459   bFrameLoaded= zLoadFrame(hF4, (LPSTR) "FRAME4.BIT");
1460   if (bFrameLoaded==FALSE) goto DISK_ERROR;
1461   bFrameLoaded= zLoadFrame(hF5, (LPSTR) "FRAME5.BIT");
1462   if (bFrameLoaded==FALSE) goto DISK_ERROR;
1463   bFrameLoaded= zLoadFrame(hF6, (LPSTR) "FRAME6.BIT");
1464   if (bFrameLoaded==FALSE) goto DISK_ERROR;
1465   bFrameLoaded= zLoadFrame(hF7, (LPSTR) "FRAME7.BIT");
1466   if (bFrameLoaded==FALSE) goto DISK_ERROR;
1467   bFrameLoaded= zLoadFrame(hF8, (LPSTR) "FRAME8.BIT");
1468   if (bFrameLoaded==FALSE) goto DISK_ERROR;
1469   bFrameLoaded= zLoadFrame(hF9, (LPSTR) "FRAME9.BIT");
1470   if (bFrameLoaded==FALSE) goto DISK_ERROR;
1471   bFrameLoaded= zLoadFrame(hF10, (LPSTR) "FRAME10.BIT");
1472   if (bFrameLoaded==FALSE) goto DISK_ERROR;
1473   bFrameLoaded= zLoadFrame(hF11, (LPSTR) "FRAME11.BIT");
1474   if (bFrameLoaded==FALSE) goto DISK_ERROR;
1475   bFrameLoaded= zLoadFrame(hF12, (LPSTR) "FRAME12.BIT");
1476   if (bFrameLoaded==FALSE) goto DISK_ERROR;
1477   bFrameLoaded= zLoadFrame(hF13, (LPSTR) "FRAME13.BIT");
1478   if (bFrameLoaded==FALSE) goto DISK_ERROR;
1479   bFrameLoaded= zLoadFrame(hF14, (LPSTR) "FRAME14.BIT");
1480   if (bFrameLoaded==FALSE) goto DISK_ERROR;
1481   bFrameLoaded= zLoadFrame(hF15, (LPSTR) "FRAME15.BIT");
1482   if (bFrameLoaded==FALSE) goto DISK_ERROR;
1483   bFrameLoaded= zLoadFrame(hF16, (LPSTR) "FRAME16.BIT");
1484   if (bFrameLoaded==FALSE) goto DISK_ERROR;
1485   bFrameLoaded= zLoadFrame(hF17, (LPSTR) "FRAME17.BIT");
1486   if (bFrameLoaded==FALSE) goto DISK_ERROR;
1487   bFrameLoaded= zLoadFrame(hF18, (LPSTR) "FRAME18.BIT");
1488   if (bFrameLoaded==FALSE) goto DISK_ERROR;
1489   bFrameLoaded= zLoadFrame(hF19, (LPSTR) "FRAME19.BIT");
1490   if (bFrameLoaded==FALSE) goto DISK_ERROR;
1491   goto DISK_OK;
1492   DISK_ERROR:
1493     DeleteObject(hF1); DeleteObject(hF2); DeleteObject(hF3);
```

```
1494    DeleteObject(hF4); DeleteObject(hF5); DeleteObject(hF6);
1495    DeleteObject(hF7); DeleteObject(hF8); DeleteObject(hF9);
1496    DeleteObject(hF10); DeleteObject(hF11); DeleteObject(hF12);
1497    DeleteObject(hF13); DeleteObject(hF14); DeleteObject(hF15);
1498    DeleteObject(hF16); DeleteObject(hF17); DeleteObject(hF18);
1499    DeleteObject(hF19); DeleteDC(hFDC);
1500    return;
1501
1502    /* ------------------- tidy up and return -------------------- */
1503    DISK_OK:
1504    hPrevF= SelectObject(hFDC,hF1);                    /* select bitmap */
1505    bAnimationLoaded= TRUE;
1506    AnimationReady= TRUE;
1507    bAnimationSaved= TRUE;
1508    MessageBeep(0);
1509    LoadString(hInst,IDS_AnimReady,lpCaption,Max);
1510    LoadString(hInst,IDS_Disk7,lpMessage,MaxText);
1511    MessageBox(GetFocus(),lpMessage,lpCaption,MB_OK);
1512    return;
1513    }
1514    /*
1515    --------------------------------------------------------------------
1516                      Reset the animation frame rate.
1517    --------------------------------------------------------------------
1518                                                                       */
1519    static void zSetFrameRate(HWND hWnd, WORD wNewRate)
1520    {
1521    if (TimerExists==FALSE)
1522      {
1523      wFrameRate= wPrevRate;
1524      MessageBeep(0);
1525      LoadString(hInst,IDS_NotReady,lpCaption,Max);
1526      LoadString(hInst,IDS_NoReset,lpMessage,MaxText);
1527      MessageBox(GetFocus(),lpMessage,lpCaption,MB_OK);
1528      return;
1529      }
1530    switch (wPrevRate)
1531      {
1532      case 55:  CheckMenuItem(hMenu,IDM_FPS182,MF_UNCHECKED); break;
1533      case 110: CheckMenuItem(hMenu,IDM_FPS91,MF_UNCHECKED); break;
1534      case 165: CheckMenuItem(hMenu,IDM_FPS61,MF_UNCHECKED); break;
1535      case 220: CheckMenuItem(hMenu,IDM_FPS45,MF_UNCHECKED); break;
1536      case 275: CheckMenuItem(hMenu,IDM_FPS36,MF_UNCHECKED); break;
1537      case 330: CheckMenuItem(hMenu,IDM_FPS30,MF_UNCHECKED); break;
1538      }
1539    KillTimer(hWnd,1);
1540    TimerID1= SetTimer(hWnd,1,wNewRate,(FARPROC) NULL);
1541    if (TimerID1==0)
1542      {
1543      LoadString(hInst,IDS_NotReady,lpCaption,Max);
1544      LoadString(hInst,IDS_CannotReset,lpMessage,MaxText);
1545      MessageBox(GetFocus(),lpMessage,lpCaption,MB_OK);
1546      TimerExists= FALSE;
1547      return;
1548      }
1549    switch (wFrameRate)
1550      {
1551      case 55:  CheckMenuItem(hMenu,IDM_FPS182,MF_CHECKED); break;
1552      case 110: CheckMenuItem(hMenu,IDM_FPS91,MF_CHECKED); break;
1553      case 165: CheckMenuItem(hMenu,IDM_FPS61,MF_CHECKED); break;
1554      case 220: CheckMenuItem(hMenu,IDM_FPS45,MF_CHECKED); break;
```

```
1555    case 275: CheckMenuItem(hMenu,IDM_FPS36,MF_CHECKED); break;
1556    case 330: CheckMenuItem(hMenu,IDM_FPS30,MF_CHECKED); break;
1557    }
1558  return;
1559  }
1560  /*
1561  -------------------------------------------------------------------
1562                  Load one frame file from disk.
1563  -------------------------------------------------------------------
1564                                                                   */
1565  static BOOL zLoadFrame(HBITMAP hBitmap, LPSTR lpFileName)
1566  {
1567    BITMAP bmImage;                          /* bitmap data structure */
1568    short BytesPerLine;                          /* width of bitmap */
1569    short RasterLines;                          /* height of bitmap */
1570    BYTE NumPlanes;                         /* number of bitplanes */
1571    LPSTR lpImageData;    /* pointer to buffer that holds bit array */
1572    GLOBALHANDLE hMem;    /* handle to buffer that holds bit array */
1573    WORD NumBytes;                         /* length of array, in bytes */
1574    LONG TestLength;                                 /* hash value */
1575    DWORD BytesCopied;    /* value returned by GetBitmapBits() */
1576    int hFile;                                 /* DOS file handle */
1577    OFSTRUCT FileStruct;                    /* data structure for file */
1578
1579  if(DisplayBits==8)              /* if running in 256-color mode... */
1580    {
1581    MessageBeep(0); MessageBox(GetFocus(),
1582    "Reset your system to 16-color mode to run this animation.
1583        Otherwise recompile the source files to run in 256-color mode.
1584          See the book for source code changes or use Windows Setup to
1585          change to a 16-color display.",
1583    "256-color support", MB_OK|MB_ICONINFORMATION);
1584    return FALSE;
1585    }
1586
1587  if (FrameReady==FALSE)              /* if no hidden-frame exists... */
1588    {
1589    MessageBeep(0);
1590    LoadString(hInst,IDS_Unexpected,lpCaption,Max);
1591    LoadString(hInst,IDS_Disk18,lpMessage,MaxText);
1592    MessageBox(GetFocus(),lpMessage,lpCaption,MB_OK);
1593    return FALSE;
1594    }
1595
1596  RetVal= GetObject(hBitmap,              /* grab bitmap data structure */
1597            sizeof(BITMAP),(LPSTR)&bmImage);
1598  if (RetVal==0)
1599    {
1600    MessageBeep(0);
1601    LoadString(hInst,IDS_Unexpected,lpCaption,Max);
1602    LoadString(hInst,IDS_Disk10,lpMessage,MaxText);
1603    MessageBox(GetFocus(),lpMessage,lpCaption,MB_OK);
1604    return FALSE;
1605    }
1606
1607  BytesPerLine= bmImage.bmWidthBytes;               /* width of bitmap */
1608  RasterLines= bmImage.bmHeight;                    /* height of bitmap */
1609  NumPlanes= bmImage.bmPlanes;              /* number of bitplanes */
1610  TestLength=                          /* calculate length of data */
1611            (LONG)(BytesPerLine * RasterLines * NumPlanes);
1612  if (TestLength > 60000)      /* if larger than hardcoded value... */
```

```
1613      {                                 /* ...of a 400x300x16-color frame */
1614      MessageBeep(0);
1615      LoadString(hInst,IDS_Unexpected,lpCaption,Max);
1616      LoadString(hInst,IDS_Disk19,lpMessage,MaxText);
1617      MessageBox(GetFocus(),lpMessage,lpCaption,MB_OK);
1618      return FALSE;
1619      }
1620   NumBytes= (WORD) TestLength;       /* initialize arg for _lread() */
1621
1622   hMem= GlobalAlloc(GMEM_MOVEABLE, NumBytes);   /* create a buffer */
1623   if (hMem==0)
1624      {
1625      MessageBeep(0);
1626      LoadString(hInst,IDS_Unexpected,lpCaption,Max);
1627      LoadString(hInst,IDS_Disk20,lpMessage,MaxText);
1628      MessageBox(GetFocus(),lpMessage,lpCaption,MB_OK);
1629      return FALSE;
1630      }
1631   lpImageData= GlobalLock(hMem);     /* lock buffer and grab pointer */
1632
1633   hFile= OpenFile(lpFileName,&FileStruct,OF_READ);
1634   if (hFile==-1)
1635      {
1636      MessageBeep(0);
1637      LoadString(hInst,IDS_Unexpected,lpCaption,Max);
1638      LoadString(hInst,IDS_Disk21,lpMessage,MaxText);
1639      MessageBox(GetFocus(),lpMessage,lpCaption,MB_OK);
1640      GlobalUnlock(hMem); GlobalFree(hMem); return FALSE;
1641      }
1642
1643   RetVal= _lread(hFile,lpImageData,NumBytes);     /* read from disk */
1644   if (RetVal==-1)
1645      {
1646      MessageBeep(0);
1647      LoadString(hInst,IDS_Unexpected,lpCaption,Max);
1648      LoadString(hInst,IDS_Disk22,lpMessage,MaxText);
1649      MessageBox(GetFocus(),lpMessage,lpCaption,MB_OK);
1650      _lclose(hFile);
1651      GlobalUnlock(hMem); GlobalFree(hMem); return FALSE;
1652      }
1653   if ((unsigned)RetVal < NumBytes)
1654      {
1655      MessageBeep(0);
1656      LoadString(hInst,IDS_Unexpected,lpCaption,Max);
1657      LoadString(hInst,IDS_Disk23,lpMessage,MaxText);
1658      MessageBox(GetFocus(),lpMessage,lpCaption,MB_OK);
1659      _lclose(hFile);
1660      GlobalUnlock(hMem); GlobalFree(hMem); return FALSE;
1661      }
1662
1663   RetVal= _lclose(hFile);                          /* close the file */
1664   if (RetVal==-1)                        /* if unable to close file... */
1665      {
1666      MessageBeep(0);
1667      LoadString(hInst,IDS_Unexpected,lpCaption,Max);
1668      LoadString(hInst,IDS_Disk24,lpMessage,MaxText);
1669      MessageBox(GetFocus(),lpMessage,lpCaption,MB_OK);
1670      GlobalUnlock(hMem); GlobalFree(hMem); return FALSE;
1671      }
1672
1673   BytesCopied= SetBitmapBits(hBitmap,NumBytes,lpImageData);
```

```
1674   if (BytesCopied==0)         /* if unable to copy bits to bitmap... */
1675     {
1676     MessageBeep(0);
1677     LoadString(hInst,IDS_Unexpected,lpCaption,Max);
1678     LoadString(hInst,IDS_Disk25,lpMessage,MaxText);
1679     MessageBox(GetFocus(),lpMessage,lpCaption,MB_OK);
1680     GlobalUnlock(hMem); GlobalFree(hMem); return FALSE;
1681     }
1682
1683   GlobalUnlock(hMem);         /* discard the pointer to the buffer */
1684   GlobalFree(hMem);                       /* discard the buffer */
1685   return TRUE;
1686   }
1687   /*
1688   ----------------------------------------------------------------
1689                       End of the C source file
1690   ----------------------------------------------------------------
1691                                                               */
```

# Part three

# Cel animation

# 9
# *Cel animation and Windows*

The Microsoft Windows graphical environment is particularly well-suited to *computer-assisted traditional animation* (CATA). This form of animation, which is also known as cel animation and drawn animation, offers a programming model that is rich with creative potential. Cel animation offers a ready-made banquet of solutions for many projects. Implementation and control of this animation programming model are straightforward to put in place, yet sophisticated in the results they produce.

**Implementation**   The cel animation programming model, or paradigm, can be efficiently and effectively implemented using the timer-based message-handler method described in chapter 6, Animating in Windows.

**Control**   Cel animation can be controlled using the scripted animation method, which can produce arresting animation sequences for entertainment, education, training, software tutorials, games, cartoons, spot animation, business presentations, point-of-purchase displays, disk-based advertising, television graphics, simulation, visualization, and other purposes. Scripted animation is also called cast-based animation. Refer back to the discussion in chapter 6, Animating in Windows, for a full description of various methods of implementation and control for computer animation.

## Cel animation paradigm

*Here's Why...*   The cel animation paradigm that provides the programming model for this method of computer animation is directly derived from traditional animation. For many years the display mechanism used by traditional animation was 35mm or 16mm movie film, as shown in FIG. 9-1. A movie camera capable of single-frame exposure provided an ideal

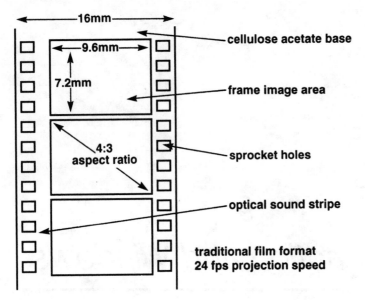

**9-1** Film specifications for traditional cel animation. Shown here is 16mm format.

**9-2** A conceptual schematic for a multiplane camera.

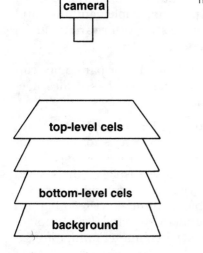

environment for the multilayered approach used by traditional animations to build a scene. By drawing individual actors, props, scene elements, and the background on separate cels (celluloid sheets), the animators could place a number of cels over the background. Because the cels are transparent except where images have been inked and painted by the animators, various scene elements could be animated independently in front of the background (by replacing cels), and the background itself could be panned and zoomed (by moving the camera). This juxtaposition of cels, background, and camera is depicted in FIG. 9-2.

## Computer animation paradigm

The same multilayered methods used by traditional animation studios like Warner, Disney, Columbia, Metro-Goldwyn-Mayer, Hanna-Barbera, and others can be easily implemented in the Windows environment.

*Here's How...* The computer animation paradigm is comprised of three elements. These animation production elements are build, save, and playback, as shown in FIG. 9-3. The build function is sometimes called the pen, ink, and paint engine. The save function is sometimes called the authoring engine. The playback function is sometimes called the playback engine or delivery engine. Together, these components of the computer-assisted traditional animation paradigm are called the animation engine. They are best implemented in a form similar to the prototype frame animation engine described and demonstrated in chapter 8, Frame animation engines.

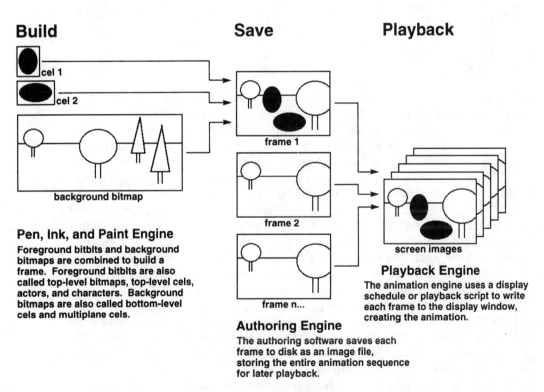

**Build**

cel 1

cel 2

background bitmap

**Pen, Ink, and Paint Engine**

Foreground bitblts and background bitmaps are combined to build a frame. Foreground bitblts are also called top-level bitmaps, top-level cels, actors, and characters. Background bitmaps are also called bottom-level cels and multiplane cels.

**Save**

frame 1

frame 2

frame n...

**Authoring Engine**

The authoring software saves each frame to disk as an image file, storing the entire animation sequence for later playback.

**Playback**

screen images

**Playback Engine**

The animation engine uses a display schedule or playback script to write each frame to the display window, creating the animation.

**9-3**  A conceptual representation of animation logistics for Windows applications.

## Digitization methods

Traditional animators produced the drawings they needed by using pencil and onionskin paper. The pencil allowed quick, creative expression. The onionskin paper allowed the animator to place one sheet over another and quickly trace any elements of the drawing that remain constant from one frame to the next. These unchanged components are called *tracebacks*.

The resulting onionskin drawings were filmed using single-frame exposure and were then reviewed by the animator for accuracy in timing, movement, shape, and so on. This prototype is called a pencil test. Finally, the finished onionskin drawings were transferred to cels, where they were inked and painted by assistant artists. All in all, the process was—and in many animation studios still is—very time-consuming and labor-intensive.

By computerizing the process, significant savings in time and labor can be realized, but a new set of challenges are introduced. Deciding how to create the drawings or images that will be animated is perhaps the most prominent of these new challenges. As shown in FIG. 9-4, six methods for creating or capturing images are:

- Scanner.
- Custom software.
- Grid.
- Digital camera.
- Video camera.
- Tablet.

The grid method is the approach that was used to build the demonstration programs in Part Three of this book. Although the other methods provide a more high-tech solution capable of volume production (as explained in FIG. 9-4), the grid method provides an animation environment ideally suited for teaching purposes. No special hardware is needed for the grid method.

*Hands on* During preparation of the sample animations in this part of the book, the individual drawings that make up the cels were sketched with pencil on professional layout paper. The paper was translucent and allowed tracebacks to be used by placing two drawings over a portable light table. When all the pencil drawings for an animation sequence were complete, each drawing in turn was placed over an animation grid. See FIG. 7-2 in chapter 7, Real-time animation engines, and FIG. 8-2 in chapter 8, Frame animation engines, for examples of sample grids.

The grid corresponds directly to the display window of the sample application. The X-Y coordinates of key elements for each pencil drawing were noted and were used later during program development and testing. The program listings in chapter 7 and chapter 8 contain X-Y coordinates that were derived in exactly this manner.

*Code* You can use the code fragment presented in chapter 7, Real-time animation engines, to build your own grid and customize it to meet the requirements of your animation project.

| METHODS FOR DIGITIZING AN ANIMATION CEL | |
| --- | --- |
| **SCANNER** | Scan images of pencil drawings that you have tested using thumb flip. |
| **CUSTOM SOFTWARE** | Use interactive drawing software to create cels. Use software-simulated motion-test. |
| **GRID** | Place pencil drawing over a scaled grid to obtain xy coordinates. Use hardcoded coordinates and hardcoded drawing functions to create the cels at runtime. |
| **DIGITAL CAMERA** | Use a digital camera like Logitech Foto Man to capture a still image in a bitmap. |
| **VIDEO** | Use a frame-grabber board to capture individual frames from a live video camera or from VTR playback. |
| **TABLET** | Place a pencil drawing on a digitizing tablet and trace with the stylus or crosshair cursor. |

**9-4** Six common methods for acquisition of digital images for use in animation sequences.

## Inbetweening

The essence of animation is motion—and the science of originating a series of drawings that depict motion is called inbetweening (or tweening). Three types of drawings of used during inbetweening. They are:

- Key drawings.
- Breakdown drawings.
- Inbetween drawings.

**Key drawings** *Key drawings* are images that represent key moments in the motion being animated. As the first example in FIG. 9-5 demonstrates, two key drawings might be used to portray the motion of a ball falling from a ledge. The first key drawing depicts the ball about to fall over the edge of the ledge. The second key drawing depicts the ball as it strikes the ground. In a traditional animation studio, key drawings are usually prepared by a layout artist or by the master animator.

**Breakdown drawings** *Breakdown drawings* are images that begin to break down the path followed by the object or actor being animated. As shown in the second example in FIG. 9-5, a breakdown drawing provides an important rough guide that indicates the characteristics of the motion being animated. A breakdown drawing defines the type of interpolation that will be

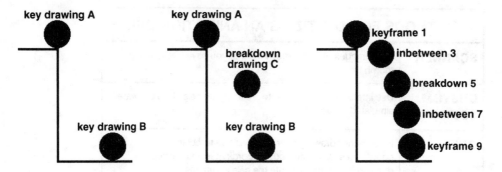

**9-5** Samples of inbetweens and breakdown drawings. At left, two keyframes or key drawings depict a ball falling from a ledge. At center, an inbetween drawing is inserted between the two key drawings. At right, a group of tweens is used.

used to generate all the drawings that will appear between the two key drawings. Different types of interpolation include linear, curved, and random.

**Inbetween drawings**  *Inbetween drawings* are interpolated from the key drawings and breakdown drawings, as shown in the third example in FIG. 9-5. When all the inbetween drawings have been completed, the entire motion sequence is complete, ready for smooth animation. In a traditional animation studio, breakdown drawings and inbetween drawings are produced by assistants called inbetweeners.

## Inbetweening charts

*Inbetweening charts*, like those shown in FIG. 9-6, are used by the animator to instruct the assistant on how to sketch the breakdown drawings and inbetween drawings. Inbetweening charts are also called spacing charts or timing charts. In the examples shown in FIG. 9-6, items 1 and 9 represent key drawings, item 5 denotes a breakdown drawing, and items 3 and 7 are inbetween drawings.

*Expert*  Inbetweening charts provide a powerful method for controlling the timing and pacing of an animation sequence. The two examples in FIG. 9-7 illustrate how to manage the speed of an object's movement. By using more inbetweens, the action will slow down during animation, but it will appear smoother. When fewer inbetweens are used, the action is quicker, more dramatic, and jerkier.

## The storyboard

In the beginning stages of an animation project, traditional animation studios will create a storyboard. A *storyboard* is a visual layout of the entire animation sequence in comic book style. This grand overview of the entire

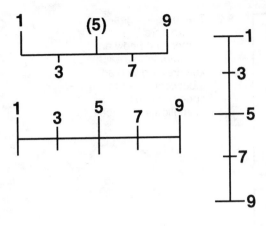

**9-6** Examples of inbetween charts, also called spacing charts. Drawings 1 and 9 are key drawings. Drawing 5 is a breakdown drawing. Images 3 and 7 are tweens.

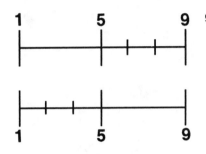

**9-7** The top chart produces an animated sequence where the movement is started rapidly and then slowly finishes. The bottom chart results in an animation sequence where the action begins slowly and accelerates at the end.

animation helps give the animators the sense of perspective, scale, and pacing they need to produce a quality product.

As a computer animator, you too should use a storyboard when you begin to assemble and collate your ideas into a concrete form. You can use the storyboard to create the key drawings that define your cel animation sequence. The illustration in FIG. 9-8 (see next page) demonstrates how to number your key drawings and how to place inbetweening charts on the key drawings.

This irresistible combination of key drawings and inbetweening charts gives you complete creative control over the computer animation sequence. The quality that results from this control is demonstrated by sample applications in the next few chapters in this part of the book.

**key drawing 24**

24
25
26
27
28

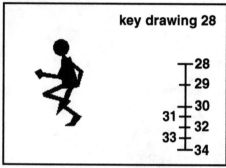

**key drawing 28**

28
29
30
31
32
33
34

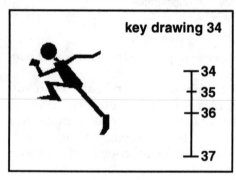

**key drawing 34**

34
35
36
37

**9-8** The three images shown here demonstrate how an animator labels each key drawing with an inbetween chart to specify the full animation sequence.

# 10
# *Characters*

Character animation is one of the most challenging aspects of computer animation. It is also one of the most rewarding and satisfying. Whether the character is realistic, caricature, or cartoon makes no difference to the tremendous impact that character animation can produce on a computer display. Your clients, customers, and end users will be spellbound and enthralled—they will give your software their undiverted attention during character animation sequences. There is something irresistible about the human face that captivates an audience—even an audience of one.

Character animation requires characters to be animated. Designing and drawing those characters is a significant undertaking that requires careful planning and hard work, even if you are a natural artist, and even more so if you are not. No matter how efficient your animation engine, no matter how elegant your source code, no matter how clever your algorithms, the success of your animation is tightly bound to the quality of the character you are animating. Knowing how to animate is not enough; you must also know what to animate. The computer and your program are the stage upon which the character will perform. You simply must have a professional-quality drawing of the character that you plan to animate.

Designing, creating, and drawing characters for computer animation sequences is a manageable part of the production process if you adopt a methodical approach. Even if you have little or no art experience, this chapter will teach you how to:

- Draw heads and faces.
- Draw hands.
- Draw arms, legs, and bodies.
- Animate eyes.

- Animate speech and dialog.
- Draw facial expressions.
- Animate a turning head.

The chapter also provides a sample application that demonstrates facial animation. It presents a character that displays a range of expressions ranging from a simple smile to a diabolical scowl—and includes wide-eyed surprise using an industry-standard double take.

Many of the tips, lessons, and principles that you will discover in this chapter are adapted from the sketchpads, light tables, and screening rooms of traditional film animators. Much of the material is distilled from drawing techniques that were introduced and perfected in the 1930s and 1940s by working illustrators and artists in the commercial art industry. The timeless quality of those drawing techniques is evidenced by the number of illustrators and artists who continue to use them today.

## How to draw heads and faces

 The ability to draw professional-looking heads and faces is a marketable skill in high demand, especially in computer animation programmers. You can perfect this skill by following an approach that uses construction elements to build character heads and faces.

**Construction elements**   The examples in FIG. 10-1 show some of the construction elements you need to build character heads. The idea of attaching a jaw to a spherical skull to build a lifelike head is promoted by many art teachers, commercial artists, cartoonists, and animators—but the concept first received widespread attention in the now-legendary art instruction book, *Figure Drawing For All It's Worth*, by advertising illustrator Andrew Loomis (published by The Viking Press in 1943, now out of print). World-famous Spanish illustrator Jose Parramon further explored the technique in his book, *Drawing The Human Head And Portraits* (published by Fountain Press in 1972, translated from the original 1950s Spanish edition). Film animation studios were also using this construction element approach, as evidenced by pencil sketches of Elmer Fudd in a model sheet created in 1948 by artists working at Warner Bros. animation studios (see *That's All Folks! The Art of Warner Bros. Animation*, by Steve Schneider, published by Henry Holt and Company in 1988).

**Male and female constructions**   The construction element method can be adapted for male and female characters. The examples in FIG. 10-2 show the difference between male and female construction elements. By using a smaller jaw with a sharper point, a female character can be developed. The male and female characters in FIG. 10-3 show how to use the construction elements from FIG. 10-2 to build finished characters. The construction elements ensure that you have the fundamental shape correct, while the finish-

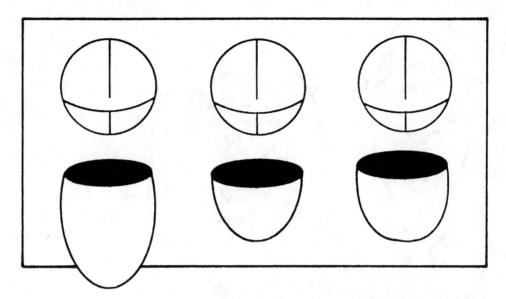

**10-1** Construction elements for cartoon character heads, a technique promoted by many art teachers, commercial artists, cartoonists, and animators.

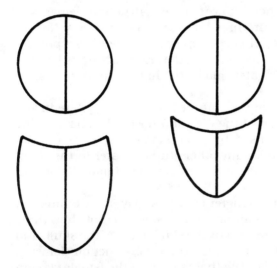

**10-2** At left, construction elements for male cartoon characters. At right, construction elements for female cartoon characters.

ing details like eyes, mouth, nose, and hair bring the character to completion.

**Different views** Few animation sequences are produced using only frontal views of characters, however. Fortunately, the construction element method makes it easy to design and build your own characters in front, three-quarter, and profile views.

**10-3**  Detail of male and female cartoon characters showing how the construction elements from FIG. 10-2 are used to build the finished drawing.

The model sheet in FIG. 10-4 shows how to use construction elements to build your own original characters in three-quarter and front views. Note in particular the three-quarter views, where a semi-sphere is used to represent the back of the skull. This set of three construction elements gives you the underlying shape you need to accurately model the hairline of your characters.

Observe also how the latitude and longitude lines on the sphere in FIG. 10-4 assist in the correct placement of the eyes and nose. The shape of the mouth is a common type much used by professional artists at Hanna-Barbera, Warner Bros., Disney, and many other studios. Later in the chapter you will see how to modify and adapt the mouth to animate dialog and speech.

Creating a profile view of your character is just as easy. The examples in FIG. 10-5 show construction elements for profile views. Again, note how three construction elements are used to represent the skull, back of the skull, and the jaw. Observe how a nose is added when the three construction elements are combined. Notice also the smaller jaw that is used in the female version of the profile views in FIG. 10-5.

**Finishing styles**   You can use many different styles to finish your characters, ranging from simple and Spartan to complex and detailed. The examples in FIG. 10-6 illustrate the difference between simple design and highly detailed character heads. Simple designs are sometimes easier to animate, but detailed designs often produce more authentic and lifelike animation sequences.

No matter what approach you take to finishing your character designs,

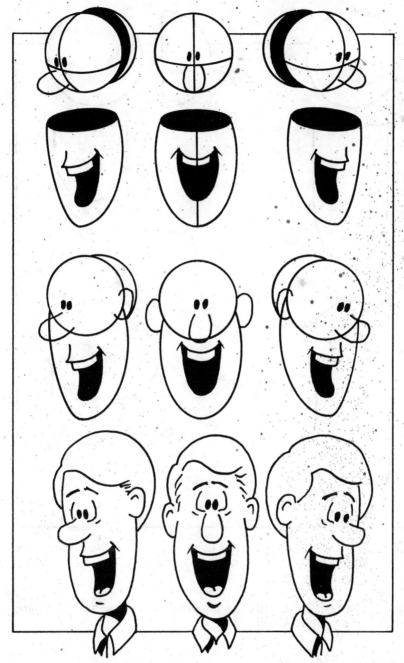

**10-4** How to develop your own original cartoon characters for animation. The top row depicts the individual construction elements in frontal and ¾ views. The center row illustrates how the construction elements are attached to each other to form the fundamental shape of the cartoon character's head. The bottom row shows the finishing details for front and ¾ views. Note the semi-sphere are the back of the head.

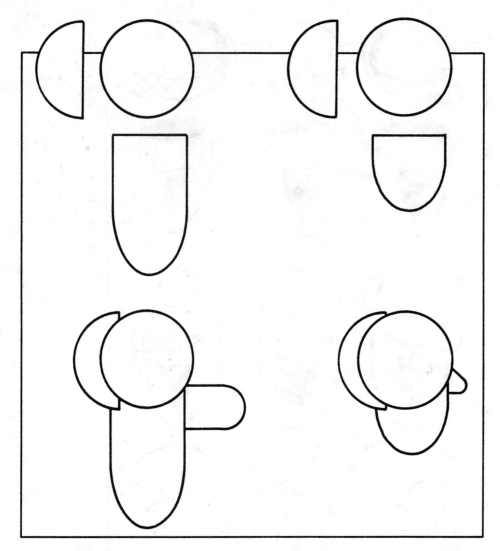

**10-5** Construction elements for profile views of cartoon characters. Male variation is shown at left. Female version shown at right.

just remember to always begin with the construction elements. They are your guarantee of professional results.

## How to draw hands

 Learning to draw hands is no more difficult than drawing heads and faces if you use the construction approach. The examples in FIG. 10-7 show how to use construction elements to build hands. First you assemble a boxlike hand, then you add the curves that give it life.

**10-6** The amount of detailing in a drawing affects the viewer's perception and the amount of production time required.

The examples in FIG. 10-8 illustrate a variety of useful hand positions, each of which was built from a prototype comprised of construction elements.

If your animation sequence uses characters that are caricatures or cartoons, then you should use the industry-standard, three-fingered hand shown in FIG. 10-7 and FIG. 10-8. If your character is realistic or semi-realistic you may wish to consider using the four-fingered hand, which is more lifelike, but much more difficult to draw and animate.

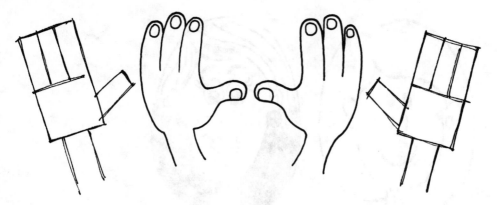

**10-7**   Construction elements for hands of animated cartoon characters.

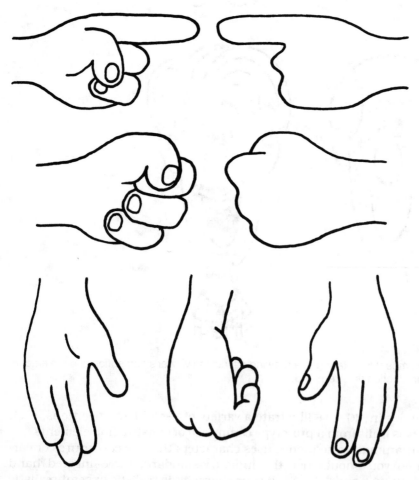

**10-8**   A sampling of hand positions useful for computer animation of cartoon characters.

# How to draw arms, legs, and bodies

**Here's How...** The examples in FIG. 10-9 show how to use stick construction elements to build arms, legs, and torsos. Note how the female figure is created with broader hips and narrower shoulders than the male figure. The female figure is shorter overall, with her back being significantly shorter than the male, but her legs being nearly the same length as the male figure.

**Expert** **Opposing shoulders and hips** You can pose your character bodies much more realistically if you grasp the principle of opposing shoulders and hips, as shown by the two examples in FIG. 10-10. If, for example, you draw the shoulders sloping down towards the right, then

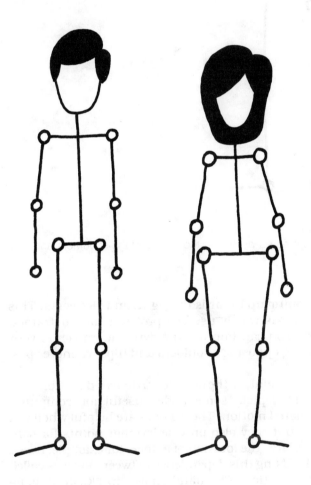

**10-9**  Stick construction elements for animated characters.

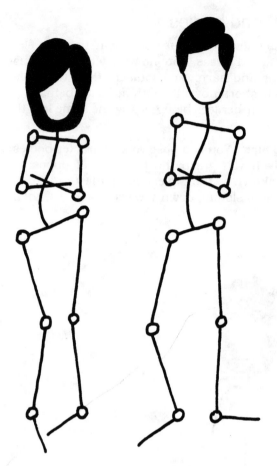

**10-10** Realistic posture can be created by setting the angles of the shoulders and hips to opposing angles.

you should draw the hips sloping up towards the right, and vice versa. This is an important principle that is widely used by professional illustrators, cartoonists, and animators. You can improve the dynamic impact of your character animations by using opposing shoulders and hips whenever possible.

Using stick figures is also useful for the study of articulated motion. The android shown in FIG. 10-11 depicts some nodes useful for computer-assisted animation of articulated motion. These nodes are helpful when you are drawing your character, but they also provide leverage points for software that automatically calculates the location of a knee, for example, based on the position of a hip node. Using this dependency between nodes is called the animation of articulated motion. The hand shown in FIG. 10-12 illustrates some nodes and angles useful for computer-assisted animation of articulated motion.

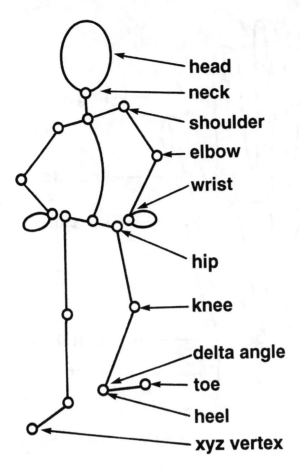

**head**

**neck**

**shoulder**

**elbow**

**wrist**

**hip**

**knee**

**delta angle**

**toe**

**heel**

**xyz vertex**

**10-11**   Nodes of a skeletal structure that can be used for computer-animated articulated motion of androids.

**Scale of character bodies**   The characters shown in FIG. 10-13 are drawn four heads tall. This is an industry-standard scale. A lifelike drawing of a human is often sized at five or six heads tall. A comic book rendering of a superhero is usually scaled at eight or nine heads tall. Cartoon characters, whether in comic book format or film animation, are usually drawn three or four heads tall.

## How to animate eyes

*Here's How...*   The eyes of a character are often the most important element, especially in animation. Numerous studies by advertising agencies have demonstrated that subjects spend more time looking at the eyes of a portrait than at any other part of the face in the photograph.

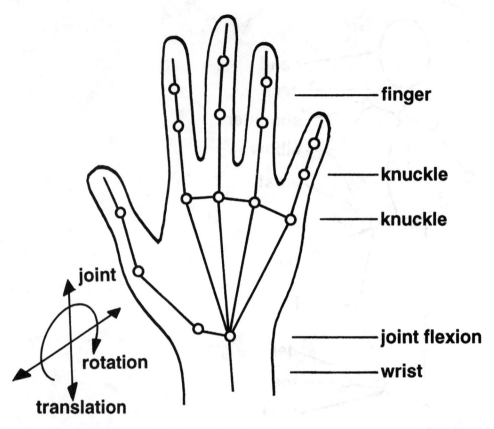

finger

knuckle

knuckle

joint flexion

wrist

joint

rotation

translation

**10-12** Skeletal structure of the human hand can be used to animate the articulated motion of androids.

Two types of eye movement are especially important for computer animation of characters. They are eye sweeps and blinks. Both are easy to do, but difficult to do well.

**The sweeping gaze**   The eye movement shown in FIG. 10-14 illustrates the correct way to animate a sweeping gaze. As the curved tweening line shows, the pupils must follow the curve of the eyeball if the eye movement is to appear lifelike. Even so, there is still one more trick you can add to your sweeping gaze animation to make it even more effective. If you carefully observe the people around you, you will notice that they often blink at the beginning of a sweeping eye movement. Researchers believe that this pre-movement blink is regulated by the subconscious mind and plays an important role in lubricating the eye just prior to movement. If you add a standard blink at the beginning of each major eye sweep in your animation, you can add a significant measure of professionalism to your work.

**The standard blink**   The difference between a standard blink and a sleepy blink is shown in FIG. 10-15. In a standard blink, the upper lid passes over

**10-13** A proper scale can be achieved by drawing your cartoon characters four heads tall.

the pupils, which themselves remain stationary. During a sleepy blink, the pupils are dragged downward as the upper lid passes over them.

The example in FIG. 10-5 shows two inbetweens and two key frames. As a general rule of thumb, blinks should be animated quickly, with as few inbetweens as possible. The more inbetweens you add to the standard blink, the less bright your character will look. The maximum recommended cycle is two key frames (fully open and fully closed), one breakdown drawing, and two inbetween drawings.

*Expert* **Double takes** A double take is a staged overreaction to some event. The character notices the event, looks away, then looks again with exaggerated surprise. The four elements of a standard double take blink are illustrated in FIG. 10-16. The sample animation in the demo program later in this chapter provides a working example of a standard double take. The first three elements shown in FIG. 10-16 should be animated

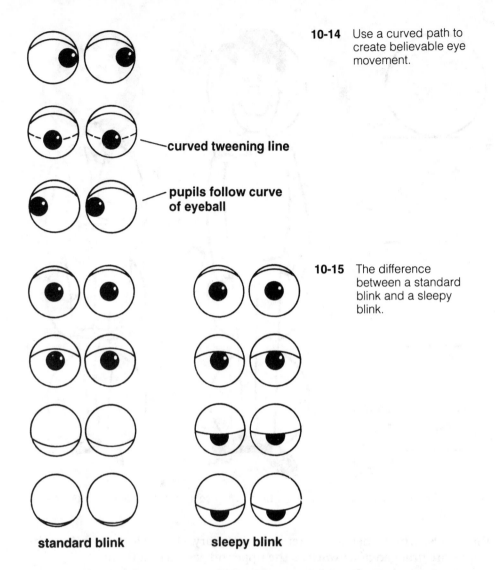

**10-14** Use a curved path to create believable eye movement.

curved tweening line

pupils follow curve of eyeball

**10-15** The difference between a standard blink and a sleepy blink.

**standard blink**     **sleepy blink**

quickly, and the final element of wide-eyed surprise should be held on-screen for a longer duration.

## How to animate speech and dialog

*Here's How...* The multimedia extensions for the Windows graphical environment make it possible to animate speech and dialog. Provided your computer is equipped with a multimedia-compatible sound card and multimedia software development tools, you can add a soundtrack to your character animations.

Two criteria must be met in order to successfully animate speech. First, the timing of the character animation must by in synch (synchronized) with

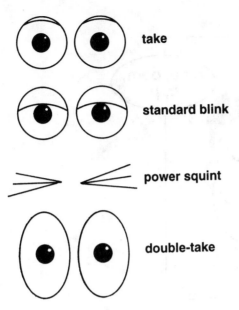

take

standard blink

power squint

double-take

**10-16** A blink double-take, often used to depict shock or surprise.

the audio track. Second, the shape of the character's mouth must accurately suggest the vowels and consonants that are being spoken by the character (via the audio track).

Professional animation studios have long known the correct mouth shapes for animating speech, but they have closely guarded the knowledge in order to maintain their competitive advantage in the marketplace. The illustrations in this chapter give you the inside information you need to successfully animate speech.

**Consonants** Four examples of consonant-vowel combinations spoken at normal speed and inflection are depicted in FIG. 10-17. It is important to understand that the actual consonant sound never takes more than two exposures in traditional film animation. If you refer back to FIG. 6-3 in chapter 6, Animating in Windows, you will see that this means a consonant should never exceed one frame in Windows-based animation applications.

Three examples of consonants spoken slowly and deliberately are shown in FIG. 10-18. As you study these examples, note that many elements of the character's mouth play equally important roles in simulating speech, including the shape of the lips, position of the tongue, visibility of the teeth, and the shape of the opening of the mouth.

**Vowels** Two examples of vowels spoken slowly and deliberately are illustrated in FIG. 10-19. Mouth shapes for the commonly used *oh* and *ooh* vowels are shown in FIG. 10-20.

**10-17** Mouth shapes for common combinations of vowels and consonants spoken at normal speed and inflection.

## How to draw facial expressions

*Here's How...* The best source for samples of facial expressions for characters—no matter whether realistic, caricature, or cartoon—is life itself. The people with whom you work and play can provide a never-ending supply of ideas. Being able to capture the essence of a facial expression is not always as easy as it seems, however. The sample expressions in this chapter give you a working inventory of facial expressions that you can use as you build your own character animation sequences.

**10-18**  Mouth shapes for consonants spoken slowly and deliberately.

**10-19**  Mouth shapes for vowels spoken slowly and deliberately.

**10-20**　Mouth shapes for the commonly used oh and ooo vowel sounds.

**Facial expression front-views**　Examples of male and female front-view facial expressions for unemotional, happy, surprise, and anger are shown in FIG. 10-21. Examples of diabolical, embarassed, affectionate, and apprehensive facial expressions in front-view are depicted in FIG. 10-22.

**Facial expression three-quarter views**　Examples of male and female three-quarter view facial expressions for lovestruck, diabolical, sad, and shame are illustrated in FIG. 10-23. Examples of three-quarter view facial expressions for distasteful, fright, determination, and smugness are shown in FIG. 10-24.

**Facial expression techniques**　By recognizing the various essential ingredients of facial expressions, you can quickly learn to draw your own from life or from mirror. The two most important elements are the eye/eyebrow combination and the mouth. Note the surprise and anger expressions in FIG. 10-21, for example. The eyes spring open, the eyebrows rise dramatically, and the mouth opens wide in the surprise expression. In the anger expression, the eyes also spring open, but the eyebrows drop, and the mouth line stretches across the face in an arc. Observe also how the jawline in these two expressions differs. The jaw stretches down to accommodate the open mouth in the surprise expression, while the jaw is wider for the grimacing mouth of the anger expression.

Detailing around the eyes can also play an important role in facial expressions. Note the detail in the diabolical expression shown in FIG. 10-22. Also note the lines around the eyes in the apprehension expression. However, the mouth does all the work in the embarassment expression in FIG. 10-22, although the height and position of the eyebrows is also a factor.

**unemotional**

**happy**

**surprise**

**anger**

**10-21** Frontal view of fundamental facial expressions useful for computer-animated cartoon characters.

*Expert* The position and orientation of the head is also important, as illustrated by the shame expression in FIG. 10-23. The uplifted eyes and eyebrows are just one part of the overall impression, with the head tilted forward, the chin tucked in, and the shoulders shrugged. Contrast this with the smug expression in FIG. 10-24, where the head is thrown back, the jaw thrust forward, and the neck stretched out. The position and shapes of the eyes, eyebrows, and mouth are not enough to suggest smugness, the orientation of the head itself is a key factor.

## How to animate a turning head

*Here's How...* One of the most frequently animated head movements is the turn. Sample key drawings and an inbetweening chart for a head turn are shown in FIG. 10-25. Like eye movements, a turning head is easy to animate, but difficult to animate well. The example shown in FIG. 10-26 shows how to use eye movement and a curved tweening line to make the head turn more authentic.

**10-22** Frontal view of some specialized facial expressions useful for computer-animated cartoon characters.

*Expert* You can use three tricks to make your animated head turns more professional. First, have the character's head tilt slightly forward and follow a curved path during the turn, as depicted in FIG. 10-26. Second, make sure the character blinks at the beginning of the head turn. And, third, use a slight sweep of the eyes to lead the movement of the head during the turn, as shown by the middle tween in FIG. 10-26.

## Preparing for the sample application

**Inbetweens**   During preparation of the sample animation presented later in the chapter, a set of key drawings and an inbetweening chart was devised, as shown in FIG. 10-27. The five keyframes shown represent the five essential expressions that the character displays during the animation sequence. Developing a computer animation involves some trial and error during the creative process, just like traditional film animation. After plotting a total of 13 key drawings and inbetweens, as illustrated in FIG. 10-27, the author's oversight became obvious. (As the saying goes, hindsight is always 20/20.) Another tween was needed after the final keyframe shown in FIG. 10-27 in order to make the transition back to the smiling expression of the first keyframe.

**10-23** Useful facial expressions shown in ¾ view for computer-animated cartoon characters.

**Tracebacks**   The grid and character silhouette shown in FIG. 10-28 illustrate how tracebacks were used during the design of the sample animation presented in this chapter. Although the sample application presents a dramatic example of facial animation, only the eyes and mouth are redrawn from one cel to the next, proving the point made previously about the importance of these two elements. In point of fact, the same block of code is called to draw the traceback portions of the character for each cel. As you evaluate the animation sequence on your own personal computer you can judge for yourself whether the author made the best decision about which facial elements to keep constant (as tracebacks) and which to animate.

## Sample application

The screen image in FIG. 10-29 shows the first frame from the sample application blink.exe. This program demonstrates facial animation techniques, including a double take. The interactive editor allows you to experiment with different animation playback options, including full forward, full reverse, pause, freeze-frame, single-step forward,

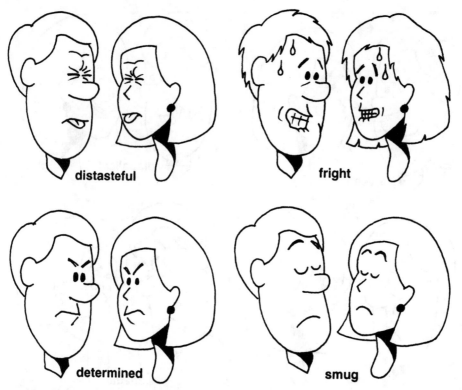

**distasteful**

**fright**

**determined**

**smug**

**10-24** Specialized facial expressions suitable for computer-animated cartoon characters shown in ¾ view.

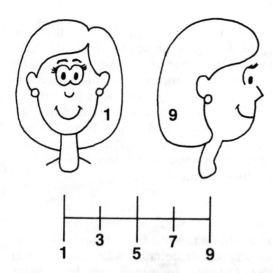

**10-25** Key drawings and an inbetween chart for a head turn.

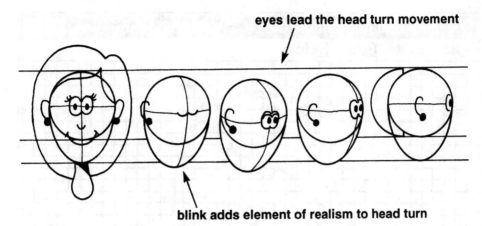

**eyes lead the head turn movement**

**blink adds element of realism to head turn**

**10-26** How to use a curve to plot the positioning of inbetweens in order to produce a believable head turn.

## Keyframes and tweens

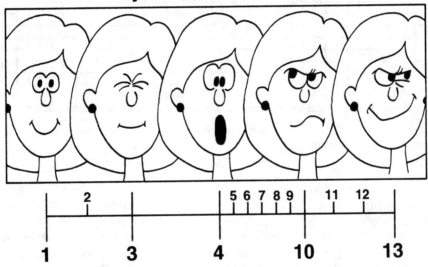

**10-27** The key drawings and inbetween chart used to create the sample application presented in this chapter.

and single-step reverse. The animation will continue to play even if the window is partly covered by another window or if the window is partly clipped by the edge of the screen.

The blink.exe demo is built from six modules, including a .def module definition file, an .h #include file, an .rc resource script file, and a .c source file—in addition to an .h #include file and a .c source file for the storage.c

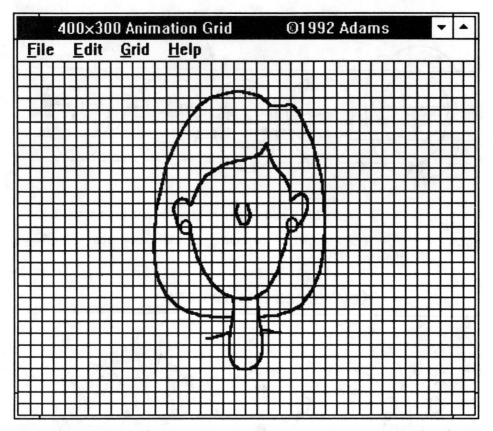

**10-28** The traceback portion of the cels, positioned on the grid template used to derive the X-Y display coordinates.

module that provides disk read/write functions for binary image files. All of these production files are presented as ready-to-use source code in the program listings later in this chapter. The source files are also provided on the companion disk. See the appropriate appendix for instructions on how to build blink.exe with QuickC for Windows, Turbo C++ for Windows, Borland C++, Zortech C++, WATCOM C, and Microsoft C and the SDK.

## What the program does: A user's guide

The sample application provides an interactive platform for experimenting with frame animation of cartoon facial expressions. You can use either a mouse or the keyboard to experiment with the demo program. The menus also support mnemonic keys. To view a runtime help message, select Help from the Help menu.

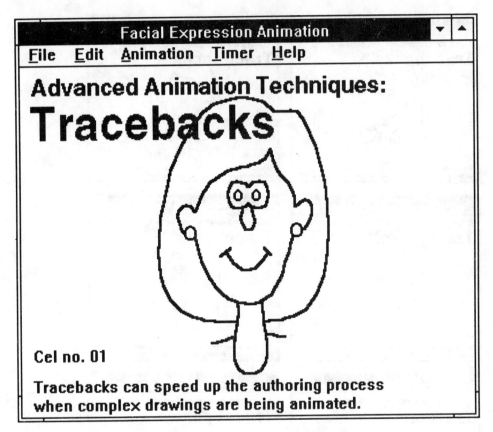

**10-29** A freezeframe from the animated sample application. Compare this computer rendering with the hand-drawn key drawing shown in FIG. 10-27.

## Initializing the system

Select Initialize system from the Animation menu to initialize the hidden frame. None of the authoring or playback features of blink.exe will function until the hidden frame has been created.

## Creating the frames

Select Create Frames from the Animation menu to create the animation sequence and store it on disk. The 15 frames that comprise the animation are illustrated in FIG. 10-30 and FIG. 10-31. The sample application will build each frame in turn on the hidden page, copy the completed frame to the display window, and then save the image to disk as a binary image file. If you have already saved the 15 frames to disk, the demo program will present a warning message and will give you the option of overwriting the existing files

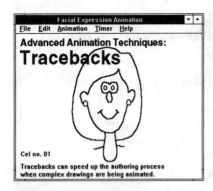

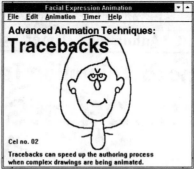

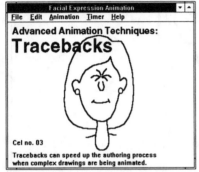

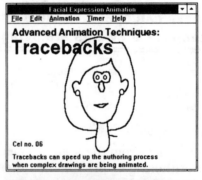

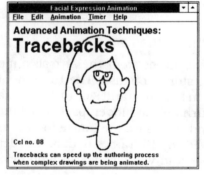

**10-30** The first 8 frames of the animation loop produced by the sample application at runtime.

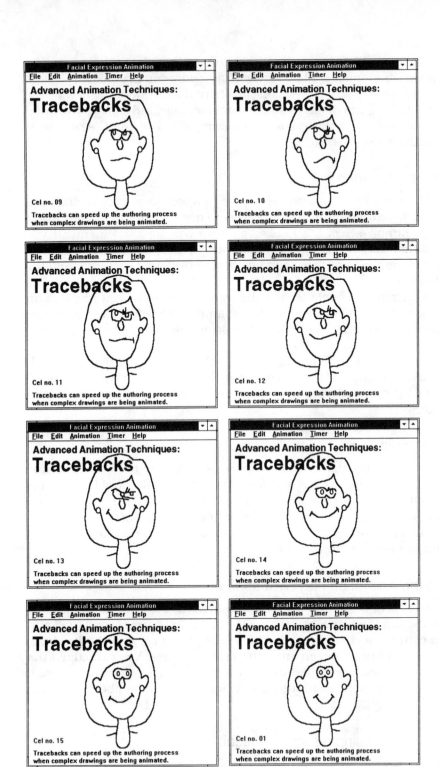

**10-31** The final eight frames of the animation loop.

with the new image files. If you choose not to overwrite the existing files, the build sequence is stopped and no further frames are constructed.

If not enough free space exists on your hard disk to store the new image files, the demo program displays an advisory message and cancels the build process. The program reports successful completion of the Create Frames function with a message box.

## Loading the animation

Before you can play the animation sequence that you have saved to disk, you must load it. If you saved the animation sequence during the current working session, simply select Load Animation from the Animation menu. If you saved the animation during a previous working session, you must select Initialize system from the Animation menu before selecting Load Animation from the Animation menu.

If the software is unable to find the frame files on disk, it displays an advisory message. If you attempt to play an animation before loading it from disk or before initializing the system, the demo program will display a hint message.

Under normal circumstances the sample application will load each frame file into the hidden frame and from there into memory. After all 15 frames have been loaded from disk, the program displays a message box to report success.

## Playing the animation

To play the animation sequence, select Run Forward from the Animation menu. A character's face is animated through a smile, double take, surprise, disgust, mischievious contemplation, and then returns to a smile. Sample runtime images from the animation sequence are shown in FIG. 10-30 and FIG. 10-31. The character will continue to exhibit facial expressions until you stop the animation.

## Adjusting the animation playback speed

You can increase or decrease the animation speed by selecting from the Timer menu. At startup the playback rate is set to 18 frames per second (fps) and the menu exhibits a check mark beside 18 fps. If you select 6 fps the check mark moves and the on-screen animation rate changes. You can adjust the playback speed when the animation is running forward, reverse, or paused. See chapter 8, Frame animation engines, for a discussion about playback rates on slower computers.

## Freeze-frame and single-step animation

**Pause**  To pause the animation, select Pause from the Animation menu. To resume animation playback in forward mode, select Run Forward from the

Animation menu. To resume animation playback in reverse mode, select Run Reverse from the Animation menu.

**Single-step**  While the animation is paused, you can activate single-step playback. Press the right arrow key on the direction keypad to display the next frame in the animation sequence. Keep pressing the right arrow key to step through the entire animation. To single-step in reverse, press the left arrow key on the direction keypad. To resume full animation playback, select either Run Forward or Run Reverse from the Animation menu.

## Persistent graphics

**Moving the window**  To test the persistent graphics features of the animation sequence, start the animation playback and then move the window by clicking on the caption bar and draggin the window to another location on the screen. Even if the window is clipped by the edge of the screen the animation will continue to play.

**Covering the window**  To confirm the cooperative multitasking features of the animation, position the window partially over a program group box and then click on the program group box. The program group box will move to the foreground, partly covering the sample application, but the animation will continue to run.

## Using the Help menu

You can use the Help menu to discover various facts about your system at runtime, including the current screen mode, the maximum number of available colors, the runtime memory mode (real, standard, or enhanced), and other information.

**Checking the screen resolution**  To find out the current screen mode, select Screen resolution from the Help menu. A message box will display the horizontal-by-vertical resolution. The blink.exe sample application supports 640 × 480, 640 × 350, 800 × 600, and 1024 × 768 resolution displays.

**Maximum displayable colors**  To determine the maximum available colors that can be displayed simultaneously, select Available colors from the Help menu. A message box will indicate the mode. In its current implementation, blink.exe supports 16-color and 2-color displays. If you want to modify the source code to support 256-color displays, see the discussion in chapter 3, Blitting.

**Determining the runtime memory mode**  To examine the current Windows runtime memory mode, select Memory mode from the Help menu. A message box will appear, containing an advisory notice describing the mode and its capabilities. The blink.exe demo program supports real, standard, and enhanced memory modes.

**Animation memory requirements**   To view some notes about animation memory requirements, select Memory notes from the Help menu.

 **Animation timing considerations**   To view an informative message about animation playback rates, select Timing notes from the Help menu.

**General help**   For a general help message at runtime, select Help from the Help menu. All of the messages provided by the Help menu are available during animation playback, and the animation will continue to play beneath any menu or message box.

# How the source code works: A programmer's guide

*Hands On*  The blink.exe demonstration program is a dedicated implementation of the prototype frame animation engine that was described and demonstrated in chapter 8, Frame animation engines. Using the techniques presented in the program listings for blink.exe, you can easily add facial expression animation capabilities to your own applications. You can also use the storage.c module to add disk input/output services to your own animation applications.

The organization of the blink.h #include file and the blink.rc resource script file follow the format established in earlier sample applications. In particular, see chapter 8, Frame animation engines, for a prototype program listing for frame animation applications.

## How the .c file works

*.c*  The .c file adheres closely to the format presented in the program listing for the prototype frame animation engine in chapter 8, Frame animation engines. The discussion that follows is intended to address only the modifications that have been made to the prototype code.

**Static variables**   The global variables that are visible throughout the blink.c file are declared at lines 0047 through 0351. Although 15 cels are used by the program, the zFINALFRAME constant is defined as 67 at line 0110. This discrepancy between 15 and 67 occurs because many of the 15 cels are held on-screen for longer than one frame's duration. By varying the length of time of display for each cel, the timing of the facial expressions and the intervening pauses can be accurately controlled during playback.

**Cels**   The bitmap handles for the 15 cels are declared at lines 0122 and 0123. The X-Y coordinates that are required to draw each of the 15 cels are provided in arrays Cel1[] through Cel15[] at lines 0137 through 0351. This smart database is encyphered with tokens to indicate whether a particular set of coordinates refers to a polyline or an ellipse. The comments at lines 0128 through 0135 explain how these tokens work. The drawing code that deciphers the smart data is located later in the program listing at lines 1079 through 1142.

**Building the 15 frames**   The function that manages the building and storage of the 15 frames is located at lines 0929 through 1000. Note in particular lines 0961 through 0990 and the use of the file names BLINK1.BIT through BLINK15.BIT.

**Drawing the 15 cels**   The function that draws each cel is located at lines 1079 through 1142. The nPolyline, nEllipse, and nEnd variables that are declared and initialized at lines 1086 through 1088 correspond directly to the tokens encyphered in the database arrays at lines 0137 through 0351.

By checking the contents of the array against these variables, the drawing code can determine whether it should draw a polyline or an ellipse. Bundling the tokens into the data makes it possible to use the same drawing code to draw each of the 15 different cels that are used by this sample application.

Before beginning to read the data in the cel arrays, the code calls zDrawTraceback() at line 1091. This function draws all elements in the character that do not change from frame to frame, as shown previously in FIG. 10-28.

The loop that fetches data and draws a graphic primitive is located from line 1098 START_OF_LOOP: to line 1127. The statement at line 1099 reads a token from the array. Then the if() block at lines 1101 through 1110 draws an ellipse if the test at line 1101 is true. Otherwise the if() block at lines 1112 through 1127 draws a polyline if the test at line 1112 is true. Finally, when the if() statement at line 1129 determines that the end of the data has been reached, the code tidies up and returns to the caller. Note the boilerplate code at lines 1131 through 1135, which displays a message box that is helpful during debugging.

**Drawing the tracebacks**   The zDrawTraceback() function at lines 1148 through 1238 draws the traceback portions of each cel. These traceback elements are those portions of the character that do not change from cel to cel. (See FIG. 10-28.) The X-Y coordinates are hard-coded into the zDrawTraceback() function—a practice which is tolerable for teaching purposes, but which would be unforgiveable in commercial code.

**Animation playback**   The zShowNextFrame() function at lines 1251 through 1461 regulates the playback of the animation sequence at runtime. Observe the switch(FrameNum) block at lines 1273 through 1342. The case 34: statement, for example, is blank. This means that the execution logic will simply fall through to the next line, and then to the next line, continuing to cascade until it encounters line 1318, where the case 44: statement provides some executable instructions. This use of blank case statements means that the hF10 image will be repeated for 11 frames during playback. The same paradigm is used by the disk-based switch block at lines 1363 through 1447. Although there are more elegant ways to code these playback delays, the approach used in blink.c results in a program listing that is easy to recognize and understand.

## How the disk input/output module works

The program listing for storage.c contains functions that provide disk input/output services for the sample animation. The program listing for storage.h simply declares zSaveFrame() and zLoadFrame(), which are functions in storage.c that can be called by other modules.

The source code in storage.c is identical to the corresponding code in the prototype frame animation engine in chapter 8, Frame animation engines. Note, however, the definition of constants at lines 0052 through 0069 and the declaration of external variables at lines 0075 through 0081. These definitions and declarations make it possible for storage.c to use text strings from blink.rc and message box variables from blink.c whenever disk-related errors are encountered at runtime.

# Program listings for the sample application

*Code* The program listings presented here contain all the source code you need to build and run the sample application. The module definition file is provided in FIG. 10-32. The #include file is found in FIG. 10-33. The resource script file is presented in FIG. 10-34. The C source file is provided in FIG. 10-35. The #include file for the disk read/write module is located in FIG. 10-36. The C source file for the read/write module is provided in FIG. 10-37.

*Disk* **Companion disk** If you have the companion disk, the six source files are presented as blink.def, blink.h, blink.rc, blink.c, storage.h, and storage.c.

*License* **License** You can paste the royalty-free source code into your own applications and distribute the resulting executable files under the conditions of the License Agreement and Limited Warranty in FIG. 10 in the introduction to this book.

**10-32** The module definition file listing for the sample application.

```
0001  NAME         DEFDEMO
0002  DESCRIPTION  'Copyright 1992 Lee Adams.  All rights reserved.'
0003  EXETYPE      WINDOWS
0004  STUB         'WINSTUB.EXE'
0005  CODE         PRELOAD MOVEABLE
0006  DATA         PRELOAD MOVEABLE MULTIPLE
0007  HEAPSIZE     1024
0008  STACKSIZE    8192
0009  EXPORTS      zMessageHandler
```

**10-33** The include file listing for the sample application.

```
0001  /*
0002  -----------------------------------------------------------------
0003              Include file BLINK.H
0004          Copyright 1992 Lee Adams.  All rights reserved.
```

```
0005       Include this file in the .RC resource script file and in the
0006       .C source file.  It contains function prototypes, menu ID
0007       constants, and string ID constants.
0008   ----------------------------------------------------------------
0009   ----------------------------------------------------------------
0010                           Function prototypes
0011   ----------------------------------------------------------------
0012                                                                  */
0013   #if !defined(zRCFILE)                     /* if not an .RC file... */
0014     LONG FAR PASCAL zMessageHandler(HWND, unsigned, WORD, LONG);
0015       int PASCAL WinMain(HANDLE,HANDLE,LPSTR,int);
0016     HWND zInitMainWindow(HANDLE);
0017     BOOL zInitClass(HANDLE);
0018   static void zClear(HWND);               /* blank the display window */
0019   static void zInitFrame(HWND);             /* creates hidden frame */
0020   static void zShowNextFrame(HWND);           /* the playback engine */
0021   static void zSetFrameRate(HWND,WORD);         /* resets the timer */
0022   static void zSaveAnimation(HWND);     /* saves animation sequence */
0023   static BOOL zBuildFrame(int *,int,HWND,LPSTR); /* builds a frame */
0024   static void zDrawTraceback(void);           /* draws the traceback */
0025   static void zDrawCel(int *);                    /* draws a cel */
0026   static void zLoadAnimation(HWND);     /* loads animation sequence */
0027   static void zCopyToDisplay(HWND);       /* copies frame to display */
0028   static void zClearHiddenFrame(void);      /* clears hidden frame */
0029   #endif
0030   /*
0031   ----------------------------------------------------------------
0032                           Menu ID constants
0033   ----------------------------------------------------------------
0034                                                                  */
0035   #define IDM_New              1
0036   #define IDM_Open             2
0037   #define IDM_Save             3
0038   #define IDM_SaveAs           4
0039   #define IDM_Exit             5
0040
0041   #define IDM_Undo             6
0042   #define IDM_Cut              7
0043   #define IDM_Copy             8
0044   #define IDM_Paste            9
0045   #define IDM_Delete           10
0046
0047   #define IDM_RunForward       11
0048   #define IDM_RunReverse       12
0049   #define IDM_StopAnimation    13
0050   #define IDM_InitFrame        14
0051   #define IDM_SaveAnimation    15
0052   #define IDM_LoadAnimation    16
0053   #define IDM_Clear            17
0054
0055   #define IDM_FPS182           18
0056   #define IDM_FPS91            19
0057   #define IDM_FPS61            20
0058   #define IDM_FPS45            21
0059   #define IDM_FPS36            22
0060   #define IDM_FPS30            23
0061
0062   #define IDM_About            24
0063   #define IDM_License          25
0064   #define IDM_Display          26
0065   #define IDM_Colors           27
```

Program listings for the sample application  **337**

```
0066    #define IDM_Mode            28
0067    #define IDM_Memory          29
0068    #define IDM_Timing          30
0069    #define IDM_GeneralHelp     31
0070    /*
0071    --------------------------------------------------------------
0072                            String ID constants
0073    --------------------------------------------------------------
0074                                                               */
0075    #define IDS_Caption         1
0076    #define IDS_Warning         2
0077    #define IDS_NoMouse         3
0078    #define IDS_About           4
0079    #define IDS_AboutText       5
0080    #define IDS_License         6
0081    #define IDS_LicenseText     7
0082    #define IDS_Help            8
0083    #define IDS_HelpText        9
0084    #define IDS_Completed       10
0085    #define IDS_Error           11
0086    #define IDS_Memory          12
0087    #define IDS_MemText         13
0088    #define IDS_Timing          14
0089    #define IDS_TimingText      15
0090    #define IDS_NotReady        16
0091    #define IDS_Ready           17
0092    #define IDS_BuildBefore     18
0093    #define IDS_Already         19
0094    #define IDS_InsufMem1       20
0095    #define IDS_InsufMem2       21
0096    #define IDS_NoTimer         22
0097    #define IDS_NoReset         23
0098    #define IDS_CannotReset     24
0099    #define IDS_Resolution      25
0100    #define IDS_ResVGA          26
0101    #define IDS_ResEGA          27
0102    #define IDS_ResCGA          28
0103    #define IDS_ResSVGA         29
0104    #define IDS_Res8514         30
0105    #define IDS_ResHerc         31
0106    #define IDS_ResCustom       32
0107    #define IDS_Color           33
0108    #define IDS_Color16         34
0109    #define IDS_Color256        35
0110    #define IDS_Color2          36
0111    #define IDS_ColorCustom     37
0112    #define IDS_Machine         38
0113    #define IDS_Enhanced        39
0114    #define IDS_Standard        40
0115    #define IDS_Real            41
0116    #define IDS_NoFrame         42
0117    #define IDS_AnimReady       43
0118    #define IDS_Unexpected      44
0119    #define IDS_Status          45
0120    #define IDS_Disk1           46
0121    #define IDS_Disk2           47
0122    #define IDS_Disk3           48
0123    #define IDS_Disk4           49
0124    #define IDS_Disk5           50
0125    #define IDS_Disk6           51
0126    #define IDS_Disk7           52
```

```
0127   #define IDS_Disk8      53
0128   #define IDS_Disk9      54
0129   #define IDS_Disk10     55
0130   #define IDS_Disk11     56
0131   #define IDS_Disk12     57
0132   #define IDS_Disk13     58
0133   #define IDS_Disk14     59
0134   #define IDS_Disk15     60
0135   #define IDS_Disk16     61
0136   #define IDS_Disk17     62
0137   #define IDS_Disk18     63
0138   #define IDS_Disk19     64
0139   #define IDS_Disk20     65
0140   #define IDS_Disk21     66
0141   #define IDS_Disk22     67
0142   #define IDS_Disk23     68
0143   #define IDS_Disk24     69
0144   #define IDS_Disk25     70
0145   #define IDS_Disk26     71
0146   #define IDS_NoBg       72
0147   #define IDS_BgAlready  73
0148   #define IDS_InsufMemBg 74
0149   /*
0150   --------------------------------------------------------------
0151                       End of include file
0152   --------------------------------------------------------------
0153                                                               */
```

**10-34**   The resource script file listing for the sample application.

```
0001   /*
0002   --------------------------------------------------------------
0003                   Resource script file BLINK.RC
0004           Copyright 1992 Lee Adams.  All rights reserved.
0005   This file defines the menu resources, the accelerator key
0006   resources, and the string resources that will be used by the
0007   demonstration application at runtime.
0008   --------------------------------------------------------------
0009                                                               */
0010   #define zRCFILE
0011   #include <WINDOWS.H>
0012   #include "BLINK.H"
0013   /*
0014   --------------------------------------------------------------
0015                       Script for menus
0016   --------------------------------------------------------------
0017                                                               */
0018   MENUS1 MENU
0019     BEGIN
0020     POPUP "&File"
0021       BEGIN
0022         MENUITEM  "&New", IDM_New, GRAYED
0023         MENUITEM  "&Open...", IDM_Open, GRAYED
0024         MENUITEM  "&Save", IDM_Save, GRAYED
0025         MENUITEM  "Save &As...", IDM_SaveAs, GRAYED
0026         MENUITEM SEPARATOR
0027         MENUITEM  "E&xit", IDM_Exit
0028       END
0029     POPUP "&Edit"
0030       BEGIN
```

```
0031        MENUITEM "&Undo\tAlt+BkSp", IDM_Undo, GRAYED
0032        MENUITEM SEPARATOR
0033        MENUITEM "Cu&t\tShift+Del", IDM_Cut, GRAYED
0034        MENUITEM "&Copy\tCtrl+Ins", IDM_Copy, GRAYED
0035        MENUITEM "&Paste\tShift+Ins", IDM_Paste, GRAYED
0036        MENUITEM "&Delete\tDel", IDM_Delete, GRAYED
0037      END
0038    POPUP "&Animation"
0039      BEGIN
0040        MENUITEM "Run &Forward", IDM_RunForward
0041        MENUITEM "Run &Reverse", IDM_RunReverse
0042        MENUITEM "&Pause", IDM_StopAnimation
0043        MENUITEM SEPARATOR
0044        MENUITEM "&Initialize system", IDM_InitFrame
0045        MENUITEM "Cr&eate Frames", IDM_SaveAnimation
0046        MENUITEM SEPARATOR
0047        MENUITEM "&Load Animation", IDM_LoadAnimation
0048        MENUITEM SEPARATOR
0049        MENUITEM "&Clear", IDM_Clear
0050      END
0051    POPUP "&Timer"
0052      BEGIN
0053        MENUITEM "&18 fps", IDM_FPS182, CHECKED
0054        MENUITEM " &9 fps", IDM_FPS91
0055        MENUITEM " &6 fps", IDM_FPS61
0056        MENUITEM " &5 fps", IDM_FPS45
0057        MENUITEM " &4 fps", IDM_FPS36
0058        MENUITEM " &3 fps", IDM_FPS30
0059      END
0060    POPUP "&Help"
0061      BEGIN
0062        MENUITEM "&About", IDM_About
0063        MENUITEM "&License", IDM_License
0064        MENUITEM SEPARATOR
0065        MENUITEM "&Screen resolution", IDM_Display
0066        MENUITEM "Available &colors", IDM_Colors
0067        MENUITEM "Memory mode", IDM_Mode
0068        MENUITEM SEPARATOR
0069        MENUITEM "&Memory notes", IDM_Memory
0070        MENUITEM "&Timing notes", IDM_Timing
0071        MENUITEM SEPARATOR
0072        MENUITEM "&Help", IDM_GeneralHelp
0073      END
0074    END
0075  /*
0076  ------------------------------------------------------------------
0077                     Script for accelerator keys
0078  ------------------------------------------------------------------
0079                                                               */
0080  KEYS1 ACCELERATORS
0081    BEGIN
0082    VK_BACK, IDM_Undo, VIRTKEY, ALT
0083    VK_DELETE, IDM_Cut, VIRTKEY, SHIFT
0084    VK_INSERT, IDM_Copy, VIRTKEY, CONTROL
0085    VK_INSERT, IDM_Paste, VIRTKEY, SHIFT
0086    VK_DELETE, IDM_Delete,VIRTKEY
0087    END
0088  /*
0089  ------------------------------------------------------------------
0090                        Script for strings
0091     Programmer's Notes:  If you are typing this listing, set your
```

```
0092        margins to a line length of 255 characters so you can create
0093        lengthy strings without embedded carriage returns.  The line
0094        wraparounds in the following STRINGTABLE script are used for
0095        readability only in this printout.
0096   --------------------------------------------------------------------
0097                                                                    */
0098   STRINGTABLE
0099     BEGIN
0100       IDS_Caption      "Facial Expression Animation"
0101       IDS_Warning      "Warning"
0102       IDS_NoMouse       "No mouse found.  Some features of this
           demonstration program may require a mouse."
0103       IDS_About        "About this program"
0104       IDS_AboutText    "This is a demo from Windcrest McGraw-Hill
           book 4114.  Copyright 1992 Lee Adams.  All rights reserved."
0105       IDS_License      "License Agreement"
0106       IDS_LicenseText "You can use this code as part of your own
           software product subject to the License Agreement and Limited
           Warranty in Windcrest McGraw-Hill book 4114 and on its
           companion disk."
0107       IDS_Help         "How to use this demo"
0108       IDS_HelpText     "The Animation menu manages the animation
           engine.  Select Initialize System then Create Frames to build
           frames and save to disk.  Select Load Animation then Run
           Forward to play animation.  See the book for advanced
           features."
0109       IDS_Completed    "Task completed OK"
0110       IDS_Error        "Runtime error"
0111       IDS_Memory       "Animation memory requirements"
0112       IDS_MemText      "The hidden frame for the animation is stored
           as a bitmap in global memory.  The demo will advise you if a
           memory shortage occurs.  To make more global memory available
           you can close other applications."
0113       IDS_Timing       "Animation timing"
0114       IDS_TimingText   "The Timer menu sets the animation display
           rate to 18.2, 9.1, 6.1, 4.5, 3.6, or 3 frames per second.
           Actual performance is limited by your computer's processor
           (25MHz or faster is recommended).  See the book for details."
0115       IDS_NotReady     "Animation not ready"
0116       IDS_Ready        "Animation ready"
0117       IDS_BuildBefore "Animation frames not ready for playback."
0118       IDS_Already      "The hidden frame has already been created."
0119       IDS_InsufMem1    "Insufficient global memory for frame bitmap."
0120       IDS_NoTimer      "Unable to create a timer.  Close other
           applications."
0121       IDS_NoReset      "Create hidden frame before attempting to
           reset timer."
0122       IDS_CannotReset "Unable to reset the timer."
0123       IDS_Resolution  "Screen resolution"
0124       IDS_ResVGA       "Running in 640x480 mode."
0125       IDS_ResEGA       "Running in 640x350 mode."
0126       IDS_ResCGA       "Running in 640x200 mode."
0127       IDS_ResSVGA      "Running in 800x600 mode."
0128       IDS_Res8514      "Running in 1024x768 mode."
0129       IDS_ResHerc      "Running in 720x348 mode."
0130       IDS_ResCustom    "Running in custom mode."
0131       IDS_Color        "Available colors"
0132       IDS_Color16      "Running in 16-color mode."
0133       IDS_Color256     "Running in 256-color mode."
0134       IDS_Color2       "Running in 2-color mode."
0135       IDS_ColorCustom "Running in a custom color mode."
```

```
0136        IDS_Machine      "Memory mode"
0137        IDS_Enhanced      "Running in enhanced mode.  Can allocate up to
       16 MB extended physical memory (XMS) if available.  Virtual
       memory up to 4 times physical memory (maximum 64 MB) is also
       available via automatic disk swapping of 4K pages."
0138        IDS_Standard      "Running in standard mode.  Can allocate up to
       16 MB extended physical memory (XMS) if available."
0139        IDS_Real      "Running in real mode.  Can allocate blocks of
       memory from the first 640K of RAM.  Can also allocate blocks
       from expanded memory (EMS) if available."
0140        IDS_NoFrame      "Hidden frame not yet created."
0141        IDS_AnimReady      "Animation ready"
0142        IDS_Unexpected    "Unexpected animation condition"
0143        IDS_Status      "Animation status"
0144        IDS_Disk1      "Animation files already saved to disk."
0145        IDS_Disk2      "Animation sequence successfully saved to
       disk."
0146        IDS_Disk3      "Unable to load next frame from disk.
       Animation halted."
0147        IDS_Disk4      "Animation sequence already loaded from disk."
0148        IDS_Disk5      "Previous load failed.  Cancelling this
       attempt."
0149        IDS_Disk6      "Not enough memory available.  Software will
       dynamically load each frame from disk during playback."
0150        IDS_Disk7      "Animation sequence successfully loaded from
       disk."
0151        IDS_Disk8      "Previous save failed.  Cancelling this
       attempt."
0152        IDS_Disk9      "No hidden-frame exists.  No frame saved to
       disk."
0153        IDS_Disk10      "Unable to retrieve bitmap data structure."
0154        IDS_Disk11      "Bit array is too long to save to disk in a
       single pass."
0155        IDS_Disk12      "Cannot create memory buffer for disk write."
0156        IDS_Disk13      "Unable to copy bits from bitmap to buffer."
0157        IDS_Disk14      "File already exists.  Overwrite existing
       file?"
0158        IDS_Disk15      "Unable to open the file for writing."
0159        IDS_Disk16      "Unable to write to the opened file."
0160        IDS_Disk17      "Unable to close the file after writing."
0161        IDS_Disk18      "No memory bitmap exists.  Unable to load from
       disk."
0162        IDS_Disk19      "Image file is larger than animation frame.
       No file loaded."
0163        IDS_Disk20      "Cannot create memory buffer for file read."
0164        IDS_Disk21      "Unable to open the file for reading.  Be sure
       you have saved an animation sequence to disk before attempting
       to load it."
0165        IDS_Disk22      "An error occurred while reading the file."
0166        IDS_Disk23      "The frame file was shorter than expected."
0167        IDS_Disk24      "Unable to close the file after reading."
0168        IDS_Disk25      "Unable to copy bits from buffer to bitmap."
0169        IDS_Disk26      "Unable to save all files.  Check if
       sufficient space available on disk."
0170        IDS_NoBg      "Hidden background image not yet created."
0171        IDS_BgAlready      "The hidden background bitmap has already been
       created."
0172        IDS_InsufMemBg  "Insufficient global memory for background
       bitmap."
0173      END
0174   /*
```

**10-34** Continued.

```
0175  ---------------------------------------------------------------
0176                    End of resource script file
0177  ---------------------------------------------------------------
0178                                                              */
```

**10-35** The C source file listing for the sample application, blink.c. This demonstration program is ready to build using QuickC for Windows, Turbo C++ for Windows, Microsoft C and the SDK, Borland C++, Symantec Zortech C++, WATCOM C, and other compilers. See FIG. 1-2 for sample command-lines to build the program. Guidelines for using your compiler are provided in the appropriate appendix at the back of the book.

```
0001  /*
0002  ---------------------------------------------------------------
0003       Sample cartoon facial expressions for Windows applications
0004       that use disk-based, hidden-page drawn, frame animation.
0005  ---------------------------------------------------------------
0006    Source file:  BLINK.C
0007    Release version:  1.00                 Programmer:  Lee Adams
0008    Type:  C source file for Windows application development.
0009    Compilers:  Microsoft C and SDK, Borland C++, Zortech C++,
0010      QuickC for Windows, Turbo C++ for Windows, WATCOM C.
0011    Memory model:  small.
0012    Dependencies:   BLINK.DEF module definition file, BLINK.H
0013                    include file, BLINK.RC resource script file,
0014                    and BLINK.C source file.  Disk I/O operations
0015                    require STORAGE.H include file and STORAGE.C
0016                    additional C source file.
0017    Output and features:  Demonstrates interactive playback of
0018      disk-based hidden-page drawn frame animation.  A cartoon
0019      character's facial expressions are animated as 67-frame loop.
0020    Publication: Contains material from Windcrest/McGraw-Hill book
0021      4114 published by TAB BOOKS Division of McGraw-Hill Inc.
0022    License:  As purchaser of the book you are granted a royalty-
0023      free license to distribute executable files generated using
0024      this code provided you accept the conditions of the License
0025      Agreement and Limited Warranty described in the book and on
0026      the companion disk.  Government users:  This software and
0027      documentation are subject to restrictions set forth in The
0028      Rights in Technical Data and Computer Software clause at
0029      252.227-7013 and elsewhere.
0030  ---------------------------------------------------------------
0031       (c) Copyright 1992 Lee Adams.  All rights reserved.
0032          Lee Adams(tm) is a trademark of Lee Adams.
0033  ---------------------------------------------------------------
0034
0035  ---------------------------------------------------------------
0036                          Include files
0037  ---------------------------------------------------------------
0038                                                              */
0039  #include <WINDOWS.H>
0040  #include "BLINK.H"
0041  #include "STORAGE.H"   /* declares callable functions in STORAGE.C
0042  /*                                                            */
0043  ---------------------------------------------------------------
0044            Static variables visible throughout this file
0045  ---------------------------------------------------------------
0046                                                              */
```

```
0047   /* -------------------- window specifications ------------------ */
0048   #define zWINDOW_WIDTH 408
0049   #define zWINDOW_HEIGHT 346
0050   #define zFRAMEWIDE 400
0051   #define zFRAMEHIGH 300
0052   int WindowX, WindowY;
0053
0054   /* -------------------- instance operations ------------------ */
0055   HANDLE hInst;
0056   HWND MainhWnd;
0057   HANDLE hAccel;
0058   HMENU hMenu;
0059   PAINTSTRUCT ps;
0060   int MessageRet;
0061
0062   /* -------------------- mouse and cursor -------------------- */
0063   HCURSOR hPrevCursor;
0064   HCURSOR hHourGlass;
0065   int MousePresent;
0066
0067   /* -------------------- runtime conditions ------------------ */
0068   int DisplayWidth, DisplayHeight;
0069   int DisplayBits;
0070   int DisplayPlanes;
0071   DWORD MemoryMode;
0072
0073   /* -------------------- message box operations ---------------- */
0074   char lpCaption[51];
0075   int Max= 50;
0076   char lpMessage[250];
0077   int MaxText= 249;
0078
0079   /* ---------------- persistent image operations -------------- */
0080   #define zBLANK 0
0081   #define zANIMATING  1
0082   int PaintImage= zBLANK;
0083
0084   /* -------------------- timer operations -------------------- */
0085   #define zTIMER_PAUSE 3
0086   int TimerCounter= zTIMER_PAUSE;
0087   BOOL TimerExists= FALSE;
0088   WORD TimerID1;
0089
0090   /* -------------------- font operations -------------------- */
0091   HFONT hFont, hPrevFont;         /* handles to new, previous font */
0092   HDC hFontDC;                          /* display-context for font */
0093
0094   /* ---------------- hidden frame operations ------------------ */
0095   HDC hFrameDC;
0096   HBITMAP hFrame;
0097   HBITMAP hPrevFrame;
0098   BOOL FrameReady= FALSE;
0099
0100   /* -------------------- animation engine -------------------- */
0101   BOOL Pause= TRUE;
0102   WORD wFrameRate= 55;
0103   WORD wPrevRate= 55;
0104   #define zFORWARD 1
0105   #define zREVERSE 0
0106   int FrameDirection= zFORWARD;
0107   BOOL Redisplay= FALSE;
```

```
0108   int FrameNum= 1;
0109   #define zFIRSTFRAME 1
0110   #define zFINALFRAME 67
0111   BOOL AnimationReady= FALSE;
0112
0113   /* ---------------- disk save/load operations ---------------- */
0114   int RetVal;                                    /* return value */
0115   BOOL bFrameSaved= FALSE;            /* frame saved to disk? */
0116   BOOL bFrameLoaded= FALSE;          /* frame loaded from disk? */
0117   BOOL bAnimationSaved= FALSE;        /* animation saved to disk? */
0118   BOOL bAnimationLoaded= FALSE;     /* animation loaded from disk? */
0119   BOOL bPrevSaveAttempt= FALSE;    /* previous save attempt made? */
0120   BOOL bPrevLoadAttempt= FALSE;     /* previous load attempt made? */
0121   HDC hFDC;                   /* memory-display context for playback */
0122   HBITMAP hPrevF,hF1,hF2,hF3,hF4,hF5,   /* bitmaps for playback... */
0123    hF6,hF7,hF8,hF9,hF10,hF11,hF12,hF13,hF14,hF15;
0124   BOOL bUseDisk= FALSE;              /* load each frame as needed? */
0125   BOOL bAnimationHalted= FALSE;     /* disk error during animation? */
0126
0127   /* ----------------- database for cel images ----------------- */
0128   /*  Note:  each array also contains drawing codes that give
0129         meaning to the coordinates in the database.  For example,
0130         a value of 1 indicates the start of a new line and the
0131         next element in the array contains the number of endpoints
0132         in the line, followed by the coordinates for the startpoint
0133         and each vertex of the polyline.  A value of 2 indicates an
0134         ellipse, followed by the diagonal coordinates.  A value of
0135         0 indicates the end of the array.                          */
0136
0137   int Cel1[]=
0138   {
0139   1,1, 175,164, 184,157,                     /* polyline (1 endpt) */
0140   1,1, 214,157, 220,163,                     /* polyline (1 endpt) */
0141   1,6, 181,161, 187,170, 194,175, 200,176,   /* polyline (6 endpts) */
0142                   206,174, 212,168, 216,163,
0143   2, 188,107, 195,116,                              /* ellipse */
0144   2, 204,107, 211,116,                              /* ellipse */
0145   1,23, 200,104, 204,100, 210,99, 215,100, /* polyline (23 endpts) */
0146                   217,105, 218,110, 216,118,
0147                   215,120, 210,122, 205,121,
0148                   202,120, 200,118, 198,120,
0149                   193,122, 188,122, 185,120,
0150                   183,115, 182,110, 183,105,
0151                   186,100, 190,99, 194,100,
0152                   198,101, 200,104,
0153   0                                    /* end of cel 1 database */
0154   };
0155   int Cel2[]=
0156   {
0157   1,1, 178,168, 183,162,
0158   1,6, 180,165, 190,170, 195,171, 200,171, 206,170, 212,167, 215,164,
0159   1,1, 215,160, 220,168,
0160   2, 188,107, 195,116,
0161   2, 204,107, 211,116,
0162   1,1, 195,96, 199,105,
0163   1,1, 205,97, 201,104,
0164   1,10, 200,110, 205,108, 210,107, 215,108, 219,112, 215,120,
0165                   212,122, 207,122, 201,121, 200,118, 200,109,
0166   1,7, 200,117, 195,121, 190,122, 185,120, 180,114, 186,108,
0167                   192,108, 200,109,
0168   0
```

```
0169   };
0170   int Cel3[]=
0171   {
0172   1,1, 179,166, 184,161,
0173   1,1, 215,159, 218,166,
0174   1,4, 181,164, 190,167, 200,167, 210,165, 216,163,
0175   1,2, 190,99, 196,102, 199,110,
0176   1,2, 211,97, 205,103, 202,109,
0177   1,3, 178,115, 183,111, 190,110, 198,113,
0178   1,3, 201,113, 210,110, 216,110, 221,114,
0179   1,3, 187,121, 189,119, 194,115, 196,115,
0180   1,3, 202,115, 208,115, 211,118, 213,121,
0181   0
0182   };
0183   int Cel4[]=
0184   {
0185   2, 195,155, 206,190,
0186   2, 194,107, 200,118,
0187   2, 201,107, 207,118,
0188   1,18, 190,121, 187,121, 182,116, 182,105, 184,96, 190,91,
0189                197,91, 199,92, 200,95, 205,92, 210,92,
0190                215,95, 218,100, 219,105, 219,110, 217,116,
0191                214,121, 210,122, 206,121,
0192   0
0193   };
0194   int Cel5[]=
0195   {
0196   2, 193,160, 204,180,
0197   2, 194,105, 200,116,
0198   2, 202,105, 209,116,
0199   1,16, 192,120, 188,120, 184,116, 184,110, 185,100, 188,96,
0200                193,95, 199,97, 200,100, 206,96, 213,96,
0201                217,98, 219,105, 218,114, 216,120, 211,122,
0202                208,121,
0203   0
0204   };
0205   int Cel6[]=
0206   {
0207   1,7, 184,168, 190,168, 213,165, 208,168, 203,172, 197,173,
0208                192,171, 184,168,
0209   2, 188,107, 195,116,
0210   2, 204,107, 211,116,
0211   1,23, 200,104, 204,100, 210,99, 215,100,
0212                217,105, 218,110, 216,118,
0213                215,120, 210,122, 205,121,
0214                202,120, 200,118, 198,120,
0215                193,122, 188,122, 185,120,
0216                183,115, 182,110, 183,105,
0217                186,100, 190,99, 194,100,
0218                198,101, 200,104,
0219   0
0220   };
0221   int Cel7[]=
0222   {
0223   1,9, 181,165, 190,166, 195,166, 210,164, 218,164, 210,166,
0224                201,169, 195,169, 190,167, 181,165,
0225   2, 188,107, 195,116,
0226   2, 204,107, 211,116,
0227   1,17, 182,102, 218,102, 218,110, 216,115, 214,120, 211,122,
0228                208,122, 202,120, 201,119, 200,115, 199,119,
0229                195,121, 192,122, 189,122, 184,118, 182,113,
```

```
0230                    182,107, 182,102,
0231  0
0232  };
0233  int Cel8[]=
0234  {
0235  1,1, 175,168, 179,162,
0236  1,5, 178,164, 186,167, 191,167, 200,165, 210,164, 218,165,
0237  2, 186,102, 192,112,
0238  2, 205,105, 212,114,
0239  1,19, 180,103, 186,101, 194,101, 200,103, 202,104, 215,103,
0240                    220,104, 219,110, 216,116, 213,120, 209,121,
0241                    206,121, 202,118, 201,111, 198,119, 193,121,
0242                    189,121, 184,116, 181,111, 181,103,
0243  0
0244  };
0245  int Cel9[]=
0246  {
0247  1,5, 180,164, 185,164, 197,162, 205,159, 212,159, 221,162,
0248  2, 185,100, 191,111,
0249  1,5, 207,105, 208,110, 209,111, 211,111, 213,109, 213,104,
0250  1,4, 177,102, 190,99, 204,105, 207,105, 212,100,
0251  1,3, 207,105, 213,104, 220,104, 225,108,
0252  1,7, 182,101, 181,109, 183,114, 187,120, 194,121, 198,121,
0253                    203,115, 204,105,
0254  1,6, 203,115, 207,120, 212,122, 216,121, 220,115, 222,110,
0255                    223,104,
0256  0
0257  };
0258
0259  int Cel10[]=
0260  {
0261  1,6, 180,170, 185,170, 200,161, 207,158, 214,158, 220,162,
0262                    222,167,
0263  1,2, 222,171, 225,165, 225,161,
0264  2, 180,99, 188,108,
0265  1,4, 205,108, 207,111, 210,112, 212,110, 212,106,
0266  1,7, 175,101, 181,98, 185,98, 192,100, 203,107, 205,108,
0267                    222,105, 226,111,
0268  1,3, 204,105, 209,104, 210,100, 210,96,
0269  1,2, 210,106, 213,103, 214,99,
0270  1,15, 180,106, 180,114, 183,120, 190,123, 195,121, 200,118,
0271                    203,112, 203,107, 203,112, 204,118, 210,121,
0272                    215,121, 219,120, 221,115, 222,110, 222,104,
0273  0
0274  };
0275  int Cel11[]=
0276  {
0277  1,6, 175,161, 185,164, 190,163, 203,160, 210,158, 207,160,
0278                    225,162,
0279  1,1, 226,158, 227,168,
0280  2, 187,100, 194,111,
0281  1,5, 210,107, 209,110, 210,113, 214,114, 216,110, 216,105,
0282  1,13, 222,109, 222,115, 220,119, 216,120, 209,120, 205,118,
0283                    202,115, 199,121, 192,122, 189,121, 182,119,
0284                    180,112, 180,104, 181,99,
0285  1,6, 175,102, 181,99, 185,98, 203,105, 207,104, 210,101,
0286                    210,95,
0287  1,2, 210,105, 204,102, 205,99,
0288  1,3, 204,108, 222,103, 225,105, 227,110,
0289  0
0290  };
```

```
0291   int Cel12[]=
0292   {
0293   1,4,  170,153,  180,161,  188,163,  195,162,  227,152,
0294   1,1,  226,145,  228,157,
0295   1,6,  194,102,  192,108,  193,110,  195,112,  199,112,  200,110,
0296                  200,107,
0297   1,6,  214,105,  213,108,  213,111,  215,113,  218,113,  220,110,
0298                  220,104,
0299   1,13,  222,108,  221,117,  220,119,  208,118,  204,116,  201,113,
0300                  200,120,  196,121,  190,121,  184,120,  180,115,
0301                  179,108,  180,102,  181,100,
0302   1,6,  176,103,  181,100,  185,99,  190,100,  203,107,  208,106,
0303                  211,95,
0304   1,2,  208,105,  213,104,  215,99,
0305   1,4,  208,105,  214,105,  220,104,  223,104,  228,107,
0306   0
0307   };
0308   int Cel13[]=
0309   {
0310   1,1,  166,151,  171,142,
0311   1,1,  226,133,  233,140,
0312   1,4,  170,148,  180,161,  190,165,  220,154,  230,135,
0313   1,6,  197,106,  196,110,  197,113,  200,115,  203,114,  204,110,
0314                  204,108,
0315   1,5,  218,106,  217,111,  219,113,  222,113,  223,111,  223,106,
0316   1,1,  202,120,  213,122,
0317   1,2,  205,116,  215,118,  225,120,
0318   1,5,  201,115,  200,120,  190,120,  185,118,  180,111,  181,102,
0319   1,6,  177,103,  186,99,  197,106,  204,108,  218,106,  223,106,
0320                  228,106,
0321   1,1,  207,107,  211,97,
0322   1,2,  207,107,  213,105,  215,100,
0323   0
0324   };
0325   int Cel14[]=
0326   {
0327   1,1,  168,158,  172,149,
0328   1,2,  226,141,  230,145,  230,150,
0329   1,5,  171,151,  185,161,  199,161,  210,158,  220,152,  228,144,
0330   2,  191,104,  198,114,
0331   2,  212,104,  219,114,
0332   1,10,  224,112,  220,119,  216,121,  210,120,  203,115,  200,119,
0333                  195,120,  188,120,  183,115,  181,110,  182,103,
0334   1,8,  179,103,  190,100,  198,100,  202,103,  205,107,  210,103,
0335                  217,102,  222,103,  225,107,
0336   1,1,  205,107,  209,100,
0337   0
0338   };
0339   int Cel15[]=
0340   {
0341   1,1,  171,165,  175,158,
0342   1,1,  220,152,  225,159,
0343   1,4,  174,161,  188,169,  200,170,  210,165,  221,156,
0344   2,  189,107,  195,116,
0345   2,  209,107,  215,116,
0346   1,19,  201,103,  210,102,  217,103,  219,106,  219,112,  216,120,
0347                  212,122,  207,122,  203,120,  200,118,  198,121,
0348                  192,122,  188,121,  184,120,  181,114,  181,107,
0349                  185,102,  190,100,  196,101,  201,103,
0350   0
0351   };
```

**10-35** Continued.

```
0352  /*
0353  ------------------------------------------------------------------
0354                   Entry point for the application
0355  ------------------------------------------------------------------
0356                                                                    */
0357  int PASCAL WinMain(HANDLE hInstance, HANDLE hPrevInstance,
0358                     LPSTR lpCmdLine, int nCmdShow)
0359  {
0360    MSG msg;
0361    HWND hWndPrev;
0362    HWND hDesktopWnd;
0363    HDC hDCcaps;
0364
0365  /* ------------ ensure only one instance is running ------------ */
0366  hWndPrev = FindWindow("DEMOCLASS", NULL);
0367  if (hWndPrev != NULL)
0368    {
0369    BringWindowToTop(hWndPrev);
0370    return FALSE;
0371    }
0372
0373  /* --------- determine capabilities of screen display ---------- */
0374  hDesktopWnd= GetDesktopWindow();
0375  hDCcaps= GetDC(hDesktopWnd);
0376  DisplayWidth= GetDeviceCaps(hDCcaps,HORZRES);
0377  DisplayHeight= GetDeviceCaps(hDCcaps,VERTRES);
0378  DisplayBits= GetDeviceCaps(hDCcaps,BITSPIXEL);
0379  DisplayPlanes= GetDeviceCaps(hDCcaps,PLANES);
0380  ReleaseDC(hDesktopWnd,hDCcaps);
0381
0382  /* ------- calculate screen position to center the window ------ */
0383  WindowX= (DisplayWidth - zWINDOW_WIDTH) / 2;
0384  WindowY= (DisplayHeight - zWINDOW_HEIGHT) /2;
0385  if (WindowX < 0) WindowX= 0;
0386  if (WindowY < 0) WindowY= 0;
0387
0388  /* ---- determine memory mode (enhanced, standard, or real) ---- */
0389  MemoryMode= GetWinFlags();
0390
0391  /* --------------- create and show the window --------------- */
0392  hInst = hInstance;
0393  if (!zInitClass(hInstance)) return FALSE;
0394  MainWnd = zInitMainWindow(hInstance);
0395  if (!MainhWnd) return FALSE;
0396  ShowWindow(MainWnd, nCmdShow);
0397  UpdateWindow(MainWnd);
0398  hAccel= LoadAccelerators(hInstance,"KEYS1");
0399  hFontDC= GetDC(MainWnd);
0400  hFont= GetStockObject(SYSTEM_FONT);
0401  hPrevFont= SelectObject(hFontDC,hFont);
0402  SetTextColor(hFontDC,RGB(191,191,191));
0403  TextOut(hFontDC,10,280,"- Copyright 1992 Lee Adams.",27);
0404  SetTextColor(hFontDC,RGB(0,0,0));
0405  SelectObject(hFontDC,hPrevFont);
0406  ReleaseDC(MainhWnd,hFontDC);
0407
0408  /* --------------------- check for mouse --------------------- */
0409  MousePresent = GetSystemMetrics(SM_MOUSEPRESENT);
0410  if (!MousePresent)
0411    {
0412    LoadString(hInst,IDS_Warning,lpCaption,Max);
```

```
0413    LoadString(hInst,IDS_NoMouse,lpMessage,MaxText);
0414    MessageBox(GetFocus(),lpMessage,lpCaption,MB_OK);
0415    }
0416
0417  /* ---------- begin retrieving messages for the window --------- */
0418  while (GetMessage(&msg,0,0,0))
0419    {
0420    if(TranslateAccelerator(MainhWnd, hAccel, &msg))
0421      continue;
0422    TranslateMessage(&msg);
0423    DispatchMessage(&msg);
0424    }
0425  return(msg.wParam);
0426  }
0427  /*
0428  -------------------------------------------------------------------
0429                  Switcher for incoming messages
0430  -------------------------------------------------------------------
0431                                                                 */
0432  LONG FAR PASCAL zMessageHandler(HWND hWnd, unsigned message,
0433                        WORD wParam, LONG lParam)
0434  {
0435    HDC hDCpaint;
0436
0437  switch (message)
0438    {
0439
0440    case WM_TIMER:
0441      TimerCounter--;
0442      if (TimerCounter > 0) break;
0443      TimerCounter++;
0444      zShowNextFrame(hWnd);
0445      break;
0446
0447    case WM_COMMAND:
0448      switch(wParam)
0449        {
0450        case IDM_New:    break;
0451        case IDM_Open:    break;
0452        case IDM_Save:    break;
0453        case IDM_SaveAs: break;
0454        case IDM_Exit:    PostQuitMessage(0); break;
0455
0456        case IDM_Undo:    break;
0457        case IDM_Cut:    break;
0458        case IDM_Copy:    break;
0459        case IDM_Paste:    break;
0460        case IDM_Delete: break;
0461
0462        case IDM_RunForward:
0463            if (AnimationReady==FALSE)
0464              {
0465              MessageBeep(0);
0466              LoadString(hInst,IDS_NotReady,lpCaption,Max);
0467              LoadString(hInst,IDS_BuildBefore,lpMessage,MaxText);
0468              TimerCounter= zTIMER_PAUSE;
0469              MessageBox(GetFocus(),lpMessage,lpCaption,MB_OK);
0470              break;
0471              }
0472            Pause= FALSE;
0473            PaintImage= zANIMATING;
```

```
0474                FrameDirection= zFORWARD;
0475                zShowNextFrame(hWnd);
0476                break;
0477           case IDM_RunReverse:
0478                if (AnimationReady==FALSE)
0479                  {
0480                  MessageBeep(0);
0481                  LoadString(hInst,IDS_NotReady,lpCaption,Max);
0482                  LoadString(hInst,IDS_BuildBefore,lpMessage,MaxText);
0483                  TimerCounter= zTIMER_PAUSE;
0484                  MessageBox(GetFocus(),lpMessage,lpCaption,MB_OK);
0485                  break;
0486                  }
0487                Pause= FALSE;
0488                PaintImage= zANIMATING;
0489                FrameDirection= zREVERSE;
0490                zShowNextFrame(hWnd);
0491                break;
0492           case IDM_StopAnimation:
0493                if (AnimationReady==FALSE)
0494                  {
0495                  MessageBeep(0);
0496                  LoadString(hInst,IDS_NotReady,lpCaption,Max);
0497                  LoadString(hInst,IDS_BuildBefore,lpMessage,MaxText);
0498                  TimerCounter= zTIMER_PAUSE;
0499                  MessageBox(GetFocus(),lpMessage,lpCaption,MB_OK);
0500                  break;
0501                  }
0502                Pause= TRUE;
0503                zShowNextFrame(hWnd);
0504                break;
0505           case IDM_InitFrame: zInitFrame(hWnd);
0506                               break;
0507           case IDM_SaveAnimation:
0508                SetCapture(hWnd); hPrevCursor= SetCursor(hHourGlass);
0509                zSaveAnimation(hWnd);
0510                SetCursor(hPrevCursor); ReleaseCapture();
0511                if (bAnimationSaved==FALSE)
0512                  {
0513                  MessageBeep(0);
0514                  LoadString(hInst,IDS_NotReady,lpCaption,Max);
0515                  LoadString(hInst,IDS_Disk26,lpMessage,MaxText);
0516                  TimerCounter= zTIMER_PAUSE;
0517                  MessageBox(GetFocus(),lpMessage,lpCaption,MB_OK);
0518                  }
0519                break;
0520           case IDM_LoadAnimation:
0521                SetCapture(hWnd); hPrevCursor= SetCursor(hHourGlass);
0522                zLoadAnimation(hWnd);
0523                SetCursor(hPrevCursor); ReleaseCapture();
0524                break;
0525           case IDM_Clear:  if (Pause==TRUE)
0526                              {
0527                              zClear(hWnd);
0528                              PaintImage= zBLANK;
0529                              }
0530                            break;
0531
0532           case IDM_FPS182: wPrevRate= wFrameRate;
0533                            wFrameRate= (WORD)55;
0534                            zSetFrameRate(hWnd, wFrameRate); break;
```

```
0535         case IDM_FPS91:  wPrevRate= wFrameRate;
0536                          wFrameRate= (WORD)110;
0537                          zSetFrameRate(hWnd, wFrameRate); break;
0538         case IDM_FPS61:  wPrevRate= wFrameRate;
0539                          wFrameRate= (WORD)165;
0540                          zSetFrameRate(hWnd, wFrameRate); break;
0541         case IDM_FPS45:  wPrevRate= wFrameRate;
0542                          wFrameRate= (WORD) 220;
0543                          zSetFrameRate(hWnd, wFrameRate); break;
0544         case IDM_FPS36:  wPrevRate= wFrameRate;
0545                          wFrameRate= (WORD) 275;
0546                          zSetFrameRate(hWnd, wFrameRate); break;
0547         case IDM_FPS30:  wPrevRate= wFrameRate;
0548                          wFrameRate= (WORD) 330;
0549                          zSetFrameRate(hWnd, wFrameRate); break;
0550
0551         case IDM_About:
0552           LoadString(hInst,IDS_About,lpCaption,Max);
0553           LoadString(hInst,IDS_AboutText,lpMessage,MaxText);
0554           TimerCounter= zTIMER_PAUSE;
0555           MessageBox(GetFocus(),lpMessage,lpCaption,MB_OK);
0556           break;
0557         case IDM_License:
0558           LoadString(hInst,IDS_License,lpCaption,Max);
0559           LoadString(hInst,IDS_LicenseText,lpMessage,MaxText);
0560           TimerCounter= zTIMER_PAUSE;
0561           MessageBox(GetFocus(),lpMessage,lpCaption,MB_OK);
0562           break;
0563
0564         case IDM_Display:
0565           if (DisplayWidth==640)
0566             {
0567             if (DisplayHeight==480)
0568               {
0569               LoadString(hInst,IDS_Resolution,lpCaption,Max);
0570               LoadString(hInst,IDS_ResVGA,lpMessage,MaxText);
0571               TimerCounter= zTIMER_PAUSE;
0572               MessageBox(GetFocus(),lpMessage,lpCaption,MB_OK);
0573               }
0574             if (DisplayHeight==350)
0575               {
0576               LoadString(hInst,IDS_Resolution,lpCaption,Max);
0577               LoadString(hInst,IDS_ResEGA,lpMessage,MaxText);
0578               TimerCounter= zTIMER_PAUSE;
0579               MessageBox(GetFocus(),lpMessage,lpCaption,MB_OK);
0580               }
0581             if (DisplayHeight==200)
0582               {
0583               LoadString(hInst,IDS_Resolution,lpCaption,Max);
0584               LoadString(hInst,IDS_ResCGA,lpMessage,MaxText);
0585               TimerCounter= zTIMER_PAUSE;
0586               MessageBox(GetFocus(),lpMessage,lpCaption,MB_OK);
0587               }
0588             break;
0589             }
0590           if (DisplayWidth==800)
0591             {
0592             LoadString(hInst,IDS_Resolution,lpCaption,Max);
0593             LoadString(hInst,IDS_ResSVGA,lpMessage,MaxText);
0594             TimerCounter= zTIMER_PAUSE;
0595             MessageBox(GetFocus(),lpMessage,lpCaption,MB_OK);
```

```
0596              break;
0597              }
0598          if (DisplayWidth==1024)
0599              {
0600              LoadString(hInst,IDS_Resolution,lpCaption,Max);
0601              LoadString(hInst,IDS_Res8514,lpMessage,MaxText);
0602              TimerCounter= zTIMER_PAUSE;
0603              MessageBox(GetFocus(),lpMessage,lpCaption,MB_OK);
0604              break;
0605              }
0606          if (DisplayWidth==720)
0607              {
0608              LoadString(hInst,IDS_Resolution,lpCaption,Max);
0609              LoadString(hInst,IDS_ResHerc,lpMessage,MaxText);
0610              TimerCounter= zTIMER_PAUSE;
0611              MessageBox(GetFocus(),lpMessage,lpCaption,MB_OK);
0612              break;
0613              }
0614          LoadString(hInst,IDS_Resolution,lpCaption,Max);
0615          LoadString(hInst,IDS_ResCustom,lpMessage,MaxText);
0616          TimerCounter= zTIMER_PAUSE;
0617          MessageBox(GetFocus(),lpMessage,lpCaption,MB_OK);
0618          break;
0619
0620      case IDM_Colors:
0621          if (DisplayBits==1)
0622              {
0623              if (DisplayPlanes==4)
0624                  {
0625                  LoadString(hInst,IDS_Color,lpCaption,Max);
0626                  LoadString(hInst,IDS_Color16,lpMessage,MaxText);
0627                  TimerCounter= zTIMER_PAUSE;
0628                  MessageBox(GetFocus(),lpMessage,lpCaption,MB_OK);
0629                  break;
0630                  }
0631              if (DisplayPlanes==1)
0632                  {
0633                  LoadString(hInst,IDS_Color,lpCaption,Max);
0634                  LoadString(hInst,IDS_Color2,lpMessage,MaxText);
0635                  TimerCounter= zTIMER_PAUSE;
0636                  MessageBox(GetFocus(),lpMessage,lpCaption,MB_OK);
0637                  break;
0638                  }
0639              }
0640          if (DisplayBits==8)
0641              {
0642              LoadString(hInst,IDS_Color,lpCaption,Max);
0643              LoadString(hInst,IDS_Color256,lpMessage,MaxText);
0644              TimerCounter= zTIMER_PAUSE;
0645              MessageBox(GetFocus(),lpMessage,lpCaption,MB_OK);
0646              break;
0647              }
0648          LoadString(hInst,IDS_Color,lpCaption,Max);
0649          LoadString(hInst,IDS_ColorCustom,lpMessage,MaxText);
0650          TimerCounter= zTIMER_PAUSE;
0651          MessageBox(GetFocus(),lpMessage,lpCaption,MB_OK);
0652          break;
0653
0654      case IDM_Mode:
0655          if (MemoryMode & WF_ENHANCED)
0656              {
```

```
0657            LoadString(hInst,IDS_Machine,lpCaption,Max);
0658            LoadString(hInst,IDS_Enhanced,lpMessage,MaxText);
0659            TimerCounter= zTIMER_PAUSE;
0660            MessageBox(GetFocus(),lpMessage,lpCaption,MB_OK);
0661            break;
0662            }
0663          if (MemoryMode & WF_STANDARD)
0664            {
0665            LoadString(hInst,IDS_Machine,lpCaption,Max);
0666            LoadString(hInst,IDS_Standard,lpMessage,MaxText);
0667            TimerCounter= zTIMER_PAUSE;
0668            MessageBox(GetFocus(),lpMessage,lpCaption,MB_OK);
0669            break;
0670            }
0671          LoadString(hInst,IDS_Machine,lpCaption,Max);
0672          LoadString(hInst,IDS_Real,lpMessage,MaxText);
0673          TimerCounter= zTIMER_PAUSE;
0674          MessageBox(GetFocus(),lpMessage,lpCaption,MB_OK);
0675          break;
0676
0677        case IDM_Memory:
0678          LoadString(hInst,IDS_Memory,lpCaption,Max);
0679          LoadString(hInst,IDS_MemText,lpMessage,MaxText);
0680          TimerCounter= zTIMER_PAUSE;
0681          MessageBox(GetFocus(),lpMessage,lpCaption,MB_OK);
0682          break;
0683        case IDM_Timing:
0684          LoadString(hInst,IDS_Timing,lpCaption,Max);
0685          LoadString(hInst,IDS_TimingText,lpMessage,MaxText);
0686          TimerCounter= zTIMER_PAUSE;
0687          MessageBox(GetFocus(),lpMessage,lpCaption,MB_OK);
0688          break;
0689        case IDM_GeneralHelp:
0690          LoadString(hInst,IDS_Help,lpCaption,Max);
0691          LoadString(hInst,IDS_HelpText,lpMessage,MaxText);
0692          TimerCounter= zTIMER_PAUSE;
0693          MessageBox(GetFocus(),lpMessage,lpCaption,MB_OK);
0694          break;
0695        default:
0696          return(DefWindowProc(hWnd, message, wParam, lParam));
0697        }
0698      break;
0699
0700    case WM_INITMENUPOPUP:
0701      TimerCounter= zTIMER_PAUSE;
0702      if (lParam == 3)
0703        hMenu= wParam;
0704      break;
0705
0706    case WM_PAINT:
0707      hDCpaint= BeginPaint(hWnd,&ps);
0708      EndPaint(hWnd, &ps);
0709      if (PaintImage==zBLANK) break;
0710      if (Pause==TRUE)
0711        {
0712        Redisplay= TRUE;
0713        zShowNextFrame(hWnd);
0714        Redisplay= FALSE;
0715        break;
0716        }
0717      zShowNextFrame(hWnd);
```

```
0718      break;
0719
0720    case WM_KEYDOWN:
0721      switch (wParam)
0722        {
0723        case VK_LEFT:    if (Pause==TRUE)
0724                           {
0725                           if (FrameDirection==zFORWARD)
0726                             {
0727                             FrameDirection= zREVERSE;
0728                             }
0729                           Pause= FALSE;
0730                           zShowNextFrame(hWnd);
0731                           Pause= TRUE;
0732                           PaintImage= zANIMATING;
0733                           }
0734                         break;
0735        case VK_RIGHT:   if (Pause==TRUE)
0736                           {
0737                           if (FrameDirection==zREVERSE)
0738                             {
0739                             FrameDirection= zFORWARD;
0740                             }
0741                           Pause= FALSE;
0742                           zShowNextFrame(hWnd);
0743                           Pause= TRUE;
0744                           PaintImage= zANIMATING;
0745                           }
0746                         break;
0747        default:
0748              return(DefWindowProc(hWnd, message, wParam, lParam));
0749        }
0750      break;
0751
0752    case WM_DESTROY:
0753      if (FrameReady==TRUE)
0754        {                            /* tidy up hidden frame bitmap... */
0755        SelectObject(hFrameDC,hPrevFrame);
0756        DeleteObject(hFrame);
0757        DeleteDC(hFrameDC);
0758        KillTimer(hWnd,1);
0759        }
0760      if (bAnimationLoaded==TRUE)
0761        {                   /* tidy up animation playback bitmaps... */
0762        SelectObject(hFDC,hPrevF);
0763        DeleteObject(hF1); DeleteObject(hF2); DeleteObject(hF3);
0764        DeleteObject(hF4); DeleteObject(hF5); DeleteObject(hF6);
0765        DeleteObject(hF7); DeleteObject(hF8); DeleteObject(hF9);
0766        DeleteObject(hF10); DeleteObject(hF11); DeleteObject(hF12);
0767        DeleteObject(hF13); DeleteObject(hF14); DeleteObject(hF15);
0768        DeleteDC(hFDC);
0769        }
0770      PostQuitMessage(0);
0771      break;
0772
0773    case WM_SYSCOMMAND:
0774      if ((wParam & 0xfff0)== SC_SIZE)
0775        {
0776        MessageBeep(0); break;
0777        }
0778      if ((wParam & 0xfff0)== SC_MINIMIZE)
```

```
0779            {
0780            MessageBeep(0); break;
0781            }
0782        if ((wParam & 0xfff0)== SC_MAXIMIZE)
0783            {
0784            MessageBeep(0); break;
0785            }
0786
0787      default:
0788        return(DefWindowProc(hWnd, message, wParam, lParam));
0789      }
0790    return FALSE;
0791    }
0792    /*
0793    ------------------------------------------------------------------
0794              Initialize the attributes of the window class
0795    ------------------------------------------------------------------
0796                                                                    */
0797    BOOL zInitClass(HANDLE hInstance)
0798    {
0799      WNDCLASS WndClass;
0800    WndClass.style= 0;
0801    WndClass.lpfnWndProc= zMessageHandler;
0802    WndClass.cbClsExtra= 0;
0803    WndClass.cbWndExtra= 0;
0804    WndClass.hInstance= hInstance;
0805    WndClass.hIcon= LoadIcon(NULL,IDI_EXCLAMATION);
0806    WndClass.hCursor= LoadCursor(NULL,IDC_ARROW);
0807    WndClass.hbrBackground= CreateSolidBrush(RGB(255,255,255));
0808    WndClass.lpszMenuName= "MENUS1";
0809    WndClass.lpszClassName= "DEMOCLASS";
0810    return RegisterClass(&WndClass);
0811    }
0812    /*
0813    ------------------------------------------------------------------
0814                        Create the main window
0815    ------------------------------------------------------------------
0816                                                                    */
0817    HWND zInitMainWindow(HANDLE hInstance)
0818    {
0819      HWND hWnd;
0820    LoadString(hInstance,IDS_Caption,lpCaption,Max);
0821    hHourGlass= LoadCursor(NULL,IDC_WAIT);
0822    hWnd = CreateWindow("DEMOCLASS",lpCaption,
0823      WS_OVERLAPPED | WS_THICKFRAME | WS_MINIMIZEBOX |
0824        WS_MAXIMIZEBOX | WS_CLIPCHILDREN,
0825      WindowX,WindowY,zWINDOW_WIDTH,zWINDOW_HEIGHT,0,0,
0826      hInstance, (LPSTR)NULL);
0827    return hWnd;
0828    }
0829    /*
0830    ------------------------------------------------------------------
0831                        GRAPHICS SYSTEM Functions
0832    ------------------------------------------------------------------
0833    ------------------------------------------------------------------
0834                        Create the hidden frame.
0835    ------------------------------------------------------------------
0836                                                                    */
0837    static void zInitFrame(HWND hWnd)
0838    {
0839      HDC hDisplayDC;
```

```
0840
0841    if (FrameReady==TRUE)
0842      {
0843      MessageBeep(0);
0844      LoadString(hInst,IDS_Ready,lpCaption,Max);
0845      LoadString(hInst,IDS_Already,lpMessage,MaxText);
0846      TimerCounter= zTIMER_PAUSE;
0847      MessageBox(GetFocus(),lpMessage,lpCaption,MB_OK);
0848      return;
0849      }
0850    GlobalCompact((DWORD)-1L);
0851    hDisplayDC= GetDC(hWnd);
0852    hFrameDC= CreateCompatibleDC(hDisplayDC);
0853    hFrame= CreateCompatibleBitmap(hDisplayDC,zFRAMEWIDE,zFRAMEHIGH);
0854    if (hFrame==NULL)
0855      {
0856      LoadString(hInst,IDS_NotReady,lpCaption,Max);
0857      LoadString(hInst,IDS_InsufMem1,lpMessage,MaxText);
0858      MessageBox(GetFocus(),lpMessage,lpCaption,MB_OK);
0859      DeleteDC(hFrameDC);
0860      TimerExists= FALSE; FrameReady= FALSE; AnimationReady= FALSE;
0861      return;
0862      }
0863    hPrevFrame= SelectObject(hFrameDC,hFrame);
0864    zClear(hWnd);
0865    BitBlt(hFrameDC,0,0,zFRAMEWIDE,zFRAMEHIGH,hDisplayDC,0,0,SRCCOPY);
0866    ReleaseDC(hWnd,hDisplayDC);
0867
0868    TimerID1= SetTimer(hWnd,1,wFrameRate,(FARPROC) NULL);
0869    if (TimerID1 == 0)
0870      {
0871      LoadString(hInst,IDS_NotReady,lpCaption,Max);
0872      LoadString(hInst,IDS_NoTimer,lpMessage,MaxText);
0873      MessageBox(GetFocus(),lpMessage,lpCaption,MB_OK);
0874      SelectObject(hFrameDC,hPrevFrame);
0875      DeleteObject(hFrame);
0876      DeleteDC(hFrameDC);
0877      TimerExists= FALSE;
0878      return;
0879      }
0880    TimerExists= TRUE;
0881    FrameReady= TRUE;
0882    FrameNum= 1;
0883    return;
0884    }
0885    /*
0886    ----------------------------------------------------------------
0887                        Clear the hidden frame.
0888    ----------------------------------------------------------------
0889                                                                    */
0890    static void zClearHiddenFrame(void)
0891    {
0892    PatBlt(hFrameDC,0,0,zFRAMEWIDE,zFRAMEHIGH,WHITENESS);
0893    return;
0894    }
0895    /*
0896    ----------------------------------------------------------------
0897            Copy the hidden frame to the display window.
0898    ----------------------------------------------------------------
0899                                                                    */
0900    static void zCopyToDisplay(HWND hWnd)
```

```
0901  {
0902    HDC hDC;
0903  hDC= GetDC(hWnd);
0904  BitBlt(hDC,0,0,zFRAMEWIDE,zFRAMEHIGH,hFrameDC,0,0,SRCCOPY);
0905  ReleaseDC(hWnd,hDC);
0906  return;
0907  }
0908  /*
0909  ------------------------------------------------------------------
0910                       Blank the display window.
0911  ------------------------------------------------------------------
0912                                                                  */
0913  static void zClear(HWND hWnd)
0914  {
0915    HDC hDC;
0916  hDC= GetDC(hWnd);
0917  PatBlt(hDC,0,0,zFRAMEWIDE,zFRAMEHIGH,WHITENESS);
0918  ReleaseDC(hWnd,hDC);
0919  return;
0920  }
0921  /*
0922  ------------------------------------------------------------------
0923                       AUTHORING SYSTEM Functions
0924  ------------------------------------------------------------------
0925  ------------------------------------------------------------------
0926                    Create 15 frames and save to disk.
0927  ------------------------------------------------------------------
0928                                                                  */
0929  static void zSaveAnimation(HWND hWnd)
0930  {
0931  if (FrameReady==FALSE)          /* if no hidden-frame available... */
0932    {
0933    MessageBeep(0);
0934    LoadString(hInst,IDS_NotReady,lpCaption,Max);
0935    LoadString(hInst,IDS_NoFrame,lpMessage,MaxText);
0936    MessageBox(GetFocus(),lpMessage,lpCaption,MB_OK);
0937    return;
0938    }
0939
0940  if (bAnimationSaved==TRUE) /* if frames already saved to disk... */
0941    {
0942    MessageBeep(0);
0943    LoadString(hInst,IDS_Unexpected,lpCaption,Max);
0944    LoadString(hInst,IDS_Disk1,lpMessage,MaxText);
0945    TimerCounter= zTIMER_PAUSE;
0946    MessageBox(GetFocus(),lpMessage,lpCaption,MB_OK);
0947    return;
0948    }
0949
0950  if (bPrevSaveAttempt==TRUE)      /* if previous attempt failed... */
0951    {
0952    MessageBeep(0);
0953    LoadString(hInst,IDS_Unexpected,lpCaption,Max);
0954    LoadString(hInst,IDS_Disk8,lpMessage,MaxText);
0955    TimerCounter= zTIMER_PAUSE;
0956    MessageBox(GetFocus(),lpMessage,lpCaption,MB_OK);
0957    return;
0958    }
0959  bPrevSaveAttempt= TRUE;
```

```
0960
0961   bFrameSaved= zBuildFrame(Cel1,1,hWnd,(LPSTR)"BLINK1.BIT");
0962   if (bFrameSaved==FALSE) return;
0963   bFrameSaved= zBuildFrame(Cel2,2,hWnd,(LPSTR)"BLINK2.BIT");
0964   if (bFrameSaved==FALSE) return;
0965   bFrameSaved= zBuildFrame(Cel3,3,hWnd,(LPSTR)"BLINK3.BIT");
0966   if (bFrameSaved==FALSE) return;
0967   bFrameSaved= zBuildFrame(Cel4,4,hWnd,(LPSTR)"BLINK4.BIT");
0968   if (bFrameSaved==FALSE) return;
0969   bFrameSaved= zBuildFrame(Cel5,5,hWnd,(LPSTR)"BLINK5.BIT");
0970   if (bFrameSaved==FALSE) return;
0971   bFrameSaved= zBuildFrame(Cel6,6,hWnd,(LPSTR)"BLINK6.BIT");
0972   if (bFrameSaved==FALSE) return;
0973   bFrameSaved= zBuildFrame(Cel7,7,hWnd,(LPSTR)"BLINK7.BIT");
0974   if (bFrameSaved==FALSE) return;
0975   bFrameSaved= zBuildFrame(Cel8,8,hWnd,(LPSTR)"BLINK8.BIT");
0976   if (bFrameSaved==FALSE) return;
0977   bFrameSaved= zBuildFrame(Cel9,9,hWnd,(LPSTR)"BLINK9.BIT");
0978   if (bFrameSaved==FALSE) return;
0979   bFrameSaved= zBuildFrame(Cel10,10,hWnd,(LPSTR)"BLINK10.BIT");
0980   if (bFrameSaved==FALSE) return;
0981   bFrameSaved= zBuildFrame(Cel11,11,hWnd,(LPSTR)"BLINK11.BIT");
0982   if (bFrameSaved==FALSE) return;
0983   bFrameSaved= zBuildFrame(Cel12,12,hWnd,(LPSTR)"BLINK12.BIT");
0984   if (bFrameSaved==FALSE) return;
0985   bFrameSaved= zBuildFrame(Cel13,13,hWnd,(LPSTR)"BLINK13.BIT");
0986   if (bFrameSaved==FALSE) return;
0987   bFrameSaved= zBuildFrame(Cel14,14,hWnd,(LPSTR)"BLINK14.BIT");
0988   if (bFrameSaved==FALSE) return;
0989   bFrameSaved= zBuildFrame(Cel15,15,hWnd,(LPSTR)"BLINK15.BIT");
0990   if (bFrameSaved==FALSE) return;
0991
0992   bAnimationSaved= TRUE;
0993   bPrevLoadAttempt= FALSE;
0994   zClear(hWnd);
0995   MessageBeep(0);
0996   LoadString(hInst,IDS_Status,lpCaption,Max);
0997   LoadString(hInst,IDS_Disk2,lpMessage,MaxText);
0998   MessageBox(GetFocus(),lpMessage,lpCaption,MB_OK);
0999   return;
1000   }
1001   /*
1002   ------------------------------------------------------------------
1003                   Build one frame and save to disk.
1004   ------------------------------------------------------------------
1005                                                                   */
1006   static BOOL zBuildFrame(int * Drawing, int Number,
1007                       HWND hWnd, LPSTR lpFileName)
1008   {               /* this function is called by zSaveAnimation() */
1009     BOOL bDiskResult;
1010     HFONT Font;
1011     HFONT PrevFont;
1012     DWORD PrevFontColor;
1013     DWORD PrevBkColor;
1014
1015   zClearHiddenFrame();                       /* clear the hidden frame */
1016
1017   /* ------------------- draw the appropriate cel --------------- */
1018   zDrawCel(Drawing);
1019
```

```
1020  /* ---------- display the titles, labels, and captions --------- */
1021  if ((DisplayBits==1)&&(DisplayPlanes==1))/* if a mono display... */
1022     {
1023     PrevFontColor= SetTextColor(hFrameDC,RGB(0,0,0));
1024     PrevBkColor=  SetBkColor(hFrameDC,RGB(255,255,255));
1025     }
1026  else                                    /* else if a color display... */
1027     {
1028     PrevFontColor= SetTextColor(hFrameDC,RGB(0,127,127));
1029     PrevBkColor=  SetBkColor(hFrameDC,RGB(0,0,0));
1030     }
1031
1032  SetBkMode(hFrameDC,TRANSPARENT);
1033  Font= CreateFont(24, 0, 0, 0, FW_BOLD, FALSE, FALSE, FALSE,
1034        ANSI_CHARSET, OUT_DEFAULT_PRECIS, CLIP_DEFAULT_PRECIS,
1035         DRAFT_QUALITY, VARIABLE_PITCH | FF_SWISS, "Helv");
1036  PrevFont= SelectObject(hFrameDC,Font);
1037  TextOut(hFrameDC,10,6,"Advanced Animation Techniques:",30);
1038  Font= CreateFont(48, 0, 0, 0, FW_BOLD, FALSE, FALSE, FALSE,
1039        ANSI_CHARSET, OUT_DEFAULT_PRECIS, CLIP_DEFAULT_PRECIS,
1040         DRAFT_QUALITY, VARIABLE_PITCH | FF_SWISS, "Helv");
1041  SelectObject(hFrameDC,Font);
1042  TextOut(hFrameDC,8,24,"Tracebacks",10);
1043  SelectObject(hFrameDC,PrevFont);
1044  TextOut(hFrameDC,10,266,"Tracebacks can speed up the authoring
            process",45);
1045  TextOut(hFrameDC,10,282,"when complex drawings are being
            animated.",41);
1046  switch (Number)
1047     {
1048     case 1:  TextOut(hFrameDC,10,240,"Cel no. 01",10); break;
1049     case 2:  TextOut(hFrameDC,10,240,"Cel no. 02",10); break;
1050     case 3:  TextOut(hFrameDC,10,240,"Cel no. 03",10); break;
1051     case 4:  TextOut(hFrameDC,10,240,"Cel no. 04",10); break;
1052     case 5:  TextOut(hFrameDC,10,240,"Cel no. 05",10); break;
1053     case 6:  TextOut(hFrameDC,10,240,"Cel no. 06",10); break;
1054     case 7:  TextOut(hFrameDC,10,240,"Cel no. 07",10); break;
1055     case 8:  TextOut(hFrameDC,10,240,"Cel no. 08",10); break;
1056     case 9:  TextOut(hFrameDC,10,240,"Cel no. 09",10); break;
1057     case 10: TextOut(hFrameDC,10,240,"Cel no. 10",10); break;
1058     case 11: TextOut(hFrameDC,10,240,"Cel no. 11",10); break;
1059     case 12: TextOut(hFrameDC,10,240,"Cel no. 12",10); break;
1060     case 13: TextOut(hFrameDC,10,240,"Cel no. 13",10); break;
1061     case 14: TextOut(hFrameDC,10,240,"Cel no. 14",10); break;
1062     case 15: TextOut(hFrameDC,10,240,"Cel no. 15",10); break;
1063     }
1064  SetBkMode(hFrameDC,OPAQUE);
1065  SetBkColor(hFrameDC,PrevBkColor);
1066  SetTextColor(hFrameDC,PrevFontColor);
1067
1068  /* ---------- display the frame and save it to disk ----------- */
1069  zCopyToDisplay(hWnd);               /* copy hidden frame to display */
1070  bDiskResult= zSaveFrame(hFrame,lpFileName);        /* save file */
1071  if (bDiskResult==FALSE) return FALSE;       /* if disk error */
1072  return TRUE;
1073  }
1074  /*
1075  ------------------------------------------------------------------
1076                  Build one frame and save to disk.
1077  ------------------------------------------------------------------
1078                                                            */
```

```
1079   static void zDrawCel(int * Drawing)
1080   {
1081     int X1,Y1,X2,Y2;                  /* temporary drawing coordinates */
1082     HPEN DrawingPen, PrevPen;                                /* pens */
1083     int Code;        /* drawing code indicates line, ellipse, or end */
1084     int NumPoints;           /* number of endpoints in a polyline */
1085     int Index;                     /* index into the database array */
1086     int nPolyline= 1;            /* used to compare value of Code... */
1087     int nEllipse= 2;
1088     int nEnd=     0;
1089     int Count;                                      /* loop counter */
1090
1091     zDrawTraceback();                   /* draw the traceback portions */
1092     DrawingPen= CreatePen(PS_SOLID,2,RGB(0,0,0));      /* create pen */
1093     PrevPen= SelectObject(hFrameDC,DrawingPen);        /* select pen */
1094
1095     /* --------- interpret the database and draw the cel ----------- */
1096     Index= 0;                  /* reset index to beginning of database */
1097
1098     START_OF_LOOP:                  /* start of loop to read database */
1099     Code= Drawing[Index];          /* read the code value (0,1,or 2) */
1100
1101     if (Code==nEllipse)                   /* if an ellipse is wanted... */
1102     {
1103       Index++; X1= Drawing[Index];      /* grab the coordinates... */
1104       Index++; Y1= Drawing[Index];
1105       Index++; X2= Drawing[Index];
1106       Index++; Y2= Drawing[Index];
1107       Ellipse(hFrameDC,X1,Y1,X2,Y2);       /* ...and draw the ellipse */
1108       Index++;                           /* increment the index... */
1109       goto START_OF_LOOP;                    /* ...and loop back */
1110     }
1111
1112     if (Code==nPolyline)                  /* if a polyline is wanted... */
1113     {
1114       Index++; NumPoints= Drawing[Index];  /* grab number of endpts */
1115       if (NumPoints<1) goto FATAL_ERROR;                /* validate */
1116       Index++; X1= Drawing[Index];          /* grab starting x coord */
1117       Index++; Y1= Drawing[Index];          /* grab starting y coord */
1118       MoveTo(hFrameDC,X1,Y1);           /* move to startpoint of line */
1119       for (Count= 1; Count <= NumPoints; Count++)
1120       {                         /* for each vertex in the polyline... */
1121         Index++; X2= Drawing[Index];               /* grab x coord */
1122         Index++; Y2= Drawing[Index];               /* grab y coord */
1123         LineTo(hFrameDC,X2,Y2);           /* draw line segment */
1124       }
1125       Index++;                           /* increment the index... */
1126       goto START_OF_LOOP;                    /* ...and loop back */
1127     }
1128
1129     if (Code==nEnd) goto FINISHED;        /* if at end of database */
1130
1131     FATAL_ERROR:         /* jump to or fall through to here if error */
1132     MessageBeep(0);
1133     MessageBox(GetFocus(),
1134     "A fatal database error has occurred in the zDrawCel() function.",
1135     "Exit now and debug the source code!", MB_OK|MB_ICONSTOP);
1136
1137     /* -------------------- tidy up and exit --------------------- */
1138     FINISHED:          /* jump to or fall through to here when done */
1139     SelectObject(hFrameDC,PrevPen);                  /* deselect pen */
```

```
1140    DeleteObject(DrawingPen);                               /* delete pen */
1141    return;
1142    }
1143    /*
1144    ----------------------------------------------------------------
1145                  Draw the traceback portions of each cel.
1146    ----------------------------------------------------------------
1147                                                                     */
1148    static void zDrawTraceback(void)
1149    {
1150       HPEN DrawingPen, PrevPen;                            /* pens */
1151
1152    DrawingPen= CreatePen(PS_SOLID,2,RGB(0,0,0));        /* create pen */
1153    PrevPen= SelectObject(hFrameDC,DrawingPen);          /* select pen */
1154
1155    Ellipse(hFrameDC,144,138,154,150);                  /* left earring */
1156    Ellipse(hFrameDC,238,136,248,148);                  /* right earring */
1157
1158    MoveTo(hFrameDC,153,148);                               /* jawline... */
1159    LineTo(hFrameDC,154,152); LineTo(hFrameDC,156,160);
1160    LineTo(hFrameDC,159,170); LineTo(hFrameDC,164,180);
1161    LineTo(hFrameDC,171,190); LineTo(hFrameDC,177,196);
1162    LineTo(hFrameDC,182,200); LineTo(hFrameDC,190,203);
1163    LineTo(hFrameDC,200,205); LineTo(hFrameDC,206,204);
1164    LineTo(hFrameDC,210,203); LineTo(hFrameDC,220,197);
1165    LineTo(hFrameDC,224,190); LineTo(hFrameDC,230,180);
1166    LineTo(hFrameDC,232,170); LineTo(hFrameDC,236,160);
1167    LineTo(hFrameDC,238,150); LineTo(hFrameDC,239,148);
1168
1169    MoveTo(hFrameDC,153,125);                               /* left ear... */
1170    LineTo(hFrameDC,149,120); LineTo(hFrameDC,145,119);
1171    LineTo(hFrameDC,142,120); LineTo(hFrameDC,138,124);
1172    LineTo(hFrameDC,137,128); LineTo(hFrameDC,139,134);
1173    LineTo(hFrameDC,141,141); LineTo(hFrameDC,144,144);
1174
1175    MoveTo(hFrameDC,241,121);                               /* right ear... */
1176    LineTo(hFrameDC,245,118); LineTo(hFrameDC,250,115);
1177    LineTo(hFrameDC,253,116); LineTo(hFrameDC,256,120);
1178    LineTo(hFrameDC,256,127); LineTo(hFrameDC,253,135);
1179    LineTo(hFrameDC,249,141);
1180
1181    MoveTo(hFrameDC,153,125);                               /* forehead... */
1182    LineTo(hFrameDC,155,120); LineTo(hFrameDC,159,110);
1183    LineTo(hFrameDC,166,100); LineTo(hFrameDC,182,90);
1184    LineTo(hFrameDC,190,88); LineTo(hFrameDC,200,86);
1185    LineTo(hFrameDC,210,83); LineTo(hFrameDC,215,80);
1186    LineTo(hFrameDC,220,72); LineTo(hFrameDC,222,80);
1187    LineTo(hFrameDC,226,90); LineTo(hFrameDC,230,95);
1188    LineTo(hFrameDC,235,100); LineTo(hFrameDC,240,109);
1189    LineTo(hFrameDC,241,115); LineTo(hFrameDC,241,121);
1190
1191    MoveTo(hFrameDC,195,124);                               /* nose... */
1192    LineTo(hFrameDC,193,130); LineTo(hFrameDC,195,136);
1193    LineTo(hFrameDC,197,140); LineTo(hFrameDC,200,141);
1194    LineTo(hFrameDC,203,140); LineTo(hFrameDC,205,136);
1195    LineTo(hFrameDC,206,133); LineTo(hFrameDC,205,130);
1196    LineTo(hFrameDC,203,123);
1197
1198    MoveTo(hFrameDC,190,203);                               /* neck... */
1199    LineTo(hFrameDC,191,210); LineTo(hFrameDC,190,220);
1200    LineTo(hFrameDC,188,230); LineTo(hFrameDC,187,240);
```

```
1201   LineTo(hFrameDC,187,250); LineTo(hFrameDC,188,255);
1202   LineTo(hFrameDC,191,260); LineTo(hFrameDC,196,264);
1203   LineTo(hFrameDC,205,264); LineTo(hFrameDC,210,261);
1204   LineTo(hFrameDC,214,256); LineTo(hFrameDC,216,248);
1205   LineTo(hFrameDC,216,239); LineTo(hFrameDC,215,230);
1206   LineTo(hFrameDC,213,220); LineTo(hFrameDC,212,203);
1207
1208   MoveTo(hFrameDC,188,232);                        /* left shoulder... */
1209   LineTo(hFrameDC,180,235); LineTo(hFrameDC,170,238);
1210   LineTo(hFrameDC,167,238);
1211
1212   MoveTo(hFrameDC,215,230);                        /* right shoulder... */
1213   LineTo(hFrameDC,225,232); LineTo(hFrameDC,232,233);
1214
1215   MoveTo(hFrameDC,190,220);                        /* hair silhouette... */
1216   LineTo(hFrameDC,170,219); LineTo(hFrameDC,160,218);
1217   LineTo(hFrameDC,150,215); LineTo(hFrameDC,140,210);
1218   LineTo(hFrameDC,130,200); LineTo(hFrameDC,125,190);
1219   LineTo(hFrameDC,122,180); LineTo(hFrameDC,121,170);
1220   LineTo(hFrameDC,120,160); LineTo(hFrameDC,121,150);
1221   LineTo(hFrameDC,122,130); LineTo(hFrameDC,129,100);
1222   LineTo(hFrameDC,131,90); LineTo(hFrameDC,140,70);
1223   LineTo(hFrameDC,150,53); LineTo(hFrameDC,160,40);
1224   LineTo(hFrameDC,170,33); LineTo(hFrameDC,190,28);
1225   LineTo(hFrameDC,200,28); LineTo(hFrameDC,215,32);
1226   LineTo(hFrameDC,224,40); LineTo(hFrameDC,238,39);
1227   LineTo(hFrameDC,244,40); LineTo(hFrameDC,250,48);
1228   LineTo(hFrameDC,260,70); LineTo(hFrameDC,268,100);
1229   LineTo(hFrameDC,270,120); LineTo(hFrameDC,271,140);
1230   LineTo(hFrameDC,270,160); LineTo(hFrameDC,267,180);
1231   LineTo(hFrameDC,260,197); LineTo(hFrameDC,250,210);
1232   LineTo(hFrameDC,240,215); LineTo(hFrameDC,230,218);
1233   LineTo(hFrameDC,213,220);
1234
1235   SelectObject(hFrameDC,PrevPen);                  /* deselect pen */
1236   DeleteObject(DrawingPen);                        /* delete pen */
1237   return;
1238   }
1239   /*
1240   ----------------------------------------------------------------------
1241                        ANIMATION PLAYBACK Functions
1242   ----------------------------------------------------------------------
1243   ----------------------------------------------------------------------
1244                        Display the next frame.
1245     This function is intelligent enough to discern between RAM-BASED
1246   FRAME ANIMATION (where all frames have already been loaded from
1247   disk and stored in RAM) and DISK-BASED FRAME ANIMATION (where
1248   each frame must be loaded from disk during playback).
1249   ----------------------------------------------------------------------
1250                                                                      */
1251   static void zShowNextFrame(HWND hWnd)
1252   {
1253     HDC hDC;
1254   if (bUseDisk==TRUE) goto DISK_PLAYBACK;
1255
1256   RAM_PLAYBACK:      /* if all frames have been loaded into RAM... */
1257   if (AnimationReady==FALSE) return;
1258   if (bAnimationLoaded==FALSE) return;
1259   if (Redisplay==TRUE) goto DISPLAY_FRAME;
1260   if (Pause==TRUE) return;
1261   if (FrameDirection==zFORWARD)
```

```
1262      {
1263      FrameNum++;
1264      if (FrameNum > zFINALFRAME) FrameNum= zFIRSTFRAME;
1265      }
1266    if (FrameDirection==zREVERSE)
1267      {
1268      FrameNum--;
1269      if (FrameNum < zFIRSTFRAME) FrameNum= zFINALFRAME;
1270      }
1271    DISPLAY_FRAME:
1272    hDC= GetDC(hWnd);
1273    switch (FrameNum)
1274      {
1275      case 1:
1276      case 2:
1277      case 3:
1278      case 4:
1279      case 5:
1280      case 6:
1281      case 7:
1282      case 8:
1283      case 9:
1284      case 10:
1285      case 11:
1286      case 12:
1287      case 13:
1288      case 14:
1289      case 15:
1290      case 16:
1291      case 17:   SelectObject(hFDC,hF1); break;
1292      case 18:   SelectObject(hFDC,hF2); break;
1293      case 19:
1294      case 20:
1295      case 21:
1296      case 22:   SelectObject(hFDC,hF3); break;
1297      case 23:
1298      case 24:
1299      case 25:
1300      case 26:
1301      case 27:
1302      case 28:   SelectObject(hFDC,hF4); break;
1303      case 29:   SelectObject(hFDC,hF5); break;
1304      case 30:   SelectObject(hFDC,hF6); break;
1305      case 31: SelectObject(hFDC,hF7); break;
1306      case 32: SelectObject(hFDC,hF8); break;
1307      case 33: SelectObject(hFDC,hF9); break;
1308      case 34:
1309      case 35:
1310      case 36:
1311      case 37:
1312      case 38:
1313      case 39:
1314      case 40:
1315      case 41:
1316      case 42:
1317      case 43:
1318      case 44: SelectObject(hFDC,hF10); break;
1319      case 45:
1320      case 46: SelectObject(hFDC,hF11); break;
1321      case 47:
1322      case 48: SelectObject(hFDC,hF12); break;
```

```
1323     case 49:
1324     case 50:
1325     case 51:
1326     case 52:
1327     case 53:
1328     case 54:
1329     case 55:
1330     case 56:
1331     case 57:
1332     case 58:
1333     case 59:
1334     case 60:
1335     case 61:
1336     case 62:
1337     case 63:
1338     case 64:
1339     case 65: SelectObject(hFDC,hF13); break;
1340     case 66: SelectObject(hFDC,hF14); break;
1341     case 67: SelectObject(hFDC,hF15); break;
1342     }
1343 BitBlt(hDC,0,0,zFRAMEWIDE,zFRAMEHIGH,hFDC,0,0,SRCCOPY);
1344 ReleaseDC(hWnd,hDC);
1345 return;
1346
1347 DISK_PLAYBACK:    /* if loading each frame from disk as needed... */
1348 if (bAnimationHalted==TRUE) return;
1349 if (Redisplay==TRUE) goto SAME_FRAME;
1350 if (Pause==TRUE) return;
1351 if (FrameDirection==zFORWARD)
1352     {
1353     FrameNum++;
1354     if (FrameNum > zFINALFRAME) FrameNum= zFIRSTFRAME;
1355     }
1356 if (FrameDirection==zREVERSE)
1357     {
1358     FrameNum--;
1359     if (FrameNum < zFIRSTFRAME) FrameNum= zFINALFRAME;
1360     }
1361 SAME_FRAME:
1362 hDC= GetDC(hWnd);
1363 switch (FrameNum)
1364     {
1365     case 1:
1366     case 2:
1367     case 3:
1368     case 4:
1369     case 5:
1370     case 6:
1371     case 7:
1372     case 8:
1373     case 9:
1374     case 10:
1375     case 11:
1376     case 12:
1377     case 13:
1378     case 14:
1379     case 15:
1380     case 16:
1381     case 17:   bFrameLoaded= zLoadFrame(hFrame, (LPSTR) "BLINK1.BIT");
1382                break;
1383     case 18:   bFrameLoaded= zLoadFrame(hFrame, (LPSTR) "BLINK2.BIT");
```

```
1384            break;
1385    case 19:
1386    case 20:
1387    case 21:
1388    case 22:  bFrameLoaded= zLoadFrame(hFrame, (LPSTR) "BLINK3.BIT");
1389            break;
1390    case 23:
1391    case 24:
1392    case 25:
1393    case 26:
1394    case 27:
1395    case 28:  bFrameLoaded= zLoadFrame(hFrame, (LPSTR) "BLINK4.BIT");
1396            break;
1397    case 29:  bFrameLoaded= zLoadFrame(hFrame, (LPSTR) "BLINK5.BIT");
1398            break;
1399    case 30:  bFrameLoaded= zLoadFrame(hFrame, (LPSTR) "BLINK6.BIT");
1400            break;
1401    case 31: bFrameLoaded= zLoadFrame(hFrame, (LPSTR) "BLINK7.BIT");
1402            break;
1403    case 32: bFrameLoaded= zLoadFrame(hFrame, (LPSTR) "BLINK8.BIT");
1404            break;
1405    case 33: bFrameLoaded= zLoadFrame(hFrame, (LPSTR) "BLINK9.BIT");
1406            break;
1407    case 34:
1408    case 35:
1409    case 36:
1410    case 37:
1411    case 38:
1412    case 39:
1413    case 40:
1414    case 41:
1415    case 42:
1416    case 43:
1417    case 44: bFrameLoaded= zLoadFrame(hFrame, (LPSTR) "BLINK10.BIT");
1418            break;
1419    case 45:
1420    case 46: bFrameLoaded= zLoadFrame(hFrame, (LPSTR) "BLINK11.BIT");
1421            break;
1422    case 47:
1423    case 48: bFrameLoaded= zLoadFrame(hFrame, (LPSTR) "BLINK12.BIT");
1424            break;
1425    case 49:
1426    case 50:
1427    case 51:
1428    case 52:
1429    case 53:
1430    case 54:
1431    case 55:
1432    case 56:
1433    case 57:
1434    case 58:
1435    case 59:
1436    case 60:
1437    case 61:
1438    case 62:
1439    case 63:
1440    case 64:
1441    case 65: bFrameLoaded= zLoadFrame(hFrame, (LPSTR) "BLINK13.BIT");
1442            break;
1443    case 66: bFrameLoaded= zLoadFrame(hFrame, (LPSTR) "BLINK14.BIT");
1444            break;
```

```
1445    case 67: bFrameLoaded= zLoadFrame(hFrame, (LPSTR) "BLINK15.BIT");
1446            break;
1447    }
1448  if (bFrameLoaded==FALSE)
1449    {
1450    bAnimationHalted= TRUE;
1451    MessageBeep(0);
1452    LoadString(hInst,IDS_Unexpected,lpCaption,Max);
1453    LoadString(hInst,IDS_Disk3,lpMessage,MaxText);
1454    TimerCounter= zTIMER_PAUSE;
1455    MessageBox(GetFocus(),lpMessage,lpCaption,MB_OK);
1456    return;
1457    }
1458  BitBlt(hDC,0,0,zFRAMEWIDE,zFRAMEHIGH,hFrameDC,0,0,SRCCOPY);
1459  ReleaseDC(hWnd,hDC);
1460  return;
1461  }
1462  /*
1463  --------------------------------------------------------------------
1464              Load the animation sequence from disk.
1465    If memory limitations prevent this function from loading the
1466    entire animation sequence into RAM, it sets a token to FALSE.
1467    In that case the playback function zShowNextFrame() will load
1468    each frame from disk as required during animation playback,
1469    otherwise all frames are expected to be in RAM.
1470  --------------------------------------------------------------------
1471                                                                    */
1472  static void zLoadAnimation(HWND hWnd)
1473  {
1474    HDC hDC;
1475
1476  if (FrameReady==FALSE)          /* if no hidden-frame available... */
1477    {
1478    MessageBeep(0);
1479    LoadString(hInst,IDS_NotReady,lpCaption,Max);
1480    LoadString(hInst,IDS_NoFrame,lpMessage,MaxText);
1481    MessageBox(GetFocus(),lpMessage,lpCaption,MB_OK);
1482    return;
1483    }
1484  if (bAnimationLoaded==TRUE)          /* if frames already loaded... */
1485    {
1486    MessageBeep(0);
1487    LoadString(hInst,IDS_Unexpected,lpCaption,Max);
1488    LoadString(hInst,IDS_Disk4,lpMessage,MaxText);
1489    TimerCounter= zTIMER_PAUSE;
1490    MessageBox(GetFocus(),lpMessage,lpCaption,MB_OK);
1491    return;
1492    }
1493  if (bPrevLoadAttempt==TRUE)         /* if previous attempt failed... */
1494    {
1495    MessageBeep(0);
1496    LoadString(hInst,IDS_Unexpected,lpCaption,Max);
1497    LoadString(hInst,IDS_Disk5,lpMessage,MaxText);
1498    TimerCounter= zTIMER_PAUSE;
1499    MessageBox(GetFocus(),lpMessage,lpCaption,MB_OK);
1500    return;
1501    }
1502  bPrevLoadAttempt= TRUE;
1503
1504  /* ----------- create bitmaps to hold the frames ----------- */
1505  GlobalCompact((DWORD)-1L);              /* maximize contiguous memory */
```

```
1506  hDC= GetDC(hWnd);
1507  hFDC= CreateCompatibleDC(hDC);
1508  hF1= CreateCompatibleBitmap(hDC,zFRAMEWIDE,zFRAMEHIGH);
1509  if (hF1==NULL) goto F1;
1510  hF2= CreateCompatibleBitmap(hDC,zFRAMEWIDE,zFRAMEHIGH);
1511  if (hF2==NULL) goto F2;
1512  hF3= CreateCompatibleBitmap(hDC,zFRAMEWIDE,zFRAMEHIGH);
1513  if (hF3==NULL) goto F3;
1514  hF4= CreateCompatibleBitmap(hDC,zFRAMEWIDE,zFRAMEHIGH);
1515  if (hF4==NULL) goto F4;
1516  hF5= CreateCompatibleBitmap(hDC,zFRAMEWIDE,zFRAMEHIGH);
1517  if (hF5==NULL) goto F5;
1518  hF6= CreateCompatibleBitmap(hDC,zFRAMEWIDE,zFRAMEHIGH);
1519  if (hF6==NULL) goto F6;
1520  hF7= CreateCompatibleBitmap(hDC,zFRAMEWIDE,zFRAMEHIGH);
1521  if (hF7==NULL) goto F7;
1522  hF8= CreateCompatibleBitmap(hDC,zFRAMEWIDE,zFRAMEHIGH);
1523  if (hF8==NULL) goto F8;
1524  hF9= CreateCompatibleBitmap(hDC,zFRAMEWIDE,zFRAMEHIGH);
1525  if (hF9==NULL) goto F9;
1526  hF10= CreateCompatibleBitmap(hDC,zFRAMEWIDE,zFRAMEHIGH);
1527  if (hF10==NULL) goto F10;
1528  hF11= CreateCompatibleBitmap(hDC,zFRAMEWIDE,zFRAMEHIGH);
1529  if (hF11==NULL) goto F11;
1530  hF12= CreateCompatibleBitmap(hDC,zFRAMEWIDE,zFRAMEHIGH);
1531  if (hF12==NULL) goto F12;
1532  hF13= CreateCompatibleBitmap(hDC,zFRAMEWIDE,zFRAMEHIGH);
1533  if (hF13==NULL) goto F13;
1534  hF14= CreateCompatibleBitmap(hDC,zFRAMEWIDE,zFRAMEHIGH);
1535  if (hF14==NULL) goto F14;
1536  hF15= CreateCompatibleBitmap(hDC,zFRAMEWIDE,zFRAMEHIGH);
1537  if (hF15==NULL) goto F15;
1538  goto BITMAPS_OK;
1539
1540  F15: DeleteObject(hF14);
1541  F14: DeleteObject(hF13);
1542  F13: DeleteObject(hF12);
1543  F12: DeleteObject(hF11);
1544  F11: DeleteObject(hF10);
1545  F10: DeleteObject(hF9);
1546  F9:  DeleteObject(hF8);
1547  F8:  DeleteObject(hF7);
1548  F7:  DeleteObject(hF6);
1549  F6:  DeleteObject(hF5);
1550  F5:  DeleteObject(hF4);
1551  F4:  DeleteObject(hF3);
1552  F3:  DeleteObject(hF2);
1553  F2:  DeleteObject(hF1);
1554  F1:  DeleteDC(hFDC); ReleaseDC(hWnd,hDC);
1555       bUseDisk= TRUE; AnimationReady= TRUE;
1556       LoadString(hInst,IDS_Status,lpCaption,Max);
1557       LoadString(hInst,IDS_Disk6,lpMessage,MaxText);
1558       MessageBox(GetFocus(),lpMessage,lpCaption,MB_OK);
1559       return;
1560  BITMAPS_OK: ReleaseDC(hWnd,hDC);
1561
1562  /* ------------ load frame files into the bitmaps ------------ */
1563  bFrameLoaded= zLoadFrame(hF1, (LPSTR) "BLINK1.BIT");
1564  if (bFrameLoaded==FALSE) goto DISK_ERROR;
1565  bFrameLoaded= zLoadFrame(hF2, (LPSTR) "BLINK2.BIT");
1566  if (bFrameLoaded==FALSE) goto DISK_ERROR;
```

```
1567  bFrameLoaded= zLoadFrame(hF3, (LPSTR) "BLINK3.BIT");
1568  if (bFrameLoaded==FALSE) goto DISK_ERROR;
1569  bFrameLoaded= zLoadFrame(hF4, (LPSTR) "BLINK4.BIT");
1570  if (bFrameLoaded==FALSE) goto DISK_ERROR;
1571  bFrameLoaded= zLoadFrame(hF5, (LPSTR) "BLINK5.BIT");
1572  if (bFrameLoaded==FALSE) goto DISK_ERROR;
1573  bFrameLoaded= zLoadFrame(hF6, (LPSTR) "BLINK6.BIT");
1574  if (bFrameLoaded==FALSE) goto DISK_ERROR;
1575  bFrameLoaded= zLoadFrame(hF7, (LPSTR) "BLINK7.BIT");
1576  if (bFrameLoaded==FALSE) goto DISK_ERROR;
1577  bFrameLoaded= zLoadFrame(hF8, (LPSTR) "BLINK8.BIT");
1578  if (bFrameLoaded==FALSE) goto DISK_ERROR;
1579  bFrameLoaded= zLoadFrame(hF9, (LPSTR) "BLINK9.BIT");
1580  if (bFrameLoaded==FALSE) goto DISK_ERROR;
1581  bFrameLoaded= zLoadFrame(hF10, (LPSTR) "BLINK10.BIT");
1582  if (bFrameLoaded==FALSE) goto DISK_ERROR;
1583  bFrameLoaded= zLoadFrame(hF11, (LPSTR) "BLINK11.BIT");
1584  if (bFrameLoaded==FALSE) goto DISK_ERROR;
1585  bFrameLoaded= zLoadFrame(hF12, (LPSTR) "BLINK12.BIT");
1586  if (bFrameLoaded==FALSE) goto DISK_ERROR;
1587  bFrameLoaded= zLoadFrame(hF13, (LPSTR) "BLINK13.BIT");
1588  if (bFrameLoaded==FALSE) goto DISK_ERROR;
1589  bFrameLoaded= zLoadFrame(hF14, (LPSTR) "BLINK14.BIT");
1590  if (bFrameLoaded==FALSE) goto DISK_ERROR;
1591  bFrameLoaded= zLoadFrame(hF15, (LPSTR) "BLINK15.BIT");
1592  if (bFrameLoaded==FALSE) goto DISK_ERROR;
1593
1594  goto DISK_OK;
1595
1596  DISK_ERROR:
1597    DeleteObject(hF1); DeleteObject(hF2); DeleteObject(hF3);
1598    DeleteObject(hF4); DeleteObject(hF5); DeleteObject(hF6);
1599    DeleteObject(hF7); DeleteObject(hF8); DeleteObject(hF9);
1600    DeleteObject(hF10); DeleteObject(hF11); DeleteObject(hF12);
1601    DeleteObject(hF13); DeleteObject(hF14); DeleteObject(hF15);
1602    DeleteDC(hFDC);
1603    return;
1604
1605  /* -------------------- tidy up and return -------------------- */
1606  DISK_OK:
1607  hPrevF= SelectObject(hFDC,hF1);                    /* select bitmap */
1608  bAnimationLoaded= TRUE;
1609  AnimationReady= TRUE;
1610  bAnimationSaved= TRUE;
1611  MessageBeep(0);
1612  LoadString(hInst,IDS_AnimReady,lpCaption,Max);
1613  LoadString(hInst,IDS_Disk7,lpMessage,MaxText);
1614  MessageBox(GetFocus(),lpMessage,lpCaption,MB_OK);
1615  return;
1616  }
1617  /*
1618  --------------------------------------------------------------------
1619                    Reset the animation frame rate.
1620  --------------------------------------------------------------------
1621                                                                    */
1622  static void zSetFrameRate(HWND hWnd, WORD wNewRate)
1623  {
1624  if (TimerExists==FALSE)
1625    {
1626    wFrameRate= wPrevRate;
1627    MessageBeep(0);
```

```
1628    LoadString(hInst,IDS_NotReady,lpCaption,Max);
1629    LoadString(hInst,IDS_NoReset,lpMessage,MaxText);
1630    MessageBox(GetFocus(),lpMessage,lpCaption,MB_OK);
1631    return;
1632    }
1633  switch (wPrevRate)
1634    {
1635    case 55:  CheckMenuItem(hMenu,IDM_FPS182,MF_UNCHECKED); break;
1636    case 110: CheckMenuItem(hMenu,IDM_FPS91,MF_UNCHECKED); break;
1637    case 165: CheckMenuItem(hMenu,IDM_FPS61,MF_UNCHECKED); break;
1638    case 220: CheckMenuItem(hMenu,IDM_FPS45,MF_UNCHECKED); break;
1639    case 275: CheckMenuItem(hMenu,IDM_FPS36,MF_UNCHECKED); break;
1640    case 330: CheckMenuItem(hMenu,IDM_FPS30,MF_UNCHECKED); break;
1641    }
1642  KillTimer(hWnd,1);
1643  TimerID1= SetTimer(hWnd,1,wNewRate,(FARPROC) NULL);
1644  if (TimerID1==0)
1645    {
1646    LoadString(hInst,IDS_NotReady,lpCaption,Max);
1647    LoadString(hInst,IDS_CannotReset,lpMessage,MaxText);
1648    MessageBox(GetFocus(),lpMessage,lpCaption,MB_OK);
1649    TimerExists= FALSE;
1650    return;
1651    }
1652  switch (wFrameRate)
1653    {
1654    case 55:  CheckMenuItem(hMenu,IDM_FPS182,MF_CHECKED); break;
1655    case 110: CheckMenuItem(hMenu,IDM_FPS91,MF_CHECKED); break;
1656    case 165: CheckMenuItem(hMenu,IDM_FPS61,MF_CHECKED); break;
1657    case 220: CheckMenuItem(hMenu,IDM_FPS45,MF_CHECKED); break;
1658    case 275: CheckMenuItem(hMenu,IDM_FPS36,MF_CHECKED); break;
1659    case 330: CheckMenuItem(hMenu,IDM_FPS30,MF_CHECKED); break;
1660    }
1661  return;
1662  }
1663  /*
1664  ----------------------------------------------------------------
1665                       End of the C source file
1666  ----------------------------------------------------------------
1667                                                              */
```

**10-36** The include file listing for the disk I/O module for the sample application.

```
0001  /*
0002  ----------------------------------------------------------------
0003                       Include file STORAGE.H
0004          Copyright 1992 Lee Adams.  All rights reserved.
0005    Include this file in the .RC resource script file and in the
0006    .C source file.  It contains function prototypes, menu ID
0007    constants, and string ID constants.
0008  ----------------------------------------------------------------
0009  ----------------------------------------------------------------
0010                       Function prototypes
0011  ----------------------------------------------------------------
0012                                                              */
0013  BOOL zSaveFrame(HBITMAP, LPSTR);        /* saves a frame to disk */
0014  BOOL zLoadFrame(HBITMAP, LPSTR);        /* loads a frame from disk*/
0015  /*
0016  ----------------------------------------------------------------
0017                       End of include file
0018  ----------------------------------------------------------------
0019                                                              */
```

**10-37** The C source file listing for the disk I/O module for the sample application.

```
0001  /*
0002  ---------------------------------------------------------------
0003      Disk routines for Windows applications that use image files
0004      for disk-based frame animation.
0005  ---------------------------------------------------------------
0006  Source file: STORAGE.C
0007  Release version: 1.00              Programmer: Lee Adams
0008  Type:  C file for multimodule Windows application development.
0009  Compilers: Microsoft C and SDK, Borland C++, Zortech C++,
0010    QuickC for Windows, Turbo C++ for Windows, WATCOM C.
0011  Memory model:  small.
0012  Dependencies:  include STORAGE.H in your main C source file.
0013    Compile STORAGE.C and link in STORAGE.OBJ to create your
0014    finished executable.
0015  Output and features:  Saves the bits of a given bitmap as a
0016    disk file.  Loads the image bits from a previously-saved
0017    disk file.
0018  Publication: Contains material from Windcrest/McGraw-Hill book
0019    4114 published by TAB BOOKS Division of McGraw-Hill Inc.
0020  License:  As purchaser of the book you are granted a royalty-
0021    free license to distribute executable files generated using
0022    this code provided you accept the conditions of the License
0023    Agreement and Limited Warranty described in the book and on
0024    the companion disk.  Government users:  This software and
0025    documentation are subject to restrictions set forth in The
0026    Rights in Technical Data and Computer Software clause at
0027    252.227-7013 and elsewhere.
0028  ---------------------------------------------------------------
0029      (c) Copyright 1992 Lee Adams.  All rights reserved.
0030         Lee Adams(tm) is a trademark of Lee Adams.
0031  ---------------------------------------------------------------
0032  .
0033  ---------------------------------------------------------------
0034                      Include files
0035  ---------------------------------------------------------------
0036                                                              */
0037  #include <WINDOWS.H>
0038  #include <SYS\TYPES.H>
0039  #include <SYS\STAT.H>
0040  /*
0041  ---------------------------------------------------------------
0042      Function prototypes (callable from outside this module).
0043  ---------------------------------------------------------------
0044                                                              */
0045  BOOL zSaveFrame(HBITMAP, LPSTR);        /* saves a frame to disk */
0046  BOOL zLoadFrame(HBITMAP, LPSTR);        /* loads a frame from disk*/
0047  /*
0048  ---------------------------------------------------------------
0049              Define necessary constants.
0050  ---------------------------------------------------------------
0051                                                              */
0052  #define IDS_Unexpected  44
0053  #define IDS_Disk9       54
0054  #define IDS_Disk10      55
0055  #define IDS_Disk11      56
0056  #define IDS_Disk12      57
0057  #define IDS_Disk13      58
0058  #define IDS_Disk14      59
0059  #define IDS_Disk15      60
0060  #define IDS_Disk16      61
0061  #define IDS_Disk17      62
0062  #define IDS_Disk18      63
```

```
0063  #define IDS_Disk19      64
0064  #define IDS_Disk20      65
0065  #define IDS_Disk21      66
0066  #define IDS_Disk22      67
0067  #define IDS_Disk23      68
0068  #define IDS_Disk24      69
0069  #define IDS_Disk25      70
0070  /*
0071  ------------------------------------------------------------------
0072                     Declare external variables.
0073  ------------------------------------------------------------------
0074                                                                 */
0075  extern BOOL FrameReady;
0076  extern HANDLE hInst;
0077  extern char lpCaption[];
0078  extern char lpMessage[];
0079  extern int Max;
0080  extern int MaxText;
0081  extern int RetVal;
0082  /*
0083  ------------------------------------------------------------------
0084                     Save a frame file to disk.
0085  ------------------------------------------------------------------
0086                                                                 */
0087  BOOL zSaveFrame(HBITMAP hBitmap, LPSTR lpFileName)
0088  {
0089    BITMAP bmImage;                      /* bitmap data structure */
0090    short BytesPerLine;                      /* width of bitmap */
0091    short RasterLines;                      /* height of bitmap */
0092    BYTE NumPlanes;                      /* number of bitplanes */
0093    LPSTR lpImageData;   /* pointer to buffer that holds bit array */
0094    GLOBALHANDLE hMem;   /* handle to buffer that holds bit array */
0095    WORD NumBytes;                      /* length of array, in bytes */
0096    LONG TestLength;                              /* hash value */
0097    DWORD BytesCopied;   /* value returned by GetBitmapBits() */
0098    int hFile;                              /* DOS file handle */
0099    OFSTRUCT FileStruct;                /* data structure for file */
0100
0101    HWND hDesktopWnd;                    /* handle to desktop display */
0102    HDC hDCcaps;                             /* a display-context */
0103    int DisplayBits;                    /* number of bits-per-pixel */
0104
0105  hDesktopWnd= GetDesktopWindow();                    /* grab handle */
0106  hDCcaps= GetDC(hDesktopWnd);            /* grab a display-context */
0107  DisplayBits= GetDeviceCaps(hDCcaps,12);    /* get bits-per-pixel */
0108  ReleaseDC(hDesktopWnd,hDCcaps);         /* release display-context */
0109  if(DisplayBits==8)               /* if running in 256-color mode... */
0110    {
0111    MessageBeep(0); MessageBox(GetFocus(),
0112    "Reset your system to 16-color mode to run this animation.
        Otherwise recompile the source files to run in 256-color mode.
         See the book for source code changes or use Windows Setup to
         change to a 16-color display.",
0113    "256-color support", MB_OK|MB_ICONINFORMATION);
0114    return FALSE;
0115    }
0116
0117  if (FrameReady==FALSE)                /* if no hidden-frame exists... */
0118    {
0119    MessageBeep(0);
0120    LoadString(hInst,IDS_Unexpected,lpCaption,Max);
```

```
0121    LoadString(hInst,IDS_Disk9,lpMessage,MaxText);
0122    MessageBox(GetFocus(),lpMessage,lpCaption,MB_OK);
0123    return FALSE;
0124    }
0125
0126  RetVal= GetObject(hBitmap,              /* grab bitmap data structure */
0127          sizeof(BITMAP),(LPSTR)&bmImage);
0128  if (RetVal==0)
0129    {
0130    MessageBeep(0);
0131    LoadString(hInst,IDS_Unexpected,lpCaption,Max);
0132    LoadString(hInst,IDS_Disk10,lpMessage,MaxText);
0133    MessageBox(GetFocus(),lpMessage,lpCaption,MB_OK);
0134    return FALSE;
0135    }
0136  BytesPerLine= bmImage.bmWidthBytes;              /* width of bitmap */
0137  RasterLines= bmImage.bmHeight;                  /* height of bitmap */
0138  NumPlanes= bmImage.bmPlanes;                 /* number of bitplanes */
0139  TestLength=                             /* calculate length of data */
0140            (LONG)(BytesPerLine * RasterLines * NumPlanes);
0141  if (TestLength > 65534) /* if too large for single-pass write... */
0142    {
0143    MessageBeep(0);
0144    LoadString(hInst,IDS_Unexpected,lpCaption,Max);
0145    LoadString(hInst,IDS_Disk11,lpMessage,MaxText);
0146    MessageBox(GetFocus(),lpMessage,lpCaption,MB_OK);
0147    return FALSE;
0148    }
0149  NumBytes= (WORD) TestLength;     /* initialize arg for _lwrite() */
0150
0151  hMem= GlobalAlloc(GMEM_MOVEABLE, NumBytes);   /* create a buffer */
0152  if (hMem==0)
0153    {
0154    MessageBeep(0);
0155    LoadString(hInst,IDS_Unexpected,lpCaption,Max);
0156    LoadString(hInst,IDS_Disk12,lpMessage,MaxText);
0157    MessageBox(GetFocus(),lpMessage,lpCaption,MB_OK);
0158    return FALSE;
0159    }
0160  lpImageData= GlobalLock(hMem);   /* lock buffer and grab pointer */
0161  BytesCopied= GetBitmapBits(hBitmap,NumBytes,lpImageData);
0162  if (BytesCopied==0)          /* if unable to copy bits to buffer... */
0163    {
0164    MessageBeep(0);
0165    LoadString(hInst,IDS_Unexpected,lpCaption,Max);
0166    LoadString(hInst,IDS_Disk13,lpMessage,MaxText);
0167    MessageBox(GetFocus(),lpMessage,lpCaption,MB_OK);
0168    GlobalUnlock(hMem); GlobalFree(hMem); return FALSE;
0169    }
0170
0171  hFile= OpenFile(lpFileName,&FileStruct,OF_EXIST);     /* exists? */
0172  if (hFile >= 0)
0173    {
0174    MessageBeep(0);
0175    LoadString(hInst,IDS_Unexpected,lpCaption,Max);
0176    LoadString(hInst,IDS_Disk14,lpMessage,MaxText);
0177    RetVal= MessageBox(GetFocus(),lpMessage,lpCaption,MB_YESNO);
0178    if (RetVal==IDNO)      /* if user does not want to overwrite... */
0179      {
0180      GlobalUnlock(hMem); GlobalFree(hMem); return FALSE;
0181      }
```

```
0182     }
0183   hFile= OpenFile(lpFileName,&FileStruct,OF_CREATE|OF_WRITE);
0184   if (hFile==-1)
0185     {
0186     MessageBeep(0);
0187     LoadString(hInst,IDS_Unexpected,lpCaption,Max);
0188     LoadString(hInst,IDS_Disk15,lpMessage,MaxText);
0189     MessageBox(GetFocus(),lpMessage,lpCaption,MB_OK);
0190     GlobalUnlock(hMem); GlobalFree(hMem); return FALSE;
0191     }
0192
0193   RetVal= _lwrite(hFile,lpImageData,NumBytes);      /* write to disk */
0194   if (RetVal==-1)
0195     {
0196     MessageBeep(0);
0197     LoadString(hInst,IDS_Unexpected,lpCaption,Max);
0198     LoadString(hInst,IDS_Disk16,lpMessage,MaxText);
0199
0200     MessageBox(GetFocus(),lpMessage,lpCaption,MB_OK);
0201     _lclose(hFile);
0202     GlobalUnlock(hMem); GlobalFree(hMem); return FALSE;
0203     }
0204
0205   RetVal= _lclose(hFile);                        /* close the file */
0206   if (RetVal==-1)                   /* if unable to close file... */
0207     {
0208     MessageBeep(0);
0209     LoadString(hInst,IDS_Unexpected,lpCaption,Max);
0210     LoadString(hInst,IDS_Disk17,lpMessage,MaxText);
0211     MessageBox(GetFocus(),lpMessage,lpCaption,MB_OK);
0212     GlobalUnlock(hMem); GlobalFree(hMem); return FALSE;
0213     }
0214
0215   GlobalUnlock(hMem);              /* discard the pointer to the buffer */
0216   GlobalFree(hMem);                        /* discard the buffer */
0217   return TRUE;
0218   }
0219   /*
0220   --------------------------------------------------------------
0221                    Load one frame file from disk.
0222   --------------------------------------------------------------
0223                                                                 */
0224   BOOL zLoadFrame(HBITMAP hBitmap, LPSTR lpFileName)
0225   {
0226     BITMAP bmImage;                      /* bitmap data structure */
0227     short BytesPerLine;                      /* width of bitmap */
0228     short RasterLines;                       /* height of bitmap */
0229     BYTE NumPlanes;                       /* number of bitplanes */
0230     LPSTR lpImageData;   /* pointer to buffer that holds bit array */
0231     GLOBALHANDLE hMem;   /* handle to buffer that holds bit array */
0232     WORD NumBytes;                    /* length of array, in bytes */
0233     LONG TestLength;                             /* hash value */
0234     DWORD BytesCopied;        /* value returned by GetBitmapBits() */
0235     int hFile;                               /* DOS file handle */
0236     OFSTRUCT FileStruct;               /* data structure for file */
0237
0238     HWND hDesktopWnd;                   /* handle to desktop display */
0239     HDC hDCcaps;                          /* a display-context */
0240     int DisplayBits;                 /* number of bits-per-pixel */
0241
0242   hDesktopWnd= GetDesktopWindow();                    /* grab handle */
```

```
0243  hDCcaps= GetDC(hDesktopWnd);              /* grab a display-context */
0244  DisplayBits= GetDeviceCaps(hDCcaps,12);    /* get bits-per-pixel */
0245  ReleaseDC(hDesktopWnd,hDCcaps);           /* release display-context */
0246  if(DisplayBits==8)              /* if running in 256-color mode... */
0247    {
0248    MessageBeep(0); MessageBox(GetFocus(),
0249    "Reset your system to 16-color mode to run this animation.
          Otherwise recompile the source files to run in 256-color mode.
           See the book for source code changes or use Windows Setup to
           change to a 16-color display.",
0250    "256-color support", MB_OK|MB_ICONINFORMATION);
0251    return FALSE;
0252    }
0253
0254  if (FrameReady==FALSE)              /* if no hidden-frame exists... */
0255    {
0256    MessageBeep(0);
0257    LoadString(hInst,IDS_Unexpected,lpCaption,Max);
0258    LoadString(hInst,IDS_Disk18,lpMessage,MaxText);
0259    MessageBox(GetFocus(),lpMessage,lpCaption,MB_OK);
0260    return FALSE;
0261    }
0262
0263  RetVal= GetObject(hBitmap,           /* grab bitmap data structure */
0264          sizeof(BITMAP),(LPSTR)&bmImage);
0265  if (RetVal==0)
0266    {
0267    MessageBeep(0);
0268    LoadString(hInst,IDS_Unexpected,lpCaption,Max);
0269    LoadString(hInst,IDS_Disk10,lpMessage,MaxText);
0270    MessageBox(GetFocus(),lpMessage,lpCaption,MB_OK);
0271    return FALSE;
0272    }
0273
0274  BytesPerLine= bmImage.bmWidthBytes;              /* width of bitmap */
0275  RasterLines= bmImage.bmHeight;                  /* height of bitmap */
0276  NumPlanes= bmImage.bmPlanes;               /* number of bitplanes */
0277  TestLength=                     /* calculate length of data */
0278          (LONG)(BytesPerLine * RasterLines * NumPlanes);
0279  if (TestLength > 60000)     /* if larger than hardcoded value... */
0280    {                         /* ...of a 400x300x16-color frame */
0281    MessageBeep(0);
0282    LoadString(hInst,IDS_Unexpected,lpCaption,Max);
0283    LoadString(hInst,IDS_Disk19,lpMessage,MaxText);
0284    MessageBox(GetFocus(),lpMessage,lpCaption,MB_OK);
0285    return FALSE;
0286    }
0287  NumBytes= (WORD) TestLength;        /* initialize arg for _lread() */
0288
0289  hMem= GlobalAlloc(GMEM_MOVEABLE, NumBytes);   /* create a buffer */
0290  if (hMem==0)
0291    {
0292    MessageBeep(0);
0293    LoadString(hInst,IDS_Unexpected,lpCaption,Max);
0294    LoadString(hInst,IDS_Disk20,lpMessage,MaxText);
0295    MessageBox(GetFocus(),lpMessage,lpCaption,MB_OK);
0296    return FALSE;
0297    }
0298  lpImageData= GlobalLock(hMem);    /* lock buffer and grab pointer */
0299
0300  hFile= OpenFile(lpFileName,&FileStruct,OF_READ);
```

```
0301   if (hFile==-1)
0302     {
0303     MessageBeep(0);
0304     LoadString(hInst,IDS_Unexpected,lpCaption,Max);
0305     LoadString(hInst,IDS_Disk21,lpMessage,MaxText);
0306     MessageBox(GetFocus(),lpMessage,lpCaption,MB_OK);
0307     GlobalUnlock(hMem); GlobalFree(hMem); return FALSE;
0308     }
0309
0310   RetVal= _lread(hFile,lpImageData,NumBytes);      /* read from disk */
0311   if (RetVal==-1)
0312     {
0313     MessageBeep(0);
0314     LoadString(hInst,IDS_Unexpected,lpCaption,Max);
0315     LoadString(hInst,IDS_Disk22,lpMessage,MaxText);
0316     MessageBox(GetFocus(),lpMessage,lpCaption,MB_OK);
0317     _lclose(hFile);
0318     GlobalUnlock(hMem); GlobalFree(hMem); return FALSE;
0319     }
0320   if ((unsigned)RetVal < NumBytes)
0321     {
0322     MessageBeep(0);
0323     LoadString(hInst,IDS_Unexpected,lpCaption,Max);
0324     LoadString(hInst,IDS_Disk23,lpMessage,MaxText);
0325     MessageBox(GetFocus(),lpMessage,lpCaption,MB_OK);
0326     _lclose(hFile);
0327     GlobalUnlock(hMem); GlobalFree(hMem); return FALSE;
0328     }
0329
0330   RetVal= _lclose(hFile);                          /* close the file */
0331   if (RetVal==-1)                        /* if unable to close file... */
0332     {
0333     MessageBeep(0);
0334     LoadString(hInst,IDS_Unexpected,lpCaption,Max);
0335     LoadString(hInst,IDS_Disk24,lpMessage,MaxText);
0336     MessageBox(GetFocus(),lpMessage,lpCaption,MB_OK);
0337     GlobalUnlock(hMem); GlobalFree(hMem); return FALSE;
0338     }
0339
0340   BytesCopied= SetBitmapBits(hBitmap,NumBytes,lpImageData);
0341   if (BytesCopied==0)        /* if unable to copy bits to bitmap... */
0342     {
0343     MessageBeep(0);
0344     LoadString(hInst,IDS_Unexpected,lpCaption,Max);
0345     LoadString(hInst,IDS_Disk25,lpMessage,MaxText);
0346     MessageBox(GetFocus(),lpMessage,lpCaption,MB_OK);
0347     GlobalUnlock(hMem); GlobalFree(hMem); return FALSE;
0348     }
0349
0350   GlobalUnlock(hMem);         /* discard the pointer to the buffer */
0351   GlobalFree(hMem);                       /* discard the buffer */
0352   return TRUE;
0353   }
0354   /*
0355   ------------------------------------------------------------------
0356                       End of the C source file
0357   ------------------------------------------------------------------
0358                                                                */
```

# 11
# *Layout*

---

Whether you call it layout or composition, it is an important element in your computer animation sequence. Layout is related to staging—and staging is directing. In the entertainment industries of television, theater, stage, and motion pictures, the director is the person responsible for deciding what prop goes where, which actors stand where, and who walks from here over to there and when. Likewise, as an animator you must decide where to place the props in the scene, where to position the characters in front of the background, what pose each character should adopt, where and when each character should move, and so on.

*Fact* **Layout and staging**  For many computer animators, layout and staging have different meanings. Layout refers to the organization of static components like background elements, props, the position of characters in a scene, and camera viewpoint. Staging refers to dynamic effects like character movement and camera movement (including pans and zooms). For many animators, layout involves static material and staging involves dynamic material. Other animators make no distinction between layout and staging.

## Layout fundamentals

By observing a few simple rules, you can make your task of laying out the scene much easier. The most important guideline for correct layouts is the rule of thirds. This rule can be applied to the two fundamental elements that are found in nearly every layout. These elements are:

- Center-of-interest.
- Horizon line.

## Center-of-interest

Every scene must have a *center-of-interest*, also called a center-of-attention or focal point. This point occurs where the most important subject in the scene is located—or where the main action is happening. You can, of course, safely place the center-of-interest in the middle of the scene, but this center-stage approach quickly becomes tiresome and boring for the users who are watching your animation sequence. You can add variation to your scenes by using the rule of thirds when deciding where to locate the center-of-interest. The grid in FIG. 11-1 shows four possible locations for a center-of-interest that will result in a balanced and interesting layout.

*Here's How...* If you are displaying a frame filled with text, perhaps supported by spot animation like a spinning logo, you should position the spot animation at one of the four center-of-interest locations suggested by FIG. 11-1. (Spot animation is a short burst of animation intended to add interest to an otherwise static image.) If your hero or heroine is speaking or gesturing, most of this action should occur at one of the four center-of-interest points, unless the character fills most of the frame.

No matter what the subject matter, you can count on professional results if you keep the rule of thirds in mind when deciding where to position the center-of-interest (either the chief character or the main action) in your scene.

## Horizon line

If your scene is set outdoors or in a large room, you will likely need a horizon line. The horizon line is where sky meets ground or where wall meets floor. Many amateurs draw the horizon line straight through the middle of the scene, but this approach results in an awkward layout that is frustrating to the eye. The horizon lines shown in FIG. 11-2 demonstrate how to apply the rule of thirds when deciding where to position your horizon.

Most scenes will use one-third ground and two-thirds sky. Enough ground is available to show detail like props and backdrops to establish the location of the scene, but the horizon line is low enough to permit the characters to remain the central attractions. They are not overwhelmed or overshadowed by the horizon line. You can add variation to your scenes,

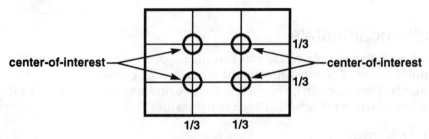

**11-1** Four possible locations for a center-of-interest that will produce a balanced layout.

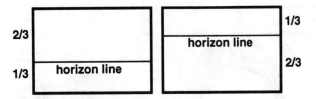

**11-2**  Set the horizon line at either a one-third or two-third height.

however, by occasionally using two-thirds ground and one-third sky. This is the same as the camera tilting down. A sense of dramatic urgency is created by this layout, but you must be careful not to overuse it.

## Staging fundamentals

Staging is often concerned with selecting a camera shot and with managing the movement of characters in a scene. Good staging adds drama and excitement to your animation sequence.

### The camera shot

The camera shot is the way the scene is captured by the camera. Examples of a long shot, a medium shot, and a close-up shot are shown in FIG. 11-3. You can also design your animation sequence using extreme close-up shots and extreme long shots, but for most projects the three shots depicted in FIG. 11-3 are sufficient.

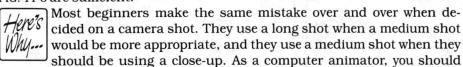 Most beginners make the same mistake over and over when decided on a camera shot. They use a long shot when a medium shot would be more appropriate, and they use a medium shot when they should be using a close-up. As a computer animator, you should not be reluctant to get right up close to your subject matter, especially if you are animating a character's face. The users of your software will be bored by tiny specks marching around the computer screen. Instead, make your animation more moving—by moving in closer.

### Managing characters

How you stage the movement of the characters in a scene depends upon how many characters are present. Most computer animation sequences involve either a one-character scene or a two-character scene.

**One-character scene**  The examples in FIG. 11-4 illustrate three ways to stage a one-person scene. The example on the right is correct; the other two examples are amateurish and do not belong in your animation projects. Television and motion picture camera operators are taught to lead the actor or actress. In the examples shown in FIG. 11-4, you can see for yourself which panel gives you the potential to add a text caption, a title, or perhaps even

**11-3** A sampling of shots. Shown from left to right, long shot, medium shot, and close-up shot (also called a tight shot).

**11-4** Three ways to frame a shot. The version shown at right is the most eye-pleasing for the viewer and the most productive for the animator.

introduce another character into the scene. Always lead your character in a one-person scene.

*Expert* **Two-character scene** Four different ways to stage a two-person scene are illustrated in FIG. 11-5. The upper left example in FIG. 11-5 is a standard medium shot. The upper right example is a reverse-angle medium shot. The lower left example is a type of reverse-angle medium shot seen often in television programming, mainly because it allows the au-

**11-5** Examples of layouts for two-subject shots. Beginners often use only the layout shown at upper-left. The frame shown at upper-right is better, but professionals often use the layouts shown at bottom-left and bottom-right.

dience to see the facial reactions of both participants. The lower right example in FIG. 11-5 is a reverse angle close-up shot, offering the most economical use of space.

When you plan a two-character scene, you need to keep in mind the impact the scene will have on the audience. If the reactions of both characters are important, then make sure that the faces of both can be seen. A general rule of thumb is, the more emotion in the scene, the more important it becomes to show each character's facial expression. The back of a character's head rarely evokes a memorable reaction from an audience.

## Layout mistakes to avoid

While you are laying out your scene, you must be your own critic. In particular, you must be especially vigilant in your battle against ambiguous lines, which often confound even experienced artists.

A scene that is burdened with three ambiguous lines is shown in FIG.

11-6. The effects that are produced by the ambiguity are trivial in this particular example, but ambiguous lines can make education, tutorial, and instructional animations much more difficult to comprehend—and they can significantly reduce the impact of an animation sequence. When there are numerous characters or props in your scene, make certain that they never just touch each other—instead make one of them distinctly behind the other in order to avoid ambiguous lines. The scene shown in FIG. 11-6, for example, could be significantly improved if there was a space between the character's shoes and the top of the puppy's head.

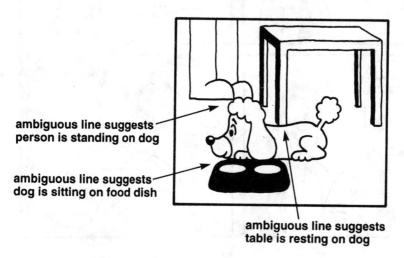

ambiguous line suggests
person is standing on dog

ambiguous line suggests
dog is sitting on food dish

ambiguous line suggests
table is resting on dog

**11-6**  Ambiguous lines resulting from a poor layout.

# 12
# *Perspective*

---

Perspective is an optical effect. In the real world, it provides cues for shape, solidity, and distance. The human eye relies upon perspective to help it make sense of the objects it encounters in the world.

 Perspective is everywhere. It is the physical manifestation of three optical effects:

- Convergence.
- Foreshortening.
- Diminution.

If you stand on a railway track, the parallel steel rails seem to get closer together the farther they go into the distance. This phenomenon is called *convergence*. The spaces between the railway ties appear to become smaller as they recede into the distance, even though each tie is equally spaced from its neighbor. The same effect occurs with fence posts that run off into the distance. This phenomenon is called *foreshortening*. In both cases, the railway ties and the fence posts appear smaller as they move off into the distance. This phenomenon is called *diminution*. Diminution means the process of diminishing. In addition to the appearance of reduced size, diminution also affects the amount of detail, tone, and color in an object—all three of these diminish as an object recedes into the distance.

Understanding how the rules of perspective work in the real world is an instinctive part of being human. Applying these rules to create an accurate, realistic sketch is called *perspective drawing*. The animator who understands perspective drawing is better equipped to produce exciting, dynamic backgrounds, props, and characters for computer animation sequences.

# Fundamentals of perspective drawing

All perspective drawings use vanishing points. Any set of parallel lines in a perspective drawing will converge at a distance location called a vanishing point. As a designer of computer animation sequences, you can choose from three types of perspective drawings:

- One-point perspective.
- Two-point perspective.
- Three-point perspective.

**One-point perspective**  A box drawn in one-point perspective is shown in FIG. 12-1. The two top edges of the box recede into the distance and theoretically converge at a point on the horizon line. That point, depicted by the small circle in FIG. 12-1, is the vanishing point. Because there is only one vanishing point in the drawing, it is called a *one-point perspective drawing*.

**Two-point perspective**  A box drawn in two-point perspective is shown in FIG. 12-2. Because the box is oriented at an angle to the viewer, the parallel lines of the two visible sides of the box converge on two different vanishing points, each located on the horizon line. Each of these two vanishing points is depicted by a small circle in FIG. 12-2. Because there are two vanishing points in the drawing, it is called a *two-point perspective drawing*.

**Three-point perspective**  A box drawn in three-point perspective is shown in FIG. 12-3. Because the box is tall and it is oriented at an angle to the viewer, the three sets of parallel edges converge on three different vanishing points. Each of these three vanishing points is depicted by a small circle in FIG. 12-3. Because there are three vanishing points in the drawing, it is called a *three-point perspective drawing*.

**Two-point vs.three-point**  If you examine the two-point perspective drawing in FIG. 12-2 and compare it to the three-point perspective drawing in FIG. 12-3, you might draw the conclusion that both drawings should have been rendered in three-point perspective. Technically, you are correct, but many drawings are rendered as two-point perspective in order to reduce the number of construction lines required and to avoid confusing

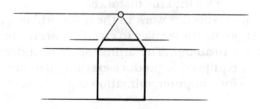

**12-1**  A box drawn in one-point perspective.

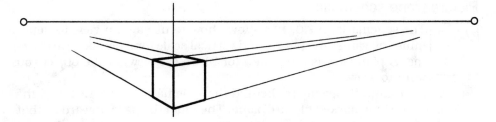

**12-2** A box drawn in two-point perspective.

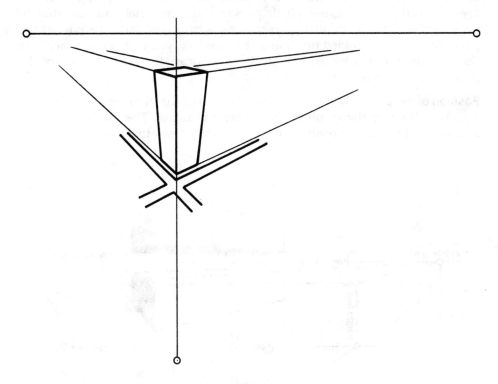

**12-3** A box drawn in three-point perspective.

the viewer's eye. The human eye finds parallel lines more pleasing and orderly than converging lines.

## Accuracy in perspective drawing

In order to achieve accuracy in a perspective drawing, you need to adopt a methodical approach. Artists, architects, and draftspersons have developed a geometry-based method for producing accurate perspective drawings. If your animation sequence requires a reasonable degree of accuracy in a perspective drawing, you can use this same approach.

## Picture plane schematic

 The schematic in FIG. 12-4 shows how to use a plan view to determine the vanishing points and vertical scale for a perspective drawing. A plan view is a top view (or bird's eye view) of the object you want to draw.

To understand the geometry behind the schematic in FIG. 12-4, fold the page along the line marked picture plane. Then fold the page upward so that the part of page containing the perspective drawing is vertical and the part of the page containing the viewpoint remains horizontal, flat on the desktop. The picture plane is the vertical plane upon which the perspective image is drawn. Now, imagine a little person about one inch tall standing on the viewpoint. What the little person sees is projected onto the part of the page that you have folded up. Using this analogy, you can begin to see how the schematic works by using sight lines to locate the critical edges of the perspective drawing.

**Position of the plan** By adjusting the position of the plan you can affect the size and shape of the resulting perspective drawing. The examples in FIG. 12-5 illustrate how the position of the plan view, relative to the viewpoint,

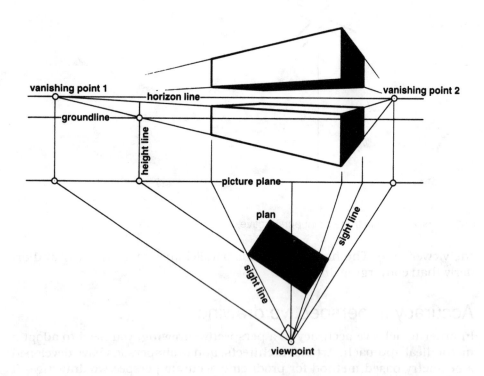

**12-4** A 3D template showing how to use a plan view to determine the correct vanishing points and vertical scale for a perspective drawing.

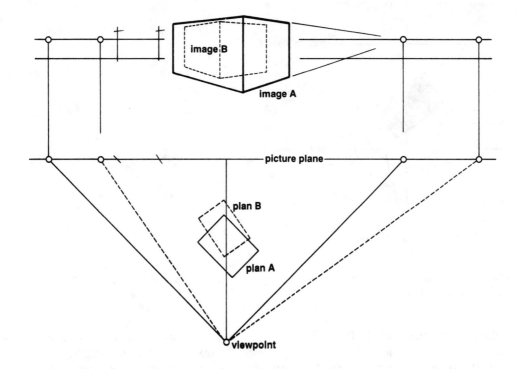

**12-5** A 3D template showing how the position of the plan view affects the resulting perspective drawing.

can produce different perspective images. Observe, for example, how two lines drawn from the viewpoint to the picture plane are employed to figure out the location of the vanishing points for plan A. These two construction lines are parallel to the sides of the plan view, of course. Note also how the dashed construction lines are used to locate the vanishing points for the dashed shape of plan B. In both instances, the position of the vanishing points is moved up onto the horizon line (refer back to FIG. 12-4) to create the vanishing points for the perspective drawings (image A and image B).

**Size**  As you inspect FIG. 12-4 and FIG. 12-5, you can see that the scale (or size) of the resulting image can be controlled by the location of the picture plane. The sight lines in FIG. 12-4 expand as they move farther from the viewpoint. This means that the farther the picture plane from the viewpoint, the larger will be the resulting image. The shape of the image does not change, only the size. The overhead view in FIG. 12-6 depicts how to use the location of the picture plane to set the scale of the resulting perspective drawing.

**Instancing**  Instancing refers to the location and orientation of an object. The concept of instancing applies to perspective drawing just like it applies to 3D programming. (Refer back to Chapter 4, Modeling, for

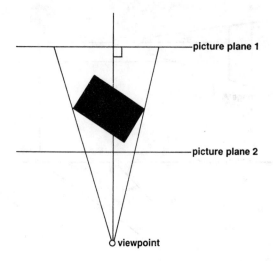

picture plane 1

picture plane 2

viewpoint

**12-6** An overhead view, showing how to use a picture plane to determine the scale of the resulting drawing.

a detailed discussion of 3D computer graphics.) You can affect and alter the instancing of an object by rotating (turning) the object, by translating (moving) the object. You can also affect the viewer's perception of the object by moving the camera. The camera is also called the *viewpoint*.

**Rotation**  The four boxes in FIG. 12-7 show how the vanishing points of a perspective drawing move when an object is rotated in the yaw plane. Refer back to FIG. 12-5 to see the corresponding rotation in the plans for the object.

**Viewpoint**  You can change the perception of the perspective image by moving the viewpoint. The effect of different viewpoint positions is suggested in FIG. 12-8. This particular effect is achieved by adjusting the height of the groundline above the picture plane, and the height of the horizon line above the groundline (see FIG. 12-4).

**Multiple instancing**  Each perspective image that results from a particular viewpoint position or plan view position is called an *instance*. If you render these perspective images on the same drawing, you are creating instances of the object. A conceptual representation of four instances of the same 3D object are shown in FIG. 12-9.

## Using the cone of vision

In order to avoid introducing distortion into your perspective drawings, you must take into account the human cone of vision. This cone defines the normal range within which the human eyes can see clearly without moving. A depiction of the human cone of vision is provided in FIG. 12-10.

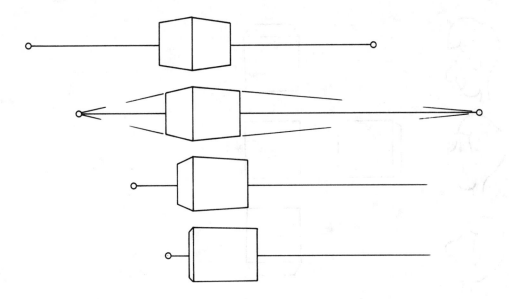

**12-7** The location of the vanishing points changes as the model is rotated. Shown here is rotation through the yaw plane.

In the real world, a scene is observed by allowing the eyes to wander over it, as shown in FIG. 12-11. Each of the circles in FIG. 12-11 represents a cone of vision. If you were standing near the four boxes you would need to shift your gaze in order to observe the entire scene. A perspective drawing, however, could easily depict the entire scene, just like in FIG. 12-11. This is where distortion can be introduced into the drawing, unfortunately.

The schematic in FIG. 12-12 illustrates how the human cone of vision can be used to choose an appropriate viewing distance. If the viewpoint is located too near the object, then parts of the object will fall outside the human cone of vision. If these rogue parts are drawn in the perspective image, they will appear angular and distorted. As FIG. 12-12 shows, however, viewpoints farther away will produce cones of vision of 60 degrees and less, resulting in more pleasing images. The perspective view (3D view) in FIG. 12-13 demonstrates explicitly how distortion is introduced into any image elements that fall outside the human cone of vision.

## Perspective problem-solving

While you work on your perspective drawing, you use vanishing points and other construction lines to help you draw edges, shapes, and volumes. You can use the rules of convergence, foreshortening, and diminution to solve many of the problems involved in perspective drawing.

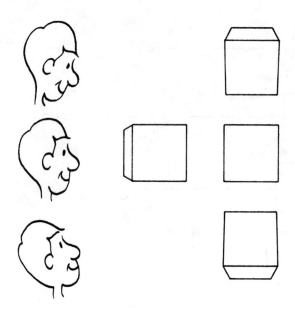

**12-8** A conceptual schematic depicting different viewpoints or camera positions.

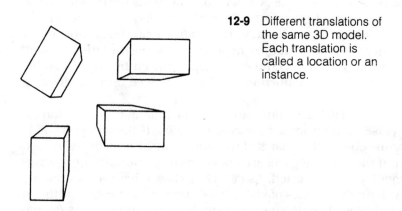

**12-9** Different translations of the same 3D model. Each translation is called a location or an instance.

*Tip* **Diagonals** Diagonal construction lines can be used to determine the correct location of breakdown drawings in a perspective drawing, as shown in FIG. 12-14. This technique is helpful for finding center positions when drawing fences, windows in buildings, telephone and power poles, and so on.

*Tip* **Lateral vanishing points** By using different vanishing points along the same horizon line, you can adjust the yaw heading of the drawing, as shown in FIG. 12-15. This technique is helpful when drawing pathways, roads, runways, ribbons, and so on.

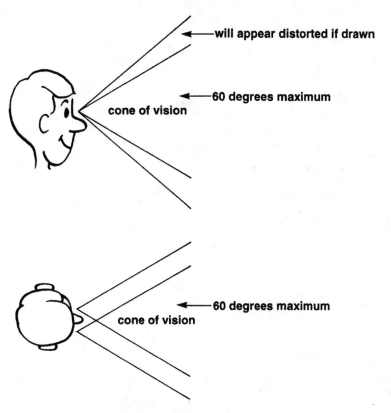

**will appear distorted if drawn**

**60 degrees maximum**

**cone of vision**

**60 degrees maximum**

**cone of vision**

**12-10**  The human cone of vision is 60 degrees or less. Using a cone of 45 degrees will result in a pleasing perspective drawing.

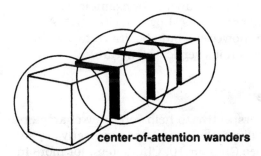

**center-of-attention wanders**

**12-11**  In the real world the center-of-attention of the eyes wanders over a scene, but a drawing must attempt to depict the entire scene in a single static layout.

[Tip] **Elevated vanishing points**  By using different elevations of the vanishing point, you can adjust the pitch heading of the drawing, as shown in FIG. 12-16. This technique is helpful when drawing pathways and roads in hilly terrain, and for illustrating freeway ramps.

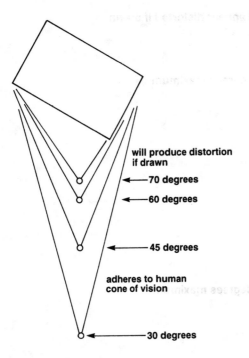

**will produce distortion
if drawn**

←—— **70 degrees**

←—— **60 degrees**

←—— **45 degrees**

**adheres to human
cone of vision**

←—— **30 degrees**

**12-12**   The human cone of vision can be used to select an appropriate viewing distance.

**Plumb lines**   The schematic in FIG. 12-17 shows the horizon line and vertical plumb line used in three-point perspective drawings. The plumb line is perpendicular to the horizon line and falls from the line of sight. If you were drawing a scene of skyscrapers, for example, each skyscraper would converge on vanishing point 3, as shown in FIG. 12-17. A landmark like the Leaning Tower of Pisa, however, would be drawn to a different vanishing point, however, because it is not a vertical structure.

## Characters in perspective

You can use the rules of perspective to help you draw characters. The examples in FIG. 12-18 illustrate how to use perspective to add volume to a stick figure. (See Chapter 10, Characters, for more information about stick figures and nodes.) After using a stick figure to get the fundamental scale correct, you can block in the figure using parallelepipeds and cylinders drawn in perspective. By using vanishing points, as shown in FIG. 12-19, you can draw a figure correctly foreshortened and in proper perspective.

**Multiple characters**   You can also use vanishing points and construction lines to correctly position multiple characters in a 3D scene, as shown in

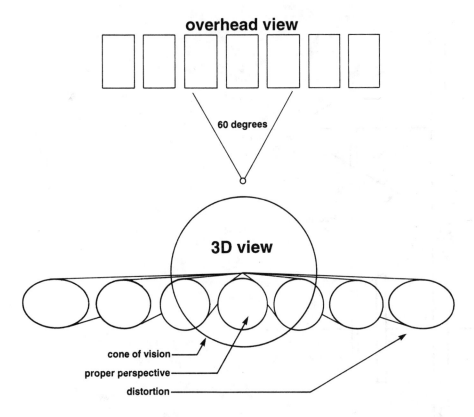

**overhead view**

60 degrees

**3D view**

cone of vision
proper perspective
distortion

**12-13**  How to use the cone of vision to select an appropriate viewpoint distance (also called camera-to-subject distance).

FIG. 12-20. Note how horizontal parallel construction lines are used with vertical height lines to translate (move) a character of known dimensions from a given location to another location. All you need is one instance of a character in order to be able to create as many instances as you want anywhere in the scene.

## Shadow in perspective

You can also use the picture plane schematic shown in FIG. 12-4 to help you add shadows to your perspective drawing. It is, after all, the tones and shadows that are used to render mass and volume in a perspective drawing. A line drawing may be technically correct, but it is the shadows that give it a lifelike quality.

**Shade and shadow**  Shadows fall into two categories: shade and shadow. Shade is found on portions of an object facing away from the light source. A shaded portion of an object is lit by ambient light, which is light reflected

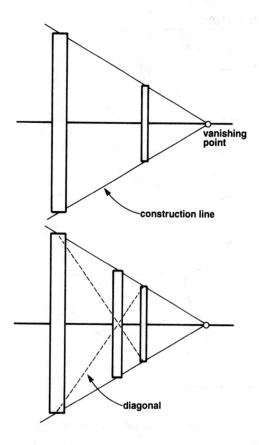

**12-14** How to use diagonals to determine the correct position of a breakdown drawing in a perspective layout.

from other objects in the scene. A shaded portion of an object is not lit by light coming directly from the light source. Shadow, on the other hand, is found on other objects or on the ground. Shadow is a result of the light source being blocked by the object. Shadows are also called *cast shadows*.

**Drawing a shadow** To determine the shape and location of a shadow, find the intersection of incoming light rays and the groundplane, as illustrated in FIG. 12-21. Observe how the edges of the shadow are either construction lines from a vanishing point, or are construction lines that join two vertices along a vanishing point construction line. The vanishing point for the shadow is derived by constructing a perpendicular down from the light source to the horizon line.

A similar approach can be used for reflections, where a mirror plane can be used to help plot reflected images, as shown in FIG. 12-22. Observe how

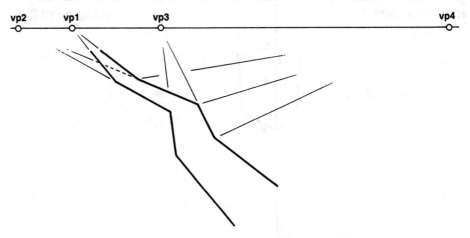

**12-15** How to adjust yaw (the heading) by using different vanishing points on the same horizon line.

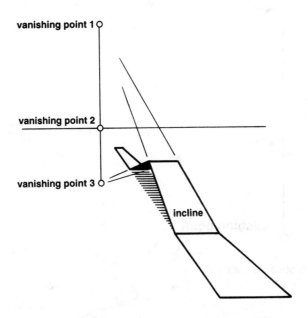

**12-16** How to adjust pitch by using different elevations of the vanishing point.

the edges of the reflection converge on the same vanishing points used by the original image. Reflected images are found on glass, mirrors, still water, metallic surfaces, glossy surfaces, and so on.

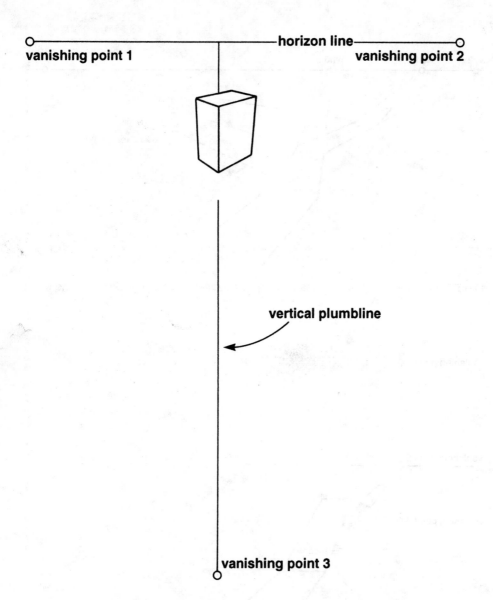

**12-17** Construction lines for three-point perspective.

**12-18** How to flesh out a stick figure in a perspective drawing.

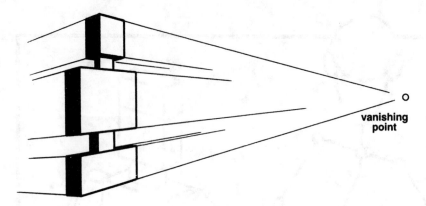

**12-19** How to guarantee that a character is correctly foreshortened and drawn in correct perspective.

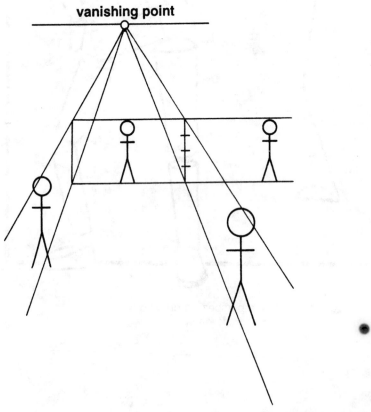

**12-20** How to use perspective to locate characters in a 3D scene layout.

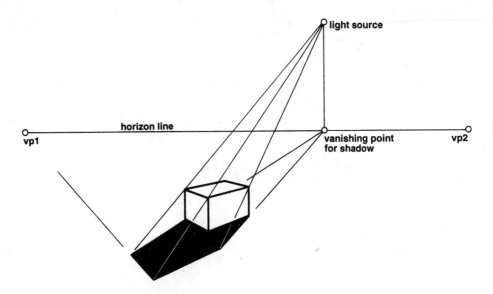

**12-21** Shadows can be derived by finding the intersection of incident light rays and construction lines on the groundplane derived from the shadow vanishing point.

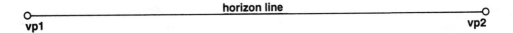

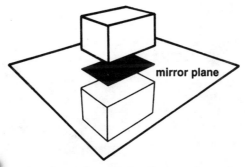

**12-22** Reflections can be drawn by constructing a mirror plane and duplicating the model.

# 13
# *Motion*

Motion is the essence of animation. During the development of an animation sequence, you might be called upon to animate bounces, collisions, walk-cycles, head-turns, flight-cycles, four-legged cycles, blinks, sneaks, staggers, double takes, and more.

Many of these words have special meanings to traditional film animators. In order to produce a convincing motion sequence, you need to understand more than merely the meanings of these effects, you need an appreciation of how to implement them in your own animation sequences.

Even as a Windows programmer, you can still take full advantage of production techniques discovered and perfected over the last 60 years by traditional film animation studios. These so-called tricks of the trade include two indispensable techniques: motion blur and squash- and-stretch.

Motion blur is often called temporal anti-aliasing and strobing by computer programmers. Squash-and-stretch is also called deformation.

## Motion blur and deformation

*Motion blur* is an optical effect related to traditional film cameras. During the filming of an object moving at high speed, the shutter opens and closes 24 times each second, advancing and exposing a fresh frame each time the shutter opens. However, if the object being filmed is moving quickly enough, it will move an appreciable distance during the 1/24th second when it is being exposed to the raw frame on the movie film. This movement results in a slightly blurred image on the film. When the developed film is projected onto a screen at 24 frames per second, however, the blur results in a realistic representation of the speeding object.

Audiences have become accustomed to this motion blur. In fact, they now demand it. If you produce a computer animation sequence of a high-speed phenomenon, you must deliberately add motion blur to the object being animated. Otherwise, the audience will perceive the object as jerky and unnatural—even if your computer animation is playing at the Windows maximum display rate of 18 frames per second.

This jerky appearance is called *temporal aliasing* by computer programmers. (Temporal means related to time; aliasing means unwanted side effects.) If the object being animated moves far enough in space (from one frame to the next) for the human eye to detect a jump, then the animation suffers from temporal aliasing—unwanted time-related side effects.

## Temporal anti-aliasing

The algorithms and processes that computer programmers employ to overcome temporal aliasing are called temporal anti-aliasing. Experienced film animators know these tricks as motion blur.

The example in FIG. 13-1 shows how to use temporal anti-aliasing to simulate the motion blur of a falling object. Note how the shape of the ball becomes more elliptical (stretched and elongated) as it accelerates. This stretching will guarantee a convincing motion sequence when the animation is played.

## Squash-and-stretch

The concept of stretching can also be applied to collisions and other movements. This technique is called squash-and-stretch. For example, the effect of mass on a bouncing ball is depicted in FIG. 13-2. In a ball of medium or light mass, acceleration is usually dramatic and some deformation occurs when the ball impacts with the floor. Consequently, you should elongate the ball when it is moving at high speed, and you should flatten it when it collides with the floor.

In a ball of heavy mass, acceleration is somewhat more sedate. Little, if any, deformation occurs at the moment of impact. Accordingly, the shape of the ball would likely remain unchanged during the animation sequence.

In addition to the effects of mass, the elasticity of an object can affect your decision whether or not to use squash-and-stretch. Two examples of the effect of elasticity on a collision are shown in FIG. 13-3.

## Practical implementations

Depending on the degree of realism that you want in your animation sequence, you can select from a number of different methods to implement motion blur. Three methods of producing temporal anti-aliasing on a computer screen are shown in FIG. 13-4.

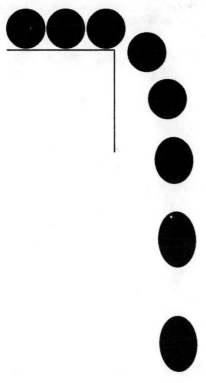

**13-1** Using temporal anti-aliasing (motion blur) to simulate speed.

The sample animation provided later in this chapter uses elongated temporal anti-aliasing—it simply stretches the object. More advanced animation engines, especially those specializing in 3D scenes, use linear-blur or logarithmic-blur temporal anti-aliasing techniques like those in FIG. 13-4. Even the simple technique of stretching the object can produce spectacular results, as demonstrated by the sample application in this chapter.

## Character motion

Animation of characters also relies heavily on motion. A typical animation sequence will use body language, walk-cycles, double takes, laugh-cycles, and more.

The four examples in FIG. 13-5 show how body language can be used to enhance the emotive content of a scene. During the animation sequence, however, your characters must use motion that smoothly moves them into and out of these poses. Traditional film animators invented and refined a technique called slow-in/slow-out to make this type of motion more believable.

*Expert* The technique of slow-in/slow-out dictates that you must program any movement to start slowly, gradually build up to full motion, and then smoothly slow down again before coming to a stop.

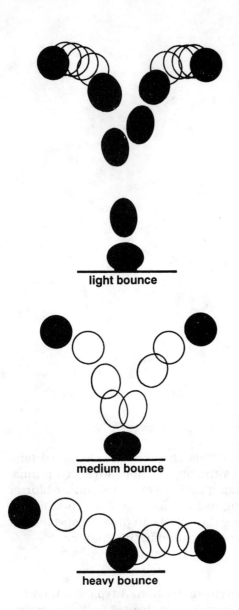

**13-2** The effects of mass on
a bounce.

**light bounce**

**medium bounce**

**heavy bounce**

Clearly, the character shown in FIG. 13-5 cannot simply snap from one pose to the next. Only by judicious use of the slow-in/slow-out technique can you animate the changeover in a way that will produce pleasing results during playback.

## Walk-cycles

Even the standard walk-cycle requires careful use of motion techniques. A geometric representation of a walk-cycle is shown in FIG. 13-6. Notice how

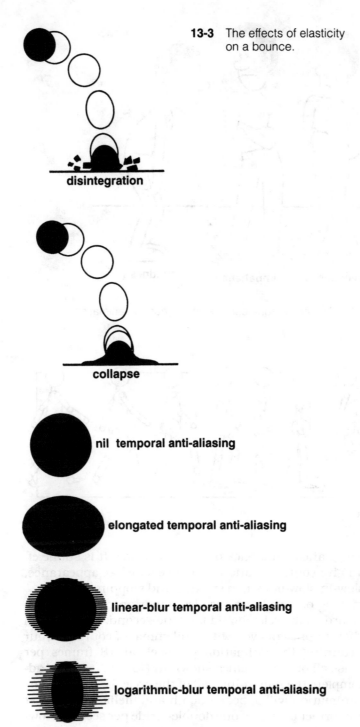

**13-3** The effects of elasticity on a bounce.

disintegration

collapse

nil temporal anti-aliasing

elongated temporal anti-aliasing

linear-blur temporal anti-aliasing

logarithmic-blur temporal anti-aliasing

**13-4** Implementations of temporal anti-aliasing suitable for computer animation.

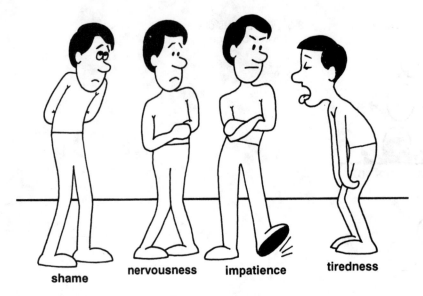

shame     nervousness     impatience     tiredness

**13-5** Body language and motion are integral components of cartoon animation.

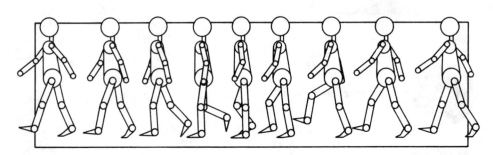

**13-6** A standard walk-cycle.

the shoulder node swings ahead and back during the stride. It is subtle effects like this that can give your animation sequence a lifelike appearance, especially if you use slow-in/slow-out when starting and stopping the walk.

*Tip*  The timing or pacing of a walk-cycle is also important. Each double-stride in a standard walk-cycle should last one second, as shown in FIG. 13-7. This dictum presents you with a dilemma, of course. If your delivery platform is running the animation playback at 18 frames per second, then you can use all of the 9 frames shown in FIG. 13-7, plus an additional 9 frames to complete the remaining half of the cycle. Using this paradigm, the resulting animation will appear smooth and lifelike, and—best of all—it will run at the correct pacing of one double-stride per second. However, if the playback computer is running the animation at 9 fps, the walk-cycle will appear as if in slow motion. You could, of course, eliminate every

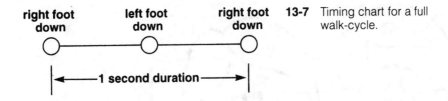

right foot down    left foot down    right foot down

|←————1 second duration————→|

**13-7** Timing chart for a full walk-cycle.

second cel from FIG. 13-7 and use only 9 frames for the double-stride. The animation will play correctly on the 9 fps machine but will appear to run in fast-forward mode on the 18 fps machine. Should you produce your animation to meet the specifications of the lowest common denominator—the slowest machine? Or should you produce different sets of frames for machines running at different speeds? You are not the first and you will not be the last computer animator to wrestle with this dilemma.

## Double takes

A double take is an exaggerated reaction. The character first notices some event, looks away, then looks back again in exaggerated surprise. Double takes are an effective way to indicate the importance of an event—in fact, audiences have come to expect double takes. Every motion picture uses them, every television situation comedy has them. The double take is a tool of the trade.

**Facial double takes**   A double take can be animated as a facial double take or as a torso double take. A standard facial double take is shown in FIG. 13-8. (Refer back to FIG. 10-16 in chapter 10, Characters, for an illustration of the take, standard blink, power squint, and double take that comprise the full standard double take sequence.)

The technique of squash-and-stretch plays an important role in the successful implementation of a facial double take. Note, the middle drawings in FIG. 13-8, for example. The jaws are flattened, the cheeks are widened, and the overall head is shorter than the top drawings. This squashing is a prelude to the stretching used in the bottom drawings, where the double take reaches climax. The jaws are stretched, giving the overall head a longer appearance.

**Torso double takes**   The motion required for a standard torso double take is shown in FIG. 13-9. You use this type of double take when you have selected a medium camera shot or a long shot of the character. Not only does the character momentarily turn away from the event, but the technique of squash-and-stretch is used. Observe the middle drawing in FIG. 13-9, for example, where the head, neck, and shoulders are squashed down. Then, in the next image, the character stretches out, adding emphasis to the double take expression on the character's face.

**13-8** A standard facial double-take.

**13-9** A standard torso double-take.

**Torso laugh-cycles**  The squashing and stretching involved in a standard torso double take can also be applied to the laugh-cycle. Laugh-cycles, like double takes, can be animated as facial laugh-cycles or as torso laugh-cycles. The motion involved in a standard torso laugh-cycle is illustrated in FIG. 13-10. Notice how the character is squashed at the beginning of the laugh, and stretches up and back during the laugh. (The hunching of the shoulders is a subtle effect used by many professional animators.) Some traditional film animators go even further and throw the character's head back near the end of the laugh-cycle.

Other motion techniques will be discussed and demonstrated later in the book, but the demo program in this chapter shows you how to use motion blur and squash-and-stretch to animate a bouncing ball in a realistic manner.

## Preparing the sample animation

The rough sketch that was used to prepare the animation sequence that is demonstrated in this chapter is shown in FIG. 13-11. The proximity of the ellipsoids to each other at the top of the sketch provides an effective method of simulating the slower speed of the ball at the apogee of each bounce cycle. The elongated ellipsoids at the middle and lower portion of the bounce cycle are used to simulate the motion blur that accompanies faster speed. The deformation of the ellipsoids at the bottom of the bounce cycle serves to simulate the ball's impact with the floor.

After completing the sketch shown in FIG. 13-11, an animation grid was used to determine the X-Y coordinates for each frame.

**13-10** A standard laugh-cycle.

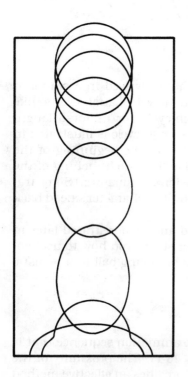

**13-11** The original rough design that was used to develop the animation sequence that is demonstrated by the sample application in this chapter.

# Sample application

The screen image in FIG. 13-12 shows the first frame from the sample application bouncing.exe. This program uses a bouncing ball to demonstrate motion blur and deformation, including stretch, squash, temporal anti-aliasing, and slow-in/slow-out. The interac-

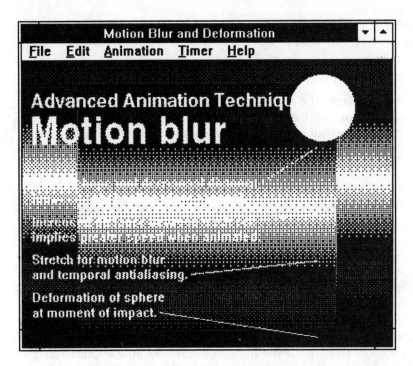

**13-12** A freezeframe from the animated sample application, showing the multicolor dithered background and the superimposed titles and captions.

tive editor allows you to experiment with different animation playback options, including full forward, full reverse, pause, freeze-frame, single-step forward, and single-step reverse. The animation will continue to play if the window is partially covered by another window or if the window is clipped by the edge of the screen.

The bouncing.exe demo is built from six modules, including a .def module definition file, an .h #include file, an .rc resource script file, and a .c source file. Also required is an .h #include file and a .c source file for the storage.c module that provides disk read/write functions. The production files for bouncing.exe are provided as ready-to-use source code in the program listings later in the chapter. The production files for the disk read/write module were provided in chapter 11. All the source files are also provided on the companion disk. You can refer to the appropriate appendix for instructions on how to build bouncing.exe with QuickC for Windows, Turbo C++ for Windows, Borland C++, Zortech C++, WATCOM C, and Microsoft C and the SDK.

## What the program does: A user's guide

The sample application provides an interactive environment suitable for experimenting with motion-based frame animation. You can use either a mouse or the keyboard to experiment with the demo program. The menus also support mnemonic keys. To view a runtime help message, select Help from the Help menu.

## Initializing the system

Select Initialize system from the Animation menu to initialize the animation environment. Neither the authoring features nor the playback features of the Animation menu will operate until the hidden frame has been created by selecting Initialize system.

## Creating the frames

Select Create Frames from the Animation menu to build the animation sequence and store it on disk. A sampling of 8 of the 13 frames that make up the animation are illustrated in FIG. 13-13. The sample application builds each frame in turn on the hidden page, copies the completed frame to the display window, and then saves the image to disk as a binary image file. If you have already saved the 13 frames to disk, the demo program displays a warning message. You have the option of overwriting the existing file with the new image file. If you choose not to overwrite the existing file, the build sequence is stopped and no other frames are built. If there is not enough free space on your hard disk for the image files, the sample application displays an advisory message and cancels the build process. The program reports successful completion of the Create Frames function with a message box.

## Loading the animation

Before you can play the animation sequence you must load it from disk. If you saved the animation sequence during the current working session, simply select Load Animation from the Animation menu. If you saved the animation during a previous working session, you must select Initialize system from the Animation menu before selecting Load Animation from the Animation menu.

If the software cannot find the frame files on disk, it displays a warning message. If you attempt to play an animation before loading it from disk (or before selecting Initialize system from the Animation menu), the demo program displays a warning message.

Under normal circumstances the sample application loads each frame file into the hidden frame, from where it copies the image to a bitmap in memory.

## Playing the animation

 To play the animation sequence, select Run Forward from the Animation menu. A bouncing ball is animated using motion blur and deformation. The motion blur simulates speed. The deformation simulates im-

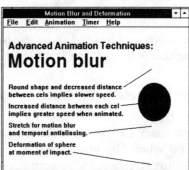
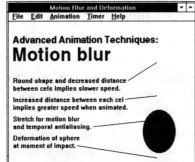
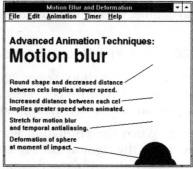
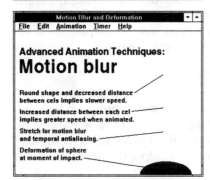
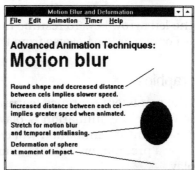
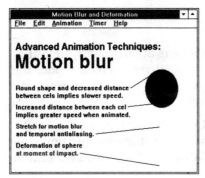
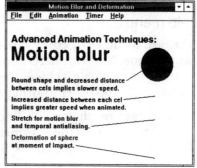

**13-13** A sampling of eight frames from the animation sequence. The dithered background has been deleted from these screen shots so the movement of the bouncing ball can be easily tracked.

pact. Sample images excerpted from the animation sequence are shown in FIG. 13-13. The ball will continue bouncing until you stop the animation.

## Adjusting the animation playback speed

You can adjust the animation speed by selecting from the Timer menu. At startup the playback rate is set to 18 frames per second. You can adjust the playback speed when the animation is playing or paused. See chapter 8, Frame animation engines, for information about playback rates on slower computers. If you try to reset the animation rate before you have initialized the animation engine, the application displays a warning message.

## Freeze-frame and single-step animation

**Pause**   To pause the animation, select Pause from the Animation menu. To resume animating in forward mode, select Run Forward from the Animation menu. To resume animating in reverse mode, select Run Reverse.

**Single-step**   When the animation is paused, you can use single-step playback. Press the right arrow key on the direction keypad to display the next frame in the animation sequence. Continue pressing the right arrow key to single-step through the entire animation. To single-step in reverse, press the left arrow key. To resume full-speed animation playback, select either Run Forward or Run Reverse from the Animation menu.

## Persistent graphics

You can test the persistent graphics features of the demo program by moving the window while the animation is playing. If the window is clipped by the edge of the screen the animation will continue to play. If the window is partly covered by a program group or by another window the animation will continue to play.

## Using the Help menu

You can use the Help menu to discover various facts about your system that are in effect at runtime. You can determine the current screen mode, the maximum number of available colors, the runtime memory mode (real, standard, or enhanced), and other information.

**Checking the screen resolution**   To find out the current screen mode, select Screen resolution from the Help menu. The sample application supports 640 × 480, 640 × 350, 800 × 600, and 1024 × 768 resolution display modes.

**Maximum displayable colors**   To determine the maximum available colors that can be displayed simultaneously, select Available colors from the Help menu. The sample application supports 16-color and 2-color displays. To modify the source code for 256-color display modes, see the discussion in chapter 3, Blitting.

**Determining the runtime memory mode**   To determine the current Windows runtime memory mode, select Memory mode from the Help menu. The sample application supports real, standard, and enhanced memory modes.

**Animation memory requirements**   To view an informative message concerning animation memory requirements, select Memory notes from the Help menu.

**Animation timing considerations**   To read an informative message about animation playback rates, select Timing notes from the Help menu.

# How the source code works: A programmer's guide

The bouncing.exe demonstration program is a dedicated implementation of the frame animation prototype that was demonstrated in chapter 8, Frame animation engines. By using the techniques presented in the program listings for bouncing.exe, you can incorporate motion-based frame animation into your own applications.

The .h #include file and the .rc resource script file follow the structure used by previous sample applications. In particular, see the discussion in chapter 8, Frame animation engines.

## How the .c file works

The .c file is derived from the prototype program listing in chapter 8, Frame animation engines. It is also closely related to the facial expression animation demo in chapter 10, Characters. The discussion here focuses on new features that have been added. Refer back to chapter 8 and chapter 10 for a detailed analysis of the code in general.

**Building the animation**   The zSaveAnimation() function at lines 0702 through 0769 manages the process than builds and saves the 13 frames of the animation sequence. The zSaveAnimation() function repeatedly calls the zBuildFrame() function, located at lines 0775 through 0869, in order to draw individual frames.

**Drawing the ellipse**   Note the switch() block at lines 0836 through 0859. This block of code draws the ellipse in the correct shape at the proper location for each frame. Notice how two variables named High and Wide are manipulated in order to adjust the shape of the ellipse as required for each frame in the animation sequence. The ellipsoid shapes were derived from the preparatory sketch illustrated earlier in FIG. 13-11. An animation grid (like the one shown in FIG. 10-28 in chapter 10) was used to calculate the location of the ellipse for each frame.

The shape of the ellipsoid provides the motion blur and temporal anti-aliasing that make the animation so effective. The shape also provides the deformation effect that simulates the impact of the ball with the floor at the bottom of each bounce cycle.

The X-Y coordinate location of each ellipse is what gives you full control over pacing and speed. The ball seems to move slower at the top of each bounce cycle, where the changes in Y coordinate values are less pronounced. It seems to accelerate while in the middle portions of each bounce cycle, where the changes in Y coordinate values are more dramatic.

**Captions and leader-lines**  The code at lines 0789 through 0827 in the zBuildFrame() function is responsible for adding text captions and leader-lines to each frame. (The leader-lines are the lines that lead from each caption to the referenced graphic element.)

The calls to TextOut() at lines 0810 through 0817 write the captions at a margin width of 10 pixels from the left edge of the client area of the window. Each line of text is written 16 raster lines below its predecessor, starting at raster line 120 (see line 0810 in the program listing). The calls to MoveTo() and LineTo() at lines 0824 through 0827 draw the leader-lines. The X-Y coordinates used here were devised by trial and error. For commercial-quality code you should instead use the font query capabilities of the GDI to calculate display-dependent coordinates at runtime. (If you are running Windows in the 800 × 600 mode the leader-lines may be slightly displaced, a consequence of the cel height of the bitmapped font characters provided by some third-party display drivers.)

# Program listings for the sample application

*Code*  The program listings presented here contain all the source code you need to build and run the sample application bouncing.exe. The bouncing.def module definition file is provided in FIG. 13-14. The bouncing.h #include file is found in FIG. 13-15. The bouncing.rc resource script file is presented in FIG. 13-16. The bouncin.c source file is provided in FIG. 13-17. The storage.h #include file for the disk read/write module is located in chapter 10, Characters, as FIG. 10-36. The storage.c source file for the read/write module is likewise provided in chapter 10, Characters, as FIG. 10-37.

*Disk*  **Companion disk**  If you have the companion disk, the six source files are presented as bouncing.def, bouncing.h, bouncing.rc, bouncing.c, storage.h, and storage.c.

*License*  **License**  You can paste the royalty-free source code into your own applications and distribute the resulting executable files under the conditions of the License Agreement and Limited Warranty in FIG. 10 in the introduction to this book.

**13-14** The module definition file listing for the sample application.

```
0001  NAME          DEFDEMO
0002  DESCRIPTION   'Copyright 1992 Lee Adams.  All rights reserved.'
0003  EXETYPE       WINDOWS
0004  STUB          'WINSTUB.EXE'
0005  CODE          PRELOAD MOVEABLE
0006  DATA          PRELOAD MOVEABLE MULTIPLE
0007  HEAPSIZE      1024
0008  STACKSIZE     8192
0009  EXPORTS       zMessageHandler
```

**13-15** The include file listing for the sample application.

```
0001  /*
0002  ----------------------------------------------------------------
0003                    Include file BOUNCING.H
0004          Copyright 1992 Lee Adams.  All rights reserved.
0005    Include this file in the .RC resource script file and in the
0006    .C source file.  It contains function prototypes, menu ID
0007    constants, and string ID constants.
0008  ----------------------------------------------------------------
0009  ----------------------------------------------------------------
0010                        Function prototypes
0011  ----------------------------------------------------------------
0012                                                                */
0013  #if !defined(zRCFILE)              /* if not an .RC file... */
0014    LONG FAR PASCAL zMessageHandler(HWND, unsigned, WORD, LONG);
0015    int PASCAL WinMain(HANDLE,HANDLE,LPSTR,int);
0016    HWND zInitMainWindow(HANDLE);
0017    BOOL zInitClass(HANDLE);
0018  static void zClear(HWND);              /* blank the display window */
0019  static void zInitFrame(HWND);           /* creates hidden frame */
0020  static void zShowNextFrame(HWND);         /* the playback engine */
0021  static void zSetFrameRate(HWND,WORD);        /* resets the timer */
0022  static void zDrawBg(HDC);               /* draws the background */
0023  static void zSaveAnimation(HWND);     /* saves animation sequence */
0024  static BOOL zBuildFrame(int,HWND,LPSTR);      /* builds one frame */
0025  static void zLoadAnimation(HWND);     /* loads animation sequence */
0026  static void zCopyToDisplay(HWND);      /* copies frame to display */
0027  static void zClearHiddenFrame(void);      /* clears hidden frame */
0028  static BOOL zSaveFrame(HBITMAP, LPSTR); /* saves a frame to disk */
0029  static BOOL zLoadFrame(HBITMAP, LPSTR);/* loads a frame from disk*/
0030  #endif
0031  /*
0032  ----------------------------------------------------------------
0033                        Menu ID constants
0034  ----------------------------------------------------------------
0035                                                                */
0036  #define IDM_New            1
0037  #define IDM_Open           2
0038  #define IDM_Save           3
0039  #define IDM_SaveAs         4
0040  #define IDM_Exit           5
0041
0042  #define IDM_Undo           6
0043  #define IDM_Cut            7
0044  #define IDM_Copy           8
0045  #define IDM_Paste          9
0046  #define IDM_Delete         10
```

```
0047
0048    #define IDM_RunForward          11
0049    #define IDM_RunReverse          12
0050    #define IDM_StopAnimation       13
0051    #define IDM_InitFrame           14
0052    #define IDM_SaveAnimation       15
0053    #define IDM_LoadAnimation       16
0054    #define IDM_Clear               17
0055
0056    #define IDM_FPS182              18
0057    #define IDM_FPS91               19
0058    #define IDM_FPS61               20
0059    #define IDM_FPS45               21
0060    #define IDM_FPS36               22
0061    #define IDM_FPS30               23
0062
0063    #define IDM_About               24
0064    #define IDM_License             25
0065    #define IDM_Display             26
0066    #define IDM_Colors              27
0067    #define IDM_Mode                28
0068    #define IDM_Memory              29
0069    #define IDM_Timing              30
0070    #define IDM_GeneralHelp         31
0071    /*
0072    ----------------------------------------------------------------
0073                            String ID constants
0074    ----------------------------------------------------------------
0075                                                                  */
0076    #define IDS_Caption        1
0077    #define IDS_Warning        2
0078    #define IDS_NoMouse        3
0079    #define IDS_About          4
0080    #define IDS_AboutText      5
0081    #define IDS_License        6
0082    #define IDS_LicenseText    7
0083    #define IDS_Help           8
0084    #define IDS_HelpText       9
0085    #define IDS_Completed      10
0086    #define IDS_Error          11
0087    #define IDS_Memory         12
0088    #define IDS_MemText        13
0089    #define IDS_Timing         14
0090    #define IDS_TimingText     15
0091    #define IDS_NotReady       16
0092    #define IDS_Ready          17
0093    #define IDS_BuildBefore    18
0094    #define IDS_Already        19
0095    #define IDS_InsufMem1      20
0096    #define IDS_InsufMem2      21
0097    #define IDS_NoTimer        22
0098    #define IDS_NoReset        23
0099    #define IDS_CannotReset    24
0100    #define IDS_Resolution     25
0101    #define IDS_ResVGA         26
0102    #define IDS_ResEGA         27
0103    #define IDS_ResCGA         28
0104    #define IDS_ResSVGA        29
0105    #define IDS_Res8514        30
0106    #define IDS_ResHerc        31
0107    #define IDS_ResCustom      32
```

**13-15** Continued.

```
0108  #define IDS_Color        33
0109  #define IDS_Color16      34
0110  #define IDS_Color256     35
0111  #define IDS_Color2       36
0112  #define IDS_ColorCustom  37
0113  #define IDS_Machine      38
0114  #define IDS_Enhanced     39
0115  #define IDS_Standard     40
0116  #define IDS_Real         41
0117  #define IDS_NoFrame      42
0118  #define IDS_AnimReady    43
0119  #define IDS_Unexpected   44
0120  #define IDS_Status       45
0121  #define IDS_Disk1        46
0122  #define IDS_Disk2        47
0123  #define IDS_Disk3        48
0124  #define IDS_Disk4        49
0125  #define IDS_Disk5        50
0126  #define IDS_Disk6        51
0127  #define IDS_Disk7        52
0128  #define IDS_Disk8        53
0129  #define IDS_Disk9        54
0130  #define IDS_Disk10       55
0131  #define IDS_Disk11       56
0132  #define IDS_Disk12       57
0133  #define IDS_Disk13       58
0134  #define IDS_Disk14       59
0135  #define IDS_Disk15       60
0136  #define IDS_Disk16       61
0137  #define IDS_Disk17       62
0138  #define IDS_Disk18       63
0139  #define IDS_Disk19       64
0140  #define IDS_Disk20       65
0141  #define IDS_Disk21       66
0142  #define IDS_Disk22       67
0143  #define IDS_Disk23       68
0144  #define IDS_Disk24       69
0145  #define IDS_Disk25       70
0146  #define IDS_Disk26       71
0147  /*
0148  ------------------------------------------------------------
0149                    End of include file
0150  ------------------------------------------------------------
0151                                                          */
```

**13-16** The resource script file listing for the sample application.

```
0001  /*
0002  ------------------------------------------------------------
0003              Resource script file BOUNCING.RC
0004        Copyright 1992 Lee Adams.  All rights reserved.
0005   This file defines the menu resources, the accelerator key
0006   resources, and the string resources that will be used by the
0007   demonstration application at runtime.
0008  ------------------------------------------------------------
0009                                                          */
0010  #define zRCFILE
0011  #include <WINDOWS.H>
0012  #include "BOUNCING.H"
0013  /*
```

**13-16** Continued.

```
0014   -------------------------------------------------------------------
0015                           Script for menus
0016   -------------------------------------------------------------------
0017                                                                    */
0018   MENUS1 MENU
0019     BEGIN
0020     POPUP "&File"
0021       BEGIN
0022         MENUITEM  "&New", IDM_New, GRAYED
0023         MENUITEM  "&Open...", IDM_Open, GRAYED
0024         MENUITEM  "&Save", IDM_Save, GRAYED
0025         MENUITEM  "Save &As...", IDM_SaveAs, GRAYED
0026         MENUITEM SEPARATOR
0027         MENUITEM  "E&xit", IDM_Exit
0028       END
0029     POPUP "&Edit"
0030       BEGIN
0031         MENUITEM  "&Undo\tAlt+BkSp", IDM_Undo, GRAYED
0032         MENUITEM SEPARATOR
0033         MENUITEM  "Cu&t\tShift+Del", IDM_Cut, GRAYED
0034         MENUITEM  "&Copy\tCtrl+Ins", IDM_Copy, GRAYED
0035         MENUITEM  "&Paste\tShift+Ins", IDM_Paste, GRAYED
0036         MENUITEM  "&Delete\tDel", IDM_Delete, GRAYED
0037       END
0038     POPUP "&Animation"
0039       BEGIN
0040         MENUITEM "Run &Forward", IDM_RunForward
0041         MENUITEM "Run &Reverse", IDM_RunReverse
0042         MENUITEM "&Pause", IDM_StopAnimation
0043         MENUITEM SEPARATOR
0044         MENUITEM "&Initialize system", IDM_InitFrame
0045         MENUITEM "Cr&eate Frames", IDM_SaveAnimation
0046         MENUITEM SEPARATOR
0047         MENUITEM "&Load Animation", IDM_LoadAnimation
0048         MENUITEM SEPARATOR
0049         MENUITEM "&Clear", IDM_Clear
0050       END
0051     POPUP "&Timer"
0052       BEGIN
0053         MENUITEM "&18 fps", IDM_FPS182, CHECKED
0054         MENUITEM " &9 fps", IDM_FPS91
0055         MENUITEM " &6 fps", IDM_FPS61
0056         MENUITEM " &5 fps", IDM_FPS45
0057         MENUITEM " &4 fps", IDM_FPS36
0058         MENUITEM " &3 fps", IDM_FPS30
0059       END
0060     POPUP "&Help"
0061       BEGIN
0062         MENUITEM "&About", IDM_About
0063         MENUITEM "&License", IDM_License
0064         MENUITEM SEPARATOR
0065         MENUITEM "&Screen resolution", IDM_Display
0066         MENUITEM "Available &colors", IDM_Colors
0067         MENUITEM "Memory mode", IDM_Mode
0068         MENUITEM SEPARATOR
0069         MENUITEM "&Memory notes", IDM_Memory
0070         MENUITEM "&Timing notes", IDM_Timing
0071         MENUITEM SEPARATOR
0072         MENUITEM "&Help", IDM_GeneralHelp
0073       END
```

**13-16** Continued.

```
0074    END
0075    /*
0076    ----------------------------------------------------------------
0077                    Script for accelerator keys
0078    ----------------------------------------------------------------
0079                                                              */
0080    KEYS1 ACCELERATORS
0081      BEGIN
0082      VK_BACK, IDM_Undo, VIRTKEY, ALT
0083      VK_DELETE, IDM_Cut, VIRTKEY, SHIFT
0084      VK_INSERT, IDM_Copy, VIRTKEY, CONTROL
0085      VK_INSERT, IDM_Paste, VIRTKEY, SHIFT
0086      VK_DELETE, IDM_Delete,VIRTKEY
0087      END
0088    /*
0089    ----------------------------------------------------------------
0090                       Script for strings
0091    Programmer's Notes:  If you are typing this listing, set your
0092    margins to a line length of 255 characters so you can create
0093    lengthy strings without embedded carriage returns.  The line
0094    wraparounds in the following STRINGTABLE script are used for
0095    readability only in this printout.
0096    ----------------------------------------------------------------
0097                                                              */
0098    STRINGTABLE
0099      BEGIN
0100        IDS_Caption     "Motion Blur and Deformation"
0101        IDS_Warning     "Warning"
0102        IDS_NoMouse     "No mouse found.  Some features of this
                demonstration program may require a mouse."
0103        IDS_About       "About this program"
0104        IDS_AboutText   "This is a demo from Windcrest McGraw-Hill
                book 4114.  Copyright 1992 Lee Adams.  All rights reserved."
0105        IDS_License     "License Agreement"
0106        IDS_LicenseText "You can use this code as part of your own
                software product subject to the License Agreement and Limited
                Warranty in Windcrest McGraw-Hill book 4114 and on its
                companion disk."
0107        IDS_Help        "How to use this demo"
0108        IDS_HelpText    "The Animation menu manages the animation
                engine.  Select Initialize System then Create Frames to build
                frames and save to disk.  Select Load Animation then Run
                Forward to play animation.  See the book for advanced
                features."
0109        IDS_Completed   "Task completed OK"
0110        IDS_Error       "Runtime error"
0111        IDS_Memory      "Animation memory requirements"
0112        IDS_MemText     "The hidden frame for the animation is stored
                as a bitmap in global memory.  The demo will advise you if a
                memory shortage occurs.  To make more global memory available
                you can close other applications."
0113        IDS_Timing      "Animation timing"
0114        IDS_TimingText  "The Timer menu sets the animation display
                rate to 18.2, 9.1, 6.1, 4.5, 3.6, or 3 frames per second.
                Actual performance is limited by your computer's processor
                (25MHz or faster is recommended).  See the book for details."
0115        IDS_NotReady    "Animation not ready"
0116        IDS_Ready       "Animation ready"
0117        IDS_BuildBefore "Animation frames not ready for playback."
0118        IDS_Already     "The hidden frame has already been created."
```

```
0119    IDS_InsufMem1    "Insufficient global memory for frame bitmap."
0120    IDS_NoTimer      "Unable to create a timer.  Close other
        applications."
0121    IDS_NoReset      "Create hidden frame before attempting to
        reset timer."
0122    IDS_CannotReset  "Unable to reset the timer."
0123    IDS_Resolution   "Screen resolution"
0124    IDS_ResVGA       "Running in 640x480 mode."
0125    IDS_ResEGA       "Running in 640x350 mode."
0126    IDS_ResCGA       "Running in 640x200 mode."
0127    IDS_ResSVGA      "Running in 800x600 mode."
0128    IDS_Res8514      "Running in 1024x768 mode."
0129    IDS_ResHerc      "Running in 720x348 mode."
0130    IDS_ResCustom    "Running in custom mode."
0131    IDS_Color        "Available colors"
0132    IDS_Color16      "Running in 16-color mode."
0133    IDS_Color256     "Running in 256-color mode."
0134    IDS_Color2       "Running in 2-color mode."
0135    IDS_ColorCustom  "Running in a custom color mode."
0136    IDS_Machine      "Memory mode"
0137    IDS_Enhanced     "Running in enhanced mode.  Can allocate up to
        16 MB extended physical memory (XMS) if available.  Virtual
        memory up to 4 times physical memory (maximum 64 MB) is also
        available via automatic disk swapping of 4K pages."
0138    IDS_Standard     "Running in standard mode.  Can allocate up to
        16 MB extended physical memory (XMS) if available."
0139    IDS_Real         "Running in real mode.  Can allocate blocks of
        memory from the first 640K of RAM.  Can also allocate blocks
        from expanded memory (EMS) if available."
0140    IDS_NoFrame      "Hidden frame not yet created."
0141    IDS_AnimReady    "Animation ready"
0142    IDS_Unexpected   "Unexpected animation condition"
0143    IDS_Status       "Animation status"
0144    IDS_Disk1        "Animation files already saved to disk."
0145    IDS_Disk2        "Animation sequence successfully saved to
        disk."
0146    IDS_Disk3        "Unable to load next frame from disk.
        Animation halted."
0147    IDS_Disk4        "Animation sequence already loaded from disk."
0148    IDS_Disk5        "Previous load failed.  Cancelling this
        attempt."
0149    IDS_Disk6        "Not enough memory available.  Software will
        dynamically load each frame from disk during playback."
0150    IDS_Disk7        "Animation sequence successfully loaded from
        disk."
0151    IDS_Disk8        "Previous save failed.  Cancelling this
        attempt."
0152    IDS_Disk9        "No hidden-frame exists.  No frame saved to
        disk."
0153    IDS_Disk10       "Unable to retrieve bitmap data structure."
0154    IDS_Disk11       "Bit array is too long to save to disk in a
        single pass."
0155    IDS_Disk12       "Cannot create memory buffer for disk write."
0156    IDS_Disk13       "Unable to copy bits from bitmap to buffer."
0157    IDS_Disk14       "File already exists.  Overwrite existing
        file?"
0158    IDS_Disk15       "Unable to open the file for writing."
0159    IDS_Disk16       "Unable to write to the opened file."
0160    IDS_Disk17       "Unable to close the file after writing."
0161    IDS_Disk18       "No memory bitmap exists.  Unable to load from
        disk."
```

**13-16** Continued.

```
0162      IDS_Disk19      "Image file is larger than animation frame.
          No file loaded."
0163      IDS_Disk20      "Cannot create memory buffer for file read."
0164      IDS_Disk21      "Unable to open the file for reading.  Be sure
          you have saved an animation sequence to disk before attempting
          to load it."
0165      IDS_Disk22      "An error occurred while reading the file."
0166      IDS_Disk23      "The frame file was shorter than expected."
0167      IDS_Disk24      "Unable to close the file after reading."
0168      IDS_Disk25      "Unable to copy bits from buffer to bitmap."
0169      IDS_Disk26      "Unable to save all files.  Check if
          sufficient space available on disk."
0170   END
0171 /*
0172 --------------------------------------------------------------------
0173                      End of resource script file
0174 --------------------------------------------------------------------
0175                                                                   */
```

**13-17** The C source file listing for the sample application, bouncing.c. This demonstration program is ready to build using QuickC for Windows, Turbo C++ for Windows, Microsoft C and the SDK, Borland C++, Symantec Zortech C++, WATCOM C, and other compilers. See chapter 10 for the program listings for storage.h and storage.c which must be linked with this application. See FIG. 1-2 for sample command-lines to build the program. Guidelines for using your compiler are provided in the appropriate appendix at the back of the book.

```
0001 /*
0002 --------------------------------------------------------------------
0003      Demonstration of motion blur (temporal antialiasing) and
0004      deformation for Windows animation applications.
0005 --------------------------------------------------------------------
0006   Source file:  BOUNCING.C
0007   Release version:  1.00                  Programmer:  Lee Adams
0008   Type:  C source file for Windows application development.
0009   Compilers:  Microsoft C and SDK, Borland C++, Zortech C++,
0010     QuickC for Windows, Turbo C++ for Windows, WATCOM C.
0011   Memory model:  small.
0012   Dependencies:  BOUNCING.DEF module definition file, BOUNCING.H
0013                  include file, BOUNCING.RC resource script file,
0014                  and BOUNCING.C source file.
0015   Output and features:  Demonstrates interactive playback of
0016     disk-based hidden-page drawn frame animation.  A bouncing
0017     sphere is subjected to motion blur and impact deformation to
0018     improve the accuracy of the simulation.  These are techniques
0019     used by traditional film animators.
0020   Publication: Contains material from Windcrest/McGraw-Hill book
0021     4114 published by TAB BOOKS Division of McGraw-Hill Inc.
0022   License:  As purchaser of the book you are granted a royalty-
0023     free license to distribute executable files generated using
0024     this code provided you accept the conditions of the License
0025     Agreement and Limited Warranty described in the book and on
0026     the companion disk.  Government users:  This software and
0027     documentation are subject to restrictions set forth in The
0028     Rights in Technical Data and Computer Software clause at
0029     252.227-7013 and elsewhere.
0030 --------------------------------------------------------------------
0031      (c) Copyright 1992 Lee Adams.  All rights reserved.
0032          Lee Adams(tm) is a trademark of Lee Adams.
```

```
0033    ----------------------------------------------------------------
0034
0035    ----------------------------------------------------------------
0036                          Include files
0037    ----------------------------------------------------------------
0038                                                                  */
0039    #include <WINDOWS.H>
0040    #include <SYS\TYPES.H>
0041    #include <SYS\STAT.H>
0042    #include "BOUNCING.H"
0043    /*
0044    ----------------------------------------------------------------
0045             Static variables visible throughout this file
0046    ----------------------------------------------------------------
0047                                                                  */
0048    /* ----------------- window specifications ---------------- */
0049    #define zWINDOW_WIDTH 408
0050    #define zWINDOW_HEIGHT 346
0051    #define zFRAMEWIDE 400
0052    #define zFRAMEHIGH 300
0053    int WindowX, WindowY;
0054
0055    /* ------------------ instance operations ------------------ */
0056    HANDLE hInst;
0057    HWND MainhWnd;
0058    HANDLE hAccel;
0059    HMENU hMenu;
0060    PAINTSTRUCT ps;
0061    int MessageRet;
0062
0063    /* -------------------- mouse and cursor -------------------- */
0064    HCURSOR hPrevCursor;
0065    HCURSOR hHourGlass;
0066    int MousePresent;
0067
0068    /* ------------------- runtime conditions ------------------- */
0069    int DisplayWidth, DisplayHeight;
0070    int DisplayBits;
0071    int DisplayPlanes;
0072    DWORD MemoryMode;
0073
0074    /* ----------------- message box operations ---------------- */
0075    char lpCaption[51];
0076    int Max= 50;
0077    char lpMessage[250];
0078    int MaxText= 249;
0079
0080    /* ---------------- persistent image operations ------------- */
0081    #define zBLANK 0
0082    #define zANIMATING  1
0083    int PaintImage= zBLANK;
0084
0085    /* -------------------- timer operations -------------------- */
0086    #define zTIMER_PAUSE 3
0087    int TimerCounter= zTIMER_PAUSE;
0088    BOOL TimerExists= FALSE;
0089    WORD TimerID1;
0090
0091    /* --------------------- font operations -------------------- */
0092    HFONT hFont, hPrevFont;          /* handles to new, previous font */
0093    HDC hFontDC;                          /* display-context for font */
```

**13-17** Continued.

```
0094
0095   /* ----------------- hidden frame operations ----------------- */
0096   HDC hFrameDC;
0097   HBITMAP hFrame;
0098   HBITMAP hPrevFrame;
0099   BOOL FrameReady= FALSE;
0100
0101   /* --------------------- animation engine -------------------- */
0102   BOOL Pause= TRUE;
0103   WORD wFrameRate= 55;
0104   WORD wPrevRate= 55;
0105   #define zFORWARD 1
0106   #define zREVERSE 0
0107   int FrameDirection= zFORWARD;
0108   BOOL Redisplay= FALSE;
0109   int FrameNum= 0;
0110   #define zFIRSTFRAME 1
0111   #define zFINALFRAME 13
0112   BOOL AnimationReady= FALSE;
0113
0114   /* ----------------- disk save/load operations --------------- */
0115   int RetVal;                                    /* return value */
0116   BOOL bFrameSaved= FALSE;            /* frame saved to disk? */
0117   BOOL bFrameLoaded= FALSE;          /* frame loaded from disk? */
0118   BOOL bAnimationSaved= FALSE;        /* animation saved to disk? */
0119   BOOL bAnimationLoaded= FALSE;     /* animation loaded from disk? */
0120   BOOL bPrevSaveAttempt= FALSE;     /* previous save attempt made? */
0121   BOOL bPrevLoadAttempt= FALSE;     /* previous load attempt made? */
0122   HDC hFDC;                   /* memory-display context for playback */
0123   HBITMAP hPrevF,hF1,hF2,hF3,hF4,hF5,   /* bitmaps for playback... */
0124     hF6,hF7,hF8,hF9,hF10,hF11,hF12,hF13;
0125   BOOL bUseDisk= FALSE;                /* load each frame as needed? */
0126   BOOL bAnimationHalted= FALSE;    /* disk error during animation? */
0127   /*
0128   --------------------------------------------------------------
0129                  Entry point for the application
0130   --------------------------------------------------------------
0131                                                                 */
0132   int PASCAL WinMain(HANDLE hInstance, HANDLE hPrevInstance,
0133                    LPSTR lpCmdLine, int nCmdShow)
0134   {
0135     MSG msg;
0136     HWND hWndPrev;
0137     HWND hDesktopWnd;
0138     HDC hDCcaps;
0139
0140   /* ------------ ensure only one instance is running ------------ */
0141   hWndPrev = FindWindow("DEMOCLASS", NULL);
0142   if (hWndPrev != NULL)
0143     {
0144     BringWindowToTop(hWndPrev);
0145     return FALSE;
0146     }
0147
0148   /* -------- determine capabilities of screen display --------- */
0149   hDesktopWnd= GetDesktopWindow();
0150   hDCcaps= GetDC(hDesktopWnd);
0151   DisplayWidth= GetDeviceCaps(hDCcaps,HORZRES);
0152   DisplayHeight= GetDeviceCaps(hDCcaps,VERTRES);
0153   DisplayBits= GetDeviceCaps(hDCcaps,BITSPIXEL);
0154   DisplayPlanes= GetDeviceCaps(hDCcaps,PLANES);
```

```
0155    ReleaseDC(hDesktopWnd,hDCcaps);
0156
0157    /* ------- calculate screen position to center the window ------ */
0158    WindowX= (DisplayWidth - zWINDOW_WIDTH) / 2;
0159    WindowY= (DisplayHeight - zWINDOW_HEIGHT) /2;
0160    if (WindowX < 0) WindowX= 0;
0161    if (WindowY < 0) WindowY= 0;
0162
0163    /* ---- determine memory mode (enhanced, standard, or real) ---- */
0164    MemoryMode= GetWinFlags();
0165
0166    /* --------------- create and show the window ---------------- */
0167    hInst = hInstance;
0168    if (!zInitClass(hInstance)) return FALSE;
0169    MainWnd = zInitMainWindow(hInstance);
0170    if (!MainhWnd) return FALSE;
0171    ShowWindow(MainhWnd, nCmdShow);
0172    UpdateWindow(MainhWnd);
0173    hAccel= LoadAccelerators(hInstance,"KEYS1");
0174    hFontDC= GetDC(MainhWnd);
0175    hFont= GetStockObject(SYSTEM_FONT);
0176    hPrevFont= SelectObject(hFontDC,hFont);
0177    SetTextColor(hFontDC,RGB(191,191,191));
0178    TextOut(hFontDC,10,280,"- Copyright 1992 Lee Adams.",27);
0179    SetTextColor(hFontDC,RGB(0,0,0));
0180    SelectObject(hFontDC,hPrevFont);
0181    ReleaseDC(MainhWnd,hFontDC);
0182
0183    /* --------------------- check for mouse -------------------- */
0184    MousePresent = GetSystemMetrics(SM_MOUSEPRESENT);
0185    if (!MousePresent)
0186      {
0187      LoadString(hInst,IDS_Warning,lpCaption,Max);
0188      LoadString(hInst,IDS_NoMouse,lpMessage,MaxText);
0189      MessageBox(GetFocus(),lpMessage,lpCaption,MB_OK);
0190      }
0191
0192    /* ---------- begin retrieving messages for the window --------- */
0193    while (GetMessage(&msg,0,0,0))
0194      {
0195      if(TranslateAccelerator(MainhWnd, hAccel, &msg))
0196        continue;
0197      TranslateMessage(&msg);
0198      DispatchMessage(&msg);
0199      }
0200    return(msg.wParam);
0201    }
0202    /*
0203    -------------------------------------------------------------------
0204                    Switcher for incoming messages
0205    -------------------------------------------------------------------
0206                                                                     */
0207    LONG FAR PASCAL zMessageHandler(HWND hWnd, unsigned message,
0208                            WORD wParam, LONG lParam)
0209    {
0210      HDC hDCpaint;
0211
0212    switch (message)
0213      {
0214
0215      case WM_TIMER:
```

```
0216      TimerCounter--;
0217      if (TimerCounter > 0) break;
0218      TimerCounter++;
0219      zShowNextFrame(hWnd);
0220      break;
0221
0222   case WM_COMMAND:
0223     switch(wParam)
0224        {
0225        case IDM_New:     break;
0226        case IDM_Open:    break;
0227        case IDM_Save:    break;
0228        case IDM_SaveAs:  break;
0229        case IDM_Exit:    PostQuitMessage(0); break;
0230
0231        case IDM_Undo:    break;
0232        case IDM_Cut:     break;
0233        case IDM_Copy:    break;
0234        case IDM_Paste:   break;
0235        case IDM_Delete:  break;
0236
0237        case IDM_RunForward:
0238           if (AnimationReady==FALSE)
0239              {
0240              MessageBeep(0);
0241              LoadString(hInst,IDS_NotReady,lpCaption,Max);
0242              LoadString(hInst,IDS_BuildBefore,lpMessage,MaxText);
0243              TimerCounter= zTIMER_PAUSE;
0244              MessageBox(GetFocus(),lpMessage,lpCaption,MB_OK);
0245              break;
0246              }
0247           Pause= FALSE;
0248           PaintImage= zANIMATING;
0249           FrameDirection= zFORWARD;
0250           zShowNextFrame(hWnd);
0251           break;
0252        case IDM_RunReverse:
0253           if (AnimationReady==FALSE)
0254              {
0255              MessageBeep(0);
0256              LoadString(hInst,IDS_NotReady,lpCaption,Max);
0257              LoadString(hInst,IDS_BuildBefore,lpMessage,MaxText);
0258              TimerCounter= zTIMER_PAUSE;
0259              MessageBox(GetFocus(),lpMessage,lpCaption,MB_OK);
0260              break;
0261              }
0262           Pause= FALSE;
0263           PaintImage= zANIMATING;
0264           FrameDirection= zREVERSE;
0265           zShowNextFrame(hWnd);
0266           break;
0267        case IDM_StopAnimation:
0268           if (AnimationReady==FALSE)
0269              {
0270              MessageBeep(0);
0271              LoadString(hInst,IDS_NotReady,lpCaption,Max);
0272              LoadString(hInst,IDS_BuildBefore,lpMessage,MaxText);
0273              TimerCounter= zTIMER_PAUSE;
0274              MessageBox(GetFocus(),lpMessage,lpCaption,MB_OK);
0275              break;
0276              }
```

```
0277                Pause= TRUE;
0278                zShowNextFrame(hWnd);
0279                break;
0280        case IDM_InitFrame: zInitFrame(hWnd); break;
0281        case IDM_SaveAnimation:
0282            SetCapture(hWnd); hPrevCursor= SetCursor(hHourGlass);
0283            zSaveAnimation(hWnd);
0284            SetCursor(hPrevCursor); ReleaseCapture();
0285            if (bAnimationSaved==FALSE)
0286              {
0287              MessageBeep(0);
0288              LoadString(hInst,IDS_NotReady,lpCaption,Max);
0289              LoadString(hInst,IDS_Disk26,lpMessage,MaxText);
0290              TimerCounter= zTIMER_PAUSE;
0291              MessageBox(GetFocus(),lpMessage,lpCaption,MB_OK);
0292              }
0293            break;
0294        case IDM_LoadAnimation:
0295            SetCapture(hWnd); hPrevCursor= SetCursor(hHourGlass);
0296            zLoadAnimation(hWnd);
0297            SetCursor(hPrevCursor); ReleaseCapture();
0298            break;
0299        case IDM_Clear:  if (Pause==TRUE)
0300                           {
0301                           zClear(hWnd);
0302                           PaintImage= zBLANK;
0303.                          }
0304                         break;
0305
0306        case IDM_FPS182: wPrevRate= wFrameRate;
0307                         wFrameRate= (WORD)55;
0308                         zSetFrameRate(hWnd, wFrameRate); break;
0309        case IDM_FPS91:  wPrevRate= wFrameRate;
0310                         wFrameRate= (WORD)110;
0311                         zSetFrameRate(hWnd, wFrameRate); break;
0312        case IDM_FPS61:  wPrevRate= wFrameRate;
0313                         wFrameRate= (WORD)165;
0314                         zSetFrameRate(hWnd, wFrameRate); break;
0315        case IDM_FPS45:  wPrevRate= wFrameRate;
0316                         wFrameRate= (WORD) 220;
0317                         zSetFrameRate(hWnd, wFrameRate); break;
0318        case IDM_FPS36:  wPrevRate= wFrameRate;
0319                         wFrameRate= (WORD) 275;
0320                         zSetFrameRate(hWnd, wFrameRate); break;
0321        case IDM_FPS30:  wPrevRate= wFrameRate;
0322                         wFrameRate= (WORD) 330;
0323                         zSetFrameRate(hWnd, wFrameRate); break;
0324
0325        case IDM_About:
0326          LoadString(hInst,IDS_About,lpCaption,Max);
0327          LoadString(hInst,IDS_AboutText,lpMessage,MaxText);
0328          TimerCounter= zTIMER_PAUSE;
0329          MessageBox(GetFocus(),lpMessage,lpCaption,MB_OK);
0330          break;
0331        case IDM_License:
0332          LoadString(hInst,IDS_License,lpCaption,Max);
0333          LoadString(hInst,IDS_LicenseText,lpMessage,MaxText);
0334          TimerCounter= zTIMER_PAUSE;
0335          MessageBox(GetFocus(),lpMessage,lpCaption,MB_OK);
0336          break;
0337
```

```
0338        case IDM_Display:
0339          if (DisplayWidth==640)
0340            {
0341            if (DisplayHeight==480)
0342              {
0343              LoadString(hInst,IDS_Resolution,lpCaption,Max);
0344              LoadString(hInst,IDS_ResVGA,lpMessage,MaxText);
0345              TimerCounter= zTIMER_PAUSE;
0346              MessageBox(GetFocus(),lpMessage,lpCaption,MB_OK);
0347              }
0348            if (DisplayHeight==350)
0349              {
0350              LoadString(hInst,IDS_Resolution,lpCaption,Max);
0351              LoadString(hInst,IDS_ResEGA,lpMessage,MaxText);
0352              TimerCounter= zTIMER_PAUSE;
0353              MessageBox(GetFocus(),lpMessage,lpCaption,MB_OK);
0354              }
0355            if (DisplayHeight==200)
0356              {
0357              LoadString(hInst,IDS_Resolution,lpCaption,Max);
0358              LoadString(hInst,IDS_ResCGA,lpMessage,MaxText);
0359              TimerCounter= zTIMER_PAUSE;
0360              MessageBox(GetFocus(),lpMessage,lpCaption,MB_OK);
0361              }
0362            break;
0363            }
0364          if (DisplayWidth==800)
0365            {
0366            LoadString(hInst,IDS_Resolution,lpCaption,Max);
0367            LoadString(hInst,IDS_ResSVGA,lpMessage,MaxText);
0368            TimerCounter= zTIMER_PAUSE;
0369            MessageBox(GetFocus(),lpMessage,lpCaption,MB_OK);
0370            break;
0371            }
0372          if (DisplayWidth==1024)
0373            {
0374            LoadString(hInst,IDS_Resolution,lpCaption,Max);
0375            LoadString(hInst,IDS_Res8514,lpMessage,MaxText);
0376            TimerCounter= zTIMER_PAUSE;
0377            MessageBox(GetFocus(),lpMessage,lpCaption,MB_OK);
0378            break;
0379            }
0380          if (DisplayWidth==720)
0381            {
0382            LoadString(hInst,IDS_Resolution,lpCaption,Max);
0383            LoadString(hInst,IDS_ResHerc,lpMessage,MaxText);
0384            TimerCounter= zTIMER_PAUSE;
0385            MessageBox(GetFocus(),lpMessage,lpCaption,MB_OK);
0386            break;
0387            }
0388          LoadString(hInst,IDS_Resolution,lpCaption,Max);
0389          LoadString(hInst,IDS_ResCustom,lpMessage,MaxText);
0390          TimerCounter= zTIMER_PAUSE;
0391          MessageBox(GetFocus(),lpMessage,lpCaption,MB_OK);
0392          break;
0393
0394        case IDM_Colors:
0395          if (DisplayBits==1)
0396            {
0397            if (DisplayPlanes==4)
0398              {
```

```
0399              LoadString(hInst,IDS_Color,lpCaption,Max);
0400              LoadString(hInst,IDS_Color16,lpMessage,MaxText);
0401              TimerCounter= zTIMER_PAUSE;
0402              MessageBox(GetFocus(),lpMessage,lpCaption,MB_OK);
0403              break;
0404              }
0405          if (DisplayPlanes==1)
0406              {
0407              LoadString(hInst,IDS_Color,lpCaption,Max);
0408              LoadString(hInst,IDS_Color2,lpMessage,MaxText);
0409              TimerCounter= zTIMER_PAUSE;
0410              MessageBox(GetFocus(),lpMessage,lpCaption,MB_OK);
0411              break;
0412              }
0413          }
0414          if (DisplayBits==8)
0415          {
0416          LoadString(hInst,IDS_Color,lpCaption,Max);
0417          LoadString(hInst,IDS_Color256,lpMessage,MaxText);
0418          TimerCounter= zTIMER_PAUSE;
0419          MessageBox(GetFocus(),lpMessage,lpCaption,MB_OK);
0420          break;
0421          }
0422      LoadString(hInst,IDS_Color,lpCaption,Max);
0423      LoadString(hInst,IDS_ColorCustom,lpMessage,MaxText);
0424      TimerCounter= zTIMER_PAUSE;
0425      MessageBox(GetFocus(),lpMessage,lpCaption,MB_OK);
0426      break;
0427
0428      case IDM_Mode:
0429          if (MemoryMode & WF_ENHANCED)
0430              {
0431              LoadString(hInst,IDS_Machine,lpCaption,Max);
0432              LoadString(hInst,IDS_Enhanced,lpMessage,MaxText);
0433              TimerCounter= zTIMER_PAUSE;
0434              MessageBox(GetFocus(),lpMessage,lpCaption,MB_OK);
0435              break;
0436              }
0437          if (MemoryMode & WF_STANDARD)
0438              {
0439              LoadString(hInst,IDS_Machine,lpCaption,Max);
0440              LoadString(hInst,IDS_Standard,lpMessage,MaxText);
0441              TimerCounter= zTIMER_PAUSE;
0442              MessageBox(GetFocus(),lpMessage,lpCaption,MB_OK);
0443              break;
0444              }
0445      LoadString(hInst,IDS_Machine,lpCaption,Max);
0446      LoadString(hInst,IDS_Real,lpMessage,MaxText);
0447      TimerCounter= zTIMER_PAUSE;
0448      MessageBox(GetFocus(),lpMessage,lpCaption,MB_OK);
0449      break;
0450
0451      case IDM_Memory:
0452          LoadString(hInst,IDS_Memory,lpCaption,Max);
0453          LoadString(hInst,IDS_MemText,lpMessage,MaxText);
0454          TimerCounter= zTIMER_PAUSE;
0455          MessageBox(GetFocus(),lpMessage,lpCaption,MB_OK);
0456          break;
0457      case IDM_Timing:
0458          LoadString(hInst,IDS_Timing,lpCaption,Max);
0459          LoadString(hInst,IDS_TimingText,lpMessage,MaxText);
```

```
0460            TimerCounter= zTIMER_PAUSE;
0461            MessageBox(GetFocus(),lpMessage,lpCaption,MB_OK);
0462            break;
0463          case IDM_GeneralHelp:
0464            LoadString(hInst,IDS_Help,lpCaption,Max);
0465            LoadString(hInst,IDS_HelpText,lpMessage,MaxText);
0466            TimerCounter= zTIMER_PAUSE;
0467            MessageBox(GetFocus(),lpMessage,lpCaption,MB_OK);
0468            break;
0469          default:
0470            return(DefWindowProc(hWnd, message, wParam, lParam));
0471        }
0472      break;
0473
0474    case WM_INITMENUPOPUP:
0475      TimerCounter= zTIMER_PAUSE;
0476      if (lParam == 3)
0477        hMenu= wParam;
0478      break;
0479
0480    case WM_PAINT:
0481      hDCpaint= BeginPaint(hWnd,&ps);
0482      EndPaint(hWnd, &ps);
0483      if (PaintImage==zBLANK) break;
0484      if (Pause==TRUE)
0485        {
0486        Redisplay= TRUE;
0487        zShowNextFrame(hWnd);
0488        Redisplay= FALSE;
0489        break;
0490        }
0491      zShowNextFrame(hWnd);
0492      break;
0493
0494    case WM_KEYDOWN:
0495      switch (wParam)
0496        {
0497        case VK_LEFT:    if (Pause==TRUE)
0498                           {
0499                           if (FrameDirection==zFORWARD)
0500                             {
0501                             FrameDirection= zREVERSE;
0502                             }
0503                           Pause= FALSE;
0504                           zShowNextFrame(hWnd);
0505                           Pause= TRUE;
0506                           PaintImage= zANIMATING;
0507                           }
0508                         break;
0509        case VK_RIGHT:   if (Pause==TRUE)
0510                           {
0511                           if (FrameDirection==zREVERSE)
0512                             {
0513                             FrameDirection= zFORWARD;
0514                             }
0515                           Pause= FALSE;
0516                           zShowNextFrame(hWnd);
0517                           Pause= TRUE;
0518                           PaintImage= zANIMATING;
0519                           }
0520                         break;
```

```
0521         default:
0522                 return(DefWindowProc(hWnd, message, wParam, lParam));
0523         }
0524     break;
0525
0526    case WM_DESTROY:
0527      if (FrameReady==TRUE)
0528        {
0529        SelectObject(hFrameDC,hPrevFrame);
0530        DeleteObject(hFrame);
0531        DeleteDC(hFrameDC);
0532        KillTimer(hWnd,1);
0533        }
0534      if (bAnimationLoaded==TRUE)
0535        {
0536        SelectObject(hFDC,hPrevF);
0537        DeleteObject(hF1); DeleteObject(hF2); DeleteObject(hF3);
0538        DeleteObject(hF4); DeleteObject(hF5); DeleteObject(hF6);
0539        DeleteObject(hF7); DeleteObject(hF8); DeleteObject(hF9);
0540        DeleteObject(hF10); DeleteObject(hF11); DeleteObject(hF12);
0541        DeleteObject(hF13); DeleteDC(hFDC);
0542        }
0543      PostQuitMessage(0);
0544      break;
0545
0546    case WM_SYSCOMMAND:
0547      if ((wParam & 0xfff0)== SC_SIZE)
0548        {
0549        MessageBeep(0); break;
0550        }
0551      if ((wParam & 0xfff0)== SC_MINIMIZE)
0552        {
0553        MessageBeep(0); break;
0554        }
0555      if ((wParam & 0xfff0)== SC_MAXIMIZE)
0556        {
0557        MessageBeep(0); break;
0558        }
0559
0560    default:
0561      return(DefWindowProc(hWnd, message, wParam, lParam));
0562    }
0563 return FALSE;
0564 }
0565 /*
0566 -------------------------------------------------------------------
0567              Initialize the attributes of the window class
0568 -------------------------------------------------------------------
0569                                                                 */
0570 BOOL zInitClass(HANDLE hInstance)
0571 {
0572    WNDCLASS WndClass;
0573 WndClass.style= 0;
0574 WndClass.lpfnWndProc= zMessageHandler;
0575 WndClass.cbClsExtra= 0;
0576 WndClass.cbWndExtra= 0;
0577 WndClass.hInstance= hInstance;
0578 WndClass.hIcon= LoadIcon(NULL,IDI_EXCLAMATION);
0579 WndClass.hCursor= LoadCursor(NULL,IDC_ARROW);
0580 WndClass.hbrBackground= CreateSolidBrush(RGB(255,255,255));
0581 WndClass.lpszMenuName= "MENUS1";
```

```
0582   WndClass.lpszClassName= "DEMOCLASS";
0583   return RegisterClass(&WndClass);
0584   }
0585   /*
0586   -----------------------------------------------------------------
0587                        Create the main window
0588   -----------------------------------------------------------------
0589                                                                   */
0590   HWND zInitMainWindow(HANDLE hInstance)
0591   {
0592     HWND hWnd;
0593   LoadString(hInstance,IDS_Caption,lpCaption,Max);
0594   hHourGlass= LoadCursor(NULL,IDC_WAIT);
0595   hWnd = CreateWindow("DEMOCLASS",lpCaption,
0596     WS_OVERLAPPED | WS_THICKFRAME | WS_MINIMIZEBOX |
0597       WS_MAXIMIZEBOX | WS_CLIPCHILDREN,
0598     WindowX,WindowY,zWINDOW_WIDTH,zWINDOW_HEIGHT,0,0,
0599     hInstance, (LPSTR)NULL);
0600   return hWnd;
0601   }
0602   /*
0603   -----------------------------------------------------------------
0604                        GRAPHICS SYSTEM Functions
0605   -----------------------------------------------------------------
0606   -----------------------------------------------------------------
0607                        Create the hidden frame.
0608   -----------------------------------------------------------------
0609                                                                   */
0610   static void zInitFrame(HWND hWnd)
0611   {
0612     HDC hDisplayDC;
0613
0614   if (FrameReady==TRUE)
0615     {
0616     MessageBeep(0);
0617     LoadString(hInst,IDS_Ready,lpCaption,Max);
0618     LoadString(hInst,IDS_Already,lpMessage,MaxText);
0619     TimerCounter= zTIMER_PAUSE;
0620     MessageBox(GetFocus(),lpMessage,lpCaption,MB_OK);
0621     return;
0622     }
0623   GlobalCompact((DWORD)-1L);
0624   hDisplayDC= GetDC(hWnd);
0625   hFrameDC= CreateCompatibleDC(hDisplayDC);
0626   hFrame= CreateCompatibleBitmap(hDisplayDC,zFRAMEWIDE,zFRAMEHIGH);
0627   if (hFrame==NULL)
0628     {
0629     LoadString(hInst,IDS_NotReady,lpCaption,Max);
0630     LoadString(hInst,IDS_InsufMem1,lpMessage,MaxText);
0631     MessageBox(GetFocus(),lpMessage,lpCaption,MB_OK);
0632     DeleteDC(hFrameDC);
0633     TimerExists= FALSE; FrameReady= FALSE; AnimationReady= FALSE;
0634     return;
0635     }
0636   hPrevFrame= SelectObject(hFrameDC,hFrame);
0637   zClear(hWnd);
0638   BitBlt(hFrameDC,0,0,zFRAMEWIDE,zFRAMEHIGH,hDisplayDC,0,0,SRCCOPY);
0639   ReleaseDC(hWnd,hDisplayDC);
0640
0641   TimerID1= SetTimer(hWnd,1,wFrameRate,(FARPROC) NULL);
0642   if (TimerID1 == 0)
```

```
0643      {
0644      LoadString(hInst,IDS_NotReady,lpCaption,Max);
0645      LoadString(hInst,IDS_NoTimer,lpMessage,MaxText);
0646      MessageBox(GetFocus(),lpMessage,lpCaption,MB_OK);
0647      SelectObject(hFrameDC,hPrevFrame);
0648      DeleteObject(hFrame);
0649      DeleteDC(hFrameDC);
0650      TimerExists= FALSE;
0651      return;
0652      }
0653   TimerExists= TRUE;
0654   FrameReady= TRUE;
0655   FrameNum= 1;
0656   return;
0657   }
0658   /*
0659   -------------------------------------------------------------------
0660                      Clear the hidden frame.
0661   -------------------------------------------------------------------
0662                                                                   */
0663   static void zClearHiddenFrame(void)
0664   {
0665   PatBlt(hFrameDC,0,0,zFRAMEWIDE,zFRAMEHIGH,WHITENESS);
0666   return;
0667   }
0668   /*
0669   -------------------------------------------------------------------
0670           Copy the hidden frame to the display window.
0671   -------------------------------------------------------------------
0672                                                                   */
0673   static void zCopyToDisplay(HWND hWnd)
0674   {
0675      HDC hDC;
0676   hDC= GetDC(hWnd);
0677   BitBlt(hDC,0,0,zFRAMEWIDE,zFRAMEHIGH,hFrameDC,0,0,SRCCOPY);
0678   ReleaseDC(hWnd,hDC);
0679   return;
0680   }
0681   /*
0682   -------------------------------------------------------------------
0683                      Blank the display window.
0684   -------------------------------------------------------------------
0685                                                                   */
0686   static void zClear(HWND hWnd)
0687   {
0688      HDC hDC;
0689   hDC= GetDC(hWnd);
0690   PatBlt(hDC,0,0,zFRAMEWIDE,zFRAMEHIGH,WHITENESS);
0691   ReleaseDC(hWnd,hDC);
0692   return;
0693   }
0694   /*
0695   -------------------------------------------------------------------
0696                      AUTHORING SYSTEM Functions
0697   -------------------------------------------------------------------
0698   -------------------------------------------------------------------
0699                 Create 13 frames and save to disk.
0700   -------------------------------------------------------------------
0701                                                                   */
0702   static void zSaveAnimation(HWND hWnd)
0703   {
```

```
0704   if (FrameReady==FALSE)          /* if no hidden-frame available... */
0705   {
0706   MessageBeep(0);
0707   LoadString(hInst,IDS_NotReady,lpCaption,Max);
0708   LoadString(hInst,IDS_NoFrame,lpMessage,MaxText);
0709   MessageBox(GetFocus(),lpMessage,lpCaption,MB_OK);
0710   return;
0711   }
0712
0713   if (bAnimationSaved==TRUE) /* if frames already saved to disk... */
0714   {
0715   MessageBeep(0);
0716   LoadString(hInst,IDS_Unexpected,lpCaption,Max);
0717   LoadString(hInst,IDS_Disk1,lpMessage,MaxText);
0718   TimerCounter= zTIMER_PAUSE;
0719   MessageBox(GetFocus(),lpMessage,lpCaption,MB_OK);
0720   return;
0721   }
0722
0723   if (bPrevSaveAttempt==TRUE)          /* if previous attempt failed... */
0724   {
0725   MessageBeep(0);
0726   LoadString(hInst,IDS_Unexpected,lpCaption,Max);
0727   LoadString(hInst,IDS_Disk8,lpMessage,MaxText);
0728   TimerCounter= zTIMER_PAUSE;
0729   MessageBox(GetFocus(),lpMessage,lpCaption,MB_OK);
0730   return;
0731   }
0732   bPrevSaveAttempt= TRUE;
0733
0734   bFrameSaved= zBuildFrame(1,hWnd,(LPSTR)"BOUNCE1.BIT");
0735   if (bFrameSaved==FALSE) return;
0736   bFrameSaved= zBuildFrame(2,hWnd,(LPSTR)"BOUNCE2.BIT");
0737   if (bFrameSaved==FALSE) return;
0738   bFrameSaved= zBuildFrame(3,hWnd,(LPSTR)"BOUNCE3.BIT");
0739   if (bFrameSaved==FALSE) return;
0740   bFrameSaved= zBuildFrame(4,hWnd,(LPSTR)"BOUNCE4.BIT");
0741   if (bFrameSaved==FALSE) return;
0742   bFrameSaved= zBuildFrame(5,hWnd,(LPSTR)"BOUNCE5.BIT");
0743   if (bFrameSaved==FALSE) return;
0744   bFrameSaved= zBuildFrame(6,hWnd,(LPSTR)"BOUNCE6.BIT");
0745   if (bFrameSaved==FALSE) return;
0746   bFrameSaved= zBuildFrame(7,hWnd,(LPSTR)"BOUNCE7.BIT");
0747   if (bFrameSaved==FALSE) return;
0748   bFrameSaved= zBuildFrame(8,hWnd,(LPSTR)"BOUNCE8.BIT");
0749   if (bFrameSaved==FALSE) return;
0750   bFrameSaved= zBuildFrame(9,hWnd,(LPSTR)"BOUNCE9.BIT");
0751   if (bFrameSaved==FALSE) return;
0752   bFrameSaved= zBuildFrame(10,hWnd,(LPSTR)"BOUNCE10.BIT");
0753   if (bFrameSaved==FALSE) return;
0754   bFrameSaved= zBuildFrame(11,hWnd,(LPSTR)"BOUNCE11.BIT");
0755   if (bFrameSaved==FALSE) return;
0756   bFrameSaved= zBuildFrame(12,hWnd,(LPSTR)"BOUNCE12.BIT");
0757   if (bFrameSaved==FALSE) return;
0758   bFrameSaved= zBuildFrame(13,hWnd,(LPSTR)"BOUNCE13.BIT");
0759   if (bFrameSaved==FALSE) return;
0760
0761   bAnimationSaved= TRUE;
0762   bPrevLoadAttempt= FALSE;
0763   zClear(hWnd);
0764   MessageBeep(0);
```

```
0765   LoadString(hInst,IDS_Status,lpCaption,Max);
0766   LoadString(hInst,IDS_Disk2,lpMessage,MaxText);
0767   MessageBox(GetFocus(),lpMessage,lpCaption,MB_OK);
0768   return;
0769   }
0770   /*
0771   -----------------------------------------------------------------
0772                   Build one frame and save to disk.
0773   -----------------------------------------------------------------
0774                                                                  */
0775   static BOOL zBuildFrame(int Number, HWND hWnd,
0776                           LPSTR lpFileName)
0777   {                      /* this function is called by zSaveAnimation() */
0778     BOOL bDiskResult;
0779     HFONT Font;                          /* handle to logical font */
0780     HFONT PrevFont;                      /* handle to default font */
0781     DWORD PrevFontColor;          /* remembers default font color */
0782     DWORD PrevBkColor;      /* remembers default background color */
0783     int X1,Y1;                      /* upper-left coord for ellipse */
0784     int Wide,High;                 /* width and depth of ellipse */
0785     HBRUSH BallBrush, PrevBrush;                     /* brushes */
0786     HPEN BallPen, LinePen, PrevPen;                     /* pens */
0787
0788   /* -------------- draw the background and captions ------------- */
0789   zClearHiddenFrame();                       /* clear hidden frame */
0790   zDrawBg(hFrameDC);            /* draw background on hidden frame */
0791   PrevFontColor=                              /* set font color */
0792             SetTextColor(hFrameDC,RGB(255,255,255));
0793   PrevBkColor=                      /* set font background color */
0794           SetBkColor(hFrameDC,RGB(0,0,0));
0795   SetBkMode(hFrameDC,TRANSPARENT);           /* use superimposition */
0796
0797   Font=                 /* set the font size and characteristics... */
0798        CreateFont(24, 0, 0, 0, FW_BOLD, FALSE, FALSE, FALSE,
0799        ANSI_CHARSET, OUT_DEFAULT_PRECIS, CLIP_DEFAULT_PRECIS,
0800        DRAFT_QUALITY, VARIABLE_PITCH | FF_SWISS, "Helv");
0801   PrevFont= SelectObject(hFrameDC,Font);       /* activate the font */
0802   TextOut(hFrameDC,10,30,"Advanced Animation Techniques:",30);
0803   Font= CreateFont(48, 0, 0, 0, FW_BOLD, FALSE, FALSE, FALSE,
0804        ANSI_CHARSET, OUT_DEFAULT_PRECIS, CLIP_DEFAULT_PRECIS,
0805        DRAFT_QUALITY, VARIABLE_PITCH | FF_SWISS, "Helv");
0806   SelectObject(hFrameDC,Font);
0807   TextOut(hFrameDC,8,48,"Motion blur",11);
0808
0809   SelectObject(hFrameDC,PrevFont);    /* activate the default font */
0810   TextOut(hFrameDC,10,120,"Round shape and decreased distance",34);
0811   TextOut(hFrameDC,10,136,"between cels implies slower speed.",34);
0812   TextOut(hFrameDC,10,160,"Increased distance between each cel",35);
0813   TextOut(hFrameDC,10,176,"implies greater speed when animated.",36);
0814   TextOut(hFrameDC,10,200,"Stretch for motion blur",23);
0815   TextOut(hFrameDC,10,216,"and temporal antialiasing.",26);
0816   TextOut(hFrameDC,10,240,"Deformation of sphere",21);
0817   TextOut(hFrameDC,10,256,"at moment of impact.",20);
0818
0819   SetBkMode(hFrameDC,OPAQUE);               /* restore overwrite mode */
0820   SetBkColor(hFrameDC,PrevBkColor);    /* restore default bg color */
0821   SetTextColor(hFrameDC,PrevFontColor);/* restore default font clr */
0822   LinePen= CreatePen(PS_SOLID,1,RGB(255,255,255));   /* line color */
0823   PrevPen= SelectObject(hFrameDC,LinePen);         /* activate pen */
0824   MoveTo(hFrameDC,258,128); LineTo(hFrameDC,320,90);
0825   MoveTo(hFrameDC,252,167); LineTo(hFrameDC,320,160);
```

```
0826  MoveTo(hFrameDC,182,224); LineTo(hFrameDC,320,210);
0827  MoveTo(hFrameDC,148,264); LineTo(hFrameDC,320,290);
0828
0829  /* ----------------- draw the appropriate cel ---------------- */
0830  X1= 290;                    /* horizontal position of bouncing ball */
0831  Wide= 70; High= 70;            /* width and height of bouncing ball */
0832  BallBrush= CreateSolidBrush(RGB(255,0,0));      /* interior color */
0833  BallPen= CreatePen(PS_SOLID,1,RGB(255,0,0));        /* edge color */
0834  PrevBrush= SelectObject(hFrameDC,BallBrush);
0835  SelectObject(hFrameDC,BallPen);
0836  switch (Number)
0837    {
0838    case 1:  Y1= 15; Ellipse(hFrameDC,X1,Y1,X1+Wide,Y1+High); break;
0839    case 2:  Y1= 25; Ellipse(hFrameDC,X1,Y1,X1+Wide,Y1+High); break;
0840    case 3:  Y1= 40; Ellipse(hFrameDC,X1,Y1,X1+Wide,Y1+High); break;
0841    case 4:  Y1= 60; Ellipse(hFrameDC,X1,Y1,X1+Wide,Y1+High); break;
0842    case 5:  Y1= 120; High= 80;
0843             Ellipse(hFrameDC,X1,Y1,X1+Wide,Y1+High); break;
0844    case 6:  Y1= 190; High= 90;
0845             Ellipse(hFrameDC,X1,Y1,X1+Wide,Y1+High); break;
0846    case 7:  Y1=253; High= 70;
0847             Ellipse(hFrameDC,X1,Y1,X1+Wide,Y1+High);
0848             Y1= 280; X1= 280; High= 40; Wide= 90;
0849             Ellipse(hFrameDC,X1,Y1,X1+Wide,Y1+High); break;
0850    case 8:  X1= 270; Y1= 272; Wide= 110; High= 56;
0851             Ellipse(hFrameDC,X1,Y1,X1+Wide,Y1+High); break;
0852    case 9:  Y1= 160; X1= 290; High= 90; Wide= 70;
0853             Ellipse(hFrameDC,X1,Y1,X1+Wide,Y1+High); break;
0854    case 10: Y1= 90; High= 80;
0855             Ellipse(hFrameDC,X1,Y1,X1+Wide,Y1+High); break;
0856    case 11: Y1= 60; Ellipse(hFrameDC,X1,Y1,X1+Wide,Y1+High); break;
0857    case 12: Y1= 40; Ellipse(hFrameDC,X1,Y1,X1+Wide,Y1+High); break;
0858    case 13: Y1= 25; Ellipse(hFrameDC,X1,Y1,X1+Wide,Y1+High); break;
0859    }
0860  SelectObject(hFrameDC,PrevBrush); SelectObject(hFrameDC,PrevPen);
0861  DeleteObject(BallBrush); DeleteObject(BallPen);
0862  DeleteObject(LinePen);
0863
0864  /* ----------- display the frame and save it to disk ----------- */
0865  zCopyToDisplay(hWnd);                /* copy hidden frame to display */
0866  bDiskResult= zSaveFrame(hFrame,lpFileName);           /* save file */
0867  if (bDiskResult==FALSE) return FALSE;           /* if disk error */
0868  return TRUE;
0869  }
0870  /*
0871  ---------------------------------------------------------------------
0872              Draw background image on the hidden frame.
0873  ---------------------------------------------------------------------
0874                                                                      */
0875  static void zDrawBg(HDC hDC)
0876  {
0877    HBRUSH hPrevBrush, hSwatchBrush;
0878    RECT rcSwatch;
0879    int iWidth= 400, iDepth= 4;
0880    int iSwatchX= 0, iSwatchY=0;
0881    BYTE bRed= 0, bGreen= 0, bBlue= 0;
0882    int iCount;
0883  if (FrameReady==FALSE)
0884    {
0885    MessageBeep(0);
0886    LoadString(hInst,IDS_NotReady,lpCaption,Max);
```

```
0887    LoadString(hInst,IDS_NoFrame,lpMessage,MaxText);
0888    MessageBox(GetFocus(),lpMessage,lpCaption,MB_OK);
0889    return;
0890    }
0891  rcSwatch.left= iSwatchX;
0892  rcSwatch.top= iSwatchY;
0893  rcSwatch.right= rcSwatch.left + iWidth;
0894  rcSwatch.bottom= rcSwatch.top + iDepth;
0895  bRed= 0; bGreen= 0; bBlue= 3;
0896  for (iCount= 0; iCount < 64; iCount++)
0897    {
0898    hSwatchBrush= CreateSolidBrush(RGB(bRed,bGreen,bBlue));
0899    hPrevBrush= SelectObject(hDC,hSwatchBrush);
0900    FillRect(hDC,&rcSwatch,hSwatchBrush);
0901    SelectObject(hDC,hPrevBrush);
0902    DeleteObject(hSwatchBrush);
0903    rcSwatch.top= rcSwatch.top + iDepth;
0904    rcSwatch.bottom= rcSwatch.bottom + iDepth;
0905    bBlue= bBlue + (BYTE) 4;
0906    }
0907  bBlue= 255; rcSwatch.bottom= 300;
0908  hSwatchBrush= CreateSolidBrush(RGB(bRed,bGreen,bBlue));
0909  hPrevBrush= SelectObject(hDC,hSwatchBrush);
0910  FillRect(hDC,&rcSwatch,hSwatchBrush);
0911  SelectObject(hDC,hPrevBrush); DeleteObject(hSwatchBrush);
0912
0913  bRed= 0; bGreen= 0; bBlue= 255;
0914  iWidth= 280; iDepth= 4;
0915  iSwatchX= 60; iSwatchY= 24;
0916  rcSwatch.left= iSwatchX;
0917  rcSwatch.top= iSwatchY;
0918  rcSwatch.right= rcSwatch.left + iWidth;
0919  rcSwatch.bottom= rcSwatch.top + iDepth;
0920  for (iCount= 0; iCount < 64; iCount++)
0921    {
0922    hSwatchBrush= CreateSolidBrush(RGB(bRed,bGreen,bBlue));
0923    hPrevBrush= SelectObject(hDC,hSwatchBrush);
0924    FillRect(hDC,&rcSwatch,hSwatchBrush);
0925    SelectObject(hDC,hPrevBrush);
0926    DeleteObject(hSwatchBrush);
0927    rcSwatch.top= rcSwatch.top + iDepth;
0928    rcSwatch.bottom= rcSwatch.bottom + iDepth;
0929    bBlue= bBlue - (BYTE) 4;
0930    }
0931  return;
0932  }
0933  /*
0934  -------------------------------------------------------------
0935                     Save a frame file to disk.
0936  -------------------------------------------------------------
0937                                                             */
0938  static BOOL zSaveFrame(HBITMAP hBitmap, LPSTR lpFileName)
0939  {
0940    BITMAP bmImage;                    /* bitmap data structure */
0941    short BytesPerLine;                     /* width of bitmap */
0942    short RasterLines;                     /* height of bitmap */
0943    BYTE NumPlanes;                     /* number of bitplanes */
0944    LPSTR lpImageData;    /* pointer to buffer that holds bit array */
0945    GLOBALHANDLE hMem;    /* handle to buffer that holds bit array */
0946    WORD NumBytes;                 /* length of array, in bytes */
0947    LONG TestLength;                           /* hash value */
```

```
0948    DWORD BytesCopied;              /* value returned by GetBitmapBits() */
0949    int hFile;                                   /* DOS file handle */
0950    OFSTRUCT FileStruct;                      /* data structure for file */
0951
0952    if (FrameReady==FALSE)              /* if no hidden-frame exists... */
0953      {
0954      MessageBeep(0);
0955      LoadString(hInst,IDS_Unexpected,lpCaption,Max);
0956      LoadString(hInst,IDS_Disk9,lpMessage,MaxText);
0957      MessageBox(GetFocus(),lpMessage,lpCaption,MB_OK);
0958      return FALSE;
0959      }
0960
0961    RetVal= GetObject(hBitmap,          /* grab bitmap data structure */
0962            sizeof(BITMAP),(LPSTR)&bmImage);
0963    if (RetVal==0)
0964      {
0965      MessageBeep(0);
0966      LoadString(hInst,IDS_Unexpected,lpCaption,Max);
0967      LoadString(hInst,IDS_Disk10,lpMessage,MaxText);
0968      MessageBox(GetFocus(),lpMessage,lpCaption,MB_OK);
0969      return FALSE;
0970      }
0971    BytesPerLine= bmImage.bmWidthBytes;          /* width of bitmap */
0972    RasterLines= bmImage.bmHeight;               /* height of bitmap */
0973    NumPlanes= bmImage.bmPlanes;              /* number of bitplanes */
0974    TestLength=                           /* calculate length of data */
0975            (LONG)(BytesPerLine * RasterLines * NumPlanes);
0976    if (TestLength > 65534) /* if too large for single-pass write... */
0977      {
0978      MessageBeep(0);
0979      LoadString(hInst,IDS_Unexpected,lpCaption,Max);
0980      LoadString(hInst,IDS_Disk11,lpMessage,MaxText);
0981      MessageBox(GetFocus(),lpMessage,lpCaption,MB_OK);
0982      return FALSE;
0983      }
0984    NumBytes= (WORD) TestLength;       /* initialize arg for _lwrite() */
0985
0986    hMem= GlobalAlloc(GMEM_MOVEABLE, NumBytes);   /* create a buffer */
0987    if (hMem==0)
0988      {
0989      MessageBeep(0);
0990      LoadString(hInst,IDS_Unexpected,lpCaption,Max);
0991      LoadString(hInst,IDS_Disk12,lpMessage,MaxText);
0992      MessageBox(GetFocus(),lpMessage,lpCaption,MB_OK);
0993      return FALSE;
0994      }
0995    lpImageData= GlobalLock(hMem);   /* lock buffer and grab pointer */
0996    BytesCopied= GetBitmapBits(hBitmap,NumBytes,lpImageData);
0997    if (BytesCopied==0)        /* if unable to copy bits to buffer... */
0998      {
0999      MessageBeep(0);
1000      LoadString(hInst,IDS_Unexpected,lpCaption,Max);
1001      LoadString(hInst,IDS_Disk13,lpMessage,MaxText);
1002      MessageBox(GetFocus(),lpMessage,lpCaption,MB_OK);
1003      GlobalUnlock(hMem); GlobalFree(hMem); return FALSE;
1004      }
1005
1006    hFile= OpenFile(lpFileName,&FileStruct,OF_EXIST);     /* exists? */
1007    if (hFile >= 0)
1008      {
```

```
1009     MessageBeep(0);
1010     LoadString(hInst,IDS_Unexpected,lpCaption,Max);
1011     LoadString(hInst,IDS_Disk14,lpMessage,MaxText);
1012     RetVal= MessageBox(GetFocus(),lpMessage,lpCaption,MB_YESNO);
1013     if (RetVal==IDNO)      /* if user does not want to overwrite... */
1014       {
1015       GlobalUnlock(hMem); GlobalFree(hMem); return FALSE;
1016       }
1017     }
1018   hFile= OpenFile(lpFileName,&FileStruct,OF_CREATE|OF_WRITE);
1019   if (hFile==-1)
1020     {
1021     MessageBeep(0);
1022     LoadString(hInst,IDS_Unexpected,lpCaption,Max);
1023     LoadString(hInst,IDS_Disk15,lpMessage,MaxText);
1024     MessageBox(GetFocus(),lpMessage,lpCaption,MB_OK);
1025     GlobalUnlock(hMem); GlobalFree(hMem); return FALSE;
1026     }
1027
1028   RetVal= _lwrite(hFile,lpImageData,NumBytes);     /* write to disk */
1029   if (RetVal==-1)
1030     {
1031     MessageBeep(0);
1032     LoadString(hInst,IDS_Unexpected,lpCaption,Max);
1033     LoadString(hInst,IDS_Disk16,lpMessage,MaxText);
1034
1035     MessageBox(GetFocus(),lpMessage,lpCaption,MB_OK);
1036     _lclose(hFile);
1037     GlobalUnlock(hMem); GlobalFree(hMem); return FALSE;
1038     }
1039
1040   RetVal= _lclose(hFile);                          /* close the file */
1041   if (RetVal==-1)                    /* if unable to close file... */
1042     {
1043     MessageBeep(0);
1044     LoadString(hInst,IDS_Unexpected,lpCaption,Max);
1045     LoadString(hInst,IDS_Disk17,lpMessage,MaxText);
1046     MessageBox(GetFocus(),lpMessage,lpCaption,MB_OK);
1047     GlobalUnlock(hMem); GlobalFree(hMem); return FALSE;
1048     }
1049
1050   GlobalUnlock(hMem);          /* discard the pointer to the buffer */
1051   GlobalFree(hMem);                          /* discard the buffer */
1052   return TRUE;
1053   }
1054   /*
1055   -------------------------------------------------------------------
1056                       ANIMATION PLAYBACK Functions
1057   -------------------------------------------------------------------
1058   -------------------------------------------------------------------
1059                         Display the next frame.
1060   This function is intelligent enough to discern between RAM-BASED
1061   FRAME ANIMATION (where all frames have already been loaded from
1062   disk and stored in RAM) and DISK-BASED FRAME ANIMATION (where
1063   each frame must be loaded from disk during playback).
1064   -------------------------------------------------------------------
1065                                                                    */
1066   static void zShowNextFrame(HWND hWnd)
1067   {
1068     HDC hDC;
1069   if (bUseDisk==TRUE) goto DISK_PLAYBACK;
```

```
1070
1071   RAM_PLAYBACK:        /* if all frames have been loaded into RAM... */
1072   if (AnimationReady==FALSE) return;
1073   if (bAnimationLoaded==FALSE) return;
1074   if (Redisplay==TRUE) goto DISPLAY_FRAME;
1075   if (Pause==TRUE) return;
1076   if (FrameDirection==zFORWARD)
1077     {
1078     FrameNum++;
1079     if (FrameNum > zFINALFRAME) FrameNum= zFIRSTFRAME;
1080     }
1081   if (FrameDirection==zREVERSE)
1082     {
1083     FrameNum--;
1084     if (FrameNum < zFIRSTFRAME) FrameNum= zFINALFRAME;
1085     }
1086   DISPLAY_FRAME:
1087   hDC= GetDC(hWnd);
1088   switch (FrameNum)
1089     {
1090     case 1:  SelectObject(hFDC,hF1); break;
1091     case 2:  SelectObject(hFDC,hF2); break;
1092     case 3:  SelectObject(hFDC,hF3); break;
1093     case 4:  SelectObject(hFDC,hF4); break;
1094     case 5:  SelectObject(hFDC,hF5); break;
1095     case 6:  SelectObject(hFDC,hF6); break;
1096     case 7:  SelectObject(hFDC,hF7); break;
1097     case 8:  SelectObject(hFDC,hF8); break;
1098     case 9:  SelectObject(hFDC,hF9); break;
1099     case 10: SelectObject(hFDC,hF10); break;
1100     case 11: SelectObject(hFDC,hF11); break;
1101     case 12: SelectObject(hFDC,hF12); break;
1102     case 13: SelectObject(hFDC,hF13); break;
1103     }
1104   BitBlt(hDC,0,0,zFRAMEWIDE,zFRAMEHIGH,hFDC,0,0,SRCCOPY);
1105   ReleaseDC(hWnd,hDC);
1106   return;
1107
1108   DISK_PLAYBACK:    /* if loading each frame from disk as needed... */
1109   if (bAnimationHalted==TRUE) return;
1110   if (Redisplay==TRUE) goto SAME_FRAME;
1111   if (Pause==TRUE) return;
1112   if (FrameDirection==zFORWARD)
1113     {
1114     FrameNum++;
1115     if (FrameNum > zFINALFRAME) FrameNum= zFIRSTFRAME;
1116     }
1117   if (FrameDirection==zREVERSE)
1118     {
1119     FrameNum--;
1120     if (FrameNum < zFIRSTFRAME) FrameNum= zFINALFRAME;
1121     }
1122   SAME_FRAME:
1123   hDC= GetDC(hWnd);
1124   switch (FrameNum)
1125     {
1126     case 1:  bFrameLoaded= zLoadFrame(hFrame, (LPSTR)"BOUNCE1.BIT");
1127              break;
1128     case 2:  bFrameLoaded= zLoadFrame(hFrame, (LPSTR)"BOUNCE2.BIT");
1129              break;
```

```
1130    case 3:  bFrameLoaded= zLoadFrame(hFrame, (LPSTR)"BOUNCE3.BIT");
1131             break;
1132    case 4:  bFrameLoaded= zLoadFrame(hFrame, (LPSTR)"BOUNCE4.BIT");
1133             break;
1134    case 5:  bFrameLoaded= zLoadFrame(hFrame, (LPSTR)"BOUNCE5.BIT");
1135             break;
1136    case 6:  bFrameLoaded= zLoadFrame(hFrame, (LPSTR)"BOUNCE6.BIT");
1137             break;
1138    case 7:  bFrameLoaded= zLoadFrame(hFrame, (LPSTR)"BOUNCE7.BIT");
1139             break;
1140    case 8:  bFrameLoaded= zLoadFrame(hFrame, (LPSTR)"BOUNCE8.BIT");
1141             break;
1142    case 9:  bFrameLoaded= zLoadFrame(hFrame, (LPSTR)"BOUNCE9.BIT");
1143             break;
1144    case 10: bFrameLoaded= zLoadFrame(hFrame, (LPSTR)"BOUNCE10.BIT");
1145             break;
1146    case 11: bFrameLoaded= zLoadFrame(hFrame, (LPSTR)"BOUNCE11.BIT");
1147             break;
1148    case 12: bFrameLoaded= zLoadFrame(hFrame, (LPSTR)"BOUNCE12.BIT");
1149             break;
1150    case 13: bFrameLoaded= zLoadFrame(hFrame, (LPSTR)"BOUNCE13.BIT");
1151             break;
1152    }
1153 if (bFrameLoaded==FALSE)
1154    {
1155    bAnimationHalted= TRUE;
1156    MessageBeep(0);
1157    LoadString(hInst,IDS_Unexpected,lpCaption,Max);
1158    LoadString(hInst,IDS_Disk3,lpMessage,MaxText);
1159    TimerCounter= zTIMER_PAUSE;
1160    MessageBox(GetFocus(),lpMessage,lpCaption,MB_OK);
1161    return;
1162    }
1163 BitBlt(hDC,0,0,zFRAMEWIDE,zFRAMEHIGH,hFrameDC,0,0,SRCCOPY);
1164 ReleaseDC(hWnd,hDC);
1165 return;
1166 }
1167 /*
1168 ------------------------------------------------------------------
1169              Load the animation sequence from disk.
1170    If memory limitations prevent this function from loading the
1171    entire animation sequence into RAM, it sets a token to FALSE.
1172    In that case the playback function zShowNextFrame() will load
1173    each frame from disk as required during animation playback,
1174    otherwise all frames are expected to be in RAM.
1175 ------------------------------------------------------------------
1176                                                                */
1177 static void zLoadAnimation(HWND hWnd)
1178 {
1179    HDC hDC;
1180
1181 if (FrameReady==FALSE)          /* if no hidden-frame available... */
1182    {
1183    MessageBeep(0);
1184    LoadString(hInst,IDS_NotReady,lpCaption,Max);
1185    LoadString(hInst,IDS_NoFrame,lpMessage,MaxText);
1186    MessageBox(GetFocus(),lpMessage,lpCaption,MB_OK);
1187    return;
1188    }
1189 if (bAnimationLoaded==TRUE)     /* if frames already loaded... */
1190    {
```

```
1191   MessageBeep(0);
1192   LoadString(hInst,IDS_Unexpected,lpCaption,Max);
1193   LoadString(hInst,IDS_Disk4,lpMessage,MaxText);
1194   TimerCounter= zTIMER_PAUSE;
1195   MessageBox(GetFocus(),lpMessage,lpCaption,MB_OK);
1196   return;
1197   }
1198   if (bPrevLoadAttempt==TRUE)        /* if previous attempt failed... */
1199   {
1200   MessageBeep(0);
1201   LoadString(hInst,IDS_Unexpected,lpCaption,Max);
1202   LoadString(hInst,IDS_Disk5,lpMessage,MaxText);
1203   TimerCounter= zTIMER_PAUSE;
1204   MessageBox(GetFocus(),lpMessage,lpCaption,MB_OK);
1205   return;
1206   }
1207   bPrevLoadAttempt= TRUE;
1208
1209   /* -------------- create bitmaps to hold the frames ------------ */
1210   GlobalCompact((DWORD)-1L);             /* maximize contiguous memory */
1211   hDC= GetDC(hWnd);
1212   hFDC= CreateCompatibleDC(hDC);
1213   hF1= CreateCompatibleBitmap(hDC,zFRAMEWIDE,zFRAMEHIGH);
1214   if (hF1==NULL) goto F1;
1215   hF2= CreateCompatibleBitmap(hDC,zFRAMEWIDE,zFRAMEHIGH);
1216   if (hF2==NULL) goto F2;
1217   hF3= CreateCompatibleBitmap(hDC,zFRAMEWIDE,zFRAMEHIGH);
1218   if (hF3==NULL) goto F3;
1219   hF4= CreateCompatibleBitmap(hDC,zFRAMEWIDE,zFRAMEHIGH);
1220   if (hF4==NULL) goto F4;
1221   hF5= CreateCompatibleBitmap(hDC,zFRAMEWIDE,zFRAMEHIGH);
1222   if (hF5==NULL) goto F5;
1223   hF6= CreateCompatibleBitmap(hDC,zFRAMEWIDE,zFRAMEHIGH);
1224   if (hF6==NULL) goto F6;
1225   hF7= CreateCompatibleBitmap(hDC,zFRAMEWIDE,zFRAMEHIGH);
1226   if (hF7==NULL) goto F7;
1227   hF8= CreateCompatibleBitmap(hDC,zFRAMEWIDE,zFRAMEHIGH);
1228   if (hF8==NULL) goto F8;
1229   hF9= CreateCompatibleBitmap(hDC,zFRAMEWIDE,zFRAMEHIGH);
1230   if (hF9==NULL) goto F9;
1231   hF10= CreateCompatibleBitmap(hDC,zFRAMEWIDE,zFRAMEHIGH);
1232   if (hF10==NULL) goto F10;
1233   hF11= CreateCompatibleBitmap(hDC,zFRAMEWIDE,zFRAMEHIGH);
1234   if (hF11==NULL) goto F11;
1235   hF12= CreateCompatibleBitmap(hDC,zFRAMEWIDE,zFRAMEHIGH);
1236   if (hF12==NULL) goto F12;
1237   hF13= CreateCompatibleBitmap(hDC,zFRAMEWIDE,zFRAMEHIGH);
1238   if (hF13==NULL) goto F13;
1239   goto BITMAPS_OK;
1240   F13: DeleteObject(hF12);
1241   F12: DeleteObject(hF11);
1242   F11: DeleteObject(hF10);
1243   F10: DeleteObject(hF9);
1244   F9:  DeleteObject(hF8);
1245   F8:  DeleteObject(hF7);
1246   F7:  DeleteObject(hF6);
1247   F6:  DeleteObject(hF5);
1248   F5:  DeleteObject(hF4);
1249   F4:  DeleteObject(hF3);
1250   F3:  DeleteObject(hF2);
1251   F2:  DeleteObject(hF1);
```

```
1252  F1:  DeleteDC(hFDC); ReleaseDC(hWnd,hDC);
1253       bUseDisk= TRUE; AnimationReady= TRUE;
1254       LoadString(hInst,IDS_Status,lpCaption,Max);
1255       LoadString(hInst,IDS_Disk6,lpMessage,MaxText);
1256       MessageBox(GetFocus(),lpMessage,lpCaption,MB_OK);
1257       return;
1258  BITMAPS_OK: ReleaseDC(hWnd,hDC);
1259
1260  /* ------------- load frame files into the bitmaps ------------- */
1261  bFrameLoaded= zLoadFrame(hF1, (LPSTR) "BOUNCE1.BIT");
1262  if (bFrameLoaded==FALSE) goto DISK_ERROR;
1263  bFrameLoaded= zLoadFrame(hF2, (LPSTR) "BOUNCE2.BIT");
1264  if (bFrameLoaded==FALSE) goto DISK_ERROR;
1265  bFrameLoaded= zLoadFrame(hF3, (LPSTR) "BOUNCE3.BIT");
1266  if (bFrameLoaded==FALSE) goto DISK_ERROR;
1267  bFrameLoaded= zLoadFrame(hF4, (LPSTR) "BOUNCE4.BIT");
1268  if (bFrameLoaded==FALSE) goto DISK_ERROR;
1269  bFrameLoaded= zLoadFrame(hF5, (LPSTR) "BOUNCE5.BIT");
1270  if (bFrameLoaded==FALSE) goto DISK_ERROR;
1271  bFrameLoaded= zLoadFrame(hF6, (LPSTR) "BOUNCE6.BIT");
1272  if (bFrameLoaded==FALSE) goto DISK_ERROR;
1273  bFrameLoaded= zLoadFrame(hF7, (LPSTR) "BOUNCE7.BIT");
1274  if (bFrameLoaded==FALSE) goto DISK_ERROR;
1275  bFrameLoaded= zLoadFrame(hF8, (LPSTR) "BOUNCE8.BIT");
1276  if (bFrameLoaded==FALSE) goto DISK_ERROR;
1277  bFrameLoaded= zLoadFrame(hF9, (LPSTR) "BOUNCE9.BIT");
1278  if (bFrameLoaded==FALSE) goto DISK_ERROR;
1279  bFrameLoaded= zLoadFrame(hF10, (LPSTR) "BOUNCE10.BIT");
1280  if (bFrameLoaded==FALSE) goto DISK_ERROR;
1281  bFrameLoaded= zLoadFrame(hF11, (LPSTR) "BOUNCE11.BIT");
1282  if (bFrameLoaded==FALSE) goto DISK_ERROR;
1283  bFrameLoaded= zLoadFrame(hF12, (LPSTR) "BOUNCE12.BIT");
1284  if (bFrameLoaded==FALSE) goto DISK_ERROR;
1285  bFrameLoaded= zLoadFrame(hF13, (LPSTR) "BOUNCE13.BIT");
1286  if (bFrameLoaded==FALSE) goto DISK_ERROR;
1287  goto DISK_OK;
1288  DISK_ERROR:
1289    DeleteObject(hF1); DeleteObject(hF2); DeleteObject(hF3);
1290    DeleteObject(hF4); DeleteObject(hF5); DeleteObject(hF6);
1291    DeleteObject(hF7); DeleteObject(hF8); DeleteObject(hF9);
1292    DeleteObject(hF10); DeleteObject(hF11); DeleteObject(hF12);
1293    DeleteObject(hF13);   DeleteDC(hFDC);
1294    return;
1295
1296  /* -------------------- tidy up and return -------------------- */
1297  DISK_OK:
1298  hPrevF= SelectObject(hFDC,hF1);                /* select bitmap */
1299  bAnimationLoaded= TRUE;
1300  AnimationReady= TRUE;
1301  bAnimationSaved= TRUE;
1302  MessageBeep(0);
1303  LoadString(hInst,IDS_AnimReady,lpCaption,Max);
1304  LoadString(hInst,IDS_Disk7,lpMessage,MaxText);
1305  MessageBox(GetFocus(),lpMessage,lpCaption,MB_OK);
1306  return;
1307  }
1308  /*
1309  ----------------------------------------------------------------
1310                  Reset the animation frame rate.
1311  ----------------------------------------------------------------
1312                                                              */
```

```
1313   static void zSetFrameRate(HWND hWnd, WORD wNewRate)
1314   {
1315   if (TimerExists==FALSE)
1316     {
1317     wFrameRate= wPrevRate;
1318     MessageBeep(0);
1319     LoadString(hInst,IDS_NotReady,lpCaption,Max);
1320     LoadString(hInst,IDS_NoReset,lpMessage,MaxText);
1321     MessageBox(GetFocus(),lpMessage,lpCaption,MB_OK);
1322     return;
1323     }
1324   switch (wPrevRate)
1325     {
1326     case 55:  CheckMenuItem(hMenu,IDM_FPS182,MF_UNCHECKED); break;
1327     case 110: CheckMenuItem(hMenu,IDM_FPS91,MF_UNCHECKED); break;
1328     case 165: CheckMenuItem(hMenu,IDM_FPS61,MF_UNCHECKED); break;
1329     case 220: CheckMenuItem(hMenu,IDM_FPS45,MF_UNCHECKED); break;
1330     case 275: CheckMenuItem(hMenu,IDM_FPS36,MF_UNCHECKED); break;
1331     case 330: CheckMenuItem(hMenu,IDM_FPS30,MF_UNCHECKED); break;
1332     }
1333   KillTimer(hWnd,1);
1334   TimerID1= SetTimer(hWnd,1,wNewRate,(FARPROC) NULL);
1335   if (TimerID1==0)
1336     {
1337     LoadString(hInst,IDS_NotReady,lpCaption,Max);
1338     LoadString(hInst,IDS_CannotReset,lpMessage,MaxText);
1339     MessageBox(GetFocus(),lpMessage,lpCaption,MB_OK);
1340     TimerExists= FALSE;
1341     return;
1342     }
1343   switch (wFrameRate)
1344     {
1345     case 55:  CheckMenuItem(hMenu,IDM_FPS182,MF_CHECKED); break;
1346     case 110: CheckMenuItem(hMenu,IDM_FPS91,MF_CHECKED); break;
1347     case 165: CheckMenuItem(hMenu,IDM_FPS61,MF_CHECKED); break;
1348     case 220: CheckMenuItem(hMenu,IDM_FPS45,MF_CHECKED); break;
1349     case 275: CheckMenuItem(hMenu,IDM_FPS36,MF_CHECKED); break;
1350     case 330: CheckMenuItem(hMenu,IDM_FPS30,MF_CHECKED); break;
1351     }
1352   return;
1353   }
1354   /*
1355   --------------------------------------------------------------------
1356                     Load one frame file from disk.
1357   --------------------------------------------------------------------
1358                                                                     */
1359   static BOOL zLoadFrame(HBITMAP hBitmap, LPSTR lpFileName)
1360   {
1361     BITMAP bmImage;                      /* bitmap data structure */
1362     short BytesPerLine;                       /* width of bitmap */
1363     short RasterLines;                       /* height of bitmap */
1364     BYTE NumPlanes;                        /* number of bitplanes */
1365     LPSTR lpImageData;   /* pointer to buffer that holds bit array */
1366     GLOBALHANDLE hMem;    /* handle to buffer that holds bit array */
1367     WORD NumBytes;                   /* length of array, in bytes */
1368     LONG TestLength;                            /* hash value */
1369     DWORD BytesCopied;       /* value returned by GetBitmapBits() */
1370     int hFile;                             /* DOS file handle */
1371     OFSTRUCT FileStruct;               /* data structure for file */
1372
1373   if (FrameReady==FALSE)          /* if no hidden-frame exists... */
```

```
1374      {
1375      MessageBeep(0);
1376      LoadString(hInst,IDS_Unexpected,lpCaption,Max);
1377      LoadString(hInst,IDS_Disk18,lpMessage,MaxText);
1378      MessageBox(GetFocus(),lpMessage,lpCaption,MB_OK);
1379      return FALSE;
1380      }
1381
1382  RetVal= GetObject(hBitmap,              /* grab bitmap data structure */
1383          sizeof(BITMAP),(LPSTR)&bmImage);
1384  if (RetVal==0)
1385      {
1386      MessageBeep(0);
1387      LoadString(hInst,IDS_Unexpected,lpCaption,Max);
1388      LoadString(hInst,IDS_Disk10,lpMessage,MaxText);
1389      MessageBox(GetFocus(),lpMessage,lpCaption,MB_OK);
1390      return FALSE;
1391      }
1392
1393  BytesPerLine= bmImage.bmWidthBytes;            /* width of bitmap */
1394  RasterLines= bmImage.bmHeight;                 /* height of bitmap */
1395  NumPlanes= bmImage.bmPlanes;              /* number of bitplanes */
1396  TestLength=                          /* calculate length of data */
1397              (LONG)(BytesPerLine * RasterLines * NumPlanes);
1398  if (TestLength > 60000)      /* if larger than hardcoded value... */
1399      {                           /* ...of a 400x300x16-color frame */
1400      MessageBeep(0);
1401      LoadString(hInst,IDS_Unexpected,lpCaption,Max);
1402      LoadString(hInst,IDS_Disk19,lpMessage,MaxText);
1403      MessageBox(GetFocus(),lpMessage,lpCaption,MB_OK);
1404      return FALSE;
1405      }
1406  NumBytes= (WORD) TestLength;        /* initialize arg for _lread() */
1407
1408  hMem= GlobalAlloc(GMEM_MOVEABLE, NumBytes);   /* create a buffer */
1409  if (hMem==0)
1410      {
1411      MessageBeep(0);
1412      LoadString(hInst,IDS_Unexpected,lpCaption,Max);
1413      LoadString(hInst,IDS_Disk20,lpMessage,MaxText);
1414      MessageBox(GetFocus(),lpMessage,lpCaption,MB_OK);
1415      return FALSE;
1416      }
1417  lpImageData= GlobalLock(hMem);    /* lock buffer and grab pointer */
1418
1419  hFile= OpenFile(lpFileName,&FileStruct,OF_READ);
1420  if (hFile==-1)
1421      {
1422      MessageBeep(0);
1423      LoadString(hInst,IDS_Unexpected,lpCaption,Max);
1424      LoadString(hInst,IDS_Disk21,lpMessage,MaxText);
1425      MessageBox(GetFocus(),lpMessage,lpCaption,MB_OK);
1426      GlobalUnlock(hMem); GlobalFree(hMem); return FALSE;
1427      }
1428
1429  RetVal= _lread(hFile,lpImageData,NumBytes);      /* read from disk */
1430  if (RetVal==-1)
1431      {
1432      MessageBeep(0);
1433      LoadString(hInst,IDS_Unexpected,lpCaption,Max);
1434      LoadString(hInst,IDS_Disk22,lpMessage,MaxText);
```

```
1435    MessageBox(GetFocus(),lpMessage,lpCaption,MB_OK);
1436    _lclose(hFile);
1437    GlobalUnlock(hMem); GlobalFree(hMem); return FALSE;
1438    }
1439  if ((unsigned)RetVal < NumBytes)
1440    {
1441    MessageBeep(0);
1442    LoadString(hInst,IDS_Unexpected,lpCaption,Max);
1443    LoadString(hInst,IDS_Disk23,lpMessage,MaxText);
1444    MessageBox(GetFocus(),lpMessage,lpCaption,MB_OK);
1445    _lclose(hFile);
1446    GlobalUnlock(hMem); GlobalFree(hMem); return FALSE;
1447    }
1448
1449  RetVal= _lclose(hFile);                        /* close the file */
1450  if (RetVal==-1)                        /* if unable to close file... */
1451    {
1452    MessageBeep(0);
1453    LoadString(hInst,IDS_Unexpected,lpCaption,Max);
1454    LoadString(hInst,IDS_Disk24,lpMessage,MaxText);
1455    MessageBox(GetFocus(),lpMessage,lpCaption,MB_OK);
1456    GlobalUnlock(hMem); GlobalFree(hMem); return FALSE;
1457    }
1458
1459  BytesCopied= SetBitmapBits(hBitmap,NumBytes,lpImageData);
1460  if (BytesCopied==0)        /* if unable to copy bits to bitmap... */
1461    {
1462    MessageBeep(0);
1463    LoadString(hInst,IDS_Unexpected,lpCaption,Max);
1464    LoadString(hInst,IDS_Disk25,lpMessage,MaxText);
1465    MessageBox(GetFocus(),lpMessage,lpCaption,MB_OK);
1466    GlobalUnlock(hMem); GlobalFree(hMem); return FALSE;
1467    }
1468
1469  GlobalUnlock(hMem);            /* discard the pointer to the buffer */
1470  GlobalFree(hMem);                        /* discard the buffer */
1471  return TRUE;
1472  }
1473  /*
1474  ----------------------------------------------------------------
1475                        End of the C source file
1476  ----------------------------------------------------------------
1477                                                              */
```

# 14
# *Backgrounds*

Backgrounds are the scenery of your animation sequence. A carefully designed, properly drawn background that is manipulated with finesse and dexterity during playback can add pizazz and panache to your animation sequence. A poorly designed, slipshod background that just hangs there is the calling card of an amateur.

Using the hidden frame technique that has been described and demonstrated in previous sample applications, you can use a background when you build your animation sequences, simply copying the background bitmap to the frame you are building.

Although you could utilize multiple hidden frames to implement numerous different backgrounds during an animation sequence, a more practical approach involves techniques originated and perfected by traditional film animators.

By using a background bitmap that is much larger than the dimensions of the display frame, you can copy selected rectangles from the oversized background to the frame you are building. By carefully choosing which portion of the oversized background to copy, you can produce pans and other camera effects. The display frame becomes, in effect, a viewport on the oversized background bitmap.

## The field-grid graticule

The single-frame camera that is used by traditional film animation studios can pan left or right across the background cel, which is held in place by a platen. It can move up and down across the background. It can move closer to the background for a close-up, and it can move farther away from the background for a long shot.

You can implement these same camera movements in your Windows animation programs. By using different arguments when you call the GDI's BitBlt() function, you can select different rectangles from the oversized bitmap, thereby simulating panning movements.

By calling the GDI's StretchBlt() function, you can produce zoom effects by taking a small rectangle from the hidden background bitmap and scaling it larger to fit the frame you are building.

## The graticule

Traditional animators use a grid to represent the working surface that holds the background image. This grid is called a *field-grid*, because the animator specifies fields on the grid that will fill the camera frame. A field-grid is also called a graticule. A 12-field grid for animation backgrounds is depicted in FIG. 14-1. Note how the dimensions of the 12-field grid preserve the 4:3 ratio of computer screens, television, and videotape. Some animation studios use a 16-field chart, but the 12-field grid is the most common.

**Specifying a field size**   During the preparation of the camera exposure sheet for an animation sequence (see chapter 15, Production), the animator uses a special notation to specify the location and size of the field to be used. This field is the rectangle that will fill the camera frame.

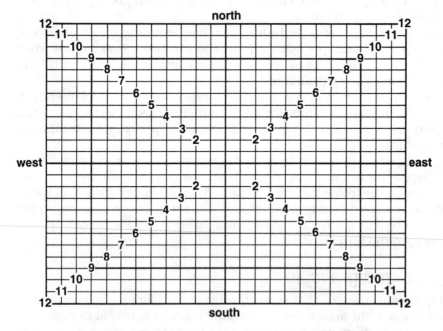

**14-1**   To ensure that animated images are visible on standard television sets, animators must keep all action and titles inside the 9-field grid (television field) of the full motion field (12-field grid).

Sample notation for specifying fields on an animation field-grid is shown in FIG. 14-2. The notation is a convenient way to describe camera position and camera movement. The conceptual schematics in FIG. 14-3 illustrate how to use an animation field-grid to specify camera zooms and camera pans.

If you look ahead to FIG. 14-5, you can see the oversized background that was used to build the camera panning demonstration in the sample application presented later in the chapter. The dimensions of the background image correspond to the field markings of the field-grid used by traditional film animators. Because the GDI's BitBlt() function takes as its arguments the origin and width and depth of the source bitmap, you can specify a rectangle at any position and at any size on the oversized bitmap. This feature of the BitBlt() function means you can simulate the effects shown in FIG. 14-3. You can also implement advanced techniques like zip pans and camera shake.

**Zip pans** A *zip pan* is a lightning-quick pan across a background scene. During a standard pan, the audience is expected to appreciate the content of the background being panned. During a zip pan, the simple act of getting the camera from here to there is what is most important. If your character has just performed a double take, for example, you might use a zip pan to quickly move the camera over to the object that surprised your character. Zip pans are also called swish pans.

**Camera shake** You can also use the GDI's BitBlt() function to implement *camera shake.* If an explosion or collision occurs in your animation, you can use a camera shake to emphasize its impact. To implement a camera

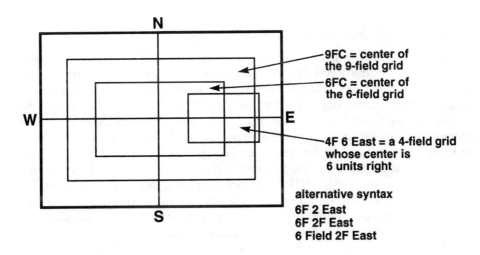

**14-2** How to specify fields on an animation field grid.

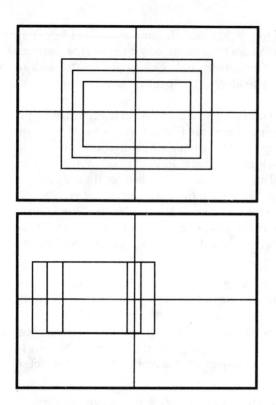

**14-3** Top, using field grids to effect a zoom in or zoom out. Bottom, using field grids to effect a pan.

shake, alternately select camera shots a bit to the left and a bit to the right of the original shot. Reduce the offset distance of each shot until you have returned to the coordinates of the original camera shot.

## Using backgrounds creatively

The creative use of backgrounds in your animation sequence can dramatically improve the marketability of your software. You can use any of the digitizing methods described in FIG. 9-4 in chapter 9, Cel animation and Windows, to capture images for use as backgrounds. By using the titling techniques described and demonstrated in chapter 5, Titling, you can build complex and arresting imagery. Even special effects like rain, snow, water, wind, and reflections can become part of your background by animating these effects on the background before you paste your actors and characters in place. The transparent PUT function described and demonstrated in chapter 3, Blitting, can be a powerful tool in helping you build your backgrounds. The sample application in this chapter provides a stable starting point for the development of your own backgrounds.

# A sample application

The screen image in FIG. 14-4 shows the first frame from the sample application panning.exe. This program demonstrates background panning techniques.

The interactive playback controller allows you to experiment with different animation playback modes, including full forward, full reverse, pause, freeze-frame, single-step forward, and single-step reverse. The animation will continue to execute if the window is partially covered by another window or if the window is partially clipped at the edge of the physical display.

The panning.exe demo is built from six modules, including a .def module definition file, an .h #include file, an .rc resource script file, and a .c source file—in addition to a storage.h #include file and a storage.c source

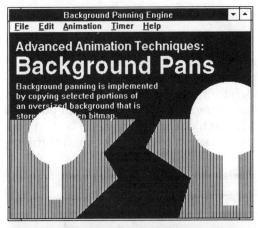

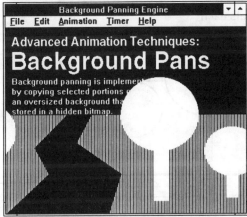

**14-4** The starting frame and ending frame from the background pan animation demo.

file for the module that provides disk read/write functions for binary image files. All panning.exe production files are presented as ready-to-use source code in the program listings in this chapter. The storage.h and storage.c production files were provided in chapter 10, Characters. All source files are also provided on the companion disk. See the appropriate appendix for instructions on how to build panning.exe with QuickC for Windows, Turbo C ++ for Windows, Borland C++, Zortech C++, WATCOM C, and Microsoft C and the SDK.

# What the program does: A user's guide

*User's Guide* The sample application provides an interactive environment for experimenting with background panning. You can use either a mouse or the keyboard to experiment with the demo program. The menus also support mnemonic keys. To view a runtime help message, select Help from the Help menu.

## Initializing the system

Select Initialize system from the Animation menu to initialize the hidden frame and to draw the hidden background shown in FIG. 14-5. The hidden background is much larger than the hidden frame and the display window. Later, during the frame-building process, the program will copy selected portions of the oversized hidden background to the hidden frame, which is then copied to the display window from where it is saved to disk. You must initialize

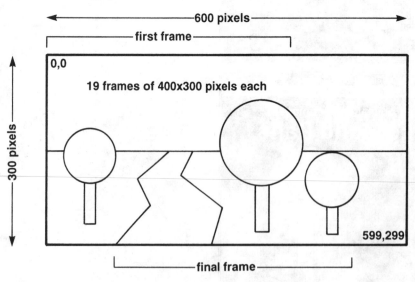

**14-5** The hidden background scene used by the sample application to demonstrate background panning.

both the hidden frame and the oversized background before building the animation.

## Creating the frames

Select Create Frames from the Animation menu to create the animation sequence and save it to disk. A sampling of four frames from the 19 frames of the animation sequence is shown in FIG. 14-6. The sample application will build each frame in turn on the hidden page, copy the completed frame to the display window, and then save the image to disk as a binary image file. If you have already saved the 19 frames to disk, the program will present a warning message. The software gives you the choice of overwriting existing files. If you choose not to overwrite an existing file, the build sequence is stopped and no more frames are constructed. If not enough free space exists on your hard disk to store the image files, the program displays a message and cancels the build process.

**14-6** The first four frames of the background pan from the animated sample application.

## Loading the animation

Before you can play the animation sequence that you have saved to disk, you must load it. If you saved the animation sequence during the current working session, select Load Animation from the Animation menu. If you saved the animation during a previous working session, you must first select Initialize system from the Animation menu and then select Load Animation from the Animation menu.

If the software is unable to find the required files on disk, it displays a message. If you attempt to play an animation before loading it from disk or before selecting Initialize system from the Animation menu, the demo program displays a hint message.

Under normal circumstances the sample application loads each frame file into the hidden frame from where it is moved to memory. After all 19 frames have been loaded from disk, the program uses a message box to report a successful load.

## Playing the animation

To play the animation sequence, select Run Forward from the Animation menu. The animation implements a background pan in 36 increments. It does this by first displaying the frames in sequence to pan from left to right, and then displaying them in reverse order to create a pan back from right to left. From the user's point of view, the camera starts at stage left, pans to stage right, and then pans back to stage left. Sample images excerpted from the animation sequence are shown in FIG. 14-6. The camera will continue panning until you stop the animation.

## Adjusting the animation playback speed

You can increase or decrease the animation speed by selecting from the Timer menu. At startup the playback rate is set to 18 frames per second, indicated by the check mark on the Timer menu. If you select 6 frames per second the check mark moves to the appropriate menu item and the animation rate changes. See chapter 8 for information about playback rates on slower computers.

## Freeze-frame and single-step animation

**Pause**   To pause the animation, select Pause from the Animation menu. To resume animation playback in forward mode, select Run Forward from the Animation menu. To resume animation playback in reverse mode, select Run Reverse from the Animation menu.

**Single-step**   When the animation is paused you can use single-step playback. First, select Pause from the Animation menu. Then press the right arrow key on the direction keypad to display the next frame in the animation sequence. Continue to press the right arrow key to single-step through the animation sequence. To single-step in reverse, press the left arrow key. To resume full animation playback, select Run Forward from the Animation menu.

## Persistent graphics

**Moving the window**   To test the persistent graphics features, start the panning and then move the window. Click on the caption bar of the window and drag it to another location. If the window is clipped by the edge of the screen the animation will continue to play.

**Covering the window**   To test the cooperative features of the animation, partly cover the window by a program group box or by another window. The animation will continue to run.

## Using the Help menu

You can use the Help menu to discover various facts about your system that are in effect at runtime. You can determine the current screen mode, the maximum number of available colors, the runtime memory mode (real, standard, or enhanced), and other information.

**Checking the screen resolution**   To find out the current screen mode, select Screen resolution from the Help menu. The sample application supports 640 × 480, 640 × 350, 800 × 600, and 1024 × 768 resolution displays.

**Maximum displayable colors**   To determine the maximum available colors that can be displayed simultaneously, select Available colors from the Help menu. The sample application supports 16-color and 2-color displays. If you want to modify the source code to support 256-color displays, see the discussion in chapter 3, Blitting.

**Determining the runtime memory mode**   To examine the current Windows runtime memory mode, select Memory mode from the Help menu. The application supports real, standard , and enhanced memory modes. Because of the number of bitmaps required at runtime, standard and enhanced memory modes provide the best performance, especially on computers equipped with 4 MB or more of memory.

**Animation memory requirements**   To view a message box about animation memory requirements, select Memory notes from the Help menu.

**Animation timing considerations**   To view a message box about animation playback rates, select Timing notes from the Help menu.

**General help**   For a general help message at runtime, select Help from the Help menu. All features of the Help menu are available during animation playback. The animation continues to play beneath any message box that Windows places on the screen.

# How the source code works: A programmer's guide

**Hands On**  The panning.exe demonstration program is a dedicated implementation of the prototype frame animation engine that was described and demonstrated in chapter 8, Frame animation engines. By excerpting the techniques presented in panning.exe, you can easily add camera pans to your own applications. By using the transparent PUT function provided in chapter 3, Blitting, you can manipulate bitblts in front of the background during the background pan.

The organization of the panning.h #include file and the panning.rc resource script file follow the format established in earlier sample applications. In particular, see chapter 8, Frame animation engines, for a prototype for frame animation.

## How the .c file works

**.C**  The .c file is derived from the prototype program in chapter 8, Frame animation engines. The .c file is also closely related to the animation demo in chapter 10, Characters. The discussion here focuses on new features that have been added to support background panning. You can refer back to chapter 8 and chapter 10 for a detailed discussion of the frame animation code in general.

**Static variables**  Global variables that are visible throughout the entire .c source file are declared and initialized at lines 0051 through 0136. Five new variables have been added at lines 0106 through 0110 in order to support the hidden bitmap for the oversized background. Compare these new variables to the variables for the hidden frame at lines 0101 through 0104. There is nothing new here, just more of the same.

The handles to the 19 frames that are used for playback are declared at lines 0133 and 0144.

**Creating the background**  When the user selects Initialize system from the Animation menu, the case IDM_InitFrame: statement at line 0290 executes. The code at line 0291 calls a function named zDrawBackground(), which is located at lines 0928 through 1025.

After first declaring some local variables and using an if() statement to ensure that the background has not already been created, the zDrawBackground() code at lines 0949 through 0963 initializes a hidden bitmap. Note the use of the zBGWIDE and zBGHIGH arguments during the call to CreateCompatibleBitmap() at line 0952. These two constants were defined at lines 0056 and 0057. Next, the if() block at lines 0953 through 0961 displays a message and then tidies up and exits if anything went wrong. The call to SelectObject() at line 0962 selects the bitmap into the newly created memory-display context.

The code located at lines 0965 through 1012 draws the background. The comments along the right side of the program listing indicate which statements create the sky, the terrain, the stream, the tree trunks, and the foliage. Note in particular the use of Polygon() at line 1000. The code at lines 0992 through 0999 loads the Points[] array with the coordinates that the GDI will use to draw the polygon that outlines the stream. The Points[] array was declared as a local variable at line 0937 using the POINT data type. This means an X and a Y integer will comprise each element of the array. Refer back to FIG. 14-5 for a sketch of the background image that is drawn by zDrawBackground().

**Building the animation** The zSaveAnimation() function at lines 0729 through 0817 manages the creation and storage of the 19 frames that make up the animation sequence. The zSaveAnimation() function calls zBuildFrame() to build each frame. The code for zBuildFrame() is located at lines 0823 through 0922. The switch() block at lines 0833 through 0892 is the essential ingredient of the build operation. Notice how the coordinates for the source bitmap are shifted during each call to BitBlt(). At lines 0853 and 0854, for example, the rectangle originating at 36,0 is copied from the oversized background to the hidden frame. To visualize this, refer again to FIG. 14-5. Next, at lines 0856 and 0857, the rectangle originating at 42,0 is copied to the hidden frame. This shifting is what creates the panning movement.

After completing the frame, line 0919 calls a core function named zSaveFrame() to save the image in the hidden frame to disk. All in all, 19 images will be stored on disk. If you are building your own panning engine for playback in real-time, you could instead copy directly from the hidden background to the screen in order to implement a pan. See FIG. 9-3 in chapter 9, Cel animation and Windows, for a suggested use of this approach.

**The animation engine** The zShowNextFrame() function at lines 1038 through 1207 manages the animation playback. In particular, the switch(FrameNum) block at lines 1060 through 1098 selects the appropriate hFn bitmap handle into the memory-display context hFDC if the computer is using RAM-based frame animation. If disk-based frame animation is being used, the switch() block at lines 1119 through 1193 loads the appropriate image file from disk during playback.

As you watch the animation running, you can see how the camera instantly changes direction at the end of a pan. This is unnatural— film cameras in the real world do not operate like this. Instead, the camera should gradually reduce the speed of the pan, come to a stop, then gradually build up the speed of the pan in the opposite direction. You might find it an interesting assignment to add slow-in/slow-out code to the animation engine. See the discussion in chapter 13, Motion, for further detail about the slow-in/slow-out technique. See lines 1271 through 1342 in the blink.c program listing in chapter 10, Characters, for a hands-on example of how to control the length of time that each frame is displayed. In its current implementation, panning.exe uses a zip pan, which is more of a special effect than a standard pan.

Note that this chapter focuses on the powerful panning capabilities of BitBlt(). For discussion and demonstration of the bitmap-scaling capabilities of the StretchBlt() function, see pages 184-187 in the author's previous book, *High-Performance C Graphics Programming for Windows* (ISBN 0-8306-3790-7, Windcrest/McGraw-Hill book 4103, published May 1992).

## Program listings for the sample application

The program listings presented here contain all the source code you need to build and run the sample application. The panning.def module definition file is provided in FIG. 14-7. The panning.h #include file is found in FIG. 14-8. The panning.rc resource script file is presented in FIG. 14-9. The panning.c source file is provided in FIG. 14-10. The storage.h #include file for the disk read/write module is located in FIG. 10-36 in chapter 10, Characters. The C source file for the read/write module is provided as storage.c in FIG. 10-37 in chapter 10, Characters.

**Companion disk**   If you have the companion disk, the six source files are presented as panning.def, panning.h, panning.rc, panning.c, storage.h, and storage.c.

**License**   You can paste the royalty-free source code into your own applications and distribute the resulting executable files under the conditions of the License Agreement and Limited Warranty in FIG. 10 in the introduction to this book.

**14-7**  The module definition file listing for the sample application.

```
0001  NAME          DEFDEMO
0002  DESCRIPTION   'Copyright 1992 Lee Adams.  All rights reserved.'
0003  EXETYPE       WINDOWS
0004  STUB          'WINSTUB.EXE'
0005  CODE          PRELOAD MOVEABLE
0006  DATA          PRELOAD MOVEABLE MULTIPLE
0007  HEAPSIZE      1024
0008  STACKSIZE     8192
0009  EXPORTS       zMessageHandler
```

**14-8**  The include file listing for the sample application.

```
0001  /*
0002  -----------------------------------------------------------------
0003                    Include file PANNING.H
0004          Copyright 1992 Lee Adams.  All rights reserved.
0005     Include this file in the .RC resource script file and in the
0006     .C source file.  It contains function prototypes, menu ID
0007     constants, and string ID constants.
0008  -----------------------------------------------------------------
0009  -----------------------------------------------------------------
0010                    Function prototypes
0011  -----------------------------------------------------------------
0012                                                                 */
```

```
0013   #if !defined(zRCFILE)                       /* if not an .RC file... */
0014     LONG FAR PASCAL zMessageHandler(HWND, unsigned, WORD, LONG);
0015     int PASCAL WinMain(HANDLE,HANDLE,LPSTR,int);
0016     HWND zInitMainWindow(HANDLE);
0017     BOOL zInitClass(HANDLE);
0018   static void zClear(HWND);                  /* blank the display window */
0019   static void zInitFrame(HWND);               /* creates hidden frame */
0020   static void zShowNextFrame(HWND);            /* the playback engine */
0021   static void zSetFrameRate(HWND,WORD);        /* resets the timer */
0022   static void zDrawBackground(HWND); /* draws oversized background */
0023   static void zSaveAnimation(HWND);        /* saves animation sequence */
0024   static BOOL zBuildFrame(int,HWND,LPSTR);    /* builds one frame */
0025   static void zLoadAnimation(HWND);    /* loads animation sequence */
0026   static void zCopyToDisplay(HWND);      /* copies frame to display */
0027   static void zClearHiddenFrame(void);       /* clears hidden frame */
0028   #endif
0029   /*
0030   ----------------------------------------------------------------
0031                        Menu ID constants
0032   ----------------------------------------------------------------
0033                                                                   */
0034   #define IDM_New              1
0035   #define IDM_Open             2
0036   #define IDM_Save             3
0037   #define IDM_SaveAs           4
0038   #define IDM_Exit             5
0039
0040   #define IDM_Undo             6
0041   #define IDM_Cut              7
0042   #define IDM_Copy             8
0043   #define IDM_Paste            9
0044   #define IDM_Delete           10
0045
0046   #define IDM_RunForward       11
0047   #define IDM_RunReverse       12
0048   #define IDM_StopAnimation    13
0049   #define IDM_InitFrame        14
0050   #define IDM_SaveAnimation    15
0051   #define IDM_LoadAnimation    16
0052   #define IDM_Clear            17
0053
0054   #define IDM_FPS182           18
0055   #define IDM_FPS91            19
0056   #define IDM_FPS61            20
0057   #define IDM_FPS45            21
0058   #define IDM_FPS36            22
0059   #define IDM_FPS30            23
0060
0061   #define IDM_About            24
0062   #define IDM_License          25
0063   #define IDM_Display          26
0064   #define IDM_Colors           27
0065   #define IDM_Mode             28
0066   #define IDM_Memory           29
0067   #define IDM_Timing           30
0068   #define IDM_GeneralHelp      31
0069   /*
0070   ----------------------------------------------------------------
0071                        String ID constants
0072   ----------------------------------------------------------------
0073                                                                   */
```

**14-8** Continued.

```
0074   #define IDS_Caption        1
0075   #define IDS_Warning        2
0076   #define IDS_NoMouse        3
0077   #define IDS_About          4
0078   #define IDS_AboutText      5
0079   #define IDS_License        6
0080   #define IDS_LicenseText    7
0081   #define IDS_Help           8
0082   #define IDS_HelpText       9
0083   #define IDS_Completed      10
0084   #define IDS_Error          11
0085   #define IDS_Memory         12
0086   #define IDS_MemText        13
0087   #define IDS_Timing         14
0088   #define IDS_TimingText     15
0089   #define IDS_NotReady       16
0090   #define IDS_Ready          17
0091   #define IDS_BuildBefore    18
0092   #define IDS_Already        19
0093   #define IDS_InsufMem1      20
0094   #define IDS_InsufMem2      21
0095   #define IDS_NoTimer        22
0096   #define IDS_NoReset        23
0097   #define IDS_CannotReset    24
0098   #define IDS_Resolution     25
0099   #define IDS_ResVGA         26
0100   #define IDS_ResEGA         27
0101   #define IDS_ResCGA         28
0102   #define IDS_ResSVGA        29
0103   #define IDS_Res8514        30
0104   #define IDS_ResHerc        31
0105   #define IDS_ResCustom      32
0106   #define IDS_Color          33
0107   #define IDS_Color16        34
0108   #define IDS_Color256       35
0109   #define IDS_Color2         36
0110   #define IDS_ColorCustom    37
0111   #define IDS_Machine        38
0112   #define IDS_Enhanced       39
0113   #define IDS_Standard       40
0114   #define IDS_Real           41
0115   #define IDS_NoFrame        42
0116   #define IDS_AnimReady      43
0117   #define IDS_Unexpected     44
0118   #define IDS_Status         45
0119   #define IDS_Disk1          46
0120   #define IDS_Disk2          47
0121   #define IDS_Disk3          48
0122   #define IDS_Disk4          49
0123   #define IDS_Disk5          50
0124   #define IDS_Disk6          51
0125   #define IDS_Disk7          52
0126   #define IDS_Disk8          53
0127   #define IDS_Disk9          54
0128   #define IDS_Disk10         55
0129   #define IDS_Disk11         56
0130   #define IDS_Disk12         57
0131   #define IDS_Disk13         58
0132   #define IDS_Disk14         59
0133   #define IDS_Disk15         60
0134   #define IDS_Disk16         61
```

**14-8** Continued.

```
0135   #define IDS_Disk17      62
0136   #define IDS_Disk18      63
0137   #define IDS_Disk19      64
0138   #define IDS_Disk20      65
0139   #define IDS_Disk21      66
0140   #define IDS_Disk22      67
0141   #define IDS_Disk23      68
0142   #define IDS_Disk24      69
0143   #define IDS_Disk25      70
0144   #define IDS_Disk26      71
0145   #define IDS_NoBg        72
0146   #define IDS_BgAlready   73
0147   #define IDS_InsufMemBg  74
0148   /*
0149   ----------------------------------------------------------------
0150                       End of include file
0151   ----------------------------------------------------------------
0152                                                                  */
```

**14-9** The resource script file listing for the sample application.

```
0001   /*
0002   ----------------------------------------------------------------
0003                   Resource script file PANNING.RC
0004           Copyright 1992 Lee Adams.  All rights reserved.
0005     This file defines the menu resources, the accelerator key
0006     resources, and the string resources that will be used by the
0007     demonstration application at runtime.
0008   ----------------------------------------------------------------
0009                                                                  */
0010   #define zRCFILE
0011   #include <WINDOWS.H>
0012   #include "PANNING.H"
0013   /*
0014   ----------------------------------------------------------------
0015                         Script for menus
0016   ----------------------------------------------------------------
0017                                                                  */
0018   MENUS1 MENU
0019     BEGIN
0020     POPUP "&File"
0021       BEGIN
0022         MENUITEM   "&New", IDM_New, GRAYED
0023         MENUITEM   "&Open...", IDM_Open, GRAYED
0024         MENUITEM   "&Save", IDM_Save, GRAYED
0025         MENUITEM   "Save &As...", IDM_SaveAs, GRAYED
0026         MENUITEM SEPARATOR
0027         MENUITEM   "E&xit", IDM_Exit
0028       END
0029     POPUP "&Edit"
0030       BEGIN
0031         MENUITEM   "&Undo\tAlt+BkSp", IDM_Undo, GRAYED
0032         MENUITEM SEPARATOR
0033         MENUITEM   "Cu&t\tShift+Del", IDM_Cut, GRAYED
0034         MENUITEM   "&Copy\tCtrl+Ins", IDM_Copy, GRAYED
0035         MENUITEM   "&Paste\tShift+Ins", IDM_Paste, GRAYED
0036         MENUITEM   "&Delete\tDel", IDM_Delete, GRAYED
0037       END
0038     POPUP "&Animation"
0039       BEGIN
```

```
0040        MENUITEM "Run &Forward", IDM_RunForward
0041        MENUITEM "Run &Reverse", IDM_RunReverse
0042        MENUITEM "&Pause", IDM_StopAnimation
0043        MENUITEM SEPARATOR
0044        MENUITEM "&Initialize system", IDM_InitFrame
0045        MENUITEM "Cr&eate Frames", IDM_SaveAnimation
0046        MENUITEM SEPARATOR
0047        MENUITEM "&Load Animation", IDM_LoadAnimation
0048        MENUITEM SEPARATOR
0049        MENUITEM "&Clear", IDM_Clear
0050      END
0051    POPUP "&Timer"
0052      BEGIN
0053        MENUITEM "&18 fps", IDM_FPS182, CHECKED
0054        MENUITEM " &9 fps", IDM_FPS91
0055        MENUITEM " &6 fps", IDM_FPS61
0056        MENUITEM " &5 fps", IDM_FPS45
0057        MENUITEM " &4 fps", IDM_FPS36
0058        MENUITEM " &3 fps", IDM_FPS30
0059      END
0060    POPUP "&Help"
0061      BEGIN
0062        MENUITEM "&About", IDM_About
0063        MENUITEM "&License", IDM_License
0064        MENUITEM SEPARATOR
0065        MENUITEM "&Screen resolution", IDM_Display
0066        MENUITEM "Available &colors", IDM_Colors
0067        MENUITEM "Memory mode", IDM_Mode
0068        MENUITEM SEPARATOR
0069        MENUITEM "&Memory notes", IDM_Memory
0070        MENUITEM "&Timing notes", IDM_Timing
0071        MENUITEM SEPARATOR
0072        MENUITEM "&Help", IDM_GeneralHelp
0073      END
0074    END
0075  /*
0076  ----------------------------------------------------------------
0077                    Script for accelerator keys
0078  ----------------------------------------------------------------
0079                                                              */
0080  KEYS1 ACCELERATORS
0081    BEGIN
0082  VK_BACK, IDM_Undo, VIRTKEY, ALT
0083  VK_DELETE, IDM_Cut, VIRTKEY, SHIFT
0084  VK_INSERT, IDM_Copy, VIRTKEY, CONTROL
0085  VK_INSERT, IDM_Paste, VIRTKEY, SHIFT
0086  VK_DELETE, IDM_Delete,VIRTKEY
0087    END
0088  /*
0089  ----------------------------------------------------------------
0090                    Script for strings
0091    Programmer's Notes: If you are typing this listing, set your
0092    margins to a line length of 255 characters so you can create
0093    lengthy strings without embedded carriage returns.  The line
0094    wraparounds in the following STRINGTABLE script are used for
0095    readability only in this printout.
0096  ----------------------------------------------------------------
0097                                                              */
0098  STRINGTABLE
0099    BEGIN
```

**14-9**  Continued.

```
0100      IDS_Caption      "Background Panning Engine"
0101      IDS_Warning      "Warning"
0102      IDS_NoMouse      "No mouse found.  Some features of this
          demonstration program may require a mouse."
0103      IDS_About        "About this program"
0104      IDS_AboutText    "This is a demo from Windcrest McGraw-Hill
          book 4114.  Copyright 1992 Lee Adams.  All rights reserved."
0105      IDS_License      "License Agreement"
0106      IDS_LicenseText "You can use this code as part of your own
          software product subject to the License Agreement and Limited
          Warranty in Windcrest McGraw-Hill book 4114 and on its
          companion disk."
0107      IDS_Help         "How to use this demo"
0108      IDS_HelpText     "The Animation menu manages the animation
          engine.  Select Initialize System then Create Frames to build
          frames and save to disk.  Select Load Animation then Run
          Forward to play animation.  See the book for advanced
          features."
0109      IDS_Completed    "Task completed OK"
0110      IDS_Error        "Runtime error"
0111      IDS_Memory       "Animation memory requirements"
0112      IDS_MemText      "The hidden frame for the animation is stored
          as a bitmap in global memory.  The demo will advise you if a
          memory shortage occurs.  To make more global memory available
          you can close other applications."
0113      IDS_Timing       "Animation timing"
0114      IDS_TimingText   "The Timer menu sets the animation display
          rate to 18.2, 9.1, 6.1, 4.5, 3.6, or 3 frames per second.
          Actual performance is limited by your computer's processor
          (25MHz or faster is recommended).  See the book for details."
0115      IDS_NotReady     "Animation not ready"
0116      IDS_Ready        "Animation ready"
0117      IDS_BuildBefore "Animation frames not ready for playback."
0118      IDS_Already      "The hidden frame has already been created."
0119      IDS_InsufMem1    "Insufficient global memory for frame bitmap."
0120      IDS_NoTimer      "Unable to create a timer.  Close other
          applications."
0121      IDS_NoReset      "Create hidden frame before attempting to
          reset timer."
0122      IDS_CannotReset "Unable to reset the timer."
0123      IDS_Resolution   "Screen resolution"
0124      IDS_ResVGA       "Running in 640x480 mode."
0125      IDS_ResEGA       "Running in 640x350 mode."
0126      IDS_ResCGA       "Running in 640x200 mode."
0127      IDS_ResSVGA      "Running in 800x600 mode."
0128      IDS_Res8514      "Running in 1024x768 mode."
0129      IDS_ResHerc      "Running in 720x348 mode."
0130      IDS_ResCustom    "Running in custom mode."
0131      IDS_Color        "Available colors"
0132      IDS_Color16      "Running in 16-color mode."
0133      IDS_Color256     "Running in 256-color mode."
0134      IDS_Color2       "Running in 2-color mode."
0135      IDS_ColorCustom "Running in a custom color mode."
0136      IDS_Machine      "Memory mode"
0137      IDS_Enhanced     "Running in enhanced mode.  Can allocate up to
          16 MB extended physical memory (XMS) if available.  Virtual
          memory up to 4 times physical memory (maximum 64 MB) is also
          available via automatic disk swapping of 4K pages."
0138      IDS_Standard     "Running in standard mode.  Can allocate up to
          16 MB extended physical memory (XMS) if available."
```

```
0139      IDS_Real          "Running in real mode.  Can allocate blocks of
          memory from the first 640K of RAM.  Can also allocate blocks
          from expanded memory (EMS) if available."
0140      IDS_NoFrame       "Hidden frame not yet created."
0141      IDS_AnimReady     "Animation ready"
0142      IDS_Unexpected    "Unexpected animation condition"
0143      IDS_Status        "Animation status"
0144      IDS_Disk1         "Animation files already saved to disk."
0145      IDS_Disk2         "Animation sequence successfully saved to
          disk."
0146      IDS_Disk3         "Unable to load next frame from disk.
          Animation halted."
0147      IDS_Disk4         "Animation sequence already loaded from disk."
0148      IDS_Disk5         "Previous load failed.  Cancelling this
          attempt."
0149      IDS_Disk6         "Not enough memory available.  Software will
          dynamically load each frame from disk during playback."
0150      IDS_Disk7         "Animation sequence successfully loaded from
          disk."
0151      IDS_Disk8         "Previous save failed.  Cancelling this
          attempt."
0152      IDS_Disk9         "No hidden-frame exists.  No frame saved to
          disk."
0153      IDS_Disk10        "Unable to retrieve bitmap data structure."
0154      IDS_Disk11        "Bit array is too long to save to disk in a
          single pass."
0155      IDS_Disk12        "Cannot create memory buffer for disk write."
0156      IDS_Disk13        "Unable to copy bits from bitmap to buffer."
0157      IDS_Disk14        "File already exists.  Overwrite existing
          file?"
0158      IDS_Disk15        "Unable to open the file for writing."
0159      IDS_Disk16        "Unable to write to the opened file."
0160      IDS_Disk17        "Unable to close the file after writing."
0161      IDS_Disk18        "No memory bitmap exists.  Unable to load from
          disk."
0162      IDS_Disk19        "Image file is larger than animation frame.
          No file loaded."
0163      IDS_Disk20        "Cannot create memory buffer for file read."
0164      IDS_Disk21        "Unable to open the file for reading.  Be sure
          you have saved an animation sequence to disk before attempting
          to load it."
0165      IDS_Disk22        "An error occurred while reading the file."
0166      IDS_Disk23        "The frame file was shorter than expected."
0167      IDS_Disk24        "Unable to close the file after reading."
0168      IDS_Disk25        "Unable to copy bits from buffer to bitmap."
0169      IDS_Disk26        "Unable to save all files.  Check if
          sufficient space available on disk."
0170      IDS_NoBg          "Hidden background image not yet created."
0171      IDS_BgAlready     "The hidden background bitmap has already been
          created."
0172      IDS_InsufMemBg    "Insufficient global memory for background
          bitmap."
0173   END
0174   /*
0175   ----------------------------------------------------------------
0176                    End of resource script file
0177   ----------------------------------------------------------------
0178                                                                */
```

**14-10** The C source file listing for the sample application, template.c. This demonstration program is ready to build using QuickC for Windows, Turbo C++ for Windows, Microsoft C and the SDK, Borland C++, Symantec Zortech C++, WATCOM C, and other compilers. See chapter 10 for the program listings for storage.h and storage.c,which must be linked with this application. See FIG. 1-2 for sample command-lines to build the program. Guidelines for using your compiler are provided in the appropriate appendix at the back of the book.

```
0001  /*
0002  ------------------------------------------------------------------
0003        BACKGROUND PANNING ENGINE for Windows applications that use
0004        disk-based, hidden-page drawn, frame animation.  The background
0005        panning engine is comprised of an authoring system for creating
0006        oversized backgrounds, frames, and disk files -- and a playback
0007        engine for loading background frames from disk files and
0008        displaying them as an animation sequence (a background pan).
0009  ------------------------------------------------------------------
0010        Source file: PANNING.C
0011        Release version: 1.00              Programmer: Lee Adams
0012        Type:  C source file for Windows application development.
0013        Compilers: Microsoft C and SDK, Borland C++, Zortech C++,
0014           QuickC for Windows, Turbo C++ for Windows, WATCOM C.
0015        Memory model:  small.
0016        Dependencies:  PANNING.DEF module definition file, PANNING.H
0017                       include file, PANNING.RC resource script file,
0018                       and PANNING.C source file.  Disk I/O operations
0019                       require STORAGE.H include file and STORAGE.C
0020                       additional C source file.
0021        Output and features:  Demonstrates interactive playback of
0022           disk-based hidden-page drawn frame animation.  A background
0023           pan is implemented.
0024        Publication: Contains material from Windcrest/McGraw-Hill book
0025           4114 published by TAB BOOKS Division of McGraw-Hill Inc.
0026        License:  As purchaser of the book you are granted a royalty-
0027           free license to distribute executable files generated using
0028           this code provided you accept the conditions of the License
0029           Agreement and Limited Warranty described in the book and on
0030           the companion disk.  Government users:  This software and
0031           documentation are subject to restrictions set forth in The
0032           Rights in Technical Data and Computer Software clause at
0033           252.227-7013 and elsewhere.
0034  ------------------------------------------------------------------
0035           (c) Copyright 1992 Lee Adams.  All rights reserved.
0036              Lee Adams(tm) is a trademark of Lee Adams.
0037  ------------------------------------------------------------------
0038
0039  ------------------------------------------------------------------
0040                            Include files
0041  ------------------------------------------------------------------
0042                                                                   */
0043  #include <WINDOWS.H>
0044  #include "PANNING.H"
0045  #include "STORAGE.H"  /* declares callable functions in STORAGE.C
            */
0046  /*
0047  ------------------------------------------------------------------
0048           Static variables visible throughout this file
0049  ------------------------------------------------------------------
0050                                                                   */
0051  /* -------------------- window specifications ----------------- */
0052  #define zWINDOW_WIDTH 408
0053  #define zWINDOW_HEIGHT 346
```

```
0054   #define zFRAMEWIDE 400
0055   #define zFRAMEHIGH 300
0056   #define zBGWIDE    600              /* width of hidden background */
0057   #define zBGHIGH    300              /* height of hidden background */
0058   int WindowX, WindowY;
0059
0060   /* ------------------ instance operations ------------------- */
0061   HANDLE hInst;
0062   HWND MainhWnd;
0063   HANDLE hAccel;
0064   HMENU hMenu;
0065   PAINTSTRUCT ps;
0066   int MessageRet;
0067
0068   /* ------------------- mouse and cursor ------------------- */
0069   HCURSOR hPrevCursor;
0070   HCURSOR hHourGlass;
0071   int MousePresent;
0072
0073   /* ------------------- runtime conditions ------------------- */
0074   int DisplayWidth, DisplayHeight;
0075   int DisplayBits;
0076   int DisplayPlanes;
0077   DWORD MemoryMode;
0078
0079   /* ------------------ message box operations ----------------- */
0080   char lpCaption[51];
0081   int Max= 50;
0082   char lpMessage[250];
0083   int MaxText= 249;
0084
0085   /* ---------------- persistent image operations -------------- */
0086   #define zBLANK 0
0087   #define zANIMATING  1
0088   int PaintImage= zBLANK;
0089
0090   /* -------------------- timer operations -------------------- */
0091   #define zTIMER_PAUSE 3
0092   int TimerCounter= zTIMER_PAUSE;
0093   BOOL TimerExists= FALSE;
0094   WORD TimerID1;
0095
0096   /* -------------------- font operations --------------------- */
0097   HFONT hFont, hPrevFont;          /* handles to new, previous font */
0098   HDC hFontDC;                              /* display-context for font */
0099
0100   /* ----------------- hidden frame operations ----------------- */
0101   HDC hFrameDC;
0102   HBITMAP hFrame;
0103   HBITMAP hPrevFrame;
0104   BOOL FrameReady= FALSE;
0105   /* --------------- hidden background operations --------------- */
0106   HDC hBackgroundDC;
0107   HBITMAP hBackground;
0108   HBITMAP hPrevBg;
0109   BOOL BgReady= FALSE;
0110   BOOL BgBitmapExists= FALSE;
0111   /* -------------------- animation engine --------------------- */
0112   BOOL Pause= TRUE;
0113   WORD wFrameRate= 55;
0114   WORD wPrevRate= 55;
```

```
0115  #define zFORWARD 1
0116  #define zREVERSE 0
0117  int FrameDirection= zFORWARD;
0118  BOOL Redisplay= FALSE;
0119  int FrameNum= 0;
0120  #define zFIRSTFRAME 1
0121  #define zFINALFRAME 36
0122  BOOL AnimationReady= FALSE;
0123
0124  /* ---------------- disk save/load operations ---------------- */
0125  int RetVal;                                    /* return value */
0126  BOOL bFrameSaved= FALSE;              /* frame saved to disk? */
0127  BOOL bFrameLoaded= FALSE;            /* frame loaded from disk? */
0128  BOOL bAnimationSaved= FALSE;        /* animation saved to disk? */
0129  BOOL bAnimationLoaded= FALSE;      /* animation loaded from disk? */
0130  BOOL bPrevSaveAttempt= FALSE;      /* previous save attempt made? */
0131  BOOL bPrevLoadAttempt= FALSE;      /* previous load attempt made? */
0132  HDC hFDC;                          /* memory-display context for playback */
0133  HBITMAP hPrevF,hF1,hF2,hF3,hF4,hF5,    /* bitmaps for playback... */
0134   hF6,hF7,hF8,hF9,hF10,hF11,hF12,hF13,hF14,hF15,hF16,hF17,hF18,hF19;
0135  BOOL bUseDisk= FALSE;                /* load each frame as needed? */
0136  BOOL bAnimationHalted= FALSE;     /* disk error during animation? */
0137  /*
0138  ------------------------------------------------------------------
0139                  Entry point for the application
0140  ------------------------------------------------------------------
0141                                                                  */
0142  int PASCAL WinMain(HANDLE hInstance, HANDLE hPrevInstance,
0143                   LPSTR lpCmdLine, int nCmdShow)
0144  {
0145    MSG msg;
0146    HWND hWndPrev;
0147    HWND hDesktopWnd;
0148    HDC hDCcaps;
0149
0150  /* ----------- ensure only one instance is running ------------ */
0151  hWndPrev = FindWindow("DEMOCLASS", NULL);
0152  if (hWndPrev != NULL)
0153    {
0154    BringWindowToTop(hWndPrev);
0155    return FALSE;
0156    }
0157
0158  /* --------- determine capabilities of screen display ---------- */
0159  hDesktopWnd= GetDesktopWindow();
0160  hDCcaps= GetDC(hDesktopWnd);
0161  DisplayWidth= GetDeviceCaps(hDCcaps,HORZRES);
0162  DisplayHeight= GetDeviceCaps(hDCcaps,VERTRES);
0163  DisplayBits= GetDeviceCaps(hDCcaps,BITSPIXEL);
0164  DisplayPlanes= GetDeviceCaps(hDCcaps,PLANES);
0165  ReleaseDC(hDesktopWnd,hDCcaps);
0166
0167  /* ------- calculate screen position to center the window ------ */
0168  WindowX= (DisplayWidth - zWINDOW_WIDTH) / 2;
0169  WindowY= (DisplayHeight - zWINDOW_HEIGHT) /2;
0170  if (WindowX < 0) WindowX= 0;
0171  if (WindowY < 0) WindowY= 0;
0172
0173  /* ---- determine memory mode (enhanced, standard, or real) ---- */
0174  MemoryMode= GetWinFlags();
0175
```

```
0176    /* --------------- create and show the window ---------------- */
0177    hInst = hInstance;
0178    if (!zInitClass(hInstance)) return FALSE;
0179    MainhWnd = zInitMainWindow(hInstance);
0180    if (!MainhWnd) return FALSE;
0181    ShowWindow(MainhWnd, nCmdShow);
0182    UpdateWindow(MainhWnd);
0183    hAccel= LoadAccelerators(hInstance,"KEYS1");
0184    hFontDC= GetDC(MainhWnd);
0185    hFont= GetStockObject(SYSTEM_FONT);
0186    hPrevFont= SelectObject(hFontDC,hFont);
0187    SetTextColor(hFontDC,RGB(191,191,191));
0188    TextOut(hFontDC,10,280,"- Copyright 1992 Lee Adams.",27);
0189    SetTextColor(hFontDC,RGB(0,0,0));
0190    SelectObject(hFontDC,hPrevFont);
0191    ReleaseDC(MainhWnd,hFontDC);
0192
0193    /* --------------------- check for mouse --------------------- */
0194    MousePresent = GetSystemMetrics(SM_MOUSEPRESENT);
0195    if (!MousePresent)
0196      {
0197      LoadString(hInst,IDS_Warning,lpCaption,Max);
0198      LoadString(hInst,IDS_NoMouse,lpMessage,MaxText);
0199      MessageBox(GetFocus(),lpMessage,lpCaption,MB_OK);
0200      }
0201
0202    /* ---------- begin retrieving messages for the window --------- */
0203    while (GetMessage(&msg,0,0,0))
0204      {
0205      if(TranslateAccelerator(MainhWnd, hAccel, &msg))
0206         continue;
0207      TranslateMessage(&msg);
0208      DispatchMessage(&msg);
0209      }
0210    return(msg.wParam);
0211    }
0212    /*
0213    --------------------------------------------------------------
0214                    Switcher for incoming messages
0215    --------------------------------------------------------------
0216                                                                 */
0217    LONG FAR PASCAL zMessageHandler(HWND hWnd, unsigned message,
0218                             WORD wParam, LONG lParam)
0219    {
0220      HDC hDCpaint;
0221
0222    switch (message)
0223      {
0224
0225      case WM_TIMER:
0226        TimerCounter--;
0227        if (TimerCounter > 0) break;
0228        TimerCounter++;
0229        zShowNextFrame(hWnd);
0230        break;
0231
0232      case WM_COMMAND:
0233        switch(wParam)
0234          {
0235          case IDM_New:    break;
0236          case IDM_Open:   break;
```

```
0237        case IDM_Save:    break;
0238        case IDM_SaveAs: break;
0239        case IDM_Exit:    PostQuitMessage(0); break;
0240
0241        case IDM_Undo:    break;
0242        case IDM_Cut:     break;
0243        case IDM_Copy:    break;
0244        case IDM_Paste:   break;
0245        case IDM_Delete: break;
0246
0247        case IDM_RunForward:
0248            if (AnimationReady==FALSE)
0249                {
0250                MessageBeep(0);
0251                LoadString(hInst,IDS_NotReady,lpCaption,Max);
0252                LoadString(hInst,IDS_BuildBefore,lpMessage,MaxText);
0253                TimerCounter= zTIMER_PAUSE;
0254                MessageBox(GetFocus(),lpMessage,lpCaption,MB_OK);
0255                break;
0256                }
0257            Pause= FALSE;
0258            PaintImage= zANIMATING;
0259            FrameDirection= zFORWARD;
0260            zShowNextFrame(hWnd);
0261            break;
0262        case IDM_RunReverse:
0263            if (AnimationReady==FALSE)
0264                {
0265                MessageBeep(0);
0266                LoadString(hInst,IDS_NotReady,lpCaption,Max);
0267                LoadString(hInst,IDS_BuildBefore,lpMessage,MaxText);
0268                TimerCounter= zTIMER_PAUSE;
0269                MessageBox(GetFocus(),lpMessage,lpCaption,MB_OK);
0270                break;
0271                }
0272            Pause= FALSE;
0273            PaintImage= zANIMATING;
0274            FrameDirection= zREVERSE;
0275            zShowNextFrame(hWnd);
0276            break;
0277        case IDM_StopAnimation:
0278            if (AnimationReady==FALSE)
0279                {
0280                MessageBeep(0);
0281                LoadString(hInst,IDS_NotReady,lpCaption,Max);
0282                LoadString(hInst,IDS_BuildBefore,lpMessage,MaxText);
0283                TimerCounter= zTIMER_PAUSE;
0284                MessageBox(GetFocus(),lpMessage,lpCaption,MB_OK);
0285                break;
0286                }
0287            Pause= TRUE;
0288            zShowNextFrame(hWnd);
0289            break;
0290        case IDM_InitFrame: zInitFrame(hWnd);
0291                            zDrawBackground(hWnd);
0292                            break;
0293        case IDM_SaveAnimation:
0294            SetCapture(hWnd); hPrevCursor= SetCursor(hHourGlass);
0295            zSaveAnimation(hWnd);
0296            SetCursor(hPrevCursor); ReleaseCapture();
0297            if (bAnimationSaved==FALSE)
```

```
0298                   {
0299                   MessageBeep(0);
0300                   LoadString(hInst,IDS_NotReady,lpCaption,Max);
0301                   LoadString(hInst,IDS_Disk26,lpMessage,MaxText);
0302                   TimerCounter= zTIMER_PAUSE;
0303                   MessageBox(GetFocus(),lpMessage,lpCaption,MB_OK);
0304                   }
0305              if (BgBitmapExists==TRUE)
0306                   {
0307                   SelectObject(hBackgroundDC,hPrevBg);
0308                   DeleteObject(hBackground);
0309                   DeleteDC(hBackgroundDC);
0310                   BgBitmapExists= FALSE;
0311                   }
0312             break;
0313         case IDM_LoadAnimation:
0314              SetCapture(hWnd); hPrevCursor= SetCursor(hHourGlass);
0315              zLoadAnimation(hWnd);
0316              SetCursor(hPrevCursor); ReleaseCapture();
0317              break;
0318         case IDM_Clear:   if (Pause==TRUE)
0319                               {
0320                               zClear(hWnd);
0321                               PaintImage= zBLANK;
0322                               }
0323                           break;
0324
0325         case IDM_FPS182: wPrevRate= wFrameRate;
0326                          wFrameRate= (WORD)55;
0327                          zSetFrameRate(hWnd, wFrameRate); break;
0328         case IDM_FPS91:  wPrevRate= wFrameRate;
0329                          wFrameRate= (WORD)110;
0330                          zSetFrameRate(hWnd, wFrameRate); break;
0331         case IDM_FPS61:  wPrevRate= wFrameRate;
0332                          wFrameRate= (WORD)165;
0333                          zSetFrameRate(hWnd, wFrameRate); break;
0334         case IDM_FPS45:  wPrevRate= wFrameRate;
0335                          wFrameRate= (WORD) 220;
0336                          zSetFrameRate(hWnd, wFrameRate); break;
0337         case IDM_FPS36:  wPrevRate= wFrameRate;
0338                          wFrameRate= (WORD) 275;
0339                          zSetFrameRate(hWnd, wFrameRate); break;
0340         case IDM_FPS30:  wPrevRate= wFrameRate;
0341                          wFrameRate= (WORD) 330;
0342                          zSetFrameRate(hWnd, wFrameRate); break;
0343
0344         case IDM_About:
0345           LoadString(hInst,IDS_About,lpCaption,Max);
0346           LoadString(hInst,IDS_AboutText,lpMessage,MaxText);
0347           TimerCounter= zTIMER_PAUSE;
0348           MessageBox(GetFocus(),lpMessage,lpCaption,MB_OK);
0349           break;
0350         case IDM_License:
0351           LoadString(hInst,IDS_License,lpCaption,Max);
0352           LoadString(hInst,IDS_LicenseText,lpMessage,MaxText);
0353           TimerCounter= zTIMER_PAUSE;
0354           MessageBox(GetFocus(),lpMessage,lpCaption,MB_OK);
0355           break;
0356
0357         case IDM_Display:
0358           if (DisplayWidth==640)
```

```
0359                     {
0360                     if (DisplayHeight==480)
0361                         {
0362                         LoadString(hInst,IDS_Resolution,lpCaption,Max);
0363                         LoadString(hInst,IDS_ResVGA,lpMessage,MaxText);
0364                         TimerCounter= zTIMER_PAUSE;
0365                         MessageBox(GetFocus(),lpMessage,lpCaption,MB_OK);
0366                         }
0367                     if (DisplayHeight==350)
0368                         {
0369                         LoadString(hInst,IDS_Resolution,lpCaption,Max);
0370                         LoadString(hInst,IDS_ResEGA,lpMessage,MaxText);
0371                         TimerCounter= zTIMER_PAUSE;
0372                         MessageBox(GetFocus(),lpMessage,lpCaption,MB_OK);
0373                         }
0374                     if (DisplayHeight==200)
0375                         {
0376                         LoadString(hInst,IDS_Resolution,lpCaption,Max);
0377                         LoadString(hInst,IDS_ResCGA,lpMessage,MaxText);
0378                         TimerCounter= zTIMER_PAUSE;
0379                         MessageBox(GetFocus(),lpMessage,lpCaption,MB_OK);
0380                         }
0381                     break;
0382                     }
0383                 if (DisplayWidth==800)
0384                     {
0385                     LoadString(hInst,IDS_Resolution,lpCaption,Max);
0386                     LoadString(hInst,IDS_ResSVGA,lpMessage,MaxText);
0387                     TimerCounter= zTIMER_PAUSE;
0388                     MessageBox(GetFocus(),lpMessage,lpCaption,MB_OK);
0389                     break;
0390                     }
0391                 if (DisplayWidth==1024)
0392                     {
0393                     LoadString(hInst,IDS_Resolution,lpCaption,Max);
0394                     LoadString(hInst,IDS_Res8514,lpMessage,MaxText);
0395                     TimerCounter= zTIMER_PAUSE;
0396                     MessageBox(GetFocus(),lpMessage,lpCaption,MB_OK);
0397                     break;
0398                     }
0399                 if (DisplayWidth==720)
0400                     {
0401                     LoadString(hInst,IDS_Resolution,lpCaption,Max);
0402                     LoadString(hInst,IDS_ResHerc,lpMessage,MaxText);
0403                     TimerCounter= zTIMER_PAUSE;
0404                     MessageBox(GetFocus(),lpMessage,lpCaption,MB_OK);
0405                     break;
0406                     }
0407                 LoadString(hInst,IDS_Resolution,lpCaption,Max);
0408                 LoadString(hInst,IDS_ResCustom,lpMessage,MaxText);
0409                 TimerCounter= zTIMER_PAUSE;
0410                 MessageBox(GetFocus(),lpMessage,lpCaption,MB_OK);
0411                 break;
0412
0413             case IDM_Colors:
0414                 if (DisplayBits==1)
0415                     {
0416                     if (DisplayPlanes==4)
0417                         {
0418                         LoadString(hInst,IDS_Color,lpCaption,Max);
0419                         LoadString(hInst,IDS_Color16,lpMessage,MaxText);
```

```
0420              TimerCounter= zTIMER_PAUSE;
0421              MessageBox(GetFocus(),lpMessage,lpCaption,MB_OK);
0422              break;
0423              }
0424            if (DisplayPlanes==1)
0425              {
0426              LoadString(hInst,IDS_Color,lpCaption,Max);
0427              LoadString(hInst,IDS_Color2,lpMessage,MaxText);
0428              TimerCounter= zTIMER_PAUSE;
0429              MessageBox(GetFocus(),lpMessage,lpCaption,MB_OK);
0430              break;
0431              }
0432            }
0433          if (DisplayBits==8)
0434            {
0435            LoadString(hInst,IDS_Color,lpCaption,Max);
0436            LoadString(hInst,IDS_Color256,lpMessage,MaxText);
0437            TimerCounter= zTIMER_PAUSE;
0438            MessageBox(GetFocus(),lpMessage,lpCaption,MB_OK);
0439            break;
0440            }
0441          LoadString(hInst,IDS_Color,lpCaption,Max);
0442          LoadString(hInst,IDS_ColorCustom,lpMessage,MaxText);
0443          TimerCounter= zTIMER_PAUSE;
0444          MessageBox(GetFocus(),lpMessage,lpCaption,MB_OK);
0445          break;
0446
0447        case IDM_Mode:
0448          if (MemoryMode & WF_ENHANCED)
0449            {
0450            LoadString(hInst,IDS_Machine,lpCaption,Max);
0451            LoadString(hInst,IDS_Enhanced,lpMessage,MaxText);
0452            TimerCounter= zTIMER_PAUSE;
0453            MessageBox(GetFocus(),lpMessage,lpCaption,MB_OK);
0454            break;
0455            }
0456          if (MemoryMode & WF_STANDARD)
0457            {
0458            LoadString(hInst,IDS_Machine,lpCaption,Max);
0459            LoadString(hInst,IDS_Standard,lpMessage,MaxText);
0460            TimerCounter= zTIMER_PAUSE;
0461            MessageBox(GetFocus(),lpMessage,lpCaption,MB_OK);
0462            break;
0463            }
0464          LoadString(hInst,IDS_Machine,lpCaption,Max);
0465          LoadString(hInst,IDS_Real,lpMessage,MaxText);
0466          TimerCounter= zTIMER_PAUSE;
0467          MessageBox(GetFocus(),lpMessage,lpCaption,MB_OK);
0468          break;
0469
0470        case IDM_Memory:
0471          LoadString(hInst,IDS_Memory,lpCaption,Max);
0472          LoadString(hInst,IDS_MemText,lpMessage,MaxText);
0473          TimerCounter= zTIMER_PAUSE;
0474          MessageBox(GetFocus(),lpMessage,lpCaption,MB_OK);
0475          break;
0476        case IDM_Timing:
0477          LoadString(hInst,IDS_Timing,lpCaption,Max);
0478          LoadString(hInst,IDS_TimingText,lpMessage,MaxText);
0479          TimerCounter= zTIMER_PAUSE;
```

```
0480            MessageBox(GetFocus(),lpMessage,lpCaption,MB_OK);
0481            break;
0482          case IDM_GeneralHelp:
0483            LoadString(hInst,IDS_Help,lpCaption,Max);
0484            LoadString(hInst,IDS_HelpText,lpMessage,MaxText);
0485            TimerCounter= zTIMER_PAUSE;
0486            MessageBox(GetFocus(),lpMessage,lpCaption,MB_OK);
0487            break;
0488          default:
0489            return(DefWindowProc(hWnd, message, wParam, lParam));
0490        }
0491      break;
0492
0493    case WM_INITMENUPOPUP:
0494      TimerCounter= zTIMER_PAUSE;
0495      if (lParam == 3)
0496        hMenu= wParam;
0497      break;
0498
0499    case WM_PAINT:
0500      hDCpaint= BeginPaint(hWnd,&ps);
0501      EndPaint(hWnd, &ps);
0502      if (PaintImage==zBLANK) break;
0503      if (Pause==TRUE)
0504        {
0505        Redisplay= TRUE;
0506        zShowNextFrame(hWnd);
0507        Redisplay= FALSE;
0508        break;
0509        }
0510      zShowNextFrame(hWnd);
0511      break;
0512
0513    case WM_KEYDOWN:
0514      switch (wParam)
0515        {
0516        case VK_LEFT:    if (Pause==TRUE)
0517                          {
0518                          if (FrameDirection==zFORWARD)
0519                            {
0520                            FrameDirection= zREVERSE;
0521                            }
0522                          Pause= FALSE;
0523                          zShowNextFrame(hWnd);
0524                          Pause= TRUE;
0525                          PaintImage= zANIMATING;
0526                          }
0527                        break;
0528        case VK_RIGHT:   if (Pause==TRUE)
0529                          {
0530                          if (FrameDirection==zREVERSE)
0531                            {
0532                            FrameDirection= zFORWARD;
0533                            }
0534                          Pause= FALSE;
0535                          zShowNextFrame(hWnd);
0536                          Pause= TRUE;
0537                          PaintImage= zANIMATING;
0538                          }
0539                        break;
```

```
0540            default:
0541                    return(DefWindowProc(hWnd, message, wParam, lParam));
0542            }
0543        break;
0544
0545    case WM_DESTROY:
0546        if (FrameReady==TRUE)
0547            {                           /* tidy up hidden frame bitmap... */
0548            SelectObject(hFrameDC,hPrevFrame);
0549            DeleteObject(hFrame);
0550            DeleteDC(hFrameDC);
0551            KillTimer(hWnd,1);
0552            }
0553        if (BgBitmapExists==TRUE)
0554            {                       /* tidy up hidden background bitmap... */
0555            SelectObject(hBackgroundDC,hPrevBg);
0556            DeleteObject(hBackground);
0557            DeleteDC(hBackgroundDC);
0558            }
0559        if (bAnimationLoaded==TRUE)
0560            {                   /* tidy up animation playback bitmaps... */
0561            SelectObject(hFDC,hPrevF);
0562            DeleteObject(hF1); DeleteObject(hF2); DeleteObject(hF3);
0563            DeleteObject(hF4); DeleteObject(hF5); DeleteObject(hF6);
0564            DeleteObject(hF7); DeleteObject(hF8); DeleteObject(hF9);
0565            DeleteObject(hF10); DeleteObject(hF11); DeleteObject(hF12);
0566            DeleteObject(hF13); DeleteObject(hF14); DeleteObject(hF15);
0567            DeleteObject(hF16); DeleteObject(hF17); DeleteObject(hF18);
0568            DeleteObject(hF19); DeleteDC(hFDC);
0569            }
0570        PostQuitMessage(0);
0571        break;
0572
0573    case WM_SYSCOMMAND:
0574        if ((wParam & 0xfff0)== SC_SIZE)
0575            {
0576            MessageBeep(0); break;
0577            }
0578        if ((wParam & 0xfff0)== SC_MINIMIZE)
0579            {
0580            MessageBeep(0); break;
0581            }
0582        if ((wParam & 0xfff0)== SC_MAXIMIZE)
0583            {
0584            MessageBeep(0); break;
0585            }
0586
0587    default:
0588        return(DefWindowProc(hWnd, message, wParam, lParam));
0589        }
0590 return FALSE;
0591 }
0592 /*
0593 -------------------------------------------------------------------
0594            Initialize the attributes of the window class
0595 -------------------------------------------------------------------
0596                                                                   */
0597 BOOL zInitClass(HANDLE hInstance)
0598 {
0599   WNDCLASS WndClass;
0600 WndClass.style= 0;
```

```
0601    WndClass.lpfnWndProc= zMessageHandler;
0602    WndClass.cbClsExtra= 0;
0603    WndClass.cbWndExtra= 0;
0604    WndClass.hInstance= hInstance;
0605    WndClass.hIcon= LoadIcon(NULL,IDI_EXCLAMATION);
0606    WndClass.hCursor= LoadCursor(NULL,IDC_ARROW);
0607    WndClass.hbrBackground= CreateSolidBrush(RGB(255,255,255));
0608    WndClass.lpszMenuName= "MENUS1";
0609    WndClass.lpszClassName= "DEMOCLASS";
0610    return RegisterClass(&WndClass);
0611    }
0612    /*
0613    -------------------------------------------------------------------
0614                        Create the main window
0615    -------------------------------------------------------------------
0616                                                                      */
0617    HWND zInitMainWindow(HANDLE hInstance)
0618    {
0619      HWND hWnd;
0620    LoadString(hInstance,IDS_Caption,lpCaption,Max);
0621    hHourGlass= LoadCursor(NULL,IDC_WAIT);
0622    hWnd = CreateWindow("DEMOCLASS",lpCaption,
0623      WS_OVERLAPPED | WS_THICKFRAME | WS_MINIMIZEBOX |
0624        WS_MAXIMIZEBOX | WS_CLIPCHILDREN,
0625      WindowX,WindowY,zWINDOW_WIDTH,zWINDOW_HEIGHT,0,0,
0626      hInstance, (LPSTR)NULL);
0627    return hWnd;
0628    }
0629    /*
0630    -------------------------------------------------------------------
0631                        GRAPHICS SYSTEM Functions
0632    -------------------------------------------------------------------
0633    -------------------------------------------------------------------
0634                        Create the hidden frame.
0635    -------------------------------------------------------------------
0636                                                                      */
0637    static void zInitFrame(HWND hWnd)
0638    {
0639      HDC hDisplayDC;
0640
0641    if (FrameReady==TRUE)
0642      {
0643      MessageBeep(0);
0644      LoadString(hInst,IDS_Ready,lpCaption,Max);
0645      LoadString(hInst,IDS_Already,lpMessage,MaxText);
0646      TimerCounter= zTIMER_PAUSE;
0647      MessageBox(GetFocus(),lpMessage,lpCaption,MB_OK);
0648      return;
0649      }
0650    GlobalCompact((DWORD)-1L);
0651    hDisplayDC= GetDC(hWnd);
0652    hFrameDC= CreateCompatibleDC(hDisplayDC);
0653    hFrame= CreateCompatibleBitmap(hDisplayDC,zFRAMEWIDE,zFRAMEHIGH);
0654    if (hFrame==NULL)
0655      {
0656      LoadString(hInst,IDS_NotReady,lpCaption,Max);
0657      LoadString(hInst,IDS_InsufMem1,lpMessage,MaxText);
0658      MessageBox(GetFocus(),lpMessage,lpCaption,MB_OK);
0659      DeleteDC(hFrameDC);
0660      TimerExists= FALSE; FrameReady= FALSE; AnimationReady= FALSE;
0661      return;
```

```
0662    }
0663    hPrevFrame= SelectObject(hFrameDC,hFrame);
0664    zClear(hWnd);
0665    BitBlt(hFrameDC,0,0,zFRAMEWIDE,zFRAMEHIGH,hDisplayDC,0,0,SRCCOPY);
0666    ReleaseDC(hWnd,hDisplayDC);
0667
0668    TimerID1= SetTimer(hWnd,1,wFrameRate,(FARPROC) NULL);
0669    if (TimerID1 == 0)
0670      {
0671      LoadString(hInst,IDS_NotReady,lpCaption,Max);
0672      LoadString(hInst,IDS_NoTimer,lpMessage,MaxText);
0673      MessageBox(GetFocus(),lpMessage,lpCaption,MB_OK);
0674      SelectObject(hFrameDC,hPrevFrame);
0675      DeleteObject(hFrame);
0676      DeleteDC(hFrameDC);
0677      TimerExists= FALSE;
0678      return;
0679      }
0680    TimerExists= TRUE;
0681    FrameReady= TRUE;
0682    FrameNum= 1;
0683    return;
0684    }
0685    /*
0686    -------------------------------------------------------------------
0687                        Clear the hidden frame.
0688    -------------------------------------------------------------------
0689                                                                    */
0690    static void zClearHiddenFrame(void)
0691    {
0692    PatBlt(hFrameDC,0,0,zFRAMEWIDE,zFRAMEHIGH,WHITENESS);
0693    return;
0694    }
0695    /*
0696    -------------------------------------------------------------------
0697              Copy the hidden frame to the display window.
0698    -------------------------------------------------------------------
0699                                                                    */
0700    static void zCopyToDisplay(HWND hWnd)
0701    {
0702      HDC hDC;
0703    hDC= GetDC(hWnd);
0704    BitBlt(hDC,0,0,zFRAMEWIDE,zFRAMEHIGH,hFrameDC,0,0,SRCCOPY);
0705    ReleaseDC(hWnd,hDC);
0706    return;
0707    }
0708    /*
0709    -------------------------------------------------------------------
0710                        Blank the display window.
0711    -------------------------------------------------------------------
0712                                                                    */
0713    static void zClear(HWND hWnd)
0714    {
0715      HDC hDC;
0716    hDC= GetDC(hWnd);
0717    PatBlt(hDC,0,0,zFRAMEWIDE,zFRAMEHIGH,WHITENESS);
0718    ReleaseDC(hWnd,hDC);
0719    return;
0720    }
0721    /*
0722    -------------------------------------------------------------------
```

```
0723                        AUTHORING SYSTEM Functions
0724   -----------------------------------------------------------------------
0725   -----------------------------------------------------------------------
0726                      Create 19 frames and save to disk.
0727   -----------------------------------------------------------------------
0728                                                                         */
0729   static void zSaveAnimation(HWND hWnd)
0730   {
0731   if (FrameReady==FALSE)              /* if no hidden-frame available... */
0732     {
0733     MessageBeep(0);
0734     LoadString(hInst,IDS_NotReady,lpCaption,Max);
0735     LoadString(hInst,IDS_NoFrame,lpMessage,MaxText);
0736     MessageBox(GetFocus(),lpMessage,lpCaption,MB_OK);
0737     return;
0738     }
0739
0740   if (BgReady==FALSE)         /* if no hidden-background available... */
0741     {
0742     MessageBeep(0);
0743     LoadString(hInst,IDS_NotReady,lpCaption,Max);
0744     LoadString(hInst,IDS_NoBg,lpMessage,MaxText);
0745     MessageBox(GetFocus(),lpMessage,lpCaption,MB_OK);
0746     return;
0747     }
0748
0749   if (bAnimationSaved==TRUE) /* if frames already saved to disk... */
0750     {
0751     MessageBeep(0);
0752     LoadString(hInst,IDS_Unexpected,lpCaption,Max);
0753     LoadString(hInst,IDS_Disk1,lpMessage,MaxText);
0754     TimerCounter= zTIMER_PAUSE;
0755     MessageBox(GetFocus(),lpMessage,lpCaption,MB_OK);
0756     return;
0757     }
0758
0759   if (bPrevSaveAttempt==TRUE)        /* if previous attempt failed... */
0760     {
0761     MessageBeep(0);
0762     LoadString(hInst,IDS_Unexpected,lpCaption,Max);
0763     LoadString(hInst,IDS_Disk8,lpMessage,MaxText);
0764     TimerCounter= zTIMER_PAUSE;
0765     MessageBox(GetFocus(),lpMessage,lpCaption,MB_OK);
0766     return;
0767     }
0768   bPrevSaveAttempt= TRUE;
0769
0770   bFrameSaved= zBuildFrame(1,hWnd,(LPSTR)"PAN1.BIT");
0771   if (bFrameSaved==FALSE) return;
0772   bFrameSaved= zBuildFrame(2,hWnd,(LPSTR)"PAN2.BIT");
0773   if (bFrameSaved==FALSE) return;
0774   bFrameSaved= zBuildFrame(3,hWnd,(LPSTR)"PAN3.BIT");
0775   if (bFrameSaved==FALSE) return;
0776   bFrameSaved= zBuildFrame(4,hWnd,(LPSTR)"PAN4.BIT");
0777   if (bFrameSaved==FALSE) return;
0778   bFrameSaved= zBuildFrame(5,hWnd,(LPSTR)"PAN5.BIT");
0779   if (bFrameSaved==FALSE) return;
0780   bFrameSaved= zBuildFrame(6,hWnd,(LPSTR)"PAN6.BIT");
0781   if (bFrameSaved==FALSE) return;
0782   bFrameSaved= zBuildFrame(7,hWnd,(LPSTR)"PAN7.BIT");
0783   if (bFrameSaved==FALSE) return;
```

```
0784  bFrameSaved= zBuildFrame(8,hWnd,(LPSTR)"PAN8.BIT");
0785  if (bFrameSaved==FALSE) return;
0786  bFrameSaved= zBuildFrame(9,hWnd,(LPSTR)"PAN9.BIT");
0787  if (bFrameSaved==FALSE) return;
0788  bFrameSaved= zBuildFrame(10,hWnd,(LPSTR)"PAN10.BIT");
0789  if (bFrameSaved==FALSE) return;
0790  bFrameSaved= zBuildFrame(11,hWnd,(LPSTR)"PAN11.BIT");
0791  if (bFrameSaved==FALSE) return;
0792  bFrameSaved= zBuildFrame(12,hWnd,(LPSTR)"PAN12.BIT");
0793  if (bFrameSaved==FALSE) return;
0794  bFrameSaved= zBuildFrame(13,hWnd,(LPSTR)"PAN13.BIT");
0795  if (bFrameSaved==FALSE) return;
0796  bFrameSaved= zBuildFrame(14,hWnd,(LPSTR)"PAN14.BIT");
0797  if (bFrameSaved==FALSE) return;
0798  bFrameSaved= zBuildFrame(15,hWnd,(LPSTR)"PAN15.BIT");
0799  if (bFrameSaved==FALSE) return;
0800  bFrameSaved= zBuildFrame(16,hWnd,(LPSTR)"PAN16.BIT");
0801  if (bFrameSaved==FALSE) return;
0802  bFrameSaved= zBuildFrame(17,hWnd,(LPSTR)"PAN17.BIT");
0803  if (bFrameSaved==FALSE) return;
0804  bFrameSaved= zBuildFrame(18,hWnd,(LPSTR)"PAN18.BIT");
0805  if (bFrameSaved==FALSE) return;
0806  bFrameSaved= zBuildFrame(19,hWnd,(LPSTR)"PAN19.BIT");
0807  if (bFrameSaved==FALSE) return;
0808
0809  bAnimationSaved= TRUE;
0810  bPrevLoadAttempt= FALSE;
0811  zClear(hWnd);
0812  MessageBeep(0);
0813  LoadString(hInst,IDS_Status,lpCaption,Max);
0814  LoadString(hInst,IDS_Disk2,lpMessage,MaxText);
0815  MessageBox(GetFocus(),lpMessage,lpCaption,MB_OK);
0816  return;
0817  }
0818  /*
0819  ------------------------------------------------------------------
0820                    Build one frame and save to disk.
0821  ------------------------------------------------------------------
0822                                                                  */
0823  static BOOL zBuildFrame(int Number, HWND hWnd, LPSTR lpFileName)
0824  {               /* this function is called by zSaveAnimation() */
0825    BOOL bDiskResult;
0826    HFONT Font;
0827    HFONT PrevFont;
0828    DWORD PrevFontColor;
0829    DWORD PrevBkColor;
0830
0831  /* --------------- perform the background pan ---------------- */
0832
0833  switch (Number)
0834    {
0835    case 1:  BitBlt(hFrameDC,0,0,zFRAMEWIDE,zFRAMEHIGH,
0836                   hBackgroundDC,0,0,SRCCOPY);
0837             break;
0838    case 2:  BitBlt(hFrameDC,0,0,zFRAMEWIDE,zFRAMEHIGH,
0839                   hBackgroundDC,6,0,SRCCOPY);
0840             break;
0841    case 3:  BitBlt(hFrameDC,0,0,zFRAMEWIDE,zFRAMEHIGH,
0842                   hBackgroundDC,12,0,SRCCOPY);
0843             break;
```

```
0844    case 4:  BitBlt(hFrameDC,0,0,zFRAMEWIDE,zFRAMEHIGH,
0845                    hBackgroundDC,18,0,SRCCOPY);
0846            break;
0847    case 5:  BitBlt(hFrameDC,0,0,zFRAMEWIDE,zFRAMEHIGH,
0848                    hBackgroundDC,24,0,SRCCOPY);
0849            break;
0850    case 6:  BitBlt(hFrameDC,0,0,zFRAMEWIDE,zFRAMEHIGH,
0851                    hBackgroundDC,30,0,SRCCOPY);
0852            break;
0853    case 7:  BitBlt(hFrameDC,0,0,zFRAMEWIDE,zFRAMEHIGH,
0854                    hBackgroundDC,36,0,SRCCOPY);
0855            break;
0856    case 8:  BitBlt(hFrameDC,0,0,zFRAMEWIDE,zFRAMEHIGH,
0857                    hBackgroundDC,42,0,SRCCOPY);
0858            break;
0859    case 9:  BitBlt(hFrameDC,0,0,zFRAMEWIDE,zFRAMEHIGH,
0860                    hBackgroundDC,48,0,SRCCOPY);
0861            break;
0862    case 10: BitBlt(hFrameDC,0,0,zFRAMEWIDE,zFRAMEHIGH,
0863                    hBackgroundDC,54,0,SRCCOPY);
0864            break;
0865    case 11: BitBlt(hFrameDC,0,0,zFRAMEWIDE,zFRAMEHIGH,
0866                    hBackgroundDC,60,0,SRCCOPY);
0867            break;
0868    case 12: BitBlt(hFrameDC,0,0,zFRAMEWIDE,zFRAMEHIGH,
0869                    hBackgroundDC,66,0,SRCCOPY);
0870            break;
0871    case 13: BitBlt(hFrameDC,0,0,zFRAMEWIDE,zFRAMEHIGH,
0872                    hBackgroundDC,72,0,SRCCOPY);
0873            break;
0874    case 14: BitBlt(hFrameDC,0,0,zFRAMEWIDE,zFRAMEHIGH,
0875                    hBackgroundDC,78,0,SRCCOPY);
0876            break;
0877    case 15: BitBlt(hFrameDC,0,0,zFRAMEWIDE,zFRAMEHIGH,
0878                    hBackgroundDC,84,0,SRCCOPY);
0879            break;
0880    case 16: BitBlt(hFrameDC,0,0,zFRAMEWIDE,zFRAMEHIGH,
0881                    hBackgroundDC,90,0,SRCCOPY);
0882            break;
0883    case 17: BitBlt(hFrameDC,0,0,zFRAMEWIDE,zFRAMEHIGH,
0884                    hBackgroundDC,96,0,SRCCOPY);
0885            break;
0886    case 18: BitBlt(hFrameDC,0,0,zFRAMEWIDE,zFRAMEHIGH,
0887                    hBackgroundDC,102,0,SRCCOPY);
0888            break;
0889    case 19: BitBlt(hFrameDC,0,0,zFRAMEWIDE,zFRAMEHIGH,
0890                    hBackgroundDC,108,0,SRCCOPY);
0891            break;
0892    }
0893
0894 /* ---------- display the titles, labels, and captions --------- */
0895 PrevFontColor= SetTextColor(hFrameDC,RGB(255,255,255));
0896 PrevBkColor=  SetBkColor(hFrameDC,RGB(0,0,0));
0897 SetBkMode(hFrameDC,TRANSPARENT);
0898 Font= CreateFont(24, 0, 0, 0, FW_BOLD, FALSE, FALSE, FALSE,
0899      ANSI_CHARSET, OUT_DEFAULT_PRECIS, CLIP_DEFAULT_PRECIS,
0900      DRAFT_QUALITY, VARIABLE_PITCH | FF_SWISS, "Helv");
0901 PrevFont= SelectObject(hFrameDC,Font);
0902 TextOut(hFrameDC,10,10,"Advanced Animation Techniques:",30);
0903 Font= CreateFont(48, 0, 0, 0, FW_BOLD, FALSE, FALSE, FALSE,
```

```
0904        ANSI_CHARSET, OUT_DEFAULT_PRECIS, CLIP_DEFAULT_PRECIS,
0905        DRAFT_QUALITY, VARIABLE_PITCH | FF_SWISS, "Helv");
0906   SelectObject(hFrameDC,Font);
0907   TextOut(hFrameDC,8,28,"Background Pans",15);
0908   SelectObject(hFrameDC,PrevFont);
0909   TextOut(hFrameDC,10,78,"Background panning is implemented",33);
0910   TextOut(hFrameDC,10,94,"by copying selected portions of",31);
0911   TextOut(hFrameDC,10,110,"an oversized background that is",31);
0912   TextOut(hFrameDC,10,126,"stored in a hidden bitmap.",26);
0913   SetBkMode(hFrameDC,OPAQUE);
0914   SetBkColor(hFrameDC,PrevBkColor);
0915   SetTextColor(hFrameDC,PrevFontColor);
0916
0917   /* ---------- display the frame and save it to disk ------------ */
0918   zCopyToDisplay(hWnd);                /* copy hidden frame to display */
0919   bDiskResult= zSaveFrame(hFrame,lpFileName);         /* save file */
0920   if (bDiskResult==FALSE) return FALSE;        /* if disk error */
0921   return TRUE;
0922   }
0923   /*
0924   --------------------------------------------------------------------
0925        Draw background image on the hidden background bitmap.
0926   --------------------------------------------------------------------
0927                                                                    */
0928   static void zDrawBackground(HWND hWnd)
0929   {
0930     HDC hDisplayDC;
0931     HBRUSH hFoliageBrush,hTrunkBrush,hSkyBrush,
0932            hTerrainBrush,hStreamBrush,hMountainBrush,
0933            hPrevBrush;
0934     HPEN hFoliagePen,hTrunkPen,hSkyPen,
0935          hTerrainPen,hStreamPen,hMountainPen,
0936          hPrevPen;
0937     POINT Points[8];
0938     int Count;
0939
0940   if (BgReady==TRUE)                        /* if already created... */
0941     {
0942     MessageBeep(0);
0943     LoadString(hInst,IDS_Ready,lpCaption,Max);
0944     LoadString(hInst,IDS_BgAlready,lpMessage,MaxText);
0945     TimerCounter= zTIMER_PAUSE;
0946     MessageBox(GetFocus(),lpMessage,lpCaption,MB_OK);
0947     return;
0948     }
0949   GlobalCompact((DWORD)-1L);
0950   hDisplayDC= GetDC(hWnd);
0951   hBackgroundDC= CreateCompatibleDC(hDisplayDC);
0952   hBackground= CreateCompatibleBitmap(hDisplayDC,zBGWIDE,zBGHIGH);
0953   if (hBackground==NULL)
0954     {
0955     LoadString(hInst,IDS_NotReady,lpCaption,Max);
0956     LoadString(hInst,IDS_InsufMemBg,lpMessage,MaxText);
0957     MessageBox(GetFocus(),lpMessage,lpCaption,MB_OK);
0958     DeleteDC(hBackgroundDC);
0959     BgReady= FALSE;
0960     return;
0961     }
0962   hPrevBg= SelectObject(hBackgroundDC,hBackground);
0963   BgReady= TRUE; BgBitmapExists= TRUE;
0964
```

```
0965   /* --------------- draw image on hidden bitmap --------------- */
0966
0967   hFoliagePen= CreatePen(PS_SOLID,1,RGB(0,255,0));   /* create pens */
0968   hTrunkPen= CreatePen(PS_SOLID,1,RGB(127,127,0));
0969   hSkyPen= CreatePen(PS_SOLID,1,RGB(0,0,255));
0970   hTerrainPen= CreatePen(PS_SOLID,1,RGB(0,127,0));
0971   hStreamPen= CreatePen(PS_SOLID,1,RGB(0,0,127));
0972   hMountainPen= CreatePen(PS_SOLID,1,RGB(127,127,127));
0973
0974   hFoliageBrush= CreateSolidBrush(RGB(0,255,0)); /* create brushes */
0975   hTrunkBrush= CreateSolidBrush(RGB(127,127,0));
0976   hSkyBrush= CreateSolidBrush(RGB(0,0,255));
0977   hTerrainBrush= CreateSolidBrush(RGB(0,127,0));
0978   hStreamBrush= CreateSolidBrush(RGB(0,0,127));
0979   hMountainBrush= CreateSolidBrush(RGB(127,127,127));
0980
0981   hPrevPen= SelectObject(hBackgroundDC,hSkyPen);           /* sky... */
0982   hPrevBrush= SelectObject(hBackgroundDC,hSkyBrush);
0983   Rectangle(hBackgroundDC,0,0,600,140);
0984
0985   SelectObject(hBackgroundDC,hTerrainPen);             /* terrain... */
0986   SelectObject(hBackgroundDC,hTerrainBrush);
0987   Rectangle(hBackgroundDC,0,140,600,300);
0988
0989   SelectObject(hBackgroundDC,hStreamPen);               /* stream... */
0990   SelectObject(hBackgroundDC,hStreamBrush);
0991   Count= 8;
0992   Points[0].x= 210; Points[0].y= 140;
0993   Points[1].x= 250; Points[1].y= 140;
0994   Points[2].x= 225; Points[2].y= 186;
0995   Points[3].x= 300; Points[3].y= 236;
0996   Points[4].x= 280; Points[4].y= 299;
0997   Points[5].x= 110; Points[5].y= 299;
0998   Points[6].x= 180; Points[6].y= 236;
0999   Points[7].x= 156; Points[7].y= 194;
1000   Polygon(hBackgroundDC,Points,Count);
1001
1002   SelectObject(hBackgroundDC,hTrunkPen);            /* tree trunks... */
1003   SelectObject(hBackgroundDC,hTrunkBrush);
1004   Rectangle(hBackgroundDC,65,180,85,270);
1005   Rectangle(hBackgroundDC,355,170,380,280);
1006   Rectangle(hBackgroundDC,475,210,496,275);
1007
1008   SelectObject(hBackgroundDC,hFoliagePen);             /* foliage... */
1009   SelectObject(hBackgroundDC,hFoliageBrush);
1010   Ellipse(hBackgroundDC,30,120,125,215);
1011   Ellipse(hBackgroundDC,300,80,430,200);
1012   Ellipse(hBackgroundDC,440,160,530,240);
1013
1014   /* -------------------- tidy up and exit -------------------- */
1015   SelectObject(hBackgroundDC,hPrevPen);
1016   SelectObject(hBackgroundDC,hPrevBrush);
1017   DeleteObject(hFoliagePen); DeleteObject(hTrunkPen);
1018   DeleteObject(hSkyPen); DeleteObject(hTerrainPen);
1019   DeleteObject(hStreamPen); DeleteObject(hMountainPen);
1020   DeleteObject(hFoliageBrush); DeleteObject(hTrunkBrush);
1021   DeleteObject(hSkyBrush); DeleteObject(hTerrainBrush);
1022   DeleteObject(hStreamBrush); DeleteObject(hMountainBrush);
1023   ReleaseDC(hWnd,hDisplayDC);
1024   return;
1025   }
```

```
1026   /*
1027   -----------------------------------------------------------------
1028                     ANIMATION PLAYBACK Functions
1029   -----------------------------------------------------------------
1030   -----------------------------------------------------------------
1031                       Display the next frame.
1032     This function is intelligent enough to discern between RAM-BASED
1033     FRAME ANIMATION (where all frames have already been loaded from
1034     disk and stored in RAM) and DISK-BASED FRAME ANIMATION (where
1035     each frame must be loaded from disk during playback).
1036   -----------------------------------------------------------------
1037                                                                   */
1038   static void zShowNextFrame(HWND hWnd)
1039   {
1040     HDC hDC;
1041   if (bUseDisk==TRUE) goto DISK_PLAYBACK;
1042
1043   RAM_PLAYBACK:          /* if all frames have been loaded into RAM... */
1044   if (AnimationReady==FALSE) return;
1045   if (bAnimationLoaded==FALSE) return;
1046   if (Redisplay==TRUE) goto DISPLAY_FRAME;
1047   if (Pause==TRUE) return;
1048   if (FrameDirection==zFORWARD)
1049     {
1050     FrameNum++;
1051     if (FrameNum > zFINALFRAME) FrameNum= zFIRSTFRAME;
1052     }
1053   if (FrameDirection==zREVERSE)
1054     {
1055     FrameNum--;
1056     if (FrameNum < zFIRSTFRAME) FrameNum= zFINALFRAME;
1057     }
1058   DISPLAY_FRAME:
1059   hDC= GetDC(hWnd);
1060   switch (FrameNum)
1061     {
1062     case 1:  SelectObject(hFDC,hF1);  break;
1063     case 2:  SelectObject(hFDC,hF2);  break;
1064     case 3:  SelectObject(hFDC,hF3);  break;
1065     case 4:  SelectObject(hFDC,hF4);  break;
1066     case 5:  SelectObject(hFDC,hF5);  break;
1067     case 6:  SelectObject(hFDC,hF6);  break;
1068     case 7:  SelectObject(hFDC,hF7);  break;
1069     case 8:  SelectObject(hFDC,hF8);  break;
1070     case 9:  SelectObject(hFDC,hF9);  break;
1071     case 10: SelectObject(hFDC,hF10); break;
1072     case 11: SelectObject(hFDC,hF11); break;
1073     case 12: SelectObject(hFDC,hF12); break;
1074     case 13: SelectObject(hFDC,hF13); break;
1075     case 14: SelectObject(hFDC,hF14); break;
1076     case 15: SelectObject(hFDC,hF15); break;
1077     case 16: SelectObject(hFDC,hF16); break;
1078     case 17: SelectObject(hFDC,hF17); break;
1079     case 18: SelectObject(hFDC,hF18); break;
1080     case 19: SelectObject(hFDC,hF19); break;
1081     case 20: SelectObject(hFDC,hF18); break;
1082     case 21: SelectObject(hFDC,hF17); break;
1083     case 22: SelectObject(hFDC,hF16); break;
1084     case 23: SelectObject(hFDC,hF15); break;
1085     case 24: SelectObject(hFDC,hF14); break;
1086     case 25: SelectObject(hFDC,hF13); break;
```

```
1087   case 26: SelectObject(hFDC,hF12); break;
1088   case 27: SelectObject(hFDC,hF11); break;
1089   case 28: SelectObject(hFDC,hF10); break;
1090   case 29: SelectObject(hFDC,hF9); break;
1091   case 30: SelectObject(hFDC,hF8); break;
1092   case 31: SelectObject(hFDC,hF7); break;
1093   case 32: SelectObject(hFDC,hF6); break;
1094   case 33: SelectObject(hFDC,hF5); break;
1095   case 34: SelectObject(hFDC,hF4); break;
1096   case 35: SelectObject(hFDC,hF3); break;
1097   case 36: SelectObject(hFDC,hF2); break;
1098   }
1099 BitBlt(hDC,0,0,zFRAMEWIDE,zFRAMEHIGH,hFDC,0,0,SRCCOPY);
1100 ReleaseDC(hWnd,hDC);
1101 return;
1102
1103 DISK_PLAYBACK:    /* if loading each frame from disk as needed... */
1104 if (bAnimationHalted==TRUE) return;
1105 if (Redisplay==TRUE) goto SAME_FRAME;
1106 if (Pause==TRUE) return;
1107 if (FrameDirection==zFORWARD)
1108   {
1109   FrameNum++;
1110   if (FrameNum > zFINALFRAME) FrameNum= zFIRSTFRAME;
1111   }
1112 if (FrameDirection==zREVERSE)
1113   {
1114   FrameNum--;
1115   if (FrameNum < zFIRSTFRAME) FrameNum= zFINALFRAME;
1116   }
1117 SAME_FRAME:
1118 hDC= GetDC(hWnd);
1119 switch (FrameNum)
1120   {
1121   case 1:  bFrameLoaded= zLoadFrame(hFrame, (LPSTR) "PAN1.BIT");
1122            break;
1123   case 2:  bFrameLoaded= zLoadFrame(hFrame, (LPSTR) "PAN2.BIT");
1124            break;
1125   case 3:  bFrameLoaded= zLoadFrame(hFrame, (LPSTR) "PAN3.BIT");
1126            break;
1127   case 4:  bFrameLoaded= zLoadFrame(hFrame, (LPSTR) "PAN4.BIT");
1128            break;
1129   case 5:  bFrameLoaded= zLoadFrame(hFrame, (LPSTR) "PAN5.BIT");
1130            break;
1131   case 6:  bFrameLoaded= zLoadFrame(hFrame, (LPSTR) "PAN6.BIT");
1132            break;
1133   case 7:  bFrameLoaded= zLoadFrame(hFrame, (LPSTR) "PAN7.BIT");
1134            break;
1135   case 8:  bFrameLoaded= zLoadFrame(hFrame, (LPSTR) "PAN8.BIT");
1136            break;
1137   case 9:  bFrameLoaded= zLoadFrame(hFrame, (LPSTR) "PAN9.BIT");
1138            break;
1139   case 10: bFrameLoaded= zLoadFrame(hFrame, (LPSTR) "PAN10.BIT");
1140            break;
1141   case 11: bFrameLoaded= zLoadFrame(hFrame, (LPSTR) "PAN11.BIT");
1142            break;
1143   case 12: bFrameLoaded= zLoadFrame(hFrame, (LPSTR) "PAN12.BIT");
1144            break;
1145   case 13: bFrameLoaded= zLoadFrame(hFrame, (LPSTR) "PAN13.BIT");
1146            break;
```

```
1147     case 14: bFrameLoaded= zLoadFrame(hFrame, (LPSTR) "PAN14.BIT");
1148             break;
1149     case 15: bFrameLoaded= zLoadFrame(hFrame, (LPSTR) "PAN15.BIT");
1150             break;
1151     case 16: bFrameLoaded= zLoadFrame(hFrame, (LPSTR) "PAN16.BIT");
1152             break;
1153     case 17: bFrameLoaded= zLoadFrame(hFrame, (LPSTR) "PAN17.BIT");
1154             break;
1155     case 18: bFrameLoaded= zLoadFrame(hFrame, (LPSTR) "PAN18.BIT");
1156             break;
1157     case 19: bFrameLoaded= zLoadFrame(hFrame, (LPSTR) "PAN19.BIT");
1158             break;
1159     case 20:  bFrameLoaded= zLoadFrame(hFrame, (LPSTR) "PAN18.BIT");
1160             break;
1161     case 21:  bFrameLoaded= zLoadFrame(hFrame, (LPSTR) "PAN17.BIT");
1162             break;
1163     case 22:  bFrameLoaded= zLoadFrame(hFrame, (LPSTR) "PAN16.BIT");
1164             break;
1165     case 23:  bFrameLoaded= zLoadFrame(hFrame, (LPSTR) "PAN15.BIT");
1166             break;
1167     case 24:  bFrameLoaded= zLoadFrame(hFrame, (LPSTR) "PAN14.BIT");
1168             break;
1169     case 25:  bFrameLoaded= zLoadFrame(hFrame, (LPSTR) "PAN13.BIT");
1170             break;
1171     case 26:  bFrameLoaded= zLoadFrame(hFrame, (LPSTR) "PAN12.BIT");
1172             break;
1173     case 27:  bFrameLoaded= zLoadFrame(hFrame, (LPSTR) "PAN11.BIT");
1174             break;
1175     case 28: bFrameLoaded= zLoadFrame(hFrame, (LPSTR) "PAN10.BIT");
1176             break;
1177     case 29: bFrameLoaded= zLoadFrame(hFrame, (LPSTR) "PAN9.BIT");
1178             break;
1179     case 30: bFrameLoaded= zLoadFrame(hFrame, (LPSTR) "PAN8.BIT");
1180             break;
1181     case 31: bFrameLoaded= zLoadFrame(hFrame, (LPSTR) "PAN7.BIT");
1182             break;
1183     case 32: bFrameLoaded= zLoadFrame(hFrame, (LPSTR) "PAN6.BIT");
1184             break;
1185     case 33: bFrameLoaded= zLoadFrame(hFrame, (LPSTR) "PAN5.BIT");
1186             break;
1187     case 34: bFrameLoaded= zLoadFrame(hFrame, (LPSTR) "PAN4.BIT");
1188             break;
1189     case 35: bFrameLoaded= zLoadFrame(hFrame, (LPSTR) "PAN3.BIT");
1190             break;
1191     case 36: bFrameLoaded= zLoadFrame(hFrame, (LPSTR) "PAN2.BIT");
1192             break;
1193     }
1194     if (bFrameLoaded==FALSE)
1195     {
1196     bAnimationHalted= TRUE;
1197     MessageBeep(0);
1198     LoadString(hInst,IDS_Unexpected,lpCaption,Max);
1199     LoadString(hInst,IDS_Disk3,lpMessage,MaxText);
1200     TimerCounter= zTIMER_PAUSE;
1201     MessageBox(GetFocus(),lpMessage,lpCaption,MB_OK);
1202     return;
1203     }
1204     BitBlt(hDC,0,0,zFRAMEWIDE,zFRAMEHIGH,hFrameDC,0,0,SRCCOPY);
1205     ReleaseDC(hWnd,hDC);
1206     return;
1207     }
```

```
1208  /*
1209  -------------------------------------------------------------------
1210              Load the animation sequence from disk.
1211  If memory limitations prevent this function from loading the
1212  entire animation sequence into RAM, it sets a token to FALSE.
1213  In that case the playback function zShowNextFrame() will load
1214  each frame from disk as required during animation playback,
1215  otherwise all frames are expected to be in RAM.
1216  -------------------------------------------------------------------
1217                                                                    */
1218  static void zLoadAnimation(HWND hWnd)
1219  {
1220    HDC hDC;
1221
1222    if (FrameReady==FALSE)         /* if no hidden-frame available... */
1223      {
1224      MessageBeep(0);
1225      LoadString(hInst,IDS_NotReady,lpCaption,Max);
1226      LoadString(hInst,IDS_NoFrame,lpMessage,MaxText);
1227      MessageBox(GetFocus(),lpMessage,lpCaption,MB_OK);
1228      return;
1229      }
1230    if (bAnimationLoaded==TRUE)      /* if frames already loaded... */
1231      {
1232      MessageBeep(0);
1233      LoadString(hInst,IDS_Unexpected,lpCaption,Max);
1234      LoadString(hInst,IDS_Disk4,lpMessage,MaxText);
1235      TimerCounter= zTIMER_PAUSE;
1236      MessageBox(GetFocus(),lpMessage,lpCaption,MB_OK);
1237      return;
1238      }
1239    if (bPrevLoadAttempt==TRUE)      /* if previous attempt failed... */
1240      {
1241      MessageBeep(0);
1242      LoadString(hInst,IDS_Unexpected,lpCaption,Max);
1243      LoadString(hInst,IDS_Disk5,lpMessage,MaxText);
1244      TimerCounter= zTIMER_PAUSE;
1245      MessageBox(GetFocus(),lpMessage,lpCaption,MB_OK);
1246      return;
1247      }
1248    bPrevLoadAttempt= TRUE;
1249
1250    /* -------------- create bitmaps to hold the frames ------------ */
1251    GlobalCompact((DWORD)-1L);            /* maximize contiguous memory */
1252    hDC= GetDC(hWnd);
1253    hFDC= CreateCompatibleDC(hDC);
1254    hF1= CreateCompatibleBitmap(hDC,zFRAMEWIDE,zFRAMEHIGH);
1255    if (hF1==NULL) goto F1;
1256    hF2= CreateCompatibleBitmap(hDC,zFRAMEWIDE,zFRAMEHIGH);
1257    if (hF2==NULL) goto F2;
1258    hF3= CreateCompatibleBitmap(hDC,zFRAMEWIDE,zFRAMEHIGH);
1259    if (hF3==NULL) goto F3;
1260    hF4= CreateCompatibleBitmap(hDC,zFRAMEWIDE,zFRAMEHIGH);
1261    if (hF4==NULL) goto F4;
1262    hF5= CreateCompatibleBitmap(hDC,zFRAMEWIDE,zFRAMEHIGH);
1263    if (hF5==NULL) goto F5;
1264    hF6= CreateCompatibleBitmap(hDC,zFRAMEWIDE,zFRAMEHIGH);
1265    if (hF6==NULL) goto F6;
1266    hF7= CreateCompatibleBitmap(hDC,zFRAMEWIDE,zFRAMEHIGH);
1267    if (hF7==NULL) goto F7;
1268    hF8= CreateCompatibleBitmap(hDC,zFRAMEWIDE,zFRAMEHIGH);
```

```
1269  if (hF8==NULL) goto F8;
1270  hF9= CreateCompatibleBitmap(hDC,zFRAMEWIDE,zFRAMEHIGH);
1271  if (hF9==NULL) goto F9;
1272  hF10= CreateCompatibleBitmap(hDC,zFRAMEWIDE,zFRAMEHIGH);
1273  if (hF10==NULL) goto F10;
1274  hF11= CreateCompatibleBitmap(hDC,zFRAMEWIDE,zFRAMEHIGH);
1275  if (hF11==NULL) goto F11;
1276  hF12= CreateCompatibleBitmap(hDC,zFRAMEWIDE,zFRAMEHIGH);
1277  if (hF12==NULL) goto F12;
1278  hF13= CreateCompatibleBitmap(hDC,zFRAMEWIDE,zFRAMEHIGH);
1279  if (hF13==NULL) goto F13;
1280  hF14= CreateCompatibleBitmap(hDC,zFRAMEWIDE,zFRAMEHIGH);
1281  if (hF14==NULL) goto F14;
1282  hF15= CreateCompatibleBitmap(hDC,zFRAMEWIDE,zFRAMEHIGH);
1283  if (hF15==NULL) goto F15;
1284  hF16= CreateCompatibleBitmap(hDC,zFRAMEWIDE,zFRAMEHIGH);
1285  if (hF16==NULL) goto F16;
1286  hF17= CreateCompatibleBitmap(hDC,zFRAMEWIDE,zFRAMEHIGH);
1287  if (hF17==NULL) goto F17;
1288  hF18= CreateCompatibleBitmap(hDC,zFRAMEWIDE,zFRAMEHIGH);
1289  if (hF18==NULL) goto F18;
1290  hF19= CreateCompatibleBitmap(hDC,zFRAMEWIDE,zFRAMEHIGH);
1291  if (hF19==NULL) goto F19;
1292  goto BITMAPS_OK;
1293  F19: DeleteObject(hF18);
1294  F18: DeleteObject(hF17);
1295  F17: DeleteObject(hF16);
1296  F16: DeleteObject(hF15);
1297  F15: DeleteObject(hF14);
1298  F14: DeleteObject(hF13);
1299  F13: DeleteObject(hF12);
1300  F12: DeleteObject(hF11);
1301  F11: DeleteObject(hF10);
1302  F10: DeleteObject(hF9);
1303  F9:  DeleteObject(hF8);
1304  F8:  DeleteObject(hF7);
1305  F7:  DeleteObject(hF6);
1306  F6:  DeleteObject(hF5);
1307  F5:  DeleteObject(hF4);
1308  F4:  DeleteObject(hF3);
1309  F3:  DeleteObject(hF2);
1310  F2:  DeleteObject(hF1);
1311  F1:  DeleteDC(hFDC); ReleaseDC(hWnd,hDC);
1312       bUseDisk= TRUE; AnimationReady= TRUE;
1313       LoadString(hInst,IDS_Status,lpCaption,Max);
1314       LoadString(hInst,IDS_Disk6,lpMessage,MaxText);
1315       MessageBox(GetFocus(),lpMessage,lpCaption,MB_OK);
1316       return;
1317  BITMAPS_OK: ReleaseDC(hWnd,hDC);
1318
1319  /* ------------ load frame files into the bitmaps ------------ */
1320  bFrameLoaded= zLoadFrame(hF1, (LPSTR) "PAN1.BIT");
1321  if (bFrameLoaded==FALSE) goto DISK_ERROR;
1322  bFrameLoaded= zLoadFrame(hF2, (LPSTR) "PAN2.BIT");
1323  if (bFrameLoaded==FALSE) goto DISK_ERROR;
1324  bFrameLoaded= zLoadFrame(hF3, (LPSTR) "PAN3.BIT");
1325  if (bFrameLoaded==FALSE) goto DISK_ERROR;
1326  bFrameLoaded= zLoadFrame(hF4, (LPSTR) "PAN4.BIT");
1327  if (bFrameLoaded==FALSE) goto DISK_ERROR;
1328  bFrameLoaded= zLoadFrame(hF5, (LPSTR) "PAN5.BIT");
1329  if (bFrameLoaded==FALSE) goto DISK_ERROR;
```

```
1330 bFrameLoaded= zLoadFrame(hF6, (LPSTR) "PAN6.BIT");
1331 if (bFrameLoaded==FALSE) goto DISK_ERROR;
1332 bFrameLoaded= zLoadFrame(hF7, (LPSTR) "PAN7.BIT");
1333 if (bFrameLoaded==FALSE) goto DISK_ERROR;
1334 bFrameLoaded= zLoadFrame(hF8, (LPSTR) "PAN8.BIT");
1335 if (bFrameLoaded==FALSE) goto DISK_ERROR;
1336 bFrameLoaded= zLoadFrame(hF9, (LPSTR) "PAN9.BIT");
1337 if (bFrameLoaded==FALSE) goto DISK_ERROR;
1338 bFrameLoaded= zLoadFrame(hF10, (LPSTR) "PAN10.BIT");
1339 if (bFrameLoaded==FALSE) goto DISK_ERROR;
1340 bFrameLoaded= zLoadFrame(hF11, (LPSTR) "PAN11.BIT");
1341 if (bFrameLoaded==FALSE) goto DISK_ERROR;
1342 bFrameLoaded= zLoadFrame(hF12, (LPSTR) "PAN12.BIT");
1343 if (bFrameLoaded==FALSE) goto DISK_ERROR;
1344 bFrameLoaded= zLoadFrame(hF13, (LPSTR) "PAN13.BIT");
1345 if (bFrameLoaded==FALSE) goto DISK_ERROR;
1346 bFrameLoaded= zLoadFrame(hF14, (LPSTR) "PAN14.BIT");
1347 if (bFrameLoaded==FALSE) goto DISK_ERROR;
1348 bFrameLoaded= zLoadFrame(hF15, (LPSTR) "PAN15.BIT");
1349 if (bFrameLoaded==FALSE) goto DISK_ERROR;
1350 bFrameLoaded= zLoadFrame(hF16, (LPSTR) "PAN16.BIT");
1351 if (bFrameLoaded==FALSE) goto DISK_ERROR;
1352 bFrameLoaded= zLoadFrame(hF17, (LPSTR) "PAN17.BIT");
1353 if (bFrameLoaded==FALSE) goto DISK_ERROR;
1354 bFrameLoaded= zLoadFrame(hF18, (LPSTR) "PAN18.BIT");
1355 if (bFrameLoaded==FALSE) goto DISK_ERROR;
1356 bFrameLoaded= zLoadFrame(hF19, (LPSTR) "PAN19.BIT");
1357 if (bFrameLoaded==FALSE) goto DISK_ERROR;
1358 goto DISK_OK;
1359 DISK_ERROR:
1360   DeleteObject(hF1); DeleteObject(hF2); DeleteObject(hF3);
1361   DeleteObject(hF4); DeleteObject(hF5); DeleteObject(hF6);
1362   DeleteObject(hF7); DeleteObject(hF8); DeleteObject(hF9);
1363   DeleteObject(hF10); DeleteObject(hF11); DeleteObject(hF12);
1364   DeleteObject(hF13); DeleteObject(hF14); DeleteObject(hF15);
1365   DeleteObject(hF16); DeleteObject(hF17); DeleteObject(hF18);
1366   DeleteObject(hF19); DeleteDC(hFDC);
1367   return;
1368
1369 /* ------------------- tidy up and return -------------------- */
1370 DISK_OK:
1371 hPrevF= SelectObject(hFDC,hF1);                    /* select bitmap */
1372 bAnimationLoaded= TRUE;
1373 AnimationReady= TRUE;
1374 bAnimationSaved= TRUE;
1375 MessageBeep(0);
1376 LoadString(hInst,IDS_AnimReady,lpCaption,Max);
1377 LoadString(hInst,IDS_Disk7,lpMessage,MaxText);
1378 MessageBox(GetFocus(),lpMessage,lpCaption,MB_OK);
1379 return;
1380 }
1381 /*
1382 -----------------------------------------------------------------
1383                   Reset the animation frame rate.
1384 -----------------------------------------------------------------
1385                                                                 */
1386 static void zSetFrameRate(HWND hWnd, WORD wNewRate)
1387 {
1388 if (TimerExists==FALSE)
1389   {
1390   wFrameRate= wPrevRate;
```

```
1391    MessageBeep(0);
1392    LoadString(hInst,IDS_NotReady,lpCaption,Max);
1393    LoadString(hInst,IDS_NoReset,lpMessage,MaxText);
1394    MessageBox(GetFocus(),lpMessage,lpCaption,MB_OK);
1395    return;
1396    }
1397  switch (wPrevRate)
1398    {
1399    case 55:  CheckMenuItem(hMenu,IDM_FPS182,MF_UNCHECKED); break;
1400    case 110: CheckMenuItem(hMenu,IDM_FPS91,MF_UNCHECKED); break;
1401    case 165: CheckMenuItem(hMenu,IDM_FPS61,MF_UNCHECKED); break;
1402    case 220: CheckMenuItem(hMenu,IDM_FPS45,MF_UNCHECKED); break;
1403    case 275: CheckMenuItem(hMenu,IDM_FPS36,MF_UNCHECKED); break;
1404    case 330: CheckMenuItem(hMenu,IDM_FPS30,MF_UNCHECKED); break;
1405    }
1406  KillTimer(hWnd,1);
1407  TimerID1= SetTimer(hWnd,1,wNewRate,(FARPROC) NULL);
1408  if (TimerID1==0)
1409    {
1410    LoadString(hInst,IDS_NotReady,lpCaption,Max);
1411    LoadString(hInst,IDS_CannotReset,lpMessage,MaxText);
1412    MessageBox(GetFocus(),lpMessage,lpCaption,MB_OK);
1413    TimerExists= FALSE;
1414    return;
1415    }
1416  switch (wFrameRate)
1417    {
1418    case 55:  CheckMenuItem(hMenu,IDM_FPS182,MF_CHECKED); break;
1419    case 110: CheckMenuItem(hMenu,IDM_FPS91,MF_CHECKED); break;
1420    case 165: CheckMenuItem(hMenu,IDM_FPS61,MF_CHECKED); break;
1421    case 220: CheckMenuItem(hMenu,IDM_FPS45,MF_CHECKED); break;
1422    case 275: CheckMenuItem(hMenu,IDM_FPS36,MF_CHECKED); break;
1423    case 330: CheckMenuItem(hMenu,IDM_FPS30,MF_CHECKED); break;
1424    }
1425  return;
1426  }
1427  /*
1428  ------------------------------------------------------------------
1429                      End of the C source file
1430  ------------------------------------------------------------------
1431                                                                */
```

# 15
# *Production*

Managing the production of a computer animation sequence from start to finish involves a wide range of skills. Among many other considerations, you need to ensure that, first, you have an orderly approach to the project itself and, second, that you take advantage of the computer's ability to perform much of the tedious, repetitive work for you. An orderly approach to the project can be sustained by an understanding of the authoring process—and you can take full advantage of the computer's strengths by using interpolation. Interpolation is also called inbetweening. This chapter touches on both subjects.

## Computer animation authoring

Computer animation authoring involves three processes. The:

- Creative process.
- Production process.
- Storage process.

The creative process involves writing and preparation. The production process involves building the individual components of the animation and testing them in a trial animation. The storage process involves saving the finished animation sequence to disk, videotape, or CD-ROM.

### The creative process

 The creative process involves the writing, editing, and development of the storyline. An animation sequence is often designed using the following creative process elements:

- Write the script.
- Prepare a rough storyboard.
- Record a soundtrack.
- Make storyboard/soundtrack timing calculations (i.e. bar sheet of film animation).
- Prepare a detailed storyboard that correlates the action, dialog, and soundtrack timing (ie camera exposure sheet or dope sheet of traditional film animation).

**The rough storyboard**   A sample layout for a storyboard is shown in FIG. 15-1. It is at this stage where the idea you have been nurturing really begins to germinate. The storyboard is where you visualize in a concrete way the animation sequence that you have in mind. The storyboard forces upon you the discipline that you need in order to bring the project under your control. And, perhaps best of all, many of the rough sketches that you use to illustrate your storyboard will eventually be used as keyframes, from which in-

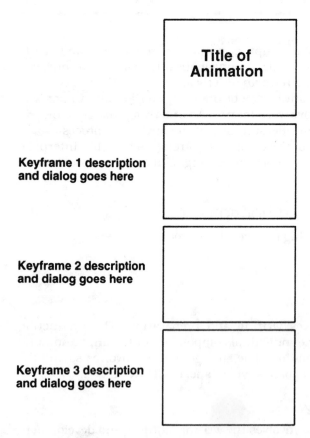

**15-1**   A conceptual schematic of a storyboard for an animation sequence.

betweens will be interpolated (either by human inbetweeners or by computer-assisted interpolation).

**The soundtrack**  If your animation sequence does not use either dialog or music to support the storyline, then you likely will not need to develop an audio track. If there are no spoken words or musical punctuation points to synchronize (or synch, pronounced *sink*) with the animation frames, then you will not need to make any timing calculations. If your animation does use audio, however, you must build the audio track into your prototype as one of the first things you do, because the visual elements are dictated by the pacing of the audio. You must synch the animation of your character's lips to the spoken audio track, because you simply cannot expect to stretch or compress the spoken audio track to match the movement of your character's lips. If you do, you will end up with a distorted audio track. Further, if the audio track consists of a musical score, your animation will be much more effective if the collision you are animating, for example, occurs precisely at the crescendo point in the music.

The audio track is the anchor that keeps the visual elements of your animation sequence from drifting. See the discussion in Appendix H, Adding an audio track, for further information about programming sound for your animation sequences.

**The detailed storyboard**  The detailed storyboard is called a camera exposure sheet, a camera instruction sheet, and a dope sheet by traditional film animation studios. You use the detailed storyboard (refer back to FIG. 15-1) to correlate the script, the keyframes, the actions of the characters and objects, the camera shot (close-up, medium, long shot, panning, or zooming), and the background.

The detailed storyboard is where you work out all the production details. The more work you put into the detailed storyboard, the fewer problems you will encounter in the production stage and the storage stage of the authoring process.

## The production process

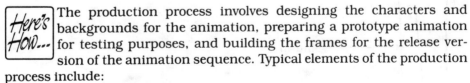

The production process involves designing the characters and backgrounds for the animation, preparing a prototype animation for testing purposes, and building the frames for the release version of the animation sequence. Typical elements of the production process include:

- Finalizing the detailed storyboard/layout.
- Preparing model sheets for each character.
- Designing the backgrounds.
- Preparing the keyframes.
- Interpolating the inbetween drawings.

- Producing a trial animation (ie pencil test).
- Correcting errors found in trial animation.
- Producing finished frames (inking and painting).

**Model sheets**   A typical color model for a character is illustrated in FIG. 15-2. If more than one programmer is working on your animation project, model sheets are essential. In addition to the color model shown in FIG. 15-2, you will need multi-pose model sheets, showing the character in a variety of poses and using a range of different facial expressions—especially the ones likely to occur in the animation sequence. See chapter 10, Characters, for a selection of useful expressions that you can use to develop your own characters.

**Backgrounds**   By referring to the script and the detailed storyboard, you can develop the backgrounds that your animation sequence needs. The more work you put into designing and drawing your backgrounds, the more professional the resulting animation will appear at runtime.

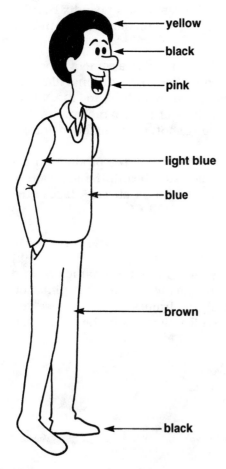

**15-2**   A color model for top-level cels.

Images for backgrounds can be created or captured from a variety of sources, including:

- Scanned images.
- Paint program (bitmap-based drawing).
- Illustration program (vector-based drawing).
- CADD drafting software.
- 3D CAD software.
- Pencil sketches laid on a grid sheet.
- Images captured by digital camera.
- Frame-grabber board and a video camera.
- Frame-grabber board and a VTR unit.
- Digitizing tablet capture of hard copy.
- Windows GDI metafiles.

You can use these same methods to create or capture images for use as characters, objects, and props in your animation project.

**The keyframes**  Preparation of the keyframes means creating finished images. Some computer animators prefer to work in black-and-white at this stage. As you begin to build your animation, you should keep in mind the relationship between computer display area and television display area shown in FIG. 15-3. None of the main characters or essential action in your keyframes can be allowed to fall outside the safe areas of the screen. You might also find it helpful to integrate a field-grid into your planning and production at this stage. See the discussion in chapter 14, Backgrounds, for more information. A sample 12-field grid useful for planning animation sequences is shown in FIG. 15-4.

**Interpolation**  The keyframes are the guideposts that guide the production of your animation sequence. You build the required inbetweens from the keyframes. The higher the quality of your keyframes, the better the resulting tweens will be. Many animation sequences lend themselves to computer-assisted production of inbetweens.

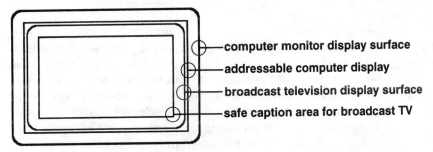

**computer monitor display surface**
**addressable computer display**
**broadcast television display surface**
**safe caption area for broadcast TV**

**15-3**  The relationships among displayable surfaces supported by personal computer displays and NTSC (videotape or broadcast television) displays.

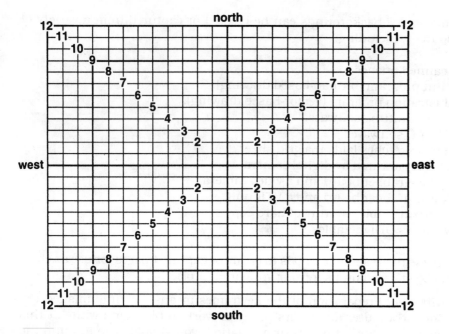

**15-4** A 12-field animation grid suitable for designing animation sequences for Windows.

The demonstration program presented later in the chapter provides some ideas on how to design your characters so that a node-based database can be created, making it possible to use smart software to generate inbetween images.

*Note* **Trial animation** Whether you deliberately build a trial animation to test specific parts of your animation sequence, or whether you use an incremental and iterative approach to gradually build towards the finished animation, you will still be using the so-called pencil-test approach that traditional animators utilize.

Very few of us get it right the first time. Fortunately, the personal computer is a forgiving assistant, always ready and willing to make a few alterations and rebuild the frames for us.

If you are working on a complex, lengthy animation sequence, you will likely find it advantageous to deliberately build a trial animation test into your production plans. Trial animations can produce many dividends, especially when you consider that time is money in the competitive world of commercial software development. Trial animations can also produce many surprises. It is more productive to pretest a walk-cycle, for example, before you insert the character into the main animation sequence. Segments that involve lip-synch dialog should also be pretested in trial animation clips.

Many programmers find it helpful to build a trial animation encompassing the entire sequence, in order to ensure that the action matches the audio track, and to get a feeling for the pacing and cadence of the animation sequence as a whole. These full-length trial animations are usually built using black-and-white images in order to keep production time under control. The foreground color and the backgrounds are added at the finishing stages when all the wrinkles have been ironed out.

*Expert* Preparing a trial animation also gives you an opportunity to test your software under different runtime conditions like different graphics modes, CPU speed, RAM configurations, and Windows runtime memory modes (real, standard, or enhanced). The more delivery platforms you support, the larger your potential market. Refer to Appendix G for tips on testing your software in different graphics modes and under different runtime memory modes.

## Preparing the sample animation

The sample animation presented in this chapter depicts a four-legged run-cycle. During preparation for the demo program, a set of eight wire-frame drawings was sketched on translucent layout paper. Each wireframe drawing represents one cel in the eight-cel animation sequence.

Nodes were placed at key locations on each drawing, usually on joints like the shoulder, knee, wrist, and so on. The distance between adjacent nodes was carefully maintained from one wire-frame drawing to the next. The illustration in FIG. 15-5 shows how this node-based approach can be used to help build a fully formed character. The snippet of source code in FIG. 15-5 demonstrates how nodes (vertices) can be manipulated to generate inbetweens, thereby relieving the computer programmer of much of the hands-on tedium of animation development. The code fragment in FIG. 15-5

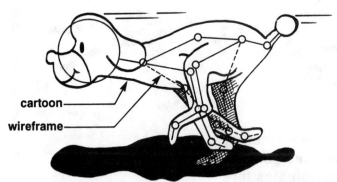

```
X1 = Cel1[16];  Y1 = Cel1[17];  /* grab first vertex */
X2 = Cel2[16];  Y2 = Cel2[17];  /* grab second vertex */
TweenX = (X1 + X2) / 2;         /* calculate tweens... */
TweenY = (Y1 + Y2) / 2;
```

**15-5**  How the cartoon dog is built from an underlying wire-frame skeletal structure. Shown here is cel number 7 from the sample application presented in this chapter.

employs *linear interpolation*, also called lerping, which is interpolation along the straight line that connects the two positions of the node being analyzed. You could also use a curve to plot the interpolation.

## Sample application

The screen image in FIG. 15-6 shows one frame excerpted from the sample application running.exe. This program demonstrates a four-legged run-cycle, using a format suitable for computer-controlled tweening. The interactive playback interface allows you to experiment with different animation playback options, including full forward, full reverse, pause, freeze-frame, single-step forward, and single-step reverse. The animation will continue to run even if the window is partly covered by another window or partly clipped by the edge of the screen.

The running.exe demo is built from six modules, including a .def module definition file, an .h #include file, an .rc resource script file, and a .c source file, in addition to an .h #include file and a .c source file for the stor-

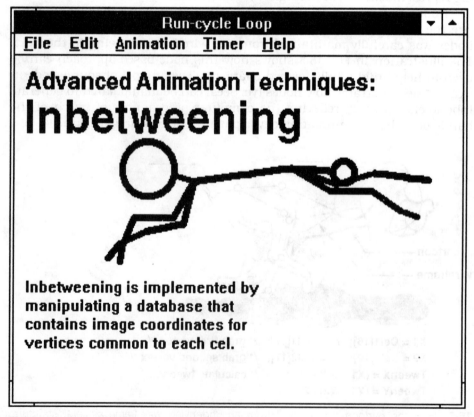

**15-6** A freezeframe from the animated sample application.

age.c module that provides disk read/write functions. All running.exe production files are provided as ready-to-use source code in the program listings in this chapter. The program listings for storage.h and storage.c were provided in chapter 10. All of the source files are also provided on the companion disk. Refer to the appropriate appendix for instructions on how to build running.exe with QuickC for Windows, Turbo C++ for Windows, Borland C++, Zortech C++, WATCOM C, and Microsoft C and the SDK.

## What the program does: A user's guide

*User's Guide* The sample application provides an interactive display for experimenting with the frame animation of a four-legged run-cycle. You can use either a mouse or the keyboard to experiment with the demo program. The menus also provide support for mnemonic keys. To see a runtime help message, choose Help from the Help menu.

### Initializing the system

Select Initialize system from the Animation menu to initialize the hidden frame. None of the authoring or playback features of the Animation menu will be active unless the hidden frame has been created.

### Creating the frames

Select Create Frames from the Animation menu to create the animation sequence and store it on disk. The eight frames that comprise the animation are illustrated in FIG. 15-7. The sample application builds each frame in turn on the hidden page, copies the completed frame to the display window, and then saves the image to disk. If you have already saved the eight frames to disk, the demo program will present a warning message. The software gives you the option of overwriting the existing file with the new image file. If you choose not to overwrite the file, the build sequence is stopped and no further frames are constructed. If not enough free disk space exists to store the image files, the demo program displays an advisory message and cancels the build process.

### Loading the animation

Before you can play the animation sequence that you have saved, you must load it into memory from disk. If you saved the animation sequence during the current working session, select Load Animation from the Animation menu. If you saved the animation during a previous working session, then select Initialize system from the Animation menu before selecting Load Animation from the Animation menu.

If the software is unable to find the animation files on disk, it displays a message. If you attempt to play an animation before loading it from disk or

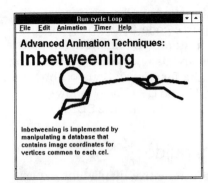

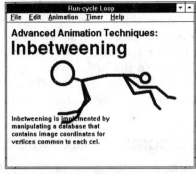

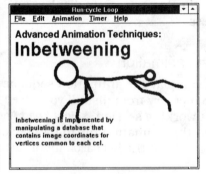

**15-7** The complete run-cycle loop from the animated sample application.

before selecting Initialize system from the Animation menu, the demo program will display a hint message prompting you to complete the required actions first.

Under normal circumstances the sample application will load each frame file into the hidden frame, from where it is copied to memory. After all eight frames have been loaded from disk, the program uses a message box to report success.

**Playing the animation** To play the animation sequence, select Run Forward from the Animation menu. A four-legged run-cycle is animated at 18 fps. The eight frames that make up the complete run-cycle are illustrated in FIG. 15-7. The four-legged creature continues running until you stop the animation.

Notice in particular the exaggerated movement of the four-legged run-cycle. The position of the legs generally preserves the essential elements of a four-legged run-cycle as it appears in animals in the real world. However, the animation purposely exaggerates the curvature of the spine and the elevation of the hind hips (see frames 3 and 4 in FIG. 15-7) in order to increase the dramatic impact of the run-cycle. You can use the images produced by the demo program or the screen shots provided in FIG. 15-7 as a guide when you design your own four-legged run-cycle.

## Adjusting the animation playback speed

You can increase or decrease the animation playback speed by selecting from the Timer menu. By default, at startup the playback rate is set to 18 fps. You can adjust the playback speed when the animation is running or paused. (See chapter 8, Frame animation engines, for a discussion about playback rates on slower computers.)

## Freeze-frame and single-step animation

**Pause** To pause the animation, select Pause from the Animation menu. To resume animation playback select Run Forward from the Animation menu.

**Single-step** While the animation is in the pause mode you can activate single-step playback. Press the right arrow key on the direction keypad to display the next frame in the animation sequence. Keep pressing the right arrow key to single-step through the entire animation. To single-step in reverse, press the left arrow key. To restore full speed animation playback, select Run Forward from the Animation menu.

## Persistent graphics

You can test and verify the persistent graphics capabilities of the demonstration program by moving the window during animation playback, and by partially covering the window with a program group or with another window. In either case, the animation continues to play uninterrupted.

## Using the Help menu

You can use the Help menu to discover various facts about your system that are in effect at runtime. You can identify the current screen mode, the maximum number of available colors, the runtime memory mode—real, standard, or enhanced—and other information. See the discussion in chapter 8, Frame animation engines, for a complete description of the features provided by the Help menu.

# How the source code works: A programmer's guide

*Hands On* The running.exe demonstration program is a dedicated implementation of the prototype animation engine that was described and demonstrated in chapter 8, Frame animation engines. The organization of the .h #include file and the .rc resource script file follow the format established in earlier sample applications.

## How the .c file works

*.C* The .c file for running.exe is a minor modification of the .c file for the frame.exe prototype animation engine provided in chapter 8. The discussion here is limited to the changes that have been made to the program listing in order to support a node-based approach to a four-legged run-cycle. Refer back to chapter 8 for a general discussion of other portions of the code.

**Database**   The database of X-Y coordinates for the cel images of the four-legged creature is contained in the arrays that are initialized at lines 0127 through 0207. The comments along the right side of the elements of Cel1[] at lines 0130 through 0136 indicate the purpose of each block of X-Y coordinates. Except for the ellipse that makes up the head (see line 0130), the remaining X-Y doublets describe the nodes shown earlier in FIG. 15-5. Because the data in each of the arrays is organized in a similar manner, the same block of drawing code can be used to draw each cel in the animation sequence. The actual X-Y coordinate values were derived by placing the pencil sketches over an animation grid similar to the sample shown in FIG. 10-28 in chapter 10, Characters.

**Building the animation**   The zSaveAnimation() function at lines 0783 through 0840 manages the building and saving of the frames that make up the animation sequence. Notice the calls to zBuildFrame() at lines 0815 through 0830, where files named RUN1.BIT through RUN8.BIT are saved to disk.

In order to draw each cel, the zBuildFrame() function at lines 0846 through 0897 repeatedly calls zDrawCel(), which is located at lines 0903 through 0957. The head of the creature being animated is drawn by a call to Ellipse() at line 0915. The tail is likewise drawn by another call to Ellipse() at line 0928. The remaining spine, hind legs, and forelegs are drawn by calls to MoveTo() and LineTo(). Note in particular how zBuildFrame() calls zDrawCel()

with a pointer argument indicating which array to use. This pointer is called Drawing inside the zDrawCel() function. The array[element] notation is used to extract the appropriate X-Y coordinates from the array.

## Program listings for the sample application

The program listings presented here contain all the source code you need to build and run the sample application. The running.def module definition file is provided in FIG. 15-8. The running.h #include file is found in FIG. 15-9. The running.rc resource script file is presented in FIG. 15-10. The running.c source file is provided in FIG. 15-11. The storage.h #include file for the disk read/write module is located in FIG. 10-36 in chapter 10, Characters. The storage.c source file for the read/write module is provided in FIG. 10-37 in chapter 10, Characters.

**Companion disk**  If you have the companion disk, the six source files are presented as running.def, running.h, running.rc, running.c, storage.h, and storage.c.

**15-8**  The module definition file listing for the sample application.

```
0001  NAME          DEFDEMO
0002  DESCRIPTION   'Copyright 1992 Lee Adams.  All rights reserved.'
0003  EXETYPE       WINDOWS
0004  STUB          'WINSTUB.EXE'
0005  CODE          PRELOAD MOVEABLE
0006  DATA          PRELOAD MOVEABLE MULTIPLE
0007  HEAPSIZE      1024
0008  STACKSIZE     8192
0009  EXPORTS       zMessageHandler
```

**15-9**  The include file listing for the sample application.

```
0001  /*
0002  --------------------------------------------------------------------
0003                    Include file RUNNING.H
0004            Copyright 1992 Lee Adams.  All rights reserved.
0005    Include this file in the .RC resource script file and in the
0006    .C source file.  It contains function prototypes, menu ID
0007    constants, and string ID constants.
0008  --------------------------------------------------------------------
0009  --------------------------------------------------------------------
0010                    Function prototypes
0011  --------------------------------------------------------------------
0012                                                                   */
0013  #if !defined(zRCFILE)                     /* if not an .RC file... */
0014     LONG FAR PASCAL zMessageHandler(HWND, unsigned, WORD, LONG);
0015     int PASCAL WinMain(HANDLE,HANDLE,LPSTR,int);
```

```
0016    HWND zInitMainWindow(HANDLE);
0017    BOOL zInitClass(HANDLE);
0018  static void zClear(HWND);                /* blank the display window */
0019  static void zInitFrame(HWND);               /* creates hidden frame */
0020  static void zShowNextFrame(HWND);          /* the playback engine */
0021  static void zSetFrameRate(HWND,WORD);          /* resets the timer */
0022  static void zSaveAnimation(HWND);       /* saves animation sequence */
0023  static BOOL zBuildFrame(int *,int,HWND,LPSTR); /* builds a frame */
0024  static void zDrawCel(int *);                    /* draws a cel */
0025  static void zLoadAnimation(HWND);       /* loads animation sequence */
0026  static void zCopyToDisplay(HWND);       /* copies frame to display */
0027  static void zClearHiddenFrame(void);      /* clears hidden frame */
0028  #endif
0029  /*
0030  -----------------------------------------------------------------
0031                          Menu ID constants
0032  -----------------------------------------------------------------
0033                                                                  */
0034  #define IDM_New            1
0035  #define IDM_Open           2
0036  #define IDM_Save           3
0037  #define IDM_SaveAs         4
0038  #define IDM_Exit           5
0039
0040  #define IDM_Undo           6
0041  #define IDM_Cut            7
0042  #define IDM_Copy           8
0043  #define IDM_Paste          9
0044  #define IDM_Delete         10
0045
0046  #define IDM_RunForward     11
0047  #define IDM_RunReverse     12
0048  #define IDM_StopAnimation  13
0049  #define IDM_InitFrame      14
0050  #define IDM_SaveAnimation  15
0051  #define IDM_LoadAnimation  16
0052  #define IDM_Clear          17
0053
0054  #define IDM_FPS182         18
0055  #define IDM_FPS91          19
0056  #define IDM_FPS61          20
0057  #define IDM_FPS45          21
0058  #define IDM_FPS36          22
0059  #define IDM_FPS30          23
0060
0061  #define IDM_About          24
0062  #define IDM_License        25
0063  #define IDM_Display        26
0064  #define IDM_Colors         27
0065  #define IDM_Mode           28
0066  #define IDM_Memory         29
0067  #define IDM_Timing         30
0068  #define IDM_GeneralHelp    31
0069  /*
0070  -----------------------------------------------------------------
0071                          String ID constants
0072  -----------------------------------------------------------------
0073                                                                  */
0074  #define IDS_Caption    1
0075  #define IDS_Warning    2
0076  #define IDS_NoMouse    3
```

```
0077  #define IDS_About          4
0078  #define IDS_AboutText      5
0079  #define IDS_License        6
0080  #define IDS_LicenseText    7
0081  #define IDS_Help           8
0082  #define IDS_HelpText       9
0083  #define IDS_Completed      10
0084  #define IDS_Error          11
0085  #define IDS_Memory         12
0086  #define IDS_MemText        13
0087  #define IDS_Timing         14
0088  #define IDS_TimingText     15
0089  #define IDS_NotReady       16
0090  #define IDS_Ready          17
0091  #define IDS_BuildBefore    18
0092  #define IDS_Already        19
0093  #define IDS_InsufMem1      20
0094  #define IDS_InsufMem2      21
0095  #define IDS_NoTimer        22
0096  #define IDS_NoReset        23
0097  #define IDS_CannotReset    24
0098  #define IDS_Resolution     25
0099  #define IDS_ResVGA         26
0100  #define IDS_ResEGA         27
0101  #define IDS_ResCGA         28
0102  #define IDS_ResSVGA        29
0103  #define IDS_Res8514        30
0104  #define IDS_ResHerc        31
0105  #define IDS_ResCustom      32
0106  #define IDS_Color          33
0107  #define IDS_Color16        34
0108  #define IDS_Color256       35
0109  #define IDS_Color2         36
0110  #define IDS_ColorCustom    37
0111  #define IDS_Machine        38
0112  #define IDS_Enhanced       39
0113  #define IDS_Standard       40
0114  #define IDS_Real           41
0115  #define IDS_NoFrame        42
0116  #define IDS_AnimReady      43
0117  #define IDS_Unexpected     44
0118  #define IDS_Status         45
0119  #define IDS_Disk1          46
0120  #define IDS_Disk2          47
0121  #define IDS_Disk3          48
0122  #define IDS_Disk4          49
0123  #define IDS_Disk5          50
0124  #define IDS_Disk6          51
0125  #define IDS_Disk7          52
0126  #define IDS_Disk8          53
0127  #define IDS_Disk9          54
0128  #define IDS_Disk10         55
0129  #define IDS_Disk11         56
0130  #define IDS_Disk12         57
0131  #define IDS_Disk13         58
0132  #define IDS_Disk14         59
0133  #define IDS_Disk15         60
0134  #define IDS_Disk16         61
0135  #define IDS_Disk17         62
0136  #define IDS_Disk18         63
0137  #define IDS_Disk19         64
```

```
0138   #define IDS_Disk20      65
0139   #define IDS_Disk21      66
0140   #define IDS_Disk22      67
0141   #define IDS_Disk23      68
0142   #define IDS_Disk24      69
0143   #define IDS_Disk25      70
0144   #define IDS_Disk26      71
0145   #define IDS_NoBg        72
0146   #define IDS_BgAlready   73
0147   #define IDS_InsufMemBg  74
0148   /*
0149   -----------------------------------------------------------------
0150                     End of include file
0151   -----------------------------------------------------------------
0152                                                                   */
```

**15-10** The resource script file listing for the sample application.

```
0001   /*
0002   -----------------------------------------------------------------
0003                  Resource script file RUNNING.RC
0004            Copyright 1992 Lee Adams.  All rights reserved.
0005   This file defines the menu resources, the accelerator key
0006   resources, and the string resources that will be used by the
0007   demonstration application at runtime.
0008   -----------------------------------------------------------------
0009                                                                   */
0010   #define zRCFILE
0011   #include <WINDOWS.H>
0012   #include "RUNNING.H"
0013   /*
0014   -----------------------------------------------------------------
0015                        Script for menus
0016   -----------------------------------------------------------------
0017                                                                   */
0018   MENUS1 MENU
0019     BEGIN
0020     POPUP "&File"
0021       BEGIN
0022         MENUITEM  "&New", IDM_New, GRAYED
0023         MENUITEM  "&Open...", IDM_Open, GRAYED
0024         MENUITEM  "&Save", IDM_Save, GRAYED
0025         MENUITEM  "Save &As...", IDM_SaveAs, GRAYED
0026         MENUITEM SEPARATOR
0027         MENUITEM  "E&xit", IDM_Exit
0028       END
0029     POPUP "&Edit"
0030       BEGIN
0031         MENUITEM  "&Undo\tAlt+BkSp", IDM_Undo, GRAYED
0032         MENUITEM SEPARATOR
0033         MENUITEM  "Cu&t\tShift+Del", IDM_Cut, GRAYED
0034         MENUITEM  "&Copy\tCtrl+Ins", IDM_Copy, GRAYED
0035         MENUITEM  "&Paste\tShift+Ins", IDM_Paste, GRAYED
0036         MENUITEM  "&Delete\tDel", IDM_Delete, GRAYED
0037       END
0038     POPUP "&Animation"
0039       BEGIN
0040         MENUITEM "Run &Forward", IDM_RunForward
0041         MENUITEM "Run &Reverse", IDM_RunReverse
0042         MENUITEM "&Pause", IDM_StopAnimation
```

```
0043        MENUITEM SEPARATOR
0044        MENUITEM "&Initialize system", IDM_InitFrame
0045        MENUITEM "Cr&eate Frames", IDM_SaveAnimation
0046        MENUITEM SEPARATOR
0047        MENUITEM "&Load Animation", IDM_LoadAnimation
0048        MENUITEM SEPARATOR
0049        MENUITEM "&Clear", IDM_Clear
0050      END
0051    POPUP "&Timer"
0052      BEGIN
0053        MENUITEM "&18 fps", IDM_FPS182, CHECKED
0054        MENUITEM " &9 fps", IDM_FPS91
0055        MENUITEM " &6 fps", IDM_FPS61
0056        MENUITEM " &5 fps", IDM_FPS45
0057        MENUITEM " &4 fps", IDM_FPS36
0058        MENUITEM " &3 fps", IDM_FPS30
0059      END
0060    POPUP "&Help"
0061      BEGIN
0062        MENUITEM "&About", IDM_About
0063        MENUITEM "&License", IDM_License
0064        MENUITEM SEPARATOR
0065        MENUITEM "&Screen resolution", IDM_Display
0066        MENUITEM "Available &colors", IDM_Colors
0067        MENUITEM "Memory mode", IDM_Mode
0068        MENUITEM SEPARATOR
0069        MENUITEM "&Memory notes", IDM_Memory
0070        MENUITEM "&Timing notes", IDM_Timing
0071        MENUITEM SEPARATOR
0072        MENUITEM "&Help", IDM_GeneralHelp
0073      END
0074    END
0075 /*
0076 ----------------------------------------------------------------
0077                   Script for accelerator keys
0078 ----------------------------------------------------------------
0079                                                              */
0080 KEYS1 ACCELERATORS
0081    BEGIN
0082    VK_BACK, IDM_Undo, VIRTKEY, ALT
0083    VK_DELETE, IDM_Cut, VIRTKEY, SHIFT
0084    VK_INSERT, IDM_Copy, VIRTKEY, CONTROL
0085    VK_INSERT, IDM_Paste, VIRTKEY, SHIFT
0086    VK_DELETE, IDM_Delete,VIRTKEY
0087    END
0088 /*
0089 ----------------------------------------------------------------
0090                      Script for strings
0091    Programmer's Notes:  If you are typing this listing, set your
0092    margins to a line length of 255 characters so you can create
0093    lengthy strings without embedded carriage returns.  The line
0094    wraparounds in the following STRINGTABLE script are used for
0095    readability only in this printout.
0096 ----------------------------------------------------------------
0097                                                              */
0098 STRINGTABLE
0099    BEGIN
0100    IDS_Caption      "Run-cycle Loop"
0101    IDS_Warning      "Warning"
0102    IDS_NoMouse      "No mouse found.  Some features of this
                         demonstration program may require a mouse."
```

```
0103     IDS_About        "About this program"
0104     IDS_AboutText    "This is a demo from Windcrest McGraw-Hill
         book 4114.  Copyright 1992 Lee Adams.  All rights reserved."
0105     IDS_License      "License Agreement"
0106     IDS_LicenseText "You can use this code as part of your own
         software product subject to the License Agreement and Limited
         Warranty in Windcrest McGraw-Hill book 4114 and on its
         companion disk."
0107     IDS_Help         "How to use this demo"
0108     IDS_HelpText     "The Animation menu manages the animation
         engine.  Select Initialize System then Create Frames to build
         frames and save to disk.  Select Load Animation then Run
         Forward to play animation.  See the book for advanced
         features."
0109     IDS_Completed    "Task completed OK"
0110     IDS_Error        "Runtime error"
0111     IDS_Memory       "Animation memory requirements"
0112     IDS_MemText      "The hidden frame for the animation is stored
         as a bitmap in global memory.  The demo will advise you if a
         memory shortage occurs.  To make more global memory available
         you can close other applications."
0113     IDS_Timing       "Animation timing"
0114     IDS_TimingText   "The Timer menu sets the animation display
         rate to 18.2, 9.1, 6.1, 4.5, 3.6, or 3 frames per second.
         Actual performance is limited by your computer's processor
         (25MHz or faster is recommended).  See the book for details."
0115     IDS_NotReady     "Animation not ready"
0116     IDS_Ready        "Animation ready"
0117     IDS_BuildBefore "Animation frames not ready for playback."
0118     IDS_Already      "The hidden frame has already been created."
0119     IDS_InsufMem1    "Insufficient global memory for frame bitmap."
0120     IDS_NoTimer      "Unable to create a timer.  Close other
         applications."
0121     IDS_NoReset      "Create hidden frame before attempting to
         reset timer."
0122     IDS_CannotReset "Unable to reset the timer."
0123     IDS_Resolution  "Screen resolution"
0124     IDS_ResVGA       "Running in 640x480 mode."
0125     IDS_ResEGA       "Running in 640x350 mode."
0126     IDS_ResCGA       "Running in 640x200 mode."
0127     IDS_ResSVGA      "Running in 800x600 mode."
0128     IDS_Res8514      "Running in 1024x768 mode."
0129     IDS_ResHerc      "Running in 720x348 mode."
0130     IDS_ResCustom    "Running in custom mode."
0131     IDS_Color        "Available colors"
0132     IDS_Color16      "Running in 16-color mode."
0133     IDS_Color256     "Running in 256-color mode."
0134     IDS_Color2       "Running in 2-color mode."
0135     IDS_ColorCustom "Running in a custom color mode."
0136     IDS_Machine      "Memory mode"
0137     IDS_Enhanced     "Running in enhanced mode.  Can allocate up to
         16 MB extended physical memory (XMS) if available.  Virtual
         memory up to 4 times physical memory (maximum 64 MB) is also
         available via automatic disk swapping of 4K pages."
0138     IDS_Standard     "Running in standard mode.  Can allocate up to
         16 MB extended physical memory (XMS) if available."
0139     IDS_Real         "Running in real mode.  Can allocate blocks of
         memory from the first 640K of RAM.  Can also allocate blocks
         from expanded memory (EMS) if available."
0140     IDS_NoFrame      "Hidden frame not yet created."
0141     IDS_AnimReady    "Animation ready"
```

**15-10** Continued.

```
0142       IDS_Unexpected    "Unexpected animation condition"
0143       IDS_Status        "Animation status"
0144       IDS_Disk1         "Animation files already saved to disk."
0145       IDS_Disk2         "Animation sequence successfully saved to
disk."
0146       IDS_Disk3         "Unable to load next frame from disk.
Animation halted."
0147       IDS_Disk4         "Animation sequence already loaded from disk."
0148       IDS_Disk5         "Previous load failed.  Cancelling this
attempt."
0149       IDS_Disk6         "Not enough memory available.  Software will
dynamically load each frame from disk during playback."
0150       IDS_Disk7         "Animation sequence successfully loaded from
disk."
0151       IDS_Disk8         "Previous save failed.  Cancelling this
attempt."
0152       IDS_Disk9         "No hidden-frame exists.  No frame saved to
disk."
0153       IDS_Disk10        "Unable to retrieve bitmap data structure."
0154       IDS_Disk11        "Bit array is too long to save to disk in a
single pass."
0155       IDS_Disk12        "Cannot create memory buffer for disk write."
0156       IDS_Disk13        "Unable to copy bits from bitmap to buffer."
0157       IDS_Disk14        "File already exists.  Overwrite existing
file?"
0158       IDS_Disk15        "Unable to open the file for writing."
0159       IDS_Disk16        "Unable to write to the opened file."
0160       IDS_Disk17        "Unable to close the file after writing."
0161       IDS_Disk18        "No memory bitmap exists.  Unable to load from
disk."
0162       IDS_Disk19        "Image file is larger than animation frame.
No file loaded."
0163       IDS_Disk20        "Cannot create memory buffer for file read."
0164       IDS_Disk21        "Unable to open the file for reading.  Be sure
you have saved an animation sequence to disk before attempting
to load it."
0165       IDS_Disk22        "An error occurred while reading the file."
0166       IDS_Disk23        "The frame file was shorter than expected."
0167       IDS_Disk24        "Unable to close the file after reading."
0168       IDS_Disk25        "Unable to copy bits from buffer to bitmap."
0169       IDS_Disk26        "Unable to save all files.  Check if
sufficient space available on disk."
0170       IDS_NoBg          "Hidden background image not yet created."
0171       IDS_BgAlready     "The hidden background bitmap has already been
created."
0172       IDS_InsufMemBg    "Insufficient global memory for background
bitmap."
0173    END
0174  /*
0175  ------------------------------------------------------------------
0176                   End of resource script file
0177  ------------------------------------------------------------------
0178                                                                 */
```

**15-11**  The C source file listing for the sample application, running.c. This demonstration program is ready to build using QuickC for Windows, Turbo C++ for Windows, Microsoft C and the SDK, Borland C++, Symantec Zortech C++, WATCOM C, and other compilers. See chapter 10 for the program listings for storage.h and storage.c,which must be linked with this application. See FIG. 1-2 for sample command-lines to build the program. Guidelines for using your compiler are provided in the appropriate appendix at the back of the book.

```
0001   /*
0002   --------------------------------------------------------------------
0003          STANDARD RUN CYCLE for Windows applications that use
0004          disk-based, hidden-page drawn, frame animation.
0005   --------------------------------------------------------------------
0006   Source file: RUNNING.C
0007   Release version: 1.00                      Programmer:  Lee Adams
0008   Type:  C source file for Windows application development.
0009   Compilers: Microsoft C and SDK, Borland C++, Zortech C++,
0010     QuickC for Windows, Turbo C++ for Windows, WATCOM C.
0011   Memory model:  small.
0012   Dependencies:  RUNNING.DEF module definition file, RUNNING.H
0013                  include file, RUNNING.RC resource script file,
0014                  and RUNNING.C source file.  Disk I/O operations
0015                  require STORAGE.H include file and STORAGE.C
0016                  additional C source file.
0017   Output and features:  Demonstrates interactive playback of
0018     disk-based hidden-page drawn frame animation.  A consistent
0019     database suitable for tweening is demonstrated as a run cycle.
0020   Publication: Contains material from Windcrest/McGraw-Hill book
0021     4114 published by TAB BOOKS Division of McGraw-Hill Inc.
0022   License:  As purchaser of the book you are granted a royalty-
0023     free license to distribute executable files generated using
0024     this code provided you accept the conditions of the License
0025     Agreement and Limited Warranty described in the book and on
0026     the companion disk.  Government users:  This software and
0027.    documentation are subject to restrictions set forth in The
0028     Rights in Technical Data and Computer Software clause at
0029     252.227-7013 and elsewhere.
0030   --------------------------------------------------------------------
0031          (c) Copyright 1992 Lee Adams.  All rights reserved.
0032          Lee Adams(tm) is a trademark of Lee Adams.
0033   --------------------------------------------------------------------
0034
0035   --------------------------------------------------------------------
0036                          Include files
0037   --------------------------------------------------------------------
0038                                                                  */
0039   #include <WINDOWS.H>
0040   #include "RUNNING.H"
0041   #include "STORAGE.H"  /* declares callable functions in STORAGE.C
0041         */
0042   /*
0043   --------------------------------------------------------------------
0044          Static variables visible throughout this file
0045   --------------------------------------------------------------------
0046                                                                  */
0047   /* -------------------- window specifications ----------------- */
0048   #define zWINDOW_WIDTH 408
0049   #define zWINDOW_HEIGHT 346
0050   #define zFRAMEWIDE 400
0051   #define zFRAMEHIGH 300
0052   int WindowX, WindowY;
0053
```

```
0054   /* ---------------- instance operations ----------------- */
0055   HANDLE hInst;
0056   HWND MainhWnd;
0057   HANDLE hAccel;
0058   HMENU hMenu;
0059   PAINTSTRUCT ps;
0060   int MessageRet;
0061
0062   /* ---------------- mouse and cursor ----------------- */
0063   HCURSOR hPrevCursor;
0064   HCURSOR hHourGlass;
0065   int MousePresent;
0066
0067   /* ---------------- runtime conditions ----------------- */
0068   int DisplayWidth, DisplayHeight;
0069   int DisplayBits;
0070   int DisplayPlanes;
0071   DWORD MemoryMode;
0072
0073   /* ---------------- message box operations ----------------- */
0074   char lpCaption[51];
0075   int Max= 50;
0076   char lpMessage[250];
0077   int MaxText= 249;
0078
0079   /* ---------------- persistent image operations ---------------- */
0080   #define zBLANK 0
0081   #define zANIMATING  1
0082   int PaintImage= zBLANK;
0083
0084   /* ---------------- timer operations ----------------- */
0085   #define zTIMER_PAUSE 3
0086   int TimerCounter= zTIMER_PAUSE;
0087   BOOL TimerExists= FALSE;
0088   WORD TimerID1;
0089
0090   /* ---------------- font operations ----------------- */
0091   HFONT hFont, hPrevFont;          /* handles to new, previous font */
0092   HDC hFontDC;                       /* display-context for font */
0093
0094   /* ---------------- hidden frame operations ----------------- */
0095   HDC hFrameDC;
0096   HBITMAP hFrame;
0097   HBITMAP hPrevFrame;
0098   BOOL FrameReady= FALSE;
0099
0100   /* ---------------- animation engine ----------------- */
0101   BOOL Pause= TRUE;
0102   WORD wFrameRate= 55;
0103   WORD wPrevRate= 55;
0104   #define zFORWARD 1
0105   #define zREVERSE 0
0106   int FrameDirection= zFORWARD;
0107   BOOL Redisplay= FALSE;
0108   int FrameNum= 1;
0109   #define zFIRSTFRAME 1
0110   #define zFINALFRAME 8
0111   BOOL AnimationReady= FALSE;
0112
0113   /* ---------------- disk save/load operations ---------------- */
0114   int RetVal;                                    /* return value */
```

*Increase. Cel. table. 13 per frame.*
*15 × 64*
*× 48.2*

```
0115   BOOL bFrameSaved= FALSE;                    /* frame saved to disk? */
0116   BOOL bFrameLoaded= FALSE;                   /* frame loaded from disk? */
0117   BOOL bAnimationSaved= FALSE;                /* animation saved to disk? */
0118   BOOL bAnimationLoaded= FALSE;               /* animation loaded from disk? */
0119   BOOL bPrevSaveAttempt= FALSE;               /* previous save attempt made? */
0120   BOOL bPrevLoadAttempt= FALSE;               /* previous load attempt made? */
0121   HDC hFDC;                          /* memory-display context for playback */
0122   HBITMAP hPrevF,hF1,hF2,hF3,hF4,hF5,     /* bitmaps for playback... */
0123    hF6,hF7,hF8;
0124   BOOL bUseDisk= FALSE;                       /* load each frame as needed? */
0125   BOOL bAnimationHalted= FALSE;       /* disk error during animation? */
0126
0127   /* ----------------- database for cel images ----------------- */
0128   int Cel1[]=
0129   {
0130   120,110, 24,                                        /* head */
0131   143,119, 160,123, 211,112, 248,114, 270,118, 295,110,  /* spine */
0132   10,                                              /* tail */
0133   282,141, 315,151, 336,174, 350,178,          /* far hindleg */
0134   196,137, 198,174, 211,193, 222,196,          /* far foreleg */
0135   193,147, 161,162, 162,187, 170,191,          /* near foreleg */
0136   258,158, 276,188, 270,213, 260,213           /* near hindleg */
0137   };
0138   int Cel2[]=
0139   {
0140   120,103, 24,
0141   144,111, 161,115, 215,117, 250,112, 272,111, 300,109,
0142   10,
0143   290,129, 327,120, 354,130, 368,133,
0144   176,150, 146,170, 142,193, 146,204,
0145   163,158, 126,163, 110,182, 108,196,
0146   283,140, 320,148, 340,166, 342,181
0147   };
0148   int Cel3[]=
0149   {
0150   120,98, 24,
0151   145,103, 161,108, 212,101, 249,96, 270,97, 296,100,
0152   10,
0153   284,116, 321,116, 346,133, 360,138,
0154   142,140, 107,140, 96,165, 94,178,
0155   152,145, 118,152, 93,163, 83,175,
0156   289,110, 323,100, 353,104, 370,106
0157   };
0158   int Cel4[]=
0159   {
0160   120,106, 24,
0161   144,116, 161,121, 213,110, 250,109, 273,110, 297,116,
0162   10,
0163   273,148, 307,143, 318,170, 328,180,
0164   177,160, 152,185, 127,190, 111,190,
0165   169,160, 152,195, 133,208, 119,208,
0166   285,135, 321,135, 345,155, 360,158
0167   };
0168   int Cel5[]=
0169   {
0170   120,128, 24,
0171   145,133, 164,131, 201,96, 231,80, 251,76, 278,76,
0172   10,
0173   229,122, 260,109, 270,131, 282,140,
0174   196,160, 180,195, 170,212, 160,212,
0175   201,146, 212,181, 209,203, 200,203,
```

*Suggest. 15. cels.*
*per.*
*frame.*

```
0176   247,122, 280,110, 304,124, 320,124
0177   };
0178   int Cel6[]=
0179   {
0180   120,122, 24,
0181   145,131, 161,135, 200,102, 233,98, 255,97, 279,90,
0182   10,
0183   228,140, 220,171, 208,194, 195,195,
0184   190,163, 216,190, 235,205, 248,208,
0185   201,149, 232,166, 254,176, 266,176,
0186   215,131, 250,138, 245,163, 247,175
0187   };
0188   int Cel7[]=
0189   {
0190   120,119, 24,
0191   145,128, 162,131, 210,110, 244,114, 265,120, 282,103,
0192   10,
0193   230,155, 233,191, 219,212, 205,214,
0194   198,152, 222,181, 245,192, 258,191,
0195   202,139, 210,175, 220,199, 229,200,
0196   205,132, 212,170, 188,180, 184,191
0197   };
0198   int Cel8[]=
0199   {
0200   120,115, 24,
0201   145,124, 163,127, 212,111, 245,115, 268,120, 290,109,
0202   10,
0203   270,153, 301,170, 308,200, 319,205,
0204   199,143, 192,180, 215,192, 229,193,
0205   201,132, 179,161, 179,186, 182,195,
0206   237,160, 264,182, 253,212, 240,214
0207   };
0208
0209   /*
0210   ------------------------------------------------------------------
0211                    Entry point for the application
0212   ------------------------------------------------------------------
0213                                                                  */
0214   int PASCAL WinMain(HANDLE hInstance, HANDLE hPrevInstance,
0215                      LPSTR lpCmdLine, int nCmdShow)
0216   {
0217     MSG msg;
0218     HWND hWndPrev;
0219     HWND hDesktopWnd;
0220     HDC hDCcaps;
0221
0222   /* ------------ ensure only one instance is running ------------ */
0223   hWndPrev = FindWindow("DEMOCLASS", NULL);
0224   if (hWndPrev != NULL)
0225     {
0226     BringWindowToTop(hWndPrev);
0227     return FALSE;
0228     }
0229
0230   /* --------- determine capabilities of screen display --------- */
0231   hDesktopWnd= GetDesktopWindow();
0232   hDCcaps= GetDC(hDesktopWnd);
0233   DisplayWidth= GetDeviceCaps(hDCcaps,HORZRES);
0234   DisplayHeight= GetDeviceCaps(hDCcaps,VERTRES);
0235   DisplayBits= GetDeviceCaps(hDCcaps,BITSPIXEL);
0236   DisplayPlanes= GetDeviceCaps(hDCcaps,PLANES);
```

```
0237   ReleaseDC(hDesktopWnd,hDCcaps);
0238
0239   /* ------- calculate screen position to center the window ------ */
0240   WindowX= (DisplayWidth - zWINDOW_WIDTH) / 2;
0241   WindowY= (DisplayHeight - zWINDOW_HEIGHT) /2;
0242   if (WindowX < 0) WindowX= 0;
0243   if (WindowY < 0) WindowY= 0;
0244
0245   /* ---- determine memory mode (enhanced, standard, or real) ---- */
0246   MemoryMode= GetWinFlags();
0247
0248   /* --------------- create and show the window --------------- */
0249   hInst = hInstance;
0250   if (!zInitClass(hInstance)) return FALSE;
0251   MainhWnd = zInitMainWindow(hInstance);
0252   if (!MainhWnd) return FALSE;
0253   ShowWindow(MainhWnd, nCmdShow);
0254   UpdateWindow(MainhWnd);
0255   hAccel= LoadAccelerators(hInstance,"KEYS1");
0256   hFontDC= GetDC(MainhWnd);
0257   hFont= GetStockObject(SYSTEM_FONT);
0258   hPrevFont= SelectObject(hFontDC,hFont);
0259   SetTextColor(hFontDC,RGB(191,191,191));
0260   TextOut(hFontDC,10,280,"- Copyright 1992 Lee Adams.",27);
0261   SetTextColor(hFontDC,RGB(0,0,0));
0262   SelectObject(hFontDC,hPrevFont);
0263   ReleaseDC(MainhWnd,hFontDC);
0264
0265   /* --------------------- check for mouse --------------------- */
0266   MousePresent = GetSystemMetrics(SM_MOUSEPRESENT);
0267   if (!MousePresent)
0268     {
0269     LoadString(hInst,IDS_Warning,lpCaption,Max);
0270     LoadString(hInst,IDS_NoMouse,lpMessage,MaxText);
0271     MessageBox(GetFocus(),lpMessage,lpCaption,MB_OK);
0272     }
0273
0274   /* ---------- begin retrieving messages for the window --------- */
0275   while (GetMessage(&msg,0,0,0))
0276     {
0277     if(TranslateAccelerator(MainhWnd, hAccel, &msg))
0278       continue;
0279     TranslateMessage(&msg);
0280     DispatchMessage(&msg);
0281     }
0282   return(msg.wParam);
0283   }
0284   /*
0285   ------------------------------------------------------------------
0286                     Switcher for incoming messages
0287   ------------------------------------------------------------------
0288                                                                   */
0289   LONG FAR PASCAL zMessageHandler(HWND hWnd, unsigned message,
0290                          WORD wParam, LONG lParam)
0291   {
0292     HDC hDCpaint;
0293
0294   switch (message)
0295     {
0296
0297     case WM_TIMER:
```

*NB. Red not realtime - go for unenhanced, 8086 mode.*

```
0298        TimerCounter--;
0299        if (TimerCounter > 0) break;
0300        TimerCounter++;
0301        zShowNextFrame(hWnd);
0302        break;
0303
0304    case WM_COMMAND:
0305        switch(wParam)
0306            {
0307        case IDM_New:       break;
0308        case IDM_Open:      break;
0309        case IDM_Save:      break;
0310        case IDM_SaveAs:    break;
0311        case IDM_Exit:      PostQuitMessage(0); break;
0312
0313        case IDM_Undo:      break;
0314        case IDM_Cut:       break;
0315        case IDM_Copy:      break;
0316        case IDM_Paste:     break;
0317        case IDM_Delete:    break;
0318
0319        case IDM_RunForward:
0320            if (AnimationReady==FALSE)
0321                {
0322                MessageBeep(0);
0323                LoadString(hInst,IDS_NotReady,lpCaption,Max);
0324                LoadString(hInst,IDS_BuildBefore,lpMessage,MaxText);
0325                TimerCounter= zTIMER_PAUSE;
0326                MessageBox(GetFocus(),lpMessage,lpCaption,MB_OK);
0327                break;
0328                }
0329            Pause= FALSE;
0330            PaintImage= zANIMATING;
0331            FrameDirection= zFORWARD;
0332            zShowNextFrame(hWnd);
0333            break;
0334        case IDM_RunReverse:
0335            if (AnimationReady==FALSE)
0336                {
0337                MessageBeep(0);
0338                LoadString(hInst,IDS_NotReady,lpCaption,Max);
0339                LoadString(hInst,IDS_BuildBefore,lpMessage,MaxText);
0340                TimerCounter= zTIMER_PAUSE;
0341                MessageBox(GetFocus(),lpMessage,lpCaption,MB_OK);
0342                break;
0343                }
0344            Pause= FALSE;
0345            PaintImage= zANIMATING;
0346            FrameDirection= zREVERSE;
0347            zShowNextFrame(hWnd);
0348            break;
0349        case IDM_StopAnimation:
0350            if (AnimationReady==FALSE)
0351                {
0352                MessageBeep(0);
0353                LoadString(hInst,IDS_NotReady,lpCaption,Max);
0354                LoadString(hInst,IDS_BuildBefore,lpMessage,MaxText);
0355                TimerCounter= zTIMER_PAUSE;
0356                MessageBox(GetFocus(),lpMessage,lpCaption,MB_OK);
0357                break;
0358                }
```

```
0359              Pause= TRUE;
0360              zShowNextFrame(hWnd);
0361              break;
0362       case IDM_InitFrame: zInitFrame(hWnd);
0363                          break;
0364       case IDM_SaveAnimation:
0365          SetCapture(hWnd); hPrevCursor= SetCursor(hHourGlass);
0366          zSaveAnimation(hWnd);
0367          SetCursor(hPrevCursor); ReleaseCapture();
0368          if (bAnimationSaved==FALSE)
0369             {
0370             MessageBeep(0);
0371             LoadString(hInst,IDS_NotReady,lpCaption,Max);
0372             LoadString(hInst,IDS_Disk26,lpMessage,MaxText);
0373             TimerCounter= zTIMER_PAUSE;
0374             MessageBox(GetFocus(),lpMessage,lpCaption,MB_OK);
0375             }
0376          break;
0377       case IDM_LoadAnimation:
0378          SetCapture(hWnd); hPrevCursor= SetCursor(hHourGlass);
0379          zLoadAnimation(hWnd);
0380          SetCursor(hPrevCursor); ReleaseCapture();
0381          break;
0382       case IDM_Clear:  if (Pause==TRUE)
0383                          {
0384                          zClear(hWnd);
0385                          PaintImage= zBLANK;
0386                          }
0387                        break;
0388
0389       case IDM_FPS182: wPrevRate= wFrameRate;
0390                        wFrameRate= (WORD)55;
0391                        zSetFrameRate(hWnd, wFrameRate); break;
0392       case IDM_FPS91:  wPrevRate= wFrameRate;
0393                        wFrameRate= (WORD)110;
0394                        zSetFrameRate(hWnd, wFrameRate); break;
0395       case IDM_FPS61:  wPrevRate= wFrameRate;
0396                        wFrameRate= (WORD)165;
0397                        zSetFrameRate(hWnd, wFrameRate); break;
0398       case IDM_FPS45:  wPrevRate= wFrameRate;
0399                        wFrameRate= (WORD) 220;
0400                        zSetFrameRate(hWnd, wFrameRate); break;
0401       case IDM_FPS36:  wPrevRate= wFrameRate;
0402                        wFrameRate= (WORD) 275;
0403                        zSetFrameRate(hWnd, wFrameRate); break;
0404       case IDM_FPS30:  wPrevRate= wFrameRate;
0405                        wFrameRate= (WORD) 330;
0406                        zSetFrameRate(hWnd, wFrameRate); break;
0407
0408       case IDM_About:
0409          LoadString(hInst,IDS_About,lpCaption,Max);
0410          LoadString(hInst,IDS_AboutText,lpMessage,MaxText);
0411          TimerCounter= zTIMER_PAUSE;
0412          MessageBox(GetFocus(),lpMessage,lpCaption,MB_OK);
0413          break;
0414       case IDM_License:
0415          LoadString(hInst,IDS_License,lpCaption,Max);
0416          LoadString(hInst,IDS_LicenseText,lpMessage,MaxText);
0417          TimerCounter= zTIMER_PAUSE;
0418          MessageBox(GetFocus(),lpMessage,lpCaption,MB_OK);
0419          break;
```

```
0420
0421        case IDM_Display:
0422          if (DisplayWidth==640)
0423            {
0424            if (DisplayHeight==480)
0425              {
0426              LoadString(hInst,IDS_Resolution,lpCaption,Max);
0427              LoadString(hInst,IDS_ResVGA,lpMessage,MaxText);
0428              TimerCounter= zTIMER_PAUSE;
0429              MessageBox(GetFocus(),lpMessage,lpCaption,MB_OK);
0430              }
0431            if (DisplayHeight==350)
0432              {
0433              LoadString(hInst,IDS_Resolution,lpCaption,Max);
0434              LoadString(hInst,IDS_ResEGA,lpMessage,MaxText);
0435              TimerCounter= zTIMER_PAUSE;
0436              MessageBox(GetFocus(),lpMessage,lpCaption,MB_OK);
0437              }
0438            if (DisplayHeight==200)
0439              {
0440              LoadString(hInst,IDS_Resolution,lpCaption,Max);
0441              LoadString(hInst,IDS_ResCGA,lpMessage,MaxText);
0442              TimerCounter= zTIMER_PAUSE;
0443              MessageBox(GetFocus(),lpMessage,lpCaption,MB_OK);
0444              }
0445            break;
0446            }
0447          if (DisplayWidth==800)
0448            {
0449            LoadString(hInst,IDS_Resolution,lpCaption,Max);
0450            LoadString(hInst,IDS_ResSVGA,lpMessage,MaxText);
0451            TimerCounter= zTIMER_PAUSE;
0452            MessageBox(GetFocus(),lpMessage,lpCaption,MB_OK);
0453            break;
0454            }
0455          if (DisplayWidth==1024)
0456            {
0457            LoadString(hInst,IDS_Resolution,lpCaption,Max);
0458            LoadString(hInst,IDS_Res8514,lpMessage,MaxText);
0459            TimerCounter= zTIMER_PAUSE;
0460            MessageBox(GetFocus(),lpMessage,lpCaption,MB_OK);
0461            break;
0462            }
0463          if (DisplayWidth==720)
0464            {
0465            LoadString(hInst,IDS_Resolution,lpCaption,Max);
0466            LoadString(hInst,IDS_ResHerc,lpMessage,MaxText);
0467            TimerCounter= zTIMER_PAUSE;
0468            MessageBox(GetFocus(),lpMessage,lpCaption,MB_OK);
0469            break;
0470            }
0471          LoadString(hInst,IDS_Resolution,lpCaption,Max);
0472          LoadString(hInst,IDS_ResCustom,lpMessage,MaxText);
0473          TimerCounter= zTIMER_PAUSE;
0474          MessageBox(GetFocus(),lpMessage,lpCaption,MB_OK);
0475          break;
0476
0477        case IDM_Colors:
0478          if (DisplayBits==1)
0479            {
0480            if (DisplayPlanes==4)
```

```
0481                    {
0482                    LoadString(hInst,IDS_Color,lpCaption,Max);
0483                    LoadString(hInst,IDS_Color16,lpMessage,MaxText);
0484                    TimerCounter= zTIMER_PAUSE;
0485                    MessageBox(GetFocus(),lpMessage,lpCaption,MB_OK);
0486                    break;
0487                    }
0488                if (DisplayPlanes==1)
0489                    {
0490                    LoadString(hInst,IDS_Color,lpCaption,Max);
0491                    LoadString(hInst,IDS_Color2,lpMessage,MaxText);
0492                    TimerCounter= zTIMER_PAUSE;
0493                    MessageBox(GetFocus(),lpMessage,lpCaption,MB_OK);
0494                    break;
0495                    }
0496                }
0497            if (DisplayBits==8)
0498                {
0499                LoadString(hInst,IDS_Color,lpCaption,Max);
0500                LoadString(hInst,IDS_Color256,lpMessage,MaxText);
0501                TimerCounter= zTIMER_PAUSE;
0502                MessageBox(GetFocus(),lpMessage,lpCaption,MB_OK);
0503                break;
0504                }
0505            LoadString(hInst,IDS_Color,lpCaption,Max);
0506            LoadString(hInst,IDS_ColorCustom,lpMessage,MaxText);
0507            TimerCounter= zTIMER_PAUSE;
0508            MessageBox(GetFocus(),lpMessage,lpCaption,MB_OK);
0509            break;
0510
0511        case IDM_Mode:
0512            if (MemoryMode & WF_ENHANCED)
0513                {
0514                LoadString(hInst,IDS_Machine,lpCaption,Max);
0515                LoadString(hInst,IDS_Enhanced,lpMessage,MaxText);
0516                TimerCounter= zTIMER_PAUSE;
0517                MessageBox(GetFocus(),lpMessage,lpCaption,MB_OK);
0518                break;
0519                }
0520            if (MemoryMode & WF_STANDARD)
0521                {
0522                LoadString(hInst,IDS_Machine,lpCaption,Max);
0523                LoadString(hInst,IDS_Standard,lpMessage,MaxText);
0524                TimerCounter= zTIMER_PAUSE;
0525                MessageBox(GetFocus(),lpMessage,lpCaption,MB_OK);
0526                break;
0527                }
0528            LoadString(hInst,IDS_Machine,lpCaption,Max);
0529            LoadString(hInst,IDS_Real,lpMessage,MaxText);
0530            TimerCounter= zTIMER_PAUSE;
0531            MessageBox(GetFocus(),lpMessage,lpCaption,MB_OK);
0532            break;
0533
0534        case IDM_Memory:
0535            LoadString(hInst,IDS_Memory,lpCaption,Max);
0536            LoadString(hInst,IDS_MemText,lpMessage,MaxText);
0537            TimerCounter= zTIMER_PAUSE;
0538            MessageBox(GetFocus(),lpMessage,lpCaption,MB_OK);
0539            break;
0540        case IDM_Timing:
0541            LoadString(hInst,IDS_Timing,lpCaption,Max);
```

```
0542          LoadString(hInst,IDS_TimingText,lpMessage,MaxText);
0543          TimerCounter= zTIMER_PAUSE;
0544          MessageBox(GetFocus(),lpMessage,lpCaption,MB_OK);
0545          break;
0546        case IDM_GeneralHelp:
0547          LoadString(hInst,IDS_Help,lpCaption,Max);
0548          LoadString(hInst,IDS_HelpText,lpMessage,MaxText);
0549          TimerCounter= zTIMER_PAUSE;
0550          MessageBox(GetFocus(),lpMessage,lpCaption,MB_OK);
0551          break;
0552        default:
0553          return(DefWindowProc(hWnd, message, wParam, lParam));
0554        }
0555      break;
0556
0557    case WM_INITMENUPOPUP:
0558      TimerCounter= zTIMER_PAUSE;
0559      if (lParam == 3)
0560        hMenu= wParam;
0561      break;
0562
0563    case WM_PAINT:
0564      hDCpaint= BeginPaint(hWnd,&ps);
0565      EndPaint(hWnd, &ps);
0566      if (PaintImage==zBLANK) break;
0567      if (Pause==TRUE)
0568        {
0569        Redisplay= TRUE;
0570        zShowNextFrame(hWnd);
0571        Redisplay= FALSE;
0572        break;
0573        }
0574      zShowNextFrame(hWnd);
0575      break;
0576
0577    case WM_KEYDOWN:
0578      switch (wParam)
0579        {
0580        case VK_LEFT:    if (Pause==TRUE)
0581                           {
0582                           if (FrameDirection==zFORWARD)
0583                             {
0584                             FrameDirection= zREVERSE;
0585                             }
0586                           Pause= FALSE;
0587                           zShowNextFrame(hWnd);
0588                           Pause= TRUE;
0589                           PaintImage= zANIMATING;
0590                           }
0591                         break;
0592        case VK_RIGHT:   if (Pause==TRUE)
0593                           {
0594                           if (FrameDirection==zREVERSE)
0595                             {
0596                             FrameDirection= zFORWARD;
0597                             }
0598                           Pause= FALSE;
0599                           zShowNextFrame(hWnd);
0600                           Pause= TRUE;
0601                           PaintImage= zANIMATING;
0602                           }
```

```
0603                          break;
0604          default:
0605                  return(DefWindowProc(hWnd, message, wParam, lParam));
0606          }
0607       break;
0608
0609    case WM_DESTROY:
0610      if (FrameReady==TRUE)
0611        {                          /* tidy up hidden frame bitmap... */
0612        SelectObject(hFrameDC,hPrevFrame);
0613        DeleteObject(hFrame);
0614        DeleteDC(hFrameDC);
0615        KillTimer(hWnd,1);
0616        }
0617      if (bAnimationLoaded==TRUE)
0618        {                          /* tidy up animation playback bitmaps... */
0619        SelectObject(hFDC,hPrevF);
0620        DeleteObject(hF1); DeleteObject(hF2); DeleteObject(hF3);
0621        DeleteObject(hF4); DeleteObject(hF5); DeleteObject(hF6);
0622        DeleteObject(hF7); DeleteObject(hF8); DeleteDC(hFDC);
0623        }
0624      PostQuitMessage(0);
0625      break;
0626
0627    case WM_SYSCOMMAND:
0628      if ((wParam & 0xfff0)== SC_SIZE)
0629        {
0630        MessageBeep(0); break;
0631        }
0632      if ((wParam & 0xfff0)== SC_MINIMIZE)
0633        {
0634        MessageBeep(0); break;
0635        }
0636      if ((wParam & 0xfff0)== SC_MAXIMIZE)
0637        {
0638        MessageBeep(0); break;
0639        }
0640
0641    default:
0642      return(DefWindowProc(hWnd, message, wParam, lParam));
0643      }
0644  return FALSE;
0645  }
0646  /*
0647  -------------------------------------------------------------------
0648            Initialize the attributes of the window class
0649  -------------------------------------------------------------------
0650                                                                    */
0651  BOOL zInitClass(HANDLE hInstance)
0652  {
0653    WNDCLASS WndClass;
0654  WndClass.style= 0;
0655  WndClass.lpfnWndProc= zMessageHandler;
0656  WndClass.cbClsExtra= 0;
0657  WndClass.cbWndExtra= 0;
0658  WndClass.hInstance= hInstance;
0659  WndClass.hIcon= LoadIcon(NULL,IDI_EXCLAMATION);
0660  WndClass.hCursor= LoadCursor(NULL,IDC_ARROW);
0661  WndClass.hbrBackground= CreateSolidBrush(RGB(255,255,255));
0662  WndClass.lpszMenuName= "MENUS1";
0663  WndClass.lpszClassName= "DEMOCLASS";
```

```
0664   return RegisterClass(&WndClass);
0665   }
0666   /*
0667   ------------------------------------------------------------------
0668                        Create the main window
0669   ------------------------------------------------------------------
0670                                                                 */
0671   HWND zInitMainWindow(HANDLE hInstance)
0672   {
0673      HWND hWnd;
0674   LoadString(hInstance,IDS_Caption,lpCaption,Max);
0675   hHourGlass= LoadCursor(NULL,IDC_WAIT);
0676   hWnd = CreateWindow("DEMOCLASS",lpCaption,
0677      WS_OVERLAPPED | WS_THICKFRAME | WS_MINIMIZEBOX |
0678        WS_MAXIMIZEBOX | WS_CLIPCHILDREN,
0679      WindowX,WindowY,zWINDOW_WIDTH,zWINDOW_HEIGHT,0,0,
0680      hInstance, (LPSTR)NULL);
0681   return hWnd;
0682   }
0683   /*
0684   ------------------------------------------------------------------
0685                      GRAPHICS SYSTEM Functions
0686   ------------------------------------------------------------------
0687   ------------------------------------------------------------------
0688                        Create the hidden frame.
0689   ------------------------------------------------------------------
0690                                                                 */
0691   static void zInitFrame(HWND hWnd)
0692   {
0693      HDC hDisplayDC;
0694
0695   if (FrameReady==TRUE)
0696      {
0697      MessageBeep(0);
0698      LoadString(hInst,IDS_Ready,lpCaption,Max);
0699      LoadString(hInst,IDS_Already,lpMessage,MaxText);
0700      TimerCounter= zTIMER_PAUSE;
0701      MessageBox(GetFocus(),lpMessage,lpCaption,MB_OK);
0702      return;
0703      }
0704   GlobalCompact((DWORD)-1L);
0705   hDisplayDC= GetDC(hWnd);
0706   hFrameDC= CreateCompatibleDC(hDisplayDC);
0707   hFrame= CreateCompatibleBitmap(hDisplayDC,zFRAMEWIDE,zFRAMEHIGH);
0708   if (hFrame==NULL)
0709      {
0710      LoadString(hInst,IDS_NotReady,lpCaption,Max);
0711      LoadString(hInst,IDS_InsufMem1,lpMessage,MaxText);
0712      MessageBox(GetFocus(),lpMessage,lpCaption,MB_OK);
0713      DeleteDC(hFrameDC);
0714      TimerExists= FALSE; FrameReady= FALSE; AnimationReady= FALSE;
0715      return;
0716      }
0717   hPrevFrame= SelectObject(hFrameDC,hFrame);
0718   zClear(hWnd);
0719   BitBlt(hFrameDC,0,0,zFRAMEWIDE,zFRAMEHIGH,hDisplayDC,0,0,SRCCOPY);
0720   ReleaseDC(hWnd,hDisplayDC);
0721
0722   TimerID1= SetTimer(hWnd,1,wFrameRate,(FARPROC) NULL);
0723   if (TimerID1 == 0)
0724      {
```

```
0725    LoadString(hInst,IDS_NotReady,lpCaption,Max);
0726    LoadString(hInst,IDS_NoTimer,lpMessage,MaxText);
0727    MessageBox(GetFocus(),lpMessage,lpCaption,MB_OK);
0728    SelectObject(hFrameDC,hPrevFrame);
0729    DeleteObject(hFrame);
0730    DeleteDC(hFrameDC);
0731    TimerExists= FALSE;
0732    return;
0733    }
0734  TimerExists= TRUE;
0735  FrameReady= TRUE;
0736  FrameNum= 1;
0737  return;
0738  }
0739  /*
0740  ---------------------------------------------------------------
0741                   Clear the hidden frame.
0742  ---------------------------------------------------------------
0743                                                              */
0744  static void zClearHiddenFrame(void)
0745  {
0746  PatBlt(hFrameDC,0,0,zFRAMEWIDE,zFRAMEHIGH,WHITENESS);
0747  return;
0748  }
0749  /*
0750  ---------------------------------------------------------------
0751           Copy the hidden frame to the display window.
0752  ---------------------------------------------------------------
0753                                                              */
0754  static void zCopyToDisplay(HWND hWnd)
0755  {
0756     HDC hDC;
0757  hDC= GetDC(hWnd);
0758  BitBlt(hDC,0,0,zFRAMEWIDE,zFRAMEHIGH,hFrameDC,0,0,SRCCOPY);
0759  ReleaseDC(hWnd,hDC);
0760  return;
0761  }
0762  /*
0763  ---------------------------------------------------------------
0764                   Blank the display window.
0765  ---------------------------------------------------------------
0766                                                              */
0767  static void zClear(HWND hWnd)
0768  {
0769     HDC hDC;
0770  hDC= GetDC(hWnd);
0771  PatBlt(hDC,0,0,zFRAMEWIDE,zFRAMEHIGH,WHITENESS);
0772  ReleaseDC(hWnd,hDC);
0773  return;
0774  }
0775  /*
0776  ---------------------------------------------------------------
0777                   AUTHORING SYSTEM Functions
0778  ---------------------------------------------------------------
0779  ---------------------------------------------------------------
0780               Create 8 frames and save to disk.
0781  ---------------------------------------------------------------
0782                                                              */
0783  static void zSaveAnimation(HWND hWnd)
0784  {
0785  if (FrameReady==FALSE)          /* if no hidden-frame available... */
```

```
0786    {
0787    MessageBeep(0);
0788    LoadString(hInst,IDS_NotReady,lpCaption,Max);
0789    LoadString(hInst,IDS_NoFrame,lpMessage,MaxText);
0790    MessageBox(GetFocus(),lpMessage,lpCaption,MB_OK);
0791    return;
0792    }
0793
0794    if (bAnimationSaved==TRUE) /* if frames already saved to disk... */
0795    {
0796    MessageBeep(0);
0797    LoadString(hInst,IDS_Unexpected,lpCaption,Max);
0798    LoadString(hInst,IDS_Disk1,lpMessage,MaxText);
0799    TimerCounter= zTIMER_PAUSE;
0800    MessageBox(GetFocus(),lpMessage,lpCaption,MB_OK);
0801    return;
0802    }
0803
0804    if (bPrevSaveAttempt==TRUE)        /* if previous attempt failed... */
0805    {
0806    MessageBeep(0);
0807    LoadString(hInst,IDS_Unexpected,lpCaption,Max);
0808    LoadString(hInst,IDS_Disk8,lpMessage,MaxText);
0809    TimerCounter= zTIMER_PAUSE;
0810    MessageBox(GetFocus(),lpMessage,lpCaption,MB_OK);
0811    return;
0812    }
0813    bPrevSaveAttempt= TRUE;
0814
0815    bFrameSaved= zBuildFrame(Cel1,1,hWnd,(LPSTR)"RUN1.BIT");
0816    if (bFrameSaved==FALSE) return;
0817    bFrameSaved= zBuildFrame(Cel2,2,hWnd,(LPSTR)"RUN2.BIT");
0818    if (bFrameSaved==FALSE) return;
0819    bFrameSaved= zBuildFrame(Cel3,3,hWnd,(LPSTR)"RUN3.BIT");
0820    if (bFrameSaved==FALSE) return;
0821    bFrameSaved= zBuildFrame(Cel4,4,hWnd,(LPSTR)"RUN4.BIT");
0822    if (bFrameSaved==FALSE) return;
0823    bFrameSaved= zBuildFrame(Cel5,5,hWnd,(LPSTR)"RUN5.BIT");
0824    if (bFrameSaved==FALSE) return;
0825    bFrameSaved= zBuildFrame(Cel6,6,hWnd,(LPSTR)"RUN6.BIT");
0826    if (bFrameSaved==FALSE) return;
0827    bFrameSaved= zBuildFrame(Cel7,7,hWnd,(LPSTR)"RUN7.BIT");
0828    if (bFrameSaved==FALSE) return;
0829    bFrameSaved= zBuildFrame(Cel8,8,hWnd,(LPSTR)"RUN8.BIT");
0830    if (bFrameSaved==FALSE) return;
0831
0832    bAnimationSaved= TRUE;
0833    bPrevLoadAttempt= FALSE;
0834    zClear(hWnd);
0835    MessageBeep(0);
0836    LoadString(hInst,IDS_Status,lpCaption,Max);
0837    LoadString(hInst,IDS_Disk2,lpMessage,MaxText);
0838    MessageBox(GetFocus(),lpMessage,lpCaption,MB_OK);
0839    return;
0840    }
0841    /*
0842    -------------------------------------------------------------------
0843                    Build one frame and save to disk.
0844    -------------------------------------------------------------------
0845                                                                     */
0846    static BOOL zBuildFrame(int * Drawing, int Number,
```

```
0847                        HWND hWnd, LPSTR lpFileName)
0848   {                   /* this function is called by zSaveAnimation() */
0849     BOOL bDiskResult;
0850     HFONT Font;
0851     HFONT PrevFont;
0852     DWORD PrevFontColor;
0853     DWORD PrevBkColor;
0854
0855   zClearHiddenFrame();                        /* clear the hidden frame */
0856
0857   /* ---------- display the titles, labels, and captions --------- */
0858   if ((DisplayBits==1)&&(DisplayPlanes==1))/* if a mono display... */
0859     {
0860     PrevFontColor= SetTextColor(hFrameDC,RGB(0,0,0));
0861     PrevBkColor=  SetBkColor(hFrameDC,RGB(255,255,255));
0862     }
0863   else                              /* else if a color display... */
0864     {
0865     PrevFontColor= SetTextColor(hFrameDC,RGB(0,0,255));
0866     PrevBkColor=  SetBkColor(hFrameDC,RGB(0,0,0));
0867     }
0868
0869   SetBkMode(hFrameDC,TRANSPARENT);
0870   Font= CreateFont(24, 0, 0, 0, FW_BOLD, FALSE, FALSE, FALSE,
0871        ANSI_CHARSET, OUT_DEFAULT_PRECIS, CLIP_DEFAULT_PRECIS,
0872        DRAFT_QUALITY, VARIABLE_PITCH | FF_SWISS, "Helv");
0873   PrevFont= SelectObject(hFrameDC,Font);
0874   TextOut(hFrameDC,10,10,"Advanced Animation Techniques:",30);
0875   Font= CreateFont(48, 0, 0, 0, FW_BOLD, FALSE, FALSE, FALSE,
0876        ANSI_CHARSET, OUT_DEFAULT_PRECIS, CLIP_DEFAULT_PRECIS,
0877        DRAFT_QUALITY, VARIABLE_PITCH | FF_SWISS, "Helv");
0878   SelectObject(hFrameDC,Font);
0879   TextOut(hFrameDC,8,28,"Inbetweening",12);
0880   SelectObject(hFrameDC,PrevFont);
0881   TextOut(hFrameDC,10,192,"Inbetweening is implemented by",30);
0882   TextOut(hFrameDC,10,208,"manipulating a database that",28);
0883   TextOut(hFrameDC,10,224,"contains image coordinates for",30);
0884   TextOut(hFrameDC,10,240,"vertices common to each cel.",28);
0885   SetBkMode(hFrameDC,OPAQUE);
0886   SetBkColor(hFrameDC,PrevBkColor);
0887   SetTextColor(hFrameDC,PrevFontColor);
0888
0889   /* ------------------ draw the appropriate cel --------------- */
0890   zDrawCel(Drawing);
0891
0892   /* ---------- display the frame and save it to disk ----------- */
0893   zCopyToDisplay(hWnd);              /* copy hidden frame to display */
0894   bDiskResult= zSaveFrame(hFrame,lpFileName);        /* save file */
0895   if (bDiskResult==FALSE) return FALSE;        /* if disk error */
0896   return TRUE;
0897   }
0898   /*
0899   ------------------------------------------------------------------
0900                   Build one frame and save to disk.
0901   ------------------------------------------------------------------
0902                                                                  */
0903   static void zDrawCel(int * Drawing)
0904   {
0905     int X1,Y1,X2,Y2;              /* temporary drawing coordinates */
0906     HPEN DrawingPen, PrevPen;                            /* pens */
0907
```

```
0908  DrawingPen= CreatePen(PS_SOLID,6,RGB(0,0,0));        /* create pen */
0909  PrevPen= SelectObject(hFrameDC,DrawingPen);          /* select pen */
0910
0911  X1= Drawing[0] - Drawing[2];                    /* draw the head... */
0912  Y1= Drawing[1] - Drawing[2];
0913  X2= Drawing[0] + Drawing[2];
0914  Y2= Drawing[1] + Drawing[2];
0915  Ellipse(hFrameDC,X1,Y1,X2,Y2);
0916
0917  MoveTo(hFrameDC,Drawing[3],Drawing[4]);            /* draw spine... */
0918  LineTo(hFrameDC,Drawing[5],Drawing[6]);
0919  LineTo(hFrameDC,Drawing[7],Drawing[8]);
0920  LineTo(hFrameDC,Drawing[9],Drawing[10]);
0921  LineTo(hFrameDC,Drawing[11],Drawing[12]);
0922  LineTo(hFrameDC,Drawing[13],Drawing[14]);
0923
0924  X1= Drawing[13] - Drawing[15];                  /* draw the tail... */
0925  Y1= Drawing[14] - Drawing[15];
0926  X2= Drawing[13] + Drawing[15];
0927  Y2= Drawing[14] + Drawing[15];
0928  Ellipse(hFrameDC,X1,Y1,X2,Y2);
0929
0930  MoveTo(hFrameDC,Drawing[9],Drawing[10]);   /* draw far hindleg... */
0931  LineTo(hFrameDC,Drawing[16],Drawing[17]);
0932  LineTo(hFrameDC,Drawing[18],Drawing[19]);
0933  LineTo(hFrameDC,Drawing[20],Drawing[21]);
0934  LineTo(hFrameDC,Drawing[22],Drawing[23]);
0935
0936  MoveTo(hFrameDC,Drawing[5],Drawing[6]);    /* draw far foreleg... */
0937  LineTo(hFrameDC,Drawing[24],Drawing[25]);
0938  LineTo(hFrameDC,Drawing[26],Drawing[27]);
0939  LineTo(hFrameDC,Drawing[28],Drawing[29]);
0940  LineTo(hFrameDC,Drawing[30],Drawing[31]);
0941
0942  MoveTo(hFrameDC,Drawing[5],Drawing[6]);    /* draw near foreleg... */
0943  LineTo(hFrameDC,Drawing[32],Drawing[33]);
0944  LineTo(hFrameDC,Drawing[34],Drawing[35]);
0945  LineTo(hFrameDC,Drawing[36],Drawing[37]);
0946  LineTo(hFrameDC,Drawing[38],Drawing[39]);
0947
0948  MoveTo(hFrameDC,Drawing[9],Drawing[10]);   /* draw near hindleg... */
0949  LineTo(hFrameDC,Drawing[40],Drawing[41]);
0950  LineTo(hFrameDC,Drawing[42],Drawing[43]);
0951  LineTo(hFrameDC,Drawing[44],Drawing[45]);
0952  LineTo(hFrameDC,Drawing[46],Drawing[47]);
0953
0954  SelectObject(hFrameDC,PrevPen);                  /* deselect pen */
0955  DeleteObject(DrawingPen);                          /* delete pen */
0956  return;
0957  }
0958  /*
0959  --------------------------------------------------------------------
0960                    ANIMATION PLAYBACK Functions
0961  --------------------------------------------------------------------
0962  --------------------------------------------------------------------
0963                       Display the next frame.
0964    This function is intelligent enough to discern between RAM-BASED
0965  FRAME ANIMATION (where all frames have already been loaded from
0966  disk and stored in RAM) and DISK-BASED FRAME ANIMATION (where
0967  each frame must be loaded from disk during playback).
0968  --------------------------------------------------------------------
```

```
0969                                                                    */
0970  static void zShowNextFrame(HWND hWnd)
0971  {
0972    HDC hDC;
0973  if (bUseDisk==TRUE) goto DISK_PLAYBACK;
0974
0975  RAM_PLAYBACK:       /* if all frames have been loaded into RAM... */
0976  if (AnimationReady==FALSE) return;
0977  if (bAnimationLoaded==FALSE) return;
0978  if (Redisplay==TRUE) goto DISPLAY_FRAME;
0979  if (Pause==TRUE) return;
0980  if (FrameDirection==zFORWARD)
0981    {
0982    FrameNum++;
0983    if (FrameNum > zFINALFRAME) FrameNum= zFIRSTFRAME;
0984    }
0985  if (FrameDirection==zREVERSE)
0986    {
0987    FrameNum--;
0988    if (FrameNum < zFIRSTFRAME) FrameNum= zFINALFRAME;
0989    }
0990  DISPLAY_FRAME:
0991  hDC= GetDC(hWnd);
0992  switch (FrameNum)
0993    {
0994    case 1:  SelectObject(hFDC,hF1);  break;
0995    case 2:  SelectObject(hFDC,hF2);  break;
0996    case 3:  SelectObject(hFDC,hF3);  break;
0997    case 4:  SelectObject(hFDC,hF4);  break;
0998    case 5:  SelectObject(hFDC,hF5);  break;
0999    case 6:  SelectObject(hFDC,hF6);  break;
1000    case 7:  SelectObject(hFDC,hF7);  break;
1001    case 8:  SelectObject(hFDC,hF8);  break;
1002    }
1003  BitBlt(hDC,0,0,zFRAMEWIDE,zFRAMEHIGH,hFDC,0,0,SRCCOPY);
1004  ReleaseDC(hWnd,hDC);
1005  return;
1006
1007  DISK_PLAYBACK:    /* if loading each frame from disk as needed... */
1008  if (bAnimationHalted==TRUE) return;
1009  if (Redisplay==TRUE) goto SAME_FRAME;
1010  if (Pause==TRUE) return;
1011  if (FrameDirection==zFORWARD)
1012    {
1013    FrameNum++;
1014    if (FrameNum > zFINALFRAME) FrameNum= zFIRSTFRAME;
1015    }
1016  if (FrameDirection==zREVERSE)
1017    {
1018    FrameNum--;
1019    if (FrameNum < zFIRSTFRAME) FrameNum= zFINALFRAME;
1020    }
1021  SAME_FRAME:
1022  hDC= GetDC(hWnd);
1023  switch (FrameNum)
1024    {
1025    case 1:  bFrameLoaded= zLoadFrame(hFrame, (LPSTR) "RUN1.BIT");
1026             break;
1027    case 2:  bFrameLoaded= zLoadFrame(hFrame, (LPSTR) "RUN2.BIT");
1028             break;
1029    case 3:  bFrameLoaded= zLoadFrame(hFrame, (LPSTR) "RUN3.BIT");
```

```
1030           break;
1031  case 4:  bFrameLoaded= zLoadFrame(hFrame, (LPSTR) "RUN4.BIT");
1032           break;
1033  case 5:  bFrameLoaded= zLoadFrame(hFrame, (LPSTR) "RUN5.BIT");
1034           break;
1035  case 6:  bFrameLoaded= zLoadFrame(hFrame, (LPSTR) "RUN6.BIT");
1036           break;
1037  case 7:  bFrameLoaded= zLoadFrame(hFrame, (LPSTR) "RUN7.BIT");
1038           break;
1039  case 8:  bFrameLoaded= zLoadFrame(hFrame, (LPSTR) "RUN8.BIT");
1040           break;
1041  }
1042  if (bFrameLoaded==FALSE)
1043  {
1044  bAnimationHalted= TRUE;
1045  MessageBeep(0);
1046  LoadString(hInst,IDS_Unexpected,lpCaption,Max);
1047  LoadString(hInst,IDS_Disk3,lpMessage,MaxText);
1048  TimerCounter= zTIMER_PAUSE;
1049  MessageBox(GetFocus(),lpMessage,lpCaption,MB_OK);
1050  return;
1051  }
1052  BitBlt(hDC,0,0,zFRAMEWIDE,zFRAMEHIGH,hFrameDC,0,0,SRCCOPY);
1053  ReleaseDC(hWnd,hDC);
1054  return;
1055  }
1056  /*
1057  ------------------------------------------------------------------
1058              Load the animation sequence from disk.
1059   If memory limitations prevent this function from loading the
1060   entire animation sequence into RAM, it sets a token to FALSE.
1061   In that case the playback function zShowNextFrame() will load
1062   each frame from disk as required during animation playback,
1063   otherwise all frames are expected to be in RAM.
1064  ------------------------------------------------------------------
1065                                                                  */
1066  static void zLoadAnimation(HWND hWnd)
1067  {
1068  HDC hDC;
1069
1070  if (FrameReady==FALSE)          /* if no hidden-frame available... */
1071  {
1072  MessageBeep(0);
1073  LoadString(hInst,IDS_NotReady,lpCaption,Max);
1074  LoadString(hInst,IDS_NoFrame,lpMessage,MaxText);
1075  MessageBox(GetFocus(),lpMessage,lpCaption,MB_OK);
1076  return;
1077  }
1078  if (bAnimationLoaded==TRUE)          /* if frames already loaded... */
1079  {
1080  MessageBeep(0);
1081  LoadString(hInst,IDS_Unexpected,lpCaption,Max);
1082  LoadString(hInst,IDS_Disk4,lpMessage,MaxText);
1083  TimerCounter= zTIMER_PAUSE;
1084  MessageBox(GetFocus(),lpMessage,lpCaption,MB_OK);
1085  return;
1086  }
1087  if (bPrevLoadAttempt==TRUE)          /* if previous attempt failed... */
1088  {
1089  MessageBeep(0);
1090  LoadString(hInst,IDS_Unexpected,lpCaption,Max);
```

```
1091    LoadString(hInst,IDS_Disk5,lpMessage,MaxText);
1092    TimerCounter= zTIMER_PAUSE;
1093    MessageBox(GetFocus(),lpMessage,lpCaption,MB_OK);
1094    return;
1095    }
1096    bPrevLoadAttempt= TRUE;
1097
1098    /* ------------- create bitmaps to hold the frames ----------- */
1099    GlobalCompact((DWORD)-1L);          /* maximize contiguous memory */
1100    hDC= GetDC(hWnd);
1101    hFDC= CreateCompatibleDC(hDC);
1102    hF1= CreateCompatibleBitmap(hDC,zFRAMEWIDE,zFRAMEHIGH);
1103    if (hF1==NULL) goto F1;
1104    hF2= CreateCompatibleBitmap(hDC,zFRAMEWIDE,zFRAMEHIGH);
1105    if (hF2==NULL) goto F2;
1106    hF3= CreateCompatibleBitmap(hDC,zFRAMEWIDE,zFRAMEHIGH);
1107    if (hF3==NULL) goto F3;
1108    hF4= CreateCompatibleBitmap(hDC,zFRAMEWIDE,zFRAMEHIGH);
1109    if (hF4==NULL) goto F4;
1110    hF5= CreateCompatibleBitmap(hDC,zFRAMEWIDE,zFRAMEHIGH);
1111    if (hF5==NULL) goto F5;
1112    hF6= CreateCompatibleBitmap(hDC,zFRAMEWIDE,zFRAMEHIGH);
1113    if (hF6==NULL) goto F6;
1114    hF7= CreateCompatibleBitmap(hDC,zFRAMEWIDE,zFRAMEHIGH);
1115    if (hF7==NULL) goto F7;
1116    hF8= CreateCompatibleBitmap(hDC,zFRAMEWIDE,zFRAMEHIGH);
1117    if (hF8==NULL) goto F8;
1118    goto BITMAPS_OK;
1119
1120    F8:  DeleteObject(hF7);
1121    F7:  DeleteObject(hF6);
1122    F6:  DeleteObject(hF5);
1123    F5:  DeleteObject(hF4);
1124    F4:  DeleteObject(hF3);
1125    F3:  DeleteObject(hF2);
1126    F2:  DeleteObject(hF1);
1127    F1:  DeleteDC(hFDC); ReleaseDC(hWnd,hDC);
1128         bUseDisk= TRUE; AnimationReady= TRUE;
1129         LoadString(hInst,IDS_Status,lpCaption,Max);
1130         LoadString(hInst,IDS_Disk6,lpMessage,MaxText);
1131         MessageBox(GetFocus(),lpMessage,lpCaption,MB_OK);
1132         return;
1133    BITMAPS_OK: ReleaseDC(hWnd,hDC);
1134
1135    /* ------------ load frame files into the bitmaps ------------- */
1136    bFrameLoaded= zLoadFrame(hF1, (LPSTR) "RUN1.BIT");
1137    if (bFrameLoaded==FALSE) goto DISK_ERROR;
1138    bFrameLoaded= zLoadFrame(hF2, (LPSTR) "RUN2.BIT");
1139    if (bFrameLoaded==FALSE) goto DISK_ERROR;
1140    bFrameLoaded= zLoadFrame(hF3, (LPSTR) "RUN3.BIT");
1141    if (bFrameLoaded==FALSE) goto DISK_ERROR;
1142    bFrameLoaded= zLoadFrame(hF4, (LPSTR) "RUN4.BIT");
1143    if (bFrameLoaded==FALSE) goto DISK_ERROR;
1144    bFrameLoaded= zLoadFrame(hF5, (LPSTR) "RUN5.BIT");
1145    if (bFrameLoaded==FALSE) goto DISK_ERROR;
1146    bFrameLoaded= zLoadFrame(hF6, (LPSTR) "RUN6.BIT");
1147    if (bFrameLoaded==FALSE) goto DISK_ERROR;
1148    bFrameLoaded= zLoadFrame(hF7, (LPSTR) "RUN7.BIT");
1149    if (bFrameLoaded==FALSE) goto DISK_ERROR;
1150    bFrameLoaded= zLoadFrame(hF8, (LPSTR) "RUN8.BIT");
1151    if (bFrameLoaded==FALSE) goto DISK_ERROR;
```

```
1152  goto DISK_OK;
1153
1154  DISK_ERROR:
1155    DeleteObject(hF1); DeleteObject(hF2); DeleteObject(hF3);
1156    DeleteObject(hF4); DeleteObject(hF5); DeleteObject(hF6);
1157    DeleteObject(hF7); DeleteObject(hF8); DeleteDC(hFDC);
1158    return;
1159
1160  /* ------------------- tidy up and return -------------------- */
1161  DISK_OK:
1162  hPrevF= SelectObject(hFDC,hF1);                    /* select bitmap */
1163  bAnimationLoaded= TRUE;
1164  AnimationReady= TRUE;
1165  bAnimationSaved= TRUE;
1166  MessageBeep(0);
1167  LoadString(hInst,IDS_AnimReady,lpCaption,Max);
1168  LoadString(hInst,IDS_Disk7,lpMessage,MaxText);
1169  MessageBox(GetFocus(),lpMessage,lpCaption,MB_OK);
1170  return;
1171  }
1172  /*
1173  -------------------------------------------------------------------
1174                     Reset the animation frame rate.
1175  -------------------------------------------------------------------
1176                                                                     */
1177  static void zSetFrameRate(HWND hWnd, WORD wNewRate)
1178  {
1179  if (TimerExists==FALSE)
1180    {
1181    wFrameRate= wPrevRate;
1182    MessageBeep(0);
1183    LoadString(hInst,IDS_NotReady,lpCaption,Max);
1184    LoadString(hInst,IDS_NoReset,lpMessage,MaxText);
1185    MessageBox(GetFocus(),lpMessage,lpCaption,MB_OK);
1186    return;
1187    }
1188  switch (wPrevRate)
1189    {
1190    case 55:  CheckMenuItem(hMenu,IDM_FPS182,MF_UNCHECKED); break;
1191    case 110: CheckMenuItem(hMenu,IDM_FPS91,MF_UNCHECKED); break;
1192    case 165: CheckMenuItem(hMenu,IDM_FPS61,MF_UNCHECKED); break;
1193    case 220: CheckMenuItem(hMenu,IDM_FPS45,MF_UNCHECKED); break;
1194    case 275: CheckMenuItem(hMenu,IDM_FPS36,MF_UNCHECKED); break;
1195    case 330: CheckMenuItem(hMenu,IDM_FPS30,MF_UNCHECKED); break;
1196    }
1197  KillTimer(hWnd,1);
1198  TimerID1= SetTimer(hWnd,1,wNewRate,(FARPROC) NULL);
1199  if (TimerID1==0)
1200    {
1201    LoadString(hInst,IDS_NotReady,lpCaption,Max);
1202    LoadString(hInst,IDS_CannotReset,lpMessage,MaxText);
1203    MessageBox(GetFocus(),lpMessage,lpCaption,MB_OK);
1204    TimerExists= FALSE;
1205    return;
1206    }
1207  switch (wFrameRate)
1208    {
1209    case 55:  CheckMenuItem(hMenu,IDM_FPS182,MF_CHECKED); break;
1210    case 110: CheckMenuItem(hMenu,IDM_FPS91,MF_CHECKED); break;
1211    case 165: CheckMenuItem(hMenu,IDM_FPS61,MF_CHECKED); break;
1212    case 220: CheckMenuItem(hMenu,IDM_FPS45,MF_CHECKED); break;
```

15-11 Continued.

```
1213    case 275: CheckMenuItem(hMenu,IDM_FPS36,MF_CHECKED); break;
1214    case 330: CheckMenuItem(hMenu,IDM_FPS30,MF_CHECKED); break;
1215    }
1216  return;
1217  }
1218  /*
1219  -------------------------------------------------------------------
1220                         End of the C source file
1221  -------------------------------------------------------------------
1222                                                                  */
```

# Part four

# Physically based animation

# 16
# *Simulation animation*

The animation implementation methods that were described and demonstrated in Part Two of the book—real-time animation and frame animation—can be managed by three different methods of animation control:

- Scripted animation.
- Procedural animation.
- Physically based animation.

The sample applications in Part Three of the book explored, in one way or another, different aspects of scripted animation and procedural animation. However, the powerful animation capabilities provided by the Windows graphical environment can also be put to work producing more serious applications using physically based animation. This form of animation is often called *simulation* or *visualization*.

## Constraint-based animation

Physically based animation uses the laws of physics to govern the motion of objects during an animation sequence. During playback (or during the production of frame images) the motion is regulated by so-called limiting conditions or forces. These limiting conditions are called *constraints*. Hence, physically based animation is also called constraint-based animation.

Physically based animation consists of four categories of control:

- Forward kinematics.
- Forward dynamics.

- Inverse dynamics.
- Inverse kinematics.

The words kinematic and dynamics have special meaning to developers of physically based animation sequences. The study of positions and velocities of objects is called kinematics. The study of forces and mass of objects is called dynamics.

## Methods of control

**Forward kinematics**  If you are using forward kinematics to control your physically based animation sequence, then your program calculates the result of the application of velocity or acceleration to an object in the scene. Your algorithms do not address the issues of force and mass.

**Forward dynamics**  If you are using forward dynamics to control your physically based animation sequence, then your code calculates the result of the application of force or constraints to an object in the scene.

**Inverse kinematics**  If you are using inverse kinematics to control your physically based animation sequence, then your application calculates the velocity or acceleration required to move an object from one position to another during a specified period of time.

**Inverse dynamics**  If you are using inverse dynamics to control your physically based animation sequence, then your program calculates the force or constraints required to move an object of a specified mass from one position to another over a specified period of time.

## The laws of motion: a primer

Physically based animation application development is wholly dependent on algorithmic control. Simply stated, it is the algorithms, the math, and the C **Visual Basic** code that you utilize to control the objects being animated that provides the backbone of your physically based animation sequence. Whereas scripted animation and procedural animation place emphasis on the display, the priority in physically based animation is the authentic movement of objects in the scene. Every effort is directed towards making these movements as lifelike as possible.

Newton's three laws of motion play a central role in planning your physically based animation sequence. The first law says that an object at rest will continue to remain at rest until some force acts upon it. The second law says that when a force is applied to an object, the object accelerates. The third law says that for every force there is an equal and opposite reacting force.

By taking these three laws into account, and by considering gravity, friction, mass, conservation of energy, momentum, velocity, work, torque, and other constraints, you can use your Windows-based animation sequence to accurately simulate events in the real world.

This chapter limits itself to demonstrating a prototype animation that you can use as a platform to design and build your own physically based 3D animation sequences. Each discipline of science and medicine, each research project, each simulation environment, and each design mandate has its own set of algorithms and formulae for controlling the motion of objects. It would be unrealistically presumptuous for this book to purport to teach you the subtleties of your own craft. The sample animation presented later in the chapter, however, provides a powerful tool for you to begin using the algorithms and formulae of your field to produce physically based animation.

Further material is also available in other books in the Applied C Graphics series from Windcrest/McGraw-Hill. For discussion and source code for a 3D sphere bouncing inside the confines of a rigid container, see page 302 in my earlier book, *Visualization Graphics in C* (ISBN 0-8306-3487-8, Windcrest/McGraw-Hill book 3487, published in 1991). For discussion and source code for an elastic collision between two spheres, see page 349 in my previous book, *High-Performance C Graphics Programming for Windows* (ISBN 0-8306-3790-7, Windcrest/McGraw-Hill book 4103, published in 1992). For discussion and source code for drawing 3D spheres, cylinders, and meshes, see my earlier book, *High-Performance CAD Graphics in C* (ISBN 0-8306-9359- 9, Windcrest/McGraw-Hill book 3059, published in 1989).

## Sample application

The screen image in FIG. 16-1 shows a frame from the sample application spatial.exe. This program demonstrates physically based animation techniques, including the disassembly and reassembly of a solid object.

The interactive controls let you experiment with different animation playback options, including full forward, full reverse, pause, freeze-frame, single-step forward, and single-step reverse. The animation continues to run even if the window is partly covered by another window or partly clipped by the edge of the screen.

The spatial.exe demo is built from eight modules, including a .def module definition file, an .h #include file, an .rc resource script file, and a .c source file. Also required is the storage.h #include file and the storage.c source file for the module that provides disk read/write functions for binary image files. Also required is the lib3d.h #include file and the lib3d.c source file for the 3D library. The production files for spatial.exe are presented as ready-to-use source code in the program listings later in this chapter. The production files for storage.h and storage.c were provided in chapter 10, Characters. The production files for lib3d.h and lib3d.c were provided in chapter 4, Modeling. All of the source files are also provided on the companion disk. You can refer to the appropriate appendix for instructions on how to build spatial.exe with QuickC for Windows, Turbo C++ for Windows, Borland C++, Zortech C++, WATCOM C, and Microsoft C and the SDK.

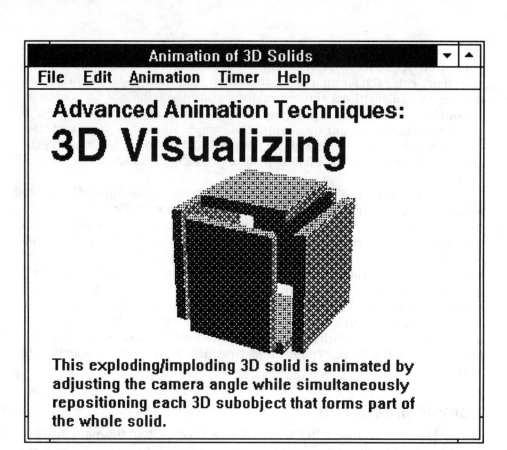

File   Edit   **Animation**   Timer   Help

## Advanced Animation Techniques:
# 3D Visualizing

**This exploding/imploding 3D solid is animated by adjusting the camera angle while simultaneously repositioning each 3D subobject that forms part of the whole solid.**

**16-1**   A freezeframe from the animated sample application.

## What the program does: A user's guide

The sample application provides an interactive environment suitable for experimenting with the disassembly and reassembly of a solid object using physically based animation. You can use either a mouse or the keyboard to experiment with the demo program. The menus also support mnemonic keys. To view a runtime help message, select Help from the Help menu.

### Initializing the system

Select Initialize system from the Animation menu to initialize the 3D library and the hidden frame. None of the authoring or playback features of the Animation menu will function until the system has been initialized.

### Creating the frames

Select Create Frames from the Animation menu to create the animation sequence and store it on disk. The eight frames that comprise the animation are illustrated in FIG. 16-2. The sample application will use the 3D library to build each frame in turn on the hidden page, copy the completed frame to the display window, and then save the image to disk as a binary image file. If you have already saved the eight frames to disk, the demo program will present a message to advise you. The software gives you the option of overwriting the existing image file. If you choose not to overwrite the existing file, the build sequence is stopped and no further frames are constructed. If not enough free space exists on your hard disk to store the image files, the demo program displays an advisory message and cancels the build process.

## Loading the animation

Before you can play an animation sequence that you have saved to disk, you must load it. If you saved the animation during the current working session, select Load Animation from the Animation menu. If you saved the animation during a previous working session, select Initialize system from the Animation menu before selecting Load Animation.

If the software is unable to find the frame files on disk, it displays an advisory message. If you attempt to play an animation before loading it from disk or before selecting Initialize system, the demo program will display a hint message.

During a normal load process the sample application will load each frame file into the hidden frame, from where it is copied to a buffer in memory. After all eight frames have been loaded from disk, the program uses a message box to report the successful load.

## Playing the animation

To play the animation sequence, select Run Forward from the Animation menu. A 3D solid box is disassembled into eight components and then reassembled. The entire animation sequence is depicted in FIG. 16-2. The 3D solid will continue to disassemble and reassemble until you stop the animation.

## Adjusting the animation playback speed

You can increase or decrease the animation speed by selecting from the Timer menu. At startup the playback rate is set to 18 frames per second.

## Freeze-frame and single-step animation

**Pause**   To pause the animation, select Pause from the Animation menu. To resume animation playback select Run Forward from the Animation menu.

**Single-step**   While the animation is paused, you can invoke single-step playback. Press the right arrow key on the direction keypad to display the next frame in the animation sequence. Keep pressing the right

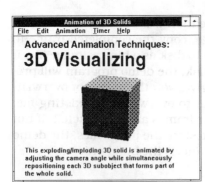
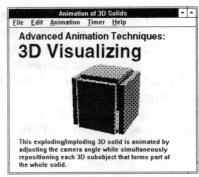

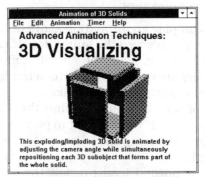

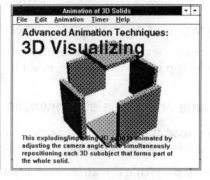

**16-2** A sampling of eight frames from the animated sample application.

row key to step through the entire animation. To resume full animation playback, select Run Forward from the Animation menu.

## Persistent graphics

**Moving the window**   To test the persistent graphics features of the animation sequence, start the animation playback and then move the window.

**Covering the window**   To test the cooperative multitasking capabilities of the animation, partially cover the window with a program group box or another window. The animation will continue to play.

## Using the Help menu

You can use the Help menu to discover various facts about your system that are in effect at runtime. You can find out the current screen mode, the maximum number of available colors, the runtime memory mode (real, standard, or enhanced), and other information. The sample application spatial.exe supports 640 × 480, 640 × 350, 800 × 600, and 1024 × 768 resolution displays. In its current implementation the demo program supports 16-color and 2-color displays. If you want to modify the source code to support 256-color displays, see the discussion in chapter 3, Blitting. The sample animation supports real, standard, and enhanced memory modes.

# How the source code works: A programmer's guide

*Hands On*   Using the programming techniques presented in the program listings for spatial.exe along with the functions contained in the 3D graphics library lib3d.c, you can easily add physically based animation capabilities to your own applications.

The demo program is a descendent of the prototype 3D program and the prototype frame animation engine described and demonstrated previously in the book. See chapter 8, Frame animation engines, for a prototype program listing for frame animation applications. See chapter 4, Modeling, for a prototype program listing for 3D modeling and shading applications.

## How the .c file works

*.C*   This discussion is limited to portions of the source code that affect the disassembly and reassembly of the 3D solid. For a discussion of the code in general see the two chapters noted in the previous paragraph.

**Building the animation**   The zSaveAnimation() function at lines 0707 through 0764 manages the building and saving of the eight frames that make up the animation sequence. The calls to zBuildFrame() at lines 0739 through 0754 specify the file names to be used, ranging from OBJ3D1.BIT through OBJ3D8.BIT.

The function zBuildFrame(), located at lines 0770 through 0828, is called eight times by zSaveAnimation(). After calling zDrawCel() at line 0783, the code at lines 0791 through 0821 uses TextOut() to write the titles and captions on each frame.

Note in particular the code at lines 0792 through 0801, which carefully adjusts the font colors so that the image will appear legible even on two-color (monochromatic) displays. This is an important consideration for software intended for release as commercial product, and not all of the preceding demonstration programs took the trouble to take care of this compatibility issue.

The function zDrawCel() at lines 0834 through 0890 is responsible for managing the calls to the 3D routines in lib3d.c. Notice how the switch() block at lines 0843 through 0853 sets the camera pitch and camera heading based upon the number of the frame being built. Then the switch() block at lines 0856 through 0876 sets a variable named Locate. This variable determines how far from the center of the 3D object are its components. As Locate is increased, so is the 3D object disassembled. Note the case 1: statement at line 0858, which is an exception that handles the solid before any disassembly beings to occur.

The code at lines 0877 through 0888 manipulates the routines in lib3d.c in order to draw the eight components of the 3D solid. Refer back to chapter 4, Modeling, for a more detailed discussion of interfacing with the lib3d.c library.

**The animation engine**   The zShowNextFrame() function at lines 0903 through 1036 manages the playback of the animation sequence. Note how blank case statements are used to control the pacing of the animation, which pauses at the fully disassembled stage and at the fully assembled stage of the animation sequence. If the case 3: statement at line 0929 is called, for example, the program logic falls through to the case 6: statement at line 0932.

# Program listings for the sample application

*Code*   The program listings presented here contain all the source code you need to build and run the sample application. The spatial.def module definition file is provided in FIG. 16-3. The spatial.h #include file is found in FIG. 16-4. The spatial.rc resource script file is presented in FIG. 16-5. The spatial.c source file is provided in FIG. 16-6. The storage.h #include file for the disk read/write module is located in FIG. 10-36 in chapter 10, Characters. The storage.c source file for the read/write module is provided in FIG. 10-37 in chapter 10, Characters. The lib3d.h #include file for the 3D routines is provided in FIG. 4-11 in chapter 4, Modeling. The lib3d.c source file for the 3D routines is located in FIG. 4-12 in chapter 4, Modeling.

**16-3**   The module definition file listing for the sample application.

```
0001  NAME          DEFDEMO
0002  DESCRIPTION   'Copyright 1992 Lee Adams.  All rights reserved.'
0003  EXETYPE       WINDOWS
0004  STUB          'WINSTUB.EXE'
0005  CODE          PRELOAD MOVEABLE
0006  DATA          PRELOAD MOVEABLE MULTIPLE
0007  HEAPSIZE      1024
0008  STACKSIZE     8192
0009  EXPORTS       zMessageHandler
```

**16-4**   The include file listing for the sample application.

```
0001  /*
0002  --------------------------------------------------------------
0003                    Include file SPATIAL.H
0004          Copyright 1992 Lee Adams.  All rights reserved.
0005     Include this file in the .RC resource script file and in the
0006     .C source file.  It contains function prototypes, menu ID
0007     constants, and string ID constants.
0008  --------------------------------------------------------------
0009  --------------------------------------------------------------
0010                    Function prototypes
0011  --------------------------------------------------------------
0012                                                              */
0013  #if !defined(zRCFILE)                   /* if not an .RC file... */
0014    LONG FAR PASCAL zMessageHandler(HWND, unsigned, WORD, LONG);
0015    int PASCAL WinMain(HANDLE,HANDLE,LPSTR,int);
0016    HWND zInitMainWindow(HANDLE);
0017    BOOL zInitClass(HANDLE);
0018  static void zClear(HWND);             /* blank the display window */
0019  static void zInitFrame(HWND);            /* creates hidden frame */
0020  static void zShowNextFrame(HWND);        /* the playback engine */
0021  static void zSetFrameRate(HWND,WORD);       /* resets the timer */
0022  static void zSaveAnimation(HWND);     /* saves animation sequence */
0023  static BOOL zBuildFrame(int,HWND,LPSTR);     /* builds a frame */
0024  static void zDrawCel(int);                   /* draws a cel */
0025  static void zLoadAnimation(HWND);     /* loads animation sequence */
0026  static void zCopyToDisplay(HWND);     /* copies frame to display */
0027  static void zClearHiddenFrame(void);     /* clears hidden frame */
0028  #endif
0029  /*
0030  --------------------------------------------------------------
0031                    Menu ID constants
0032  --------------------------------------------------------------
0033                                                              */
0034  #define IDM_New               1
0035  #define IDM_Open              2
```

```
0036   #define IDM_Save              3
0037   #define IDM_SaveAs            4
0038   #define IDM_Exit              5
0039
0040   #define IDM_Undo              6
0041   #define IDM_Cut               7
0042   #define IDM_Copy              8
0043   #define IDM_Paste             9
0044   #define IDM_Delete            10
0045
0046   #define IDM_RunForward        11
0047   #define IDM_RunReverse        12
0048   #define IDM_StopAnimation     13
0049   #define IDM_InitFrame         14
0050   #define IDM_SaveAnimation     15
0051   #define IDM_LoadAnimation     16
0052   #define IDM_Clear             17
0053
0054   #define IDM_FPS182            18
0055   #define IDM_FPS91             19
0056   #define IDM_FPS61             20
0057   #define IDM_FPS45             21
0058   #define IDM_FPS36             22
0059   #define IDM_FPS30             23
0060
0061   #define IDM_About             24
0062   #define IDM_License           25
0063   #define IDM_Display           26
0064   #define IDM_Colors            27
0065   #define IDM_Mode              28
0066   #define IDM_Memory            29
0067   #define IDM_Timing            30
0068   #define IDM_GeneralHelp       31
0069   /*
0070   --------------------------------------------------------------
0071                        String ID constants
0072   --------------------------------------------------------------
0073                                                              */
0074   #define IDS_Caption       1
0075   #define IDS_Warning       2
0076   #define IDS_NoMouse       3
0077   #define IDS_About         4
0078   #define IDS_AboutText     5
0079   #define IDS_License       6
0080   #define IDS_LicenseText 7

0081   #define IDS_Help          8
0082   #define IDS_HelpText      9
0083   #define IDS_Completed    10
0084   #define IDS_Error        11
0085   #define IDS_Memory       12
0086   #define IDS_MemText      13
0087   #define IDS_Timing       14
0088   #define IDS_TimingText   15
0089   #define IDS_NotReady     16
0090   #define IDS_Ready        17
0091   #define IDS_BuildBefore 18
0092   #define IDS_Already      19
0093   #define IDS_InsufMem1    20
0094   #define IDS_InsufMem2    21
0095   #define IDS_NoTimer      22
0096   #define IDS_NoReset      23
```

```
0097  #define IDS_CannotReset 24
0098  #define IDS_Resolution 25
0099  #define IDS_ResVGA     26
0100  #define IDS_ResEGA     27
0101  #define IDS_ResCGA     28
0102  #define IDS_ResSVGA    29
0103  #define IDS_Res8514    30
0104  #define IDS_ResHerc    31
0105  #define IDS_ResCustom  32
0106  #define IDS_Color      33
0107  #define IDS_Color16    34
0108  #define IDS_Color256   35
0109  #define IDS_Color2     36
0110  #define IDS_ColorCustom 37
0111  #define IDS_Machine    38
0112  #define IDS_Enhanced   39
0113  #define IDS_Standard   40
0114  #define IDS_Real       41
0115  #define IDS_NoFrame    42
0116  #define IDS_AnimReady  43
0117  #define IDS_Unexpected 44
0118  #define IDS_Status     45
0119  #define IDS_Disk1      46
0120  #define IDS_Disk2      47
0121  #define IDS_Disk3      48
0122  #define IDS_Disk4      49
0123  #define IDS_Disk5      50
0124  #define IDS_Disk6      51
0125  #define IDS_Disk7      52
0126  #define IDS_Disk8      53
0127  #define IDS_Disk9      54
0128  #define IDS_Disk10     55
0129  #define IDS_Disk11     56
0130  #define IDS_Disk12     57
0131  #define IDS_Disk13     58
0132  #define IDS_Disk14     59
0133  #define IDS_Disk15     60
0134  #define IDS_Disk16     61
0135  #define IDS_Disk17     62
0136  #define IDS_Disk18     63
0137  #define IDS_Disk19     64
0138  #define IDS_Disk20     65
0139  #define IDS_Disk21     66
0140  #define IDS_Disk22     67
0141  #define IDS_Disk23     68
0142  #define IDS_Disk24     69
0143  #define IDS_Disk25     70
0144  #define IDS_Disk26     71
0145  #define IDS_NoBg       72
0146  #define IDS_BgAlready  73
0147  #define IDS_InsufMemBg 74
0148  /*
0149  --------------------------------------------------------------
0150                        End of include file
0151  --------------------------------------------------------------
0152                                                              */
```

**16-5** The resource script file listing for the sample application.

```
0001   /*
0002   ------------------------------------------------------------------
0003                   Resource script file SPATIAL.RC
0004              Copyright 1992 Lee Adams.  All rights reserved.
0005      This file defines the menu resources, the accelerator key
0006      resources, and the string resources that will be used by the
0007      demonstration application at runtime.
0008   ------------------------------------------------------------------
0009                                                                   */
0010   #define zRCFILE
0011   #include <WINDOWS.H>
0012   #include "SPATIAL.H"
0013   /*
0014   ------------------------------------------------------------------
0015                          Script for menus
0016   ------------------------------------------------------------------
0017                                                                   */
0018   MENUS1 MENU
0019     BEGIN
0020     POPUP "&File"
0021       BEGIN
0022         MENUITEM   "&New", IDM_New, GRAYED
0023         MENUITEM   "&Open...", IDM_Open, GRAYED
0024         MENUITEM   "&Save", IDM_Save, GRAYED
0025         MENUITEM   "Save &As...", IDM_SaveAs, GRAYED
0026         MENUITEM SEPARATOR
0027         MENUITEM   "E&xit", IDM_Exit
0028       END
0029     POPUP "&Edit"
0030       BEGIN
0031         MENUITEM   "&Undo\tAlt+BkSp", IDM_Undo, GRAYED
0032         MENUITEM SEPARATOR
0033         MENUITEM   "Cu&t\tShift+Del", IDM_Cut, GRAYED
0034         MENUITEM   "&Copy\tCtrl+Ins", IDM_Copy, GRAYED
0035         MENUITEM   "&Paste\tShift+Ins", IDM_Paste, GRAYED
0036         MENUITEM   "&Delete\tDel", IDM_Delete, GRAYED
0037       END
0038     POPUP "&Animation"
0039       BEGIN
0040         MENUITEM "Run &Forward", IDM_RunForward
0041         MENUITEM "Run &Reverse", IDM_RunReverse
0042         MENUITEM "&Pause", IDM_StopAnimation
0043         MENUITEM SEPARATOR
0044         MENUITEM "&Initialize system", IDM_InitFrame
0045         MENUITEM "Cr&eate Frames", IDM_SaveAnimation
0046         MENUITEM SEPARATOR
0047         MENUITEM "&Load Animation", IDM_LoadAnimation
0048         MENUITEM SEPARATOR
0049         MENUITEM "&Clear", IDM_Clear
0050       END
0051     POPUP "&Timer"
0052       BEGIN
0053         MENUITEM "&18 fps", IDM_FPS182, CHECKED
0054         MENUITEM " &9 fps", IDM_FPS91
0055         MENUITEM " &6 fps", IDM_FPS61
0056         MENUITEM " &5 fps", IDM_FPS45
0057         MENUITEM " &4 fps", IDM_FPS36
0058         MENUITEM " &3 fps", IDM_FPS30
0059       END
0060     POPUP "&Help"
0061       BEGIN
```

```
0062        MENUITEM "&About", IDM_About
0063        MENUITEM "&License", IDM_License
0064        MENUITEM SEPARATOR
0065        MENUITEM "&Screen resolution", IDM_Display
0066        MENUITEM "Available &colors", IDM_Colors
0067        MENUITEM "Memory mode", IDM_Mode
0068        MENUITEM SEPARATOR
0069        MENUITEM "&Memory notes", IDM_Memory
0070        MENUITEM "&Timing notes", IDM_Timing
0071        MENUITEM SEPARATOR
0072        MENUITEM "&Help", IDM_GeneralHelp
0073     END
0074   END
0075 /*
0076 ----------------------------------------------------------------
0077                   Script for accelerator keys
0078 ----------------------------------------------------------------
0079                                                              */
0080 KEYS1 ACCELERATORS
0081   BEGIN
0082   VK_BACK, IDM_Undo, VIRTKEY, ALT
0083   VK_DELETE, IDM_Cut, VIRTKEY, SHIFT
0084   VK_INSERT, IDM_Copy, VIRTKEY, CONTROL
0085   VK_INSERT, IDM_Paste, VIRTKEY, SHIFT
0086   VK_DELETE, IDM_Delete,VIRTKEY
0087   END
0088 /*
0089 ----------------------------------------------------------------
0090                      Script for strings
0091   Programmer's Notes:  If you are typing this listing, set your
0092   margins to a line length of 255 characters so you can create
0093   lengthy strings without embedded carriage returns.  The line
0094   wraparounds in the following STRINGTABLE script are used for
0095   readability only in this printout.
0096 ----------------------------------------------------------------
0097                                                              */
0098 STRINGTABLE
0099   BEGIN
0100     IDS_Caption      "Animation of 3D Solids"
0101     IDS_Warning      "Warning"
0102     IDS_NoMouse      "No mouse found.  Some features of this
      demonstration program may require a mouse."
0103     IDS_About        "About this program"
0104     IDS_AboutText    "This is a demo from Windcrest McGraw-Hill
      book 4114.  Copyright 1992 Lee Adams.  All rights reserved."
0105     IDS_License      "License Agreement"
0106     IDS_LicenseText "You can use this code as part of your own
      software product subject to the License Agreement and Limited
      Warranty in Windcrest McGraw-Hill book 4114 and on its
      companion disk."
0107     IDS_Help         "How to use this demo"
0108     IDS_HelpText     "The Animation menu manages the animation
      engine.  Select Initialize System then Create Frames to build
      frames and save to disk.  Select Load Animation then Run
      Forward to play animation.  See the book for advanced
      features."
0109     IDS_Completed    "Task completed OK"
0110     IDS_Error        "Runtime error"
0111     IDS_Memory       "Animation memory requirements"
0112     IDS_MemText      "The hidden frame for the animation is stored
      as a bitmap in global memory.  The demo will advise you if a
```

```
                  memory shortage occurs.  To make more global memory available
                  you can close other applications."
0113    IDS_Timing        "Animation timing"
0114    IDS_TimingText  "The Timer menu sets the animation display
                  rate to 18.2, 9.1, 6.1, 4.5, 3.6, or 3 frames per second.
                  Actual performance is limited by your computer's processor
                  (25MHz or faster is recommended).  See the book for details."
0115    IDS_NotReady      "Animation not ready"
0116    IDS_Ready         "Animation ready"
0117    IDS_BuildBefore "Animation frames not ready for playback."
0118    IDS_Already       "The hidden frame has already been created."
0119    IDS_InsufMem1    "Insufficient global memory for frame bitmap."
0120    IDS_NoTimer       "Unable to create a timer.  Close other
                  applications."
0121    IDS_NoReset       "Create hidden frame before attempting to
                  reset timer."
0122    IDS_CannotReset "Unable to reset the timer."
0123    IDS_Resolution  "Screen resolution"
0124    IDS_ResVGA        "Running in 640x480 mode."
0125    IDS_ResEGA        "Running in 640x350 mode."
0126    IDS_ResCGA        "Running in 640x200 mode."
0127    IDS_ResSVGA       "Running in 800x600 mode."
0128    IDS_Res8514       "Running in 1024x768 mode."
0129    IDS_ResHerc       "Running in 720x348 mode."
0130    IDS_ResCustom    "Running in custom mode."
0131    IDS_Color         "Available colors"
0132    IDS_Color16       "Running in 16-color mode."
0133    IDS_Color256     "Running in 256-color mode."
0134    IDS_Color2        "Running in 2-color mode."
0135    IDS_ColorCustom "Running in a custom color mode."
0136    IDS_Machine       "Memory mode"
0137    IDS_Enhanced     "Running in enhanced mode.  Can allocate up to
                  16 MB extended physical memory (XMS) if available.  Virtual
                  memory up to 4 times physical memory (maximum 64 MB) is also
                  available via automatic disk swapping of 4K pages."
0138    IDS_Standard     "Running in standard mode.  Can allocate up to
                  16 MB extended physical memory (XMS) if available."
0139    IDS_Real          "Running in real mode.  Can allocate blocks of
                  memory from the first 640K of RAM.  Can also allocate blocks
                  from expanded memory (EMS) if available."
0140    IDS_NoFrame       "Hidden frame not yet created."
0141    IDS_AnimReady    "Animation ready"
0142    IDS_Unexpected  "Unexpected animation condition"
0143    IDS_Status        "Animation status"
0144    IDS_Disk1         "Animation files already saved to disk."
0145    IDS_Disk2         "Animation sequence successfully saved to
                  disk."
0146    IDS_Disk3         "Unable to load next frame from disk.
                  Animation halted."
0147    IDS_Disk4         "Animation sequence already loaded from disk."
0148    IDS_Disk5         "Previous load failed.  Cancelling this
                  attempt."
0149    IDS_Disk6         "Not enough memory available.  Software will
                  dynamically load each frame from disk during playback."
0150    IDS_Disk7         "Animation sequence successfully loaded from
                  disk."
0151    IDS_Disk8         "Previous save failed.  Cancelling this
                  attempt."
0152    IDS_Disk9         "No hidden-frame exists.  No frame saved to
                  disk."
0153    IDS_Disk10        "Unable to retrieve bitmap data structure."
```

**16-5** Continued.

```
0154      IDS_Disk11      "Bit array is too long to save to disk in a
          single pass."
0155      IDS_Disk12      "Cannot create memory buffer for disk write."
0156      IDS_Disk13      "Unable to copy bits from bitmap to buffer."
0157      IDS_Disk14      "File already exists.  Overwrite existing
          file?"
0158      IDS_Disk15      "Unable to open the file for writing."
0159      IDS_Disk16      "Unable to write to the opened file."
0160      IDS_Disk17      "Unable to close the file after writing."
0161      IDS_Disk18      "No memory bitmap exists.  Unable to load from
          disk."
0162      IDS_Disk19      "Image file is larger than animation frame.
          No file loaded."
0163      IDS_Disk20      "Cannot create memory buffer for file read."
0164      IDS_Disk21      "Unable to open the file for reading.  Be sure
          you have saved an animation sequence to disk before attempting
          to load it."
0165      IDS_Disk22      "An error occurred while reading the file."
0166      IDS_Disk23      "The frame file was shorter than expected."
0167      IDS_Disk24      "Unable to close the file after reading."
0168      IDS_Disk25      "Unable to copy bits from buffer to bitmap."
0169      IDS_Disk26      "Unable to save all files.  Check if
          sufficient space available on disk."
0170      IDS_NoBg        "Hidden background image not yet created."
0171      IDS_BgAlready   "The hidden background bitmap has already been
          created."
0172      IDS_InsufMemBg  "Insufficient global memory for background
          bitmap."
0173  END
0174  /*
0175  -------------------------------------------------------------------
0176                      End of resource script file
0177  -------------------------------------------------------------------
0178                                                                   */
```

**16-6**  The C source file listing for the sample application, spatial.c. This demonstration program is ready to build using QuickC for Windows, Turbo C++ for Windows, Microsoft C and the SDK, Borland C++, Symantec Zortech C++, WATCOM C, and other compilers. See chapter 10 for the program listings for storage.h and storage.c,which must be linked with this application. See chapter 4 for the program listings for lib3d.h and lib3d.c which must be linked with this application. See FIG. 1-2 for sample command-lines to build the program. Guidelines for using your compiler are provided in the appropriate appendix at the back of the book.

```
0001  /*
0002  -------------------------------------------------------------------
0003      Reconfigurable 3D animation prototype for Windows applications
0004      that use disk-based, hidden-page drawn, frame animation.
0005  -------------------------------------------------------------------
0006      Source file:  SPATIAL.C
0007      Release version:  1.00              Programmer:  Lee Adams
0008      Type:  C source file for Windows application development.
0009      Compilers:  Microsoft C and SDK, Borland C++, Zortech C++,
0010         QuickC for Windows, Turbo C++ for Windows, WATCOM C.
0011      Memory model:  small.
0012      Dependencies:  SPATIAL.DEF module definition file, SPATIAL.H
```

```
0013                    include file, SPATIAL.RC resource script file,
0014                    and SPATIAL.C source file.  Disk I/O operations
0015                    require STORAGE.H include file and STORAGE.C
0016                    additional C source file.  3D graphics operations
0017                    require LIB3D.H include file and LIB3D.C
0018                    additional C source file.
0019       Output and features:  Demonstrates interactive playback of
0020          disk-based hidden-page drawn frame animation.  A consistent
0021          database suitable for tweening is demonstrated as a run cycle.
0022       Publication: Contains material from Windcrest/McGraw-Hill book
0023          4114 published by TAB BOOKS Division of McGraw-Hill Inc.
0024       License:  As purchaser of the book you are granted a royalty-
0025          free license to distribute executable files generated using
0026          this code provided you accept the conditions of the License
0027          Agreement and Limited Warranty described in the book and on
0028          the companion disk.  Government users:  This software and
0029          documentation are subject to restrictions set forth in The
0030          Rights in Technical Data and Computer Software clause at
0031          252.227-7013 and elsewhere.
0032    ----------------------------------------------------------------
0033          (c) Copyright 1992 Lee Adams.  All rights reserved.
0034             Lee Adams(tm) is a trademark of Lee Adams.
0035    ----------------------------------------------------------------
0036
0037    ----------------------------------------------------------------
0038                          Include files
0039    ----------------------------------------------------------------
0040                                                                  */
0041    #include <WINDOWS.H>
0042    #include "SPATIAL.H"
0043    #include "STORAGE.H"  /* declares callable functions in STORAGE.C
            */
0044    #include "LIB3D.H"      /* declares callable functions in LIB3D.C
            */
0045    /*
0046    ----------------------------------------------------------------
0047          Static variables visible throughout this file
0048    ----------------------------------------------------------------
0049                                                                  */
0050    /* ------------------- window specifications ----------------- */
0051    #define zWINDOW_WIDTH 408
0052    #define zWINDOW_HEIGHT 346
0053    #define zFRAMEWIDE 400
0054    #define zFRAMEHIGH 300
0055    int WindowX, WindowY;
0056
0057    /* ------------------- instance operations ------------------- */
0058    HANDLE hInst;
0059    HWND MainhWnd;
0060    HANDLE hAccel;
0061    HMENU hMenu;
0062    PAINTSTRUCT ps;
0063    int MessageRet;
0064
0065    /* -------------------- mouse and cursor -------------------- */
0066    HCURSOR hPrevCursor;
0067    HCURSOR hHourGlass;
0068    int MousePresent;
0069
0070    /* -------------------- runtime conditions ------------------- */
0071    int DisplayWidth, DisplayHeight;
```

**16-6** Continued.

```
0072    int DisplayBits;
0073    int DisplayPlanes;
0074    DWORD MemoryMode;
0075
0076    /* ----------------- message box operations ----------------- */
0077    char lpCaption[51];
0078    int Max= 50;
0079    char lpMessage[250];
0080    int MaxText= 249;
0081
0082    /* ---------------- persistent image operations -------------- */
0083    #define zBLANK 0
0084    #define zANIMATING  1
0085    int PaintImage= zBLANK;
0086
0087    /* -------------------- timer operations -------------------- */
0088    #define zTIMER_PAUSE 3
0089    int TimerCounter= zTIMER_PAUSE;
0090    BOOL TimerExists= FALSE;
0091    WORD TimerID1;
0092
0093    /* ------------------ font operations ---------------------- */
0094    HFONT hFont, hPrevFont;           /* handles to new, previous font */
0095    HDC hFontDC;                      /* display-context for font */
0096
0097    /* ---------------- hidden frame operations ----------------- */
0098    HDC hFrameDC;
0099    HBITMAP hFrame;
0100    HBITMAP hPrevFrame;
0101    BOOL FrameReady= FALSE;
0102
0103    /* -------------------- animation engine -------------------- */
0104    BOOL Pause= TRUE;
0105    WORD wFrameRate= 55;
0106    WORD wPrevRate= 55;
0107    #define zFORWARD 1
0108    #define zREVERSE 0
0109    int FrameDirection= zFORWARD;
0110    BOOL Redisplay= FALSE;
0111    int FrameNum= 1;
0112    #define zFIRSTFRAME 1
0113    #define zFINALFRAME 24
0114    BOOL AnimationReady= FALSE;
0115
0116    /* ---------------- disk save/load operations --------------- */
0117    int RetVal;                                    /* return value */
0118    BOOL bFrameSaved= FALSE;                /* frame saved to disk? */
0119    BOOL bFrameLoaded= FALSE;             /* frame loaded from disk? */
0120    BOOL bAnimationSaved= FALSE;       /* animation saved to disk? */
0121    BOOL bAnimationLoaded= FALSE;     /* animation loaded from disk? */
0122    BOOL bPrevSaveAttempt= FALSE;      /* previous save attempt made? */
0123    BOOL bPrevLoadAttempt= FALSE;      /* previous load attempt made? */
0124    HDC hFDC;                  /* memory-display context for playback */
0125    HBITMAP hPrevF,hF1,hF2,hF3,hF4,hF5,    /* bitmaps for playback... */
0126      hF6,hF7,hF8;
0127    BOOL bUseDisk= FALSE;             /* load each frame as needed? */
0128    BOOL bAnimationHalted= FALSE;   /* disk error during animation? */
0129
0130    /*
0131    ------------------------------------------------------------------
0132                        Entry point for the application
```

**16-6** Continued.

```
0133  --------------------------------------------------------------------
0134                                                                   */
0135  int PASCAL WinMain(HANDLE hInstance, HANDLE hPrevInstance,
0136                     LPSTR lpCmdLine, int nCmdShow)
0137  {
0138    MSG msg;
0139    HWND hWndPrev;
0140    HWND hDesktopWnd;
0141    HDC hDCcaps;
0142
0143  /* ----------- ensure only one instance is running ----------- */
0144  hWndPrev = FindWindow("DEMOCLASS", NULL);
0145  if (hWndPrev != NULL)
0146    {
0147    BringWindowToTop(hWndPrev);
0148    return FALSE;
0149    }
0150
0151  /* --------- determine capabilities of screen display ---------- */
0152  hDesktopWnd= GetDesktopWindow();
0153  hDCcaps= GetDC(hDesktopWnd);
0154  DisplayWidth= GetDeviceCaps(hDCcaps,HORZRES);
0155  DisplayHeight= GetDeviceCaps(hDCcaps,VERTRES);
0156  DisplayBits= GetDeviceCaps(hDCcaps,BITSPIXEL);
0157  DisplayPlanes= GetDeviceCaps(hDCcaps,PLANES);
0158  ReleaseDC(hDesktopWnd,hDCcaps);
0159
0160  /* ------- calculate screen position to center the window ------ */
0161  WindowX= (DisplayWidth - zWINDOW_WIDTH) / 2;
0162  WindowY= (DisplayHeight - zWINDOW_HEIGHT) /2;
0163  if (WindowX < 0) WindowX= 0;
0164  if (WindowY < 0) WindowY= 0;
0165
0166  /* ---- determine memory mode (enhanced, standard, or real) ---- */
0167  MemoryMode= GetWinFlags();
0168
0169  /* --------------- create and show the window ---------------- */
0170  hInst = hInstance;
0171  if (!zInitClass(hInstance)) return FALSE;
0172  MainhWnd = zInitMainWindow(hInstance);
0173  if (!MainhWnd) return FALSE;
0174  ShowWindow(MainhWnd, nCmdShow);
0175  UpdateWindow(MainhWnd);
0176  hAccel= LoadAccelerators(hInstance,"KEYS1");
0177  hFontDC= GetDC(MainhWnd);
0178  hFont= GetStockObject(SYSTEM_FONT);
0179  hPrevFont= SelectObject(hFontDC,hFont);
0180  SetTextColor(hFontDC,RGB(191,191,191));
0181  TextOut(hFontDC,10,280,"~ Copyright 1992 Lee Adams.",27);
0 82  SetTextColor(hFontDC,RGB(0,0,0));
0183  SelectObject(hFontDC,hPrevFont);
0184  ReleaseDC(MainhWnd,hFontDC);
0185
0186  /* --------------------- check for mouse --------------------- */
0187  MousePresent = GetSystemMetrics(SM_MOUSEPRESENT);
0188  if (!MousePresent)
0189    {
0190    LoadString(hInst,IDS_Warning,lpCaption,Max);
0191    LoadString(hInst,IDS_NoMouse,lpMessage,MaxText);
0192    MessageBox(GetFocus(),lpMessage,lpCaption,MB_OK);
0193    }
```

```
0194
0195    /* --------------- initialize the 3D environment --------------- */
0196    zInitialize3D(MainhWnd);              /* initialize the 3D variables */
0197
0198    /* ---------- begin retrieving messages for the window --------- */
0199    while (GetMessage(&msg,0,0,0))
0200      {
0201      if(TranslateAccelerator(MainhWnd, hAccel, &msg))
0202        continue;
0203      TranslateMessage(&msg);
0204      DispatchMessage(&msg);
0205      }
0206    return(msg.wParam);
0207    }
0208    /*
0209    -------------------------------------------------------------------
0210                    Switcher for incoming messages
0211    -------------------------------------------------------------------
0212                                                                       */
0213    LONG FAR PASCAL zMessageHandler(HWND hWnd, unsigned message,
0214                            WORD wParam, LONG lParam)
0215    {
0216      HDC hDCpaint;
0217
0218    switch (message)
0219      {
0220
0221      case WM_TIMER:
0222        TimerCounter--;
0223        if (TimerCounter > 0) break;
0224        TimerCounter++;
0225        zShowNextFrame(hWnd);
0226        break;
0227
0228      case WM_COMMAND:
0229        switch(wParam)
0230          {
0231          case IDM_New:      break;
0232          case IDM_Open:     break;
0233          case IDM_Save:     break;
0234          case IDM_SaveAs:   break;
0235          case IDM_Exit:     PostQuitMessage(0); break;
0236
0237          case IDM_Undo:     break;
0238          case IDM_Cut:      break;
0239          case IDM_Copy:     break;
0240          case IDM_Paste:    break;
0241          case IDM_Delete:   break;
0242
0243          case IDM_RunForward:
0244              if (AnimationReady==FALSE)
0245                {
0246                MessageBeep(0);
0247                LoadString(hInst,IDS_NotReady,lpCaption,Max);
0248                LoadString(hInst,IDS_BuildBefore,lpMessage,MaxText);
0249                TimerCounter= zTIMER_PAUSE;
0250                MessageBox(GetFocus(),lpMessage,lpCaption,MB_OK);
0251                break;
0252                }
0253              Pause= FALSE;
0254              PaintImage= zANIMATING;
```

```
0255                FrameDirection= zFORWARD;
0256                zShowNextFrame(hWnd);
0257                break;
0258        case IDM_RunReverse:
0259            if (AnimationReady==FALSE)
0260                {
0261                MessageBeep(0);
0262                LoadString(hInst,IDS_NotReady,lpCaption,Max);
0263                LoadString(hInst,IDS_BuildBefore,lpMessage,MaxText);
0264                TimerCounter= zTIMER_PAUSE;
0265                MessageBox(GetFocus(),lpMessage,lpCaption,MB_OK);
0266                break;
0267                }
0268            Pause= FALSE;
0269            PaintImage= zANIMATING;
0270            FrameDirection= zREVERSE;
0271            zShowNextFrame(hWnd);
0272            break;
0273        case IDM_StopAnimation:
0274            if (AnimationReady==FALSE)
0275                {
0276                MessageBeep(0);
0277                LoadString(hInst,IDS_NotReady,lpCaption,Max);
0278                LoadString(hInst,IDS_BuildBefore,lpMessage,MaxText);
0279                TimerCounter= zTIMER_PAUSE;
0280                MessageBox(GetFocus(),lpMessage,lpCaption,MB_OK);
0281                break;
0282                }
0283            Pause= TRUE;
0284            zShowNextFrame(hWnd);
0285            break;
0286        case IDM_InitFrame: zInitFrame(hWnd);
0287                            break;
0288        case IDM_SaveAnimation:
0289            SetCapture(hWnd); hPrevCursor= SetCursor(hHourGlass);
0290            zSaveAnimation(hWnd);
0291            SetCursor(hPrevCursor); ReleaseCapture();
0292            if (bAnimationSaved==FALSE)
0293                {
0294                MessageBeep(0);
0295                LoadString(hInst,IDS_NotReady,lpCaption,Max);
0296                LoadString(hInst,IDS_Disk26,lpMessage,MaxText);
0297                TimerCounter= zTIMER_PAUSE;
0298                MessageBox(GetFocus(),lpMessage,lpCaption,MB_OK);
0299                }
0300            break;
0301        case IDM_LoadAnimation:
0302            SetCapture(hWnd); hPrevCursor= SetCursor(hHourGlass);
0303            zLoadAnimation(hWnd);
0304            SetCursor(hPrevCursor); ReleaseCapture();
0305            break;
0306        case IDM_Clear:  if (Pause==TRUE)
0307                            {
0308                             zClear(hWnd);
0309                             PaintImage= zBLANK;
0310                            }
0311                        break;
0312
0313        case IDM_FPS182: wPrevRate= wFrameRate;
0314                        wFrameRate= (WORD)55;
0315                        zSetFrameRate(hWnd, wFrameRate); break;
```

```
0316          case IDM_FPS91:   wPrevRate= wFrameRate;
0317                            wFrameRate= (WORD)110;
0318                            zSetFrameRate(hWnd, wFrameRate); break;
0319          case IDM_FPS61:   wPrevRate= wFrameRate;
0320                            wFrameRate= (WORD)165;
0321                            zSetFrameRate(hWnd, wFrameRate); break;
0322          case IDM_FPS45:   wPrevRate= wFrameRate;
0323                            wFrameRate= (WORD) 220;
0324                            zSetFrameRate(hWnd, wFrameRate); break;
0325          case IDM_FPS36:   wPrevRate= wFrameRate;
0326                            wFrameRate= (WORD) 275;
0327                            zSetFrameRate(hWnd, wFrameRate); break;
0328          case IDM_FPS30:   wPrevRate= wFrameRate;
0329                            wFrameRate= (WORD) 330;
0330                            zSetFrameRate(hWnd, wFrameRate); break;
0331
0332          case IDM_About:
0333            LoadString(hInst,IDS_About,lpCaption,Max);
0334            LoadString(hInst,IDS_AboutText,lpMessage,MaxText);
0335            TimerCounter= zTIMER_PAUSE;
0336            MessageBox(GetFocus(),lpMessage,lpCaption,MB_OK);
0337            break;
0338          case IDM_License:
0339            LoadString(hInst,IDS_License,lpCaption,Max);
0340            LoadString(hInst,IDS_LicenseText,lpMessage,MaxText);
0341            TimerCounter= zTIMER_PAUSE;
0342            MessageBox(GetFocus(),lpMessage,lpCaption,MB_OK);
0343            break;
0344
0345          case IDM_Display:
0346            if (DisplayWidth==640)
0347              {
0348              if (DisplayHeight==480)
0349                {
0350                LoadString(hInst,IDS_Resolution,lpCaption,Max);
0351                LoadString(hInst,IDS_ResVGA,lpMessage,MaxText);
0352                TimerCounter= zTIMER_PAUSE;
0353                MessageBox(GetFocus(),lpMessage,lpCaption,MB_OK);
0354                }
0355              if (DisplayHeight==350)
0356                {
0357                LoadString(hInst,IDS_Resolution,lpCaption,Max);
0358                LoadString(hInst,IDS_ResEGA,lpMessage,MaxText);
0359                TimerCounter= zTIMER_PAUSE;
0360                MessageBox(GetFocus(),lpMessage,lpCaption,MB_OK);
0361                }
0362              if (DisplayHeight==200)
0363                {
0364                LoadString(hInst,IDS_Resolution,lpCaption,Max);
0365                LoadString(hInst,IDS_ResCGA,lpMessage,MaxText);
0366                TimerCounter= zTIMER_PAUSE;
0367                MessageBox(GetFocus(),lpMessage,lpCaption,MB_OK);
0368                }
0369              break;
0370              }
0371            if (DisplayWidth==800)
0372              {
0373              LoadString(hInst,IDS_Resolution,lpCaption,Max);
0374              LoadString(hInst,IDS_ResSVGA,lpMessage,MaxText);
0375              TimerCounter= zTIMER_PAUSE;
0376              MessageBox(GetFocus(),lpMessage,lpCaption,MB_OK);
```

```
0377              break;
0378              }
0379          if (DisplayWidth==1024)
0380              {
0381              LoadString(hInst,IDS_Resolution,lpCaption,Max);
0382              LoadString(hInst,IDS_Res8514,lpMessage,MaxText);
0383              TimerCounter= zTIMER_PAUSE;
0384              MessageBox(GetFocus(),lpMessage,lpCaption,MB_OK);
0385              break;
0386              }
0387          if (DisplayWidth==720)
0388              {
0389              LoadString(hInst,IDS_Resolution,lpCaption,Max);
0390              LoadString(hInst,IDS_ResHerc,lpMessage,MaxText);
0391              TimerCounter= zTIMER_PAUSE;
0392              MessageBox(GetFocus(),lpMessage,lpCaption,MB_OK);
0393              break;
0394              }
0395          LoadString(hInst,IDS_Resolution,lpCaption,Max);
0396          LoadString(hInst,IDS_ResCustom,lpMessage,MaxText);
0397          TimerCounter= zTIMER_PAUSE;
0398          MessageBox(GetFocus(),lpMessage,lpCaption,MB_OK);
0399          break;
0400
0401      case IDM_Colors:
0402          if (DisplayBits==1)
0403              {
0404              if (DisplayPlanes==4)
0405                  {
0406                  LoadString(hInst,IDS_Color,lpCaption,Max);
0407                  LoadString(hInst,IDS_Color16,lpMessage,MaxText);
0408                  TimerCounter= zTIMER_PAUSE;
0409                  MessageBox(GetFocus(),lpMessage,lpCaption,MB_OK);
0410                  break;
0411                  }
0412              if (DisplayPlanes==1)
0413                  {
0414                  LoadString(hInst,IDS_Color,lpCaption,Max);
0415                  LoadString(hInst,IDS_Color2,lpMessage,MaxText);
0416                  TimerCounter= zTIMER_PAUSE;
0417                  MessageBox(GetFocus(),lpMessage,lpCaption,MB_OK);
0418                  break;
0419                  }
0420              }
0421          if (DisplayBits==8)
0422              {
0423              LoadString(hInst,IDS_Color,lpCaption,Max);
0424              LoadString(hInst,IDS_Color256,lpMessage,MaxText);
0425              TimerCounter= zTIMER_PAUSE;
0426              MessageBox(GetFocus(),lpMessage,lpCaption,MB_OK);
0427              break;
0428              }
0429          LoadString(hInst,IDS_Color,lpCaption,Max);
0430          LoadString(hInst,IDS_ColorCustom,lpMessage,MaxText);
0431          TimerCounter= zTIMER_PAUSE;
0432          MessageBox(GetFocus(),lpMessage,lpCaption,MB_OK);
0433          break;
0434
0435      case IDM_Mode:
0436          if (MemoryMode & WF_ENHANCED)
0437              {
```

```
0438            LoadString(hInst,IDS_Machine,lpCaption,Max);
0439            LoadString(hInst,IDS_Enhanced,lpMessage,MaxText);
0440            TimerCounter= zTIMER_PAUSE;
0441            MessageBox(GetFocus(),lpMessage,lpCaption,MB_OK);
0442            break;
0443            }
0444         if (MemoryMode & WF_STANDARD)
0445            {
0446            LoadString(hInst,IDS_Machine,lpCaption,Max);
0447            LoadString(hInst,IDS_Standard,lpMessage,MaxText);
0448            TimerCounter= zTIMER_PAUSE;
0449            MessageBox(GetFocus(),lpMessage,lpCaption,MB_OK);
0450            break;
0451            }
0452         LoadString(hInst,IDS_Machine,lpCaption,Max);
0453         LoadString(hInst,IDS_Real,lpMessage,MaxText);
0454         TimerCounter= zTIMER_PAUSE;
0455         MessageBox(GetFocus(),lpMessage,lpCaption,MB_OK);
0456         break;
0457
0458       case IDM_Memory:
0459         LoadString(hInst,IDS_Memory,lpCaption,Max);
0460         LoadString(hInst,IDS_MemText,lpMessage,MaxText);
0461         TimerCounter= zTIMER_PAUSE;
0462         MessageBox(GetFocus(),lpMessage,lpCaption,MB_OK);
0463         break;
0464       case IDM_Timing:
0465         LoadString(hInst,IDS_Timing,lpCaption,Max);
0466         LoadString(hInst,IDS_TimingText,lpMessage,MaxText);
0467         TimerCounter= zTIMER_PAUSE;
0468         MessageBox(GetFocus(),lpMessage,lpCaption,MB_OK);
0469         break;
0470       case IDM_GeneralHelp:
0471         LoadString(hInst,IDS_Help,lpCaption,Max);
0472         LoadString(hInst,IDS_HelpText,lpMessage,MaxText);
0473         TimerCounter= zTIMER_PAUSE;
0474         MessageBox(GetFocus(),lpMessage,lpCaption,MB_OK);
0475         break;
0476       default:
0477         return(DefWindowProc(hWnd, message, wParam, lParam));
0478       }
0479     break;
0480
0481   case WM_INITMENUPOPUP:
0482     TimerCounter= zTIMER_PAUSE;
0483     if (lParam == 3)
0484       hMenu= wParam;
0485     break;
0486
0487   case WM_PAINT:
0488     hDCpaint= BeginPaint(hWnd,&ps);
0489     EndPaint(hWnd, &ps);
0490     if (PaintImage==zBLANK) break;
0491     if (Pause==TRUE)
0492       {
0493       Redisplay= TRUE;
0494       zShowNextFrame(hWnd);
0495       Redisplay= FALSE;
0496       break;
0497       }
0498     zShowNextFrame(hWnd);
```

```
0499      break;
0500
0501   case WM_KEYDOWN:
0502     switch (wParam)
0503       {
0504       case VK_LEFT:    if (Pause==TRUE)
0505                          {
0506                          if (FrameDirection==zFORWARD)
0507                            {
0508                            FrameDirection= zREVERSE;
0509                            }
0510                          Pause= FALSE;
0511                          zShowNextFrame(hWnd);
0512                          Pause= TRUE;
0513                          PaintImage= zANIMATING;
0514                          }
0515                        break;
0516       case VK_RIGHT:   if (Pause==TRUE)
0517                          {
0518                          if (FrameDirection==zREVERSE)
0519                            {
0520                            FrameDirection= zFORWARD;
0521                            }
0522                          Pause= FALSE;
0523                          zShowNextFrame(hWnd);
0524                          Pause= TRUE;
0525                          PaintImage= zANIMATING;
0526                          }
0527                        break;
0528       default:
0529               return(DefWindowProc(hWnd, message, wParam, lParam));
0530       }
0531     break;
0532
0533   case WM_DESTROY:
0534     if (FrameReady==TRUE)
0535       {                          /* tidy up hidden frame bitmap... */
0536     SelectObject(hFrameDC,hPrevFrame);
0537     DeleteObject(hFrame);
0538     DeleteDC(hFrameDC);
0539     KillTimer(hWnd,1);
0540       }
0541     if (bAnimationLoaded==TRUE)
0542       {                          /* tidy up animation playback bitmaps... */
0543     SelectObject(hFDC,hPrevF);
0544     DeleteObject(hF1); DeleteObject(hF2); DeleteObject(hF3);
0545     DeleteObject(hF4); DeleteObject(hF5); DeleteObject(hF6);
0546     DeleteObject(hF7); DeleteObject(hF8); DeleteDC(hFDC);
0547       }
0548     PostQuitMessage(0);
0549     break;
0550
0551   case WM_SYSCOMMAND:
0552     if ((wParam & 0xfff0)== SC_SIZE)
0553       {
0554     MessageBeep(0); break;
0555       }
0556     if ((wParam & 0xfff0)== SC_MINIMIZE)
0557       {
0558     MessageBeep(0); break;
```

```
0559          }
0560       if ((wParam & 0xfff0)== SC_MAXIMIZE)
0561          {
0562          MessageBeep(0); break;
0563          }
0564
0565    default:
0566       return(DefWindowProc(hWnd, message, wParam, lParam));
0567     }
0568 return FALSE;
0569 }
0570 /*
0571 ------------------------------------------------------------------
0572             Initialize the attributes of the window class
0573 ------------------------------------------------------------------
0574                                                                 */
0575 BOOL zInitClass(HANDLE hInstance)
0576 {
0577    WNDCLASS WndClass;
0578 WndClass.style= 0;
0579 WndClass.lpfnWndProc= zMessageHandler;
0580 WndClass.cbClsExtra= 0;
0581 WndClass.cbWndExtra= 0;
0582 WndClass.hInstance= hInstance;
0583 WndClass.hIcon= LoadIcon(NULL,IDI_EXCLAMATION);
0584 WndClass.hCursor= LoadCursor(NULL,IDC_ARROW);
0585 WndClass.hbrBackground= CreateSolidBrush(RGB(255,255,255));
0586 WndClass.lpszMenuName= "MENUS1";
0587 WndClass.lpszClassName= "DEMOCLASS";
0588 return RegisterClass(&WndClass);
0589 }
0590 /*
0591 ------------------------------------------------------------------
0592                        Create the main window
0593 ------------------------------------------------------------------
0594                                                                 */
0595 HWND zInitMainWindow(HANDLE hInstance)
0596 {
0597    HWND hWnd;
0598 LoadString(hInstance,IDS_Caption,lpCaption,Max);
0599 hHourGlass= LoadCursor(NULL,IDC_WAIT);
0600 hWnd = CreateWindow("DEMOCLASS",lpCaption,
0601   WS_OVERLAPPED | WS_THICKFRAME | WS_MINIMIZEBOX |
0602     WS_MAXIMIZEBOX | WS_CLIPCHILDREN,
0603   WindowX,WindowY,zWINDOW_WIDTH,zWINDOW_HEIGHT,0,0,
0604   hInstance, (LPSTR)NULL);
0605 return hWnd;
0606 }
0607 /*
0608 ------------------------------------------------------------------
0609                      GRAPHICS SYSTEM Functions
0610 ------------------------------------------------------------------
0611 ------------------------------------------------------------------
0612                      Create the hidden frame.
0613 ------------------------------------------------------------------
0614                                                                 */
0615 static void zInitFrame(HWND hWnd)
0616 {
0617    HDC hDisplayDC;
0618
```

```
0619   if (FrameReady==TRUE)
0620     {
0621     MessageBeep(0);
0622     LoadString(hInst,IDS_Ready,lpCaption,Max);
0623     LoadString(hInst,IDS_Already,lpMessage,MaxText);
0624     TimerCounter= zTIMER_PAUSE;
0625     MessageBox(GetFocus(),lpMessage,lpCaption,MB_OK);
0626     return;
0627     }
0628   GlobalCompact((DWORD)-1L);
0629   hDisplayDC= GetDC(hWnd);
0630   hFrameDC= CreateCompatibleDC(hDisplayDC);
0631   hFrame= CreateCompatibleBitmap(hDisplayDC,zFRAMEWIDE,zFRAMEHIGH);
0632   if (hFrame==NULL)
0633     {
0634     LoadString(hInst,IDS_NotReady,lpCaption,Max);
0635     LoadString(hInst,IDS_InsufMem1,lpMessage,MaxText);
0636     MessageBox(GetFocus(),lpMessage,lpCaption,MB_OK);
0637     DeleteDC(hFrameDC);
0638     TimerExists= FALSE; FrameReady= FALSE; AnimationReady= FALSE;
0639     return;
0640     }
0641   hPrevFrame= SelectObject(hFrameDC,hFrame);
0642   zClear(hWnd);
0643   BitBlt(hFrameDC,0,0,zFRAMEWIDE,zFRAMEHIGH,hDisplayDC,0,0,SRCCOPY);
0644   ReleaseDC(hWnd,hDisplayDC);
0645
0646   TimerID1= SetTimer(hWnd,1,wFrameRate,(FARPROC) NULL);
0647   if (TimerID1 == 0)
0648     {
0649     LoadString(hInst,IDS_NotReady,lpCaption,Max);
0650     LoadString(hInst,IDS_NoTimer,lpMessage,MaxText);
0651     MessageBox(GetFocus(),lpMessage,lpCaption,MB_OK);
0652     SelectObject(hFrameDC,hPrevFrame);
0653     DeleteObject(hFrame);
0654     DeleteDC(hFrameDC);
0655     TimerExists= FALSE;
0656     return;
0657     }
0658   TimerExists= TRUE;
0659   FrameReady= TRUE;
0660   FrameNum= 1;
0661   return;
0662   }
0663   /*
0664   ------------------------------------------------------------------
0665                     Clear the hidden frame.
0666   ------------------------------------------------------------------
0667                                                                   */
0668   static void zClearHiddenFrame(void)
0669   {
0670   PatBlt(hFrameDC,0,0,zFRAMEWIDE,zFRAMEHIGH,WHITENESS);
0671   return;
0672   }
0673   /*
0674   ------------------------------------------------------------------
0675            Copy the hidden frame to the display window.
0676   ------------------------------------------------------------------
0677                                                                   */
0678   static void zCopyToDisplay(HWND hWnd)
0679   {
```

```
0680      HDC hDC;
0681  hDC= GetDC(hWnd);
0682  BitBlt(hDC,0,0,zFRAMEWIDE,zFRAMEHIGH,hFrameDC,0,0,SRCCOPY);
0683  ReleaseDC(hWnd,hDC);
0684  return;
0685  }
0686  /*
0687  ------------------------------------------------------------------
0688                   Blank the display window.
0689  ------------------------------------------------------------------
0690                                                                  */
0691  static void zClear(HWND hWnd)
0692  {
0693      HDC hDC;
0694  hDC= GetDC(hWnd);
0695  PatBlt(hDC,0,0,zFRAMEWIDE,zFRAMEHIGH,WHITENESS);
0696  ReleaseDC(hWnd,hDC);
0697  return;
0698  }
0699  /*
0700  ------------------------------------------------------------------
0701                   AUTHORING SYSTEM Functions
0702  ------------------------------------------------------------------
0703  ------------------------------------------------------------------
0704                   Create 8 frames and save to disk.
0705  ------------------------------------------------------------------
0706                                                                  */
0707  static void zSaveAnimation(HWND hWnd)
0708  {
0709  if (FrameReady==FALSE)           /* if no hidden-frame available... */
0710    {
0711    MessageBeep(0);
0712    LoadString(hInst,IDS_NotReady,lpCaption,Max);
0713    LoadString(hInst,IDS_NoFrame,lpMessage,MaxText);
0714    MessageBox(GetFocus(),lpMessage,lpCaption,MB_OK);
0715    return;
0716    }
0717
0718  if (bAnimationSaved==TRUE) /* if frames already saved to disk... */
0719    {
0720    MessageBeep(0);
0721    LoadString(hInst,IDS_Unexpected,lpCaption,Max);
0722    LoadString(hInst,IDS_Disk1,lpMessage,MaxText);
0723    TimerCounter= zTIMER_PAUSE;
0724    MessageBox(GetFocus(),lpMessage,lpCaption,MB_OK);
0725    return;
0726    }
0727
0728  if (bPrevSaveAttempt==TRUE)       /* if previous attempt failed... */
0729    {
0730    MessageBeep(0);
0731    LoadString(hInst,IDS_Unexpected,lpCaption,Max);
0732    LoadString(hInst,IDS_Disk8,lpMessage,MaxText);
0733    TimerCounter= zTIMER_PAUSE;
0734    MessageBox(GetFocus(),lpMessage,lpCaption,MB_OK);
0735    return;
0736    }
0737  bPrevSaveAttempt= TRUE;
0738
0739  bFrameSaved= zBuildFrame(1,hWnd,(LPSTR)"OBJ3D1.BIT");
0740  if (bFrameSaved==FALSE) return;
```

Program listings for the sample application   **559**

```
0741   bFrameSaved= zBuildFrame(2,hWnd,(LPSTR)"OBJ3D2.BIT");
0742   if (bFrameSaved==FALSE) return;
0743   bFrameSaved= zBuildFrame(3,hWnd,(LPSTR)"OBJ3D3.BIT");
0744   if (bFrameSaved==FALSE) return;
0745   bFrameSaved= zBuildFrame(4,hWnd,(LPSTR)"OBJ3D4.BIT");
0746   if (bFrameSaved==FALSE) return;
0747   bFrameSaved= zBuildFrame(5,hWnd,(LPSTR)"OBJ3D5.BIT");
0748   if (bFrameSaved==FALSE) return;
0749   bFrameSaved= zBuildFrame(6,hWnd,(LPSTR)"OBJ3D6.BIT");
0750   if (bFrameSaved==FALSE) return;
0751   bFrameSaved= zBuildFrame(7,hWnd,(LPSTR)"OBJ3D7.BIT");
0752   if (bFrameSaved==FALSE) return;
0753   bFrameSaved= zBuildFrame(8,hWnd,(LPSTR)"OBJ3D8.BIT");
0754   if (bFrameSaved==FALSE) return;
0755
0756   bAnimationSaved= TRUE;
0757   bPrevLoadAttempt= FALSE;
0758   zClear(hWnd);
0759   MessageBeep(0);
0760   LoadString(hInst,IDS_Status,lpCaption,Max);
0761   LoadString(hInst,IDS_Disk2,lpMessage,MaxText);
0762   MessageBox(GetFocus(),lpMessage,lpCaption,MB_OK);
0763   return;
0764   }
0765   /*
0766   -----------------------------------------------------------------
0767                     Build one frame and save to disk.
0768   -----------------------------------------------------------------
0769                                                                   */
0770   static BOOL zBuildFrame(int Number, HWND hWnd, LPSTR lpFileName)
0771   {                   /* this function is called by zSaveAnimation() */
0772     BOOL bDiskResult;
0773     HFONT Font;
0774     HFONT PrevFont;
0775     DWORD PrevFontColor;
0776     DWORD PrevBkColor;
0777     HDC hDC;
0778
0779   zClearHiddenFrame();                     /* clear the hidden frame */
0780   zClear(hWnd);                         /* clear the display window */
0781
0782   /* ----------------- draw the appropriate cel ----------------- */
0783   zDrawCel(Number);                   /* draw on display window... */
0784   if (FrameReady==TRUE)
0785     {                             /* ...and copy to hidden frame */
0786     hDC= GetDC(hWnd);
0787     BitBlt(hFrameDC,0,0,zFRAMEWIDE,zFRAMEHIGH,hDC,0,0,SRCCOPY);
0788     ReleaseDC(hWnd,hDC);
0789     }
0790
0791   /* --------- display the titles, labels, and captions --------- */
0792   if ((DisplayBits==1)&&(DisplayPlanes==1))/* if a mono display... */
0793     {
0794     PrevFontColor= SetTextColor(hFrameDC,RGB(0,0,0));
0795     PrevBkColor=  SetBkColor(hFrameDC,RGB(255,255,255));
0796     }
0797   else                            /* else if a color display... */
0798     {
0799     PrevFontColor= SetTextColor(hFrameDC,RGB(191,191,191));
0800     PrevBkColor=  SetBkColor(hFrameDC,RGB(0,0,0));
0801     }
```

```
0802
0803   SetBkMode(hFrameDC,TRANSPARENT);
0804   Font= CreateFont(24, 0, 0, 0, FW_BOLD, FALSE, FALSE, FALSE,
0805         ANSI_CHARSET, OUT_DEFAULT_PRECIS, CLIP_DEFAULT_PRECIS,
0806         DRAFT_QUALITY, VARIABLE_PITCH | FF_SWISS, "Helv");
0807   PrevFont= SelectObject(hFrameDC,Font);
0808   TextOut(hFrameDC,10,10,"Advanced Animation Techniques:",30);
0809   Font= CreateFont(48, 0, 0, 0, FW_BOLD, FALSE, FALSE, FALSE,
0810         ANSI_CHARSET, OUT_DEFAULT_PRECIS, CLIP_DEFAULT_PRECIS,
0811         DRAFT_QUALITY, VARIABLE_PITCH | FF_SWISS, "Helv");
0812   SelectObject(hFrameDC,Font);
0813   TextOut(hFrameDC,8,28,"3D Visualizing",14);
0814   SelectObject(hFrameDC,PrevFont);
0815   TextOut(hFrameDC,10,234,"This exploding/imploding 3D solid is
             animated by",48);
0816   TextOut(hFrameDC,10,250,"adjusting the camera angle while
             simultaneously",47);
0817   TextOut(hFrameDC,10,266,"repositioning each 3D subobject that
             forms part of",50);
0818   TextOut(hFrameDC,10,282,"the whole solid.",16);
0819   SetBkMode(hFrameDC,OPAQUE);
0820   SetBkColor(hFrameDC,PrevBkColor);
0821   SetTextColor(hFrameDC,PrevFontColor);
0822
0823   /* --------- display the frame and save it to disk ----------- */
0824   zCopyToDisplay(hWnd);              /* copy hidden frame to display */
0825   bDiskResult= zSaveFrame(hFrame,lpFileName);       /* save file */
0826   if (bDiskResult==FALSE) return FALSE;        /* if disk error */
0827   return TRUE;
0828   }
0829   /*
0830   -------------------------------------------------------------------
0831                          Draw a cel.
0832   -------------------------------------------------------------------
0833                                                                    */
0834   static void zDrawCel(int Number)
0835   {
0836     int Locate= 27;
0837
0838   /* --------------- initialize the modeling color ------------- */
0839   zSetShadingColor(zBLUE);
0840
0841   /* ---------------- manage the moving viewpoint -------------- */
0842   zSetCameraDistance(360);  /* maintain camera-to-subject range... */
0843   switch (Number)
0844       {       /* ...while moving camera crane down and trucking right */
0845       case 1: zSetCameraPitch(340); zSetCameraHeading(340); break;
0846       case 2: zSetCameraPitch(338); zSetCameraHeading(335); break;
0847       case 3: zSetCameraPitch(336); zSetCameraHeading(330); break;
0848       case 4: zSetCameraPitch(334); zSetCameraHeading(325); break;
0849       case 5: zSetCameraPitch(332); zSetCameraHeading(320); break;
0850       case 6: zSetCameraPitch(330); zSetCameraHeading(315); break;
0851       case 7: zSetCameraPitch(328); zSetCameraHeading(310); break;
0852       case 8: zSetCameraPitch(326); zSetCameraHeading(305); break;
0853       }
0854
0855   /* ---------- manage the explosion/implosion of cube ---------- */
0856   switch (Number)
0857       {    /* draw single solid if cel 1, else adjust positioning... */
0858       case 1:
0859               zSetSubjectLocation(0,0,0); zSetSubjectAttitude(0,0,0);
```

```
0860          zSetSubjectSize(30,30,30); zDrawCube();
0861          return;
0862   case 2: Locate+= 4;
0863          break;
0864   case 3: Locate+= 8;
0865          break;
0866   case 4: Locate+= 12;
0867          break;
0868   case 5: Locate+= 16;
0869          break;
0870   case 6: Locate+= 20;
0871          break;
0872   case 7: Locate+= 24;
0873          break;
0874   case 8: Locate+= 28;
0875          break;
0876   }
0877 zSetSubjectLocation(0,-Locate,0); zSetSubjectSize(24,3,24);
0878 zDrawCube();                         /* component F (bottom) */
0879 zSetSubjectLocation(0,0,-Locate); zSetSubjectSize(24,30,3);
0880 zDrawCube();                         /* component D (back left) */
0881 zSetSubjectLocation(-Locate,0,0); zSetSubjectSize(3,30,30);
0882 zDrawCube();                         /* component A (back left) */
0883 zSetSubjectLocation(0,Locate,0); zSetSubjectSize(24,3,24);
0884 zDrawCube();                         /* component E (top) */
0885 zSetSubjectLocation(Locate,0,0); zSetSubjectSize(3,30,30);
0886 zDrawCube();                         /* component C (front right) */
0887 zSetSubjectLocation(0,0,Locate); zSetSubjectSize(24,30,3);
0888 zDrawCube();                         /* component B (front right) */
0889 return;
0890 }
0891 /*
0892 ------------------------------------------------------------------
0893                  ANIMATION PLAYBACK Functions
0894 ------------------------------------------------------------------
0895 ------------------------------------------------------------------
0896                     Display the next frame.
0897  This function is intelligent enough to discern between RAM-BASED
0898  FRAME ANIMATION (where all frames have already been loaded from
0899  disk and stored in RAM) and DISK-BASED FRAME ANIMATION (where
0900  each frame must be loaded from disk during playback).
0901 ------------------------------------------------------------------
0902                                                              */
0903 static void zShowNextFrame(HWND hWnd)
0904 {
0905   HDC hDC;
0906 if (bUseDisk==TRUE) goto DISK_PLAYBACK;
0907
0908 RAM_PLAYBACK:      /* if all frames have been loaded into RAM... */
0909 if (AnimationReady==FALSE) return;
0910 if (bAnimationLoaded==FALSE) return;
0911 if (Redisplay==TRUE) goto DISPLAY_FRAME;
0912 if (Pause==TRUE) return;
0913 if (FrameDirection==zFORWARD)
0914   {
0915   FrameNum++;
0916   if (FrameNum > zFINALFRAME) FrameNum= zFIRSTFRAME;
0917   }
0918 if (FrameDirection==zREVERSE)
0919   {
0920   FrameNum--;
```

```
0921      if (FrameNum < zFIRSTFRAME) FrameNum= zFINALFRAME;
0922      }
0923 DISPLAY_FRAME:
0924 hDC= GetDC(hWnd);
0925 switch (FrameNum)
0926      {
0927      case 1:
0928      case 2:
0929      case 3:
0930      case 4:
0931      case 5:
0932      case 6:   SelectObject(hFDC,hF1); break;
0933      case 7:   SelectObject(hFDC,hF2); break;
0934      case 8:   SelectObject(hFDC,hF3); break;
0935      case 9:   SelectObject(hFDC,hF4); break;
0936      case 10: SelectObject(hFDC,hF5); break;
0937      case 11: SelectObject(hFDC,hF6); break;
0938      case 12: SelectObject(hFDC,hF7); break;
0939      case 13:
0940      case 14:
0941      case 15:
0942      case 16:
0943      case 17:
0944      case 18: SelectObject(hFDC,hF8); break;
0945      case 19: SelectObject(hFDC,hF7); break;
0946      case 20: SelectObject(hFDC,hF6); break;
0947      case 21: SelectObject(hFDC,hF5); break;
0948      case 22: SelectObject(hFDC,hF4); break;
0949      case 23: SelectObject(hFDC,hF3); break;
0950      case 24: SelectObject(hFDC,hF2); break;
0951      }
0952 BitBlt(hDC,0,0,zFRAMEWIDE,zFRAMEHIGH,hFDC,0,0,SRCCOPY);
0953 ReleaseDC(hWnd,hDC);
0954 return;
0955
0956 DISK_PLAYBACK:   /* if loading each frame from disk as needed... */
0957 if (bAnimationHalted==TRUE) return;
0958 if (Redisplay==TRUE) goto SAME_FRAME;
0959 if (Pause==TRUE) return;
0960 if (FrameDirection==zFORWARD)
0961      {
0962      FrameNum++;
0963      if (FrameNum > zFINALFRAME) FrameNum= zFIRSTFRAME;
0964      }
0965 if (FrameDirection==zREVERSE)
0966      {
0967      FrameNum--;
0968      if (FrameNum < zFIRSTFRAME) FrameNum= zFINALFRAME;
0969      }
0970 SAME_FRAME:
0971 hDC= GetDC(hWnd);
0972 switch (FrameNum)
0973      {
0974      case 1:   bFrameLoaded= zLoadFrame(hFrame, (LPSTR) "OBJ3D1.BIT");
0975             break;
0976      case 2:   bFrameLoaded= zLoadFrame(hFrame, (LPSTR) "OBJ3D1.BIT");
0977             break;
0978      case 3:   bFrameLoaded= zLoadFrame(hFrame, (LPSTR) "OBJ3D1.BIT");
0979             break;
0980      case 4:   bFrameLoaded= zLoadFrame(hFrame, (LPSTR) "OBJ3D1.BIT");
0981             break;
```

```
0982    case 5:  bFrameLoaded= zLoadFrame(hFrame, (LPSTR) "OBJ3D1.BIT");
0983             break;
0984    case 6:  bFrameLoaded= zLoadFrame(hFrame, (LPSTR) "OBJ3D1.BIT");
0985             break;
0986    case 7:  bFrameLoaded= zLoadFrame(hFrame, (LPSTR) "OBJ3D2.BIT");
0987             break;
0988    case 8:  bFrameLoaded= zLoadFrame(hFrame, (LPSTR) "OBJ3D3.BIT");
0989             break;
0990    case 9:  bFrameLoaded= zLoadFrame(hFrame, (LPSTR) "OBJ3D4.BIT");
0991             break;
0992    case 10: bFrameLoaded= zLoadFrame(hFrame, (LPSTR) "OBJ3D5.BIT");
0993             break;
0994    case 11: bFrameLoaded= zLoadFrame(hFrame, (LPSTR) "OBJ3D6.BIT");
0995             break;
0996    case 12: bFrameLoaded= zLoadFrame(hFrame, (LPSTR) "OBJ3D7.BIT");
0997             break;
0998    case 13: bFrameLoaded= zLoadFrame(hFrame, (LPSTR) "OBJ3D8.BIT");
0999             break;
1000    case 14: bFrameLoaded= zLoadFrame(hFrame, (LPSTR) "OBJ3D8.BIT");
1001             break;
1002    case 15: bFrameLoaded= zLoadFrame(hFrame, (LPSTR) "OBJ3D8.BIT");
1003             break;
1004    case 16: bFrameLoaded= zLoadFrame(hFrame, (LPSTR) "OBJ3D8.BIT");
1005             break;
1006    case 17: bFrameLoaded= zLoadFrame(hFrame, (LPSTR) "OBJ3D8.BIT");
1007             break;
1008    case 18: bFrameLoaded= zLoadFrame(hFrame, (LPSTR) "OBJ3D8.BIT");
1009             break;
1010    case 19: bFrameLoaded= zLoadFrame(hFrame, (LPSTR) "OBJ3D7.BIT");
1011             break;
1012    case 20: bFrameLoaded= zLoadFrame(hFrame, (LPSTR) "OBJ3D6.BIT");
1013             break;
1014    case 21: bFrameLoaded= zLoadFrame(hFrame, (LPSTR) "OBJ3D5.BIT");
1015             break;
1016    case 22: bFrameLoaded= zLoadFrame(hFrame, (LPSTR) "OBJ3D4.BIT");
1017             break;
1018    case 23: bFrameLoaded= zLoadFrame(hFrame, (LPSTR) "OBJ3D3.BIT");
1019             break;
1020    case 24: bFrameLoaded= zLoadFrame(hFrame, (LPSTR) "OBJ3D2.BIT");
1021             break;
1022    }
1023  if (bFrameLoaded==FALSE)
1024    {
1025    bAnimationHalted= TRUE;
1026    MessageBeep(0);
1027    LoadString(hInst,IDS_Unexpected,lpCaption,Max);
1028    LoadString(hInst,IDS_Disk3,lpMessage,MaxText);
1029    TimerCounter= zTIMER_PAUSE;
1030    MessageBox(GetFocus(),lpMessage,lpCaption,MB_OK);
1031    return;
1032    }
1033  BitBlt(hDC,0,0,zFRAMEWIDE,zFRAMEHIGH,hFrameDC,0,0,SRCCOPY);
1034  ReleaseDC(hWnd,hDC);
1035  return;
1036  }
1037  /*
1038  ------------------------------------------------------------------
1039             Load the animation sequence from disk.
1040    If memory limitations prevent this function from loading the
1041    entire animation sequence into RAM, it sets a token to FALSE.
1042    In that case the playback function zShowNextFrame() will load
```

```
1043      each frame from disk as required during animation playback,
1044      otherwise all frames are expected to be in RAM.
1045   --------------------------------------------------------------
1046                                                                */
1047   static void zLoadAnimation(HWND hWnd)
1048   {
1049      HDC hDC;
1050
1051   if (FrameReady==FALSE)          /* if no hidden-frame available... */
1052      {
1053      MessageBeep(0);
1054      LoadString(hInst,IDS_NotReady,lpCaption,Max);
1055      LoadString(hInst,IDS_NoFrame,lpMessage,MaxText);
1056      MessageBox(GetFocus(),lpMessage,lpCaption,MB_OK);
1057      return;
1058      }
1059   if (bAnimationLoaded==TRUE)         /* if frames already loaded... */
1060      {
1061      MessageBeep(0);
1062      LoadString(hInst,IDS_Unexpected,lpCaption,Max);
1063      LoadString(hInst,IDS_Disk4,lpMessage,MaxText);
1064      TimerCounter= zTIMER_PAUSE;
1065      MessageBox(GetFocus(),lpMessage,lpCaption,MB_OK);
1066      return;
1067      }
1068   if (bPrevLoadAttempt==TRUE)       /* if previous attempt failed... */
1069      {
1070      MessageBeep(0);
1071      LoadString(hInst,IDS_Unexpected,lpCaption,Max);
1072      LoadString(hInst,IDS_Disk5,lpMessage,MaxText);
1073      TimerCounter= zTIMER_PAUSE;
1074      MessageBox(GetFocus(),lpMessage,lpCaption,MB_OK);
1075      return;
1076      }
1077   bPrevLoadAttempt= TRUE;
1078
1079   /* -------------- create bitmaps to hold the frames ------------ */
1080   GlobalCompact((DWORD)-1L);           /* maximize contiguous memory */
1081   hDC= GetDC(hWnd);
1082   hFDC= CreateCompatibleDC(hDC);
1083   hF1= CreateCompatibleBitmap(hDC,zFRAMEWIDE,zFRAMEHIGH);
1084   if (hF1==NULL) goto F1;
1085   hF2= CreateCompatibleBitmap(hDC,zFRAMEWIDE,zFRAMEHIGH);
1086   if (hF2==NULL) goto F2;
1087   hF3= CreateCompatibleBitmap(hDC,zFRAMEWIDE,zFRAMEHIGH);
1088   if (hF3==NULL) goto F3;
1089   hF4= CreateCompatibleBitmap(hDC,zFRAMEWIDE,zFRAMEHIGH);
1090   if (hF4==NULL) goto F4;
1091   hF5= CreateCompatibleBitmap(hDC,zFRAMEWIDE,zFRAMEHIGH);
1092   if (hF5==NULL) goto F5;
1093   hF6= CreateCompatibleBitmap(hDC,zFRAMEWIDE,zFRAMEHIGH);
1094   if (hF6==NULL) goto F6;
1095   hF7= CreateCompatibleBitmap(hDC,zFRAMEWIDE,zFRAMEHIGH);
1096   if (hF7==NULL) goto F7;
1097   hF8= CreateCompatibleBitmap(hDC,zFRAMEWIDE,zFRAMEHIGH);
1098   if (hF8==NULL) goto F8;
1099   goto BITMAPS_OK;
1100
1101   F8:  DeleteObject(hF7);
1102   F7:  DeleteObject(hF6);
1103   F6:  DeleteObject(hF5);
```

```
1104   F5:   DeleteObject(hF4);
1105   F4:   DeleteObject(hF3);
1106   F3:   DeleteObject(hF2);
1107   F2:   DeleteObject(hF1);
1108   F1:   DeleteDC(hFDC); ReleaseDC(hWnd,hDC);
1109         bUseDisk= TRUE; AnimationReady= TRUE;
1110         LoadString(hInst,IDS_Status,lpCaption,Max);
1111         LoadString(hInst,IDS_Disk6,lpMessage,MaxText);
1112         MessageBox(GetFocus(),lpMessage,lpCaption,MB_OK);
1113         return;
1114   BITMAPS_OK: ReleaseDC(hWnd,hDC);
1115
1116   /* ------------- load frame files into the bitmaps ------------- */
1117   bFrameLoaded= zLoadFrame(hF1, (LPSTR) "OBJ3D1.BIT");
1118   if (bFrameLoaded==FALSE) goto DISK_ERROR;
1119   bFrameLoaded= zLoadFrame(hF2, (LPSTR) "OBJ3D2.BIT");
1120   if (bFrameLoaded==FALSE) goto DISK_ERROR;
1121   bFrameLoaded= zLoadFrame(hF3, (LPSTR) "OBJ3D3.BIT");
1122   if (bFrameLoaded==FALSE) goto DISK_ERROR;
1123   bFrameLoaded= zLoadFrame(hF4, (LPSTR) "OBJ3D4.BIT");
1124   if (bFrameLoaded==FALSE) goto DISK_ERROR;
1125   bFrameLoaded= zLoadFrame(hF5, (LPSTR) "OBJ3D5.BIT");
1126   if (bFrameLoaded==FALSE) goto DISK_ERROR;
1127   bFrameLoaded= zLoadFrame(hF6, (LPSTR) "OBJ3D6.BIT");
1128   if (bFrameLoaded==FALSE) goto DISK_ERROR;
1129   bFrameLoaded= zLoadFrame(hF7, (LPSTR) "OBJ3D7.BIT");
1130   if (bFrameLoaded==FALSE) goto DISK_ERROR;
1131   bFrameLoaded= zLoadFrame(hF8, (LPSTR) "OBJ3D8.BIT");
1132   if (bFrameLoaded==FALSE) goto DISK_ERROR;
1133   goto DISK_OK;
1134
1135   DISK_ERROR:
1136     DeleteObject(hF1); DeleteObject(hF2); DeleteObject(hF3);
1137     DeleteObject(hF4); DeleteObject(hF5); DeleteObject(hF6);
1138     DeleteObject(hF7); DeleteObject(hF8); DeleteDC(hFDC);
1139     return;
1140
1141   /* -------------------- tidy up and return -------------------- */
1142   DISK_OK:
1143   hPrevF= SelectObject(hFDC,hF1);                    /* select bitmap */
1144   bAnimationLoaded= TRUE;
1145   AnimationReady= TRUE;
1146   bAnimationSaved= TRUE;
1147   MessageBeep(0);
1148   LoadString(hInst,IDS_AnimReady,lpCaption,Max);
1149   LoadString(hInst,IDS_Disk7,lpMessage,MaxText);
1150   MessageBox(GetFocus(),lpMessage,lpCaption,MB_OK);
1151   return;
1152   }
1153   /*
1154   -----------------------------------------------------------------
1155                      Reset the animation frame rate.
1156   -----------------------------------------------------------------
1157                                                                   */
1158   static void zSetFrameRate(HWND hWnd, WORD wNewRate)
1159   {
1160   if (TimerExists==FALSE)
1161     {
1162     wFrameRate= wPrevRate;
1163     MessageBeep(0);
1164     LoadString(hInst,IDS_NotReady,lpCaption,Max);
```

**16-6** Continued.

```
1165    LoadString(hInst,IDS_NoReset,lpMessage,MaxText);
1166    MessageBox(GetFocus(),lpMessage,lpCaption,MB_OK);
1167    return;
1168    }
1169 switch (wPrevRate)
1170    {
1171    case 55:  CheckMenuItem(hMenu,IDM_FPS182,MF_UNCHECKED); break;
1172    case 110: CheckMenuItem(hMenu,IDM_FPS91,MF_UNCHECKED); break;
1173    case 165: CheckMenuItem(hMenu,IDM_FPS61,MF_UNCHECKED); break;
1174    case 220: CheckMenuItem(hMenu,IDM_FPS45,MF_UNCHECKED); break;
1175    case 275: CheckMenuItem(hMenu,IDM_FPS36,MF_UNCHECKED); break;
1176    case 330: CheckMenuItem(hMenu,IDM_FPS30,MF_UNCHECKED); break;
1177    }
1178 KillTimer(hWnd,1);
1179 TimerID1= SetTimer(hWnd,1,wNewRate,(FARPROC) NULL);
1180 if (TimerID1==0)
1181    {
1182    LoadString(hInst,IDS_NotReady,lpCaption,Max);
1183    LoadString(hInst,IDS_CannotReset,lpMessage,MaxText);
1184    MessageBox(GetFocus(),lpMessage,lpCaption,MB_OK);
1185    TimerExists= FALSE;
1186    return;
1187    }
1188 switch (wFrameRate)
1189    {
1190    case 55:  CheckMenuItem(hMenu,IDM_FPS182,MF_CHECKED); break;
1191    case 110: CheckMenuItem(hMenu,IDM_FPS91,MF_CHECKED); break;
1192    case 165: CheckMenuItem(hMenu,IDM_FPS61,MF_CHECKED); break;
1193    case 220: CheckMenuItem(hMenu,IDM_FPS45,MF_CHECKED); break;
1194    case 275: CheckMenuItem(hMenu,IDM_FPS36,MF_CHECKED); break;
1195    case 330: CheckMenuItem(hMenu,IDM_FPS30,MF_CHECKED); break;
1196    }
1197 return;
1198 }
1199 /*
1200 ------------------------------------------------------------------
1201                        End of the C source file
1202 ------------------------------------------------------------------
1203                                                              */
```

# A

# *Compiling the sample programs with Microsoft C*

If you are using Microsoft C and the Microsoft Windows Software Development Kit (SDK) you can build all of the sample applications in the book with your compiler. Whether you are using the source files on the companion disk or working with the program listings in the book, you can build each program as is, without breaking open the source code. Each application can be compiled, linked, and stamped in its current form—no modifications are required if you are running Microsoft C and the SDK.

Each demo program has been validated using Microsoft C 6.0A and version 3.0 of the SDK. The programs are also designed to work smoothly with Microsoft C/C++ 7.0 and version 3.1 of the SDK.

This appendix explains how to access the source code, how to configure your system, and how to use your compiler's command-line to build the sample applications. The discussion attempts to be practical and hands-on, no matter whether you are a beginner, intermediate, or expert. If you are an experienced programmer, you will already be familiar with many of the topics presented here. If you are a beginner, you can find more information in the documentation for your compiler.

## Working with the source code

The source code for the demo programs is available in two formats—as production files on the companion disk and as program listings in the book. Both variations are taken directly from the production files on the author's hard disk.

If you are using the companion disk, simply copy the production files to your hard disk and you are ready to begin building the sample applications with Microsoft C and the SDK.

If you are working from the book, you must use a text editor or word processor to create production files from the program listings before you can begin building the sample applications with Microsoft C and the SDK.

## Using the companion disk

If you are working with the companion disk, use DOS or the Windows File Manager to copy the production files from the disk to an appropriate directory on your hard disk. The companion disk contains a .def module definition file, an .h #include file, an .rc resource script file, and a .c source file for each sample application. The disk also contains additional modules—.c source files that are common to many of the demo programs. The frame animation demos, for example, each use a common .c module named storage.c that provides disk input/output functions. The 3D demos use a common .c module named lib3d.c.

The .mak files on the companion disk are intended to be used with QuickC for Windows. Do not use the .mak files with Microsoft C and the SDK.

## Using the program listings

If you are working directly from the book, use your favorite text editor or word processor to create an ASCII text file from the listings. Do not type the line numbers that appear along the left margin of each program listing. These line numbers were inserted by me to make it easier for the text discussion to refer to specific portions of the source code. The line numbers are not part of the source code.

# Configuring your system

During installation of your Microsoft C and SDK packages, be sure to select both small and medium memory model libraries and choose Windows capability. This ensures that the appropriate runtime libraries are installed on your hard disk. Each sample application in the book uses the small memory model.

During a working session the Microsoft compilers and the linker must be able to find your source files, the #include files, and the library files. You can facilitate this accessibility by ensuring that your autoexec.bat and config.sys files are up to date, containing the appropriate set path, set include, and set lib statements. During installation the Microsoft setup software offers to add these statements to your autoexec.bat and config.sys files. Alternatively, you can elect to perform this chore yourself.

# Building an application

Building a Windows application with Microsoft C and the SDK is a straightforward operation that follows the three-step, compile-link-stamp process used throughout the book. This command-line approach provides a consistent, reliable development environment. See FIG. 1-2 in chapter 1 for a schematic that illustrates a generic set of command lines.

## The working directory

Before beginning the compile session, make the directory that contains the source files the current directory. For example, if the source files are in a directory named c:\source, then type the following line at the DOS prompt:

    cd c:\source <enter>

where <enter> refers to pressing the Enter key.

## Compiling the production files

To compile the production files into object code, use the following command-line:

    cl -c -AS -Os -Gsw -Zpe -W2 *file.c* <enter>

Note that the file name, *file.c*, is a placeholder for the particular file that you are compiling. If you are compiling detect.c, type detect.c instead of *file.c*. If you are building an application comprised of multiple .c source files, you must use the command line separately for each of the source modules. If you are building running.c, for example, you would execute the command line once using detect.c as the file name and once again using storage.c as the file name. If you are building spatial.c, you would run the command line once using spatial.c as the file name, once again using storage.c as the file name, and once again using lib3d.c as the file name. When typing the command line, use the same uppercase and lowercase characters shown here in the example.

If the sample application uses floating-point math, you must insert the -FPi mnemonic in the command line. The source files spatial.c, image3D.c, and lib3d.c should be compiled with the following command line:

    cl -c -AS -Os -Gsw -Zpe -W2 -FPi *file.c* <enter>

## Linking the object files

After you have successfully compiled all the .c source files that make up the application, you must link together the resulting object files with the required runtime libraries and the import library. The import library provides access to the functions built into GDI.EXE and other dynamic link libraries provided by the retail version of Windows.

Use the following command line to invoke the linker:

    link /al:16 /NOD *file.obj*, *file.exe*,,LIBW SLIBCEW,*file.def* <enter>

Use the same uppercase and lowercase characters shown here in the example. Type the command line as a single, uninterrupted string. Do not press Enter until the end of the command line, even if it wraps around to the left side of the display while you are typing.

In the example shown here, the name *file.obj* is a placeholder for the object file you created with the compiler in the previous step. If you compiled detect.c, for example, the resulting object file is named detect.obj. Insert the file name detect.obj instead of file.obj. Also insert the file name of the desired executable instead of *file.exe*, and insert the file name of the appropriate module definition file instead of *file.def*.

If you are building an application comprised of numerous object files, you must name each object file on the command line. If, for example, you are building running.c, you must name both running.obj and storage.obj. The following command line format is used:

link /al:16 /NOD *file1.obj,file2.obj,file.exe*,,LIBW SLIBCEW,*file.def* ⟨enter⟩

In the example shown here LIBW is the import library that allows your code to call functions in Windows' dynamic link libraries, gdi.exe, user.exe, and kernel.exe. SLIBCEW is the Windows-compatible C runtime library.

If you are building an application that uses floating-point math, you must add the name of the WIN87EM library file to the linker command line. Here is an example:

link /al:16 /NOD *file.obj,file.exe*,,LIBW SLIBCEW WIN87EM,*file.def* ⟨enter⟩

This rule may not apply if you wish the resulting executable to run only on machines equipped with a floating-point math coprocessor. Refer to the Microsoft C documentation for more information. Using the example linker command line shown here will produce an executable that will run on any compatible personal computer, whether or not a math coprocessor is present.

## Stamping the executable

To compile the .rc resource script file, attach the resources to the executable, and stamp the resulting executable, you should type the following command line in order to invoke the resource compiler:

rc *file.rc* ⟨enter⟩

The file name *file.rc* is a placeholder for the name of the application you are building. If you are building detect.c, for example, you would insert the file name detect.rc instead of *file.rc*. If you are building spatial.c, you would insert the file name spatial.rc instead of *file.rc*.

When it is attaching the resources to the executable, the resource compiler also stamps the executable file with the Windows version number. If the version number is missing from the header of the executable file, Windows may refuse to launch the application. An application stamped with version 3.0 can usually run under Windows 3.0, Windows 3.1, and newer versions.

## Launching the application

To launch the application and exercise its features, choose Run . . . from the File menu of Windows Program Manager. When you are prompted, type the full path name of the demo program. For example, if you used Microsoft C to compile the program into a directory named c:\source, you would type:

c:\source\*filename.exe*

Substitute the name of the appropriate executable file for the filename.exe placeholder used in this example.

# Validation suite

Every application in the book has been built using Microsoft C 6.0A and SDK 3.0 on a 33 MHz Intel 80386DX personal computer equipped with 4 MB RAM and a VGA display system.

Each resulting executable was launched in Microsoft Windows and run under the following Windows display modes: 640-×-480-×-16 color VGA, 800-×-600-×-16 color SVGA, 1024-×-768-×-16 color XGA, 640-×-480-×-2 color VGA and MCGA, 640-×-350-×-16 color EGA, 640-×-350-×-2 color EGA, and 720-×-348-×-2 color Hercules. Where appropriate, the 640-×-480-×-256 color SVGA mode was also tested.

# B
# *Compiling the sample programs with QuickC for Windows*

If you are using QuickC for Windows you can build all of the sample applications in the book with your compiler. Whether you are using the source files on the companion disk or working with the program listings in the book, you can build each program as is, without breaking open the source code. No modifications are required if you are running QuickC for Windows—each demo program has been validated using QuickC for Windows version 1.00.

## Working with the source code

The source code for the demo programs is available in two formats—as production files on the companion disk and as program listings in the book. Both variations are taken directly from the production files on the author's hard disk.

If you are using the companion disk, simply copy the production files to your hard disk and you are ready to begin building the sample applications with QuickC for Windows.

If you are working from the book, you must use a text editor or word processor to create production files from the program listings before you can begin building the sample applications with QuickC for Windows.

## Using the companion disk

If you are working with the companion disk, use DOS or the Windows File Manager to copy the production files from the disk to an appropriate directory on your hard disk. The companion disk contains a .mak project file, a .def module definition file, an .h #include file, an .rc resource script file, and a .c source file for each sample application. The disk also contains additional modules—.c source files that are common to many of the demo programs. The frame animation demos, for example, each use a common .c module named storage.c that provides disk input/output functions. The 3D demos use a common .c module named lib3d.c.

The .mak files on the companion disk are explicitly intended for use with QuickC for Windows. Simply select Open . . . from the Project menu and choose the appropriate .mak file. Choose Build from the Project menu to build the application, then click Restart from the Run menu to launch the application.

## Using the program listings

If you are working directly from the book, use the QuickC for Windows editor or your favorite word processor to create a text file from the listings. Do not type the line numbers that appear along the left margin of each program listing. These line numbers were inserted by the author to make it easier for the text discussion to refer to specific portions of the source code. The line numbers are not part of the source code.

Before you can build the application you must create a .mak file. This file contains a list of the .def, .h, .rc, and .c files that QuickC for Windows will use to build the finished application. To create the .mak file choose Open . . . from the Project menu and type the name of the new .mak file. Then use the mouse to select the various .def, .h, .rc, and .c files that make up the project. To build the application, click Build from the Project menu. Then select Restart from the Run menu to launch the application.

## Configuring your system

During installation of your QuickC for Windows package, be sure to select both small and medium memory model libraries. This ensures that the appropriate runtime libraries are installed on your hard disk and can be found by the QuickC for Windows compiler, which itself is a dynamic link library (DLL). Each sample application in the book uses the small memory model.

## Validation suite

Every application in the book was built using QuickC for Windows version 1.00 on a 33 MHz Intel 80386DX personal computer equipped with 4 MB RAM and a VGA display system.

Each resulting executable was launched in Microsoft Windows and run under the following Windows display modes: 640-×-480-×-16 color VGA, 800-×-600-×-16 color SVGA, 1024-×-768-×-16 color XGA, 640-×-480-×-2 color VGA and MCGA, and 640-×-350-×-16 color EGA. Where appropriate, the 640×480×256-color SVGA mode was also tested.

# C
# *Compiling the sample programs with Borland C++*

If you are using Borland C++ you can build all of the sample applications in the book with your compiler. Whether you are using the source files on the companion disk or working with the program listings in the book, you can build each program as is, without breaking open the source code. Each application can be compiled, linked, and stamped in its current form—no modifications are required if you are running Borland C++.

Each demo program has been validated using Borland C++ 2.0. The programs are also designed to work smoothly with Borland C++ 3.0.

This appendix explains how to access the source code, how to configure your system, and how to use your compiler's command line to build the sample applications. If you prefer instead to use the integrated development environment of the Turbo C++ editor provided with Borland C++ 3.0, you should refer to Appendix D.

The discussion here attempts to be practical and hands-on, no matter whether you are a beginner, intermediate, or expert. If you are an experienced programmer, you will already be familiar with many of the topics presented here. If you are a beginner, you can find more information in the documentation for your compiler.

## Working with the source code

The source code for the demo programs is available in two formats—as production files on the companion disk and as program listings in the book. Both variations are taken directly from the production files on the author's hard disk.

If you are using the companion disk, simply copy the production files to

577

your hard disk and you are ready to begin building the sample applications with Borland C++.

If you are working from the book, you must use a text editor or word processor to create production files from the program listings before you can begin building the sample applications with Borland C++.

## Using the companion disk

If you are working with the companion disk, use DOS or the Windows File Manager to copy the production files from the disk to an appropriate directory on your hard disk. The companion disk contains a .def module definition file, an .h #include file, an .rc resource script file, and a .c source file for each sample application. The disk also contains additional modules—.c source files that are common to many of the demo programs. The frame animation demos, for example, each use a common .c module named storage.c that provides disk input/output functions. The 3D demos use a common .c module named lib3d.c.

The .mak files on the companion disk are intended to be used with QuickC for Windows, and are not for use with Borland C++.

## Using the program listings

If you are working directly from the book, use your favorite text editor or word processor to create an ASCII text file from the listings. Do not type the line numbers that appear along the left margin of each program listing. These line numbers were inserted by the author to make it easier for the text discussion to refer to specific portions of the source code. The line numbers are not part of the source code.

# Configuring your system

During installation of your Borland C++ package, be sure to select both small and medium memory model libraries and choose Windows capability. This ensures that the appropriate runtime libraries are installed on your hard disk. Each sample application in the book uses the small memory model.

During a working session the Borland C++ compilers and the linker must be able to find your source files, the #include files, and the library files. You can facilitate this accessibility by ensuring that your autoexec.bat and config.sys files are up to date, containing the appropriate set path, set include, and set lib statements. During installation the Borland C++ setup software offers to add these statements to your autoexec.bat and config.sys files. Alternatively, you can elect to perform this chore yourself.

# Building an application

Building a Windows application with Borland C++ is a straightforward operation that follows the three-step, compile-link-stamp process used throughout the book. This command-line approach provides a consistent, reliable development environment. See FIG. 1-2 in chapter 1 for a schematic that illustrates a generic set of command lines.

## The working directory

Before beginning the compile session, make the directory that contains the source files the current directory. For example, if the source files are in a directory named c:\source, then type the following line at the DOS prompt:

    cd c:\source <enter>

where <enter> refers to pressing the Enter key.

## Compiling the production files

To compile the production files into object code, use the following command line:

    BCC -W -c file.c <enter>

Note that the file name, file.c, is a placeholder for the particular file that you are compiling. If you are compiling detect.c, type detect.c instead of file.c. If you are building an application comprised of multiple .c source files, you must use the command line separately for each of the source modules. If you are building running.c, for example, you would execute the command line once using detect.c as the file name and once again using storage.c as the file name. If you are building spatial.c, you would run the command line once using spatial.c as the file name, once again using storage.c as the file name, and once again using lib3d.c as the file name.

When typing the command line, use the same uppercase and lowercase characters shown here in the example.

## Linking the object files

After you have successfully compiled all the .c source files that make up the application, you must link together the resulting object files with the required runtime libraries and the import library. The import library provides access to the functions built into GDI.EXE and other dynamic link libraries provided by the retail version of Windows.

Use the following command line to invoke the linker:

    TLINK /Tw /c /LC:\BORLANDC\LIB C0WS.OBJ file.obj,file.exe,,IMPORT CWINS
    CS,file.def <enter>

Use the same uppercase and lowercase characters shown here in the example. Type the command line as a single, uninterrupted string. Do not press Enter until the end of the command line, even if it wraps around to the left side of the display while you are typing.

In the example shown here, the name *file.obj* is a placeholder for the object file you created with the compiler in the previous step. If you compiled detect.c, for example, the resulting object file is named detect.obj. Insert the file name detect.obj instead of *file.obj*. Also insert the file name of the desired executable instead of *file.exe*, and insert the file name of the appropriate module definition file instead of *file.def*. The /L switch denotes the directory where the C runtime libraries are found.

If you are building an application comprised of numerous object files, you must name each object file on the command line. If, for example, you are building running.c, you must name both running.obj and storage.obj. The following command line format is used:

TLINK /Tw /c /LC:\BORLANDC\LIB C0WS.OBJ *file1.obj file2.obj,file.exe,,*IMPORT CWINS CS,*file.def* <enter>

In the example shown here, IMPORT is the import library that allows your code to call functions in Windows' dynamic link libraries, gdi.exe, user.exe, and kernel.exe. CWINS and CS are Windows-compatible C runtime libraries. C0WS.OBJ contains startup code for the small memory model.

If you are building an application that uses floating-point math, you must add the name of the MATHX library file to the linker command line. Here is an example:

TLINK /Tw /c /LC:\BORLANDC\LIB C0WS.OBJ *file.obj,file.exe,,*IMPORT CWINS MATHX CS,*file.def* <enter>

This rule may not apply if you wish the resulting executable to run only on machines equipped with a floating-point math coprocessor. Refer to the Borland C++ documentation for more information. Using the example linker command line shown here will produce an executable that will run on any compatible personal computer, whether or not a math coprocessor is present.

## Stamping the executable

To compile the .rc resource script file, attach the resources to the executable, and stamp the resulting executable, you should type the following command line in order to invoke the resource compiler:

rc *file.rc* <enter>

The file name *file.rc* is a placeholder for the name of the application you are building. If you are building detect.c, for example, you would insert the file name detect.rc instead of *file.rc*. If you are building spatial.c, you would insert the file name spatial.rc instead of *file.rc*.

When it is attaching the resources to the executable, the resource compiler also stamps the executable file with the Windows version number. If the version number is missing from the header of the executable file, Windows may refuse to launch the application. An application stamped with version 3.0 can usually run under Windows 3.0, Windows 3.1, and newer versions.

## Launching the application

To launch the application and exercise its features, choose Run . . . from the File menu of Windows Program Manager. When you are prompted, type the full path name of the demo program. For example, if you used Borland C++ to compile the program into a directory named c:\source, you would type:

    c:\source\filename.exe

Substitute the name of the appropriate executable file for the filename.exe placeholder used in this example.

# Validation suite

Every application in the book has been built using Borland C++ 2.0 on a 33 MHz Intel 80386DX personal computer equipped with 4 MB RAM and a VGA display system. Each resulting executable was launched in Microsoft Windows and run under the 640-$\times$-480-$\times$-16 color display mode.

# D
# Compiling the sample programs with Turbo C++ for Windows

If you are using Turbo C++ for Windows you can build all of the sample applications in the book with your compiler. Whether you are using the source files on the companion disk or working with the program listings in the book, you can build each program as is, without breaking open the source code. No modifications are required if you are running Turbo C++ for Windows—each demo program has been validated using Turbo C++ for Windows version 3.0.

## Working with the source code

The source code for the demo programs is available in two formats—as production files on the companion disk and as program listings in the book. Both variations are taken directly from the production files on the author's hard disk.

If you are using the companion disk, simply copy the production files to your hard disk and you are ready to begin building the sample applications with Turbo C++ for Windows.

If you are working from the book, you must use a text editor or word processor to create production files from the program listings before you can begin building the sample applications with Turbo C++ for Windows.

## Using the companion disk

If you are working with the companion disk, use DOS or the Windows File Manager to copy the production files from the disk to an appropriate directory on your hard disk. The companion disk contains a .def module definition file, an .h #include file, an .rc resource script file, and a .c source file for each sample application. The disk also contains additional modules—.c source files that are common to many of the demo programs. The frame animation demos, for example, each use a common .c module named storage.c that provides disk input/output functions. The 3D demos use a common .c module named lib3d.c.

The .mak files on the companion disk are intended for use with QuickC for Windows. They will not work with Turbo C++ for Windows, which uses .prj files instead. To create a .prj file, use the Project menu and type the name of the new .prj file. Then use the mouse to select the project dependency files, which include the .c, .def, and .rc files that TurboC++ for Windows needs to build the finished executable. (Instead of the .rc file, Turbo C++ for Windows actually uses the .res file, however, which you must pre-compile using the supplied Resource Workshop tool.) Do not name the .h file in the .prj file. To build the sample application select Make from the Compile menu. Then choose Run to launch the program.

## Using the program listings

If you are working directly from the book, use the Turbo C++ for Windows editor or your favorite word processor to create a text file from the listings. Do not type the line numbers that appear along the left margin of each program listing. These line numbers were inserted by the author to make it easier for the text discussion to refer to specific portions of the source code. The line numbers are not part of the source code.

Before you can build the application you must create a .prj file. This file contains a list of the .def, .rc, and .c files that Turbo C++ for Windows will use to build the finished application. To create a .prj file, use the Project menu and type the name of the new .prj file. Then use the mouse to select the project dependency files, which include the .c, .def, and .rc files that TurboC++ for Windows needs to build the finished executable. (Instead of the .rc file, Turbo C++ for Windows actually uses the .res file, however, which must be pre-compiled using the Resource Workshop tool.) Do not name the .h file in the .prj file. To build the sample application select Make from the Compile menu. Then choose Run to launch the program.

## Using the Resource Workshop

You can use the Resource Workshop tool to pre-compile the project's .rc file into a .res file. Select Preferences from the File menu and add the paths of your include directory and source directory to Include Path. Set Multi-save .RES to on. Then choose Save Project.

The resulting .res file is used by Turbo C++ for Windows during a build, although it is the .rc file that is named in the .prj file.

## Configuring your system

During installation of your Turbo C++ for Windows package, be sure to select both small and medium memory model libraries. This ensures that the appropriate runtime libraries are installed on your hard disk and can be found by the Turbo C++ for Windows compiler. Each sample application in the book uses the small memory model.

Be sure to install the Resource Workshop. You will need this tool in order to compile the .rc files into .res files.

The first time you start Turbo C++ for Windows, select Directories from the Options menu and add the appropriate paths to Include Directory and Output Directory.

To keep your compile sessions tidy, choose Frequent errors from the Messages submenu, which appears on the Compiler submenu under the Options menu. Disable the item titled Parameter.

## Validation suite

Every application in the book was built using Turbo C++ for Windows version 3.0 on a 33 MHz Intel 80386DX personal computer equipped with 4 MB RAM and a VGA display system.

Each resulting executable was launched in Microsoft Windows and run under the following Windows display modes: 640-×-480-×-16 color VGA, 800-×-600-×-16 color SVGA, 1024-×-768×-16 color XGA, 640-×-480-×-2 color VGA and MCGA, and 640-×-350-×-16 color EGA. Where appropriate, the 640-×-480-×-256 color SVGA mode was also tested.

# E
# *Compiling sample programs with Symantec Zortech C++*

If you are using Symantec Zortech C++ you can build all of the sample applications in the book with your compiler. Whether you are using the source files on the companion disk or working with the program listings in the book, you can build each program as is, without breaking open the source code. Each application can be compiled, linked, and stamped in its current form—no modifications are required if you are running Zortech C++. Each demo program in the book has been explicitly validated using Zortech C++ 3.0.

This appendix explains how to access the source code, how to configure your system, and how to use your compiler's command line to build the sample applications.

The discussion here attempts to be practical and hands-on, no matter whether you are a beginner, intermediate, or expert. If you are an experienced programmer, you will already be familiar with many of the topics presented here. If you are a beginner, you can find more information in the documentation for your compiler.

## Working with the source code

The source code for the demo programs is available in two formats—as production files on the companion disk and as program listings in the book. Both variations are taken directly from the production files on the author's hard disk.

If you are using the companion disk, simply copy the production files to your hard disk and you are ready to begin building the sample applications with Zortech C++.

If you are working from the book, you must use a text editor or word processor to create production files from the program listings before you can begin building the sample applications with Zortech C++.

## Using the companion disk

If you are working with the companion disk, use DOS or the Windows File Manager to copy the production files from the disk to an appropriate directory on your hard disk. The companion disk contains a .def module definition file, an .h #include file, an .rc resource script file, and a .c source file for each sample application. The disk also contains additional modules—.c source files that are common to many of the demo programs. The frame animation demos, for example, each use a common .c module named storage.c that provides disk input/output functions. The 3D demos use a common .c module named lib3d.c.

The .mak files on the companion disk are intended to be used with QuickC for Windows, and are not for use with Zortech C++.

## Using the program listings

If you are working directly from the book, use your favorite text editor or word processor to create an ASCII text file from the listings. Do not type the line numbers that appear along the left margin of each program listing. These line numbers were inserted by the author to make it easier for the text discussion to refer to specific portions of the source code. The line numbers are not part of the source code.

# Configuring your system

During installation of your Symantec Zortech C++ package, be sure to select both small and medium memory model libraries and choose Windows capability. This ensures that the appropriate runtime libraries are installed on your hard disk. Each sample application in the book uses the small memory model.

During a working session the Zortech C++ compilers and the linker must be able to find your source files, the #include files, and the library files. You can facilitate this accessibility by ensuring that your autoexec.bat and config.sys files are up to date, containing the appropriate set path, set include, and set lib statements.

# Building an application

Building a Windows application with Zortech C++ is a straightforward operation that follows the three-step, compile-link-stamp process used throughout the book. This command-line approach provides a consistent, reliable development environment. See FIG. 1-2 in chapter 1 for a schematic that illustrates a generic set of command lines.

## The working directory

Before beginning the compile session, make the directory that contains the source files the current directory. For example, if the source files are in a directory named c:\source, then type the following line at the DOS prompt:

    cd c:\source <enter>

where <enter> refers to pressing the Enter key.

## Compiling the production files

To compile the production files into object code, use the following command line:

    ZTC -c -v -W file.c <enter>

Note that the file name, *file.c*, is a placeholder for the particular file that you are compiling. If you are compiling detect.c, type detect.c instead of *file.c*. If you are building an application comprised of multiple .c source files, you must use the command line separately for each of the source modules. If you are building running.c, for example, you would execute the command line once using detect.c as the file name and once again using storage.c as the file name. If you are building spatial.c, you would run the command line once using spatial.c as the file name, once again using storage.c as the file name, and once again using lib3d.c as the file name.

When typing the command line, use the same uppercase and lowercase characters shown here in the example.

## Linking the object files

After you have successfully compiled all the .c source files that make up the application, you must link together the resulting object files with the required runtime libraries and the import library. The import library provides access to the functions built into GDI.EXE and other dynamic link libraries provided by the retail version of Windows. Use the following command line to invoke the linker:

    BLINK file/al:16,file,,/NOD LIBW ZWS,file.def <enter>

Use the same uppercase and lowercase characters shown here in the example. Type the command line as a single, uninterrupted string. Do not press Enter until the end of the command line, even if it wraps around to the left side of the display while you are typing.

In the example shown here, the name *file* is a placeholder for the object file you created with the compiler in the previous step. If you compiled detect.c, for example, the resulting object file is named detect.obj. Insert the file name detect instead of *file*. Also insert the file name of the appropriate module definition file instead of *file.def*.

If you are building an application comprised of numerous object files, you must name each object file on the command line. If, for example, you are building running.c, you must name both running.obj and storage.obj. The following command-line format is used:

BLINK *file*/al:16,*file1 file2*,,/NOD LIBW ZWS,*file.def* <enter>

In the example shown here, LIBW is the import library that allows your code to call functions in Windows' dynamic link libraries, gdi.exe, user.exe, and kernel.exe. ZWS is a Windows-compatible C runtime library.

## Stamping the executable

To compile the .rc resource script file, attach the resources to the executable, and stamp the resulting executable, you should type the following command line in order to invoke the resource compiler:

rc *file.rc* <enter>

The file name *file.rc* is a placeholder for the name of the application you are building. If you are building detect.c, for example, you would insert the file name detect.rc instead of *file.rc*. If you are building spatial.c, you would insert the file name spatial.rc instead of *file.rc*.

When it is attaching the resources to the executable, the resource compiler also stamps the executable file with the Windows version number. If the version number is missing from the header of the executable file, Windows may refuse to launch the application. An application stamped with version 3.0 can usually run under Windows 3.0, Windows 3.1, and newer versions.

## Launching the application

To launch the application and exercise its features, choose Run . . . from the File menu of Windows Program Manager. When you are prompted, type the full path name of the demo program. For example, if you used Zortech C++ to compile the program into a directory named c:\source, you would type:

c:\source\*filename.exe*

Substitute the name of the appropriate executable file for the *filename.exe* placeholder used in this example.

# Validation suite

Every application in the book has been built using Zortech C++ 3.0 on a 33 MHz Intel 80386DX personal computer equipped with 4 MB RAM and a VGA display system. Each resulting executable was launched in Microsoft Windows and run under the 640- × - 480- × -16 color display mode.

# F
# *Compiling the sample programs with WATCOM C*

If you are using WATCOM C you can build all of the sample applications in the book with your compiler. Whether you are using the source files on the companion disk or working with the program listings in the book, you can build each program as is, without breaking open the source code. Each application can be compiled, linked, and stamped in its current form—no modifications are required if you are running WATCOM C. Each demo program in the book has been explicitly validated using WATCOM C 8.5.

This appendix explains how to access the source code, how to configure your system, and how to use your compiler's command line to build the sample applications.

The discussion here attempts to be practical and hands-on, no matter whether you are a beginner, intermediate, or expert. If you are an experienced programmer, you will already be familiar with many of the topics presented here. If you are a beginner, you can find more information in the documentation for your compiler.

## Working with the source code

The source code for the demo programs is available in two formats—as production files on the companion disk and as program listings in the book. Both variations are taken directly from the production files on the author's hard disk.

If you are using the companion disk, simply copy the production files to your hard disk and you are ready to begin building the sample applications with WATCOM C.

If you are working from the book, you must use a text editor or word processor to create production files from the program listings before you can begin building the sample applications with WATCOM C.

## Using the companion disk

If you are working with the companion disk, use DOS or the Windows File Manager to copy the production files from the disk to an appropriate directory on your hard disk. The companion disk contains a .def module definition file, an .h #include file, an .rc resource script file, and a .c source file for each sample application. The disk also contains additional modules—.c source files that are common to many of the demo programs. The frame animation demos, for example, each use a common .c module named storage.c that provides disk input/output functions. The 3D demos use a common .c module named lib3d.c.

The .def files on the companion disk are not needed by WATCOM C, whose linker command line provides the requisite parameters. The .mak files on the companion disk are intended to be used with QuickC for Windows, and are not for use with WATCOM C.

## Using the program listings

If you are working directly from the book, use your favorite text editor or word processor to create an ASCII text file from the listings. Do not type the line numbers that appear along the left margin of each program listing. These line numbers were inserted by the author to make it easier for the text discussion to refer to specific portions of the source code. The line numbers are not part of the source code.

# Configuring your system

During installation of your WATCOM C package, be sure to select both small and medium memory model libraries and choose Windows capability. This ensures that the appropriate runtime libraries are installed on your hard disk. Each sample application in the book uses the small memory model.

During a working session the WATCOM C compilers and the linker must be able to find your source files, the #include files, and the library files. You can facilitate this accessibility by ensuring that your autoexec.bat and config.sys files are up to date, containing the appropriate set path, set include, and set lib statements.

# Building an application

Building a Windows application with WATCOM C is a straightforward operation that follows the three-step, compile-link-stamp process used throughout the book. This command-line approach provides a consistent, reliable development environment. See FIG. 1-2 in chapter 1 for a schematic that illustrates a generic set of command lines.

## The working directory

Before beginning the compile session, make the directory that contains the source files the current directory. For example, if the source files are in a directory named c:\source, then type the following line at the DOS prompt:

```
cd c:\source <enter>
```

where <enter> refers to pressing the Enter key.

## Compiling the production files

To compile the production files into object code, use the following command line:

```
wcc -ms -oaxt -zw -W2 file.c <enter>
```

Note that the file name, *file.c*, is a placeholder for the particular file that you are compiling. If you are compiling detect.c, type detect.c in place of *file.c*. If you are building an application comprised of multiple .c source files, you must use the command line separately for each of the source modules. If you are building running.c, for example, you would execute the command line once using detect.c as the file name and once again using storage.c as the file name. If you are building spatial.c, you would run the command line once using spatial.c as the file name, once again using storage.c as the file name, and once again using lib3d.c as the file name.

When typing the command line, use the same uppercase and lowercase characters shown here in the example.

## Linking the object files

After you have successfully compiled all the .c source files that make up the application, you must link together the resulting object files with the required runtime libraries.

Use the following command line to invoke the linker:

```
wlink form win memory font opt st = 8192,heap = 1024 opt a = 16 f file.obj I windows exp zMessageHandler <enter>
```

Use the same uppercase and lowercase characters shown here in the example. Type the command line as a single, uninterrupted string. Do not press Enter until the end of the command line, even if it wraps around to the left side of the display while you are typing.

In the example shown here, the name *file.obj* is a placeholder for the object file you created with the compiler in the previous step. If you compiled detect.c, for example, the resulting object file is named detect.obj. Insert the file name detect.obj in place of *file.obj*.

If you are building an application comprised of numerous object files, you must name each object file on the command line. If, for example, you are building running.c, you must name both running.obj and storage.obj. The following command line format is used:

wlink   form   win   memory   font   opt   st=8192,heap=1024   opt   a=16   f
*file1.obj,file2.obj* | windows exp zMessageHandler <enter>

In the example shown here, zMessageHandler is the callback function that is
exported by the demo program.

    If the application you are building uses floating-point math routines,
you must add the mnemonic -fpi to the compiler command line and make
the appropriate adjustment to the link command line. See your WATCOM C
documentation for further information. If you use -fpi to compile a .c module, you must use it on all .c modules in the project.

## Stamping the executable

To compile the .rc resource script file, attach the resources to the executable,
and stamp the resulting executable, you should type the following command
line in order to invoke the resource compiler:

    rc *file.rc* <enter>

The file name *file.rc* is a placeholder for the name of the application you are
building. If you are building detect.c, for example, you would insert the file
name detect.rc instead of *file.rc*. If you are building spatial.c, you would insert
the file name spatial.rc instead of *file.rc*.

    When it is attaching the resources to the executable, the resource com-
piler also stamps the executable file with the Windows version number. If
the version number is missing from the header of the executable file, Windows may refuse to launch the application. An application stamped with
version 3.0 can usually run under Windows 3.0, Windows 3.1, and newer
versions.

## Launching the application

To launch the application and exercise its features, choose Run . . . from the
File menu of Windows Program Manager. When you are prompted, type the
full path name of the demo program. For example, if you used WATCOM C to
compile the program into a directory named c:\source, you would type:

    c:\source\\*filename.exe*

Substitute the name of the appropriate executable file for the *filename.exe*
placeholder used in this example.

# Validation suite

The applications in the book have been test-built using WATCOM C 8.5 on a
33 MHz Intel 80386DX personal computer equipped with 4 MB RAM and a
VGA display system. Each resulting executable was launched in Microsoft
Windows and run under the 640-$\times$-480-$\times$-16 color display mode.

# G
# *Testing your software*

There is no substitute for testing your prototype application on a genuine target platform identical to your customer's machine. However, you can often use your development platform to successfully mimic different display modes and memory modes.

It is a wise programmer who tests a prototype application early—and often—during the development cycle. Fonts, hues, graphics, metafiles, and window classes often produce unexpected surprises in different graphics modes. Software animation that relies on memory allocation and memory moves can suffer from unacceptable performance degradation in some memory modes, especially on RAM-starved slower machines when Windows' memory manager shuffles code and data between physical memory and disk. All of these idiosyncrasies can be overcome by source code work-arounds, but you will not even be aware a problem exists unless you test your prototype under different conditions.

## Memory modes

If you are running Windows in enhanced mode, you can use Windows 3.0 to mimic both the real mode and standard mode. You can use Windows 3.1 to mimic standard mode only, because real mode is not supported.

You normally start Windows by typing win at the operating system prompt and pressing Enter. To force Windows 3.0 to use real mode, type win/ r instead. To force Windows 3.0 to use standard mode, type win/s instead. To force Windows 3.1 to use standard mode, type win/s. When you are finished testing your prototype, return to the operating system prompt, type win, and press Enter to restart Windows in enhanced mode.

See chapter 6 for a discussion of the runtime characteristics of real, standard, and enhanced memory modes and the implications for software animation.

## Display modes

If your development platform is equipped with a so-called super VGA (SVGA) graphics adapter, you can often mimic a variety of Windows runtime display modes. Many manufacturers of graphics boards provide Windows drivers to support display modes like 640-×-480-×-256 color, 800-×-600-×-16 color, 1024-×-768-×-16 color, and others.

Windows stores information about runtime display modes in a file named setup.inf, which is usually located in the c:\windows\system directory on your hard disk. The utility program provided by the manufacturer of your SVGA graphics adapter will often automatically edit the setup.inf file to include the additional display modes supported by your graphics card.

To change to a different display mode, double-click on the Windows Setup icon in the Main program group. Choose the Options menu and then select Change System Settings. Click the Display list box and choose the display mode you want. After Windows reconfigures itself you will need to restart Windows for the new display mode to take effect.

Repeat this method each time you wish to change to a different display mode. Alternatively, after you have established a display mode, you can save your win.ini and system.ini files under new names. These two Windows startup files are usually located in your c:\windows directory. By saving a uniquely named set of win.ini and system.ini files for each display mode, you can simply copy these files into the c:\windows directory as win.ini and system.ini before starting Windows.

# H
# *Adding an audio track*

An audio track can add realism and excitement to an animation sequence. Upgrading your Windows application to support an audio card can increase its marketability, especially if your software can operate whether or not an audio card is present.

## Audio card technology

An audio card usually consists of a full-length or half-length interface card and a set of external speakers or a set of headphones. The audio card typically includes an analog-to-digital converter (ADC) for converting incoming analog audio signals into digital format that can be stored on disk. The card also includes a digital-to-analog converter (DAC) for converting digital files to an analog signal that can be used by the audio amplifier, the external speakers, and the headphones.

### Windows-compatible audio cards

Windows-compatible audio cards are shipped with a dynamic link library (DLL) containing the functions and code that drives the audio card hardware. Any Windows application wishing to use an audio effect must first register the DLL functions, load the DLL into RAM, open a so-called virtual device supported by the DLL, and then call the appropriate functions in the device to generate the audio effects. The application must close the device when finished using audio, freeing it for use by other Windows applications. When your application terminates, it should terminate the DLL.

## Software development kits

In order to make your Windows application capable of producing audio effects, you normally use a software development kit provided by the manufacturer of the audio card. The software development kit usually contains sample programs, an .h #include file, a .lib library of functions that interface with the DLL, and a copy of the DLL itself. The .h #include file contains function prototypes and data declarations, including error codes and DLL messages. The .lib library contains high-level functions for producing sophisticated audio effects. The DLL is the same dynamic link library your application expects to find on the end-user's hard drive. It provides the interface between your software and the hardware on the audio card.

A typical DLL usually supports three types of audio effects (also called devices). These devices are voice, music, and MIDI. To use one of these effects, your software must first open the device by calling a function in the DLL and passing the handle of the window that will own (be using) the device. No other application can use the device while your application's window owns it.

For example, the software development kit for Sound Blaster audio cards specifies the following syntax to activate the voice device:

```
vocOpenDevice(hWnd);
```

After using the audio effects, your application would make the following call to close the device:

```
vocCloseDevice();
```

When your application terminates, it would call another function to terminate the DLL:

```
sbcTerminateDLL();
```

## Supporting the market

Although the examples shown here are for audio cards provided by Sound Blaster, the techniques are common to other leading audio cards. Because each software development kit provides functions for detecting the presence of the manufacturer's audio card, your Windows application can easily support a number of different audio cards. At startup your application simply attempts to locate an audio card's DLL and activate it. If manufacturer A's card is found, it will be used, otherwise your application attempts to locate and activate the DLL for manufacturer B's audio card, and so on. Your software can utilize a switch() expression to call the appropriate audio functions during animation playback. The switch() block can also facilitate avoiding calling any audio functions if no audio card was detected.

## Technical limitations

Because the main CPU of the computer is involved during audio effects, your application should not attempt to synchronize dialog with animation playback. Instead, you should pause the animation while playing a lengthy sound, otherwise the animation will appear to play erratically as the CPU switches its attention from animation playback to audio effects and back again. The load on the CPU can easily degrade system performance, but by clever use of pauses and freeze-frames you can camouflage the technical limitations of synchronizing an audio track with software animation.

## DLL Considerations

Loading, using, and terminating DLLs is an advanced programming skill that is integral to using an audio card. Your application must import a function from the DLL before it can call the function. You can import functions either explicitly at link time or dynamically at runtime. Each method has its advantages and disadvantages, which are usually explained by the software development kit. For a practical example of dynamic importing, see the source code from the demonstration program in Chapter 7 of the author's previous book, *High-Performance C Graphics Programming for Windows* (Windcrest/McGraw-Hill book 4103, ISBN 0-8306-3790-7, published May 1992).

Other advanced programming techniques involve registering a unique message value for the DLL, handling DLL messages, and providing a locked memory buffer for use by functions in the DLL. The sample programs provided by most software development kits often supply the code fragments you need to build a stable application.

# I
# *Animation schools*

This appendix provides a listing of selected animation schools, including universities with computer science or art departments that provide instruction in animation techniques. The listing is not complete or comprehensive, and is provided for information purposes only.

Vancouver Film School
400 — 1168 Hamilton Street
Vancouver, BC, Canada V6B 2S2

UCLA Animation Workshop
University of California at Los Angeles
Department of Theater, Film, and Television
405 Hildgard Avenue
Los Angeles, CA 90024

California Institute of the Arts
24700 McBean Parkway
Valencia, CA 91355

American Animation Institute
4729 Lankershim Blvd.
North Hollywood, CA 91602

Sheridan College of Applied Arts
Trafalgar Road
Oakville, ON, L6H 2L1, Canada

Pratt Institute
200 Willoughby Avenue
Brooklyn, NY 11205

# J
# *PC animation equipment and supplies*

This appendix provides a list of selected sources for hardware and software tools for animation, including magazines, catalogs, and directories. The list is not complete or comprehensive and is provided for information purposes only.

## PC animation software tools

Alias Research, Inc.
110 Richmond Street East
Toronto ON, M5C 1P1, Canada

Supplier of 3D modeling and rendering software packages, Alias Animator and Power Animator.

Autodesk, Inc.
2320 Marinship Way
Sausalito, CA 94965

Supplier of PC-based animation and 3D modeling software packages, including AUTODESK ANIMATOR PRO and AUTODESK 3D STUDIO.

Macromind-Paracomp Inc.
310W-600 Townsend Street
San Francisco, CA 94103

Supplier of ACTION, a Windows-based multimedia authoring and animation software package.

AXA Corporation
17752 Mitchell, Suite C
Irvine, CA 92714

Supplier of Ink & Paint, Camera fx, and Producer for cel animation under Windows.

## PC animation hardware

VideoLogic
245 First Street
Cambridge, MA 02142

Supplier of MEDIATOR, a print-to-tape hardware device that converts VGA graphics to NTSC or PAL videocassette.

Lyon Lamb Video Animation Systems
4531 Empire Boulevard
Burbank, CA 91505

Supplier of the PC-VAS single frame recording/grabber board for interfacing PCs to videotape and videodisc.

Diaquest, Inc.
1440 San Pablo Avenue
Berkeley, CA 94702

Supplier of the SERIES II VIDEO ANIMATION CONTROLLER hardware device, used for interfacing a personal computer with frame-accurate videocassette recorders.

## Dedicated animation systems

Lyon Lamb Video Animation Systems, Inc.
4531 Empire Boulevard
Burbank, CA 91505

Supplier of broadcast-quality hardware and software systems.

Quantel Corporation
85 Old Kings Highway
Darien, CT 06820

Supplier of FLASH HARRY, a turnkey system (hardware and software) for broadcast-quality animation sequences.

Videomedia, Inc.
175 Lewis Road
San Jose, CA 95111

Supplier of broadcast-quality, frame-control hardware to be used in conjunction with a frame-accurate videocassette recorder.

Alias Research, Inc.
110 Richmond Street East
Toronto ON, M5C 1P1, Canada

Supplier of 2D and 3D modeling, rendering, and animation hardware and software systems.

Autographix Inc.
63 Third Avenue
Burlington, MA 01803

Supplier of high-end workstation hardware and software systems.

## Frame-accurate videocassette recorders

JVC Professional Video Products Co.
41 Slater Drive
Elmood Park, NJ 07407
Models CR-600U, 900U, 6650, and 8250
Models KR-M800U, M82OU, and M86OU
Models BR-S61OU, S611U, S81OU, and S811U
Model BR-S605U

Panasonic Industrial Co.
2 Panasonic Way
Secaucus, NJ 07094
Models AG-6500, 7500(A), 7510, 7650, and 7750
Models AU-60, 63, 65, and 300
Models AU-550, 620, 630, 640, 650, and 660
Models TQ-3031 and LQ-4000.

Sony Corporation of America
16550 Via Esprillo, San Diego, CA 92127
Models BVH-2000, 2000PM, and 2000PS
Models BVH-2180, 2180PM, and 2000PS
Models BVH-2500 and 2500PS
Models BVH-2700, 2800, 2800PS, and 2830PS
Models 3000 and 3100
Models BVU-800, 820, 850, 870, 900, 920, and 950
Models BVW-10, 15, 40, 60, 65, 70, and 75
Models DVR-10, C10, and 1000
Models VP-7000, 7020, and 7030
Models PVW-2600 and 2800

## Catalogs, magazines, and directories

Animation Industry Directory
P.O. Box 25547
Los Angeles, CA 90025

This annual directory contains listings for animation studios and services in North America.

Computer Graphics World
Pennwell Publishing Company
One Technology Park Drive
Westford, MA 01886

This monthly magazine provides well-illustrated, timely articles about computer graphics, visualization, and animation.

Millimeter
826 Broadway Avenue
New York, NY 10003

A trade magazine devoted to commercial animation news.

## Multimedia authoring software for Windows

Animation Works Interactive
Gold Disk Inc.
5–5155 Spectrum Way
Mississauga ON Canada L4W 5A1

Uses built-in script language. Supports Windows multimedia audio, animation, and full-motion video.

ACTION!
Macromind-Paracomp, Inc.
310W–600 Townsend St
San Francisco CA 94103

Uses built-in script language. Supports Windows multimedia audio, animation, and full-motion video.

Multimedia ToolBook
Asymetrix Corporation
700–100 110th Avenue NE
Bellevue WA 98004

Uses built-in script language. Supports Windows multimedia audio, animation, and full-motion video.

UltraGraphics
Intex Solutions, Inc.
35 Highland Circle
Needham MA 02194

Uses built-in script language. Supports Windows multimedia animation.

# Glossary

**accelerator table**  A list of accelerator keystrokes and their corresponding menu IDS. The table is a part of the resource script file for a Windows application.

**actor**  A movable 2D or 3D object in procedural animation and kinetic animation. Also called a cast member.

**additive operators**  The + operator and the − operator.

**aggregate type**  A C or C++ array, structure, or union.

**algorithm**  A method for solving a problem.

**alias**  1.  The jagged effect or jaggies produced by diagonal or curved lines on monitors with coarse resolution. See *super sampling*; 2.  The awkward jumping effect present in animations where the frame display rate is too slow to smoothly simulate actors moving at speed across the image. See *anti-aliasing, motion blur*; 3.  One of several names which refer to the same memory location or variable. See *union*.

**alphanumeric**  A set of characters containing both letters and numbers.

**ampersand**  The & character.

**animate on ones**  Animating by displaying each frame no longer than the frame rate, usually 1/30th second (TV and VTR) or 1/24th second (film). On personal computers the system timer chip issues an interrupt at 55 ms intervals (about 18.2 times per second), thereby limiting computer animation to animating on twos. See *animate on twos*.

**animate on twos**  Animating by displaying each frame for a length of time that is twice the frame rate. TV and VTR animation is usually played at 30 frames per second. If an animation sequence is animated on twos, each frame is held on display for 1/15th second instead of 1/30th second (66.7 ms). The system timer chip in personal computers issues an interrupt at 55 ms intervals, permitting a close approximation of animating on twos.

**animation**  A rapid display of separate images that deceives the human eye into perceiving motion. Animation is based on an optical illusion called image retention that is characteristic of all human eyes. Rather than seeing two separate images, the first image is retained long enough by the rods and cones of the eye to blur the transition to the next image when viewing film animation, television animation, or computer animation.

**animation control**  The process of managing the objects and events that are being animated. See *animation implementation*.

**animation engine**  A block of code or a module that loads and manages the (usually interactive) playback of an animation sequence.

**animation implementation**  The mechanics of creating the illusion of movement on the computer screen. See *animation control*.

**animation player**  See *animation engine*. (Autodesk Inc. claims the capitalized phrase Animation Player as a trademark.)

**anti-aliasing**  The process of reducing the visual impact of jagged lines or jumpy animation movement. See *aliasing, motion blur*.

**area fill**  To fill a specified region with a specified color or pattern. The color attribute surrounding the region to be filled is called the boundary.

**area process**  An image-processing functon that modifies an individual pixel or picture element as a result of considering the surrounding pixels (the neighborhood). See *neighborhood, point process*.

**argument**  A value passed to a C function or to a C++ method by the caller. The value received by a function or method is called a parameter.

**argument-type list**  The list of arguments found in a C function prototype or C++ method definition.

**arithmetic operator**  A mathematical operator such as addition ( + ), multiplication (*), and others.

**array**  A set of data elements of similar type grouped together under a single name, usually arranged in rows and columns. An array can be scalar (consisting of numeric or string data) or graphic (consisting of pixel attributes).

**assignment**  To assign a value to a variable. The C and C++ assignment operator is  =. Avoid confusion with the equality operator  ==. An arithmetic operation can be performed during the assignment process using the + = addition assignment operator, the − = subtraction assignment operator, the * = multiplication assignment operator, the / = division assignment operator, and the % = remainder assignment operator. Other assignment variations include the [[ = left-shift assignment operator, the ]]= right-shift assignment operator, the & = bitwise-AND assignment operator, and the ˆ = bitwise- XOR assignment operator.

**atom table**  A table of strings and corresponding integer ID numbers (atoms).

**audio track**  The sound component of an animation sequence or multimedia presentation. Microsoft Windows Multimedia Extensions provides support for audio from a wave audio sound file, a musical MIDI file, or directly from CD-ROM or videodisc.

**authoring**  Designing, creating, and testing an animation sequence or multimedia presentation.

**authoring platform**  The personal computer system on which an animation sequence or multimedia presentation is prototyped and tested. See *delivery platform*.

**background color**  The underlying color over which the graphics are drawn. The GDI sets the default background color for a new window to white.

**backplane removal**  The elimination of backward-facing facets from convex polyhedra like cubes, spheres, and cylinders in 3D scenes. Also called backface culling.

**bar sheet**  A written, visual representation of the sound track for an animation sequence. Used to synchronize character movement with dialog and sound effects. See *lip-synch*.

**binary file**  A file stored in binary format, as opposed to ASCII or ANSI format (text). Sometimes called a binary image in graphics programming.

**binary operator**  A C or C++ operator used in binary expressions. Binary operators include multiplicative operators (*,/), additive operators (+, −), shift operators ([[,]]), relational operators ([,],[=,]=,==,!=,), bitwise operators (&,|,), logical operators (&&,||), and the sequential-evaluation operator (,).

**bit array**  A graphic array or bitblt image.

**bitblt**  An acronym for bit block transfer. Also called block graphics and graphic array.

**bitblt animation**  Graphic array animation.

**bitblt image**  A graphic array.

**bit block transfer**  See *bitblt*.

**bitmap**  An arrangement of bytes in display memory or conventional memory representing a virtual display surface upon which graphics can be drawn. A device-dependent bitmap can be displayed on a particular device (ie a graphics adapter). A device- independent bitmap contains a generalized description of its contents, enabling the application (or Windows GDI) to modify it for display on a diverse range of devices.

**bitplane**  One of four separate buffers that are sandwiched together by VGA, EGA, Super VGA, and 8514/A hardware in order to drive video output. Also called a color plane.

**bit tiling**  Mixing pixels of different colors to create patterns or shades. Windows' built-in bit tiling is called dithering.

**bitwise operators**  &, |, and ^, which compare bits to check for true and false conditions. See C's bitwise operators are AND (&), OR (|), and XOR (^). Also see C's logical operators AND (&&), OR (||), and NOT (!).

**black box**  A block of code that has been previously tested and debugged and is assumed to operate correctly. The programmer is unconcerned with the algorithm or processes used by the black box code, only with the input and output. See *white box.*

**black-box testing**  Program testing that is concerned with input and output, not with the inner functioning of code. See *white-box testing.*

**blitting**  Using bitblts (graphic arrays) in a graphics program.

**block**  A cohesive sequence of C or C++ statements, instructions, declarations, or definitions that are enclosed within braces { }.

**block graphics**  Same as graphic array. See *bitblt.*

**bounding box**  1. In 3D computer graphics, a parallelepiped (a six-sided box) that encompasses all the vertices of a 3D model or subobject; 2. In 2D computer graphics, a rectangle that surrounds the vertices of an object. Also called a stand-in.

**bounding box test**  Using the bounding boxes of two objects to determine if a potential conflict exists.

**braces**  The { } tokens that enclose a block in a C or C++ program. See *brackets, parentheses.*

**brackets**  The [ ] tokens that are used to initialize and access the elements of arrays.

**B-rep**  Boundary representation, a method of creating images of 3D models by using planes, polygons, and facets. The outer surfaces or skin are used to model the so-called boundaries of the 3D object. See *CSG.*

**buffer**  An area of memory used for temporary storage of data or images.

**bump mapping**  The intentional random displacement of surface normals to simulate a rough surface on a 3D model.

**callback function**  A function in an application that is called by the Windows operating system. For example, the window function in an application is a callback function. See *window function.*

**camera coordinates**  The X-Y-Z coordinates that describe how a 3D model will appear to a hypothetical viewer at a given location in the 3D scene. Also called view coordinates.

**camera instruction sheet**  See *dope sheet.*

**caption bar**  The title bar of a Windows application's main window. Usually contains the name of the application.

**caret**  The ˆ character.

**cast-based animation**  An object-oriented form of animation control whereby multiple actors are independently animated in front of a scene.

**cast member**  See *actor.*

**CATA**  An acronym for computer-assisted traditional animation.

**CD-ROM**  An acronym for compact disk read-only memory. A 4.7-inch diameter plastic disc that stores digital data by pits and lands (bumps) that are etched into its surface. The data is read by interpreting the plastic surface with a laser beam. A CD-ROM disk can store 600 MB of data, representing numeric, text, sound, or graphic information.

**cel**  1. An image painted on acetate as used in traditional film animation studios; 2. The rectangular space occupied by a single character in a particular font; 3. A bitblt or bitmap used for computer cel animation sequences.

**cel animation**  Computer animation that emulates traditional methods of cel animation, where actors or scenic elements painted on transparent acetate are manipulated in front of static background art while being filmed using a single-exposure camera.

**char**  A C or C++ variable stored in one byte of memory, capable of representing values from $-128$ to $+127$. An unsigned char can represent values from 0 to 255. By default, char is signed. A char type is often used to store the integer value of a member of the ASCII or ANSI alphanumeric character set.

**chroma key**  See *key color.*

**CGI**  Computer-generated image.

**CGM**  The ANSI computer graphics metafile format for exchanging images between application programs or between computer systems.

**claymation**  A form of pixilation animation in which clay and plasticine models are used as actors and scenery. See *pixilation, stop-motion photography.*

**client area**  The interior image space of a Windows application's main window that is available for use by the application.

**clipboard**  A block of global memory that is managed by Windows in order to permit applications to pass data and images to other applications.

**clock tick**  An interrupt issued at intervals of 54.925 ms (about 18.2 times each second) by the system timer chip. See *INT 08H.*

**CMY model**  The cyan-magenta-yellow color model used primarily by printers and publishers using offset lithography.

**clipping**  See *line clipping.*

**collision detection**  Detecting the moment when a vertex or facet of one solid 3D model conflicts with the space occupied by a vertex or facet plane of another solid 3D model. Collision response refers to the action taken by the software after collision is detected.

**color cycling**  A method for producing animation by swapping palette values.

**color interpolation**  Determining the color of a pixel from its neighbors or from its distance between two pixels whose colors are known.

**common user access**  See *CUA.*

**computer visualization**  Using graphics to interpret, manipulate, or create data. Specialized fields of computer visualization include scientific visualization, 3D modeling and rendering, computer animation, biomedicine, fluid dynamics, tomography, computer vision, image processing, and others.

**constructive solid geometry**  See *CSG.*

**conventional memory**  RAM up to 640K.

**coordinate system**  The arrangement of X axis and Y axis in a 2D graphics environment or the arrangement of X axis, Y axis, and Z axis in a 3D graphics environment.

**copy** To provide a handle to the Windows clipboard.

**cosine** The cosine of an angle in a right-angle triangle defines the relationship between the hypotenuse and the adjacent side.

**cross-compiler development** Application development that ensures compatibility on different compiler products, such as Microsoft C and the SDK, QuickC for Windows, Borland C++, Zortech C++, WATCOM C, and Turbo C++ for Windows.

**CSG** Constructive solid geometry, a method of creating images of 3D models by using primitives (subobjects) such as cubes, cylinders, spheres, and cones. See *B-rep*.

**CUA** Common user access. CUA is a collection of IBM standardized specifications for developers designing user interface components for applications running under windowing operating systems like Windows, OS/2, and others. See SAA.

**cut** To instantly change from one full-frame image to another during animation playback. See dissolve.

**cycle** See loop.

**declaration** The statements that define the name and attributes of a C or C++ variable, function, structure, or class.

**decrement** To make smaller by a specified number of units.

**default** A condition assumed to exist unless defined otherwise by the user or developer.

**definition** The instructions that comprise a C function or a C++ method.

**deformation** See squashing-and-stretching.

**delivery platform** The personal computer system(s) on which a finished animation sequence or multimedia presentation is intended to be played. Also called a playback platform. See authoring platform.

**depth cuing** The use of colors or line styles to assist the viewer in interpreting depth in a computer-generated 3D image.

**depth sort** Ordering (sorting) the visible facets of a 3D scene into a sequence so that the 3D modeler draws the facets in farthest-to-nearest order (the so-called painter's algorithm).

**development platform** The configuration of hardware and software used to build a software product. See target platform.

**digital camera** A still camera that stores imagery in digital format instead of on photographic film. Dedicated software permits the image data to be exported to a personal computer via the parallel or serial port.

**digital video interactive** A combination of hardware and software methods for combining graphics, video, audio, titling, and other multimedia components into a computer-controlled presentation. See multimedia.

**digitize** To convert an analog image or signal to a corresponding series of bits and bytes.

**display context**  A Windows data structure that defines an output device and the various drawing attributes associated with it, such as drawing tools, colors, dimensions, and others.

**display coordinates**  Screen coordinates. Refers primarily to the converted camera coordinates of a 3D modeling application.

**display-independent**  Refers to algorithms, functional code, graphics, and Windows applications that perform consistently across a diverse range of different display modes and display hardware.

**display schedule**  A script that manages the playback of an animation sequence.

**dissolve**  To smoothly replace one image with another by fading out the first image while fading up the second image. Also called a cross-fade.

**dithering**  The bit tiling or patterning of pixels used to implement a shading or coloring scheme. Windows uses dithering to simulate colors beyond the limited selection available in the 16-color VGA mode. See bit tiling.

**DLL**  See dynamic link library.

**do-nothing routine**  A routine that simply returns control to the caller. Do-nothing routines are used during preliminary program development and debugging. Also called a stub.

**dope sheet**  A camera instruction sheet for animation production.

**double-buffer animation**  A method of animation whereby the software builds the next frame on a hidden bitmap while displaying the current frame on the application's display window. To display the next finished image the application copies the hidden bitmap to the screen. Double-buffer animation operates slightly differently in DOS-based applications.

**dpi**  Dots per inch. Often used to describe the graphics resolution of laser printers and scanners.

**DVI**  An acronym for digital video interactive.

**dynamic link library**  A library of routines and data that can be called or accessed by any Windows application. The Graphics Device Interface (GDI) is a dynamic link library (DLL). A DLL file may use either the DLL or EXE filename extension.

**dynamics**  The study of motion as it relates to force, mass, and other constraints in animation sequences.

**electronic darkroom**  Refers to image-processing routines that manipulate images to produce results otherwise obtained by sending negatives, transparencies, or prints to professional photography labs or retouching services.

**elegant**  See optimize.

**EMB**  Extended memory blocks.

**emulation**  1. Simulation of unavailable hardware by available hardware and software; 2. Simulation of a real-world situation or event by software.

**EMS**  Expanded memory specification. Expanded memory is used to provide additional physical RAM for computers which are otherwise limited to 640K RAM. Access is through a page manager. See *XMS*.

**enhanced mode**  Windows runtime memory mode requiring an 80286, 80386, 80486 or higher processor with more than 2MB RAM (to a maximum of 16MB), running in protected mode, and providing virtual memory via disk swapping when physical memory is exhausted.

**ensemble processing**  An image-processing function whereby the content of two images is compared.

**ergonomics**  Refers to compatibility of hardware or software with human psychology and physiology.

**error-handler**  An algorithm or routine used to handle exceptions occurring at runtime.

**error trapping**  Using a programmer-defined routine to detect and respond to errors caused by hardware or software exceptions at runtime.

**Euler operators**  Logical or boolean operators for the manipulation of 3D solids. The standard operations are join, intersection, and subtraction.

**expanded memory**  See *EMS*.

**expression**  A combination of operators acting on variables.

**extended memory**  See *XMS*.

**extrusion**  Stretching or deforming an object in a 3D scene. See *rotation*, *translation*.

**4D**  Four dimensional. Often used to refer to animated 3D computer graphics because the fourth dimension of time has been added to the image. Usually represented by (X,Y,Z,T) notation.

**4D space-time**  A display of 3D-space over time. See *4D*.

**facet**  A polygonal plane surface used to create solid 3D models constructed by the B-rep method.

**file pointer**  A variable that indicates the current position of read and write operations on a file. See *stream*.

**filtering**  A method of color interpolation useful for anti-aliasing (removal of jaggies).

**fitted curve**  A computer-generated curve.

**fixed-loop animation**  An animation sequence driven by a block of code that executes repeatedly for a fixed number of iterations. See *idle-loop animation*.

**font**  A cohesive set of alphanumeric characters in a particular point size (ie 12 pt.) of a particular typeface (ie Helv) in a particular type style (ie bold).

**font file**  A file containing the bitmap data or vector formulas required to generate and display a particular font. See *font*.

**force constraints**  The forces acting upon actors in a physically based animation sequence. See *geometric constraints*.

**forensic animation**  Computer-generated animation used as evidence in criminal proceedings or civil litigation, often in motor vehicle collision lawsuits.

**forward dynamics**   The process of calculating the result of the application of force, loads, or constraints on an object. See *inverse dynamics.*

**forward kinematics**   The process of calculating the result of the application of velocity or acceleration on an object. See *inverse kinematics.*

**fourier analysis**   Using rate of change as the discriminating factor to analyze image data.

**fourier window**   A method of anti-aliasing.

**fps**   Frames per second, used to express the display rate of animation programs. Traditional film animation uses 24 frames per second (25 fps in Europe). North American NTSC television animation uses 30 frames per second (25 fps in Europe). See *NTSC.*

**frame**   1. A single image in an animation sequence, usually intended to mean a full screen image; 2. A complete image that is being interpreted or manipulated by an image-processing function.

**frame animation**   The rapid display of previously created graphic images (frames). Frames can be stored as metafiles or as bitmaps in convention memory, extended memory, or on hard disk. See *animation engine.*

**frame grab**   Capturing a graphic image from an external source and storing it in a buffer or on disk. Typical external sources include scanners, live video, videotape players, and others.

**frame process**   An image-processing function that manipulates or combines two input images to produce a third image. Each image is called a frame.

**frames per second**   The rate of animation, expressed as new images per second. Also called fps.

**freezeframe**   To display over a period of time a single frame from an animated sequence.

**frequency**   The rate of change found by fourier analysis.

**frisket**   1. A paper or cellophane shield used by graphic artists and film animators to protect portions of artwork from being inadvertently colored during airbrushing; 2. A bitmap matte used to protect an existing background during a transparent put operation. See *transparent put.*

**function declaration**   Statements that define the name, return type, storage class, and parameter list of a C or C++ function. See *declaration.*

**function definition**   Statements that define the name, return type, storage class, parameter list, and the executable instructions which comprise a C or C++ function. See *definition.*

**GDI**   Graphics Device Interface, the host graphics engine built into Windows as a dynamic link library (DLL) whose routines can be called by any Windows application.

**GDI.EXE**   The Windows dynamic link library that provides device-independent graphics functions for Windows applications. See *KERNEL.EXE, USER.EXE.*

**geometric constraints**   The dimensional conditions affecting kinetic animation. See *force constraints.*

**geometric model**   A mathematical definition of an object.

**geometric processing**   Image processing functions such as move, copy, shear, stretch, and others.

**geometry**   Mathematics concerned with points, lines, angles, shapes, solids, and surfaces.

**global variable**   A variable in a C or C++ source file that is available to all functions in that file. A variable declared outside of any function is global by default.

**gnomon**   A visual representation of the X-Y-Z axis system in a 3D application.

**Gouraud shading**   Smooth shading.

**gradient**   A subtle transition between two hues. Also called a ramp.

**graphics device interface**   See *GDI.*

**granular**   Refers to the size of the smallest linkable element of a library, set of routines, or collection of data. In commercially available libraries the granularity is usually at the individual function level.

**granularity**   See *granular.*

**graphic array**   A rectangular image that has been saved in RAM as a bit array (bitblt) for later retrieval and display. Also called a block. See *bitblt.*

**graphic array animation**   Placing one or more graphic arrays (bitblts) onto the display in order to produce animation. Also called bitblt animation and block animation.

**graphics driver**   A module of executable code designed to interact directly with the graphics hardware. The VGA graphics driver shipped with the retail version of Windows is named VGA.DRV.

**gray scale**   Refers to images or to the palette scheme used by images displayed as a range of gray tones.

**groundplane**   A graphic representation of the orientation of the 3D environment in modeling and shading software.

**GUI**   Graphical user interface.

**handle**   An identifier that is provided by Windows to an application at runtime that permits the application to use or manipulate a window, display context, bitmap, data, or other object identified by the handle.

**hexadecimal**   The base 16 numbering system. The decimal system uses base 10. The base is also called the radix.

**hex**   Same as hexadecimal. A hexadecimal value is prefixed by the 0x symbol in C and C++. It is followed by the H symbol in assembly language.

**hidden line**   A line that should be hidden by another graphic.

**hidden surface**   A plane or facet that is hidden by other surfaces.

**hidden surface elimination**   See *hidden surface removal.*

**hidden surface removal**   The process of removing from a 3D scene all surfaces that should be hidden from view. Visible surface algorithms falls into two broad categories: image-space methods and object-space methods.

**high memory** The first 64K segment of memory in RAM physically located above 1MB on an 80286, 80386, 80486, or newer computer. Through an addressing idiosyncrasy DOS applications can access this portion of memory and can use it as a page to access simulated EMS, which is actually located in XMS.

**histogram** A table describing the distribution of gray values or color in an image being manipulated by image-processing software.

**HLS** The hue-luminance-saturation color model.

**HMA** High memory area.

**host graphics engine** The runtime graphics library being used. Windows applications use the Graphics Device Interface (GDI) as the host engine.

**HSV** The hue-saturation-value color model.

**Hungarian notation** A convention of rules for naming and capitalization of functions, variables, and constants in Windows applications source files.

**HVC** The hue-value-chroma color model.

**icon** A miniature bitmap image that represents a minimized Windows application.

**idle-loop animation** An animation sequence driven by a block of code that executes repeatedly, but only when there are no other demands on the Windows operating environment. See *fixed-loop animation.*

**illumination model** A paradigm that explains the process whereby a 3D scene is lighted.

**image file** A binary file that contains a graphic image or the algorithm for recreating the image.

**image processing** Analyzing, interpreting, and modifying a digitized image with a computer. Typical applications include photo retouching and enhancement, blur removal, edge detection, geometric processing (stretch, invert, mirror, flop), contrast adjustment, cut and paste, computer vision, morphing and tweening, pattern recognition, target recognition, ensemble processing, and others.

**image-space methods** Hidden surface algorithms that are based on 2D images. See *object-space methods.*

**include file** A text file that is logically but not physically merged into the source code at compile time.

**increment** To make larger by a specified number of units.

**indirection** Refers generally to the act of addressing a variable in memory. Specifically refers to the indirection operator (*) which is used in C and C++ to declare a pointer to another variable. See *pointer.*

**ink and paint** In traditional film animation, refers to the final rendering (or inking and painting) of cels derived from the pencil sketches used to prototype the animation sequence. In computer animation, refers to coloring the frames, whether by interactive paint software or by computer-controlled automatic methods.

**instance**   1. A single occurrence of a graphical entity in an image or scene; 2. A running copy of a Windows application. More than one copy can be executing.

**instancing**   Creating a complex 2D or 3D model by multiple occurrences of the same entity at different locations in the scene.

**int 08H**   An interrupt issued 18.2 times each second (once each 54.925 milliseconds) by the computer's system timer chip. Used by Windows' virtual timer. See *clock tick*.

**integer**   A whole number with no fractional parts or decimal point.

**interactive**   Responds to input from the user at runtime.

**interactive graphics**   Software that creates or modifies a graphical display in timely response to user input.

**interop**   Interoperability, the ability of software to operate on and share data across different hardware platforms.

**intersection**   See *Euler operators*.

**inverse dynamics**   The process of calculating the forces or constraints required to move an object of a certain mass from one position to another over a fixed period of time. See *forward dynamics*.

**inverse kinematics**   The process of calculating the velocity or acceleration required to move an object from one position to another over a fixed period of time. See *forward kinematics*.

**iterative**   See *loop*.

**jiffy**   The shortest time interval between two frames during playback of an animation sequence. Conversely, frames per second refers to the number of frames displayed per second during playback. See *fps*.

**join**   See *Euler operators*.

**KERNEL.EXE**   The Windows dynamic link library that provides system resources such as memory management and resource management to Windows applications at runtime. See *USER.EXE, GDI.EXE*.

**key color**   A color that will appear transparent when the image is overlaid on another image or background. Called chroma key by the broadcast television industry.

**keyframe**   A significant frame in an animation script, tweening session, or morphing sequence. Typically, the developer or the user provides a set of keyframes and the software provides the in-between images (tweens).

**kinematics**   The study of motion as it relates to the positions and velocities of objects in animation sequences.

**kinematic animation**   Computer animation that is managed by algorithms conforming more or less to the laws of physics. See *kinematics, procedural animation*.

**lamina**   A 3D plane that can be viewed from either side.

**language binding**   A module that calls compiler-dependent routines in a graphics library or runtime library.

**lens distortion error field**  A bitmap schematic that indicates the areas of lens distortion in images grabbed from a live video camera attached to a computer.

**lerping**  Linear interpolation.

**library**  A file containing modules of object code representing functions available for use by the developer's C or C++ program.

**LIM**  The Lotus-Intel-Microsoft technical specification for expanded memory hardware and software components.

**line clipping**  Deletion of a line segment that exceeds the physical range of the display buffer, viewport, or window.

**line styling**  Dotted or dashed lines.

**linear interpolation**  An algorithm for generating in-between images from keyframes whereby the movement of a vertex is assumed to follow a straight line. Also called lerping. See *spline interpolation*.

**lip-synch**  Synchronization of a cartoon character's mouth movements to a sound track. See *bar sheet*.

**local variable**  Same as static variable. See *global variable*.

**logical operators**  && and ||, which perform logical operations on bytes being compared. The && token is used to AND two bytes (the resulting bit will be on only if both the bits being evaluated were on). The || token is used to OR two bytes (the resulting bit will be on if either of the bits being evaluated were on).

**logical palette**  A table of colors defined by a Windows application for its own use. Where possible the colors in a logical palette are mapped by Windows to matching hues in the system palette (hardware palette). If no match is possible, Windows uses dithering to simulate the color requested by the logical palette. See *system palette*.

**look-up table**  The logical table used by the graphics adapter to match color index numbers (used by the application software) to RGB gun settings (used by the display monitor). Windows sets the values of the look-up table at startup.

**loop**  A repeating set of frames that comprises an animation cycle, as in a run cycle. In traditional film animation, lengths of film were spliced end to end to form repeating loops. See *idle loop*.

**LUT**  Look-up table.

**mach band**  An optical illusion whereby the human eye emphasizes the subtle differences between two adjacent shaded areas.

**matte**  A bitblt mask that is used in conjunction with GDI raster operations to permit an irregularly shaped, multicolor bitblt image to be cleanly placed onto a multicolored background. Also called a key matte. In traditional filmmaking a matte is a black mask that prevents a designated part of each frame from being exposed, thereby permitting other images to be added later. See *travelling matte*.

**MDK**  Multimedia development kit.

**memory model**  One of the memory-management schemes used by C and C++ to set up memory space for executable code and addressable data.

Windows applications usually employ the small model or the medium memory model.

**message loop**  The block of statements in a Windows application that retrieves input messages from the application queue maintained by the Windows operating system.

**metafile**  The GDI statements and the data necessary to reconstruct an image. A Windows metafile can exist in RAM , can be stored on disk for later use, and can be passed to the clipboard for use by other Windows applications.

**millisecond**  1/1000th of a second. Windows applications wishing to define a timer interval must do so using milliseconds (ms).

**model photography**  See *stop-motion photography.*

**model sheet**  A set of reference design drawings showing a cartoon character in typical poses.

**modeling**  Creating a geometric shape representing a 3D object.

**module**  The block of C or C++ code contained in a separate source file. Can also mean a cohesive block of code that performs a specific function.

**morgue**  A collection of reference photographs and drawings used by artists, animators, designers, and writers.

**morphing**  A gradual transformation of a graphics object to a different object. Derived from the term metamorphosis.

**motion-control model photography**  See *stop-motion photography.*

**motion blur**  In traditional film photography, image fuzziness caused by the subject moving faster than the frame rate of the camera. Animation software often employs intentional image blurring (temporal anti-aliasing) to overcome temporal aliasing. See *temporal aliasing.*

**motion dynamics**  Changes in location, orientation, and juxtaposition of objects during an animation sequence. See *update dynamics, viewing dynamics.*

**motion test**  A prototype animation sequence used to test timing, pacing, and movement before producing the final images. Traditional film animators used an animation pencil-test for the same purpose.

**MPC**  Acronym for multimedia personal computer.

**MSC**  Microsoft C.

**multimedia**  A collection of hardware and software methods for combining graphics, full-motion video, audio, titling, and other components from diverse sources into a computer-controlled presentation. See *digital video interactive.*

**multimedia personal computer**  A PC with multimedia-capable hardware components.

**multi-module programming**  Using separately compiled source files to build an executable file.

**multiplicative operators**  The * and / operators, which are multiplication and division.

**native code**  Executable code that is processor-specific.

**neighborhood** The grouping of picture elements (pixels) that surrounds the subject picture element being analyzed. Neighborhoods are considered by image-processing software functions when manipulating an image or when detecting edges. See *spatial filter*.

**nested loop** A program loop contained within another loop.

**normalized coordinates** Coordinates that have been scaled to the range $-1$ to $+1$. Normalized coordinates are considered device-independent.

**NTSC** A video signal that adheres to the accepted technical standards of the broadcast industry in the United States, Canada, Mexico, Central America, and Japan. NTSC is defined as 525 lines refreshed 30 frames per second. The PAL standard, used in Europe, Australia, and New Zealand, is 625 lines at 25 fps. See *VTR*.

**NULL** A constant that means undefined. NULL is defined as 0 by WINDOWS.H.

**null pointer** A pointer to nothing. An undefined pointer.

**nybble** Half a byte, or four bits.

**object** A cohesive 2D or 3D graphical entity.

**object file** A file containing object code. Also called an OBJ file.

**object-space methods** Hidden surface algorithms that operate on the 3D X-Y-Z coordinates of a 3D scene.

**objectification** Representing a phenomenon as form, color, texture, motion, and time. See *visualization*.

**onion skin** A feature provided by animation software, whereby the previous three or four cels can be superimposed over the current cel. See *cel animation*.

**OOP** Object-oriented programming, whereby each independent module contains both executable code and the data upon which it operates.

**operand** A constant or a variable operated on by operators in an expression.

**optimize** To improve a program's execution speed or to reduce its memory requirements at runtime.

**overlay** A module of data or executable code that is loaded from disk at runtime over an existing block of code or data.

**painter's algorithm** A method of 3D hidden object removal. See *z-buffer method*.

**PAL** See *NTSC*.

**pan** To move an image left or right. See *scroll*.

**parameter** A value that a function expects to receive when called. Also called an argument, but many technical writers and developers make a distinction between the two.

**paste** To retrieve a handle from the Windows clipboard.

**pencil-test** See *motion test*.

**persistent image** Refers to graphics displayed in the client area of a window that are preserved when the window is moved, clipped or unclipped by the edge of the screen, covered or uncovered by another application's window, or resized.

**physically based animation**  An animation sequence managed according to laws of physics. See *forward dynamics, forward kinematics, inverse dynamics, inverse kinematics.*

**pipe**  The | character.

**pixel**  Picture element. A pixel is the smallest addressable graphic on a display screen. In RGB systems, a pixel is a triad comprised of a red dot, a green dot, and a blue dot.

**pixilation**  Animation created by single-frame exposures of inanimate models. Claymation is a form of pixilation. See *claymation, stop-motion photography.*

**plane equation**  A vector formula that describes the qualities of a plane, including the location of a given point relative to the surface of the plane. Plane equations are useful for hidden surface removal.

**plane equation test**  Testing to determine if a given point is located on the inside or outside of a given facet in a 3D scene.

**platform-independent**  Refers to applications able to execute on a diverse range of hardware configurations.

**point process**  An image-processing function that modifies an individual pixel or a single picture element as a result of considering the value or location of the pixel. Neighboring pixels are not considered. See *area process, neighborhood.*

**pointer**  A variable that contains the address of another variable. See *null pointer.*

**polygon**  Usually intended to mean a plane surface used to create a 3D solid model constructed by the B-rep method. Also used to describe a multi-sided, closed geometric shape.

**POV**  Point of view, also called viewpoint.

**preprocessor directive**  An instruction that modifies the behavior of a C or C++ compiler at compile time. Common preprocessor directives are #if, #elif, #endif, and #include.

**procedural animation**  Object-oriented animation. See *cast-based animation.*

**prototype**  1. The initial declaration of a function in a C or C++ program, usually containing the return type and argument list of the function; 2. A tentative mock-up of a program for project-planning purposes.

**quadric primitive**  A 3D subobject.

**RAD**  Rapid applications development, a method of efficient software development that stresses preliminary prototypes, client feedback, and clearly defined goals.

**radian**  A length of arc based upon the relationship between elements of a unit circle (whose radius equals one unit).

**radiosity**  An algorithm that considers the overall energy levels from different light sources in a 3D scene.

**radix**  The base of a numbering system. The radix of the hexadecimal numbering system is 16, of the decimal system is 10.

**ramp**  See *gradient.*

**rapid applications development** See *RAD*.

**raster operations** Boolean operators that affect bitmap operations performed by GDI functions. Some common raster operations are XOR, AND, OR, and overwrite.

**ray tracing** An algorithm that calculates the illumination level of a model by tracing a ray of light back from the viewer's eye to the model and eventually to the light source.

**real mode** Windows runtime memory mode using an 8086, 8088 or higher processor with 1MB RAM maximum, using EMS as a global heap for applications.

**real-time animation** 1. An animation sequence that is being created and displayed at runtime; 2. An animation sequence intended to correspond to or react to events occurring in the real world at runtime.

**reflection mapping** Mathematically projecting onto the surface of a 3D model a previously defined bitmap containing a visual reflection of other objects in the scene. The reflection bitmap is acquired by temporarily placing the viewpoint on the surface of the mirrored object.

**refresh buffer** The display buffer. The display hardware uses the display buffer to refresh the display monitor.

**regen** Regeneration of a graphic entity or image. The instructions necessary to implement regen are sometimes stored in a metafile.

**registration points** The user-specified coordinates in keyframes that will be used to create tweens. See *tweening*.

**relational operators** The operators [, ], [=, ]=, ==, and !=, which in C and C++ mean less-than, greater-than, less-than-or-equal-to, greater-than-or-equal-to, equal-to, and not-equal-to. A relational operator compares the relationship between two values.

**rendering** Adding illumination, shading, and color to a 3D scene.

**reveal** See *wipe*.

**RGB model** The color model used by most personal computer graphics adapters and monitors.

**rotation** Adjusting the yaw, roll, or pitch attitude of an object in a 3D scene. See *extrusion, translation*.

**rotoscoping** Deriving realistic images for use in animated sequences by tracing the shapes found in live-action films.

**rubber banding** The rapid erasing and redrawing of guidelines that represent the shape and position of a graphical entity to be drawn by the software if the user's current selection were used.

**run-cycle** A loop of frames that can be repeated in order to produce a running actor in an animated sequence. Static run cycles are usually overlayed on a panning background. Dynamic run cycles often use bitblts to move the actor across a static background.

**runtime** The time when the application is executing.

**SAA** Systems application architecture. SAA is a set of IBM specifications for standardized protocols, interfaces, and conventions to be used by applications running under windowing operating systems like Windows, OS/2, and others. CUA is one of four topics covered in SAA documents. See *CUA*.

**scalar** A mathematical quantity that has quantity but not direction. A vector has quantity and direction.

**scanner** A peripheral device capable of grabbing a continuous tone hardcopy image and storing it in computer memory as a digitized image.

**scientific visualization** The graphical representation of formulas or phenomena for the purpose of scientific research.

**scripted animation** The computer-assisted equivalent of traditional cel animation.

**scroll** To move an image upwards or downwards. See *pan*.

**SDK** The Microsoft Windows Software Development Kit.

**section** A cross-section, cutaway view of a 3D object.

**semantically implemented** A phrase used by compiler manufacturers to indicate that their compiler recognizes a keyword but does not implement it. Syntactically implemented keywords are fully functional.

**sequential-evaluation operator** (,) used to separate a series of sequentially evaluated expressions.

**sfx** Sound effects.

**shading** Adding the effects of illumination, shadow, and color to a 3D model. Sometimes called rendering.

**shift operators** [[ and ]], which shift the bits in a byte to the left or to the right.

**simulation** An imitation of a real-world event.

**simulator** A program that imitates a real-world event.

**sine** The sine of an angle in a right-angle triangle defines the relationship between the hypotenuse and the side opposite.

**single-step** To advance to and pause at the next frame of an animation sequence after receiving explicit input (usually a keystroke) from the user. See *freeze frame*.

**slow-in/slow-out** The avoidance of unnatural instant-start and instant-stop events in computer animation sequences.

**solid model** A 3D model with hidden surfaces removed. It can be constructed by the constructive solid geometry method (CSG) or the boundary representation method (B-rep).

**spatial filter** A matrix calculation used by image-processing routines to manipulate images. See *neighborhood*.

**specular reflection** A highlight on the surface of a 3D model.

**spline interpolation** An algorithm for generating in-between images from keyframes whereby the movement of a vertex is assumed to follow a fitted curve or freeform curve. See *linear interpolation*.

**squashing-and-stretching** Deformation of an object or actor as a result of movement, acceleration, deceleration, collision, or other events.

**staging** Choreographing or directing an animation sequence or an individual frame.

**stamp** A field of data in the header of a Windows application file. The resource compiler stamps each application with the Windows version for which the executable file is intended. Windows will not launch any application that does not contain the appropriate stamp.

**standard mode**   Windows runtime memory mode requiring an 80286, 80386, 80486 or higher processor with less than 2MB RAM, running in protected mode.

**stand-in**   A bounding box.

**statement**   A C or C++ instruction. Sometimes called an expression.

**static variable**   A variable that is available to only the function in which it has been declared. Also called a local variable. See *global variable.*

**stereo vision**   Computer vision implemented with two video cameras.

**stereo lithography**   A process that uses 3D software to drive lasers that sculpt prototype solids from plastic, acrylic, wood, or light metal. Used for industrial prototyping.

**stock font**   A font that is built into the retail versions of Windows. Stock fonts are guaranteed to be available for use by an application at runtime. See *font.*

**stop-motion photography**   A method for production animation whereby inanimate models are photographed a few frames at a time and manually moved between each exposure. Also called model animation and motion-control model animation. See *claymation, pixelation.*

**stream**   The flow of data to or from a file or other output device.

**structure**   A set of items grouped under a single name. The elements may be of different types. In an array, the elements must be of similar type.

**stub**   See *do-nothing routine.*

**subtraction**   See *Euler operators.*

**super sampling**   Creating an image at a resolution that is greater than the actual screen resolution. When the image is scaled down to fit into the display buffer, many digital artifacts like jagged lines are suppressed as a convenient by-product of the scaling mathematics.

**Super VGA**   Graphics adapters that extend the capabilities of the original IBM VGA. Typical Super VGAs provide a 640-×-480-×-256 color mode, 800-×-600-×-16 color mode, 1024-×-768-×-16 color mode, and 1024-×-768-×-256 color mode. Software drivers that enable Windows to run the Super VGA in these modes are usually provided by the hardware manufacturer.

**surface normal**   A line that is perpendicular to the surface of a plane in a 3D environment. The illumination level of a surface can be derived by comparing the surface normal to the angle of incidence of incoming light rays.

**swish pan**   A rapid pan. Also called a zip pan.

**syntactically implemented**   The full functional implementation of a particular keyword or statement by a C or C++ compiler. See *semantically implemented.*

**systems application architecture**   See *SAA.*

**system palette** The current hardware palette, composed of a look-up table (LUT) that correlates a specified color index (usually an integer) with a particular triad of voltage settings for the RGB guns of the display monitor. A VGA running Windows can provide a system palette of 16 distinct and simultaneously displayable hues. A Super VGA, 8514/A, or XGA running Windows can provide a system palette of 256 hues. See *logical palette.*

**3D** Three dimensional. Refers to computer images representing objects possessing the three dimensions of width, height, and depth. See *4D.*

**target platform** The group of personal computers and operating system configuration versions for which a software product is developed.

**temporal aliasing** Refers to an awkward jumping effect present in computer-animated sequences when the frame rate is too slow to smoothly simulate actors moving at speed across the image. See *anti-aliasing, motion blur.*

**tilde** The character, which C and C++ use to mean one's complement.

**timer** A logical timing device maintained by Windows in order to send a WM_TIMER message to the application at an interval defined by the application. See *animate on twos.*

**timer-based animation** An animation sequence driven by WM_TIMER timer messages from the Windows API.

**titling** Adding titles, production credits, and labels to an animated sequence or multimedia presentation.

**toon** An actor (cartoon character) in a computer-animated cartoon sequence.

**touring** See *walk-through.*

**traceback** The portion of an animation frame that is unchanged from the previous frame.

**translation** Repositioning of an object in a 3D scene. See *rotation, extrusion.*

**transparent put** The graphics effect of cleanly placing a random-shaped, multicolored bitblt image over a multicolored background scene. See *frisket.*

**travelling matte** A matte whose shape changes as it accompanies a moving image. See *matte.*

**trigonometry** Mathematics concerned with the relationship of two sides opposite a specific angle in a right-angle triangle. Sine and cosine are particularly useful for 3D computer graphics.

**tween** An in-between image that software has interpolated from keyframes provided by the user or developer. See *keyframe.*

**tweening** Generating tweens.

**UAE** Unrecoverable application error. Windows 3.0 displays a UAE message box when it can no longer continue to manage the execution of an application because of memory conflicts , a corrupted block of memory, an illegal pointer, or an incorrect function address.

**UMB** Upper memory blocks.

**unary operator** An operator that manipulates a single variable. C and C++ provide the following unary operators: logical NOT (!), bitwise compliment (), arithmetic negation ($-$), indirection (*), address-of (&), and unary plus (or arithmetic increment) ($+$).

**union** A C or C++ structure that allocates the same memory space to different variables. The variables are often of different types.

**unrecoverable application error** See *UAE*.

**update dynamics** Changes in shape, color, and texture during an animation sequence. See *motion dynamics, viewing dynamics*.

**USER.EXE** The Windows dynamic link library that provides window management functions for Windows applications at runtime. See *GDI.EXE, KERNEL.EXE*.

**vector** A mathematical value that has quantity and direction. A scalar value has only quantity.

**VGA** Video graphics array. Windows runs in the 640-×-480-×-16 color mode on VGA adapters.

**videodisc** A large-format plastic disc used to store digital or analog information. Read by laser beam. Often used to store and play full-motion video and audio. Similar in concept to CD-ROM.

**view coordinates** See *camera coordinates*.

**viewing dynamics** Changes in lighting, camera, and viewpoint during an animation sequence. See *motion dynamics, update dynamics*.

**viewport** A subset of the display screen.

**visibility** Describes whether or not a function or a variable can be used by other parts of a C or C++ program.

**visual algorithm** The graphical representation of a computer function or algorithm.

**visualization** Using graphics to interpret, manipulate, or create data. Specialized fields of computer visualization include scientific visualization, 3D modeling and rendering, computer animation, biomedicine, fluid dynamics, tomography, computer vision, image processing, and others. See *objectification*.

**visualization graphics** The graphics used for computer visualization. See *visualization*.

**void** Undefined. See *NULL*.

**volume visualization** Using 3D objects to represent data. See *scientific visualization*.

**VTR** Videotape recorder or videotape recording. See *NTSC*.

**walk-through** Animation of a 3D architectural model, intended to simulate a walk-through by the viewer. Also called touring.

**weighted sum** An image-processing operation whereby the sum of values of a pixel and its neighbors are calculated in compliance with a spatial filter.

**white box** A block of code currently under development and whose algorithms and processes are being adjusting during testing. See *black box*.

**white-box testing**  Program testing that requires access to the inner workings of a block of code. See *black-box testing.*

**window**  1. The display space used by a Windows application; 2. A viewport on the display screen; 3. The logical relationship between the display screen and the world coordinates in 3D graphics programming.

**window class**  A logical definition describing the attributes of a window. A window class is used to create the main window of a Windows application.

**window function**  A callback function in a Windows application, responsible for interpreting incoming messages and directing program flow to the appropriate core functions of the application. See *callback function.*

**windows.h**  The include file that contains definitions and declarations for Windows variables, data structures, functions, and constants that are available for use by a Windows application.

**WinMain()**  The entry-point function of a Windows application. WinMain() contains the message loop.

**wipe**  Revealing the next image by selectively manipulating the image buffer. Similar in concept to opening a set of venetian blinds to reveal a scene or opening a sliding door to reveal a room. Also called a reveal.

**wire-frame**  A 3D object modeled with edges, with no hidden surfaces removed.

**WM_COMMAND**  The runtime variable that contains an incoming message that identifies the user's actions in navigating through and selecting from the application's menus.

**world coordinates**  The X-Y-Z coordinates that describe the position and orientation of an object in a 3D environment.

**XGA**  Extended graphics adapter. As defined by IBM, an XGA adapter provides a 640-$\times$-480-$\times$-256 color mode, 1024-$\times$-768-$\times$-256 color mode, a 640-$\times$-480-$\times$-65536 color mode, and all VGA modes.

**XMS**  Extended memory specification. XMS memory is physical memory located above 1MB which can be accessed by an 80286, 80386, 80486, or newer microprocessor. See *EMS.*

**YIQ model**  The color model used by commercial television components.

**z-buffer**  A buffer containing the depth values for each pixel in a scene, allowing the software to draw only the nearest object at any particular location.

**z-buffer method**  A method of hidden surface removal. See *z-buffer.* Also called the painter's algorithm.

**zip pan**  See *swish pan.*

**zoom**  To move the camera closer to or farther away from the objects in a 3D scene.

**zoom axis**  The 3D axis that represents the near/far context in a 3D scene. The zoom axis is perpendicular to the image plane. The 3D routines in the demonstration programs in this book use the Z axis to represent near/far.

# Index

# Special Preview

Watch for Lee Adams' next book in the high-performance Windows graphics series, coming soon from Windcrest/McGraw-Hill. It's entitled *Windows Visualization Programming with C/C++: Visualization, Simulation, and Virtual Reality* (book #4115).

Learn how to create Windows applications that can manipulate and display solid, shaded 3D models. Explore hidden surface removal. Investigate multiple light sources and use advanced rendering techniques like facet shading, Gouraud shading, and Phong shading. Create textures using professional techniques like surface mapping, bump mapping, and others. Use shadows and transparency for dramatic effect.

Then use the 3D images you have created to assemble dramatic animation sequences that run from your hard disk. Explore kinematics, dynamics, visualization, and simulation.

Lee Adams' next book can turn your personal computer into a 3D production studio. It's coming soon from Windcrest/McGraw-Hill . . . *C for Windows: 3D Visualization Programming* (book 4115), featuring over 20,000 lines of program listings—nearly 900K of royalty-free source code you can paste into your own applications. And it's from one of the most trusted names in computer graphics programming, the bestselling author of *Visualization Graphics in C* and *High Performance C Graphics Programming for Windows* (book 4103).

See for yourself why other books and articles often list a Lee Adams book as their source. Read the author the other authors read.

# Other Bestsellers of Related Interest

**BUILD YOUR OWN 386/386SX
COMPATIBLE AND SAVE A BUNDLE
—2nd Edition**—Aubrey Pilgrim

Assemble an 80386 microcomputer at home using mail-order parts that cost a lot less today than they did several years ago. Absolutely no special technical know-how is required—only a pair of pliers, a couple of screwdrivers, and this detailed, easy-to-follow guide. 248 pages, 79 illustrations. Book No. 4089, $18.95 paperback, $29.95 hardcover

**BIT-MAPPED GRAPHICS**—Steve Rimmer

This is one of the first books to cover the specific graphic file formats used by popular paint and desktop publishing packages. It shows you how to pack and unpack bit-map image files so you can import and export them to other applications. And, it helps you spot through available file formats, standards, patches, and revision levels, using commercial-quality C code to explore bit-mapped graphics and effectively deal with image files. 504 pages, 131 illustrations. Book No. 3558, $26.95 paperback, $38.95 hardcover

**MACINTOSH SYSTEM 7: The Complete
Sourcebook**—Gordon M. Campbell

Campbell shows off some of the exciting new features of System 7 and offers tips for upgrading your hardware and software. This is your best guide to the first major development in the Macintosh since its introduction in 1984. With this book by your keyboard, you can count on clear skies and smooth sailing, for either upgrade or installation. 320 pages, illustrated. Includes 3.5″ disk. Book No. 4074, $32.95 paperback only

**THE CONCISE PC NOTEBOOK AND
LAPTOP USER'S GUIDE**—Dan Gookin

Here, you'll find complete information on computers designed to leave the office and follow you on the road. Useful tips are furnished throughout to help make laptop computing easier and more productive for you, no matter what your technical skill. With this book in hand, your initiation to laptop computing will be virtually painless! 304 pages, 40 illustrations. Includes 3¹/₂″ disk. Book No. 3921, $22.95 paperback only

**MS-DOS® BATCH FILE PROGRAMMING
—3rd Edition**—Ronny Richardson

Now updated to cover DOS 5.0, this book explores the power of .BAT—the PC user's key to total system control. Richardson shows how to boost productivity dramatically with simple step-saving programs. He discusses two of the most often customized system batch files, AUTOEXEC.BAT and CONFIG.SYS and then shows you how to create your own batch files. 440 pages, 186 illustrations. 5.25″ disk included. Book No. 3916, $26.95 paperback, $36.95 hardcover

**MS-DOS® BATCH FILE UTILITIES
—Ronny Richardson**

Featuring more than 200 of the best batch file programs available for the PC, this is the most complete source of documentation available for batch file utilities currently offered as shareware or in the public domain. Arranged alphabetically and meticulously cross-referenced by category, this valuable reference features detailed descriptions and instructions for ALL commercial batch files on the DOS market today. 368 pages, 275 illustrations. 5.25″ disk included. Book No. 3915, $29.95 paperback, $36.95 hardcover

**FOXPRO®: The Master Reference
—2nd Edition**—Robin Stark
and Shelley Satonin

Design and run powerful, customized databases in no time using all the exciting new features of FoxPro. This alphabetical guide to every FoxPro command and function covers all versions through 2.0—more than 350 entries in all. Its innovative three-part indexing system leads you quickly to all commands, functions, and examples found in the book. 512 pages, 135 illustrations. Book No. 4056, $24.95 paperback only